中国研究
China Studies

青年汉学家研修计划论文集（北京·郑州）

2017

A Collection of Research Papers of
the Visiting Program for Young Sinologists
2017（Beijing·Zhengzhou）

文化和旅游部对外文化联络局
中外文化交流中心　编

中国社会科学出版社

图书在版编目（CIP）数据

2017青年汉学家研修计划（北京·郑州）论文集.汉英对照/文化和旅游部对外文化联络局，中外文化交流中心编.—北京：中国社会科学出版社，2018.7
ISBN 978-7-5203-2823-4

Ⅰ.①2… Ⅱ.①文…②中… Ⅲ.①汉学—文集—汉、英
Ⅳ.①K207.8-53

中国版本图书馆CIP数据核字（2018）第150906号

出 版 人	赵剑英
责任编辑	夏　侠
责任校对	郭　莹
责任印制	王　超

出　　版	中国社会科学出版社
社　　址	北京鼓楼西大街甲158号
邮　　编	100720
网　　址	http://www.csspw.cn
发 行 部	010-84083685
门 市 部	010-84029450
经　　销	新华书店及其他书店
印刷装订	环球东方（北京）印务有限公司
版　　次	2018年7月第1版
印　　次	2018年7月第1次印刷
开　　本	710×1000　1/16
印　　张	37.75
字　　数	678千字
定　　价	298.00元

凡购买中国社会科学出版社图书，如有质量问题请与本社联系调换
电话：010-84083683
版权所有　侵权必究

2017青年汉学家研修计划（北京）
（2017.09.11～09.29）

2017年9月11日，2017青年汉学家研修计划（北京）开班仪式在国家图书馆举行，图为嘉宾与全体学员合影

Group photo of distinguished guests and the participants in the Visiting Program for Young Sinologists (Beijing) at the opening ceremony held in the National Library on September 11, 2017

2017年9月11日，2017青年汉学家研修计划（北京）开班仪式在国家图书馆举行，图为开班仪式会场

At the opening ceremony of the Visiting Program for Young Sinologists (Beijing) held in the National Library on September 11, 2017

2017年9月13日，学员们在专家授课现场

Young Sinologists listen to the lecture on September 13, 2017

2017年9月20日，部分学员参观郭沫若故居

Some of the participants on a visit to former residence of Guo Moruo on September 20, 2017

2017年9月24日,赴江西省景德镇考察的学员们参观中国陶瓷博物馆

Participants on a visit to Chinese Porcelain Museum in Jingdezhen, Jiangxi Province on September 24, 2017

2017年9月25日,青年汉学家体验中国民乐

Young Sinologists experiencing Chinese folk music on September 25, 2017

2017 青年汉学家研修计划（郑州）
（2017.07.10 ~ 07.28）

2017年7月10日，2017青年汉学家研修计划（郑州）开班仪式在郑州大学举办，图为嘉宾与全体学员合影

Group photo of distinguished guests and the participants in the Visiting Program for Young Sinologists (Zhengzhou) at the opening ceremony held in Zhengzhou University on July 10, 2017

2017年7月10日，2017青年汉学家研修计划（郑州）开班仪式在郑州大学举办，图为开班仪式会场

At the opening ceremony of the Visiting Program for Young Sinologists (Zhengzhou) held in Zhengzhou University on July 10, 2017

2017年7月12日，学员们按专业被分到各个研修单位研修，图为郑州大学历史学院小组导师见面会现场

Some of the participants undergoing training in the Academy of History of Zhengzhou University on July 12, 2107; Young Sinologists are distributed to different research institutes according to majors

2017年7月13日，学员们参观大河村遗址博物馆

Participants on a visit to Dahe Village Site Museum on July 13, 2017

2017 年 7 月 16 日晚，学员们在郑州大学体育馆学习中国武术

Participants practiced Wushu in the gymnasium of Zhengzhou University on July 13, 2017

2017 年 7 月 25 日，学员们在北京参加"汉学与当代中国"座谈会，图为嘉宾与全体学员合影

Group photo at the closing ceremony of the "Symposium on China Studies" on July 25, 2017

编辑委员会

编委会主任：谢金英
编委会副主任：朱 琦 于 芃 李 蕊 韩国河
编委会委员：梁 川 徐逊吉 孙 杰 贾 锟
　　　　　　黄卓明

主办：中华人民共和国文化和旅游部　中国社会科学院
承办：中外文化交流中心

Hosts: Ministry of Culture and Tourism of the People's Republic of China
　　　 Chinese Academy of Social Sciences
Organizer: Network of International Culturalink Entities

| 目 录 |

"一带一路"倡议

3　埃塞俄比亚和马来西亚与中国交往的比较分析：以"一带一路"倡议为例
　　林鎝淡　【马来西亚】
　　新加坡南洋理工大学南洋公共管理研究生院博士后研究员
　　吉迪恩·贾拉塔　【埃塞俄比亚】
　　乐施会中非对话论坛项目经理

11　中国从"改革开放"到"一带一路"
　　基恩·博里奇　【阿尔巴尼亚】
　　阿尔巴尼亚历史研究中心学者

35　南亚各国对中国"一带一路"倡议的态度及其原因浅析
　　萨尔波塔姆·什雷斯塔　【尼泊尔】
　　尼泊尔阿尼哥协会主席、临床神经内科医生

49　论文化遗产在"一带一路"构建中的作用
　　魏骏骁　【德国】
　　德国考古研究院欧亚考古研究所博士

71　中国在智利的文化外交
　　玛丽缘　【智利】
　　智利教育部汉语研究项目研究员

89　在"一带一路"倡议下对中国与拉丁美洲的思考
　　侯赛　【秘鲁】
　　秘鲁天主教大学孔子学院讲师

文学、文化、文字

113　浅论张抗抗长篇小说《作女》中卓尔形象
　　穆罕默德·谢赫　【埃及】
　　明亚大学语言学院中文系讲师

138 拉丁美洲汉译文学概览
　　马安娜 【墨西哥】
　　绿宝石语言中心教师

160 汉字文化与中越传统丧葬礼俗研究
　　张家权 【越南】
　　胡志明市国家大学人文与社会科学大学中国语文系副主任

189 从外国人的角度对中国文化色彩词语初探
　　——以《现代汉语词典》中含"气"、"道"、"德"、"阴"和"阳"等汉字的语词为例
　　约万诺维奇·安娜 【塞尔维亚】
　　贝尔格莱德大学语言学院东方语言系中文专业讲师

210 汉语"一定、肯定、当然、绝对"与泰语"แน่นอน"的语义辨析
　　陈昌旭 【泰国】
　　泰国皇太后大学汉语教师

242 对外古汉语教学的重要性和方法探索
　　吴淑铃 【美国】
　　美国南伊利诺大学

255 论现当代文学在对外汉语教学中的作用
　　丹妮 【印度】
　　都安大学助理教授

274 对词块教学法中文化教学问题的思考
　　——以西班牙大学为例
　　赵婧萱 【西班牙】
　　西班牙格拉纳达大学教师

290 "青年汉学家研修计划"研修成果
　　蔼孙那檀 【美国】
　　北卡罗来纳州立大学副教授

303	经验、记忆与写作的叙事：马原1987年短篇小说《错误》的叙事学分析 高伟林 【澳大利亚】 澳大利亚布里斯班昆士兰大学语言及文化学系中文翻译讲师

中国传统文化

347	论古琴美学思想与儒道家修身养性的作用 菲李普 【意大利】 乌比诺大学副教授
370	中国古代先秦音乐和乐器研究 宋镇烈 【韩国】 庆星大学中文博士在读
397	中国20世纪20—30年代摄影理论研究 罗飞 【意大利】 巴塞罗那自治大学客座讲师

中国与世界

423	中国与南非经济关系（1990—2010） 布拉西马·迪亚凯特 【科特迪瓦】 费利克斯乌弗埃博瓦尼大学讲师、研究员
446	有中国特色的负责任核主权国 麦克斯韦尔·莱纳德·乔纳森·多曼 【英国】 英美安全信息委员会、上议院
474	非洲重建：来自中国快速发展的经验 黑豹 【马拉维】 马拉维国家税务局专员
505	从军事合作到经济外交：中国与安哥拉关系变化的研究 托科库·英纳森特·奥可可 【尼日利亚】 阿布贾大学历史外交研究讲师

523　纵向重叠与实施差距：加拿大与中国的气候战略比较
　　　米凯拉·彼得森-麦克纳布 【加拿大】
　　　加拿大英属哥伦比亚大学硕士研究生

545　中国国际关系理论的兴起：对西方其他国家范式的挑战？
　　　保罗 【菲律宾】
　　　菲律宾综合科技大学社会学系讲师

563　中国在全球应对气候变化的作用：对其贡献的评估
　　　李开 【加拿大】
　　　加拿大亚太基金会中国研究伙伴关系项目专员

CONTENTS

The "Belt and Road" Initiative

6 **Comparative Perspectives of Ethiopian and Malaysian Engagement with China: the Case of the "Belt and Road" Initiative**
Guanie Lim Cia Lit / Malaysia
Postdoctoral Fellow of the Nanyang Centre for Public Administration, Nanyang Technological University, Singapore
Gedion Jalata / Ethiopia
Program Manager of the Africa-China Dialogue Platform(ACDP), Oxfam International

20 **China since the Reform and Opening of 1978 to the "Belt and Road" Initiative**
Gjon Boriçi /Albania
Scholar in the Institute of History, Center of Albanian Studies

41 **The South Asian Countries' Attitude to Chinese the "Belt and Road" Initiative and Reason Analysis**
Sarbottam Shrestha / Nepal
Chairman of the Argentinean Association, Clinical Neurologist, Nepal

58 **On the Role of Cultural Heritage in the Construction of the "Belt and Road" Initiative**
Patrick Wertmann / Germany
Doctor, Eurasian Archaeological Institute, German Archaeological Academy

78 **China's Cultural Diplomacy in Chile**
María Elvira Ríos Peñafiel / Chile
Researcher of the Ministry of Education of Chile

97   **Reflections about China and Latin America under the "Belt and Road" Initiative**
        Feliciano José / Peru
        Lecturer of the Confucius Institute at Catholic Pontifical University of Peru; Founder and Director of Seed International China Ltd.

Literature, Culture and Language

123   **On the Image of Zhuo'er in Zhang's Novel, *Women on the Edge***
        Mohanmed Anwar Elmadny Elshikh / Egypt
        Lecturer of the Chinese and Literature Department, School of Language, Minya University

146   **A Brief Panoramic Revision of Latin American Chinese to Spanish Literary Translators**
        Adriana Martínez González / Mexico
        Teacher of the Emerald Language Center

173   **The Study of Chinese Culture and the Traditional Funeral Etiquette and Customs Between China and Vietnam**
        Truong Gia Quyen / Vietnam
        Deputy Director, Chinese Language Department, National University of Humanities and Social Sciences, Ho Chi Minh City

196   **A Preliminary Study on Chinese Cultural Terms from the Perspective of Foreigners**
        Ana Jovanović / Serbia
        Docent at the Department of Oriental Languages, Literature and Cultures, Faculty of Philology, University of Belgrade

224   **The Semantics Analysis of "Yiding, Kending, Dangran, Juedui" in Chinese and "Naenon" in Thai**
        Teeraparp Predeepoch / Thailand
        Chinese Teacher of Mae Fah Luang University, Thailand

247 **Exploration of the Importance and Methods of Ancient Chinese Teaching**
Shu-ling Wu / United States of America
Chinese Assistant Professor and China Program Leader, Southern Illinois University in Carbondale

262 **On the Role of Modern and Contemporary Literature in Teaching Chinese as A Foreign Language**
Tanvi Negi Malla / India
Assistant Professor of Doon University

280 **On Culture Teaching in the Teaching Method of Word Chunks**
Isabel Maria Balsas Urena / Spain
Lecturer, University of Granada

295 **Research Accomplishments of the Visiting Program for Young Sinologists**
Nathaniel Isaacson / United States of America
Associate Professor of North Carolina State University

318 **The Narrative of Experience, Memory and Writing: A Narratological Analysis of Ma Yuan's 1987 Short Story *Mistakes***
William Gatherer / Australia
Lecturer in Chinese Translation, School of Languages and Cultures, University of Queensland, Brisbane, Australia

Chinese Traditional Culture

356 **On the Aesthetic Thought of Guqin and the Role of Confucianism and Taoist in Self-Cultivation**
Fillippo Costantini / Italy
Associate Professor, University of Urbino

381 **A Study on the Music and Musical Instruments in the Ancient Qin Dynasty**
Jinyeul Song / Republic of Korea
Doctoral Candidate of Chinese Department, Kyungsung

405   An Introduction to Theoretical Aspects of Photography in China During the '20 and '30
       Roberto Figliulo / Italy
       Guest Lecturer of the Autonomous University of Barcelona

China and the World

431   The China-South Africa Economic Relations (1990-2010)
       Brahima Diakite / Cote d'lvoire
       Teacher & Researcher of Felix Houphouet-Boigny University, Cote d'lvoire

456   Responsible Nuclear Sovereignty with Chinese Characteristics
       Maxwell Leonard Jonason Downman / United Kingdom of Great Britain and Northern Ireland
       British American Security Information Council, House of Lords

486   Re-constructing Chinese Model Into Africa: Experience from Chinese Rapid Development
       Donasius Pathera / Malawi
       Compliance &Business Analyst, Domestic Taxes, Malawi Revenue Authority

512   From Military Cooperation to Economic Diplomacy: A Study of the Changing Relations Between China and Angola
       Tochukwu Innocent Okeke / Nigeria
       Lecturer of the Department of History and Diplomatic Studies, University of Abuja

530   Vertical Overlap and the Enforcement Gap: A Comparison of Canadian and Chinese National Climate Strategies
       Michaela Celeste Pedersen-Macnab / Canada
       Master Degree Candidate, University of British Columbia, Canada

551   The Rise of a Chinese International Relations Theory: Challenge to the West of a Paradigm for the Rest?
       Paulo Benedicto Villar / Philippines
       Lecturer, Department of Sociology, University of Science and Technology, Philippines

573 **China's Role in the Global Fight on Climate Change: An Assessment of its Contribution**
Charles-Louis Labrecque / Canada
Project Specialist for the China Research Partnership, Asia Pacific Foundation of Canada

「一带一路」倡议

The "Belt and Road" Initiative

埃塞俄比亚和马来西亚与中国交往的比较分析：
以"一带一路"倡议为例

林鑽溁 【马来西亚】
新加坡南洋理工大学南洋公共管理研究生院博士后研究员
吉迪恩·贾拉塔 【埃塞俄比亚】
乐施会中非对话论坛项目经理

自中国于 2013 年提出"一带一路"倡议以来，埃塞俄比亚和马来西亚一直处于各自地区（即东非和东南亚）与中国合作的前沿。尽管埃塞俄比亚和马来西亚彼此似乎共同点并不多，但是我们认为，特别是在吸引中国投资方面两国均拥有支持增长的体制来借助中国这一经济引擎的力量。两国同时也都善于处理与地区和全球大国的外交关系以维护各自的主权。我们并不鼓励其他经济体建立类似的"亲中"体制，但是本文所讨论的原则，为渴望就"一带一路"倡议与中国建立紧密关系的其他发展中经济体提供了政策借鉴，或者至少说是一些初步指导。

一 简述

自从 2013 年"一带一路"倡议宣布以来，中国企业在海外的扩张被广泛报道。其中一个最常见的分析思路认为，中国企业，特别是中国国有企业，体现了中国日益娴熟的外交手腕。这一看法宣扬"中国威胁论"的认识，（通常）选择孤立的事件以证明，中国政府利用其大批国有跨国公司作为与其他国家接触的手段，最终实现在诸如东非和东南亚这样的周边地区提升其政治影响力以抗衡美国霸权的目的（Naím，2007 年）。然而，实际情况要比之复杂得多，因为这些边缘地区的国家（通常）拥有足够的能力对来自中国的资本加以管理和调和，使之用于促进其自身目标的实现。对埃塞俄比亚和马来西亚这两个在各自地区积极支持（同时也对其保持谨慎）"一带一路"倡议的国家而言，更是如此。这两个国家为何如此擅长与中国打交道？换句话说，它们成功的关键因素是什么？除了它们各自独特的地理位置之外（两国均处于东西方之间的战略地理位置），对肤浅的观察者而言，两国之间的共同点确实乏善可陈。然而，如果我们深入研究这一问题，会逐渐发现有助于两国对中国的政治和经济力量加以调和从而使其服务于促进各自发展议程这一目标的某些共同特点。

二　主要内容

虽然与日本这样典型的发展国家和"亚洲四小龙"这样的一线经济体比较起来相对较弱，但是埃塞俄比亚和马来西亚拥有推动工业化发展的十分有效的体系。尤其是两国均善于吸引外国直接投资（包括但不仅限于中国投资）以促进其经济增长。对外资的开放无疑促进了其经济的增长。埃塞俄比亚为其作为东非地区增长最快的经济体而引以为傲——自 1991 年重建和平以来其国内生产总值以惊人的速度不断增长。而马来西亚也自 1957 年独立以来实现了从一个农业经济体发展成为一个相对成熟经济体的跨越，巩固了其作为"亚洲四小虎"这样的二线经济体之一的地位。

近来，埃塞俄比亚和马来西亚迅速地抓住了"一带一路"倡议的机会，在中国企业的支持下实施了一系列需要较长孕育期的资本密集型项目。在埃塞俄比亚，中铁集团和中国土木工程集团利用 3 家中国国有银行的融资，联合承建了亚的斯亚贝巴至吉布提的铁路。在马来西亚，马来西亚—中国关丹产业园区项目（MCKIP）于 2013 年启动，这是位于广西的中国—马来西亚钦州工业园区的姊妹项目。上述两个工业园区常被视为"一带一路"倡议在该地区的旗舰项目，甚至在更广泛的领域作为面向东南亚其他国家的示范案例。它们也是由中国国有企业与马来西亚联合承建的。

另一个支撑上述成功的关键因素是两国对地缘政治的精通。两国均位于东西方的十字路口，备受全球和地区大国的关注。埃塞俄比亚更具有作为进入非洲之角的跳板这一战略位置的优势。其成功地发挥了对邻国的吉布提港的影响力，从而减轻了其作为内陆国的劣势，开拓了一条连接中东与东非市场的重要贸易通道。而马来西亚则毗邻世界最重要的航运通道之一的马六甲海峡。特别是中国长期以来一直在寻求克服对马六甲海峡的过度依赖，即所谓的"马六甲困局"。目前中国 80% 的能源供给需要通过这一狭窄航道的运输。

尽管拥有地理上的战略位置，两国都极为精明地利用多个地区安全和政治安排机制来维护各自主权。具体而言，两国都精于拉拢强大盟友以维护其政治上的自主性。西方大国（包括与其结盟的国家）是两国首选的安全合作伙伴，比如两国迅速地加入了诸如美国领导的全球反恐战争这样的倡议。两国虽然在经济发展方面日益依赖中国，但是却在平衡中美利益方面展现出各自的灵活性，同时并未牺牲各自主权的完整。鉴此，埃塞俄比亚和马来西亚两国的政治精英必须为其同时与华盛顿和北京保持密切关系所做出的贡献而得到赞赏[1]。比如，埃塞俄比亚已故总理梅莱斯·泽纳维（Meles Zenawi）因其在埃塞内战期间（1974—1991）以及和平时期（1991 年后）与美国和中国同时建立了合作关系而闻名。他所提出的东非发展模式借鉴了中国的发展经验（Cheru，2016）。而马来西亚总理纳吉布·拉扎克（Najib Razak）同样善于处理与中美两国的外交关系。他同时也从已故总理敦·阿卜杜勒·拉扎克（Tun Abdul Razak）在其任内与中国建立的特殊关系中受益——当时，马来西亚于 1974 年成为首个与中国建立外交关系的东南亚国家。在之后历任的马来西亚总理任内，特别是在现任总理纳吉布的领导下，中马双边关系得到了不断的发展（Negeow，2017 年）。

三 结语

总之，埃塞俄比亚和马来西亚两国具有支持增长的体制以吸引来自中国的外国直接投资，特别是需要较长偿还期的资金密集型项目。两国同时也在处理与地区和全球大国（比如中国）的外交关系从而维护国家主权方面展现出了能力。这些体制具有历史渊源，并不容易复制，从而使得两国在参与"一带一路"倡议时相比地区竞争对手具有独特的优势。更为重要的是，两国的能动性和自主性对大众媒体宣扬的"中国威胁论"起到了削弱的作用。

---

[1] 需要指出的是，许多国家也是这么做的，但却不如埃塞俄比亚和马来西亚做得那么精到和高效。

Comparative Perspectives of Ethiopian and Malaysian Engagement with China: the Case of the "Belt and Road" Initiative

Guanie Lim Cia Lit / Malaysia

Postdoctoral Fellow of the Nanyang Centre for Public Administration, Nanyang Technological University, Singapore

Gedion Jalata / Ethiopia

Program Manager of the Africa-China Dialogue Platform(ACDP), Oxfam International

Since China's 2013 announcement of the "Belt and Road" Initiative (BRI), Ethiopia and Malaysia have been at the forefront in collaborating with China in their respective subcontinents (East Africa and Southeast Asia, respectively). While there appears to be few similarities between Ethiopia and Malaysia, we argue that both countries possess pro-growth institutions to tap into China's economic engine, especially in attracting Chinese investment. They are also adept in managing their foreign relationship with regional and global powers to maintain their sovereignty. While we stop short of exhorting other economies to construct similar "pro-China" institutions, the principles discussed provide policy lessons, or at least some initial guidance, for other developing economies aspiring to forge closer ties with China in relation to the Belt and Road Initiative.

I. Introduction

Since the BRI was announced in 2013, there has been wide coverage of the overseas expansion of Chinese firms. One of the most common line of analysis portrays Chinese firms, especially the state-owned enterprises (SOEs), as manifestations of China's increasingly skillful diplomacy. This portrayal propagates the "China Threat" belief, picking out (often) isolated cases to argue that the Chinese state uses its large cohort of SOEs' transnational businesses as a means to engage with other countries, with the ultimate aim of bolstering its political influence against US domination in peripheral regions such as East Africa and Southeast Asia (see Naím, 2007).

Nevertheless, the on-the-ground reality is considerably more complex as states in these marginal regions do (and often) possess ample capacity to manage and mediate Chinese capital, utilizing the latter to further their own goals. This is especially true in Ethiopia and Malaysia, two of the more active (yet cautious) proponents of the BRI in their respective sub-regions. What makes these two countries so adept at dealing with China? In other words, what are their critical success factors? Beyond their unique geopolitical locations (both are strategically located between East and West), they share very little commonalities to the casual observer. However, if we delve deeper into the issue, we begin to observe some common features that help both countries mediate Chinese political economic might to further their own agenda.

II. Content

While relatively weak compared to the archetypical developmental states of Japan and the first-tier Asian tiger economies, both Ethiopia and Malaysia possess fairly effective institutions in driving industrialization. In particular, they are good at attracting foreign direct investment (FDI), including but not limited to Chinese capital, to bolster growth. The openness to foreign capital has certainly helped them grow their economies. Ethiopia prides itself on being the fastest-growing economy of East Africa, expanding its gross domestic product (GDP) at an impressive pace since peace resumed in 1991 (Oqubay, 2016; Alemu and Scoones, 2013). For Malaysia, it has also transformed its previously agrarian economy to a relatively sophisticated one since its independence in 1957, cementing its position as a second-tier Asian tiger economy (Lim, 2014).

In recent times, the Ethiopians and Malaysians have been noticeably quick to seize upon the BRI, implementing capital-intensive projects with long gestation period with the support of Chinese firms. For Ethiopia, the Addis Ababa-Djibouti Railway was built by the state-owned China Railway Group and the China Civil Engineering Construction Corporation, with financing provided by three state-owned Chinese banks. For Malaysia, the MCKIP Malaysia-China Kuantan Industrial Park (MCKIP) was launched in 2013 as the sister park of China-Malaysia Qinzhou Industrial Park (CMQIP) in Guangxi province. Both industrial parks are often earmarked as flagship BRI projects in the region and more generally, the ideal demonstrative case studies for other Southeast Asian countries (Kong, 2016). They are also jointly constructed by the SOEs of China and Malaysia.

Another key factor undergirding their success is their mastery of geopolitics. Both countries are situated at the crossroads of East and West, granting them the attention of global and regional powers. Ethiopia's location gives it strategic dominance as a jumping off point in the Horn of Africa. It has managed to leverage the neighboring Port of Djibouti, alleviating its landlocked status ad granting it a critical trading route interconnecting the markets of the Middle East and Eastern Africa. For Malaysia, it enjoys direct access to the Strait of Malacca, one of the most important shipping lanes in the world. In particular, Beijing has long sought to bridge its over-reliance on the Strait of Malacca, what it calls the "Malacca Dilemma". In terms of energy supplies, about 80% of current Chinese energy needs pass through this narrow waterway.

Notwithstanding their geostrategic locations, both Ethiopia and Malaysia are savvy enough to maintain their sovereignty through several regional security and political arrangements. More specifically, they are astute in drawing in powerful allies to maintain their political autonomy. Western powers (and those aligned to them) are the preferred security partners as they have swiftly joined initiatives such as the US-led Global War on Terror (see Noor and Qistina, 2017). Despite an increasing reliance on China for economic growth, Ethiopia and Malaysia have displayed their resilience in "balancing" the interests of US and China, without compromising their integrity. To this end, the Ethiopian and Malaysian political elites must be credited for maintaining a close relationship with both Washington and Beijing.[1] For instance, Meles Zenawi, the late Ethiopian Prime Minister, was famed for forging cooperative ties with US and China both during the Ethiopian civil war (1974-1991) and peaceful times (post-1991). He is known to advocate an East Asian style of development, often borrowing the development experience of China (Cheru, 2016). For Malaysia, Prime Minister Najib Razak is just as adept in handling foreign affairs with respect to US and China. He also benefits from Malaysia's special relationship with China when, under the Prime Ministership of Tun Abdul Razak, it became the first Southeast Asian country to establish diplomatic ties with the Chinese in 1974. The bilateral tie has blossomed under successive Prime Ministers, especially under the leadership of Prime Minister Najib (the son of Tun Abdul Razak) (Ngeow, 2017).

III. Conclusion

In summary, we have made the case that Ethiopia and Malaysia possess pro-growth institutions to attract Chinese FDI, especially in capital-intensive projects with long payoff period. Both countries have also displayed competence in managing their foreign relationship with regional and global powers (such as China) to maintain their sovereignty. These institutions have historical origins and are not

---

[1] It must be mentioned that many small states do this, but often without the subtlety and efficiency of Ethiopia and Malaysia.

easily replicable, granting them a distinct advantage over their regional rivals in tapping into the BRI. More importantly, the agency and autonomy of these two states weaken the "China Threat" thesis promulgated by the popular media.

References

Alemu, D., & Scoones, I. (2013). Negotiating New Relationships: How the Ethiopian State is Involving China and Brazil in Agriculture and Rural Development. *IDS Bulletin*, 44(4), 91-100.

Cheru, F. (2016). Emerging Southern Powers and New Forms of South–South Cooperation: Ethiopia's Strategic Engagement with China and India. *Third World Quarterly*, 37(4), 592-610.

Kong, T. Y. (2016). China's 21st Century Maritime Silk Road: Malaysian Perspectives. In T. W. Lim, H. Chan, K. Tseng, & W. X. Lim (Eds.), China's One Belt One Road Initiative (pp. 289- 306). London: Imperial College Press.

Lim, G. (2014). The Internationalisation of Mainland Chinese Firms into Malaysia: From Obligated Embeddedness to Active Embeddedness. *Journal of Current Southeast Asian Affairs*, 33(2), 59-90.

Naím, M. (2007). Rogue Aid. *Foreign Policy*, March/April 2007(159), 95-96.

Ngeow, C. B. (2017). Barisan Nasional and the Chinese Communist Party: A Case Study in China's Party-Based Diplomacy. *The China Review: An Interdisciplinary Journal on Greater China*, 17(1), 53-82.

Noor, E., & Qistina, T. (2017). Great Power Rivalries, Domestic Politics and Malaysian Foreign Policy. *Asian Security*, 13(3), 200-219.

Oqubay, A. (2016). Made in Africa: Industrial Policy in Ethiopia, Oxford: Oxford University Press.

中国从"改革开放"到"一带一路"

基恩·博里奇 【阿尔巴尼亚】
阿尔巴尼亚历史研究中心学者

一 引言

中国过去 40 年迅速发展的城市化是以大量农村剩余劳动力涌入城市为主要特点的。中国城市化水平从 1978 年的 17.9% 增至 2015 年的 56.1%，年增长率约 1%。2011 年，城市人口首度超过农村人口，达到 6.8 亿（联合国经济和社会事务部，2012 年），其中包括约 1.23 亿农民工（中国国务院发展研究中心项目组，2010 年）。过去 30 年，中国经历了快速的经济增长，成为世界增速最快的经济体，年均经济增长率约 9%。

2013 年对中国外交而言是不平凡的一年。世界经历了重大变革和深刻调整，涉及增长模式的转变、区域贸易安排机制、地缘政治格局演变和国际治理体系。中国外交采取主动，根据国际环境新的趋势和中国国内改革和发展议程，提出新的理念，开拓新的领域。中国正在探索一条具有中国特色的大国外交之路（中国外交部长王毅，2014 年 3 月）。

二 中国与全球治理新时代

全球治理涉及如何治理世界的问题，即在没有一个占据支配地位的中央权威或世界政府的情况下，如何处理全球性问题？如何确保世界的秩序和稳定？在理解全球治理这一概念时，首先需要回答一下问题：什么是全球性？什么是治理？

治理的概念在哪些方面与传统的政治和政府的概念有所不同？我们今天为什么要研究全球治理？

"全球性"这一词语通常指超越国际秩序或国家间体系的情形，涉及广泛而不同的世界事务主要参与者——除了国家，还包括个人、社会组织、国际组织等等。什么是"治理"？也许关于"治理"最为权威的定义来自全球治理委员会编写的一份报告。该委员会由来自世界各地的26位杰出人士组成，主席为瑞典前首相英瓦尔·卡尔松和前英联邦秘书长斯里达斯。这一题为"我们的全球家园"的报告于1995年发布，其中对全球背景下的治理定义如下：

"全球治理是包括公共和私人领域的个人和机构管理其共同事务的多种方式的总和。这是一个持续的进程，彼此冲突和不同的利益可在其中进行调节，同时可在其中采取合作行动。全球治理包括授权实施强制执行的正式机构和体制，也包括人民和机构认可的或认为符合其利益的非正式安排机制。"

我们需要记住的一点是，中国可以成为一个问题，也可以成为一个解决方案；中国可能仍旧对制度性的多边主义存有强烈的保留态度，也可能并不愿意放弃在规则制定和实施上的主权控制。

自20世纪70年代末以来，中国已经放开了大多数价格，对农业实施了非集体化经营，并融入了世界市场。这些变化推动了经济前所未有的增长——人均国内生产总值从1978年的674美元增加至2004年的5086美元。取得这一成功的因素是什么？第一，一些人士关注于中国经济在改革前的单元型组织结构。中国这一经济体此前是由平行的、多样的省级经济体构成，而不是单一的全国性的层级结构。当引入市场机制后，这一体系避免了混乱并促进了竞争。第二，一些人士提出，政治上的权力下放鼓励了地方的改革试验，使得新的理念从基层迸发出来。第三，一些人士认为，权力下放对中央政府形成了政治制约，限制了争利行为，并使得投资者相信改革将会持续。第四，一些人士指出，财政权下放极大地激发了地方官员促进经济增长的积极性。最后，一些人士认为，权力下放有助于强化对企业的预算约束，从而迫使它们进行重组改制。

中国经济自1978年开始，以一种特别有利于市场化的方式进行了构建——至少与其北方的共产主义邻邦相比而言。在苏联，地区经济体是相互依存、专一领域的单元，在国家分工体系中扮演不同角色并由中央计划部门加以协调。因为担心军事入侵，毛泽东鼓励地方自给自足，将大量计划和行政管理权力下放给省级干部。

与其他社会主义国家相比，中国的经济管理1978年之后相对非中央集权化。在20世纪80年代，中国的成功与更加集权化的苏联失败的改革形成对比。然而，到20世纪89年末，苏联在政治上的权力下放明显超过了中国。波罗的海的加盟共和国竞相独立，以至于到1991年初，戈尔巴乔夫努力挽救苏联保持一个松散的邦联整体。在1990年实行政党在地区的自由选举后，俄罗斯在政治上也较中国更为非集权化，各地区的经济政策各不相同。如果权力下放可以解释为什么20世纪80年代改革在中国比在苏联进展得更好，那么它却无法解释在20世纪90年代中国比俄罗斯发展得更好。相反的结局本应发生。管理权的下放在20世纪80年代与改革同时发生，一部分是因为权力下放本身就是邓小平及其支持者倡导的一项改革举措，另一部分是因为邓小平力图以向其在各省的盟友提供权力的方式，避开中央层面的改革反对派。但是，尽管对财政收入再次实施了中央集中控制这一转变，经济改革在20世纪90年代持续进行并在某些领域提速。

尽管在政治改革上明显落后于东方集团国家和苏联，但是可以证明的是，中国是实施经济改革最为成功的社会主义国家。1965至1980年，中国的实际国民生产总值年均增长率仅为6.4%；而1980至1988年，这一数字增至10.4%。1978至1988年，中国国民生产总值增长了两倍，人均国民生产总值翻了一倍。最为显著的进步体现在农村经济领域。按可比价格计算，1978至1990年，农业生产总值年均增长率达6.04%，农村集体企业生产总值增长了26.7%，农民人均纯收入从133.57元增至629.79元，年均增长额41.4元，而此前的28年期间，这一数字仅为3.2元。

在评价有关中国的地区角色和战略的文献时，我们可以发现这样一种渐进的叙述。这一叙述将中国的地区参与描述为3个阶段的进程：在处理地区关系时，中国的方式变得不再怀疑和保守；进而积极地参与地区多边平台；当前则变得缺乏一致性，这似乎导致了一种看法，即（至少是）中国正在变得更加强硬。尽管这一叙述呈现了关于中国在地区参与方面的一种线性演进过程，但是我们认为，这三种不同的参与方式实际上是针对不同的对象和情况，同时运作的。需要关注这其中矛盾和复杂的问题，以便为理解中国的地区参与提供有益的分析依据，而不是简单的将其分为不同的历史阶段。

三 新中国的外交政策

1977年8月中共十一大之后的一段时间，中国领导人仍然试图坚持毛泽东关于"三个世界"的理论。1977年11月1日，《人民日报》发表了题为"毛主席关于三个世界划分的理论是对马列主义的重大贡献"的长篇社论文章。文章重申，两个超级大国是全人类的共同敌人，第三世界是反对帝国主义、殖民主义和霸权主义的主要力量，第二世界是在反对超级大国霸权的最广泛的国际统一战线中可以联合的力量。值得注意的是，文章首次在理论基础上解释了为什么作为对世界和平的威胁，苏联比美国更加危险。

在经济改革启动后，"四个现代化"成为中国领导层最重要的目标。四个现代化是指农业、工业、国防和科技的现代化。这是已故的周恩来总理当时根据毛主席的指示，在1964至1965年以及1975年召开的第四届和第五届全国人大上分别倡议的关于中国经济发展的宏大概念。1978年2至3月召开的第五届全国人大特别重申了这一概念，自此实现现代化成为国家的主要任务。在这一时期，实现现代化和提高人民生活水平的要求成为指导中国外交政策的最重要因素。就经济改革而言，中国最初试图向南斯拉夫学习，之后又向匈牙利学习，后来又向"亚洲四小龙"学习。其对外交政策的影响是，中国必须接受由西方国家制定规则的国际经济秩序。而西方国家和日本也准备向中国的现代化提供友好的支持。独立自主的和平外交政策于是能够得到进一步的加强。

中国的对外关系大概在1992至1993年得到了全面恢复。中国政府努力构建和恢复其所理解的公正的世界和平。因此，中国领导层可以更好地重新定义对世界的看法。随着苏联的解体和两极格局的式微，中国领导人相信，一个新的国际关系格局正在形成。但是，"一超多强"的这一力量格局仅仅是短暂的过渡。与20世纪70年代和20世纪80年代不同的是，中国领导人关于外交政策的权威表述不再对世界大战的威胁进行评论。对这一话题保持沉默可以被解读为不再认为其是迫在眉睫的问题。相反地，中国应当将重心放在发展综合国力的当前和长期的竞争上，不能在这一激烈的竞争中落后。

中国的经济成功和不断上升的国际影响力强化了其对现行国际组织的接受，如联合国、世界银行、国际货币基金组织等，而之前中国认为它们不过是西方帝国列强的工具。此外，中国进一步期望这些国际组织发挥更为重要的作用，并试图通过这些国际组织表达并促进其利益。中国成为利用世界银行贷款最多的国家：截至1995年6月，共获得224亿美元的世界银行贷款。但是，中国仍然回避在这些组织内发挥积极的领导作用。首先，中国认为自己既是一个主要大国同时也是一个发展中国家，因此无意于领导第三世界。其次，中国当时依然缺乏经验丰富的外交官和国际公务员。中国所有的外交政策专家几乎毫无例外地认为，中国必须融入现行的国际体系，以便实现和平崛起。事实上，中国越发展，越需要参与国际体系及其制度安排。和平崛起意味着和平竞争，即基于规则开展竞争；尽管这些规则可能对中国并不公平，但是中国可能并不愿意扮演规则制定者的角色。

当前的国际体系主要是为代表和促进美国的利益而设计的。随着中国以及其他外来国家（如印度）实力的增强，美国将不得不调整这一体系及其制度安排，以适应前者的要求和期望。但是，正如国际货币基金组织甚至是G8集团缓慢改革进程所体现的，美国和欧洲很不情愿进行改革和调整。随着中国开始崛起成为全球大国，其不断增长的力量将以什么形式呈现？换句话说，成为全球霸权国家的中国将会是什么样？在过去的两个世纪，世界出现了两个全球超级大国：1850至1914年的英国和1945年至今的美国。

四 中国经济改革的成功

中国经济改革取得了令人瞩目的成功——在过去15年里，实现了年均9%的经济增速。

中国的权力下放与西方的联邦制在多个重要方面都是不同的。首先，西方的联邦制植根于保护私人权利的明确体系。其次，西方联邦制具有坚实和明确的宪法基础。第三，西方的联邦制几乎总是与政治自由、选举制和民主化相联系。

最近，中国的迅速崛起让分析家开始质疑美国是否能够继续维持霸权。中国现在是世界第二大经济体，能源的消费量已超过美国。中国在2020年之前成为世界最大的经济体似乎可能只是时间问题。此外，与日本和德国不同，中国不只是一个主要的经济大国，它还是一个拥有核武器的国家，也是联合国安理会的五个常任理事国之一。

五 走向"一带一路"倡议

中共十五大提出实施全面改革，对国有企业所有制进行改制。尽管这一方案的官方名称为"共同所有制",但是其被认为是私有化的代号。考虑到中国经济的体量,这也许是世界上最为宏伟的私有化方案。由于中国经济在近半个世纪的时期始终由国有部门所主导,当这一方案宣布时,其在国内外所产生的巨大震惊效果也就是可以理解的了。对一些人而言,中国的私有化预示着一场波澜壮阔的改革运动。

我们的问题是:为什么中国最终变得比巴西更重要?这是地理位置的原因:即便假设与中国经济增长水平和人口数量相当,巴西也没有与中国同样的连接海洋和陆地的主要海洋线路,而且也不像中国一样主要位于疾病更少、气候更加适宜的温带地区。中国毗邻西太平洋,陆地纵深广阔,与石油和天然气资源丰富的中亚地区相邻。巴西的比较优势相比更少:其位于南美洲,与其他陆地在地理上隔绝。中国已在中亚地区的投资额达 250 亿美元,投资修建了横跨哈萨克斯坦的一条 2000 英里的公路。哈萨克斯坦的阿拉木图与中国西部城市乌鲁木齐每日均有航班往来,中国商品充斥中亚市场。

中国在地理上的得天独厚是一个如此基本和明显的因素,以至于在关于近几十年来中国经济活力和国家自信的所有讨论中容易被忽略。

正如在东西伯利亚一样,中国与俄罗斯在中亚地区激烈地争夺势力范围。中国与属于苏联的中亚地区之间的贸易额从 1992 年的 5.27 亿美元增至 2009 年的 259 亿美元。然而,北京当前体现其影响力的方式则是修建了两条主要管道,一条是从里海横跨哈萨克斯坦抵达新疆的石油管道,另一条是从土库曼斯坦和乌兹别克斯坦边境横跨乌兹别克斯坦和哈萨克斯坦抵达新疆的天然气管道。这再一次证明,大中华挺进英国地缘政治学家麦金德爵士所称的欧亚大陆腹地时,军队是不必要的;重点是其对能源的无尽需求和其少数民族造成的内部危险。中国正在利用各种形式的国家力量,包括军事、外交、经济、商业、军事和人口实力,向其合法陆地和海洋边界之外扩张,从而涵盖中华帝国在其历史鼎盛时期的疆域范围。

中国是世界上最古老的文明之一,文字记载历史可追溯至 4000 年前。中国人创造的工程奇迹包括三峡大坝、长城、兵马俑等。火药、指南针、造纸术和印刷术是中国古代的四大发明。一位在多个世界 500 强公司董事会任职的华人投资家兼企业高管说,一个企业的权力与权威取决于其是国有企业、合资企业、外资全资企业还是民营企业。自 1978 年以来,中国逐步减少了国有企业的数量;国有企业的工业产出占比从30年前的75%降至如今的46%。在许多方面，对改革之前时代的中国政治经济的研究要比对今天的研究简单地多。可以确认的是，中国从来都不是一个纯粹的极权国家。分析家花费了大量时间和精力，试图找到权力的真正中心，特别是对精英派别、军队作用和各省领导权力给予了重点关注。当然，中国领导人在制定国内发展战略时，总是会考虑与超级大国的关系。尽管如此，中国政治不断增长的自主性使得完全在国内层面上研究中国的政治经济成为可能。

就许多方面而言，中国是从1993年开始崛起为全球贸易大国的。从1993年开始，中国的出口额在两年时间里猛增了60%（实际增长率为53%），在五年时间里翻了一倍。这一时期，中国实现了从1993年122亿美元的贸易逆差到次年的54亿美元贸易顺差的转变，到1997年，贸易顺差已增至403亿美元。中国作为全球出口大国的迅速发展，特别是中国与美国和其他发达国家之间贸易顺差的规模，可能无法避免地使得中国面临了改革其双轨制结构并按照"更加公平的"国际规则行事的外部压力。在2001年加入WTO时，中国政府同意取消多年来一直采用的保护其国内行业的多个机制。欧盟成员国中与中国经济关系最为紧密的无疑是德国，其在中国与欧洲整体关系中的分量达47%。这一指标清晰地表明，中国的目标是与世界上最重要的那些国家开展竞争。

六 "一带一路"倡议

"一带一路"倡议是中国国家主席习近平在访问哈萨克斯坦期间于2013年9月7日在纳扎尔巴耶夫大学演讲时提出来的。演讲的主旨是通过经济合作加强欧亚国家间的关系。"一带一路"倡议完全是中国提出的倡议。但是"一带一路"倡议的核心是什么？在2017年9月青年汉学家访华研修计划期间的授课中，笔者了解到该倡议自提出之初一直坚持如下五项原则：

相互尊重、互不侵犯、互不干涉、平等和互惠、和平共处。

在研修期间与中国社会科学院的学者交流过程中，笔者了解到"一带一路"倡议同时建立在以下五项基础上：

- 政治协调
- 基础设施互联互通
- 提升贸易

- 货币支持（货币兑换）
- 和平共处、文化外交

中国有一项全球经济复苏计划。该计划始自中国。从2012年至2020年，中国将完成国家现代化进程和构建中产阶级社会的任务。但是走向世界需要面临更大的挑战。在与中国社科院国际政治理论研究所和国际战略研究所的交流中，笔者了解到，中国实现上述战略，拥有的是行动的实力，而不是进攻的实力。基于这一愿景，中国的"一带一路"倡议完全是一项改善世界各民族之间关系的和平战略。其目标是在经济倡议的基础上将亚洲、欧洲和非洲和平地连接在一起。鉴于世界经济正在缓慢复苏，如果"一带一路"倡议能够成功，其所覆盖的人口将达46亿，占世界的60%，所覆盖的国内生产总值将达20万亿美元，占全球的三分之一。

"一带一路"倡议背景下的国际产能合作基于新的发展理念。中国国家主席习近平在阐述这一倡议时，同时提到了二十国集团杭州峰会期间为达成共识所明确的"五个决心"，即：

- 决心一：为世界经济指明方向，规划路径
- 决心二：创新增长模式，为世界经济注入新动力
- 决心三：完善全球经济金融治理，提高世界经济抗风险能力
- 决心四：重振国际贸易和投资这两大引擎的作用，构建开放型世界经济
- 决心五：推动包容和联动式发展，让二十国集团合作成果惠及全球

对某些学者而言，"一带一路"倡议是对西方全球化的回应，旨在建立一个更加美好的世界。随着中国的崛起和美国全球主导力的相对衰落，中美之间的竞争日益激化。尽管中美经济彼此依存并希望实现双赢而不是零和结局，历史经验显示，大国之间的竞争容易受到非理性因素的影响，从而导致意外甚至是对立的结果。根据西方的理论和国家关系的经验，崛起大国通常会挑战守成大国，而守成大国通常因为担心而针对崛起大国采取防范行动，这就导致了被称为"修昔底德陷阱"（古希腊历史学家修昔底德以其名字创造的术语）的情况发生。如果我们知道古代斯巴达和雅典之间以及一个世纪前英国与德国之间发生的战争，我们就会非常希望中美之间避免冲突。

一般来说，中国的政治哲学倾向于将完整的战略格局作为单一整体的一个组成部分加以考虑。基于这一特点，中国进入21世纪后，寻求的是其文化和制度

与世界的文化和制度之间的全球相关性。而"一带一路"倡议则确认了这一点。

七 结语

中国在提出"一带一路"倡议后，其未来的成功将体现哪些特点？通过2017年9月青年汉学家研修计划的学习，笔者在本文列出以下七大特点：

1. 中国称其为民族国家，但是准确地说中国是一个以文明为纽带组成的国家；
2. 就与亚洲各国以及其他地区国家之间的关系而言，中国倾向于成为未来世界经济的支点；
3. 中国对待世界的态度是和平的；
4. 中国不仅是亚洲大陆的一个国家，而且是亚洲大陆的一个友好国家；
5. 中国政策非常明确；自1949年以来形成了由共产党的坚强领导所代表的十分有效的制度；
6. 中国的现代化与其工业化速度是匹配的；
7. 中国的政权自1949年以来是稳定和坚实的。换句话说，中国实行的是"具有中国特色的社会主义道路"。

最后一个特点在2017年10月18至25日召开的中共十九大上也得到了重申和确认。中共中央总书记习近平在十九大报告中宣布，中国特色的社会主义进入了新时代。

这是一个不仅对中国而且对世界都无比重要的时代，因为，正如习近平主席指出的，这是一个充满希望同时也充满挑战的时代，没有一个国家可以单独面对。因此他号召各国共同努力，一起构建人类命运共同体。习主席说，中国将与世界各国一同构建人类命运共同体，为全人类和平与发展的崇高事业做出新的更大贡献。

China since the Reform and Opening of 1978 to the "Belt and Road" Initiative

Gjon Boriçi /Albania

Scholar in the Institute of History, Center of Albanian Studies

I. Introduction

China's rapid urbanization over the past four decades has been characterized by a massive amount of surplus rural labor flooding into cities. The level of urbanization in China rose from 17.9 percent in 1978, to 56.1 percent in 2015, with an annual increase of approximately 1.0 percent.[1] The size of the urban population first surpassed the rural population in 2011, when it reached 680 million (UN Department of Economics and Social Affairs, 2012). Approximately 123 million included in that number were migrant workers (Project Team of the Development Research Center of the State Council, 2010).[2] Over the past 30 years China has experienced rapid economic growth and become the world's fastest growing economy, with an average

---

1 Guangzhong Cao, Kai Li, Ruimin Wang, Tao Liu, "Consumption structure of migrant worker families in China", in China & World Economy, vol. 25, No. 5, Institute of World Economics and Politics, Chinese Academy of Social Sciences, July-August 2017, p. 1.
2 Ibid.

growth rate of approximately 9 percent.[1]

The year 2013 was an extraordinary year for China's diplomacy. The world went through greater changes with profound adjustment going on across the globe involving the shift of the growth model, regional trade arrangements, evolution of the geopolitical landscape and the system of international governance. China's diplomacy took the initiative to develop fresh ideas and break new ground in light of new trends in the international environment and China's domestic reform and development agenda. China is exploring a path of conducting major-country diplomacy with Chinese characteristics.(Wang Yi, Minister of Foreign Affairs, March 2014).[2]

II. China and the New Era of Global Governance

Global governance concerns the issue of how the world is governed; that is how global problems are handled and how global order and stability can be ensured, in the absence of an overarching central authority or world government to regulate. To understand global governance, the following question need to be asked: What is global? What is governance? In what ways does governance differ from the conventional notions of politics and government? Why do we study global governance today?[3]

The word global usually refers to a situation that goes beyond the international order or the inter-state system. Its use evokes a wide array of actors in world affairs ranging from individuals and social groups to international organizations and others, apart from states, as a major set of actors. What is governance? Perhaps the most authoritative definition of governance comes from a report compiled but the

---

1 Ailun Xiong, Hans Westlund, Hongyi Li, Yonggjian Pu, "Social capital and total factor productivity: evidence from Chinese provinces", in China & World Economy, vol. 25, No. 5, Institute of World Economics and Politics, Chinese Academy of Social Sciences, July-August 2017, p. 22.
2 China's Foreign Affairs, Department of Policy Planning, Ministry of Foreign Affairs, People's Republic of China, Beijing: World Affairs Press, 2013, p. 103.
3 Gerald Chan, Pak K. Lee and Lai-Ha Chan, "Global governance", in China Engages Global Governance; a new world order in the making?, Oxon: Routledge, 2012, p. 9.

commission on global governance, consisting of twenty-six prominent members from around the world, chaired by Ingvar Carlsson a former Swedish prime minister, and Shridath Rampal, a former secretary-general of the British Commonwealth. the report, entitled Our Global Neighborhood, published 1995[1], defines governance in a global context as:

"The sum of the many ways individuals and institutions, public and private, manage their common affairs. It is a continuing process through which conflicting or diverse interests may be accommodated and co-operative action may be taken. It includes formal institutions and regimes empowered to enforce compliance, as well as informal arrangements that people and institutions either have agreed to or perceive to be in their interest".[2]

We need to bear in mind that China can be a problem or it can be the solution, and China may still harbor strong reservations about institutional multilateralism and may not be willing to surrender its sovereign control over rule-making and implementations.[3]

Since the late 1970s China has liberalized most prices, decollectivized agriculture and integrated into world markets. These changes fueled an unprecedented period of growth that increased GDP per capita from $674 in 1978 to $5,086 in 2004.[4] What made this possible? First, some focus on the pre-reform economy's cellular organization. Rather than a specified, nationwide hierarchy, China's economy consisted of parallel, diversified provincial economies. This situation reduced dislocations and stimulated competition when markets were introduced. Second, some believe political decentralization encouraged local reforms' experiments that allowed new ideas to percolate up from the grass roots. Third, some argue

---

1 Ibid, op. cit., p. 9.
2 Ibid, op. cit. p. 9.
3 Ibid, p. 22.
4 Hongbin Cai and Daniel Treisman, "Did government decentralization cause China's economic miracle", in Politics of Modern China, vol. II, ed. by, Yongnian Zheng, Yiyi Lu and Lynn T. White III, London & New York: Routledge, 2010, op. cit, p. 85.

decentralization created political checks on the central authorities, limiting predation and convincing investors that reforms would last. Fourth, some suggest fiscal decentralization gave local officials strong incentives to stimulate economic growth. Finally, some contend decentralization helped harden budget constraints on enterprises, forcing them to restructure.[1]

China's economy as of 1978 was structured in a way particularly conductive to marketization, at least as compared with its northern communist neighbor.[2] In the Soviet Union regional economies were mutually dependent, specialized units that played different roles in the national divisions of labor and were coordinated by central planners.[3] In China, by contrast, provincial economies were most self-sufficient and internally diversified. Fearing military invasion, Mao encouraged local self-sufficiency and devolved much planning and administration to provincial cadres.[4]

Among communist countries, it is true China's economic administration was relatively decentralized after 1978. For the next decade, one could contrast China's successes with the reform failures of the more centralized USSR. However, by late 1989 political decentralization in the Soviet Union had clearly outstripped in China. The Baltic republics were racing toward independence, and by early 1991 Gorbatchev was trying to save the Soviet Union as a loose confederation. After its party free regional elections in 1990, Russia was also more politically decentralized than China, with economic policies diverging in the regions. If decentralized explains why reforms worked better in China than the Soviet Union in 1980s, it cannot explain why China fared better Russia in the 1990s. The opposite should have occurred.[5] Administrative decentralization coincided with reform in the 1980s, in part because decentralization was itself a reform promoted by Deng Xiaoping and

---

1 Ibid, p. 85.
2 Ibid, op. cit., p. 88.
3 Ibid.
4 Ibid, op. cit.
5 Ibid, p. 93.

his supporters, in part because Deng sought to circumvent opposition at the center by empowering his allies in the provinces. but economic reforms continued in the 1990s, accelerating in some areas, despite a shift toward recentralization of control of revenues.[1]

While clearly lagging behind the Eastern bloc countries and the former Soviet Union in political reform, China is arguably the most successful of the socialist states in implementing economic reform.[2] Real GNP grew at an average annual rate of 10.4 percent from 1980 to 1988 compared with only 6.4 percent during 1965-1980; total GNP grew more than twofold between 1978 and 1988.[3] During 1978-88 per capita GNP doubled in real terms.[4] The most impressive strides were in the rural economy. Calculated on the basis of comparable prices, total agricultural output value increased by an average annual rate of 6.04 percent between 1978 and 1990.[5] Output value of rural collective enterprises increased 26.7 percent for that same twelve-year period.[6] Per capita net income among peasants increased from 133.57 to 629.79 Yuan, with an average annual increase of 41.4 Yuan, as compared with only a 3.2 Yuan increase on average for the previous twenty-eight years.[7]

In assessing the literature on China's regional role and strategy, we can identify an evolving narrative that suggests a three stage process: China's approach has moved from being skeptical and conservative in its relations with the region.[8] Towards active engagement in the regional multilateral forums, and on to the current lack of consistency that seems to lead to a perception (at least) that China is becoming more

---

1　Ibid, op. cit., p. 106.
2　Jean C. Oi, "Fiscal reform and the economic foundations of the local state corporatism in China", in Politics of Modern China, vol. II, ed. by, Yongnian Zheng, Yiyi Lu and Lynn T. White III, London & New York: Routledge, 2010, p. 33.
3　Ibid, op. cit.
4　Ibid.
5　Ibid.
6　Ibid.
7　Ibid, op. cit.
8　Catherine Jones and Shaun Breslin, "China in East Asia; confusion on the horizon?", ed. Jamie Gaskarth, Oxon: Routledge, 2015, op. cit., p. 117.

assertive.[1] Although this narrative is presented here as a linear evolution of China's regional engagement, we argue that these three different approaches actually operate simultaneously over time, and across different actors and different situation. Rather, than seeking simplicity and discrete historical epochs, it is the contradictions and complexities that need to be highlighted in order to provide a useful analysis for understanding China's regional engagements.[2]

III. The New China's Foreign Policy

In the Eleventh Party Congress held in August 1977, Chinese leaders still attempted to embrace Mao Zedong's theory of the three worlds. On 1 November 1977, the editorial department of Renmin Ribao (*People's Daily*) published a lengthy article entitled "Chairman Mao's Theory of the differentiation of the Three Worlds is a major contribution to Marxism-Leninism".[3] It reaffirmed that the two superpowers were the common enemy of mankind that the Third World was the main force against imperialism, colonialism and hegemonic, and that the Second World was the force that could be united within the broadest possible international united front against superpower hegemony. The article advocated the exploitation of the contradiction between two superpowers.[4] What was noteworthy was that the article provided for the first time, on a theoretical basis, about why the Soviet Union was more dangerous than the US relations as threat to the world peace.[5]

The idea of Four Modernizations became the most important goal of the Chinese leadership after economic reforms had been launched. The four modernizations are the modernization of agriculture, industry, national defense, and science & technology. It was the grand concept for the development of the Chinese economy advocated by the late Premier Zhou Enlai on the instructions of Chairman Mao at

---

1　Ibid, op. cit.
2　Ibid.
3　Joseph Yu-shek Cheng, China's foreign Policy; challenges and prospects, Singapore: World Scientific Publishing Co., 2016, p. 3.
4　Ibid.
5　Ibid, op. cit., p. 4.

the Third and Fourth NPC held in 1964-1965 and 1975 respectively. The concept was emphatically reaffirmed at the fifth NPC in February to march 1978 and modernization has since been depicted as the main task of the country.[1] In this period, the demand of modernization and improving people's living standards became the most important factor guiding China's foreign policy. In terms of economic reforms, China first tried to learn from Yugoslavia, then from Hungary, and then from the "four little dragons of Asia". The impact of foreign policy was that China had to accept the international economic order whose rules had been defined be the western countries. The Western Countries and Japan, however, were ready to offer China friendly support for its modernization efforts. The independent foreign policy of peace line was able to consolidate.[2]

China's foreign relations were probably back in full swing by 1992-1993. The Chinese government worked hard at building or restoring its perceived rightful place in the world.[3] And the leadership was then in a better position to redefine the world view. With the disintegration of the Soviet Union and the fading away of bipolarity, Chinese leaders believed that a new pattern of international relations was in the process of emerging. But, this power configuration of "one superpower, a number of major powers" was only transitional. Unlike in the 1970's and the 1980's, the Chinese leaders' authoritative statements on foreign policy did not comment on the danger of a world war. Silence on this topic might be construed as treating this as non-pressing issue. Instead, in its view, China should concentrate on the intermediate and long-term completions in building "comprehensive national power", and it should not allow itself to fall behind in this fierce completion.

China's economic success and rising international influence reinforced its acceptance of the existing international organizations, such as the United Nations, World Bank, International Monetary Fund, etc., which it previously considered to be tools of Western imperialist powers; it further expected these organizations to play

---

1 Ibid.
2 Ibid, p. 6.
3 Ibid, op. cit. p. 7.

a more significant role and intended to articulate and promote its interests through them. It became the recipient of most loans from World Bank, US$22.4 billion by the end of June 1995.[1] However, it was still shying away from active leadership in these organizations. In the first place, it considered itself a major power and a developing country, and it had no intention of leading the Third World. Second, it still suffered from lack of seasoned diplomats and international civil servants.[2] China's foreign policy experts, almost without exception, argue that China has to integrate with existing international system un order to realize its peaceful rise. In fact, the more developed China becomes, the greater the need to participate in the international system and its institutions. Peaceful rise implies peaceful competition, i.e., competition according to the rules, although the rules may not be fair to China, and China may not enjoy any role in defining the rules.[3]

The present international system is designed primarily to represent and promote American interests. As China's power grows, together with that of other outsiders like India, the United States will be obliged to adapt the system and its institutions to accommodate their demands and aspirations, but, as demonstrated be the slowness of reform in the IMF and even the G8, there is great reluctance on the part of both US and Europe.[4] As China begins to emerge as a global power, what forms will its growing strength take? Or, to put it another way, what will a globally hegemonic China look like? Over the past two centuries, there have been two globally dominant powers: Britain between 1850 and 1914, and the United States from 1945 to the present.[5]

IV. The Success of China's Economic Reforms

The remarkable success of China's economic reforms - fostering economic

---

1 Ibid, op. cit. p. 9.
2 Ibid, p. 9.
3 Ibid, op. cit., p. 11.
4 Martin Jacques, When China rules the world; the end of the Western world and the birth of a New Global Order, New York: The Penguin Press, 2012, op. cit. p. 360
5 Ibid, pp. 496-497.

growth averaging 9 percent per year over the past fifteen years - seems to defy conventional wisdom.

The decentralization in China differs from Western federalism in several important respects. First, the latter virtually always roots federalism in an explicit system for protecting individual rights. Second, Western federalism typically has strong, explicit constitutional foundations, third, it is almost always associated with political freedom, representation, and democratization.

More recently, the meteoric rise of China has made analysts question whether the United States still retains hegemony. China's economy is now the second largest in the world, and already consumes more energy than the United States. It seems only a matter of time until it is the world's largest economy perhaps prior to 2020. Additionally, unlike Japan and Germany, China's power is not primary economic - it is a nuclear power with a large army and is one of the five permanent members of the UN Security Council.

V. Towards "Belt and Road" Initiative

The Fifteenth Congress of the Chinese Communist Party inaugurated a sweeping reform that has been transforming the ownership of state-owned enterprises (SOEs). Though a term "common ownership" was the official name given to the scheme, it was regarded as a coded reference to privatization. Given the size of China's economy, this is probably the most ambitious privatization plan ever in the world. Bearing in mind that for nearly half a century the Chinese economy has remained based on the dominance of the state sector, it is understandable that the scheme had a shocking psychological effect at home and abroad the moment it was officially declared. For some people, China's privatization foretold a crusade.[1]

Let's make the question: why China ultimately more important than Brazil?

---

1 Qingjiang Kong, "Quest for constitutional justification; privatization with Chinese characteristics", in Politics of Modern China, vol. II, ed. by, Yongnian Zheng, Yiyi Lu and Lynn T. White III, London & New York: Routledge, 2010, p. 144.

Because of geographical location: even supposing the same level of economic growth as China and a population of equal size, Brazil does not command the main sea lines of communication connecting oceans and continents as China does; nor does it mainly lie in the temperate zone like China, with a more disease-free and invigorating climate. China fronts the Western Pacific and has depth on land reaching to oil-and natural-gas-rich Central Asia. Brazil offers less of a comparative advantage. It lies isolated in South America, geographically removed from other landmasses.[1] China has invested over $25 billion in Central Asia. It is paying for a two-thousand-mile highway across Kazakhstan. There are daily flights between the Kazakh city of Almaty and the western Chinese city of Urumqi, and Chinese goods fill Central Asian markets.[2]

The fact that China is blessed by geography is something so basic and obvious that it tends to be overlooked in all the discussions about its economic dynamism and national assertiveness over recent decades.[3]

In Central Asia, as in eastern Siberia, China competes fiercely with Russia for a sphere of influence. Trade between China and former Soviet Central Asia has risen from 527 million $ in 1992 to 25.9 billion $ in 2009.[4] But the means of Beijing's sway will for the moment be two major pipelines, one carrying oil from the Caspian Sea across Kazakhstan to Xinjiang, and the other transportation natural gas from the Turkmenistan-Uzbekistan border, across Uzbekistan and Kazakhstan to Xinjiang. Again, no troops will be necessary as Greater China extends into Mackinder's Eurasian heartland, the upshot of an insatiable demand for energy and the internal danger posed by its own ethnic minorities.[5] China is using all forms of its national power - political, diplomatic, economic, commercial, military, and demographic - to expand virtually beyond its legal land and sea borders in order to encompass the

---

1 Robert Kaplan, The revenge of geography; what the map tells us about coming conflicts and the battle against fate, New York: Random House, 2013, op.cit., p. 31.
2 Ibid, op. cit., p. 184.
3 Ibid, p. 189.
4 Ibid, op. cit., p. 205.
5 Ibid.

borders of imperial China at its historic high points.[1]

China is one of the oldest civilizations worldwide, with a written history dating over 4,000 years. Engineering feats include the Three Gorges Dam, the Great Wall of China, and the Terracotta Warriors. China is the birthplace of gunpowder, the compass, papermaking, and printing.[2] According to one Chinese investor and executive who serves on the board of several Fortune 500 companies, where power and authority reside depends on whether it is a state-owned enterprise (SOE), joint venture, wholly-owned company, or private company.[3] Since 1978, China has gradually reduced the number of SOEs, down from over 75 % of China's industrial output thirty years ago to 46% today.[4] In many respects, studying China's political economy in the pre-reform era was much simpler than it is today. To be sure, China was never a purely totalitarian state, and analysts have spent considerable time and effort trying to find the real locus of power, with particular emphasis on elite factionalism, the role of the military, and the power of provincial leaders. And of course, China's leaders always had relations with the superpowers in mind when defining domestic development strategies. Nevertheless, the increasingly autarkic nature of Chinese politics made it possible to study China's political economy almost entirely in domestic terms.[5]

In many respects, it was only in 1993 that China began to emerge as a global trading power. From 1993, exports increased by 60 percent in two years (53 percent in real terms), and doubled in the space of five years.[6] In the process, a US$12.2 billion trade deficit in 1993 was transformed into a US$5.4 billion surplus the

---

1　Ibid, p. 221.
2　Sharon Schweitzer & Liz Alexander, "Access to Asia, your multicultural guide to building trust, inspiring respect, and creating long-lasting business relationship", New Jersey: John Wiley & Sons, 2016, op. cit., p. 68.
3　Ibid, p. 86.
4　Ibid, op. cit.
5　Shaun Breslin, "Globalization, international coalitions and domestic reform", in Politics of Modern China, vol. II, ed. by Yongnian Zheng, Yiyi Lu and Lynn T. White III, London & New York: Routledge, 2010, p. 202.
6　Ibid, op. cit., p. 207.

following year, with the trade surplus rising to US$40.3 billion in 1997.[1] The rapid growth of China as a global exporter - and in particular, the size of the Chinese trade surplus with the United States and other developed states - has perhaps inevitably brought external pressure for China to reform its dualistic structure and to behave by "fairer" international rules.[2] In joining WTO in 2001, Chinese authorities agreed to give up many of the mechanisms that had been used to protect domestic actors in previous years. Among the countries within the EU that China has more economic relations is beyond any doubt Germany with 47% of the whole package of China's relations in Europe.[3] This is a clear index that China aims to compete with the most important countries in the world.

VI. "Belt and Road" Initiative

Belt and Road initiative was initiated as an process on September 7th 2013, from President Xi Jinping's speech made during a visit in Kazakhstan, at the Nazarbayev University.[4] The main theme of the speech was the aim to strengthen the Eurasian relations through economic cooperation. The Belt and Road initiative is totally a Chinese initiative. But what essentially is Belt and Road initiative? During the classes in the China Studies program in September 2017, this initiative as is in its beginnings upholds five principles which are:

Mutual respects; Mutual-nonaggression; Mutual non-interference; Equality and mutual benefit; Peaceful coexistence.[5]

---

1 Ibid, op. cit., p. 207.
2 Ibid, p. 210.
3 Kjeld Erik Brødsgaard, "China and the EU; will China come to the rescue of troubled economies?, in China: Development and Governance, ed. by, Wang Gungwu & Zheng Yongnian, Singapore: World Scientific Publishing Co., 2013, p. 458.
4 Liudmila Bialkovich, "China-Belarus relations based on cross-cultural communication", in A Collection of Research Papers of the Visiting Program for Young Sinologists 2016, China Studies, Beijing, 2016, p. 47.
5 Nadia Helmy, "The Role of Arab and foreign students in China in disseminating the Political Culture for Chinese B&R initiative", in A Collection of Research Papers of the Visiting Program for Young Sinologists 2016, China Studies, Beijing, 2016, p. 112.

During the talking's in the VPYS program in the Chinese Academy of Social Sciences, B&R initiative is also based on five fields:

Political Coordination; Infrastructure connectivity; Enhanced trade; Currency support (exchange); People's exchange, cultural diplomacy.

China has a global economy recover plan. This plan starts with China. From 2012 to 2020, China would conclude the process of its society modernization and the enforcement of middle class structure. But to take on the world, requires to face big challenges. With the conversation I've made with the Department of International Politics Theory and with the Department of International Strategy in CASS, China to fulfill this strategy, has the power to act but not the power to attack. Based on this vision, China's Belt and Road initiative is totally a peaceful strategy to improve the relations among the peoples of the world. The goal is to peacefully connect, Asia, Europe and Africa based on economic initiative. As the world economy is slowly recovering the Belt and Road initiative if it succeeds, would cover a population of nearly 4.6 billion which is more than 60% of the world's population, and would a have a total GDP of $20 trillion, about 1/3 of the global GDP.[1]

International cooperation on production capacity against the background of the Belt and Road initiative is a based on a new philosophy of development. The Chinese president Xi Jinping, during the presentation of this initiative also spoke about five "determinations" of the G20 parties to introduce consensus during the Hangzhou Summit. These determinations were to:

1. Be determined to identify the direction of the world's economy and plan routes;
2. Be determined to innovate the manner of growth so as to inject new impetus into world's economy;
3. Be determined to improve the global economy and economic governance so as to enhance the capability of the world's economy for withstanding risks;

---

[1] Tian Feng, "China's role and international cooperation on production capacity under background of the Belt and Road initiative", in The Collection of Work at the Symposium on China studies 2016, Beijing, p. 383.

4. Be determined to re-invigorate two engines, which are international trade and investment, so as to build and open world economy;

5. Be determined to promote inclusive and interdependent development, and render the cooperation achievements made by the G20 beneficial to the whole world.[1]

For some scholars, Belt and Road initiative is a response to Western globalization to build a better world.[2] With the rise of China and the relative decline of the US's global dominance, the competition between China and the US has intensified. Despite the interdependence and the hope for arriving at a win-win situation instead of a zero-sum game, historical experiences show that competition among major countries can easily be affected by irrational factors, with unexpected and even adverse results. According to Western theories and experiences of international relations, rising powers often challenge established ones, and the latter often fear and take precautions against the former, leading to a situation known as the Thucydides trap, a term coined by a Greek historian.[3] If we see what happened in ancient times between Sparta and Athens, or a century ago between England and Germany, is well hoped to avoid a clash between China and USA.

In general, Chinese statesmanship has a tendency to view the entire strategic landscape as a part of a single whole.[4] With this distinction China enters the XXI century as a country claiming global relevance for the proper culture and institutions with the culture and world institutions. The Belt and Road initiative confirms this.

VII. Conclusion

What will be the characteristics of China's success following Belt and Road

---

1 Ibid, pp. 388-389.
2 Martin Albrow, "Philosophical social science as a bridge from" Belt and Road "to global governance", in The Collection of Work at the Symposium on china studies 2016, Beijing, p. 11.
3 Yongnian Zheng, "The 'Belt and Road' initiative: China's grand diplomacy", in The Collection of Works at the Symposium on China studies 2016, Beijing, p.37.
4 Henry Kissinger, On China, London: Allen Lane 2011, p. 31.

initiative? There are seven characteristics that I would like to collocate in this paper which I learned during my China studies in September 2017:

1. China describes itself a nation-state, but in true is a civilization-state

2. China in its relations in Asia and not only there, tends to promote itself as the fulcrum of the future world's economy;

3. China's attitude towards the world is shown peaceful;

4. China is more than a state within a continent; China represents the good part of the Asian continent;

5. China's policy is very much specific; it's a highly competent institution represented by a strong party leadership since 1949;

6. The modernity in China is matched by the speed of the country's industrialization;

7. China's regime since 1949 is stable and concrete. In other words, was promoted "Socialism with Chinese characteristics".

The last characteristic was also affirmed and confirmed by the 19th Party Congress which was held in Beijing in October 18-25, 2017.[1] In the report he delivered at the opening of the 19th National Congress of the Communist Party of China, Xi Jinping, the general secretary of the CPC Central Committee, announced that socialism with Chinese characteristics has entered a new era.

It is an era that is not only of tremendous importance to China but also to the world. For it is an era that, as President Xi Jinping pointed out, is not only full of hope but also full of challenges, which no country alone can tackle. Hence his call for countries to work together to build a community of shared future for all mankind.[2] President Xi said China will work with other nations to build a global community with a shared future, and make new and greater contributions to the noble cause of peace and development for all humanity.[3]

1　China Daily, 25/10/2017. www.chinadaily.com.
2　Ibid.
3　Xinhua, 25/10/2017.

南亚各国对中国"一带一路"倡议的态度及其原因浅析

萨尔波塔姆·什雷斯塔 【尼泊尔】
尼泊尔阿尼哥协会主席、临床神经内科医生

2013年9月7日和10月2日中国国家主席习近平分别在哈萨克斯坦纳扎尔巴耶夫大学和印度尼西亚国会大厦演讲时提出共同建设"丝绸之路经济带"和"21世纪海上丝绸之路"的战略构想,之后全球多个国家作出不同的回应。南亚国家在不同时期也作出不同的回应。

一 南亚各国对"一带一路"倡议的态度

印度: 印度领导人对"一带一路"倡议的态度和回应是混合型的,在有利于印度自身的合作项目上印度并没有断然拒绝。比如印度在加入亚洲基本设施建设投资银行(亚投行)方面表现非常积极。在中国还没有正式提出"一带一路"倡议之前,2013年5月19日李克强总理访问印度时,提出了与印度、孟加拉国和缅甸共同建设"印中孟缅经济走廊"的倡议,并得到印度的赞同。2014年9月习近平对印度进行国事访问时,虽然印度总理莫迪对"印中孟缅经济走廊"做出积极回应,但印度领导人并没有明确表示积极支持"一带一路"倡议,而是在2014年提出了"季风""香料之路"等自己的计划。

巴基斯坦: 巴基斯坦是南亚甚至全球国家中对"一带一路"倡议态度最积极、合作愿望最真诚的一个。2013年9月24日中方领导第一次就"一带一路"的相关事宜与巴基斯坦领导举行会谈以后,在两年的时间内两国高层领导人对此进行了近 15 次会谈，每次会谈都有一些新的内容。巴基斯坦领导人表示支持中国提出的"一带一路"倡议，支持亚投行和丝路基金。中国与巴基斯坦的合作从共同建设中巴经济走廊提升到打造中巴命运共同体。

孟加拉国： 2014 年 6 月 9 日孟加拉国总理哈西娜访华时表示孟加拉国将积极参与"一带一路"与"孟中印缅经济走廊"建设。在此之后，孟加拉国高层领导人与中国国家领导人又进行过四五次会谈，每次会谈孟加拉国领导都表示了对"一带一路"倡议和"孟中印缅经济走廊"建设的支持。但不像巴基斯坦，孟加拉国与中国的合作内容没有增加，合作也没有升级。

阿富汗： 阿富汗领导人对中国提出的"一带一路"倡议具有浓厚的兴趣，认为倡议对阿富汗至关重要，甚至认为"一带一路"倡议能够拯救阿富汗。所以 2014 年 10 月 28 日阿富汗总统加尼访华时，在北京明确表示愿意积极参与丝绸之路经济带建设，加强双方在油气、矿产、基础设施建设和民生等领域的合作。

尼泊尔： 中国正式出台"一带一路"倡议后一年的时间内，尼泊尔对此没有做出任何回应，尼泊尔国内媒体上也没有出现过任何相关的报道或新闻。2015 年 3 月中国国家主席会见来华参加博鳌论坛的尼泊尔总统亚达夫，当时总统亚达夫表示尼泊尔坚定地支持"一带一路"倡议和"亚投行"建设。与此同时，尼泊尔驻华大使在接受采访时也表示尼泊尔应该支持"一带一路"倡议，但是尼泊尔政府一直没有正式表态，媒体上仍然没有出现有关报道或文章。直到 2017 年初尼泊尔才开始了解"一带一路"倡议，当地媒体也开始介绍"一带一路"。2017 年 5 月尼泊尔政府表示愿意参与"一带一路"建设，并与中国签署了"一带一路"框架协议。

斯里兰卡： 斯里兰卡是对"一带一路"倡议很早就表示其支持态度的一个南亚国家。2014 年 2 月 11 日，斯里兰卡总统特使、外长佩里斯表示支持"21 世纪海上丝绸之路"，时任斯里兰卡总统拉贾帕克萨也一直对"一带一路"倡议表示支持，而且斯里兰卡是首个以政府声明的形式支持中国"一带一路"倡议的国家。2015 年 3 月，斯里兰卡新政府上台，中国和斯里兰卡关系受挫，科伦坡港口城项目被停止，但新政府仍然表示支持"21 世纪海上丝绸之路"的建设。

马尔代夫： 2014 年 8 月和 9 月，马尔代夫与中国国家主席分别在中国和马尔代夫举行会谈时都表示愿意积极响应中国"21 世纪海上丝绸之路"的建设倡议。

不丹：不丹至今没有直接对"一带一路"倡议做出过任何回应，但不丹总理策林托杰于 2015 年 7 月 31 日表示，现阶段不丹没有加入亚投行的必要，因为不丹第 11 个五年计划建设所需资金已经筹备齐全。

二 南亚各国对"一带一路"倡议回应之浅析

从以上的描述不难看出南亚各国对"一带一路"的回应和态度非常不同。其中有回应和行动都非常积极的巴基斯坦，有始终都不做回应的不丹，也有对"一带一路"的某些部分表示反对的印度。其余几个政治上表示支持但又没有实际行动或项目的国家，情况也不尽相同。

南亚也被称为印度次大陆，从这个名称就不难看出印度在南亚的地位。南亚北接中亚，衔接丝绸之路经济带的主要国家，东面与中国和东南亚为邻，西面是西亚和整个中东地区，南面通过浩瀚的印度洋与包括非洲海岸在内的"21 世纪海上丝绸之路"沿线国家遥相呼应，可以说南亚是中国"一带一路"倡议相当关键的地区。

印度是南亚最大国，也是唯一的大国。印度比南亚其他任何国家在国土面积和人口方面都大至少四倍。南亚其他国家跟印度有着不可忽略的关系，但其他国家之间的往来又不多。这是南亚国际关系的基本状态。

中国虽然不是南亚国家，但跟南亚的多个国家拥有共同边界，是比较关注南亚的一个大国，同时中国也是南亚联盟的观察国。中国跟其南亚邻国的关系不尽相同。中国和印度存在着边境问题，1962 年为此发生了中印战争。除了边境问题，中国和印度在一些国际问题上也存在分歧。印度认为南亚是它的影响范围，害怕中国在南亚的势力扩张，担心中国跟印度周边的南亚国家之间的合作加强而包围自己。近些年来，中国与印度之间的贸易总额虽然大幅度增长，两国之间的交往也比过去频繁，但两国之间的外交关系并没有真正地改善。其主要原因是，印度认为，中国在国际舞台上的地位虽然明显提高，而且中国开始宣讲自己是一个"负责任的大国"，但中国在南亚地区的角色并没有随之改变，依然按照过去的"传统友好"模式只跟印度的敌国巴基斯坦合作，忽略了比巴基斯坦大几十倍的贸易伙伴国印度。

南亚各国对中国提出的"一带一路"倡议的回应主要由两个因素决定：第一是这个国家跟印度的关系；第二是自己国家的内部安全和发展等状况。

巴基斯坦跟印度的关系自两个国家独立之时就一直剑拔弩张，曾因边境问题发生过三次战争，目前仍然存在着宗教、领土争端和核武器等问题，两国边境上仍经常发生摩擦。所以巴基斯坦对"一带一路"倡议支持的热诚除了抓住这个难得的机会发展自己国家的经济以外，还有进一步接近中国以平衡与印度的关系的意图。

印度为孟加拉国的独立战争做了贡献，认为自己是孟加拉国的"解放者"。尽管如此，孟加拉国和印度的关系并不算很好，两国之间存在着恒河水资源分配、边界管理、难民问题等方面的问题。孟加拉国虽然只有印度一个邻国，但它拥有自己的海岸线，并非内陆国家。孟加拉国对"一带一路"倡议的支持态度主要是为了给自己国家寻求经济发展的机会，对平衡来自印度的压力这一面的考虑比较次要。但孟加拉国海上和陆地上的地理位置完全被印度包围，所以在"孟中印缅经济走廊"建设中，印度的消极表现无法让孟加拉国更好地参与"一带一路"建设。

马尔代夫的情况与孟加拉国有些相似。印度曾经派兵干涉马尔代夫的内政，扮演着马尔代夫国家"保护者"的角色。马尔代夫为自己国家的经济发展表示支持"一带一路"倡议，积极参与"21世纪海上丝绸之路"的建设，但因为其地理位置等因素也未能开展大型项目。

阿富汗跟印度的关系可以说是"若即若离"，印度对阿富汗局势的影响力非常有限，阿富汗也没有需要去依附印度的地缘政治压力。阿富汗是为了自己国家的经济建设对"一带一路"倡议表示出浓厚的兴趣，但因为阿富汗国内的安全等因素而没有在"一带一路"下开展大型项目。

尼泊尔的情况比较特殊。大多数尼泊尔人在民族、语言、宗教、文化传统等方面跟印度比较接近，所以对印度有种亲近感，尼泊尔南方一些民族不少人跟印度人有联姻关系。尽管如此，因为印度对尼泊尔政治的干涉、对尼泊尔主流媒体的控制、为控制尼泊尔水资源而施加的各种压力等，导致尼泊尔人反印度情绪比较高。因为尼泊尔主流媒体在印度的控制之下，所以媒体上很难看到尼泊尔人的反印度报道。虽然尼泊尔是一个民主国家，每届政府都是通过民主投票产生，但印度在尼泊尔新政府的产生过程中往往能够起到很重要的作用，所以无论哪个政党执政都不会轻易做出可能导致印度不高兴的事情来，这给一些学者造成了尼泊尔是一个完全依附于印度的国家的错觉，一些学者甚至把尼泊尔与印度的关系同不丹与印度的关系之间画等号。实际上尼泊尔人民是希望跟自己的两个邻国保持同等距离来发展自己的外交关系，只是在印度的强大压力下，尼泊尔往往无法抵挡。但是印度的压力越大，尼泊尔人民的反印情绪越强。尼泊尔对"一带一路"倡议迟缓的回应主要是因为初期宣传很少，除了一些对华友好组织的有限宣传外，尼泊尔媒体没有做过任何有关报道。后来尼泊尔一旦了解到"一带一路"倡议的意义，"一带一路"很快就成为尼泊尔知识分子和政客们的主要话题，于是尼泊尔顶着印度的压力在很短的时间内下定决心签署了"一带一路"框架性协议。尼泊尔的确会通过接近中国、加强跟中国的合作来平衡来自印度的压力，印度把这种现象称之为"玩中国牌"。

不丹是个特殊的国家，它不仅面积小、人口少，而且已经失去自己的国防和外交权，由印度负责其国家安全和外交。不丹跟中国没有建交。中国政府出台"一带一路"倡议后，不丹一直没有做出任何回应，对此很多学者认为不丹有参加"一带一路"建设的意愿，只是迫于印度的压力而没有参与。但是根据不丹国家的状况，它没有对中国的"一带一路"倡议做出回应，其主要不是因为印度，不丹内部似乎都没有对此问题进行过讨论，因为"一带一路"是发展之路、建设之路，而不丹仍然是把非工业化、宗教生活和原始愚昧看作是幸福的一个国家。

三　结论

南亚国家与印度的关系在该国对"一带一路"倡议的态度和回应方面起到了非常重要的作用，跟印度关系越紧张对倡议的态度越积极，巴基斯坦和近期尼泊尔的表现可以证实这一点。

南亚国家对经济建设的渴望程度也影响着该国对倡议的态度和回应，阿富汗和不丹的表现可以证实这一点。

参考文献

1. 孙红旗:《"一带一路"战略构思与南亚国际关系的重构》,《江苏师范大学学报》(哲学社会科学版),2016年第1期。
2. 杨思灵:《一带一路:南亚地区国家间关系分析视角》,《印度洋经济体研究》,2015年第5期。
3. 杜幼康:《"一带一路"与南亚地区国际合作前瞻》,《学术前沿》2017年4月下。

4. 王欢欢、李忠林：《"一带一路"视野下的中国—南亚区域合作进展及挑战》《求是》，2016 年第 2 期。

5. [新加坡] 赵洪：《中国的"一带一路"倡议：争论综述》，《边界与海洋研究》，2016 年第 11 期。

The South Asian Countries' Attitude to Chinese the "Belt and Road" Initiative and Reason Analysis

Sarbottam Shrestha / Nepal

Chairman of the Argentinean Association, Clinical Neurologist, Nepal

On September 7 and October 2, 2013, Chinese President Xi Jinping proposed the initiative — "Silk Road Economic Belt" and the "21st Century Maritime Silk Road" during his speeches at the Nazarbayev University in Kazakhstan and the Indonesian Capitol. Soon afterwards, countries around the world responded differently. The countries of Southern Asia also made different responses at different times.

I. The Attitude of Countries in Southern Asia to the "Belt and Road" Initiative

India: Indian leaders present mixed attitudes and responses to the "Belt and Road" Initiative, and do not categorically reject the cooperation projects favorable for India. For example, India has been very active in joining the Asian Infrastructure Investment Bank (AIIB). Before China officially proposed the "Belt and Road" Initiative, Premier Li Keqiang proposed the initiative to build the "Bangladesh-China-India-Myanmar Economic Corridor" jointly with India, Bangladesh and Myanmar during his visit to India on May 19, 2013, which was much agreed to by India. Although Indian Prime Minister Modi responded positively to the "Bangladesh-China-India-Myanmar Economic Corridor" during the state visit to India by Xi Jinping in September 2014, the Indian leaders did not explicitly express their active support for the "Belt and Road" Initiative but, on the contrary, they put forward their own plans, such as "Monsoon" and the "Spice Road" in 2014.

Pakistan: Pakistan holds the most active and sincere attitude towards the "Belt and Road" Initiative in Southern Asia and even all over the world. Since the Chinese leaders held talks with the Pakistani leaders on the "Belt and Road" Initiative for the first time on September 24, 2013, senior leaders of the two countries conducted nearly 15 talks during the two years, talking about different contents in each talk. Pakistani leaders expressed their support for the "Belt and Road" Initiative proposed by China, as well as the AIIB and the Silk Road Fund. The cooperation between China and Pakistan has been expanded from the joint construction of the China-Pakistan Economic Corridor to the establishment of a China-Pakistan community with a shared future common destiny.

Bangladesh: During his visit to China on June 9, 2014, Hasina, the Prime Minister of Bangladesh, stated that Bangladesh would actively participate in the construction of the "Belt and Road" Initiative and the Bangladesh-China-India-Myanmar Economic Corridor. Afterwards, senior leaders of Bangladesh and China held four or five more talks. In each talk, Bangladeshi leaders expressed their support for the "Belt and Road" Initiative and the construction of the Bangladesh-China-India-Myanmar Economic Corridor. Unfortunately, unlike Pakistan, the cooperation between Bangladesh and China has neither been increased in content nor upgraded in nature.

Afghanistan: The Afghan leaders have a keen interest in the "Belt and Road" Initiative proposed by China, and they believe that the initiative is of paramount importance to Afghanistan and it could even save Afghanistan. During his visit to China on October 28, 2014, Afghan President Ghani made it clear in Beijing that he was willing to actively participate in the construction of the Silk Road Economic Belt to strengthen the cooperation of both sides on oil and gas, minerals, the construction of infrastructure and people's livelihood.

Nepal: Nepal has not yet made any response, and it has been one year after China officially launched the "Belt and Road" Initiative. Besides, there have been no reports or news in Nepal's domestic media. In March 2015, the Chinese President met with Nepalese President Yadav who had come to China to attend the Boao Forum for Asia. At that time, President Yadav declared that Nepal would firmly support the "Belt and Road" Initiative and the construction of the "Asian Infrastructure Investment Bank". At the same time, the Nepali ambassador to China also said during an interview, that Nepal should support the "Belt and Road" Initiative. However, the Nepalese government had not stated its stand clearly, and no reports or articles had been released in the media until Nepal began to understand the "Belt and Road" Initiative; local media began to introduce the Initiative in early 2017. In May 2017, the Nepalese government expressed its willingness to participate in the "Belt and Road" Initiative and signed a framework agreement for the "Belt and Road" Initiative with China.

Sri Lanka: Sri Lanka is a South Asian country that has early expressed its supportive attitude to the "Belt and Road" Initiative. On February 11, 2014, Peiris, the Special Envoy of Sri Lanka's President and Foreign Minister, expressed support for the 21st-Century Maritime Silk Road. Rajapaksa, then the Sri Lankan President, also expressed support for the "Belt and Road" Initiative. Sri Lanka is the first country that has expressed its support for China's "Belt and Road" Initiative in the form of a government statement. When the new Sri Lankan government came to power in March 2015, the relations between China and Sri Lanka were tense, and the port city project of Colombo was stopped. However, the new administration expressed again its support for the construction of the 21st-Century Maritime Silk Road.

Maldives: In August and September 2014, the Maldives and Chinese Presidents expressed their willingness to respond positively to China's initiative of the 21st-Century Maritime Silk Road when they held talks in China and in the Maldives.

Bhutan: Bhutan has not made any direct response to the "Belt and Road" Initiative. However, Clintonjee, the Prime Minister of Bhutan, on July 31, 2015 said that Bhutan did not have the need to join the AIIB at that stage, because the funds required for the construction of the 11th five-year plan had not been fully prepared.

II. Analysis of the Response of the Countries of Southern Asia to the "Belt and Road" Initiative

It is not difficult to see from the foregoing information that the countries of Southern Asia have very different responses and attitudes towards the "Belt and Road" Initiative. Pakistan has responded and acted very positively, Bhutan has never responded, and India has expressed opposition to certain parts of the "Belt and Road" Initiative. The remaining countries have expressed support politically, but they have not engaged in practical actions or projects. The situation is varied from country to country.

Southern Asia is also known as the Indian subcontinent, revealing the important position of India in Southern Asia. Southern Asia is bordered by Central Asia in the north to connect the main countries of the Silk Road Economic Belt. Besides, it is bordered by China and Southeast Asia to the east, and West Asia and the entire Middle East to the west. Through the vast Indian Ocean to the south, it faces the countries along the 21st Century Maritime Silk Road, including the African coast. It can be said that Southern Asia is a critical area for China's "Belt and Road" Initiative.

India is the largest country and the only great power in Southern Asia. India is at least four times larger in both land area and population than any other country in Southern Asia. Other countries in Southern Asia have a non-negligible relationship with India. However, India does not have many exchanges with other countries.

This is the basic status of South Asian international relations.

Although China is not a country of Southern Asia, it has a common border with many countries of Southern Asia. China is a big country that cares more about Southern Asia, as well as an observer of the South Asian Alliance. China's relations with its South Asian neighbors are varied. Border issues exist between China and India. In 1962, the Sino-Indian War broke out. Apart from the border issue, China and India also have controversies on some international issues. India believes that Southern Asia is in its sphere of influence, and fears the expansion of China's power in Southern Asia, and worries that China's cooperation with the South Asian countries surrounding India is strengthened in order to surround India. Though the total volume of trade between China and India has increased substantially in recent years, and the exchanges between the two countries have also been more frequent than in the past, the diplomatic relations between the two countries have not really improved. It is mainly because of the fact that India believes that although China has improved its position on the international stage and preached itself as a "responsible big country," China has not changed its role in Southern Asia and still follows the past "traditional friendship" model to cooperate only with Pakistan, an enemy country to India, neglecting India, a country that is a trading partner which is dozens of times larger than Pakistan.

The response of South Asian countries to China's "Belt and Road" Initiative mainly depends on two factors, namely, one country's relationship with India, and its internal security and development.

The relations between Pakistan and India have maintained a state of tension since the independence of the two countries. Three wars took place because of the border issue. Now, conflicts still exist in terms of religion, territorial disputes and nuclear weapons. Friction at the border between the two countries is still frequent. Therefore, Pakistan's enthusiasm for supporting the "Belt and Road" Initiative is not only aimed at developing its national economy by taking advantage of the rare opportunity, but it is also aimed at trying to further approach China so as to balance its relations with India.

Due to the contribution to the war of independence in Bangladesh, India considers itself to be the "liberator" of Bangladesh. Despite this, the relations between Bangladesh and India are not good. There are conflicts in the distribution of water resources in the Ganges, border management, and refugee issues between the two countries. Although India is the only neighboring country of Bangladesh, Bangladesh is not a landlocked country because of its own coastline. Bangladesh's support for the "Belt and Road" Initiative is mainly to seek opportunities for its own economic development, followed by the mitigation of the pressure from India. However, Bangladesh is completely surrounded by India on the sea and on land in terms of its geographical location. Therefore, the negative performance of India in the construction of the Bangladesh-China-India-Myanmar Economic Corridor makes it impossible for Bangladesh to participate to its best in the "Belt and Road" Initiative.

The situation in the Maldives is somewhat similar to that in Bangladesh. India sent troops to interfere in the internal affairs of the Maldives and played the role of "protector" of the Maldives. The Maldives expressed support for the "Belt and Road" Initiative for its own economic development and actively participated in the construction of the 21st Century Maritime Silk Road. However, due to its geographical location and other factors, the Maldives has not been able to carry out large-scale projects.

The relations between Afghanistan and India can be said to be "neither friendly nor aloof". India has a very limited influence on the situation in Afghanistan, and Afghanistan has no need to rely on India's geopolitical pressure. Afghanistan also expressed strong interest in the "Belt and Road" Initiative for its own national economic construction. However, due to factors such as security, Afghanistan has not carried out large-scale projects under the "Belt and Road" Initiative.

Nepal has a relatively special situation. Most Nepalese people are closer to India in terms of ethnicity, language, religion, and cultural traditions, so that they have a sense of intimacy with India. Moreover, many people in southern Nepal have a marriage relationship with Indians. Despite this, the anti-Indian sentiment of the Nepalese people remains relatively high due to India's interference in Nepal's politics, control over Nepal's mainstream media and various pressures placed on the control of Nepal's water resources. Because the mainstream Nepali media are under the control of India, it is very difficult to see anti-Indian reports in Nepalese media. Although Nepal is a democracy, every administration is created through democratic voting, but India often plays a critical role in the process of the generation of the new administration in Nepal. As a result, no matter which political party is in power, it is less likely for it to take any action that could possibly provoke India. This causes some scholars to create the illusion that Nepal is a country totally dependent on India. Some scholars even consider the relationship between Nepal and India equivalent to the relationship between Bhutan and India. As a matter of fact, the Nepalese people hope to develop their own diplomatic relations by keeping the same distance with their two neighboring countries. Unfortunately, Nepal always remains susceptible under the pressure of India. However, the greater the pressure on India is, the stronger the anti-Indian sentiment of the Nepali people becomes. The slow response of Nepal to the "Belt and Road" Initiative was mainly due to the little publicity at the initial stage. The Nepali media did not make any reports, except the limited publicity by some friendly organizations towards China. Later, once Nepal understood the significance of the "Belt and Road" Initiative, the Initiative quickly became a major topic for Nepal's intellectuals and politicians. Therefore, with pressure from India, Nepal decided in a short time to sign the framework agreement for the "Belt and Road" Initiative. As a result, Nepal indeed balances the pressure from India by approaching China and strengthening cooperation with China. India calls the phenomenon as "playing the China card".

Bhutan is a special country, with a small area and a small population. It has lost its own defense and diplomatic rights. India is responsible for Bhutan's national security and diplomacy. Bhutan has not established diplomatic relations with China. After the Chinese government introduced the "Belt and Road" Initiative, Bhutan has not yet made any response. For this reason, many scholars believe that Bhutan has the willingness to participate in the "Belt and Road" Initiative, but it fails to do so only due to pressure from India. However, according to the present situation in Bhutan, the failure of response to China's "Belt and Road" Initiative is not mainly attributable to India. Bhutan has not discussed this issue internally. The "Belt and Road" Initiative is a road of development and a road of construction. However, Bhutan still regards non-industrialization, religious life, and primitive ignorance as criteria that will lead to well-being.

III. Conclusions

For South Asian countries, the relationship with India plays a very important role in the attitude and response to the "Belt and Road" Initiative. A more nervous relationship with India leads to a more active attitude towards the Initiative, which can be proved by the recent reaction of Pakistan and Nepal.

For South Asian countries, the eagerness for economic construction also affects the attitude and response to the Initiative, which can be proved by the conduct of Afghanistan and Bhutan regarding the Initiative.

论文化遗产在"一带一路"构建中的作用[1]

魏骏骁　【德国】
德国考古研究院欧亚考古研究所博士

　　在"一带一路"国际合作高峰论坛即将召开之前，新华社、孔子学院总部和国务院国资委联合编撰出版了《"一带一路"100个全球故事》丛书[2]。该丛书以七种语言通过一百个故事来展现2013年提出的"一带一路"倡议以来对沿线国家的影响。其中一篇介绍的是中国与乌兹别克斯坦两项考古发掘合作项目之一——撒马尔罕古代月氏人墓葬的发掘，文章写道："文化交流是人类文明发展的重要动力，乌兹别克和中国人民由于古代丝绸之路相知了，新丝绸之路无疑将两个老朋友重聚在一起。"[3] 实际上，自古以来，陆路和海上丝绸之路对欧亚大陆政治、文化和经济交流的影响就意义深远，两千多年后，"一带一路"的构建将续写这一历史的辉煌。本文通过对《2018欧洲文化遗产年》项目以及欧盟其他相关文化项目的对比研究，梳理中国近期国际考古合作项目，尝试讨论中国文化遗产在当下"一带一路"建设中所扮演的角色。

一　"一带一路"倡议与古代丝绸之路

　　习近平在发出"一带一路"倡议时，重点提到了两千一百多年前，汉代的张

---

[1] 在此非常感谢郑州大学考古系徐玲教授给出的指导和宝贵意见。
[2] 新华通讯社、国务院国资委、孔子学院总部：《"一带一路"100个全球故事》，新华出版社2017年版。
[3] 《千年丝路上的新交流》，同上书，新华出版社2017年版，第97—100页。

骞肩负和平友好使命，两次出使中亚，开启了中国同中亚各国友好交往的大门，开辟出一条横贯东西、连接欧亚的丝绸之路。指出："两千多年的交往历史证明，只要坚持团结互信、平等互利、包容互鉴、合作共赢，不同种族、不同信仰、不同文化背景的国家完全可以共享和平，共同发展。为了加强经济关系，深化合作而共同建设好丝绸之路经济带，人民之间的频繁交流，互相的了解和友谊是必要的，因此需要进一步地巩固加强"[1]。表明"一带一路"倡议是在古代丝绸之路的精神感召下的一种创新。该倡议被描述为"中国到目前为止提出最重大而影响最深远的倡议"[2]。它呼吁通过在未来数十年进行的基础设施建设，文化交流的促进和贸易的扩展使一带一路沿线国家融合成为一个有凝聚力的经济区。

实际上，类似的跨国倡议或者项目同样也可以在全世界各地找到。比如欧洲联盟《欧洲文化线路》标识项目[3]。这个标识是欧洲理事会授予那些促进欧洲共享文化、历史、纪念和一体化的文化线路。这些线路一定要符合欧洲理事会倡导的一些基本价值，如民主、人权以及跨文化交流等。目标是促进人民之间的频繁交流及通过文化旅游促进当地的经济。当下欧盟的整体概念因极端主义、欧洲怀疑主义等面临着一系列政治、经济和社会等方面的巨大挑战，这样的倡议对欧洲联盟发展显然十分重要。

古代丝绸之路的名称命名是后发生的，是德国地理学家李希霍芬（Ferdinand Freiherr von Richthofen 1833—1905）在19世纪末才提出命名的，指约公元前一世纪汉代开始的丝绸贸易之路[4]。从现有材料看，李希霍芬的丝绸之路的命名并不准确。丝绸之路既非单一的丝绸贸易，也非单一的一条线路，而是古代连接东西南北、跨越欧亚，涉及沿线国家政治、经济及文化的一个大规模的历史网络。因此其英文"Silk Road"的名称应用作复数"Silk Roads"。而流通内容上，尽管丝绸是大宗，但绝不限于丝绸，应还包括瓷器、皮毛、玉和香料，以及来自于异域的

---

1 参见 http://cpc.people.com.cn/n/2013/0908/c64094-22843712.html，2017年12月28日。

2 J.M., Wu: "One Belt and One Road", Far-reaching Initiative, 2015 年。请参见 https://www.chinausfocus.com/finance-economy/one-belt-and-one-road-far-reaching-initiative/，2017年12月28日。

3 《欧洲文化线路》的英文名称为 "Cultural Routes of the Council of Europe"，参见该项目的官方网站：http://www.culture-routes.net/cultural-routes，2017年12月28日。

4 关于丝绸之路历史的出版物很多，其中可参考：Ch. I. Beckwith: *Empires of the Silk Road: A History of Central Eurasia from the Bronze Age to the Present*, New Jersey 2011; P. Frankopan: *The Silk Roads: A New History of the World*. Vintage Books, New York 2016; J.A. Millward: *The Silk Road: A Very Short Introduction*. Oxford University Press, New York, 2013; F. Wood: *The Silk Road: Two Thousand Years in the Heart of Asia*, University of California Press, Oakland 2004.

马、金器和玻璃器等货物。除此之外，还有宗教、技术甚至像瘟疫之类的疾病流通。而时间上，丝绸之路实际发生的时间更早，据考证约在公元前第二个千年就已存在了，当时沿着跨越中亚北部草原地区的路线已有活跃的交易活动。在公元前第一个千年中旬，即波斯阿契美尼德王朝（公元前500—前330），已形成了一条在每隔一段距离就有驿站和客栈的路线。这条长达3000多公里，连接着现在的伊朗苏萨城（Susa）和土耳其士麦那港（Smyrna）的路线促进了长途贸易。当时每一个驿站均提供马匹和驿使，从而保证官方的公文在9天之内就可传递全程，普通信件大约3个月的时间也可到达。开辟丝绸之路的下一步应该是亚历山大大帝在公元前4世纪初向东的迁移。亚历山大马其顿帝国的崛起导致了希腊文化的扩张以及古希腊和东方文明之间经济和文化的交流促进。亚历山大大帝从西方迁移东方的时候，也正是东方的汉武帝（公元前40—前87）和他在公元前138年派遣出使西域的张骞开辟了到达中亚的路线。

随着丝绸之路贸易的发展，中国因为提供的丝绸和其他奢侈品，最远到达罗马帝国。根据历史文献可以发现当时富有的罗马妇女非常喜欢丝绸，不惜花重金购买。唐太宗（627—649），中国经历了贸易和文化交流前所未有的增长。欧亚各地的使者参访了唐朝宫廷，异域商人带来了各地的货物，外来的宗教日益繁荣。唐代是中国历史上最开放，文化最多元的一个王朝。中国的领土在唐朝时一直扩张到波斯帝国的边界。影响所及，丝绸之路更加繁荣。当时的唐朝都城长安，成为源源不断输出丝绸、瓷器等货物的影响最大城市之一。

与古代陆地丝绸之路相对应的是长期被忽略的"海上丝绸之路"。"海上丝绸之路"的开辟大约在公元1世纪[1]。据《汉书·地理志》记载，当时的中国船队通过南海和斯里兰卡远航到印度以东的孟加拉湾。与此同时，罗马帝国的航海者也出发探索阿拉伯海岸并建立与亚洲各国人民之间的贸易关系。如果天气好赶上顺风时，当时的船有时能一直远航到印度西岸或者西北岸。在这里，来自欧洲的船装着中国来的货物，然后将其运送回罗马帝国。同时，来自罗马船队的货物被运到中国。此已从中国南方，如广东、广西发现的罗马玻璃器文物中得到了证实[2]。至唐代，阿拉伯和中国之间的贸易更加频繁。当时像宁波、泉州、扬州和广州等港口城市甚至建了外国居民区，来自马来、越南、印度、波斯和阿拉伯等地的人

1　国家文物局：《海上丝绸之路》，文物出版社2014年版；R. Ptak: *Die maritime Seidenstrasse: Küstenräume, Seefahrt und Handel in vorkolonialer Zeit*, C.H.Beck, München 2007.

2　熊昭明、李青公：《广西出土汉代玻璃器的考古学与科技研究》，文物出版社2011年版。

们在此开设商店，并在当地定居下来，建造宗教性建筑和墓地。从那时起开始了大规模生产和通过陆路和海路出口陶器。至宋代，中国的城市对所有的社会阶层开放。在当时的城市中里发现了购物街、居住区、手工作坊、医院和养老院等。宋代对南太平洋的兴趣更加强烈，一度建立了远至非洲东部的贸易关系。13世纪蒙古人掌握权力和建立元代后，随着陆路丝绸之路的功能逐渐下降，同时，海上丝绸之路却因丝绸的巨大收益而日益兴盛。

二 文化遗产与"一带一路"倡议构建

"一带一路"倡议除了明确的政治、经济目标外，另一个重要目标就是增进新时代沿线人民之间的交流。2015年习近平讲话中强调："该倡议将促进文明之间的交流，架起人民友谊的桥梁，推动人类发展和维护世界和平。"[1] 不过，与那些在媒体上占据主流报道，价值超过几百亿美元的基础建设工程不同，此目标在国际上未能得到应有的重视。

实际上，中国众多的与古代丝绸之路相关的历史、文化，当下多被认为在"文化遗产外交"方面是一种重要的"软实力"[2]。中国在有关丝绸、瓷器和其他古代物质文化的介绍，以及一些关于相互交流的文明和全球历史的理念，在未来几年将在提高跨国贸易、完善基础设施和安全方面起着决定性的作用。从近年来中国政府不断加大对古代历史，特别是考古和文化遗产研究方面经费的投入来看，就很容易理解由于对古代历史的重视，也使中国在今天的国际事务中起着潜移默化的作用，并由此教育人民和影响未来。其中，建造新的博物馆和每年推出的无数展览就是其中一种途径。影响较大的，如2014年11月至2015年1月在中国国家博物馆举办了迄今为止规模最大的丝绸之路展览，汇集了来自全国16个省、市、自治区44家文博单位的400余件文物。正如展览策展人所介绍的："今天，'丝绸之路'一词早已超越其历史含义，成为一种精神和象征，为当今世界的和平与发展提供了价值典范。"[3] 希望通过该展览"多层面立体地向世人展示丝绸之路的历史文化与灿烂成就，以史为鉴，提倡人类平等、包容、交流、互鉴的共同发展理念"。

---

1 参见 http://news.xinhuanet.com/politics/2015-03-28/c_1114794507.htm，访问时间：2017年12月28日。

2 参见 http://www.gov.cn/ldhd/2010-10/18/content_1723271.htm，2017年12月28日；http://www.china.com.cn/international/txt/2009-09/10/content_18501006.htm，2017年12月28日；http://www.cssn.cn/kgx/kgdt/201712/t20171225_3792921.shtml，2017年12月28日。

3 国家文物局：《丝绸之路》，文物出版社北京2014年版。

展览前言明确涉及合作、交流、互鉴、共享和集体应对挑战的"一带一路"倡议。近年,类似中国国家博物馆举办此类丝绸之路展览近年十分集中。展览文物多来自全国各地与丝绸之路有关的遗址中。不过,近期也有越来越多一带一路沿线国家的博物馆合作举办的展览。如在故宫博物院举办的《浴火重光——来自阿富汗国家博物馆的宝藏》展览以及中国国家博物馆举办的《阿拉伯之路——沙特出土文物》展览等。2016年12月至2017年2月在宁波博物馆举办《中马关系——从古代到未来》展览。除此类专题展览外,古代丝绸之路沿线的一些城镇还开始建立专门的博物馆,如喀什、和田、若羌、且末、库尔勒等,近年均建成了博物馆,尝试通过新建博物馆展示本地的历史和文化遗产。

与陆路丝绸之路的情况一样,中国政府近年提供巨大资金来保护和展示海上丝绸之路高峰时期相关的文化遗迹。大部分曾在海上丝绸之路充当重要贸易港口的海岸城市都建立了博物馆。最为典型的是宋代南海一号沉船的打捞和广东阳江海上丝绸之路博物馆的建设[1]。南海一号沉船的发现是在1987年,当时的考古专家在24米深的海底发现一艘掩埋在海底1米深的淤泥中,装载有8万余件保存完好的宋代瓷器、生活用具等文物,重达3000吨的中国沉船,命名为"南海一号"。尝试采用"整体打捞"的方案将其转移至博物馆中,为此专门新建广东海上丝绸之路博物馆。"南海一号"沉船的发现为研究中国古代长途贸易和国际关系提供了珍贵资料,在"一带一路"倡议中扮演着十分重要的角色。这些历史遗存在一定程度上在今天与上述地区的交流中也起着重要的作用。中国近年还在斯里兰卡和肯尼亚两国投资寻找郑和船队遗存的项目。这两个国家在21世纪海上丝绸之路基础设施网络中非常关键。中国在两国提供资金来修建深水港,包括斯里兰卡的科伦坡和汉班托塔和肯尼亚的拉穆岛[2]。改善当地基础设施(港口和铁路)后的非洲东部在这个倡议中将起到重要作用。2005年12月,中国国家文物局与肯尼亚官方签署了在肯尼亚拉穆群岛进行合作考古的有关协议,是第一次由中国政府出资,中国学者主导的海外考古[3]。与肯尼亚的这项合作项目经过了5年的调查、论证和筹备,并得到了商务部提供的2000万元左右的经费支持。2010年,中国和肯尼亚签署了由中国国家博物馆、肯尼亚国家博物馆和北京大学考古文博学院

---

[1] 参见广东省文物考古研究所《2011年"南海一号"的考古试掘》,科学出版社2011年版;国家文物局《海上丝绸之路》,文物出版社2014年版。

[2] http://beltandroad.zaobao.com/beltandroad/news/story20170217-725636,2017年12月28日。

[3] http://www.kaogu.cn/cn/xianchangchuanzhenlaoshuju/2013/1025/36168.html,2017年12月28日。

合作"中国和肯尼亚合作实施拉穆群岛地区考古项目"[1]。考古专家在肯尼亚马林迪市附近的曼布鲁伊村一个遗址上发现了明朝"永乐通宝"钱币[2],成为中国在数百年前与非洲有过贸易交易的有力证据。除此之外,发掘的过程中还出土了明初御用的龙泉窑瓷器[3]。2011年5月,中国社会科学院考古研究所王巍所长会见了来访的斯里兰卡贵宾,双方交流了两国海洋考古的情况,并就两国之间的考古合作项目进行了磋商[4]。

"一带一路"倡议中通过介绍丝绸、航海、文化与宗教交流方面的历史来促进跨区域政治、经济的发展和国家友好关系也值得关注。新的软实力观念注重一个国家通过自己的文化和商品的出口来保障自身的影响力。通过重新倡导历史上陆路和海上丝绸之路的概念将给跨国、跨区域贸易,以及丝路沿线的人与人之间的交流带来一种新的活力。近期,每年在联合国教科文组织委员会会议上,与丝绸之路有关的提名有越来越多的趋势,"一带一路"很明显地改变了文化产业合作方面的政治意义。联合国教科文组织阐述丝绸之路说:"丝绸之路以前在东、西之间起着经济和文化桥梁的作用。在它形成的过程中,古代世界的宗教和文化之间的沟通,交流和融合很广泛,使人们创造了一个灿烂而有影响力的文明和留下了珍贵的文化遗存。这些文化遗址现在能促进和鼓励丝绸之路沿线的人们更好地理解不同文明之间的多样性,共处和交流。"[5] 实际上,早在1998年联合国教科文组织就开展了一次丝绸之路的研究项目来促进欧亚各地文化传播的了解和文化遗产的保护[6]。2006年,联合国教科文组织和中国国家文物局在吐鲁番共同举办了一次高规格的研讨会,决定联合起草丝绸之路世界文化遗产的申请[7]。当时参与的共有6个国家,除中国外还有哈萨克斯坦、吉尔吉斯斯坦、塔吉克斯坦、乌兹别克斯坦和土库曼斯坦等中亚国家。由于涉及的地区广泛,最终决定把申请分成几个走廊。最后是中国同哈萨克斯坦和吉尔吉斯斯坦联合申请"丝绸之路:长安—天山廊道的路网"。2014年,在卡塔尔首都多哈召开的第38届联合国教科文组织世

1　http://www.chnmuseum.cn/tabid/1312/InfoID/90053/frtid/1243/Default.aspx,2017年12月28日。
2　http://www.kaogu.cn/cn/xianchangchuanzhenlaoshuju/2013/1026/39068.html,2017年12月28日。
3　http://www.kaogu.cn/cn/xianchangchuanzhenlaoshuju/2013/1026/39237.html,2017年12月28日。
4　http://www.kaogu.cn/cn/xueshudongtai/zhongwaijiaoliu/youpengziyuanfa/2013/1026/43465.html,2017年12月28日。
5　http://whc.unesco.org/en/tentativelists/6093/,2017年12月28日。
6　http://finance.people.com.cn/n/2014/0623/c1004-25185125.html,2017年12月28日。
7　http://finance.people.com.cn/n/2014/0623/c1004-25185125.html,2017年12月28日。

界遗产委员会会议上，中国和哈萨克斯坦、吉尔吉斯斯坦联合申报的"丝绸之路：长安—天山廊道路网"顺利进入世界文化遗产名录，成为首例跨国合作、成功申遗的项目[1]。2015年11月，丝绸之路协调委员会在哈萨克斯坦阿拉木图开会时筹备了今后的申遗和旅游发展战略。未来可以预见到更多的丝绸之路包括海上丝绸之路的遗址的申报项目。

三 中欧文化遗产实践的比较观察

"一带一路"倡议延续了中国政府重视文化建设和文化外交的一贯思路。从古代丝绸之路了解到当时的跨边界贸易是基于相互的信任和尊重。对多数人来说，丝绸之路的故事充满了和平贸易，丰富多元的宗教，友好和谐的文化交流。"一带一路"倡议就建立在此观念之上，即不同地区之间文化和经济方面的连接可以减少猜疑和促进共同繁荣。实际上，该政治文化理念已被更多的国家用来处理涉及国内外事务的诸多方面。

1987年由欧洲理事会发起的《欧洲文化线路》项目，目前已经超越欧盟边界，甚至超越了欧洲的边界。一些文化线路延伸到了北非或者中东地区。该项目由总部设在卢森堡的欧洲文化线路协会管理，主要负责各个文化线路上相关组织、大学与欧洲理事会之间的交流。当年，通过的《圣地亚哥—德康波斯特拉宣言》(*Santiago de Compostela Declaration*)设立了圣地亚哥朝圣的线路，是欧洲当时第一个文化线路[2]。此后，欧洲理事会为了让更多民众了解欧洲的历史和文化，逐步认证了一系列具有文化、社会和历史价值的线路。截至2017年初，数量达到了32个。其中代表性的文化线路除圣地亚哥朝圣线路外，还有汉莎同盟文化线路（1991）[3]、王者大道（Via Regia, 2005）[4]、史前岩画艺术线路（2010）[5]等。汉莎同盟文化线路非常值得关注，与"一带一路"倡议一样，它也是一个跨地区甚至是跨国的贸易网络。该文化线路基于13世纪中期德国航海商人成立的

---

1 http://news.sina.com.cn/c/2014-06-24/130930414025.shtml，2017年12月28日。

2 https://www.coe.int/en/web/cultural-routes/the-santiago-de-compostela-pilgrim-routes，2017年12月28日。

3 https://www.coe.int/en/web/cultural-routes/the-hansa，2017年12月28日。

4 王者大道是欧洲古代主要贸易网络之一，起点是波兰的克拉科夫市，终点是法国巴黎。该贸易网络证明欧洲几个世纪长的跨欧洲文化迁移。请参见：https://www.coe.int/en/web/cultural-routes/via-regia，访问时间：2017年12月28日。

5 https://www.coe.int/en/web/cultural-routes/prehistoric-rock-art-trails，2017年12月28日。

汉莎同盟贸易网络，直到 17 世纪一直对欧洲经济、政治和贸易等事务有着非常重要影响。此网络沿着北欧的海岸延伸，主要围绕波罗的海沿岸，涉及城市多达 225 个。目前，共有 16 个国家的 185 个城市参与了汉莎同盟文化线路，其中有不少联合国教科文组织列出的世界文化遗产地。从一定意义上，可以说汉莎同盟是现在欧洲联盟的中世纪先驱，呈现了古代欧洲一种无价的共同文化遗产。

另外值得一提的是《欧洲文化之摇篮》项目[1]。该项目由 9 个欧洲合作国家组成，目的在于追寻弗朗西亚媒体（Francia Media）的遗迹——从公元 841 年至 1033 年欧洲中世纪的政治构建。与《欧洲文化线路》项目相似，《欧洲文化之摇篮》项目的目标也是试图揭示中世纪早期欧洲这个构想的根源，以加强人们对这一时期文化遗产的认知，并发掘它对当下欧洲的重大意义。《欧洲文化之摇篮》官方明确表示，"参观欧洲不同国家的博物馆或者遗址时，我们注意到他们的介绍主要着重于这个国家的历史，却很少提及组成今天欧盟的很多国家所共享的历史。这一点令人遗憾，因为这一文化遗产很好地强调了我们几个世纪以来的文化共同点；通过更好地了解这些历史，能够让我们在动荡时期增进欧洲境内的凝聚力和团结。从更长远的角度来看，强调欧洲共有的文化遗产将增进文化交流，激发新理念并在科学的欧洲共同体内加以实践。"[2] 上述项目中多采取跨边界的举措，意在强调共享文化、历史和欧洲一体化，近年的欧洲工业遗产线路（总共 16 条线路）[3]、欧洲皇家住宅协会[4]、欧洲花园遗产网络[5]等，甚至如 Europeana.eu 这样的视觉化博物馆项目[6]，通过数字化方式将欧洲各国博物馆的藏品链接起来。而项目的最终目的，是能够让人们更容易地获取文化遗产有关的资源，提高人们对欧洲历史和文化的认知，加强对新欧洲的认同感，并培养人们对文化遗产的保护意愿。

总之，在"一带一路"倡议的框架内，复杂的跨边界文化、历史被浓缩为一系列文化遗产的追溯，并直接与官方的外交政策和贸易目标相联系。文化在当下

---

1 《欧洲文化之摇篮》的英文名称为 "Cradles of European Culture"，http://www.cradlesec.eu/CEC2014/default.aspx，2017 年 12 月 28 日。
2 http://www.cradlesec.eu/CEC2014/Project.aspx，2017 年 12 月 28 日。
3 欧洲工业遗产线路 (European Route of Industrial Heritage)，http://www.erih.net，2017 年 12 月 28 日。
4 欧洲皇家住宅协会 (European Royal Residences Association) http://www.europeanroyalresidences.eu，2017 年 12 月 28 日。
5 欧洲花园遗产网络 (European Garden Heritage Network) https://wp.eghn.org/en/european-garden-heritage-network-eghn，2017 年 12 月 28 日。
6 Europeana，https://www.europeana.eu/portal/en，2017 年 12 月 28 日。

全球化世界里显而易见和国际外交舞台密切相关。通过"一带一路"倡议所注重的陆路和海上的线路、贸易区域和走廊，相关的国家会继续寻找共同的文化、历史，通过一个共享的文化遗产语言，将得到区域影响力从而促进外交、经济、政治和人和人之间的进一步交流。

On the Role of Cultural Heritage in the Construction of the "Belt and Road" Initiative[1]

Patrick Wertmann / Germany

Doctor, Eurasian Archaeological Institute, German Archaeological Academy

Before the upcoming of Belt and Road Forum for International Cooperation, the Xinhua News Agency, the Confucius Institute Headquarters and the State-owned Assets Supervision and Administration Commission of the State Council have jointly compiled and published the book series, *The Belt and Road: People with Stories*.[2] This book series shows the influence of the "Belt and Road" Initiative proposed in 2013 on the countries along the route through a hundred stories in seven languages. One of the stories describes the excavation of the ancient Yueh-chih tombs in Samarkand, one of the two archaeological excavation cooperation projects between China and Uzbekistan. As stated in the article, "Cultural exchange is an important driving force for the development of human civilization. The ancient Silk Road allows the Uzbekistan and the Chinese people to get to know

---

[1] I would like to express sincere gratitude to Professor Xu Ling of the Department of Archaeology of Zhengzhou University for her guidance and valuable opinions.

[2] Xinhua News Agency, State-owned Assets Supervision and Administration Commission of the State Council, Confucius Institute Headquarters: New Exchanges on the Millennium Silk Road, *The Belt and Road: People with Stories*, Xinhua Publishing House, 2017.

each other. The new Silk Road undoubtedly reunites two old friends."[1] In fact, since ancient times, the Land and Maritime Silk Road have exerted far-reaching influences on the political, cultural and economic exchanges in Eurasia. Over two thousand years later, the construction of the "Belt and Road" Initiative will continue to make historical glory. Through a comparative study of the "2018 European Cultural Heritage Year" project and other EU-related cultural projects, China's recent international archaeological cooperation projects have been sorted out to try to discuss the role of Chinese cultural heritage in the construction of the "Belt and Road" Initiative.

I. The "Belt and Road" Initiative and the Ancient Silk Road

When Xi Jinping put forward the "Belt and Road" Initiative[2], he focused on the fact that more than 2,100 years ago, Zhang Qian in the Han Dynasty took up the mission of peace and friendship to serve as an envoy to Central Asia, opening a door for friendly exchanges between China and Central Asian countries and a silk road that links Europe and Asia across the east and west. He pointed out that: "The history of two thousand years of communication proves that as long as we adhere to solidarity and mutual trust, equality and mutual benefit, inclusiveness and mutual understanding, and win-win cooperation, countries of different races, beliefs, and cultural backgrounds can fully share peace and achieve common development. To enhance economic links, deepen cooperation and jointly build the Silk Road Economic Belt, frequent exchanges, mutual understanding and friendship between

---

1 Xinhua News Agency, State-owned Assets Supervision and Administration Commission of the State Council, Confucius Institute Headquarters: New Exchanges on the Millennium Silk Road, *The Belt and Road: People with Stories*, Beijing: Xinhua Publishing House, 2017, pp.97-100.

2 In the speech of *Promote Friendship between Our People, Work Together for a Bright Future* at the Nazarbayev University in Kazakhstan on September 7, 2013, Xi Jinping proposed for the first time an initiative to jointly build the "Silk Road Economic Belt". In the initiative, Xi Jinping specifically emphasized the traditional friendship between China and Kazakhstan, and gave a comprehensive discussion of the good-neighbourly and friendly cooperative relations between China and the countries in Central Asia. Subsequently, Xi Jinping also proposed to jointly build the "Silk Road Economic Belt" characterized by the innovative model so as to benefit the people along the route.

people are indispensable and need to be consolidated further."[1] This shows that the "Belt and Road" Initiative is an innovation inspired by the spirit of the ancient Silk Road, and is described as "China's most significant and far-reaching initiative to date."[2] It calls for the integration of the countries along the Belt and Road into a cohesive economic zone through the construction of infrastructure in the coming decades, the promotion of cultural exchanges and the expansion of trade.

In fact, similar transnational initiatives or projects can also be found throughout the world, such as the logo project of the "European Cultural Route" of the European Union.[3] The logo is awarded by the Council of Europe to the cultural route that promotes European shared culture, history, commemoration and integration. These routes must meet the basic values advocated by the Council of Europe, such as democracy, human rights and cross-cultural communication. The goals are to promote frequent exchanges among peoples and boost the local economy through cultural tourism. Currently, the overall concept of the European Union is facing a series of political, economic and social challenges due to extremism and European skepticism. This initiative is obviously very important to the development of the European Union.

The ancient Silk Road was named after the proposal by Ferdinand Freiherr von Richthofen (1833-1905) at the end of the 19th century, a German geographer. It refers to the Silk Trade Road that began during the Han Dynasty in the first century B.C..[4] According to the existing information, the naming of Richthofen's Silk Road

---

1 http://cpc.people.com.cn/n/2013/0908/c64094-22843712.html, accessed on 2017-12-28.
2 J.M., Wu: "One Belt and One Road", Far-reaching Initiative, 2015. https://www.chinausfocus.com/finance-economy/one-belt-and-one-road-far-reaching-initiative/,accessed on 2017-12-28.
3 Cultural Routes of the Council of Europe, http://www.culture-routes.net/cultural-routes, accessed on 2017-12-28.
4 There are many publications on the history of the Silk Road, for examples: Ch. I. Beckwith: *Empires of the Silk Road: A History of Central Eurasia from the Bronze Age to the Present*, New Jersey 2011; P. Frankopan: *The Silk Roads: A New History of the World*. Vintage Books, New York 2016; J.A. Millward: *The Silk Road: A Very Short Introduction*. Oxford University Press, New York, 2013; F. Wood: *The Silk Road: Two Thousand Years in the Heart of Asia*, University of California Press, Oakland 2004.

is not accurate. The Silk Road is neither a single occasion of silk trade nor a single route. It is a large-scale historical network that links the East and the West, and the North and the South across Europe and Asia, and involves the politics, economics and culture of the countries along the route. Therefore, the English name, Silk Road, should be changed to the plural form, Silk Roads. In terms of the contents circulated, though silk accounts for a large proportion, the goods should include porcelain, fur, jade and spices, horses, goldsmiths and glassware from exotic lands, without limitation to silk. In addition, religion, technology and even diseases such as the plague have also been circulated. In terms of time, the Silk Road came into being earlier. According to research, it had already existed around the second millennium B.C.. There were active trading activities along the route that spanned the grasslands of northern Central Asia. In the middle of the first millennium B.C., the reign of the Persian Achaemenid Dynasty (B.C. 500-330), a route for stations and inns at intervals was formed. Over a distance of more than 3,000 kilometers, the route connecting the current Susa, Iran and Smyrna, Turkey greatly promoted long-distance trade. At that time, each station provided horses and emissaries to make sure that the official documents could be delivered throughout the whole journey within nine days, and ordinary letters could also be served in about three months. The next step in the history of the opening of the Silk Road should be the route that Alexander the Great followed in his military campaigns towards the East in the early 4th century B.C.. The rise of Alexander's Macedonian Empire led to the expansion of Greek culture and the economic and cultural exchange between the ancient Greek and Eastern civilizations. When Alexander the Great moved from the West to the East, the Emperor Wudi (B.C.156-86) of the Eastern Han Dynasty sent Zhang Qian to visit the Western Regions in B.C. 138, opening up a route to Central Asia (beyond the Hexi Corridor and the Tarim Basin).

With the development of trade along the Silk Road, China's wealth increased due to the supply of silk and other luxury goods going to the Roman Empire at the farthest end of the Road. According to historical documents, it can be found that rich Roman women at that time liked silk very much and did not hesitate to spend a lot of money to buy it. After the Emperor Taizong of Tang took office (627-649), China experienced an unprecedented growth of trade and cultural exchanges. The messengers from all over European and Asian countries visited the court of the Tang Dynasty. Exotic businessmen brought goods from all over the countries, leading to increasingly prosperous foreign religions. The Tang Dynasty is the most open and the most culturally diverse dynasty in Chinese history. In the Tang Dynasty, China's territory was expanded to the border of the Persian Empire. Within the scope of influence, the Silk Road was more prosperous. At that time, Chang'an, the capital of the Tang Dynasty, became one of the most influential cities that continuously exported silk, porcelain and other goods.

Compared with the ancient Land Silk Road, the Maritime Silk Road has long been neglected. The Maritime Silk Road was opened around the first century A.D..[1] According to the *History of the Han Dynasty · Geography*, the Chinese fleets at that time sailed through the South China Sea and Sri Lanka to the Bay of Bengal to the east of India. At the same time, the sailors of the Roman Empire departed to explore the Arabian coast and establish trade relations with the peoples of Asian countries. If the weather was good enough to meet with the following wind, the ship at that time could sometimes sail to the west coast or the northwest coast of India. Here, ships from Europe carried the goods from China and shipped them back to the Roman Empire. Meanwhile, the goods from the Roman fleets were shipped to China. This has been confirmed by the Roman glassware found in southern China, such as Guangdong and Guangxi.[2] By the Tang Dynasty, the trade between the Arabs and the Chinese had become more frequent. At the time, port cities like Ningbo, Quanzhou, Yangzhou, and Guangzhou even established foreign residential

---

1 For publications on the history of the Maritime Silk Road, refer to: State Administration of Cultural Heritage, *Maritime Silk Road*, Cultural Relics Publishing House, Beijing, 2014; R. Ptak: *Die maritime Seidenstrasse: Küstenräume, Seefahrt und Handel in vorkolonialer Zeit*, C.H.Beck, München 2007.

2 Xiong Zhaoming, Li Qinggong, *Archaeology and Technology Research of the Han Dynasty Glassware Unearthed in Guangxi*, Cultural Relics Publishing House, Beijing, 2011.

areas, where people from Malay, Vietnam, India, Persia and Arabia settled to set up shops and build religious buildings and cemeteries. Since then, the production and exportation of pottery by land and sea have been going on on a large scale. In the Song Dynasty, Chinese cities were open to all social classes. Shopping streets, residential areas, workshops, hospitals, and nursing homes were found in the cities at that time. The Song Dynasty became more interested in the South Pacific and once established trade relations with eastern Africa. After the Mongolians took power in the 13th century and established the Yuan Dynasty, the economics and culture of large countries along the route were gradually separated with the gradual decline in the function of the Land Silk Road. While the Land Silk Road was disintegrating, the Martime Silk Road began to flourish increasingly due to the tremendous benefits of silk.

II. Cultural Heritage and the Construction of the "Belt and Road" Initiative

In addition to clear political and economic goals, another important goal of the "Belt and Road" Initiative is to increase the exchanges between peoples along the route in the new era. In his speeches in 2015, Xi Jinping emphasized that: "This initiative will promote the exchanges among civilizations, build bridges for people's friendship, promote human development and safeguard world peace."[1] However, unlike the infrastructure projects worth more than 10 billion USD in the media mainstream reports, due attention has not been given internationally to this goal.

In fact, China's history and culture related to the ancient Silk Road are now considered to be an important "soft power"[2] in terms of "cultural heritage diplomacy". China's introduction of silk, porcelain, and other ancient material cultures, as well as some ideas on mutual civilization and global history, will

---

1 http://news.xinhuanet.com/politics/2015-03/28/c_1114794507.htm, State Administration of Cultural Heritage, *Silk Road*, Cultural Relics Publishing House, Beijing, 2014.
2 http://www.gov.cn/ldhd/2010-10/18/content_1723271.htm, accessed on 2017-12-28; http://www.china.com.cn/international/txt/2009-09/10/content_18501006.htm, accessed on 2017-12-28; http://www.cssn.cn/kgx/kgdt/201712/t20171225_3792921.shtml, accessed on 2017-12-28.

play a decisive role in enhancing cross-border trade and improving infrastructure and security in the coming years. According to the increasing investment of the Chinese government in ancient history in recent years, especially archaeological and cultural heritage research, it is easy to understand that fact due to the emphasis on ancient history. Further, China also plays a subtle role in today's international affairs, thus educating the people and influencing the future. Among them, one way is to construct new museums and launch numerous exhibitions each year. The most influential exhibitions, such as the largest Silk Road exhibition ever held at the National Museum of China from November 2014 to January 2015, brought together more than 400 cultural relics from 44 heritage institutions in 16 provinces, municipalities and autonomous regions across the country. As introduced by the exhibition curator: "Today, the term 'Silk Road' has long surpassed its historical meaning and has become a symbol of the spirit of and a model for the peace and development of today's world." [1] It is hoped, through this exhibition, to "present the historical culture and splendid achievements of the Silk Road to the world in a multi-level and three-dimensional manner, draw lessons from history and advocate the concepts of human equality, inclusiveness, communication, mutual understanding, and common development." The preface to this exhibition makes it clear that the "Belt and Road" Initiative involves cooperation, exchange, mutual learning, sharing, and collective response to challenges. In recent years, the National Museum of China has held similar Silk Road exhibitions successively, where most of the cultural relics exhibited came from sites related to the Silk Road all over the country. What's more, there have been more and more exhibitions jointly organized by the museums in the countries along the Belt and Road, such as the *Blooming Light - Treasures from the National Museum of Afghanistan* held at the Palace Museum and the *Road to Arab - Saudi Excavated Cultural Relics* held by the National Museum of China, and *China-Malaysia Relations - From Ancient Times to the Future* held from December 2016 to February 2017 at the Ningbo Museum.

---

1 State Administration of Cultural Heritage, *Silk Road*, Cultural Relics Publishing House, Beijing, 2014.

In addition to these thematic exhibitions, some towns along the ancient Silk Road have also begun to establish special museums. For instance, Kashgar, Khotan, Ruoqiang, Qiemo and Korla have built museums in recent years to try to display local historical and cultural heritage through a new museum.

As in the case of the Land Silk Road, the Chinese government has provided huge funds in recent years to protect and demonstrate the cultural heritages associated with the peak of the Maritime Silk Road. Most of the coastal cities that once served as important trading ports on the Maritime Silk Road had established museums. The most typical examples are the salvage of the Nanhai No.1 sunken ship during the Song Dynasty and the construction of the Yangjiang Maritime Silk Road Museum in Guangdong.[1] The Nanhai No.1 sunken ship was discovered in 1987, when Archaeologists discovered a sunken Chinese ship, weighing 3,000 tons, which was buried under 1m of mud on the seabed at a depth of 24m and had a load more than 80,000 well-preserved Song Dynasty porcelains, living utensils and other cultural relics. It was named Nanhai No.1. The "whole salvage" program was adopted to transfer the sunken ship to the museum, and for this reason, the Guangdong Maritime Silk Road Museum was specially built. The discovery of the "Nanhai No.1" sunken ship had provided valuable information for the study of ancient Chinese long-distance trade and international relations, and played a vital role in the "Belt and Road" Initiative. This historical legacy also play an important role in today's exchanges with these regions. In recent years, China has also invested in the projects of seeking the Zheng He' fleet in Sri Lanka and Kenya. Sri Lanka and Kenya are critical in the network of infrastructure of the 21st Century Maritime Silk Road. China has provided funds for the construction of deep-water ports in the two countries, including Colombo and Hambantota in Sri Lanka and Lamu in Kenya.[2] After improvement of local infrastructure (ports and railroads),

---

1 Please refer to Guangdong Provincial Institute of Cultural Relics and Archaeology, *2011 'Nanhai No. 1' Archeological Excavation*, Science Press, Beijing, 2011; State Administration of Cultural Heritage, *Maritime Silk Road*, Cultural Relics Publishing House, Beijing, 2014.
2 http://beltandroad.zaobao.com/beltandroad/news/story20170217-725636, accessed on 2017-12-28.

eastern Africa will play an important role in this initiative. In December 2005, the State Administration of Cultural Heritage and the Kenyan government signed an agreement on cooperative archaeology in the Lamu Islands in Kenya, which was the first overseas archaeology project funded by the Chinese government and led by the Chinese scholars.[1] The cooperation project with Kenya underwent five years of investigation, demonstration and preparation, and received the financial support of about 20 million RMB from the Ministry of Commerce. In 2010, China and Kenya signed an agreement on the cooperation project *China and Kenya Work Together to Implement the Archaeological Project in the Lamu Islands*[2] carried out by the National Museum of China, the National Museum of Kenya and the School of Archeology and Museology of Peking University. Archaeologists discovered the Ming Dynasty "Yongle Tongbao" coins[3] at a historic site in the Mambrui Village near the Malindi City of Kenya, becoming some powerful evidence that China had traded with Africa hundreds of years ago. In addition, the Longquan kiln porcelain[4] for the use of emperors at the beginning of the Ming Dynasty was also unearthed during the excavations. In May 2011, Wang Wei, the Director of the Institute of Archaeology of the Chinese Academy of Social Sciences, met with the guests from Sri Lanka to exchange information on the maritime archaeology of the two countries and conduct consultations on the archeological cooperation projects between the two countries.[5]

Through the introduction of the history of silk, navigation, culture and religion exchanges, the "Belt and Road" Initiative promotes cross-regional political and economic development and pays attention to national friendly relations. The new concept of soft power focuses on a country's protection of its own influence through its own culture and exportation of goods. The re-initiation of the concept

---

1 http://www.kaogu.cn/cn/xianchangchuanzhenlaoshuju/2013/1025/36168.html, 2017-12-28.
2 http://www.chnmuseum.cn/tabid/1312/InfoID/90053/frtid/1243/Default.aspx, 2017-12-28.
3 http://www.kaogu.cn/cn/xianchangchuanzhenlaoshuju/2013/1026/39068.html, 2017-12-28.
4 http://www.kaogu.cn/cn/xianchangchuanzhenlaoshuju/2013/1026/39237.html, 2017-12-28.
5 http://www.kaogu.cn/cn/xueshudongtai/zhongwaijiaoliu/youpengziyuanfa/2013/1026/43465.html, 2017-12-28.

of the Land and Maritime Silk Roads in history will bring new vitality to cross-border and cross-regional trade, and people-to-people exchanges. Recently, at the UNESCO committee meeting, the annual nominations related to the Silk Road have demonstrated an increasing trend. The "Belt and Road" Initiative has obviously changed the political significance of cooperation regarding the cultural industry. In UNESCO's explanation of the Silk Road, it is stated: "Since the Silk Road had played the role of a bridge between the economy and culture of the east and the west. In the process of formation, the communication, exchange and integration between the religion and culture of the ancient world were extensive, so that people created a splendid and influential civilization and left precious cultural relics. Now, these cultural sites can promote and encourage people along the Silk Road to better understand the diversity among civilizations, enable them to coexist and communicate with one another." [1] In fact, as early as 1998, UNESCO launched a research project on the Silk Road to promote the understanding of cultural transmission and the protection of cultural heritage throughout Europe and Asia [2]. In 2006, UNESCO and the State Administration of Cultural Heritage jointly organized a high-profile seminar in Turpan and decided to jointly draft an application for the Silk Road World Cultural Heritage.[3] At that time, there were a total of six countries involved, namely, China, Kazakhstan, Kyrgyzstan, Tajikistan, Uzbekistan and Turkmenistan. Due to the extensive area involved, it was finally decided to make a division into several corridors in the application. Lastly, China jointly applied for the "Silk Road: The Chang'an-Tianshan Corridor Road Network" with Kazakhstan and Kyrgyzstan. In 2014, at the 38th UNESCO World Heritage Committee Meeting held in Doha, Qatar, the "Silk Road: The Chang'an - Tianshan Corridor Road Network" jointly applied for by China, Kazakhstan and Kyrgyzstan successfully entered the World Cultural Heritage List, becoming the first transnational cooperation and successful application project.[4] In November 2015, the Coordinating Committee

---

1　http://whc.unesco.org/en/tentativelists/6093/, 2017-12-28.
2　http://finance.people.com.cn/n/2014/0623/c1004-25185125.html, 2017-12-28.
3　http://finance.people.com.cn/n/2014/0623/c1004-25185125.html, 2017-12-28.
4　http://news.sina.com.cn/c/2014-06-24/130930414025.shtml, 2017-12-28.

of the Silk Road prepared the subsequent application for the list of a strategy for the development of world heritage and tourism during the meeting in Alma-Ata, Kazakhstan. In the future, there are expected to be more applications made regarding parts of the Silk Road, including the ruins of the Maritime Silk Road.

III. Comparative Observation of Cultural Heritage Practices in China and in Europe

The "Belt and Road" Initiative carries forward the Chinese government's consistent line of thought regarding an emphasis on cultural construction and cultural diplomacy. It has been learned from the ancient Silk Road that cross-border trade is based on mutual trust and respect. For most people, the stories of the Silk Road are full of peaceful trading experiences, rich and diverse religions, and friendly and harmonious cultural exchanges. The "Belt and Road" Initiative is based on the conceptual heritages, that is, cultural and economic connections among different regions can reduce suspicion and promote common prosperity. In fact, this political and cultural concept has been used by many countries to deal with many domestic and foreign affairs.

The *European Cultural Route* project initiated by the Council of Europe in 1987 has now surpassed the EU borders and even the European borders. Some cultural routes extend to Northern Africa or to the Middle East. The project is managed by the Association of European Cultural Routes, headquartered in Luxembourg. The Association is responsible for the exchanges among relevant organizations, universities and the European Council on various cultural routes. Previously, the Santiago pilgrimage route was established, according to the *Santiago de Compostela Declaration*, becoming the first cultural route[1] in Europe at that time. Since then, the Council of Europe has gradually certified a series of routes with cultural, social and historical values in order to allow more people to understand the history and culture of Europe. By the beginning of 2017, the number of routes

---

1 https://www.coe.int/en/web/cultural-routes/the-santiago-de-compostela-pilgrim-routes，2017-12-28.

has reached up to 32. The typical cultural routes are the Santiago Pilgrimage Route, Lufthansa Alliance Cultural Route (1991)[1], Via Regia (2005)[2] and Prehistoric Rock Art Route (2010)[3], etc. Among them, the Lufthansa Alliance Cultural Route, which is a trans-regional or even transnational trade network just as the "Belt and Road" Initiative, is very noteworthy. Based on the Lufthansa Alliance trade network established by German maritime merchants in the mid-13th century, the cultural route had continued to exert a very important influence on European economic, political and trade affairs until the 17th century. The network extends along the coast of northern Europe, and involves as many as 225 cities mainly along the coast of the Baltic Sea. At present, a total of 185 cities in 16 countries participate in the Lufthansa Alliance Cultural Route, including many World Heritage Sites listed by UNESCO. In a sense, it can be said that the Lufthansa Alliance is the medieval pioneer of the European Union, presenting an invaluable common cultural heritage in ancient Europe.

The project called the "Cradle of European Culture" should also be mentioned.[4] Involving nine European cooperative countries, the project aims to trace the remains of Francia Media — the political construction of medieval Europe from A.D. 841 to A.D. 1033. Similar to the project called the "Route of European Culture", the project called the "Cradle of European Culture" is also aimed at revealing the root causes of the concept, in Europe in the early Middle Ages, of increasing people's awareness of the cultural heritage of this period and discovering its great significance for contemporary Europe. Concerning the "Cradle of European Culture", it is officially stated that "when visiting museums or sites in different European countries, we notice that their introduction mainly focuses only on the history of the country in which the museum or site is located, and seldom mentions

---

1　https://www.coe.int/en/web/cultural-routes/the-hansa, 2017-12-28.
2　Via Regia is one of the major trading networks of ancient Europe, which starts from Krakow, Poland and ends at Paris, France. The trade network proves the centuries-long trans-European cultural migration of Europe. https://www.coe.int/en/web/cultural-routes/via-regia, 2017-12-28.
3　https://www.coe.int/en/web/cultural-routes/prehistoric-rock-art-trails, 2017-12-28.
4　Cradles of European Culture, http://www.cradlesec.eu/CEC2014/default.aspx, 2017-12-28.

the history shared by many countries that make up the European Union today. It is a real pity, because the cultural heritage is a good example of the cultural elements that we have had in common for centuries; a better understanding of history can enable us to increase the cohesion and unity in Europe during turbulent times. In the long run, the emphasis on the European shared cultural heritage will contribute to enhancing cultural exchanges, stimulating new ideas and practicing them in the European scientific community."[1] For instance, the project adopts many cross-border initiatives and is designed to emphasize shared culture, history and European integration. In recent years, the European Industrial Heritage Route (a total of 16 routes)[2], the European Royal Residential Association,[3] the European Garden Heritage Network,[4] and even the Europeanana[5] as a project for the visualisation of museums, have brought together the collections of European museums digitally. The ultimate goal of the project is to make it easier for people to acquire cultural heritage-related resources, raise people's awareness of European history and culture, strengthen their sense of identity with the New Europe, and cultivate people's willingness to protect their own and others' cultural heritage.

To sum up, complicated cross-border cultural history is condensed into numerous elements of the traceability of cultural heritage and directly linked to official foreign policy and trade goals within the framework of the "Belt and Road" Initiative. In the current globalized world, culture is increasingly prominent and closely related to the international diplomatic arena. Through the land and sea routes, trade areas, and corridors emphasized in the "Belt and Road" Initiative, relevant countries will continue to seek common cultural history and share the language of heritage to gain regional influence, thereby further promoting the diplomatic, economic, political and people-to-people exchanges.

---

1 http://www.cradlesec.eu/CEC2014/Project.aspx,2017-12-28.
2 European Route of Industrial Heritage,http://www.erih.net,2017-12-28.
3 European Royal Residences Association,http://www.europeanroyalresidences.eu,2017-12-28.
4 European Garden Heritage Network,https://wp.eghn.org/en/european-garden-heritage-network-eghn, 2017-12-28.
5 Europeana, https://www.europeana.eu/portal/en, 2017-12-28.

中国在智利的文化外交

玛丽缘 【智利】
智利教育部汉语研究项目研究员

  笔者与智利发展大学政府学院国际关系研究中心的伊莎贝尔（Isabel Rodríguez）教授共同对中国在智利的文化外交活动进行了考察，特别是针对中文的教学。本文是关于这一调研项目和2017年9月青年汉学家访华研修计划的研究报告的一部分。

  中国与智利良好的历史关系符合智利社会对中国这一亚洲国家的看法。日益扩大的交流，不仅使得两国于1954年成立了友好协会，而且在1970年两国建交之前就建立了商贸关系。智利是拉丁美洲继古巴之后第二个与中国建交的国家，也是南美洲最早与中国建交的国家。两国议会之间建立了交流机制；智利于2005年与中国签署了自由贸易协定，这是拉美国家与中国签署的首个自贸协定（Lizama, 2013: 228）。此外，智利与中国保持着全方位的外交关系，"涉及智利的地区和市级政府以及中国的省级、省辖市和直辖市政府"（Lizama, 2013: 233）。

  中智关系的发展也体现了中国正在寻求的经济与文化的交汇。两国在经济和文化领域签署的众多协定和协议明显地体现了这一点；2012年中智两国建立战略合作伙伴关系，形成了经济与文化的交汇发展。关于中国树立其形象的具体方面，笔者认为，在经济层面主要是突出现代和科技元素，而在文化层面则是强调传统元素。在文化上，两国在政府层面的双边合作得到了社会团体之间交流的有益补充。正如在其他拉美国家一样，中国文化在智利的推广不仅通过中国政府而且通过一系列文化中心开展，这使得智利人民得以了解中国传统文化的各个方面——武术、戏曲、中医、舞蹈和中文等。这也表明，针对别国的公共外交必须同时有政府和非政府层面的参与。

在过去十年，智利的中国文化和语言教学成为了一个革命性的案例，其发端于智利教育部与中国孔子学院共同开展的一个合作项目。

笔者在此补充跨越太平洋集团公司董事 Rodrigo Fábrega 提到的一个因素。他强调，与拉丁语、法语和英语等其他语言形成对比的是，中文教学纳入智利公立学校的教学计划。这一举措意味着不再只是智利精英阶层在学习中文，而是改变了语言融入智利社会的方式。

从 2004 年至今，中文学习在智利开展得非常迅速。合作在智利推广中文，源自拉戈斯政府的前教育部长 Sergio Bitar 的个人兴趣，他在访华期间考察了中文与世界的相关联系。2004 年 5 月 1 日，智利共和国教育部与中华人民共和国教育部签署了《教育领域合作谅解备忘录》。备忘录为在智利教育部国际关系办公室设立中文教学计划铺平了道路。中文教学计划的运作需要依靠中国政府（通过国家汉办）和智利政府（通过教育部和各市政府）的合作。2016 年，智利全国几乎所有省份都开设了中文课程，学习中文的学生人数超过 3000 人。

鉴于学习中文的学生众多，笔者希望更深入地了解这些年轻人心目中的中国和中国社会形象以及影响他们对中国看法的因素。就此而言，我们认为"想象"在社会关系中扮演的角色是很重要的："……想象的含义在人类行为和社会关系中扮演着组织者的角色，是既定社会的想象产物。通过想象产生的含义，社会对与其自身存在相关的基本'问题'给出了'答案'。"（Kavoulakos, 1987: 145-164）

2014 年，笔者对位于 Valparaiso、Metropolitana 和 Bio-Bio 地区的 7 个教育机构进行了考察。通过参与智利多个城市的中文教学过程和儿童经历，笔者发现了一系列影响教学开展和学生想象的因素。其中最突出的影响因素之一也许是学校的位置。在首都的学生关于中国的看法、经历和想象与在各省或小镇的学生是不同的。在首都中心地区的机构与中国人的联系和接触更多，因为首都的亚洲人明显要比其他城市多得多。同时，城市的经济活动也是一个重要影响因素，比如在 Valparaiso 和 Coronel 这两座港口城市，每个月都有中国货船往来。

同样地，中文老师的作用也是根本性的。中文老师是连接中国与学生的桥梁。大多数情况下，中文老师是学生们认识的唯一的中国人，因此他们在文化传播中的作用和方式是理解中国的关键。在开设中文课程之前,许多学生对中国只有非常笼统的认知。然而,通过老师的教学,中文课程激发了他们对中国的兴趣,使他们建立了对中国的想象。笔者所采访的学生中,没有一个对中国的看法是负面或充满问题的。除了根据老师传授的知识所建立的对中国的想象,一些学生还提到了对智利华人的传统印象:严肃、有教养、勤奋好学。不过,对中国人的这一印象也会根据他们接触到的最近的例子而得到确认或发生变化:有些学生不再这么看待中国人,因为他们的中文老师并未表现出这些特征;而另外一些学生则产生或强化了这一印象,因为他们的老师具有这些特征。从以上调查可以看出,老师的责任和引导是重要的。

老师接受的培训包括 5 个方面:普通话教学、课程准备(包括书目资料的准备)、课程分析和反馈、中国文化教学(特别是剪纸、书法和太极教学)和跨文化适应(如何融入其他国家的文化中)。他们同时还要选出一名自己最优秀的学生参加著名的"汉语桥"比赛——各国选出最优秀的中文学生(包括孔子学院和其他公共机构的学员)到中国参加每年一届的国际性中文比赛。

在这一方面,笔者将提到一个特别的案例——"汉语桥——世界大学生中文比赛"。2016 年智利赛区的比赛是由圣托马斯大学与智利教育部和中国国家汉办合作组织的。来自智利中小学和大学的学生参加了这一比赛。比赛的主题为"点亮未来的梦想"(这与习近平提出的"中国梦"相关)。笔者选取了 Biobio 地区的圣尼古拉斯才艺卓越学校(Multi-Talented Excellence School of San Nicolas)的一名参赛学生为例,阐述这一比赛的意义和影响。该名女同学来自 Cobquecura,这是 2010 年地震海啸中受灾最严重的地区之一。在演讲中,她提到了她的家庭在地震海啸中经历的困境,随后展示了一幅照片,上面是一个中国人走下飞机向当地居民提供人道主义援助的场景。她指出,从那一刻起,她对这些帮助他们的人产生了极大的敬仰并希望了解他们。随后,这个女孩开始对中国感兴趣并开始学习中文和中国文化。在演讲中,她对中国的钦佩是显而易见的;她在才艺表演中对中国和中国传统文化展现出的强烈兴趣吸引了在场的观众。同时,她还在比赛中扮成一个身着红衣的中国姑娘,演唱中国的传统歌曲,模仿中国女孩的举手投足。

这位参加"汉语桥"比赛的年轻选手的案例体现了中国文化外交的几个特点:第一,中国政府向智利提供人道主义援助所体现出的具有人情味的政策。中国政府提供的援助惠及了智利经济匮乏和发展落后的脆弱地区，进入到了乡村居民的心中。第二，语言教学同样遍布智利全国，包括远离城市的教育机构。第三，笔者提到的这名学生是在 Biobio 地区的圣尼古拉斯才艺卓越学校学习的中文。该校提倡素质教育，包括语言教学方面的素质教育。该校要求学生学习两门外语，包括中文。

除了以上特点，有必要强调的另一点是，学生在比赛中的角色转变。一个最为突出的例证就是才艺表演。在这一环节，参赛选手通常会身着中国传统服饰。在许多情况下，参赛选手似乎完全成为一个真正的中国人。就这一点而言，海瑟·施密特（Heather Schmidt）所采用的其称为"再东方主义"的方法，是令人感兴趣的；尤其是通过传统和古老文化中的这些东方的、异国的和神秘的形象来打破东方主义理论的想法：

"中国的代表形象突出的是传统和古老：身着旗袍的女子弹奏琵琶和古琴；身着皇家服饰和头饰的女子表演精致的茶道；男子身着长衫或唐装在舞台上推广孔子学院；身着绸缎的男子表演太极。孔子学院中的这些东方形象体现了西方社会对中国形象长期以来的东方主义观点：迷人、神秘、异国、诱惑而且肯定是'不同的'。"（Schmidt, 2013: 657）

"汉语桥"比赛毫无疑问是对希望继续学习中文的学生提供的一座有形桥梁。这座桥梁最为重要的帮助是中国政府提供的奖学金。这一支持对智利这样的国家具有更大的意义，因为智利没有汉学研究学科，没有中国研究的研究生专业，研究中国和亚洲的教师应当在大学中的某些亚洲研究中心寻求拓展知识的途径或将这一领域的课程纳入某些本科专业。中国对智利很重要，智利需要在这一领域培养更多的汉学家、翻译家和专家。

就孔子学院而言，笔者了解到其做了大量的努力，在世界各地推广中文教学。2008年以来智利建立了两所孔子学院，不仅在其所在的大学而且在众多教育机构拓展中文教学。但是，除了由孔子学院拉美地区中心（总部位于智利）组织的翻译和文学传播活动之外，孔子学院对中国文化在智利的传播还不够，也未能更深入地开展活动，以促进智利对中国社会有更好的了解。其还可以拓展研讨领域，就思想、文学、美学和历史等课题进行思考，并开展旨在使年轻人更好了解中国的学术对话。参与智利教育部中国语言计划的学生也感受到了这一点。

2017年第一个学期，智利教育部在16个开设中文课程的公立教育机构对其中文课程进行了调研。在调研和沟通中，学生们强调需要更多地学习中国文化，更广泛和更具体地了解中国社会的各个方面。同样，笔者也对在北京学习的智利学生进行了采访。他们说，因为对中国文化缺乏了解，他们在智利所想象的中国与实际看到的中国完全不同，这在很大程度上对他们面对真实的中国造成了困难——事实上，中国与所有国家一样，既有优点也有不足。

面对学生们的关切，智利教育部与一个专家组合作制定了名为"从文化的角度教授中文"的为期4年的一项中文教学计划。该计划包含了教授中国文化的内容，从而使得学生能够对这个从语言和文化上对东亚产生最大影响的国家有更多的了解。通过学习中国语言和文化，智利学生能够掌握关于中国和亚洲其他地区的基本知识。同样，文化与语言的结合可以使教学内容更加跨学科，这也是智利国家教学大纲方案和计划的核心目标。

除此之外，我们也探讨了中共十九大之后孔子学院和中国国家汉办将在中国文化对外传播方面发挥什么作用。在习近平提出的"新时代"，是否会提出将中国古代哲学传统理想与国际惯例相结合的论述？上述论述中的某些部分已经在一些文化活动的题目中体现出来，比如2016年的"汉语桥"比赛就体现了习近平主席提出的"中国梦"。2017年，中国国家汉办号召成立一个教师联盟推进"一带一路"倡议的持续进展。同样地，孔子学院的汉语教师要在国家汉办接受培训，培训内容包括强调中国特色社会主义以及有关中国政治论述的概念，如和谐、民族复兴和爱国主义。

就上述问题，孙吉胜提到了中共十九大和传统文化，强调了对外文化关系中的中国特点。她指出，中国人强调集体，而西方人强调个人。同样地，她补充道，西方强调二元对立，从分歧而不是统一的角度出发持续创造对立，产生不可调和的两级对立。她说，尽管西方可能与中国对立，但是双方也可以彼此合作、支持甚至转变，用中国哲学中的阴阳理论实现和谐。

孙进行了一个有趣的比较，显示了中国外交的叙事和文化论述所使用的方式，即寻求说服世界接受其被动、合作和非军事的立场。然而，Sun在提到"西方"的时候，并未明确她到底指的是哪个西方，因为从笔者角度，世界上存在多个"西方"；有的"西方"长期在脆弱和质疑的状态中存在，超出了虚幻的构建认知。比如拉丁美洲就是这样。这个大洲先后被"欧洲的西方"和美国帝国所殖民，现在又以美国文化的方式被"西方化"。这个地区正在与其自身的身份认同做斗争。笔者知道，中国认为拉丁美洲有其独特性，但是在其话语体系中却常常将拉美视作"西方"，而未考虑到事实上有多个"西方"同时存在；而中国作为"东方"的说法也是欧洲殖民者创造的。

关于孙所强调的中国思想，笔者想到黄卓越提出的观点。他在比较两种不同的对意识形态的理解方法时，提到阿尔都塞（Althusser）的思想：一种是强调观点和话语，另一种是强调行动和社会（黄卓越，2012: 235）。关于这一点，他补充道，我们必须考察界线和社会差别的存在以及意识形态概念的有用性，以便考虑其他的"微观政治"角度，并通过这一方式，观察社会和意识形态形成的层级复杂性和多元素互动，以更接近现实地去进行分析（黄卓越，2012: 237）。他认为应当用"社会意识形态"这样的说法，将意识形态作为一个由不同社会力量（也包括国家的意志）构成的理论和实践领域："我们认同福柯（Foucault）的观点，即教育、法律、文化、学术和宗教有它们各自的领域（话语模式），但是当某个支配性的意识形态足够强大的时候，它就将成为可以重塑其他领域的基本规则。"（黄卓越，2012: 248）

在这一方面，同时将社会差别与孙所提到的中国思想的文化论述以及中国文化传播方式相联系，则有必要关注中国社会当前的变化与孙所提到的社会理想之间的关系。和其他发展中国家一样，中国经历了一场赛跑，这场赛跑因为一系列竞争者的参与而变得激烈。我们也在谈论中国千百万的年轻人必须通过竞争，以取得高分进入大学：

"在由过渡膨胀的发展理论所导致的秩序混乱的竞争背景下，老师、家长和学生不得不遵守学校按照市场规则制定的规定；随之而来的是，学生不得不面对学校强加给他们的竞争，家长渴望确保他们的孩子在市场竞争中不落后，于是他们将自己的焦虑转嫁到孩子的身上。"（黄卓越，2012:246）

综上所述，在语言和文化传播领域，中国为世界做了大量的工作，在全球各地创建了孔子学院，通过每年提供数万个奖学金名额的方式开展文化传播活动。随着中国国家汉办与智利教育部于2004年签署了双边协定，中文教学以惊人的速度在智利迅速发展。孔子学院向智利全国各地的教育机构敞开了大门，为它们提供语言教学指导。孔子学院拉美地区中心在该地区中国语言和文化的传播上起到了根本作用，特别是在组织与中国文化传播和鼓励中文著作翻译相关的活动方面。所有这些机构已经有了一个坚实的平台，可以在此基础上建立研究中心，从而对中国文化有更深入的了解，并与智利文化进行知识方面的合作，开展涉及广泛讨论和具有社会代表性的研究、思考和分析活动，组织涉及这一领域学科的学术会议和研讨会。通过这种方式，这些机构不仅能够合作提升中国文化在智利的发展，而且能够提升针对中国和中国社会的文化研究水平。

China's Cultural Diplomacy in Chile

María Elvira Ríos Peñafiel / Chile

Researcher of the Ministry of Education of Chile

Together with Professor Isabel Rodríguez, from the International Relations Center (Faculty of Government of the University of Development), we have carried out an investigation of China's cultural diplomacy in Chile, specifically the teaching of the Chinese language.

This report is part of this and of the research carried out during the Young Sinologists Meeting held in September 2017.

The good historical relations between China and Chile have been conformed the perceptions of the Chilean society towards this Asian country. The exchange between both countries was increasing every day and resulted in the Friendship Association, which was founded in 1954 and subsequently led to the establishment of commercial relations that preceded the diplomatic relations of 1970. Chile was the second country in Latin America and the first in South America with which China established formal diplomatic relations after Cuba; a mechanism was created between the parliaments and Chile was the first country in Latin America to sign a free trade agreement with China in 2005 (Lizama, 2013: 228). In addition, Chile and China maintain a para-diplomatic relationship, which "involves regional governments and municipalities in the case of Chile, and, in the case of China, provincial governments, municipalities within the provinces and municipalities under central jurisdiction" (Lizama, 2013: 233).

This also responds to the economic and cultural convergence that China is seeking, which in the case of Chile is evident in the numerous treaties and agreements that are being signed in both areas, that converged in 2012, with the status of strategic partner that China gave to Chile. In the concrete aspects of the image that China seeks to project, we emphasize that in the economic sphere the interest is on highlighting the modern and technological element, while in the culture sphere is emphasize the traditional elements of culture. This has given support to a bilateral cooperation narrative at the level of governments, which has been complemented with relations between societies on cultural issues. In the case of Chile, like many other Latin American countries, the presence of Chinese culture is not only developing from the work of the Chinese government, but also from a series of cultural centers, which invite to know the traditional culture from different aspects; martial arts, theater, medicine, dance or language. This reflects that the public diplomacy directed towards other societies necessarily involves governmental actors and non-governmental actors.

In the last ten years, there has been an almost revolutionary case of teaching Chinese culture and language in Chile, which had been originated from a project created by the Ministry of Education of Chile and then, from the Confucius Institute.

I would like to add a factor mentioned by the director of the Crossing the Pacific Corporation, Rodrigo Fábrega, who emphasize that, in contrast to other languages such as Latin, French and English, the teaching of Chinese is incorporated as a teaching program in public schools. That is to say Chinese learning does not begin in the Chilean elite sector, an issue that overturns the way in which languages have been inserted into Chilean society.

From 2004 until today, the studies on Chinese language in Chile was extended very fast. The mutual collaboration in dissemination of the Chinese language in Chile arises from the interest of the former Minister of Education of the Government of Ricardo Lagos, Sergio Bitar, who in a visit to China observes the relevance of the Chinese language in the world. On May 1, 2004, the Memorandum of Understanding for Cooperation in the Field of Education was signed between the Ministry of Education of the Republic of Chile (MINEDUC) and the Ministry of Education of the People's Republic of China. This Memorandum gave way to the creation of the Chinese Language Teaching Program in the Office of International Relations (ORI). The functioning of the Chinese Language Program depends on the Chinese government, through the HANBAN office and the Chilean government, through MINEDUC and the municipalities. In 2016 there were more than 3,000 students studying Chinese in almost all Province of the country.

Given the high number of Chinese language students we wanted to know more closely the image that these young people were building in their minds about China and its society and what were the factors that influenced that look. In this regard, we think the role played by the imaginary in social relationships is significant; "…imaginary significations play an organizing role in human behavior and in social relations, and are an imaginary creation of the given society. Through the imaginarily created significations, each society gives 'answers' to the basic 'questions' which have to do with its own existence"(Kavoulakos, 1987: 145-164).

In 2014, we carried out an investigation in seven educational establishments, located in Valparaiso, Metropolitana and Bio-Bio regions. By entering into the processes of teaching Chinese and the experience of children from various cities in Chile, we discovered a series of factors that influence both the way in which the studies are carried out and the imaginary of the students. Perhaps one of the most distinctive factors is the place where the schools are located. The perception, experience and imagination about China of students in the capital differ from that of students who are in provinces or small towns. The establishments located in the center of the capital manifest a greater link or contact with Chinese, because in the capital the presence of Asians is considerably higher than the cities of the other schools mentioned. Also, the economic activity of the city is also another important factor; an example is Valparaiso and Coronel, both port cities, where Chinese ships arrive every month.

Likewise, the role of the teacher is fundamental. The teacher is the bridge between China and the students; in most of the case, the teachers are the only Chinese persons they know, therefore, their role and way of transmitting the cultural is the key to understand China. Prior to the Chinese courses, many of the students had a very general picture of China. However, the classes aroused their interest and created an imaginary around that country through the teachings of their teachers. None of the students interviewed mentioned something negative or problematic about China. Apart from the imaginary created from the information transmitted by the teacher, some students mention a stereotype of the Chinese in Chile: serious, cultured and studious people. However, this image of the Chinese also occurs or varies according to the closest example for them: there are students who no longer follow that stereotype because the Chinese teacher does not represent it, while for other students it is created or intensified due to that the teacher has those characteristics. From the above we observe the great responsibility and leadership of teachers.

Teachers receive a training that is divided into five parts: Mandarin Chinese teaching, preparation of classes with bibliographic material, analysis and reflection of the classes, teaching of Chinese culture (specifically learning the art of paper cutting, calligraphy and *taiji*) , and adaptation to an intercultural medium (how to insert yourself in the culture of another country). They also have the mission of preparing one of their best students to compete in the famous Chinese Bridge competition. This contest brings together the best Chinese students at a national level (including Confucius Institute students and public institutions) to compete and be selected for the international competition that takes place every year in China.

In this regard, we will refer to a specific case: the Chinese Bridge. This competition was held in 2016, organized by the Confucius Institute of the University of Santo Tomas in conjunction with the Ministry of Education and Hanban. The students from the schools as well as from the universities participated in the competition. The contest was titled "Dreams that illuminate the future" (related to the Chinese Dream proposed by Xi Jinping). We would like to exemplify the relevance and influence of this competition with one of the students of the Multi-Talented Excellence School of San Nicolas, of the Biobio Region. The girl is from Cobquecura, one of the areas most affected by the tsunami that occurred in the 2010 earthquake. In her presentation, she referred to that difficult situation that her family lived in the earthquake and tsunami, and then she showed an image of the Chinese coming down from an airplane, arriving to deliver humanitarian support. She pointed out that, from that moment, she felt a great admiration and curiosity to know who those people that helped them were. Since then, the young woman became interested in China and began studying Chinese language and culture. Her admiration for this country was evident in the presentations that she made during the Chinese Bridge competition; the great fascination that this student expressed in her performance towards China and her traditional culture drew attention to the spectators of the competition. Also, the student characterized a Chinese girl, dressed in red, who sang traditional songs, making gestures and movements that, at first glance, simulated a real Chinese girl.

The case of this young participant of the Chinese Bridge contest brings together several elements of Chinese cultural diplomacy. First of all, the affective policy that emerges from the humanitarian aid of the Chinese government to Chile. The support given by the Chinese government reached vulnerable places, economic scarcity and underdevelopment, permeating the hearts of the villagers. Secondly, the teaching of the language, which has also spread throughout the country, includes educational establishments far from the cities. The student we have mentioned is studying Chinese at Multi-Talented Excellence School of San Nicolas, one of the establishments located in the Bio-Bio region. This establishment advocates quality education, with the seal in the languages. Their students learn two foreign languages and among the options they have the teaching of the Chinese language.

In addition to the aforementioned, is necessary to emphasize the "transformation" of the student during his presentation at the Chinese Bridge. One of the most striking evidence is the artistic act; in this presentation, it is common to see the competitors dressed in typical Chinese costumes. In many cases it happens that the degree of characterization is such that the competitors seems to be a true Chinese. According to this characterization, it's interesting the Heather Schmidt's approach, which she calls "re-orientalism"; Above all, from the intention to break with the theory of Orientalism, through those orientalist, exotic and mythical images of traditional and ancient culture:

> Representations of China highlight the traditional and ancient: women clad in *qipaos* (traditional form-fitting dresses) playing *pipas* (a stringed instrument similar to a lute) and *guzhengs* (similar to a zither); women dressed in imperial garments and headdress performing elaborate tea ceremonies; men wearing *changshan*-style costumes (traditional male garments worn like a robe the length of the body) or *Tang*-style jackets (made from colourful brocades) at display booths promoting Confucius Institutes; men in silk martial arts uniforms performing tai chi. Such Orientalist representations in CIs play on and play into long-held Orientalist ideas in the West about what China is: intriguing, mysterious, exotic, enticing, and most definitely "Other" (Schmidt, 2013: 657).

The Chinese Bridge has been, without a doubt, a tangible bridge for those who intend to continue their studies of Chinese language. The most important support to cross that bridge are the scholarships awarded by the Chinese government.

This support acquires greater relevance in countries like ours, which do not have sinology studies, where there are no postgraduate studies on China and where teachers dedicated to the study of China or Asia should look for ways to develop their knowledge in some Asian Study Centers in universities or incorporating courses of the area in some bachelor degree. Despite the importance that China has for the country, Chile still needs to prepare sinologists, translators and experts in the field.

With respect to the Confucius Institutes, we know of the enormous effort to expand the teaching of the language throughout the world. In Chile, two Confucius Institutes have been installed since 2008, which have extended the teaching of the language not only in their universities but in different educational establishments in the country. However, the dissemination of the culture carried out in the Confucius Institute, except for the work of translation and literary dissemination organized by the Regional Center of the CI in Latin America (CRICAL) with its headquarters in Chile is not enough. It fails delve deeper into topics that allow a greater understanding of Chinese society, opening spaces for discussion, reflection on thought, literature, aesthetics, history for example, or intercultural dialogue that allows young people to know China. This observation is also perceived among students who belong to the Ministry's Chinese Language Program.

During the first semester of 2017, the Ministry of Education made observations of the Chinese language classes in the 16 public educational establishments that carry out the Chinese program. In these observations and conversations with the students, they emphasized to study more the culture, knowing more widely and in detail various topics that allow them to understand Chinese society. In the same way, we interviewed a group of young Chileans students in Beijing. They commented that, due to the lack of knowledge of Chinese culture, the image with which they had arrived from Chile to the Asian country had completely changed, producing, for the most part, a difficulty in facing what would become the real China, a country like all, with virtues and defects.

Faced with the concern of the students, the Ministry, together with a group of experts, has developed a 4-year program of teaching the language entitled "Teaching the Chinese Language from Culture". This Mandarin Chinese Language Teaching Program incorporates the teaching of Chinese culture, which allows us to expand knowledge about the country that has most influence, both in language and cultural aspects, in East Asia. Studying the Chinese language and culture allows us to understand fundamental elements not only of China, but of a wide area of Asia. Likewise, the cultural and idiomatic combination allows its contents to be interdisciplinary, which is a key objective of the plans and programs of the National Curriculum.

In addition to the above, and in relation to China's political contingency in 2017, we ask ourselves what will be the role of the Confucius Institute and Hanban in cultural dissemination after the 19th National Congress of the Communist Party; In the New Era of Xi Jinping, will it try to bring the discourse that evokes ideals of the ancient Chinese philosophical tradition to international practice, to develop an ideology that not only contributes to a positive view or vision towards China, but also towards a harmonious spirit among civilizations? Some of that discourse is manifested in titles of cultural activities, such as Chinese Bridge of 2016, whose title evokes President Xi Jinping's Chinese Dream. In 2017, Hanban opened a call for work to form a group of teachers to develop and sustain the "Belt and Road" Initiative. In the same way, at the time of going abroad to do Chinese language classes, teachers receive training in Hanban whose program, among other things, incorporates lectures that emphasize the ideals of socialism with Chinese characteristics, pointing concepts that have been central in Chinese political ideological discourse, such as harmony, revitalization and patriotism.

Regarding the above, Sun Jisheng refers to the 19th National Congress of the Communist Party and traditional culture, emphasizing the Chinese characteristics in the cultural relations with the exterior. Sun points out that the Chinese emphasize community while the West emphasizes individuality. In the same way, Sun adds that the West highlights the binary opposition, starting from the division and not the unity, creating opposites in a constant way, generating incompatible poles opposites. Although West can be an opposite of China, she said, the two sides can collaborate, support and even transform, evoking the Chinese philosophy of yin and yang and in this way, achieves harmony (Sun, 2017: 7-8).

Sun makes an interesting comparison that shows the way in which the narrative and cultural discourse of Chinese diplomacy operates, seeking to convince the world of its passive, cooperative and non-military position. However, when Sun refers to "the West" it does not make clear to which West it refers, because from our perspective there are several "Wests" which, beyond their illusory construction, manifest themselves and live in a constant fragility and questioning. This is the case with Latin America, a continent colonized by that "European West" that was later "colonized" by the US empire, again being "Westernized" but in the American cultural style. And now, it is a region that lives in the struggle of its own identity. We know that China considers Latin America with its distinctions, but in the discourse, it constantly falls into the concept of *xifang*, without taking into account that there are several "Wests" and, at the same time, they place themselves in that "East" term also created by European colonizers.

Now, returning to the Chinese thought that Sun emphasizes, I would like to refer to what Huang Zhuoyue points out, who alludes to Althusser's thought, when he refers to two methods of understanding what is understood by ideology: one emphasizes ideas and speech and the other in actions and society (Huang, 2012: 235). To this he adds that, together with the usefulness of the concept of ideology, we must examine the existence of demarcations and social differentiations to consider other "micropolitical" perspectives and in this way, observe the hierarchical complexity and the multi-elemental interaction of the society / ideology formation and perform an analysis closer to reality (Huang, 2012: 237). Huang suggests talking, rather, of a "social ideology", so as to take ideology as the conceptual and practical field composed of various social forces (including state's will also):

"We agree with Foucault that education, law, culture, academia, and religion have their own fields (discursive modes), but when certain dominant ideology is strong enough, it will become a basic rule capable of reshaping various fields" (Huang, 2012: 248).

In this regard, and considering linking the social differentiation with the cultural discourse of Chinese thought that Sun Jisheng mentioned, and the way of transmitting the Chinese culture, it is necessary to attend, for example, the current changes of the Chinese society versus the ideals of the society posed by Sun. China, like other developing countries, has experienced a race that is exacerbated by the number of competitors; we talk about the thousands of young people who must compete to achieve a score that allows them to enter universities:

> "In the context of badly ordered competition caused by the overexpansion of the ideology of development, teachers, parents, and students have to obey the rules of the school, which has to adopt the market law, and in the wake of that, students have to face the competition imposed on them by the school; parents are eager to ensure that their children will not fall behind in the market-principle-to-be, so they transfer their own anxiety to their children" (Huang, 2012: 246).

In conclusion, in the field of the dissemination of language and culture, China has done a generous work to the world, creating Confucius Institutes that have spread across all continents, carrying out cultural dissemination activities by delivering thousands of scholarships annually. In Chile, the teaching of the language had an extraordinary boom with the agreement that Hanban and Mineduc signed in 2004, developing the teaching of the language at the national level. The Confucius Institute opens its doors to educational establishments throughout the country, to offer language instruction. CRICAL has been fundamental in the extension of the language and culture in the region, specifically on the activities related to the dissemination of Chinese literature and encouraging the translation of works.

All these entities already have a solid platform, in which they could set up study centers that allow to know the culture in greater depth, that collaborate in a mutual knowledge with the Chilean culture, making studies, reflections and analysis that involve enriching discussions and most representative of society, conducting academic meetings, seminars, involving academics in the area. In this way, not only would they collaborate in improving the development of culture in the country, but also in raising cultural studies to levels of our understanding of China and her society.

References

Fábrega, Rodrigo, Fábrega, Jorge, Piña, Karina, *¿Por qué el aprendizaje del chino mandarín puede generar beneficios de larga duración en el bienestar de un país como Chile?* Santiago, Universidad Adolfo Ibáñez, junio de 2011.

Huang, Zhuoyue, "The Competition of Two Discourses: The Making of a New Ideology in China, *Cultural Politics* Vol 8, Issue 2, Duke University Press, Duke University, 2012.

Kavoulakos, Konstantinos, "Cornelius Castoriadis on Social Imaginary and Truth", *Ariadne 12*, 2006, pp. 201-213.

Lizama, Natalia, El estado de la paradiplomacia sino-chilena", en Isabel, Rodríguez y Yang Shouguo (eds.), *La diplomacia pública de China en América Latina*, Santiago de Chile, RIL Editores, 2013.

Ríos, María Elvira, "El proceso de inserción del "carácter" chino en Chile: La experiencia del aprendizaje del idioma chino, *Entre Espacios: La historia latino-americana en el contexto global, Actas del XVII Congreso Internacional de AHILA,* Berlín, Freie Universität Berlín, 9-13 de septiembre de 2014.

Schmidt, Heather, "China's Confucius Institutes and the "Necessary White Body", *The Canadian Journal of Sociology / Cahiers canadiens de sociologie,* Vol. 38, No. 4, Par / Santos Special Issue, 2013.

孙吉胜：《传统文化与十八大以来中国外交话语体系构建》，《外交评论》，2017年第4期。

在"一带一路"倡议下对中国与拉丁美洲的思考

侯赛 【秘鲁】

秘鲁天主教大学孔子学院讲师

一 引言

我曾以商人和学生身份到过中国,我想就"一带一路"倡议及其对拉美国家未来几年的影响分享一些个人观点。此外,本文旨在回顾研修期间我们与各位专家深入研讨及我们青年汉学家之间讨论的各种概念和话题。

二 "一带一路"倡议及中国的世界角色

"一带一路"倡议实质上是一项旨在成为全球经济发展新动力的宏伟经济发展计划。其主要目标是促进曾参与"古丝绸之路"和"海上丝绸之路"的地区和国家之间的贸易、合作和发展。通过为项目、基础设施、互联互通和发展提供开放的平台,中国正在提倡建设"命运共同体",即各国共同探索和建设经济繁荣,既为本国人民谋福祉,也创造一个和谐的世界。

"一带一路"倡议的灵感来源于古丝绸之路。正如习近平主席所言:"历史就是最好的老师",古丝绸之路清楚地说明了不同文明如何能够互相联系、共同兴旺、搭建通向共识的桥梁并帮助不同文化互取所长。在这样的环境下,中国在古丝绸之路中的作用显得尤为重要,因其不仅开创了这一商贸路线,更成为了中西之间交流与合作的主要推动者。千百年来,中国作为区域强国支持了许多亚洲王国和国家的发展,而"一带一路"倡议也让人回想起这种积极的方式。但是,这一倡议并不是古丝绸之路的复兴，不应被视为古丝绸之路，两者也不具有可比性。与古丝绸之路相比，这一新平台旨在联系起的不光是许多世纪前古丝绸之路沿线的国家，甚至是跨越全球不同地区的国家。

此外，这一倡议的另一重要作用在于能够促进参与国家间的和平与稳定。在过去几个世纪，古丝绸之路沿线国家经历着影响当地和区域发展的冲突。中东、非洲和亚洲的一些特定区域遭受着纷争，对合作、商业和文化交流而言，这些地区是有风险的。从这一角度而言，像"一带一路"这样的倡议让很多这些国家有机会寻求共同点，在谈判桌上与中国一起规划并执行对他们的人民有利的项目。"一带一路"倡议有一个明确的重心，即"开放与包容"。而中国作为该倡议的核心，为国际合作提供了另一源泉。这一倡议更符合发展中国家的实际需求，因为中国本身在公众决策、公众谋划和大规模基础设施项目执行方面取得了成功。正因为如此，到目前为止，100多个国家和国际组织已同意支持该倡议，50多个国家已与中国签署"一带一路"框架下的合作协议。

此外，我们也看到，该倡议启动4年以来，越来越多的国家、机构和国际组织表现出真正参与的兴趣。但是，所有已参与成员和潜在参与者都应该意识到，"一带一路"是长期框架下的倡议，至少会在未来30年展开。因此，所有国家和利益攸关方都应制定和规划好各自的路线图，以期从这一合作平台获得最大利益。大多数发展中国家缺少长期发展计划，因而在需要提出为期30年的项目或愿景时遭遇现实挑战。我认为这一倡议为这些国家提供了绝佳机会，借此他们可以放眼长远，与中国一道创造极具意义且行之有效的国际合作框架。当然，他们也需要考虑另一个方面，即这一倡议仍在建设中。我指的是，它可能依实际情况而改变或调整。基于这一考虑，各国甚至中国都应保持适应变化的灵活性，并着眼于"一带一路"的主要目标，即经济合作和一体化。

在青年汉学家研修计划的一次会议中，我们回顾分析了"一带一路"倡议与"马歇尔计划"的不同之处。我们一致认为，与"马歇尔计划"相比，"一带一路"倡议存在四个原则上的不同。第一，本质不同。"一带一路"倡议对所有国家开放，每个国家拥有是否参与的最终决定权；第二，更具灵活性。之前已提到，此倡议可能会根据未来中国或世界形势的变化而变化；第三，更具包容性。"一带一路"不区别对待政治观点或利益不同的国家。相反，它尽力使未得到其他国际合作支持的国家参与其中；第四，过程渐进。前文也有提到，随着中国成为第一大经济体并实现到2020年全面建成小康社会、到2050年成为伟大的社会主义现代化强国的目标，"一带一路"将有所改变，其影响力也会逐渐增强。

在该倡议的发展过程中，我们也应当思考一下中国的对外交往原则，这也是中国建立国际合作体的指导方针。这些指导方针非常重要，因为能帮助我们理解中国处理国际事务的策略及其影响。第一也是最重要的原则是采取经济手段。中国希望通过合作和支持不同国家来建设经济繁荣。从这一点来说，中国并非想压迫或侵略其他国家，而是视经济兴旺为创造和平与理解的最可靠方式。第二条原则是远离争端和冲突。中国认为一个国家的命运由其人民的意志决定，因此，中国不会干涉任何国家间的争端，会尊重各国主权。第三，中国将有有所保留地利用其日益增强的国际影响力，无意控制或压迫国际社会。

但是，为什么"一带一路"倡议对中国未来几十年的发展如此重要？由于中国正在追求一种"新常态"（其含义是注重GDP增长的质量而非速度），因此通过维持最低经济增长标准来保持经济稳定，并由此实现里程碑式的发展和繁荣就显得尤为重要。"一带一路"倡议因此成为这种经济增长模式的主要部分，因为中国需要通过更多国际项目消化其过剩产能。另外，中国在某些行业的发展无疑已经达到了世界标准，尤其是基础设施、太阳能、电子商务、移动和城市化相关的产业。因此，中国也有能力出口技术和专业技能，为发展中经济体提供更多发展方法。中国在厄瓜多尔的基础设施项目就是一个很好的例子。中国在厄瓜多尔开展了很多基础设施项目，助其防御自然灾害。因此，与之前相比，厄瓜多尔的洪灾及经济、人力损失大幅降低。得益于中国的防御知识和灾害管理技术，厄瓜多尔现在比秘鲁和哥伦比亚等邻国更能应对气候挑战和灾害。

"一带一路"倡议具有相关性的另一重要原因是，中国希望在国际社会扮演更积极的角色并增强"人类命运共同体"的理念。过去几年，中国为国际社会做出了更大的贡献，这是有目共睹的。这也能通过以下事实证明：中国是各种国际组织和平台的主要贡献者，如联合国基金会、联合国安保部队、世界银行和国际货币基金组织。然而，这些组织大部分都由西方大国和某些国家掌控，他们意在为这些国际组织的合作设立工作框架和规则，所以即使中国想贡献更多，也面临着这些国家所设的限制。考虑到这一情况，中国没有让自己陷于被动，而是开始在整个国际社会扮演更加积极的角色并发起了旨在为区域和国际社会增加更多价值的国际倡议。比如，中国发起创立的亚洲基础设施投资银行、新开发银行等项目已吸引了国际社会的广泛关注和兴趣，同时也对"一带一路"的融资起到重要作用。而且，这些多边机构是在中国的运行框架下产生的，因而中国起着主导作用，取代了一般传统多边组织中的西方规则。中国提高国际影响力的另一策略是组织和举办国际活动。这些活动使中国在为解决世界主要挑战建言献策时更有发言权。过去几年，我们看到，在亚太经合组织、二十国集团首脑峰会、博鳌论坛等平台上，中国不断提倡通过贸易和合作建立一个全球化、互联互通的世界。值得特别注意的是去年5月14至15日中国在北京举办的"一带一路"国际合作高峰论坛。首次举办"一带一路"国际合作高峰论坛，中国的目标是增加各国和社会对这一倡议的认识并在国家间建立更加稳固的合作网络。这次活动取得显著的成功，29位国家元首和130多位国家和国际组织的代表参与其中。亚洲和欧洲国家是主要参与者；但美国和日本也派了代表或代表团参加。这展示了中国想要通过"一带一路"促进的开放精神。

在青年汉学家研修计划中我们有机会了解"一带一路"倡议的不同重点，总结如下：

——政策沟通：作为倡议的重要目标之一，与各国政府的合作与协调是倡议实施各步骤和各项目的主要基础。

——贸易畅通："一带一路"是全球经济复苏计划的中国版本，因此，建立经济走廊、贸易平台和提倡国家间自由贸易生态系统有利于实现这一倡议。

——民心相通：同古丝绸之路一样，"一带一路"倡议也以促进文化联系和文明交流为目标。同时，它提供了极好的机会，有助于在众多国家间传播中国文化，增强世界对中国软实力的认识和其自身的建设。

——设施联通：举国建设基础设施一直是中国经济发展的动力之一，因而，在倡议参与国连接和建设基础设施比其他举措更能促进当地和区域的贸易和发展。

——资金融通：为了实现互联互通和经济繁荣的目标，"一带一路"倡议还旨在建立基金会和金融支援项目、丰富跨境资金流动和支付方式。此外，同倡议参与国的资金融通也有助于扩大人民币使用范围，为处理国际事务提供另一种货币选择。

三 拉丁美洲与"一带一路"倡议

随着"一带一路"倡议的广度和力度在未来几年、几十年里逐渐加强，中国与拉美国家的关系也会增强。由于大多时候中国是拉美的主要商业伙伴和外商直接投资的主要来源，在"一带一路"倡议开始阶段，许多拉美国家就已明确表现出参与和贡献的意愿。例如，智利共和国总统和阿根廷共和国总统参加了 2017 年 5 月在北京举办的"一带一路"国际合作高峰论坛，秘鲁、巴西、哥伦比亚和其他拉美国家也派出部长级代表参加。这体现了"一带一路"倡议对拉美的重要性。

如果我们把古丝绸之路当作发展"一带一路"倡议的唯一初始框架，那么拉美地区并非此商贸路线的一部分。尽管有学者称中国和拉美在几世纪前由于"马尼拉大帆船"商贸路线——即一条由马尼拉（菲律宾）出发，穿越整片太平洋，运送各种货物商品到墨西哥的路线——而有过贸易关系，但我认为这个观点有点牵强，因为这条路线主要是前西班牙殖民地（墨西哥和菲律宾）之间的贸易路线。不可否认，它是一条在贸易方面连接亚洲和拉丁美洲的重要路线，我们也确实能在它通行的年间找到许多中国产品和元素，但我认为它同古丝绸之路没有联系。

我们在前文已有论及，"一带一路"倡议是长期框架下的倡议，旨在促进各国和各地区的经济繁荣。并且，它是一个开放包容的平台，不区别对待任何国家。但是，拉美国家有必要尽早表现出加入的兴趣并做出承诺。由于它是长期的项目，早期加入的国家和组织就能享受到长期参与的福利并获得更多有利于自身发展的资源。正如所有成功的企业和项目一样，创始人或者在初期提供支持的人更能利用好机会。因此，我认为拉美国家应该增加对该倡议的兴趣和参与，并培养当地的"一带一路"专家，为与中国建立联系提供建议和支持。到 2017 年，亚洲基础设施投资银行已包括以下拉丁美洲非区域性的潜在成员：巴西、秘鲁、委内瑞拉、玻利维亚、智利和阿根廷，这本身就说明了拉美国家与中国结好和支持该倡议的明确意向。

拉美各国在收入和基础设施建设方面水平悬殊，由于地理条件和自然地貌原因，要在国内高效通行或流动难度非常大。该地区还面临诸多问题，如腐败、低效公共管理和环境问题，当然，还有贫穷和犯罪问题（这两个问题与经济发展直接相关）。另外，由于过去这些年缺少长期规划和政治稳定，该地区为达到我们都想达到的经济繁荣正在苦苦挣扎。也有经济正在成长的国家，比如智利、秘鲁、阿根廷、哥伦比亚和墨西哥，但他们也面临着内部政治问题的挑战，比如总统选举，越来越多的人对现状不满而寻求极端解决方式（如意识形态极端的政治候选人或者想要改变整个经济和社会框架的政党）。拉美目前的局势非常不稳定，我相信"一带一路"倡议确实能提供一个共同平台，让所有国家通过计划与中国的合作和项目来克服他们面临的问题和挑战。显然，中国和拉美作为发展中的经济体存在许多相似之处，因此，拉美国家将中国视为一个成功的例子，并学习中国为建成小康社会所采取的经济和政治举措。

拉美国家有责任制定"一带一路"2050愿景，将他们的所有方案和合作与中国对接。如果拉美国家能够创造出共同的愿景和与中国合作的路线图，我认为其成果将对中国和拉美双方都十分有益。

在建设"一带一路"框架下的中拉关系时还有一个理念值得探讨，即创建"数字一带一路"。双方都应探索连接各市场领域的机制，包括商业、文化和知识；从这一层面来说，结合中国电子产业的先进水平及中国企业的全球化程度这两个重要因素，双方都应创造更多项目来促进电子商务、教育、文化传播的发展，交流最佳实践、案例和知识。利用数字互联，国家间可以克服距离限制而变得更紧密。

问题不在于距离，而在于知识和理解。因此，更多拉美国家的公司应该利用已在中国发展起来的平台宣传他们的产品和服务。中国是全世界最重要的消费市场之一，甚至是最重要的消费市场，拥有最大的中产阶级群体，且这个群体还在增长。越来越多的中国公民了解到来自拉美国家的产品和服务。拉美的食品、饮料和旅游服务通过中国的许多网络平台得到了宣传，但许多新产品和服务，包括卫生产业、时尚产业、教育等，都还有很大的发展空间。同时，中国企业和初创公司越来越重视拉美市场，对其兴趣也在增加，这主要是因为中国国内竞争十分激烈，所以越来越多的公司寻求扩张海外市场，并带上了自己的技术。滴滴出行和摩拜单车就是两个很有代表性的例子。前者是亚洲利用共享经济概念最为成功的公司之一。作为优步在不同市场的主要竞争者，滴滴出行计划将它的技术和专业知识输送到像墨西哥这样城市交通问题严重的国家。类似地，摩拜也是中国共享单车模式的先锋之一，正在进入智利和墨西哥等市场，为拉美地区的城市流动带来一种环保的方案。

这两个例子都充分体现了中国创新和公司创新是如何将新方法和独特的专业知识带到城市并帮助我们解决主要问题的。我认为，中国的创新企业会有更多机会进入拉美市场，为更多领域带来发展，比如农业、网络教育、农村经济和环境。通过"数字一带一路"，我们能把"中国创新"带到拉美国家，应用中国的成功方法，并按照当地的实际予以调整。中国一直在试验不同的社会创新方法，很多方法在许多年后催生了数百万的小企业，包括大量农村企业，提供了共同的发展和脱贫基础。为什么拉美不能效仿呢？

许多专家一致认为，对于"一带一路"倡议，短期内只有在拉美地区建设基础设施才能促进双边合作并推动更多国家参与这一倡议。如果看一下拉美国家的差异，我们会发现各届政府都关注通信技术和和基础设施。但是，由于我们的地理条件限制，尤其是在安第斯山附近的国家，发展、建设及与农村联通的速度非常之慢。因此，中国的建筑技术和专业技能切实地为支持拉美地区互联互通提供可靠的选择。中国广袤而多样的领土正是由伟大的基础设施连接起来的，比如高速公路、高铁系统、机场、港口。由于这些年持续的发展和提高，中国的建筑技术已名列世界前茅，且能应用于世界上大多数难度高的地区。

最后，如果有合作的机会和需要，商业和政府关系会按照自己的节奏前进。不过，如果我们想让这个关系更加持久，我们需要将目光转向人文交流，教育和文化交流对双方都很重要。中国的奖学金数量、教育机会和培训项目在过去几年中有很大提升，给成千上万的拉美人来华学习创造了条件。例如，仅在2017年，就有超过350名秘鲁学生获得奖学金，为了学习和培训漂洋过海来到中国。这个数字使中国成为迄今为止向秘鲁提供最多奖学金的国家。而事实是，中国对其他国家也是如此，包括智利、哥伦比亚、哥斯达黎加、巴西。但是当拉美的学术和商业精英决定专业深造和硕士研究的目的地时，主要的选择还是美国和欧洲国家。我们应该更加重视中国教育和发展的机会，这样高质量的人才才会前往中国接受培养。一旦这些人才成为关键的决策者，他们就能和中国建立联系。我们不能否认中国（通过孔子学院）在提升文化、语言和教育付出的巨大努力，但是拉美国家为吸引中国人才做出的努力、相关的项目和倡议都是非常有限的。拉美国家需要在促进中国文化、教育机会和语言中扮演一个更积极主动的角色，才会有越来越多的中国学生将我们国家视为一个潜在合作之地。

四 结论

本文旨在反馈和分享关于"一带一路"倡议现状及拉美与中国潜在合作的一些想法。基于上述观点，我们可以得出结论，我们双方还要做很多事情。但是，我相信，由于目前双方努力合作、共创发展蓝图，在接下来的几年里双边合作会扩大。从这方面来说，我很乐观，相信很快就能看到"一带一路"倡议对我们国家的影响。中国在过去几年增加了对拉美地区发展的支持，如今它不仅是我们产品和服务的主要进口国，在处理拉美某些最具挑战性的社会问题方面，中国也是我们的亲密盟友。我们感激中国向我们输送了许多资源，以及为加强双边关系所做的努力，但与此同时，我们期待拉美地区向中国迈出更积极主动的步伐。

我们与中国社科院专家、地方与中央政府代表进行了交谈，召开了会议，从中能感受到中国对于拉美了解甚多。另一方面，拉美国家缺乏中国专家，政治精英对"一带一路"倡议了解不多，这都是显而易见的。因此，作为"青年汉学家"，我们现在更有必要加强国人对中国的了解，宣传中国的形象，并让他们加深对"一带一路"倡议的了解。我们国家也需要更加积极主动，在"一带一路"倡议框架下发展一个中国蓝图，创造支撑我们经济体的双赢局面，同时支持中国在2050年实现目标。

我们的国家应当做出努力，我认为中国同样也应该增强其软实力和在拉美的国家品牌推广。例如，中国品牌获得质量和技术水平认可的过程非常漫长，很多公司品牌，甚至是大部分中国创新和独角兽企业（市值超过十亿美元的私营企业）仍然不为拉美市场所知。在交通、航天、建造、公共政策、能源与创业等方面中国也取得了巨大的进展，这应该作为范例在拉美地区推广，借此说明中国如何发展创新驱动型经济，及"一带一路"倡议如何发挥重要作用。

最后，大部分拉美国家将在接下来几年里庆祝独立两百周年纪念，这是我们历史的伟大里程碑。但是到成立两百年时，我们仍未将发展和繁荣带给大多数人民，想到这点我感到非常难过。中国决心在百年华诞时建成一个伟大的社会主义现代化强国，并在30年前就开始为此愿景付诸行动，我受到了极大的鼓舞。随着"一带一路"倡议的推进，中国不仅会在2050年实现目标，而且在实现的过程中，也将弘扬共同的价值观念，推进项目，帮助国际社会加深联系，促进不同地区的和平与发展。

Reflections about China and Latin America under the "Belt and Road" Initiative

Feliciano José / Peru

Lecturer of the Confucius Institute at Catholic Pontifical University of Peru; Founder and Director of Seed International China Ltd.

With my deepest gratitude to the Government of the People's Republic of China, The Ministry of Culture of the Peoples Republic of China, the Chinese Academy of Social Sciences and the Chinese Embassy in Peru, I would like express some of my thoughts and conclusions after taking part in the "Beijing Young Sinologist program of September 2017". As a participant of this program I was able to share with a group of brightest sinologist from around the world, different learning sessions, meetings and visits in Beijing and Jiangxi province, allowing me to increase my awareness about China and the Belt and Road initiative in a complete different level. I also want to extend my words of gratitude to the professors, local scholars and staff that accompanied us during the days of the program and helped us to experience China at a completely different level.

I. Introduction

As someone who has experience about China as a businessmen and student, I would like to share my views on the Belt and Road Initiative and how I see this initiative impacting Latin-American in the next years. In addition, this essay aims to recall the different concepts and topics that were discussed during our days in the program from the insightful sessions we had with different experts and the discussions we had among the Young Sinologists.

II. The "Belt and Road" initiative and China's Role in the World

The Belt and Road initiative or the "Belt and Road" Initiative is essentially an ambitious economic development plan that aims to become the new engine for global economic growth. The main goal of this initiative is to promote trade, partnership and development across the different regions and countries that used to be part of the "Ancient Silk Road" and the "Ancient Maritime Route". By providing an open platform for projects, infrastructure, connectivity and development; China is promoting the idea of a "common shared destiny" in which countries can explore and build together economic prosperity for their own people and in this way, create a harmonious world.

The Ancient Silk Road is the inspiration for this initiative and as president Xi Jinping said: "History is the best teacher". The Ancient Silk Road was a clear example of how different civilizations can connect and thrive together, building bridges of common understanding and helping cultures to exchange the best of them together. In this context, the role of China in the Ancient Silk Road was more than important, not only as the start of this trading and commerce route, but also as the main promoter of exchange and cooperation between the east and the west. For many centuries, China as a regional power supported the development of the different kingdoms and countries in Asia and the Belt and Road Initiative also recalls that proactive approach, however the initiative is not the renaissance of the ancient Silk Road. While it should be taken or compared with the previous Silk Road, it is a new platform that aims to connect not only the countries that used to belong to this trading route centuries ago, but countries across different regions in the world.

In addition, another important aspect of this initiative is the promotion of peace and stability across the countries in which the initiative is taking place. From centuries till recent years, countries across the Ancient Silk Road have been experiencing conflicts that affects their development from local and regional level. Specific zones in the Middle East, Africa and Asia, have been suffering disputes which creates a risky environment for cooperation, business and cultural connection. In that sense, an initiative like the "Belt and Road" offers an opportunity to work in a common ground for many of these countries and seat in the same table to plan and execute projects with China that can be beneficial for their own people. The "Belt and Road" initiative has a clear focus on "Openness and Tolerance". China, as the center of this initiative, provides an alternative source for international cooperation, which is more align with the real needs of the developing countries since China is a success story of public policies, strategies and execution of massive infrastructure projects. It is because of these reasons that till today, over 100 countries and international organizations have agreed in supporting this initiative and over 50 countries have signed agreements of cooperation with China in the framework of the initiative.

Furthermore, as we have seen in these four years since the initiative was in place, more and more countries, institutions and international organizations are showing genuine interest to take part in the initiative. However all current members and potential participants of the initiative need to realize that the "Belt and Road" has a very long time framework, at least for the next 30 years. For this reason, countries and all interest parties need to plan and create their unique roadmap to take full benefits from this platform of cooperation. Most of the developing countries are lack of long term planning and they face real challenges when they need to create a project or a vision for the next 30 years, I personally believe that this initiative offers them a great opportunity to develop a long term perspective, creating a meaningful and effective international cooperation framework with China. However, one aspect that they also need to take in consideration is that the initiative is still under construction, what I mean is that it can change or be modified based on the circumstances. For this reason countries and even China need to be flexible to adapt and keep aiming for the main goal of the initiative which is economic integration and partnership.

During one of the sessions of the Young Sinologist Program we reviewed the differences between the "Belt and Road" Initiative and the "Marshall Plan" and we all agree that there are four principles that made these two international initiatives different. First, the nature, the Belt and Road is open for everyone, countries have the ultimate decision to join or not join. Second, flexibility. As we mentioned, the initiative can change based on the future circumstances that China or the world can face. Third, inclusiveness. The initiative doesn't discriminate anyone based on different political views or benefits, on the contrary, it tries to involved countries which doesn't received support from other international sources. Finally, gradualness. As we mentioned before, the initiative will be changing and its impact will be increasing in the next years as China becomes the largest economy in the world and achieve its goals of a moderately prosperous society by 2020 and becomes a great, modern, socialist country by 2050.

Under the development of the initiative, we also need to reflect on what are the international foreign principles of China, which are basically the guidelines in which China aims to build its international cooperation community. These guidelines are very important since they help us to understand the foreign affairs strategies of China and its implications. The first and most important principle of China's international affairs is the economic approach, China aims to build economic prosperity through cooperation and supporting different countries. In this sense, China doesn't aim to oppress or be invade, China sees the economic thriving as the most sustainable way to create peace and understanding. The second principle is about keeping distance from disputes and conflicts; China believes that the destiny of one country depends on its people's will, for this reason, China will not interfere in any dispute between countries and will respect the sovereignty of countries.

Third, China will use its rising influence in the world with reserve and with no intentions to control or oppress the international community.

However, why the Belt and Road initiative is so important for China in the next decades? As China is following a "New Normal" (which implies the focus on quality over quantity in terms of GDP growth), it is more relevant than ever to keep the economy stable by maintaining a minimum growth standard and in this way to achieve their milestones in terms of development and prosperity. The Belt and Road initiative is a main component in this economic growth since China needs to place its overcapacity in more projects around the world. In addition, China's development of certain industries has reached certainly world standard, especially in the ones related to infrastructure, solar industry, ecommerce, mobility and urbanization. For this reason China is also in the capacity to exports its technology and know-how to other countries, offering a diverse range of solutions for developing economies. This is the case about for example, China's infrastructure projects in Ecuador; China built different infrastructure projects in Ecuador, in order to prevent natural disasters in the country, this allowed Ecuador to reduce their emergencies in terms of floods, economic and human losses dramatically, in comparison to previous years. China's risk and disaster management has helped Ecuador to overcome and prepare much more for the climate challenges disaster than its neighbor countries, including Peru and Colombia.

Another reason for the relevance of the "Belt and Road" initiative is China's wish to play a more proactive role in the international community and enhance the concept of a "Community of Common Shared Destiny". As we can see, over the past years, China's effort to contribute to the global community have been increasing considerably and we can testify that based on the following facts: China is currently a main contributor to the different international organization and platforms, including, UN Funds, UN Security forces, the World Bank, the International Monetary Fund. Nevertheless, most of these organizations are under control of the western powers and certain countries, so even if China wants to contribute more, there is a restriction imposed by those countries who aim to establish the framework of work and rules of operation of these international organizations. Due to this circumstance, China instead of being reactive to this situation, has started to play a more proactive role in the international community and has create international initiatives that aims to add more value to the regional and global communities. For instance, China's AIIB (Asian Infrastructure Investment Bank), The New Development Bank and so on, are projects that has received a lot of attention and interest from the international community, playing also an important role in terms of financing the Belt and Road initiative. In addition, these multilateral institutions were created under China's working framework, allowing China to play a leading role, replacing for instance the common western rules in the traditional multilateral organizations. Another strategy of China to increase their influence in the world is organizing and hosting different events that can allow them to raise their voice and propose solutions and ideas to the world's main challenges. During the past years, we have witness how China is proposing the idea of a globalized and connected world through trade and cooperation in different platforms like APEC, G20 and also the Boao Forum. A special note should be dedicated to the Belt and Road Forum hosted by China in Beijing in May 14-15, as the first Belt and Road Forum, China's goal was to increase the awareness of the initiative among the international community and also build a stronger partnership network among countries. This first event was an outstanding success as it drew 29 heads of state and over more than 130 representatives of countries and international organization. Asian and European countries were the majority of participants; however, United States and Japan also send delegations and representatives, showing this spirit of openness that China is aiming to build with the initiative.

During the "Young Sinologist Program" we have the opportunity to understand the different priorities of the "Belt and Road" initiative that can be summarize in the followings:

- Political Coordination, as an important column of the initiative, the cooperation and coordination with different governments is the main foundation of every step and project of the initiative.

- Unimpeded Trade, the Belt and Road initiative is the Chinese version for the global economic recovery plan, for this reason, creating economic corridors, commerce platforms and proposing a free trading ecosystem across countries will help to the achievement of the initiative.

- People to People Diplomacy, like the Ancient Silk Road, the Belt and Road initiative also aims for cultural connection and civilization exchanges. It also provides a great opportunity to promote Chinese culture across different nations, increasing the awareness and the construction of the Chinese Soft power around the world.

- Facilities Connectivity, China's experience on building infrastructure across its nation has been one of the reasons for the development of the economy, for this reason, connecting and building infrastructure projects across the countries that are part of the initiative can support the trade and the development of local and regional economies more than any other.

- Financial Integration, in order to achieve the goals of connectivity and economic prosperity, the creation of funds, financial support projects, cross-border flow of capital and payment solutions are fundamental solutions that this initiative also looks at. In addition, the financial integration with different countries that are part of the initiative also helps to expand the RMB scope, offering an alternative currency for international matters.

III. Latin-America and the "Belt and Road"

The relationship between Latin-America and the Belt and Road Initiative will enhance as the initiative develops in scope and power in the next years and decades. Since the beginning of the "Belt and Road", many countries in Latin-American have shown their clear intentions to join and to contribute to the initiative, since China in most of the cases is the main commercial partner and also one of the main foreign direct investment sources for Latin-American countries. For example, during the Belt and Road Forum hosted in May 2017, the presidents of the Republic of Chile and the Republic of Argentina attended the meeting held in Beijing, in addition, Peru, Brazil, Colombia and other Latin countries, send ministry level representatives which showed the importance of this initiative to the region.

If we take the Ancient Silk Road as the only initial framework to build the Belt and Road initiative, the Latin-American region was not part of this commercial route, even though some scholars claim that China and Latin-America has some trading connection centuries ago, due to the "Galleon of Manila" a commercial route that start in Manila (Philippines) and cross the whole Pacific Ocean in order to reach Mexico transporting different goods and commodities. This view is a little bit forced, since it was mostly a trading route between former Spanish Colonies (Mexico and The Philippines). We cannot deny that it was an important route to connect Asia with the Latin-America in terms of trading, and that for sure we can find many Chinese elements and products across its years of operation, but I believe it was not an ancient route that has a connection with the ancient Silk Road.

As we discuss in previous paragraphs, the "Belt and Road" initiative has a long term framework and aims to provide economic prosperity for different countries and regions. In addition, it is an open and inclusive platform that does not discriminate countries, It is important that countries in Latin-America have the commitment and interest in joining the initiative as early as possible. Since it's a long term project, countries and organizations that join the initiative in the early stage can receive the benefits of having a long term participation and get more resources for its own development. Like any successful company or project, the founders and the ones who bet in favor of the project as early as possible are the ones who take more advantage of the opportunity, in this sense, I believe that countries in Latin-America need to increase their interest and participation in the initiative and also develop local Belt and Road experts which can provide ideas and support to the connection of the countries with China. By 2017, The AIIB (Asian Infrastructure Investment Bank) has involved the following non-regional prospective members from Latin-America: Brazil, Peru, Venezuela, Bolivia, Chile and Argentina. This also speaks of the clear intentions of Latin-American countries to be closer to China and to support the initiative.

Latin-America is a region with a high disparity in terms of income and infrastructure, due to the geographical conditions and natural landscapes, it is very challenging to connect the cities in a country with efficient transportation and mobility. In addition, the region faced problems like corruption, public management inefficiency, and environmental issues and of course, poverty and delinquency (these two are direct connected with the economic development). Also the lack of long term vision and the political instability in these past year are leading the region to struggle in order to achieve the economic prosperity that we all aim at. There are interesting growing economies like Chile, Peru, Argentina, Colombia and Mexico, however, all of these countries also face different internal political challenges, including presidential elections and an increasing population that is not satisfied with the current status quo and that is looking for more extreme solutions (including for example political candidates with extreme ideologies or parties that would like change the whole economic and social framework). As the current situation in Latin-America is very uncertain, I believe that the Belt and Road initiative really offers a common platform for all the countries to propose projects and cooperation with China in order to solve the issues and the challenges that they faced. The similarities of China and Latin-American as developing economies are very obvious, for this reason, is even more than accurate that countries in the region look at China as a successful story and learn from the economic and government solutions that is bringing China to become a moderate prosper society.

Its responsibility of the Latin-American countries to develop a Belt and Road vision 2050, in which they can align all their initiative and cooperation with China. If countries in Latin-America are able to create a common vision and a roadmap of cooperation with China I think the results will be more than beneficial for both, China and Latin-America.

Another concept that can be explored in the construction of the relationship between China and Latin-America in the framework of the Belt and Road Initiative is the creation of a "Digital Belt and Road". Both regions should look into mechanisms that allow their markets to connect in different fields, from business, culture and knowledge; in this sense, and taking in consideration two important factors like the advanced level of the digital industry in China and the globalization process of Chinese companies, both regions should look into create more projects that enhance the E-commerce, education, cultural promotion and exchanges of best case practices and knowledge. By using the digital connectivity, countries can overcome the distances and be closer.

Distance is not the problem but knowledge and awareness are. For this reason, more countries and companies in Latin-America should promote their products and services to the Chinese market by using digital platforms that have already developed in China. The Chinese market is one of the most, if not the most important consumer market of the world, with a largest growing middle class, more and more Chinese citizens are aware of international products and services from Latin-America. Food and beverage and travelling services are promoted by different online platforms in China, but there is still a huge room for new products and services including for example: health industry, fashion Industry, and education, among others. Furthermore, Chinese companies and Start Ups are also looking at the Latin-American market with more emphasis and interest, this is mainly because the local competition is extremely furious, so more companies are looking for option to reach new markets and bring their technology with them. This is the case for example of two very famous companies in China: Didi Chuxing（滴滴出行） and Mobike. The first one is one of the most successful companies in Asia using the concept of shared economy. As the main competitor of UBER (U.S. peer-to-peer ridesharing technology company) in different markets, Didi Chuxing aims to bring its know-how and technology to markets like Mexico in which the transportation is one of the most severe problems in cities. Following that line, the second company Mobike, also one of the pioneers in the bike-sharing model in China, is entering markets like Chile and Mexico, providing an environment friendly solution for mobility in Latin-American cities.

These two cases are clear examples of how China Innovation and China's Start Ups companies can bring solutions and their unique know-how to help solve the main challenges in our cities. I believe that there are more opportunities for Chinese innovative companies to come to Latin-America and to bring development in fields like: agriculture, online education, rural economy and environment. Through the "Digital Belt and Road" we can promote the expansion of "Innovation made in China" to the Latin-American countries and in this way, adapt solutions that have shown a great success in China into our local realities. China has been a laboratory of different social innovation solutions that have helped the creation of millions of small entrepreneurs, including a large number in the rural areas, providing them with common development based to overcome poverty. Why can't Latin-Americans do the same?

Many experts agree that in the short-term period of the "Belt and Road" Initiative, it is the construction of infrastructure in Latin-America that can boost the cooperation between our regions and also promote the involvement of more countries in to the initiative. When we look at Latin-American disparity, communication technology and infrastructure are the focus of the different governments in turn. However, since our geography is very challenging, especially for the Andean countries, the speed of development, construction and connection with the rural areas is very slow. For this, China's construction technology and know-how, really offers a genuine alternative to the support of a connected Latin-America. China's large and challenging territory has been connected with great infrastructure, including highways, high-speed train systems, airports, ports, etc. The construction technology that China has develop in these years is one of the most advanced in the world and can be utilize in the most difficult areas in the world.

Last but not least, business and government relationship follows its own pace if there are opportunities and needs for cooperation. Nevertheless, if we want to make this relationship more sustainable in time, we need to look at the people to people connection and here, education and cultural exchange plays an important role for both sides. The scholarships, education opportunities and training in China have increased a lot in the past years, allowing thousands of Latin-Americans to come to China to study. Just to give an example, only in the year 2017, over 350 students from Peru received scholarships and travel to China in order to study and receive training, this number made China the country that offers more scholarships in Peru by far. The reality of the scholarships is the same in other countries, including for instance, Chile, Colombia, Costa Rica, Brazil, etc. But when we look at where the academic or business elite in Latin-America go to study their specialization or master studies, the main options are USA and Europe. China's opportunities in education and development should be promoted with more emphasis in our region so the best talent can come to China and be trained so once these talents become key decision makers they can be connected with China. We cannot deny the great efforts of China to promote her culture, language and education (through the Confucius Institutes), however when we look at the effort that the Latin-American countries do to attract Chinese talents, the projects or initiatives are very limited. Countries in Latin-American need to play a more proactive role promoting the culture, education opportunities and language in China, so that more and more Chinese students see our region as a potential land for cooperation.

IV. Conclusion

This article was aiming to reflect and share some ideas about the current situation of the Belt and Road Initiative and the Latin-America's potential cooperation with China. Based on the ideas shared, we can conclude that there is still so much to do between our regions, I believe that the cooperation will be enhanced in the next years, due to the current efforts of both regions to cooperate and co-create a common roadmap, in this way I am very optimistic that we will see the impact of the Belt and Road initiative in our countries very soon. China's support for the developing of the Latin-America region has increased over the past years, China now is not only the main destination for our products and services, but also as a closer ally in solving some of our most challenging social issues in our region. We are thankful to China for putting many resources and effort to be closer to our region, but at the same time, we expect that Latin-America will take a more proactive approach with China.

China's knowledge about Latin-America is very wide, we have witnessed this through our talks and meetings with the experts of Chinese Academy of Social Sciences and also with many representatives from local and central government in China. On the other hand, the lack of China experts in Latin-America countries is very obvious as well as the Belt and Road awareness in the political elite of Latin-America. For this reason, it's more than important that we as Young Sinologists, to promote the knowledge, the image of China and the implications of the Belt and Road initiative among our countrymen. We also need our country in Latin-America to be more proactive and develop a China Roadmap in the framework of the Belt and Road Initiative in order to create a win-win situation that support our economies but at the same time support China to achieve its goal by 2050.

Besides the efforts that for sure our countries should make, I believe that China should also increase its soft power and country branding in Latin-America. Just as an example, the process of Chinese brands in order to become recognized by its quality and technology level has been tremendous. However, a lot of brands are still unknown by the Latin-America market. Furthermore, China Innovation and Chinese Unicorns (private companies whose value is above one billion USD), are mostly unknown in the Latin-American countries. Other great developments of China in the fields of transportation, aerospace industry, construction, public policy, energy and start up should be promoted across the Latin-American region as an example of how China is aiming at creating an innovation-based economy and how the Belt and Road initiative also plays an important role on it.

Finally, most of the countries in Latin-America will celebrate its 200 years of independence in the next years, which is a great milestone for our history, but it is extremely difficult to think that in 200 years we as a region has not been able to bring development and prosperity to the majority of our population. It is very inspiring to see how The People's Republic of China aims to become a great modern socialist country by its centenary and put this vision into action more than 30 years before. With the creation of the Belt and Road Initiative, China will not only achieve its goal by 2050, but in the way of doing so, it will provide common shared values and projects that will help the international community to be closer, promoting peace and development across different regions.

文学、文化、文字

Literature, Culture and Language

浅论张抗抗长篇小说《作女》中卓尔形象

穆罕默德·谢赫 【埃及】
明亚大学语言学院中文系讲师

一 张抗抗

张抗抗，1950年7月3日出生，中国当代著名女作家，她创造了许多作品，如《隐形伴侣》《残忍》《白罂粟》《北极光》《情爱画廊》《赤彤丹朱》等，这些作品不但受到中国人的喜爱，而且还被译成多个国家的文字，享誉国内外。她的小说大都涉及爱情、婚姻、家庭，表现了自己的爱情理想和婚姻观念，有着深刻的生命体验和丰富的人生意蕴。张抗抗是一位女性写作最纯粹的作家，她的小说以反映社会现实的丰富性和深刻性，其所包蕴的丰富深邃的思想内涵和精湛高超的艺术表现手法，显示了文学革命的实绩。她对许多文学作品女性形象问题都有着自己独到的见解。

2002年，张抗抗发表的长篇小说《作女》，是一部具有当代意识和女性意识的小说，真实地描写白领女性生存现状及理想蓝图，她们独立自主，不要婚姻，衣食无忧，不靠男人却活得滋润，活得张扬，活得淋漓尽致。这部小说的女主人公叫卓尔，她个性张扬，有现代年轻人理想的彻底的独立精神——离道、藐视金钱、穷毕生之力挑战传统。当她的要求与社会观念发生冲突的时候，她内心就会有一种跃动，即对社会规则的挑衅和对自我生命意识的肯定。作者让'卓尔'这个女人，排除万难摒弃社会伦理和道德法律的约束，做到精神的绝对自由。张抗抗试图通过一批独立不羁卓尔不群的"作"女挣脱现存的道德标准的约束，追求理想快乐，建立一个美丽的自由的"她世界"。

二 所谓"作女"

张抗抗小说"作女"中的所谓"作"要读平声，"存在于北京、东北、上海、浙江一带，方言中都是有这个'作'字的。原意专指女性中那些不安分守己、特立独行、自不量力、任性而天性热爱折腾的女人。可以肯定不是褒义词"[1]。有论者评价她"身上兼而具有新新人类和独立女性的气质，言语行为都挺酷"[2]。"作"在方言中，把那些违反常规、不安分守己的行为叫"作"，而且这个字专指女性。但在张抗抗看来，"作"是男性按照自己的价值标准加给女性的一个贬义词，她要通过《作女》正名，遂赋予了"作"字新的含义，认为"作"是个褒义词，对当今女性生存状态的高度概括，体现了新时代的女性不安于现状、勇于拼搏、追求并实现人生的自我价值。"作"形容女性不安于现状，在生活中主动出击和挑战以获得更为自我的空间，是女性解放的表现，不是被动地接受命运的安排，而是希望由自己来选择或者面对自己的生存状况，一旦达到目标，她们或将停止"作"的步伐，按照自己追求的生活方式生活；或者选择继续"作"下去，在她们看来，"作"就是不断地放弃与不断地开始。张抗抗是一位极有个性的作家，她不仅本人具有精神的独立性，而且一再呼吁女性自主、自立、自强，是一个女性意识很强的作家。在她身上，散发着知识女性的端庄与利落。她以女性独特的视角，描写生活中的"作女"，她写"作女"来为这群"作"出了自我却为意识规范所不容的新女性正名，告诉人们，对于今日女性来说，"作"不是一个坏词。"她用一支纯熟流畅的笔描绘现代富有挑战精神的女性。她们的生命力和创造力同样绚目夺人，经济独立、人格独立、情感独立是她们的生活的状态"[3]。她们总是精神饱满地去迎接生活的挑战，并且乐于不断尝试肉体和精神的冒险，渴望在男权社会中争取独立的自我，渴望自由和理想的生活。张抗抗为什么写"作女"？因为"作"成为张抗抗小时候一个明显的性格特征，如她自己所说的："我想我少女的时候，少女时代，那时候曾经是青春叛逆期，肯定有一个特别强烈的'作欲'发作的时期，我觉得在那个时候可能是比较'作'，包括我到黑龙江去……"[4]连张抗抗本人

1　张抗抗：《作女》，华艺出版社，2002年版，第72页。
2　张抗抗：《我们为什么而作》，《北京青年报》2002年7月3日。
3　张抗抗：《女人说话（三）——我作故我在》，中央电视台《百家讲坛》栏目组。
4　张抗抗：《女人说话（三）——我作故我在》，中央电视台《百家讲坛》栏目组。

都解释不清楚去黑龙江的具体原因，她就放弃了离外婆家很近的知青点，因为她当时"已无法安于一隅，她的内心的骚动无法停止——外面的世界，雅苑的北国，无时无刻不在吸引着我。也许是为了文学，也许是为了'革命'，也许是为了爱情，甚至连我自己也不知道为了什么，反正我一定要到远方去，去开拓自己的未来"[1]。她在《你是先锋吗？》书中（158 页），强调"作女"形象的精神面貌、人生观和价值观，正如她所说："写作迫使我走向内心去寻求自由，写作能够促使我对人、人生和社会发问，通过发问来整理和慰藉自己，并为自己创造想象的空间。[2]"她还认为，因为我们生活中已经有很多"作女"这类人物：近二十来她发现在自己周围，有许多女性朋友，越来越不安于以往那种传统的生活式，她们的行为常常不合情理，她们不认命，不知足，不甘心，对于生活不再是被迫无奈的承受，而是主动的出击和挑衅，她们更注重个人的价值实现和精神享受，为此不惜一次次碰壁、一次次受伤……我把这样的女人誉为"作女"[3]。她们在社会生活的各个领域中，所表现出来的狂热以及盲目的"作"态，其实是女性的自我肯定，自我宣泄、自我拯救的别样方式；是现代女性在新的历史条件下，对自己能力的检测和发问。从 20 世纪 90 年代到 21 世纪，都市女性中"作女"越来越多的现象，也许可视为中国女性解放的标志之一："作"是立足于中国本土文化、一个充满弹性的女性生长点[4]，"作女"都是充满创造力的人，她们之所以"作"，是因为她们现在的发展空间还太小，当她们的要求与社会观念发生冲突时，内心就会有一种跃动，就是对社会规则的挑衅和对自我生命意识的肯定。"作女"的出现，并不仅因为外来的西方女权文化的影响，更是因为中国本土文化的某种继承性、共同性，同时又有着各自突出的特征，其中最为明显的则是对待婚姻、家庭的态度，她们不满既定的婚姻、家庭的内容与模式，于中感受到了制约，对于那些"作女"而言，婚姻、家庭有时候是一种重新追求、而有时候则是一个包袱，她们会根据自身的需要做出选择，这都为今天"作女"的诞生和生长奠定了深厚的基础。

小说展示主人公及其女友的部分生活，塑造了一批独特甚至有些别类的女性形象。以 35 岁成熟女性的卓尔为代表的"作女"们，个性异常突出，就是一群对什么都感兴趣却又喜新厌旧的女性形象。作女们的"作"主要体现在以下几个

1　张抗抗：《大荒冰河》，吉林人民出版社 1998 年版，第 36 页。
2　参见张抗抗《眼中笔下的作女》《光明日报》2002 年版。
3　张抗抗：《女人说话（三）——我作故我在》，中央电视台《百家讲坛》栏目组。
4　张抗抗：《我为什么写〈作女〉》，《文艺报》(文学周刊) 2002 年 6 月 25 日第 2 版。

方面：

1. 对自由渴望和追寻

张抗抗评述自己历年的创作时说道："尽管在叙述方法上有许多变化，但有一些实质性的东西是始终延续，并被我自己所坚持的，这就是对人的精神世界的关注。"[1] 体现在《作女》对自由的不懈追求。卓尔为了去南极故意放弃待遇丰厚的美编工作，她放弃工作并非求职的艰难或者下岗的苦难，相反，她总在辞职，她总会以各种原因辞职，比如卓尔想去南极，她放弃工作的理由是："你以为我每天写写画画就活得轻松自在了？那活儿我早就干够了，给人配图画版，一点创造性都没有。上班下班，看人眼色，重复、每天的日子没完没了的重复，就像一颗被送入轨道的人造卫星，绕着地球一圈圈转，一直转到报废……我够了，再这样下去，我迟早会死掉的！"（《作女》18页）上班的路上，她从不走相同的固定路线，她喜欢依照每天的心情，来选择一条不一定最近，也许比较令人愉快的途径，她也喜欢用小巧的车型，因其掉头灵活。她的发型也是千变万化，结婚那天还是长发飘逸，过了些日子又理成短发。在吃饭的问题上，卓尔是无穷无尽的变化，草莓炒鸡蛋、牛肉加鸡肉清炖、蜂蜜萝卜豆腐，另外还特别喜欢搬家。卓尔需要按照自身的意愿去选择、创造一种适合自己的生活，她们需要自由自在地呼吸，自由自在地行动。在张抗抗看来，"作"本身是一种创造力。张抗抗说过："没有选择便没有自由，更没有创造。"[2]

卓尔相貌普通、略带男孩子气质，内心世界丰富，有着很强的独立意识和社会适应能力，同时深藏着一种很坚定的意志。对卓尔的前夫刘博，用世俗的眼光来评判的话，应该算是比较优秀的，但是卓尔因为与其性情的不能兼容，决然选择了放弃这段婚姻。然而面对一个萍水相逢却互相吸引的观鸟人，她却能够真情相待。在与男性之间的交往中，包括已经事业有成、腰缠万贯的郑达磊，她一直若即若离，始终保持自己的独立性。她从不把自己的幸福寄托在男性身上，男人对她而言也只是生活的一部分，是解决单身生活的伴侣，或是一起打拼的伙伴，或者是惺惺相惜的朋友。她对贤妻良母的社会规则不屑一顾，全权主导自己的思想和生活，充分的保持着自己的完整和独立性。卓尔没有固定的工作，生活漂泊甚至居无定所，但是她凭着自己的兴趣和"作"的劲头，生活的自在随意。她去

---

[1] 张抗抗：《我们为什么而作》，《北京青年报》2002年7月3日。
[2] 张抗抗：《大荒冰河》，吉林人民出版社1998年版第319页。

天琛公司工作，真正吸引她的，并不是丰厚的物质待遇；真正使她发生兴趣的，恰恰是想象——否定——再想象——再否定，这个令人着迷的颠三倒四的过程。

在为"天琛"做的广告策划中，卓尔响亮地提出了"我是我自己"这样一个口号，这其实也是很多女性很想发出的声音。很显然，卓尔是在不断选择和放弃中寻求自我，寻找自我的价值和证实自己的存在，用自己独特的生活态度对社会规范做出反抗并实现自身的价值。她走沙漠、去南极、开荒山，任意的折腾，生活的随心所欲。正如张抗抗所说的那样，在很多时候，一个人的个性比性别更重要。在很多方面，卓尔有着年轻人的彻底的独立自由的精神，甚至是有些离经叛道，她有着很强的个体和自我存在的意识。

按照自己的逻辑生存，价值观和生活态度、行为方式都带着卓尔自身的特色和气质，独树一帜甚至有些标新立异。以消费为中心的都市对她来说，只不过是实现自我的舞台，卓尔就是卓尔，无人可替代，在享受着消费文化的同时她又保持着高度的自由，清楚知道自己想要什么，真正能束缚她的因素，少之又少。同一心想保持自己窈窕淑女的形象并成为郑太太但实际上却被消费文化侵蚀和淹没的陶桃比起来，陶桃是属于画地为牢，且自以心为形役，卓尔却独立、自由，活的率性而恣意。

2. 全新的婚姻爱情观

卓尔对待爱情有自己的主见，绝不依靠男人养活，绝不当第三者，但频繁的离婚及约会，对爱情与婚姻的立场没有以往女性的被动，她不遵循传统的爱情与婚姻、家庭的既定路线，也没有一味地迎合父母、未婚夫和社会的婚恋标准，她有着自己的选择，更多地考虑自己的思想、情感的需要。昔日的传统婚姻主要根据"父母之命，媒妁之言"，或者是某种利益交换的产物，讲究"门当户对"，在这种婚姻里，女性几乎没有发言权。《作女》中的卓尔是一个无处不作、无时不作与无事不敢作的女性。为了"作"得有声有色，她首先把一个家庭"作"没了，她稀里糊涂地从一开始就没有领会"家"的内涵，连她自己都不明白为什么和刘博结婚，每天只吃醋溜白菜，所有物件必须放在固定的位置，对于这样一个墨守成规的刘博，卓尔毅然放弃了拥有美国绿卡的机会，与大男人主义化身的丈夫刘博离婚。关于婚姻，"作女"们有着自己的独特见解。卓尔说："结婚？我看不出究竟是为了什么？"[1] 张抗抗也分析"作女们"的婚姻立场："……就说'作女'吧，

1　参见张抗抗《中国当代作家自选集大系——张抗抗》，现代出版社2006年版。

会给自己带来很多麻烦，也给别人带来一大堆麻烦。那么通常我们正常的家庭秩序是很难容忍这样的生活方式的，所以，她们为了使自己能够坚守自己的这样一种信念和尊重自己的愿望，那么她们只能选择独身。这其实是一种无奈。这种无奈来自于实际上男性还不能够完全地接受女性的这种极强烈的或者说这种独立精神，所以她得有一个过程。还有一个就是在整个社会进步过程中，婚姻它也逐渐变得不是那么像以前那样只是独一无二的一种情感方式，或者说生活方式。也不是了。"[1] 虽说"作女"的出现给社会带来一系列的麻烦，如对传统伦理道德的颠覆等。但是那些伦理道德在某种程度上是以牺牲女性的自然欲望为前提的，是一种不公平的准则。

笔者一直认为"作女"这个名称是贬义词，在日常生活中，倘若某某人在异性面前表现的过于矫情扭捏，或者有事没事表现的异于普通人，或与平时行为大相径庭，那这个词就派上用场了；然而，作家张抗抗却赋予了这个词语新的含义，尤指那些不安分、追求自由而又天生爱折腾的女子。很显然，这个词这时褒贬难分，例如："进入21世纪的自由经济时代，城市女性的境遇发生了深刻的变化，我发现自己周围的那些女子，越来越多地不安于以往那种传统的生活方式，她们不认命、不知足、不甘心，对生活不再是被动的无奈接受，而是主动的出击和挑衅，她们更注重个人价值的实现和精神享受，为此不惜一次次碰壁、一次次受伤，直到头破血流、筋疲力尽……我把这样的女人誉为'作女'"。

卓尔一向我行我素，与刘博离婚，和火锅店的老板老乔保持着婚外关系，不顾道德谴责，甚至因为某些原因与自己的老板、闺蜜陶桃的男友发生了关系，她的爱情婚姻观念可以说是无拘无束，甚至有违伦理，这是我不喜欢的一点。

3. 女性意识的蜕变

解读20世纪90年代中国女性文学，可以发现其女性作品经历了一个蜕变期，从早期对男性的追随都有一个相似之处，就是崇拜男性偶像，放弃自己思想上的自主权，将自己托付给男性偶像，骨子里还有"夫唱妇随"[2]的旧观念，是男性的崇拜者与服从者，在爱情婚姻中，女人经常受到男朋友或者她的男人的伤害与欺骗，哪怕一天碰上了心里爱的男人，也是不能选择的，因为有父权安排，一直是父系文化占据统治地位，女人们处在文化的边缘地带。美国著名的女性主义

---

1 参见张抗抗《中国当代作家自选集大系——张抗抗》，现代出版社2006年版。
2 参见郭海鹰《丛〈作女〉看张抗抗女性意识的蜕变》，《湖北师范学院学报》2008年第1期。

者阿德里安娜·里奇曾经指出:"父权就是父亲的权力,父权制指一种家庭社会的、意识形态的和政治体系,在此体系中,男人通过强力和直接的压迫,或通过仪式、传统、法律、语言、习俗、礼仪、教育和劳动来决定妇女应起什么作用,同时把女性处处置于男性的统辖之下……"[1]只有到了"五四"新文化运动,中国文学史上的第一个女作家群终于向社会发出了呐喊,要求打破性别歧视,争取人格独立,提倡女性在精神上的完全独立,体现出经济独立、思想开放、生命力旺盛、不断冒险尝试、自强、自我解放、大胆的现代女性,就是反抗她们一直以来受限制的处境,摆脱男权社会加之于妇女长期生理、心理、情感上的一切束缚,不能容忍任何来自世俗世界的束缚,她们希望想做什么就做什么,她们想从自己的真实感受出发去实践自己的想法,还想逃避男性世界,激烈地反叛几千年的中国封建社会和男权主义对女性的身心压抑,表现出对传统价值观念的彻底蔑视,寻找一条向未来的路,创造自己的未来,希望每天能活得有滋有味。因为长期受到中国儒家文化对一家中一对夫妇和家庭男女不平等的思想束缚,正如"父为子纲,夫为妻纲",要求儿女服从于父亲,妻子服从于老公,在几千年强大传统文化的制约下,女性的"力气不够顶开头上沉重的盖板,所以只能一点点地拱动,拱动就成为女人'作'的姿态与形状"[2]。只有到了五四时期女作家在作品中表现出鲜明的妇女解放、独立自主的思想,才开始了真正意义上的女性文学。女性主义代表人物弗吉尼亚·伍尔夫强调女性们需要"一间自己的屋子",这样才能够独立自主地思考。而在张抗抗看来,"一间自己的屋子"有更深刻的含义:"它不是一个牢笼,不是一个封闭的禁地。那间屋当然有一扇通往外界的门,可以使我们来来往往出出进进,随时出门走到广阔的田野山川去……"[3]随着改革开放的不断深入人心,女性们也开始了她们的个性解放。特别是西方女权思想的灌输,让中国女性开始关注自身,开始有意识地寻求自身的价值,其独立意识开始觉醒。由于当代中国女作家的实力足以在精神上、智力上代表中国女性的觉醒程度和现代地位,中国女性文学便负载着对女性意识不断深入的把握过程,负载着对女性解放道路的求索,负载着对整个世界的认识、思考和参与,以及对人类普遍生存意义及精神家园的探索与追寻。毫无疑问,张抗抗在她的创作中充分展示了当代女作家对女性意识

---

[1] 阿德里安娜·里奇:《生来是女人》,转引自康正果《女权主义与文学》,中国社会科学出版社1993年版,第3页。
[2] 张抗抗:《张抗抗散文集》,新华出版社2004年版,第206页。
[3] 张抗抗:《打开自己那间屋的门窗》,《中国青年报》,2001年10月11日。

的觉悟与自己的女性意识的蜕变，充分展现了新时期的女性对女性灵魂的自审，在她的长篇小说《作女》中，强烈的女性的情感态度和生活态度，通过《作女》中女主人公卓尔表达了对爱情婚姻独特的看法和见解，就是反对无爱的婚姻，她说："相爱的双方，谁也没有权利让对方为自己牺牲，无论是感情还是事业，我可不喜欢牺牲这个词儿。"她还要求女主人公千万不能依靠男人养活，自己必须有自己生存能力，让自己活得更像自己，正如张抗抗所说的："我在卓尔身上给予我的女性理想，我希望中国女性能够更具独立意识，有一种阳光心态，有足够的力量抵挡外界对我们的伤害"[1]。张抗抗的小说《作女》突破了传统女性意识，塑造了卓尔富有挑战精神的都市女性形象，表现了她不安于现状的理想追求、生命活力和精神状态。开创了女性的新天地，使女性逐渐地从依赖的地位走向独立的地位。虽然女主人公卓尔有稳定的工作、稳定的收入、有良好的教育背景，她完全可以过着平静的生活，找个爱人安分守己地过日子。但这一切恰恰是卓尔厌倦的，她带有独立的精神气质和叛逆性性格。在她的生活中，没有什么是男人能做而她不能做的事，只要愿意做自己想要的，不做也是叛逆，内心涌动着对已有的生活状态的厌倦以及对新鲜生命的渴望，比如阿不这个人物，无论跟谁说一件事，她吐出来的第一个字是"不"，卓尔也对女性的传统价值观念表现出叛逆，她还是要活得有声有色、有滋有味。卓尔进入婚姻生活之后，不久发现实现不了她情感渴望，就逃避婚姻了，因为对婚姻生活各方面带来的不适应和失望，她怎么努力也找不到她寻找的爱情，卓尔逃避婚姻不只是因为找不到理想爱情，卓尔的丈夫刘博是她大学时候的同学，在加拿大读博士，但他安于现状，喜欢每天的日子一成不变，按照固定不变的程式进行。而卓尔则喜欢追求动态的新鲜感，二十多年来，刘博一直吃着白菜和红烧肉成长，而且居然百吃不厌，卓尔的原则却是饭菜好坏无所谓，但不能重复，因为她讨厌每天吃同样的东西。她还拒绝性爱总是由男性把握主动，反抗男性的性霸权，要求所有的女性成为自己性爱的主角，从被动变为主动。卓尔一次去北海寻找投资项目，一位朋友介绍她到邻省的一个小城。她得知离那个城市一百多公里之外有一个著名的风景地，于是坐上旅游巴士独自一人到了那个被称为小镇的村子，第二天她就背上新购置的睡袋出去玩了一整天，天黑回到了帐篷那儿，卓尔入睡了不久感到好像正在发生什么，就是那位同游的青年男子猛烈地抱住了她，对卓尔说："我要你！"她脑子立刻蹦出"这

---

1 赵淑琴：《从张抗抗〈作女〉看女性生存理想的期待》，《大理学院学报》，2009 年第 9 期。

句话被男人说了千年，从来都属于男人专用的话语，为什么只能是他们要，而不能是我要呢"诘问。卓尔虽然被他深深吸引，两人在帐篷里发生了刻骨铭心的一夜情，但是分手的时候，卓尔没有给他留电话号码，她担心重逢会破坏了这一夜美好的感觉。卓尔在床上还拒绝刘博。她拒绝的原因更多是由于厌倦，婚后不久，卓尔就发现，刘博每次做爱的程序都是一模一样的。卓尔与男人之间的关系，卓尔不仅是主动的，她还要处处占上风，从不肯委曲求全，她讨厌花男人的钱，更讨厌花与自己关系接近的男人的钱。她有着很强的自我意识。有一次和几个女性朋友去一个酒店喝酒，卓尔看到了一幅画，画面上一个女人亲热地挽着一个男人，一只手伸在他的衣兜里，画面上有一行大字：教你如何花光男人的钱。卓尔的脑袋一下子涨得大大，心里有一股邪火冒出来。她马上意识到这是对全体女性的侮辱，当场要求经理取下这幅画，就在餐馆与一群"作女们"大打出手，她说："卓尔说请你把这幅东西拿下来，你以为女人都是花男人的钱吗？你看看那一桌女人，都是 AA 制自己埋单，我是女人但我不花男人的钱。"因为经理没同意把那幅画取下，卓尔和几个伙伴们抄起酒瓶大打出手。

女性意识是女性对自身价值的思考，它既是一种对性别意识的觉醒又带有社会属性。随着不同的时代发展，女性对自身的认识也逐渐深刻。并不像 20 世纪之前的女性，被三纲五常、四书五经约束得惟丈夫马首是瞻，争取经济与社会地位的平等是女性意识觉醒初期的主要诉求，女性意识的内容也不断得以补充和丰富。女性意识的启蒙期已经过去，女性对自我的认知也相应发生新的变化，她们不再把女性的困境简单地归之于现实生活中男性的压制，而更重视对女性地位之所以形成、改变的社会、历史因素的挖掘。张抗抗的《作女》正是从女性视角挖掘潜在的女性意识。

三 结语

张抗抗推出的《作女》赫然写着："本书献给她世纪"，这本小说以"作女"命名和正名，为女性意识极度张扬的"她世纪"留下了一部"作女"档案。小说中，张抗抗不光重新梳理了女性的生理、心理和情感特质，还重新探讨了女人的优点和弱点，它创造出的一个新词——"作女"，已然成为新世纪之初一个时髦的词语，其创作是"与时俱进"的，她那令人瞩目的女性意识，其实经历了一个明显的蜕变过程，从早期对男性偶像的追随、仰视到女性自主、自立、自强，可见作者呼吁女性意识的觉醒，做新时代女性，追求自由和内心的梦想。

《作女》小说中那些女性角色都能给人们留下深刻的印象。作品受到社会时代和思想背景影响，笔下的人物形象的命运和性格都是具有社会基础和思想基础的。无论是肆无忌惮，放肆"作"的卓尔，还是随波逐流，安分守己的陶桃，还是一堆说不上名的 A 小姐、B 小姐，都具有北京城各个群体的代表性，对于张抗抗《作女》女性地位的异化的研究不仅具有重要的历史意义，也具有积极的现代意义。

笔者通读了小说后，感触颇深，从作者幽默诙谐又不失精彩的文字中了解了这个时代不同女性的心理特征、思想观念、爱情观、生活情况，似乎身在北京众多"作女"中，感受着她们对循规蹈矩的生活的厌烦，有人选择妥协，无奈，而有人却极力反抗，寻找乐趣。其实，这些所谓的"作女"只是某个群体在那个年代中的代表，她们放大了人群中那些不喜欢安分守己，苟延残喘，屈服于百无聊赖的生活的每个人。

我想，作者想表达的无非是对平庸而缺乏个性、媚俗而哗众取宠的群体的嗤之以鼻，对那些不甘平庸，乐于享受生活，不在乎旁人眼光，为自己而活的"作女"们以支持，像书中的主人公卓尔，毕竟卓尔不群，类似那句简单却不失真诚的名言"我是我自己"，随意"作"。

On the Image of Zhuo'er in Zhang's Novel, *Women on the Edge*

Mohanmed Anwar Elmadny Elshikh / Egypt

Lecturer of the Chinese and Literature Department, School of Language, Minya University

I. Zhang Kangkang

Zhang Kangkang, born on July 3, 1950, a famous contemporary female writer in China, has created many works, such as *Stealth Companion, Cruelty, White Poppy, Northern Lights, Love Gallery, Chitong Danzhu* and so on, which have not only been popular among Chinese people, but they have also been translated into many languages, gaining worldwide recognition. Most of her novels are related to love, marriage and family, showing her own ideal of love and her concept of marriage, and they have profound life experiences and rich life connotations. Zhang Kangkang is the purest writer among all female writers. Her novels reflect the richness and profundity of social reality, and there are rich and profound ideological connotations and an exquisite method of artistic expression in her novels, which shows the achievements of the literary revolution. She has her own unique views on the female images of many literary works.

Women on the Edge (《作女》), published by Zhang Kangkang in 2002, is a novel with a contemporary consciousness and a female consciousness. It is a real description of the current living situation and ideal blueprint of white-collar women. They are independent. They need no marriage and live with nothing to worry about. They do not live off men, but they live well and vividly. The heroine of this novel is called Drow, who has an assertive personality, and has the complete independent spirit that modern youth desire — rebelling against the orthodoxy, despising money and taking a lifetime to challenge traditions. When her demands conflict with social concepts, she will be excited inwardly, that is, the provocation of social rules and the affirmation of her own consciousness of life. The woman Drow described by the author can overcome all difficulties and abandon the restrictions of social ethics and moral law in order to achieve absolute freedom of spirit. Zhang Kangkang tries to establish a beautiful and free "she world" through the independent and excellent "*Women on the Edge*(which is also called zuo nv, 《作女》)" who struggle to free themselves from the existing moral standards and seek the ideal and happiness.

II. *Woman on the Edge*

The word "zuo (作)" in the novel *Women on the Edge* (《作女》) written by Zhang Kangkang should be pronounced with level tone, one of the four tones in classical Chinese.The pronunciation exists in Beijing, the Northeast, Shanghai and Zhejiang, and this word is used in the dialects. It originally specifically refers to the women who do not abide by law and behave themselves, who are independent, who overestimate themselves and who are capricious and love to mess about. It is certain that the word is not a commendatory term.[1] Some commentators appraise Zhang Kangkang as "both a new human being and an independent woman with a pretty cool speech and behaviors"[2]. In the dialect, the behavior of violating routine and not abiding by law and behaving themselves is called "zuo (作)", which is used exclusively for women. However, in Zhang Kangkang's view, "zuo (作)" is

---

1　Zhang Kangkang, *Women on the Edge*, Beijing: Huayi Publishing House, 2002, p.72.
2　Zhang Kangkang, Why Are We on the Edge?, *BeijingYouth Daily*, July 3, 2002.

a derogatory term that is imposed on women by men according to their own value standards. So she desires to rectify the meaning of the word through *Women on the Edge* (《作女》), and gives the word a new meaning, thinking that "zuo (作)" is a commendatory term, which has greatly summarized the current living condition of women, and has reflected the fact that women in the new age are not content with the status quo, they strive to struggle, pursue and realize their value of life. "zuo (作)" is used to describe women who are not content with the status quo. They are proactive, and actively challenge life to gain more self-involved space, which manifests female liberation. Instead of passively accepting the arrangement of fate, they want to choose or face their own living conditions by themselves. Once they achieve the goal, they will either stop the pace of "zuo (作)" and live according to the way of life they pursue, or choose to continue to "zuo (作)"; in their view, "zuo (作)" means giving up and starting continuously.

Zhang Kangkang is a writer with a real individuality. She herself has spiritual independence, and at the same time she also appeals to women to be independent, self-reliant and self-improved. As a writer with a strong female consciousness, she exudes the dignity and agility of intellectual women. She describes these "zuo nv (作女)" in life from the unique female perspective. She writes "zuo nv (《作女》)" to rectify the names for these new women who are "zuo (作)" in their own way, but not allowed by consciousness and standard, telling people that "zuo (作)" is not a bad word for today's women. "She fluently depicts the modern women with a challenging spirit. Their vitality and creativity are equally brilliant, and economic independence, an independent personality and an emotional independence are the state of their lives"[1]. They are always full of spirit and energy to meet the challenges of life, are willing to constantly try physical and spiritual adventures, strive for independence in a male-dominated society, and are eager for a free and ideal life. Why did Zhang Kangkang write *Women on the Edge* 《作女》? Because "zuo (作)" was an obvious character trait when she was young, as she said, "I think when I was

---

1 Zhang Kangkang, Lady Talk (3)—I Zuo Therefore I Am, CCTV *Lecture Room* column group.

a girl, I mean, in my girlhood, the rebellious period of my youth, there must have been a period when I particularly wanted to 'zuo (作)' something, and I think I may have been very "zuo (作)" at that time, including my going to Heilongjiang..."[1]. Even Zhang Kangkang herself could not clearly explain the specific reason for her going to Heilongjiang, she just gave up the post of educating youth near her grandmother's house, because she was "unable to be in a corner, and she could not stop her inner turmoil — the outside world, the northern part of our country, were attracting me all the time". "Perhaps for literature, perhaps for 'revolution', perhaps for love, even I myself did not know for what. Anyway, I had to go far away to open up my own future"[2]. She stressed the spiritual outlook, the outlook on life and the value of "zuo nv (作 女)" in the book *Are You a Pioneer?* (p.158). As she said, "Writing forces me to seek freedom towards my inner heart and it can motivate me to ask people, life and society, by which I can organize and console myself and then create room for my own imagination." She also thinks that because there are many "zuo nv (作女)" in our life: I have found during the past two decades that many female friends around me are increasingly dissatisfied with the traditional way of life, they often behave unreasonably, they are not resigned to fate, not content and not reconciled, and they actively face and provoke life instead of being forced to helplessly accept it. They pay more attention to the realization of personal value and spiritual enjoyment regardless of being rebuffed or injured time and time again… I call them "zuo nv (作女)"[3]. The fanaticism and the blind behaviors of "zuo (作)" they have shown in every field of social life are actually another way of female self-affirmation, self-catharsis and self-salvation. Modern women test and question their own abilities under the new historical conditions. From the 1990s to the 21st century, more and more "zuo nv (作女)" among urban women appear, which may be seen as one of the symbols of Chinese female liberation: "zuo (作)" is a flexible female

---

1 Zhang Kangkang, Lady Talk (3)—I Zuo Therefore I Am, CCTV *Lecture Room* column group.
2 Zhang Kangkang, *Wild Glacier*, Jilin People's Publishing House, 1998, p.36.
3 See The View of Women on the Edge by Zhang Kangkang, *Guangming Daily*, 2002.

growing point based on local Chinese culture[1], "zuo nv (作 女)" are all creative, and the reason for their "zuo (作)" is that their developmental space now is too small. When their demands are in conflict with social ideas, they will be excited about provoking social rules and affirming their own life consciousness. "zuo nv (作 女)" appear due to the influence of Western feminist culture, as well as the inheritance and common character of local Chinese culture which also has its own prominent characteristics, of which the most obvious one is the attitude towards marriage and family. They are dissatisfied with the contents and pattern of the established marriage and family; for those "zuo nv (作女)", marriage and family are sometimes a new pursuit, and sometimes a burden. They will make a choice according to their own needs, which lays a solid foundation for the birth and growth of today's "zuo nv (作女)". The novel shows part of the life of the heroine and her female friends, and shapes a group of unique or even special female images. The "zuo nv (作 女)" represented by Drow, a 35-year-old mature woman, have extremely outstanding personalities, that is, they are a group of women who are interested in everything but always abandon the old for the new. Their "zuo (作)" are mainly reflected in the following aspects:

1. Desire and pursuit of freedom

When Zhang Kangkang commented on her writings over the years, she said, "although there are many changes in the narrative method, there are still some substantial things that always continue, and I myself also insist on them, that is the attention to the human being's spiritual world."[2] It is reflected in the persistent pursuit of freedom by the *Women on the Edge*. In order to go to the Antarctic, Drow deliberately gave up a well-paid job as an art editor, but not because of the difficulty of finding a job or the misery of being laid-off. On the contrary, she was always resigning. She always resigned for a variety of reasons. For example, Drow wanted to go to the Antarctic, and then she gave up her high-paying job for the following

---

[1] Zhang Kangkang, Why Did I Write the *Women on the Edge?*, *Journal of Literature and Art* (Saturday Review of Literature) June 25, 2002, Page 2.

[2] Zhang Kangkang, Why Are We on the Edge?, *Beijing Youth Daily*, July 3, 2002.

reason: "You think I live comfortably, just draw and write every day? I've already done enough for that job. I've just illustrated pictures for others, with no creation at all. Go to work and get off work, look at others' attitude, repeat, repeat every day without end, I feel that I am like an artificial satellite sent into orbit, rotating around the earth in a circle till scrapped... I have had enough of it. I will die sooner or later if it continues!" (Page 18 of *Women on the Edge*) She never takes the same fixed route on her way to work. She likes to choose a way that may not be the nearest, but more pleasurable, and she likes to use a small and flexible vehicle model which is convenient for changing directions. Her hairstyle is also always changing. She still has long hair on the day of her marriage, later on, she has a haircut. In addition, Drow is always changing her food, scrambled eggs with strawberries, stewed beef and chicken, honey and radishes with bean curd. She especially likes moving house. Drow needs to choose and create a suitable life according to her own will. She needs to breathe and act freely. In Zhang Kangkang's view, "zuo" itself is a kind of creativity. Zhang Kangkang always said: "No choice means no freedom, no creation."[1]

Drow is average-looking with a little boy's temperament, she has a rich inner world, a strong sense of independence and social adaptability, and a very strong will. Drow's ex-husband, Liu Bo, seems to be comparatively excellent when judged by conventional standards, but Drow chose to give up the marriage because of their incompatible temperament. However, faced with a bird-watcher that she met by chance but with whom there is a mutual attraction, she can sincerely relate to him. In her contact with men, including Zheng Dalei who has already made a successful career and is very wealthy, she always keeps them at arm's length and maintains her independence. She never puts her happiness on a man. Men are only part of her life, a companion to a single life, a partner to struggle together with or a friend to appreciate. She disdains the social rules of a good wife and a loving mother, fully dominates her own thoughts and life, and fully maintains her integrity

---

1　Zhang Kangkang, *Wild Glacier*, Jilin People's Publishing House, 1998, p.319.

and independence. Drow has no fixed job, her life is one of wandering and even itinerant without a fixed residence, but she lives comfortably and casually with her interest and "zuo (作)". She worked at Tian Chen Company not because of the abundant material benefits: "What really made her interested in that job was just imagination—negation—re-imagination—re-negation, a fascinating process."

In the advertising planning for "Tian Chen", Drow resoundingly comes up with a slogan "I am myself", which is actually a voice that many women want to have. It is obvious that Drow is searching for her self-identity in constantly choosing and giving up, is seeking her own value and wants to confirm her existence; and she uses her own unique attitude towards life to resist the social norms and realize the value of her own. She goes to the desert and Antarctic and cultivates the barren hills; she freely tosses about, and lives at her own will. As Zhang Kangkang said, in many cases, a person's personality is more important than gender. In many respects, Drow has a young person's spirit of complete independence and freedom, and she is sometimes even deviant with a strong sense of individuality and self-existence. Drow is living according to her own logic, values, life attitudes and behavioral pattern, which are all unique and even unorthodox, with Drow's own characteristics and temperament. The consumption-centered city is only a stage for her to realize herself. Drow is herself, and no one can replace her; she maintains a high degree of freedom while enjoying the culture of consumption, knowing exactly what she wants, almost nothing can really restrict her. Compared with Tao Tao, who is bent on being a fair lady and becoming Mrs. Zheng but is actually corroded and inundated by the culture of consumption, Drow is independent and free, unruly and willful while Tao Tao is restricted by herself.

2. The brand new view of marriage and love

Drow has her own opinion of love; she never relies on men and never becomes the other woman. However, she frequently divorces and dates, and does not treat love and marriage passively like the previous women. She neither follows the established route of traditional love, marriage and family nor blindly caters to the marriage and love standard of parents, fiancé and society; she makes her own choices, and more consideration is given to her own needs of thought and emotion. In the past, the traditional marriage was mainly based on the "dictates of parents and words of matchmakers", or just a product of the exchange of a certain interest, seeking a perfect match. Women hardly had any say in it. Drow is a woman who dares to "zuo (作)" anything, everywhere, at any time. For "zuo (作)" impressively, she first lost a family by "zuo (作)". She was muddleheaded, and did not understand the connotation of "family" at the beginning. Even she herself did not know why she married Liu Bo. Drow gave up her chance to own the green card of the United States and divorced her husband Liu Bo, who had male chauvinism and was conventional when they only ate cabbage with sweet and sour sauce every day and things had to be put in the fixed place. As for marriage, "zuo nv (作女)" had their own unique views. Drow said, "Marriage? I can't see what it is for?"[1] Zhang Kangkang also analyzed the marriage standpoint of "zuo nv (作女)": "… Just say 'zuo nv (作女)', they will bring a world of trouble to themselves as well as to others. So, usually it is hard for our normal family order to tolerate such a lifestyle, so they can only choose to be single in order to make themselves stick to such a belief and respect their wishes. This is actually a kind of helplessness. This helplessness comes from the fact that men cannot fully accept the strong or independent spirit of women, so she must have a process. Another reason is that in the progress of whole society, marriage has gradually become a less unique emotional way or a lifestyle than before"[2]. Although the emergence of "zuo nv (作女)" will bring a series of troubles to society, such as the subversion of traditional ethics and morality, to some extent, those ethics and morality are a kind of unfair criterion at the cost of the natural desire of women.

I have always believed that the name "zuo nv (作女)" is a derogatory term. If a person is too affected in front of the opposite sex, or is different from the ordinary

---

1 See Zhang Kangkang, *Contemporary Chinese Writer Selection—Zhang Kangkang* [M], Beijing: Modern Press, 2006.
2 Zhang Kangkang, Lady Talk (3)—I Zuo Therefore I Am, CCTV *Lecture Room* column group.

person at ordinary times, or acts totally differently from the usual behavior, then we can use this word. However, Zhang Kangkang, the author of *Women on the Edge* in this article, gives the word a new meaning, referring especially to the women who are discontented with life, pursue freedom and love to mess about. Clearly, it is hard to distinguish whether the word is derogatory or commendatory. "In the era of a free economy in the 21st century, the situation of urban women has changed profoundly. I find that the women around me are more and more discontented with the traditional way of life. They are not resigned to fate, not content and not reconciled, and they actively face and provoke life instead of being forced to helplessly accept it. They pay more attention to the realization of their own personal values and spiritual enjoyment regardless of being rebuffed or injured time and time again… I call them 'zuo nv (作女)'".

Drow has always gone her own way, divorced Liu Bo, kept extramarital relations with Joe, the boss of the hot pot restaurant, ignored moral condemnation, and even had an affair with her own boss, the boyfriend of her ladybro Tao Tao. Her love and marriage values could be said to be unrestrained and even unethical, which I dislike.

3. The transformation of the female consciousness

According to Chinese female literature in the 20th Century, we can find that the female works have undergone a period of transformation. From the early pursuit of men, there is a similarity, that is, the worship of male idols, the abandonment of their own ideological autonomy, their entrusting themselves to male idols, and the old idea that "A wife is her husband's echo" in their hearts[1]. They are men's worshippers and followers, and women are often hurt and deceived by a boyfriend or a man in love and marriage, they even cannot choose the man they love, because their marriages are arranged by their fathers. The patriarchal culture has always occupied a dominant position, and women are on the edge of culture. The famous

---

1 See Guo Haiying, An Exploration of the Transformation of Zhang Kangkang's Feminine Consciousness from the Perspective of *Women on the Edge*, *Journal of Hubei Normal University*, 2008(1), p.5.

American feminist Adriana Ricci once pointed out: "Paternity is the power of a father, and patriarchy refers to a family and a social, ideological and political system, in which men decide the role of women by force and direct oppression, or through ritual, tradition, law, language, custom, etiquette, education, and labor, and put women under the governance of men…"[1] It was only after the new cultural movement on "May 4th" that the first female group of writers in the history of Chinese literature eventually cried out to the society, demanding the breaking of sex discrimination, the independence of the personality, and the full spirit of independence for women, which embodies the modern women with economic independence, open-mindedness, vigorous vitality, in search of constant adventure, self-improvement, self-liberation and boldness. That is, they resist the restrictive situation they have always been in, they shed all of the long-term physiological, psychological and emotional constraints of women by a patriarchal society, and cannot tolerate any constraints from the secular world. They do what they want to do. They want to practice their own ideas from their true feelings. They want to escape from the male world and rebel fiercely against the women's physical and mental depression due to thousands of years of Chinese feudal society and male chauvinism. They show a thorough disdain for the traditional values, they are looking for a way to the future, and want to create their own future, hoping to live wonderfully every day. Because they have long been subject to the Chinese culture of Confucianism for a couple and a family of gender inequality, like "father guides son, and husband guides wife", demanding that children are obedient to their father, a wife is obedient to her husband. Restricted by thousands of years of a strong traditional culture, women's "strength is not strong enough to open up the heavy cover overhead, so they can only move a little bit, and that movement becomes the pose and shape of women's 'zuo (作)'"[2]. It was only after the "May 4th" Period that women writers expressed their distinct ideas of women's liberation and independence in their works, when they began to feel a true sense of women's

---

1 Adriana Ricci: *Born a Woman*, quoted from Kang Zhengguo: *Feminism and Literature,* China Social Sciences Press, 1993, p.3.
2 Zhang Kangkang, *Prose Works of Zhang Kangkang*, Xinhua Publishing House, 2004, p.206.

literature. Virginia Woolf, a feminist representative, emphasizes that women need "a room of their own" so that they can think independently. In Zhang Kangkang's view, "a room of their own" has a more profound meaning: "It is not a cage, not a closed, forbidden place. There is, of course, a door to the outside, which allows us to come and go, in and out, and go out to the vast fields and mountains at any time..."[1] As the reform and opening up gradually wins support among the people, women have begun to emancipate their individuality. In particular, the instillation of Western feminism made Chinese women begin to focus on themselves and begin to consciously seek their own values, and their independence consciousness began to awaken. As the strength of the contemporary Chinese women writers is enough to represent the awakening degree and modern status of Chinese women in spirit and intelligence, Chinese women's literature bears the progress in their grasping the constant deepening of the feminine consciousness, the search for a way to achieve women's liberation, and the understanding of, thinking about and participation in the whole world, as well as the exploration and pursuit of the universal meaning of human existence and spiritual home. There is no doubt that Zhang Kangkang has fully displayed the contemporary writers' awareness of female consciousness and the transformation of her own female consciousness in her works, the self-examination of women in the new era, to women's soul. In her novel *Women on the Edge*, she has a strong female emotional attitude and attitude towards life. The heroine Drow in the novel has expressed her unique view and opinion about love and marriage, which is opposed to a loveless marriage. She said, "no one in love has the right to let each other sacrifice for himself/herself, whether in emotion or career, I do not like the word sacrifice." She has also described in the novel that the heroine does not rely on men, she must have the ability to survive by herself and live as herself, just as Zhang Kangkang said: "I give my female ideal to Drow, I hope that Chinese women can be more independent, have a kind of healthy psychology, and be strong enough to resist outside harm"[2]. The novel *Women on the Edge* written by

---

1 Zhang Kangkang, A Door to the Outside World, *China Youth News*, October 11, 2001.
2 Zhao Shuqi, See Expectation of Female Survival Ideal from *Women on the Edge* Written by Zhang Kangkang, *Journal of Dali University*, 2009(9), p.44.

Zhang Kangkang has broken through the traditional female consciousness and portrayed the city image of Drow with a challenging spirit, showing her ideal pursuit, life vitality and mental state in which she is not comfortable with the status quo. This has created a new world for women, and enabled women to gradually move from a dependent status to an independent status. Although Drow has a stable job, a stable income, and a good educational background, she can absolutely live a quiet life and live in peace with a lover. However, all these are exactly what Drow is tired of. She is independent and rebellious, and she is very sexy. Nothing in her life is what men can do but she can't do, she is only willing to do what she wants, not doing is also a kind of rebellion. She is tired of the existing state of life and is inwardly eager for a fresh life, such as the character Ah Bu, the first word she always says is "bu (不) (which means No)", no matter to whom; Drow also rebels against the traditional values of women, but she still lives wonderfully and delightfully. Drow found that her emotional desire could not be realized soon after she got married, so she escaped from marriage; all aspects of marriage were full of inadaptation and disappointments, and she tried to find her love, but failed. Besides the reason that she could not find ideal love, Drow escaped marriage also because her husband Liu Bo, her university schoolmate who had studied for a doctorate in Canada, was content with the status quo and liked a changeless every-day life. But Drow wanted the pursuit of dynamic freshness. For more than 20 years, Liu Bo had always had Chinese cabbage and braised meat and had not gotten tired of them; Drow does not care about the quality of food, but it cannot be repeated because she hates eating the same food every day. She also refuses the sex hegemony of men when they make love, asking all women to become the masters of their own sex love, from passivity to initiative. Once Drow sought investment projects in Beihai; a friend introduced her to a small town of the neighboring province. She knew that there was a famous scenic spot more than 100 kilometers away from the city, so she alone took a tourist bus to the village called a town, and the next day she carried a newly-bought sleeping bag and spent the whole day playing, and she went back to the tent when it got dark. Drow fell asleep, and soon after something seemed to be happening. It was the young bird-watcher who hugged her fiercely and said, "I want you!". "The words have been said by men for thousand years. It has always been a man's special words. Why is it only they who want, but not I want?" was what immediately came to her mind. Although she was deeply attracted by him, and they had an unforgettable one-night stand in the tent, but when they separated, Drow did not give him her phone number. She worried that the reunion might destroy the good feeling of the night. Drow also refused Liu Bo, in bed. She refused him more because of boredom: soon after their marriage, Drow found that Liu Bo had the same process for making love every time. In her relationship with men, Drow was very active and always prevailed over men. She was never willing to stoop to compromise. She hated to spend men's money, especially that of those men who were close to her. She had a strong self-consciousness. Once Drow went to a hotel to drink with a few female friends, she saw a picture where a woman was holding on to a man's arm intimately with the other hand in his pocket. There was a line of big characters on the picture: Teach yourself how to spend all of a man's money. Drow was extremely angry. She immediately realized that it was an insult to all women, and then she asked the manager to take down the picture. She fought with a group of "zuo nv (作女)" in this restaurant. Drow said, "Please take it down. Do you think all women spend men's money? Look at the women at that table, they are all going Dutch. I'm a woman. But I never spend men's money." Because the manager did not agree to taking down the picture, Drow grabbed the wine bottles and started to fight with her partners. She completely acted on her own, regardless of the social ethics and moral.

I think that the name "zuo nv (作女)" is a derogatory term. In ordinary life, if someone is too affected before the opposite sex, then we can use this word. However, Zhang Kangkang, the author of *Women on the Edge* in this article, gives the word a new meaning, referring especially to the women who are discontented with life, pursue freedom and love to mess about. Clearly, it is hard to distinguish whether the word is derogatory or commendatory. "In the era of free economy in the 21st century, the situation of urban women has changed profoundly. I find that the women around me are more and more discontented with the traditional way of life. They are not resigned to fate, not content and not reconciled, and they actively face and provoke life instead of being forced to helplessly accept it. They pay more attention to the realization of their personal values and spiritual enjoyment regardless of being rebuffed or injured time and time again… I call them 'zuo nv (作女)'".

Female consciousness is a reflection of a woman's own values. It is an awakening of gender consciousness and it also has a social attribute. With the development of different times, women's understanding of themselves is becoming more and more profound. The women before the 20th century were restrained by the principles of feudal moral conduct and Four Books and Five Classics, and they followed the leadership of their husband, their son and their seniors, but unlike these women, today's women have awakened their female consciousness; the main appeal initially is to strive for the equality in economic and social status, with the contents of female consciousness being constantly supplemented and enriched. The enlightenment period of female consciousness has passed, and women's self-cognition has changed correspondingly. They no longer simply attribute the predicament of women to the suppression of men in real life, and more attention is paid to the exploration of social and historical factors that have formed and changed the status of women. *Women on the Edge* written by Zhang Kangkang uniquely explores the potential female consciousness from the female perspective.

III. Conclusion

The sentence "This book is dedicated to the SHE century" is written in the novel *Women on the Edge* launched by Zhang Kangkang. This novel is named after "zuo nv (作女)" and rectifies the name of "zuo nv (作女)", leaving a "zuo nv (作女)" file for the "she century" when female consciousness is highly publicized. In the novel, the author not only re-analyzes the physiological, psychological and emotional characteristics of women, but also re-explores the strengths and weaknesses of women. The newly-created word — "zuo nv (作女)", became a fashionable word at the beginning of the new century. Her creation is "keeping pace with the times", and her remarkable female consciousness has actually undergone an obvious process of transformation, that is, from the early pursuit and admiration of male idols to female autonomy, self-reliance and self-improvement, which shows that the author calls for the awakening of a female consciousness, being modern women of the times, and with the pursuit of freedom and dreams in their hearts.

All the female characters in the novel are deeply impressive. The work is influenced by the social era and the ideological background, and the fate and features of the characters in this work have their social and ideological basis. All the characters are typical of various groups of Beijing, whether it is Drow, who is an unscrupulous and wantonly "zuo (作)", or Tao Tao who always drifts with the current and behaves herself, or many Miss As and Miss Bs whose names are unknown. The study of the alienation of the female status in *Women on the Edge* is not only of great historical significance but also of positive modern significance.

After reading through the novel, I am touched deeply. I understand the psychological characteristics, ideas, views of love and living conditions of different women of this age from the author's humorous and wonderful style of writing. It seems that I myself am accompanied by many "zuo nv (作女)" of Beijing, and feel their hatred for the rules of life, to which some of them choose to make a compromise, and some are struggling to find fun. Actually, these so-called "zuo nv (作女)" are only representatives of a group in this age, and they magnify every one of us who does not like sticking to their last, lingering out and succumbing to the bored life.

What the author wants to express, I think, is nothing but her sniffing at the group that is mediocre, lacking in personality, vulgar and seeks popularity, and her support for those who do not want to be mediocre, enjoy life, do not care about the others, and live for themselves, like the heroine Drow (the Chinese name is 卓尔). After all, 卓尔不群 means excellent and unrivaled, which is similar to the simple but sincere saying "I am myself", randomly "zuo (作)".

拉丁美洲汉译文学概览

马安娜 【墨西哥】
绿宝石语言中心教师

中译西的文学翻译历史很短。大多数中文到西语的直接翻译是由母语为汉语的人士或西班牙人完成的。这是因为中国学西语的人数有明显的优势，而西班牙的中文翻译研究机构数量领先世界。截至2018年2月，墨西哥学院是拉丁美洲唯一一个历史悠久、专门从事汉学研究的机构，也是唯一一个持续从事中国文学翻译的中心。拉丁美洲还有其他专门的汉学研究中心，如委内瑞拉梅里达的亚非研究中心和墨西哥国立自治大学的墨西哥中国研究中心；但他们的研究主要集中在政治和经济方面，至今还没有发表过中西文学译作。尽管如此，还是有几位拉美译者编写了一个翻译语料库，包含中国古典文学和当代作品。迄今为止，从中文到西语的拉美文学译者还不清楚他们前辈及当代同事的历史。这有以下几个原因。第一，出版的作品很难跨越国界，因为出版社不一定能遵守出口条例；第二，一些译者在社交媒体和互联网上知名度有限，无论是普通读者还是学术专家要找到他们的作品更难。综上所述，信息方面还存在各种各样的空白。一方面，拉美的汉学研究，特别是与文学有关的汉学研究不是很多，另一方面，拉美译者缺乏群体身份定位，并且现在才开始写下他们自己的历史："拉美的翻译遗产至今仍然是未知的，并且被忽略了"。因此，本文的目的是全全概述直接将中文译成西语的拉丁美洲文学译者。

这项工作将"拉丁美洲译者"限定在出生在该地区、母语为西班牙语、出版了两本或两本以上的中译西译作的人。本文也考虑了这项工作具体和困难的记录。本文将回顾译者的教育背景、汉语学习、作品写作环境以及文学类型和具体文本。最后，本文总体评估他们是否有共同的任务愿景，或者他们是否有明确的个人立场。

值得注意的是，由于缺乏之前的类似作品，写这篇文章有一定的困难。如前所述，信息是分散的。大多数可用数据尚未由汉学家或专门从事文学翻译的学者汇编。也有大量的新闻采访，但其中一些不够准确。还有许多提供矛盾信息的非正式档案。基于上述原因，本文优先选择直接引用译者的话。毫无疑问，这仅仅是广阔全景的概述，欢迎其他出版物提供更多细节和解释。

第一个开始这项研究的是秘鲁人吉叶墨·亚历杭德罗·达尼诺·里瓦托（Guillermo Alejandro Dañino Ribatto）。1929年12月2日，他出生在特鲁希略的一个富裕商人家庭，是14个孩子中最小的一个。8岁时，他的父亲去世，母亲把家搬到了利马。然后他开始去由基督教兄弟协会领导的宗教学校学习。17岁时，他被正式接纳为基督学校修士会会员。他从小就对人文学科感兴趣，自学了英语、法语和意大利语。他的上级派他到阿雷基帕，将他培训成为一名宗教教育工作者。因为其他候选人受到青睐，他的高等教育陷入停滞。在某种程度上，这使他陷入了深深的沮丧之中，卧床一年。后来他获准继续学业，后毕业于秘鲁罗马天主教大学。他学习语言学和符号学，并在巴黎社会科学高等学院获得博士学位。除了在国立圣马尔科斯大学教书期间偶尔读了一些中国诗歌，认识一些华裔学生之外，他前半生中，也没有过多地考虑中国。1979年，他接到电话，让他到中国大使馆参加会议。他受邀在南京大学教授了两年西班牙语。他在五十岁时飞去北京，那时对中文没有任何了解："世界上使用最广的口语，历史上最古老的语言，对我来说是宇宙中最令人费解的、最难以逾越的、也是最有吸引力的语言"（吉叶墨）。在去中国的途中，经过贝尔格莱德时，他遇到一位中国绅士，向他学习了一些基本词汇。到达北京机场后，他决定学习中文："我一直在想，我前进的道路很漫长（需要顽强和心）。千里之行，始于足下。我迈出这一步，不知道自己要去哪里，也不知道要付出多少努力，但想到回报，就觉得为自己的工作而努力非常值得"（吉叶墨）。他发现周围的人一律穿着蓝色中山装。邓小平提出的改革开放政策刚刚开始实施，其作用在中国人的生活中尚未显现。街上仍然以自行车为主，他骑着一辆自行车去发现南京。他受到了学生的热烈欢迎，学生下午去看望他，以免他觉得孤独。他与另一位教授家共住，生活条件较好。他有司机、导游和厨师，吃得很丰盛，在口译人员的陪同下去了很多历史古迹，翻译对他敏锐的观察和问题进行解释。他记录了旅行中听到的一切，并在《中国：迷人之境》一书中描述了这些经历。有人给他取了中文名字叫吉叶墨，这是吉祥的名字，伴随着他以后的生活，并预示着他的作家生涯。为期两年的合同结束时，他已经深深喜欢上了这个国家，因此又续签了四年合约，为西班牙语系的15名中国教授传授《文学》《语言学》和《文化概论》课程，教本科生《口语》《笔译》和《语法》课程。在此期间，他自学中文，在全国各地旅行。他决定留在中国几十年，有两个因素起了关键作用："首先是中国人带给他的温暖，其次是丰富多彩的中国文化"（Navarro）。1980年，一个摄制组在南京大学寻找外国志愿者，参演在马德里拍摄的电影。吉叶墨教授后来在回忆录中以"我现在是谁？一个秘鲁演员在中国的经历"为题详述了他的首演。作为一个首批出演中国电影的外国人，他在中国也经常被要求签名。除了电影之外，他还参演短片、纪录片和肥皂剧。1985年，他住在北京大钟寺的酒店，门卫用简短的中文字和汉语拼音诗集作为礼物送给他。语言学的训练对他深入研究诗歌帮助很大。因此，他开始翻译中国文学作品。他的大部分作品集中在诗歌翻译上，因为"我喜欢诗歌，尤其是这种类型的诗歌。这些诗歌表达和平、团结、对人类的深刻感情、对自然的爱、超越等。我相信这些诗歌是值得传播的，特别是其表情达意的形式"（Ciurlizza）。吉叶墨诗歌翻译的一个显著特征是其表现形式：诗歌以中文印刷，左页是拼音，翻译版本在对面，提醒读者他最初是以这种方式接触这些作品的。另一个特征是有丰富的脚注和大量的参考书目。当时，吉叶墨的翻译开创了先河。在他之前，只有古巴的黄玛塞（Marcela de Juan）从事中文到西语的翻译，而且翻译量很少。除了诗歌，他还翻译了民间故事，谚语和短篇小说。为了满足年轻读者的需求，他撰写了《20个中国故事和黄龙》。至于古汉语，他认为古汉语能将大量信息集中在几个字中。除了翻译之外，他还撰写了一些关于中国的书籍，其中最重要的一本是《中国文化百科全书》，这是西班牙语中的一部先锋彩色插图作品，汇集了他30多年来积累的中国文化，涵盖了中国的物质文化和非物质文化、传统和传说、中国历史名人、领导人、作家以及利玛窦等影响中国历史的外国人等多个主题。针对教讲西班牙语的人汉语的这个问题，他编写了三本书，帮助学习者熟悉文字、习惯用语和谚语。2002年，他回到秘鲁，在国立圣马尔科斯大学、秘鲁罗马天主教大学和安东尼奥·蒙托亚德大学任教数年。除了中国的相关工作外，吉叶墨还出版了面向儿童的《圣经》以及中小学生道德准则的介绍性文章。吉叶墨教授是一个非常谦虚的人。当被问及他的汉语水平时，他回答道："这是一种丰富而难度极高的语言，有无穷无尽的汉字。必须要记住三万个汉字。我可以用中文进行对话，也可以阅读，但要付出辛苦"（Pajares）。他的作品集以及他对理解和传播中国文化的贡献使他获得了多项奖项，其中最重要的奖项是利马华人授予他的"名誉中国人"。2016年11月21日，习近平主席在利马国家人类学博物馆举行的中国、拉丁美洲和加勒比海文化交流年活动的讲话中，认可了吉叶墨教授的毕生贡献。直到今天，吉叶墨教授还在继续翻译和写作工作。他计划在不久的将来出版一本关于中国艺术的书。

芦苇（Wilfredo Carrizales）1951年出生于委内瑞拉的卡瓜。12岁时，他通过一部美国电影《北京55日》第一次了解中国，电影讲的是义和团运动。1972年，他买了一本《中国画报》，被"所谓文化大革命时期（中国）农民的新生活"所吸引。出于对共产主义的浓厚兴趣，他阅读了毛泽东的著作，并试图用各种方式来了解中国。1976年10月，他获得了中文学习的奖学金。1977至1982年，他在北京大学学习古汉语、当代汉语和中国文化。那时北京的公交还不发达，仍然有狭窄的传统胡同，他曾骑自行车探索这些胡同。他第一次来到中国就交了朋友，在全国各地旅行，品尝中国美食。1992至2001年，他负责协调委内瑞拉阿拉瓜文化部的文学和出版工作。2001年9月至2008年9月，他担任委内瑞拉驻华使馆文化专员。他的外交工作凸显了他在中国推广委内瑞拉文化的努力。2009至2011年，他在北京担任讲师。2009至2010年，他在北京大学教授拉美文学和翻译。2010至2011年，他在北京师范大学教授中译西的翻译课程和拉美概况课程。回国后，他花了很多时间在委内瑞拉的各所大学里推介中国文化。他的翻译作品很多，从古典和现代短篇小说到诗歌和当代小说，无所不包。正如吉叶墨教授一样，他既不否认学习汉语的困难，也不忽视文化差异："我可以告诉那些正在开始学习中文的人和中国人，他们必须抛弃已有的关于两种语言的所有偏见，并且敢于冒险。大胆无畏地理解困难的汉语，然后逐渐发现中国思想文化的基石"。关于中译西翻译方面存在的具体困难，他强调了结构上的差异，特别是古汉语："时间越久远，中文书写的独特方式越难理解，越难翻译准确。最难翻译的是古典诗歌和哲学。翻译的困难源于中文的特点：中文联系紧密、单音节构成、一词多义，没有性数变化，无动词时态变化……尽管增加了新的特征，现代中文仍然具有其中的一些特征，这一点在文学和诗歌中特别明显"（Bravo）。除此之外，芦苇还将英文诗歌译为西语，并做过摄影师、诗人和短篇小说作家。2006年，包含一系列散文诗的电子版《我的住所》获得委内瑞拉中西部地区第四届国家图书奖。他的翻译作品发表在他的家乡——中国和西班牙。他现在居住在委内瑞拉的图梅罗，在那里他继续自己的写作和摄影创作。他不断发表关于在中国拍摄的照片的文章。

伊西德罗·埃斯特拉达（Isidro Estrada）1958年出生于古巴哈瓦那的一个普通家庭。1976年，他在哈瓦那的巴勃罗拉法格外语研究中心完成了英西笔译和口译学习。年轻时，他曾在古巴拉丁新闻社工作。1995年，上述机构与中国新华社签署了一项合同，由此他首次来到中国并担任外国专家。2000年，他搬到了北京，目前他和妻子一直住在北京。直到今天，他仍担任新华社的编辑，为电子版的《北京报道》、《今日中国》杂志和《古巴直播》、中国日报、人民网、中国国际广播电台西班牙语广播和中央电视台西班牙语频道工作。他同时不定期为《哈瓦那时报》和《走进中国》提供短篇文章和图片。作为一名记者，他工作成绩突出，因为他有兴趣报道中古关系，关注古巴的华人社区和北京的拉美侨民。在古巴生活过后，他对中国特色社会主义有着非常敏锐的看法。2007年，郭翎霞和他花费一年时间研究和拍摄纪录片《中国萨尔萨舞》。纪录片回顾了中国这种特殊类型的舞蹈的历史，采访了很多这种舞蹈的代表者，并探讨了在中国不同城市这种舞蹈的存在情况。2009年，他与帮助他制作电影的同事艾丽西亚（Alicia）结婚。直到今天，他在翻译时还会咨询她，这在中文翻译中是一种非常普遍的现象。像吉叶墨和芦苇一样，他发现汉语很难理解，他的汉语不熟练："我承认，尽管我在中国，特别是在北京待了17年，但我的普通话非常不合格，马马虎虎都谈不上，尤其是发音。我认为（中文的）四个声调一直在与我的记忆和舌头打架"。2012年，他和妻子翻译了《当代中国文学三部曲》短篇小说集。2013年，他再次联手妻子参加2013年国际汉语翻译大赛，并以迟子建的短篇故事翻译取得第一名的成绩。2017年，两人翻译了1954年至2014年间发表的16篇中文短篇小说，题为《中国文学卷1和2》以及为陕西省作家协会成立60周年出版的《陕西故事》。埃斯特拉达总是与母语人士合作翻译，他认为翻译应忠实于原文，同时目的语应该地道并具有高度可读性："一开始，我记住了艾丽西亚（Alicia）关于这个问题的看法，想要严格遵守原文，害怕不能表达出原文的感觉。我认为这项工作的成功，关键在于两位译者都达到理想的中间立场，一方面忠实于原文，特别是体验作者在中文中表达的感觉，另一方面以目标语言实现最终产出和无缝阅读，好像文章本来就是用目的语写的一样"。

陈雅轩（Mónica Alejandra Ching Hernández）1960年出生于墨西哥城。1981至1985年，她在特佩亚克大学学习通讯科技。从姓氏中可以得知，她的祖父是广东人。他于1900年离开中国，开始了前往墨西哥的旅程。与大多数墨西哥华人一样，祖先的语言已经传给后代。1997年，陈雅轩辞去了广告公司的工作，开始在墨西哥国立自治大学外语研究中心学习中文。她想找到自己的根，去了解和理解他们。直到今天，她的生活还围绕着中国的语言和文学。2000至2002年，她在墨西哥学院亚非研究中心获得硕士学位，那时她也关注中国。2005至2006年，中国政府授予她奖学金，让她继续在北京语言大学学习中文。2006至2008年，她在中央电视台做翻译。她拥有一个名为Literación的文学机构。该公司旨在促进西班牙语作家和中国作家之间的交流，并发现新的人才，发表他们的作品。她在《环球亚洲》和《自由写作》等出版物中撰写了针对普通大众的文章。2007年，她以漫画书的形式出版了《红楼梦》的改编本。该书由墨西哥国家文学翻译基金会提供的奖学金资助。1008幅插图采用了中国"宫廷插画"的绘画技巧。她选择高度视觉化的版本说明她有兴趣吸引年青一代，因为年青一代是在充满图像且缺乏长篇文字的世界中长大的。这种试图吸引年轻观众的尝试得到了出版社的充分支持，出版社添加了"推荐给15岁以上读者"的推荐语。对于这项特殊工作，她获得了几位中国的墨西哥文学教授，特别是赵振江教授的建议。这本书在不同场合向公众展示，面向北京、墨西哥城和巴塞罗那三个城市的不同受众。完成这本书后，她想要改编《西游记》，她也承认这需要长时间的工作，只有在译者时间充足时才有可能。截至2018年初，这一计划尚未实现。2011年，她出版了《月光》，以诗的形式收录了48首歌曲和短篇小说，描写了中国女诗人黄庆云的乡村诗歌。这种格式让读者了解了吉叶墨教授所喜欢的方式：整页用于彩色插图，而下一页分为3栏：一栏是中文原文，另一栏是拼音，第三栏为西语翻译。使用中国传统绘画技法"泼墨"的中国艺术家梁培龙表示，整部作品都明显考虑了讲西班牙语的孩子的兴趣倾向。顾名思义，墨水滴在宣纸上："结果是一幅幅抽象的画，通过墨迹和不完美的线条赋予角色生命：画上的孩子脸是倾斜的，服装是模糊的"（"序言"）。翻译时，她遇到了以下困难："中文的拟声词充满了意义，很优雅。其他困难还有土语，婴幼儿语言和极其常见的典型的四字结构"。她试图以一种对年轻读者有吸引力的方式来捕捉原文的本质，以摆脱这些障碍："我冒昧地将中文原文的意思添加到西语中，而没有直译。直译可能会使文本无法理解"（Ching）。2013年，她在蒙特雷科技大学库埃纳瓦卡校区教中文。2014年，她回到北京担任讲师。2015年，五洲传播出版社出版了她的译作《安魂》，这是周大新的一篇文章，讲的是作者个人失去儿子的经历。截至2018年初，她在北京语言大学教文学翻译和中国文化翻译。她继续翻译并积极参与在讲西班牙语的世界推广中国文学。

明雷（Miguel Ángel Petrecca）1979年出生于阿根廷。他在布宜诺斯艾利斯大学获得文学学位。此后他开始对中国诗歌产生兴趣，经过一番徒劳的尝试，即和一群朋友用一本字典逐字翻译，于2004年正式开始研究中文。同年，他出版了自己的诗集 *El gran furcio*。2007年，他出版了另一本诗集 *El maldonado*。2008年，他获得了一年的奖学金，在北京语言大学学习中文。2011年，他发表了他的第一本中文译作《精神的国度：中国当代诗歌一百首》，旨在向读者介绍中国文学鲜为人知的一面："中国古诗中有'中国性'概念的结构。因此我乐于与此概念背道而行，走向当代。这部作品中的所有诗人都是50后。他们中的一些人在60年代末开始写作，但其中大部分都在80年代和90年代创作，他们构建了不同发展和风格的全景"（Halfon）。2013至2015年，他在国立东方语言文化学院攻读中国研究硕士学位。截至2018年，他继续在这个项目中做博士论文的研究，研究的主题是当代中国诗歌，导师是何碧玉（Isabelle Rabut）。2013年，他出版了另一本诗集《意愿》。他曾担任中文口译员，并将法语翻译成西语。2015年，他和他的商业合作伙伴马斯洛朱利亚（Marcelo Jouliá）开办了CienFuegos，这是巴黎的一家书店，其特色是推广独立出版社，并组织活动向公众介绍不太知名的作家。对他而言，翻译是一项创新活动："翻译是重新写作，呈现新工具，新程序，新观点，声音等"（Semino）。谈到将中文译成西语的具体困难，他补充道："中文措辞与西班牙语大不相同。中文大多使用短语和并列。中文标点符号的误导性与西语不同，对重复的容忍度更大（例如重复主语）。将它翻译成西语时，很多情况下需要以某种方式重构"（Tentoni）。2015年，五洲传播出版社出版了他翻译的于坚的诗《卡他出塔的石头》。同年，Adriana Hidalgo出版社出版了由他编辑和翻译的《当代中国叙述者文集》。2016年，他出版了鲁迅短篇小说集《呐喊》

的译本和格非的小说《隐身衣》。他还出版了自己的诗集《墙上的记忆》。2017 年，Pre-textos 编辑部出版了一本旅行书籍，记录了他在北京生活的经历。他翻译并出版了阿乙的犯罪小说《下面，我该干些什么》。截至 2018 年初，他居住在巴黎，在那里他继续翻译并完成他的博士学位论文。

虽然这些拉美译者在时间上相隔了 50 多年，但得益于奖学金或工作机会，他们能够弥补拉美没有专门研究和翻译中国文学的空白。他们中大多数人在北京生活了很长时间，致力于翻译和加强本国与中国的文化交流。他们的不同之处在于，吉叶墨喜欢中国古典文学，而年轻人则喜欢当代文学和古典文学。吉叶墨的宗教职业很好地解释了他想要翻译道德范例文本的渴望，希望提出另一种道德体系。芦苇和明雷等年轻译者则不然，芦苇选择自杀诗人的文本，而明雷则喜欢将杀手等反英雄作为文本主角。只有具有宗教背景的吉叶墨和作为母亲的陈雅轩努力出版针对年轻读者的文章。他们中大多数人从事中译西的翻译之前，都从事学术界或新闻业的相关工作。他们既要翻译，同时又要工作来维持生活。芦苇和明雷的翻译受益于以母语出版的诗歌。在他们开始学习中文时，他们也都精通至少另一种外语。他们都承认母语和中文的巨大差异。他们中大多数人一致认为，中译西的翻译更接近改编和文化调和，而不是字面翻译。虽然忙于其他作品、翻译和角色，但可以说中国已经成为他们生活的指南针。

A Brief Panoramic Revision of Latin American Chinese to Spanish Literary Translators

Adriana Martínez González / Mexico

Teacher of the Emerald Language Center

The history of Chinese to Spanish literary translation is rather short. Most direct translations in this particular combination have been carried out either by native Chinese speakers or by Spanish nationals. This is due to the fact that the People's Republic of China has a clear advantage in terms of the number of hispanists[1], while Spain leads the Spanish speaking world in terms of the number of institutions where Chinese translation studies can be found. As of February 2018, the only country in Latin America with a long history of a training facility devoted to sinology is College of Mexico. It is also the only center to have a relatively continuous output of Chinese literature in translation. There are other centers dedicated to the study of sinology across the continent, such as Center of African and Asian Studies in Mérida, Venezuela and Cechimex (Center of Chinese Studies in Mexico) in UNAM, Mexico. Their research, however, is mainly focused on politics and economy

---

1 Though Spanish language faculties in China are also rather recent (Spanish clases began formally in China in 1952), the country has now a large number of experts in both Spanish language and literature.

so to this day they have yet to publish Chinese to Spanish literay translations. Nonwithstanding all the above, there have been several Latin American translators who have produced a corpus of translations that cover both classical Chinese literature and contemporary works. To this day, Latin American literary translators working from Chinese to Spanish lack a clear knowledge of the history of those who preceded them and who their contemporary colleages are. This is due to several factors, the first one being that published works have a hard time crossing borders, as publishing houses don't always have the capacity to comply with export regulations, the second one being that some translators have a relatively limited presence in social media and on the internet, so their work is more difficult to find, both for the common reader as well as for the academic specialist. There are, then, various gaps of information yet to be filled in. On the one hand, Sinology studies in Latin America, specially those pertaining to literature are not very numerous, on the other hand, Latin American translators lack a sense of identity as a group and are only nowadays starting to write their own history: "Latin America's translation legacy is still to this day practically unknown and ignored" (Montoya 16). It is therefore the purpose of this essay to outline a brief panoramic vision of Latin American literary translators who produce direct Chinese to Spanish translations.

This work has limited the category "Latin American translators" to native Spanish speakers born inside the region who have published two or more books in direct translation from Mandarin Chinese to Spanish. Also taken into account for this article is to have some sort of record of the specific difficulties faced in the course of this work. This essay will review the translator's educational background, study of Chinese language, circumstances in which the work has been written, as well as the literary genres and the specific texts produced. Lastly, there will be an overall evaluation to see if they share a vision of their task or if they have clearly marked individual postures.

It is worth noting that because of the lack of previous similar works, writing this article has posed certain difficulties. As has already been noted, information is fragmented. Most of the available data has not been compiled by sinologists or by academics specializing in literary translation. There is an abundance of press interviews, some of them lacking in accuracy. There are also numerous informal profiles that provide contradictory information. For the above reasons, direct quotes from the translators have been prioritized. It goes without saying that this is nothing but a brief sketch of a vast panorama. The author welcomes details and clarification for further publications.

The first to head this study is Peruvian Guillermo Alejandro Dañino Ribatto, born in Trujillo on December 2, 1929 into a wealthy merchant family, the youngest of 14 children. When he was 8 years old his recently widowed mother moved her numerous brood to Lima. He then began attending a religious school led by the Association of Christian Brothers. At 17 years old he was formally accepted as a member of the Congregation of Brothers of La Salle. From the earliest of times he was interested in humanities. He self-taught himself English, French and Italian. His superiors sent to him to Arequipa to train to become a religious educator. His higher education was stalled because other candidates were favored at his expense. At some point this sunk him into a deep depression that kept him in bed for an entire year. He was later granted consent to continue his studies and graduated at the Pontifical Catholic University of Peru. He read linguistics and semiotics and obtained his Ph.D at the School of Advanced Studies in the Social Sciences in Paris. Other than the occasional reading of some Chinese poetry and the acquaintance of some students of Chinese descent[1] whilst teaching at the National University of San Marcos, he spent half his life without sparing much thought for China. In 1979, a call was put through to him to attend a meeting at the Chinese embassy. He was there invited to teach Spanish for a period of two years at Nanjing University. He flew to Beijing the very day he turned fifty years old without any previous knowledge of the language: "The most spoken tongue in the world, the most ancient

---

1 As of 2018, the Chinese community in Peru is the largest of it's kind in Latin America. They constitute an important part of Peruvian society, with their own set of institutions, traditions and contributions to the rest of the country's society.

one in History and to me the most impenetrable, kilometric and attractive in the universe" (Dañino). On the way to the Chinese capital he passed Belgrade, met a Chinese gentleman and learnt some basic words. Upon arriving at Beijing airport he set his mind on learning Chinese: "I supposed and I keep thinking that I had a long road (forged by tenacity and patience) up ahead. A journey of a thousand miles begins by a simple step. I took this step without knowing where I was headed, nor the effort it would require, but anticipating the rewards that awaited me were well worthy of the work I had set myself out to do" (Dañino). He found himself immerse amidst a people wearing the mandatory blue Mao suit. Deng Xiaoping's Opening and Reform policy had barely just begun and was marginally apparent in Chinese people's lives. The streets were still dominated by bicycles and he rode one to discover Nanjing. He was warmly welcomed by his students, who visited him during the afternoons to keep him from loneliness. He led a privileged existence at the home of another professor. He was provided with a chauffeur, a tourist guide and a cook to tend to his needs. He was lavishly dined and taken to multiple places of historical importance, accompanied by interpreters who responded to his keen observations and questions. He took note of all that was said to him and described these first experiences in the book *China, a Fascinating and Misterious Country*. He was given the Chinese name 吉叶墨, an auspicious sign that has accompanied him in the latter part of his existence and that foreshadowed his career as a writer. At the end of the two-year contract he had already developed a profound liking of his host country, thus extending his stay for an additional four years at the same institution teaching literature, linguistics and general culture to 15 Chinese professors of the Department of Spanish Language, as well as speaking, translation and grammar to undergraduates. During this time he studied Chinese on his own, while traveling extensively throughout the country (out of a total of 34 provinces he visited 33). Two factors played a key role in his decision to remain in China for several decades: "First and foremost, the warmth he found in Chinese people; secondly, the rich vastness of Chinese culture" (Navarro). In 1980 a film crew showed up at Nanjing University looking for foreigners to volunteer as actors for a film where the action was set in Madrid. The professor made his debut in what would later be detailed in the memoir entitled *Who am I now? Experiences of a Peruvian Actor in China*. As one of the first foreigners featured in Chinese films he is still regularly stopped and asked for autographs while in China. In addition to movies he performed in short films, documentaries and soap operas. In 1985, whilst living at The Great Bell Temple Monastery Hotel in Beijing, the doorman gifted him with a short collection of Chinese poetry written in Chinese characters and pinyin. His training as a linguist helped him decipher the poems. Thus began his work as a translator of Chinese literature. The majority of his oeuvre is centered around the translation of verse because "I like poetry, (particularly) this type that conveys peace, solidarity, profound feelings for humanity, love of Nature, transcendency, etc. I believe these poems are well worth being known, particularly in the poetic form that they were being phrased" (Ciurlizza). A distinctive feature of Dañino's poetry translations is the format they are presented in: the poem is printed in Chinese and pinyin in the left page, the translated version is on the opposite page, reminding the reader of the way the professor himself first came in contact with these works. Another distinctive feature of his books is the use of abundant footnotes and an extensive list of bibliographical references. At the time, Dañino's translations were trailblazing. Before him, only Cuban born Marcela de Juan[1] had produced direct translations from Chinese to Spanish and in a much minor amount. In addition to verse, he has translated folk tales, proverbs and short stories. He has also addressed the needs of younger readers in a book entitled *20 Chinese Stories and a Yellow Dragon*. On the subject of Classical Chinese, he emphasizes it's capacity to concentrate large amounts of information in a couple of characters. He has also written a couple of books about China, the most important one being *An Encyclopedia of Chinese Culture*, a pioneeringcolor-illustrated work in Spanish that compiles the sum of over 30 years of life devoted to learning about this culture. It covers multiple topics, which go from material culture to intangible culture,

---

1 Although born in Cuba, Marcela de Juan held Chinese and Spanish nationalities, which is why she is not included in this work.

traditions and legends, to famous characters in Chinese history, ranging from historical leaders and writers to foreigners that had great impact in Chinese history, such as Matteo Ricci. On the subject of teaching Chinese as a foreign language to Spanish speakers, he has written a series of three books to help learners get acquainted with words, idiomatic expressions and proverbs[1]. In 2002 he returned to Peru, where he taught for a number of years at the National University of San Marcos, at the Pontifical Catholic University of Peru and at the Antonio Ruiz de Montoya University. In addition to his China related work, Dañino has also published a book aimed to introduce *The Holy Bible* to children and an introductory text to ethics aimed at middle schools. On a personal level, professor Dañino is an extremely humble man. When asked about his level of proficiency in Chinese he answers: "It is a rich and extremely difficult language, it's characters are endless. There is a 30, 000 character dictionary that one has to commit to memory. I will say I can hold a conversation in Chinese and can also read it, but through hard, painstaking work" (Pajares). The corpus of his work and his numerous contributions to the understanding and dissemination of Chinese culture have made him recipient of several awards, the most important one being the tittle of "Honoris Causa Chinese", a price bestowed on him by the Chinese community in Lima. On November 21 2016, his lifework contributions were acknowledged by President Xi Jinping in a speech read out at the National Museum of Anthropology in Lima on the ocasion of the Year of Cultural Interchange between China, Latin America and the Caribean. To this day, professor Dañino continues his work as a translator and writer. He plans to publish a book on Chinese art in the near future.

Wilfredo Carrizales was born in Cagua la Vieja, Venezuela in 1951. At age twelve he first came in contact with China via an American movie, *55 days in Beijing*, a depiction of the Boxer Rebellion. In 1972 he bought some copies of *China Illustrated* and was attracted by "the new life of the (Chinese) peasants during the so-called Cultural Revolution" (Bravo). His keen interest in communism

---

1 Yet to be published as of February 2018.

led him to read up on Mao's work and to try by every conceivable means to set foot in the country of his interest. On October 1976 he obtained a scholarship to study Chinese language. From 1977 to 1982 he attended Peking University where he read Classical and Contemporary Chinese, as well as Chinese culture. His stay in Beijing occurred at a time when public transport was not well developed, and the city still consisted of traditional narrow alleyways, which he explored on bike. From his very first trip to China he cultivated friendships and travelled vastly across the country, developing a taste for Chinese cuisine. From 1992 to 2001 he coordinated the section of Literature and Publishing for the Venezuelan Ministry of Culture in Aragua, Venezuela. From September 2001 to September 2008 he worked as a cultural attaché to the Venezuelan embassy in China. His diplomatic work stands out for his efforts to promote his country's culture in China. From 2009 to 2011 he worked as a lecturer in Beijing. For the 2009 to 2010 period he taught Latin American literature and translation at Peking University. From 2010 to 2011 he taught a Chinese to Spanish translation course in Beijing Normal University, as well as a panoramic course on Latin America. During his trips back home he devotes time to delivering conferences to introduce Chinese culture at various Venezuelan universities. His work as a translator is extremely varied, ranging from classical and contemporary short stories to poetry and contemporary novels. In a similar fashion to Guillermo Dañino, he neither denies the difficulty of learning Chinese language, nor does he disregard cultural differences: "I would tell those beginning to study Chinese language and China that they must leave behind all their pre-existing prejudices about any of the two of them and to be adventurous (in the good sense of the word). To boldly and fearlessly apprehend the difficult Chinese language and secondly to gradually discover the keystones of Chinese thought and culture" (Bravo). On the subject of the specific difficulties of Chinese to Spanish translation, he highlights differences in structure, particularly in Classical Chinese: "The further away in time a peculiar way of writing in Chinese is, the more difficult it is to understand it and to translate it correctly. The hardest to translate are classical poetry and philosophy. The difficulties of Chinese translation derive from it's characteristics proper: an agglutinating, monosyllabic, polysemic language, lacking number and gender distinction, tenseless verbs...Modern Chinese still has some of these features, though new traits have been added, this is specially noticeable in literature and poetry" (Bravo). In addition to the above mentioned, Carrizales has also translated poetry from English to Spanish and has worked as a photographer, poet and short story writer. In 2006 the digital edition of *The house that inhabits me*, a series of poetic proses written by him, was awarded the Fourth National Book Award for the Mid-Western Region of Venezuela. His translations have been published in his homeland, China and Spain. He now resides in Turmero, Venezuela where he continues his own creative work as a writer and a photographer. He constantly posts articles and photographs related to China.

Isidro Estrada was born in 1958 in La Habana, Cuba in a family of modest means. In 1976 he finished his studies in translation and interpreting of English to Spanish at the Center of Studies of Foreign Languages ISPLE Pablo Lafargue in La Habana. During his youth he worked for the Cuban agency Latin Press. In 1995 the aforementioned agency arranged for a joint contract with the Chinese agency Xinhua and he made his first trip to China to work as a foreign expert. In the year 2000 he moved to Beijing, where he currently resides with his wife. To this day, he continues his work as an editor in Xinhua, on the digital version of the weekly newspaper *Beijing reports*, in the magazines *China Today* and *Cuba Now*, in the Chinese newspaper *People Online*, and at the Spanish division of CRI and Spanish CCTV while simultaneously contributing occasional articles and photographs to *Havana Times* and *Hands out of China*. His work as a journalist stands out because of his interest in covering Chinese-Cuban relationships, the Chinese community in Cuba and Latin American expatriates in Beijing. Having lived in Cuba allows him to have an an extremely perceptive view of the specific features of Chinese socialism. In 2007, Guo Lingxia and he devoted the year to researching and filming the documentary *A touch of Chinese salsa*, which goes over the history of this particular type of dance in China, interviews it's maximum exponents and explores the appropriation of the dance in different Chinese cities. In 2009 he married Alicia, the colleague who helped him develop the film. To this day he consults her on his Chinese translations, a very common phenomenon in Chinese translation[1]. Like Guillermo Dañino and Wilfredo Carrizales, he finds Chinese language difficult and is extremely modest on his level of proficiency: "I confess that in spite of my (spending) over 17 years in China, specifically in the city of Beijing, my Putonghua is very substandard. Slightly less than *"mama huhu"*, they'd say here. Particularly in terms of pronunciation. I think (Chinese's) four tones are at perennial war with my memory and my tongue" (Yang). In 2012 he and his wife translated a collection of short stories entitled *Trilogy of Contemporary Chinese Literature*. In 2013 he once again teamed up with his other half and won the 2013 International Contest of Chinese Translation and came out in first place with a Chi Zijian short story. In 2017 the two translated 16 shorts stories written between 1954 and 2014 published under the title *Chinese Literature Volumes 1 and 2, Stories from Shaanxi* published on the 60th anniversary of Shaanxi's Writers Association. Estrada, who always works in collaboration with a native speaker, believes translation should be faithful to the original, while at the same time being idiomatic and highly readable in the target language: "At the beginning I wanted to adhere too closely to the original text, bearing in mind Alicia's thoughts on the subject, fearful of not reflecting the original feeling. I believe the key to success in this work is that both translators reach an ideal middle ground that allows, on the one hand, fidelity to the original text and specially to experience the author's feeling in Chinese while, on the other hand, achieving a final product in the target language that allows for a seamless reading, as if the text had been conceived in that language" (Rosales).

Mónica Alejandra Ching Hernández was born in Mexico City in 1960. From 1981 to 1985 she read Communication Sciences and Techniques at Tepeyac

---

1 Another example of this kind of collaborations would be Phoenix, wife to American-born Chinese to English translator, Sydney Shapiro.

University. As can be inferred from her lastname, her grandfather was Cantonese. He left China and embarked on a journey to Mexico in the year 1900. As most Mexicans of Chinese descent, the ancestor's language was lost to the descendants, but in 1997 Mónica quit her job at an advertising agency and began to study Chinese language at the Center for studies of Foreign Languages, UNAM. Her intention was to go back to her roots and gain knowledge and understanding of them. To this day, her life revolves around Chinese language and literature. From 2000 to 2002 she pursued her masters at the Center of Asian and African Studies at College of Mexico, where she focused on China. From 2005 to 2006 the Chinese government bestowed her a scholarship that allowed her to continue studying Chinese language at Beijing Language and Culture University. From 2006 to 2008 she worked as a translator for CCTV. She owns a literary agency called Literación. The company aims to promote exchange between Spanish speaking and Chinese writers, as well as to find new talents and publish them. She has written articles aimed at the general public in publications such as *Globalasia* and *Free writing*. In 2007 she published an adaptation of *Dream of Red Mantions* in an fully illustrated comic book format. The book was bankrolled by a scholarship provided by the (Mexican) National Fund of Literary Translation. The 1008 illustrations were done using the Chinese drawing technique called "imperial illustration". Her choice of a highly visual edition speaks about her interest to attract the younger generations that have grown up in a world overfilled with images and lacking in lengthy written texts. This attempt to reach the teenage market has been fully supported by the publishing house, which added the label "recommended for readers age 15 and up." For this particular work she was advised by several Chinese professors specializing in Mexican Literature, particularly professor Zhao Jengjia. The book was presented to the public in different venues aimed at diverse publics in 3 cities: Beijing, Mexico City and Barcelona. Upon completion of this work she announced her interest to produce a similar adaptation of *Journey to the West,* though she also acknowledged it would require lenghty work and dedication, which is only possible when time is of no concern for the translator. As of early 2018, this plan is yet to be fulfilled. In 2011 she published *Moonlight*, a compilation of 48 songs and short stories in verse depicting the Chinese countryside written by the Chinese poetess, Huang Qingyun. The format reminds the reader of the one favored by professor Dañino: a full page is devoted to a colored illustration while the following page is divided in 3 different columns: one for the original text in Chinese characters, another one for pinyin and a third one for the Spanish translation. Monica's keen interest in reaching Spanish speaking children is evident throughout the work, illustrated by the Chinese artist Liang Peilong, who used the traditional Chinese painting technique "spilled ink." As the name implies, drops of ink are splashed on rice paper: "The result being an abstract drawing that through stains and imperfect lines breathes life into it´s characters: children with oblique faces, vague costumes" ("Preface"). While doing this translation she encountered the following difficulties: "Chinese's onomatopoeias, filled with meaning and grace. Other difficulties were regionalisms, infantile language and the extremely common four sylable structure, typical of the Chinese language" (Ching). Her response was to capture the essence of the original in a manner attractive to young readers: "I took the liberty to adapt the original meaning of the Chinese text into the Spanish language, leaving behind all literal translation. A literal translation would have rendered an almost unintelligible text" (Ching). In 2013 she taught Chinese language at TEC de Monterrey, Cuernavaca. In 2014 she moved back to Beijing to work as a lecturer. In 2015 China Intercontinental Press published her translation of *Requiem*, a Zhou Daxin text that deals with the author's personal experience of losing a son. As of early 2018 she teaches literary translation and translation of Chinese culture at Beijing Language and Culture University. She continues to translate and is actively involved in the promotion of Chinese literature in the hispanic speaking world.

Miguel Ángel Petrecca was born in Argentina in 1979. He graduated with a degree in Literature from Buenos Aires University. He became interested in Chinese poetry and after a few futile attempts to traslate it word by word with a dictionary with a group of friends he began his formal study of the language in 2004. That very same year he published a collection of his own poetry, *El gran furcio*. In 2007 he published another book of poems, *El maldonado*. In 2008 he obtained a one year scholarship to study Chinese language at Beijing Language and Culture University. In 2011 he published his first Chinese language translation, *A Mental Country: 100 ContemporaryChinese Poems*, a collection intended to present the reader with a little known facet of Chinese literature: "There is a crystallization of the vision of the 'Chineseness' concept in classical Chinese poetry. This is why I was interested in going against this notion, in moving towards the contemporary. All the poets included in this work were born after the 50's. Some of them began to write by the end of the 60's, but the majority of them belong to the 80's and 90's and they build up a panorama of different moves and styles of the last period"(Halfon). From 2013 to 2015 he read a masters program in Chinese studies at the National Institute of Oriental Languages and Civilization. As of 2018 he continues to research his Ph.D. dissertation in the same program. His subject of study is contemporary Chinese poetry and the dissertation is supervised by Isabelle Rabut. In 2013 he published another poetry book, *Will*. He has worked as a Chinese interpreter and also translates French into Spanish. In 2015 he and his business partner Marcelo Jouliáopened up Cien Fuegos, a parisian bookstore distinguished by it´s promotion of independent publishing houses and for organizing events to introduce less known writers to the public. For him, translation is an innovative activity: "Translation is a way to revitalize writing, to present new tools, procedures, points of view, voices, etc" (Semino). As to the specific difficulties of translating Chinese into Spanish he adds: "Chinese phrasing greatly differs from Spanish. Chinese language works mostly with short phrases and juxtaposition. Chinese punctuation is misleadingly different from ours, with much greater tolerance to repetition (for example, repetition of subjects). When rendering it into Spanish there are many occasions where you have to, in a certain way, build the phrase" (Tentoni). In 2015 China Intercontinental Press published *The stone of* Kata-Tjuta, a translation of Yu Jian's poetry. That very same year, Adriana Hidalgo published an anthology of contemporary Chinese narrators compiled and translated by him. In 2016 he published a translation of Luxun's short stories, *Kong Yiji and other stories* and a novel by Ge Fei, *The invisible*. He also published a collection of his own poems, *The memory of a wall*. In 2017 Pre-textos published a travel book he wrote on his experiences living in the capital, *Beijing*. He translated and published *A touch of evil*, a crime novel by Ah Yi. As of early 2018 he resides in Paris, where he continues to translate and finish his Ph.D. dissertation.

Though separated by more than 50 years of history, these Latin American translators have all benefited from scholarships or positions that have allowed them to compensate the fact that there are no permanent and continuous programs in Latin America devoted to the study and translation of Chinese literature. Most of them have spent a large part of their existence in Beijing and have devoted their life to translation and to cultural interchange between their home countries and China. As to the differences between them, Dañino favours classical Chinese literature, while the younger ones embrace both contemporary and classical literature. Dañino's religious vocation may very well explain his eagerness to translate texts based on their moral exemplarity. This is fascination with presenting an alternative moral system is lost in younger translators, such as Carrizales and Petrecca, the first chosing suicide poets, the second one favouring texts with antiheroes, such as killers, as their protagonists. Only Guillermo Dañino, a man with a religious background, and Mónica Ching, a mother, have made great efforts to publish texts aimed at younger readers. Most of them worked in jobs related with academia or journalism prior to doing Chinese to Spanish translation. They have all translated while keeping a day job to pay the bills. Carrizales and Petrecca's translations benefit from being published poets in their native language.They were also all proficient in at least another foreign language[1] at the time they began their study of Chinese. They all acknowledge the vast differences between their native language and Chinese. Most of them coincide in the fact that Chinese to Spanish translation is

---

1 They are all fluent in English. Petrecca and Dañino are the polyglots of the group.

closer to adaptation and a cultural mediation than to a literal rendition. Though busy with other works, translations and roles, it may be said that China has become the compass of their existence.

References

Dañino, Guillermo. *Desde China, un país fascinante y misterioso.* Perú: Protoperú, 2002.
Bravo, Guillermo. "Entrevista al sinólogo venezolano Wilfredo Carrizales" *China Files.* Web. 9 February 2018.
Ching Hernández, Mónica. "Prólogo" *Claro de luna.* México: Factoría K, 2011.
Ciurlizza, Naguib. "Naguib Ciurlizza entrevista a Guillermo Dañino." Online video clip. Youtube. Willax Televisión, February 8 2013. Web. 9 February 2018.
Halfon, Mercedes. "Miguel Ángel Petrecca, un poeta que traduce poesía china contemporánea." *Club de traductores literarios de Buenos Aires.* Web. 9 February 2018.
Montoya, Paula, y Juan Guillermo Ramírez, y Claudia Ángel. "Una investigación en historia de la traducción: cuatro traductores colombianos del siglo XIX." *Íkala, revista de lenguaje y cultura*, vol. 11, no. 17, 2006, pp. 13-30, Editorial Universidad de Antioquía.
Navarro, Susana. "Guillermo Dañino resume sus 35 años en China en una nueva enciclopedia." *Pontificia Universidad Católica de Perú.edu* Web. 9 February 2018.
Pajares, Gonzalo. "En China, por distinto, la gente me seguía" *Perú21*. Web. 9 February 2018.
Rosales, Abel. "Que la literatura de ficción de China hable en mil lenguas al resto del mundo" *CRI Online.* Web. 9 February 2018.
Semino, Darío. "La parada latinoamericana en París. Entrevista con Miguel Ángel Petrecca." *Lalibrearteylibros.* Web. 9 February 2018.
Tentoni, Valeria. "Un oriente argentino" *Eterna Cadencia.* Web. 9 February 2018.
Yang, Elena. "Entrevista Exclusiva: Feliz vida en Beijing de un cubano y su esposa china." *China.org.cn* Web. 9 February 2018.

汉字文化与中越传统丧葬礼俗研究

张家权 【越南】

胡志明市国家大学人文与社会科学大学中国语文系副主任

一 《说文解字》中所展现的丧葬礼俗

1. 丧葬礼仪

（1）初终之礼

初死之时，要迁尸于牖下。《说文·片部》："牖，穿壁以木为交窗也。从片、户、甫。"此字为会意字。本义为窗户。"迁尸于牖下"就是指把死者的遗体安置在正寝的北窗下，即所谓"寝东首于北牖下"。

当有人病危时，家人要把房子打扫干净，撤去乐器，把病人迁到僻静之处。然后换上新衣服，再用属纩放在死者的口鼻前"以俟绝气"，若确定绝气，就开始为死者招魂，这个仪式称作"复"。《说文·彳部》："复，往来也。从彳复声。"《段注》曰："往来也。辵部曰：'返，还也。还，复也'。皆训往而仍来。"本义为返回、回来。希望灵魂能归于肉体，从而苏醒。当"复而不苏"时，就可以治办丧事了。

首先，要设帏堂、设奠。《说文·丌部》："奠，置祭也。从酋。酋，酒也。下其丌也。《礼》有奠祭者。""奠"是个会意字。金文字形的上面是"酋"(即"酒"，《段注》曰："酋，酒也。"），下面像放东西的基物。本义为设酒食以祭，特指初死时的备供品敬礼。丧礼中把作为酒食等祭品放在地上的祭祀称为奠祭。古人把从始死到棺柩落葬之前的祭祀统称为"奠"。现代的社会的丧礼上，也写着"奠"字，正是古代奠祭的孑遗。

在治丧中，对死者举行招魂仪式，确认正式死亡后，就要发丧，即讣告，让远方的亲人赶回家奔丧。《说文》未收"讣"字，但收"赴"。而"讣"与"赴"、"报"同源，《集韵》曰："讣，通作赴。"《正字通》云："与报通。"《玉篇·言部》："讣，告丧也。"本义为报丧，通告某人逝世的消息。《说文·走部》："赴，趋也。从走，仆省声。"表示奔走，急速奔向凶险之处或紧急之事。有人死了，这个噩耗要赶紧通知亲戚朋友，可以用书信、传话来告知，所以后来演变为从言，写作"讣"。汉代的奔丧习俗，一直延续至今。

另外，凡病危之人，一定要居住在正室，其正室之名为寝，寝谓居住之室，亦称为正寝，所以才有"寿终正寝"一词。《说文·宀部》释："寝，卧也。"

当迁尸于牖下之后，脱去衣服，还要用角柶插入死者的口中，把上下齿撑开，以便行饭含之礼。同时还要用一种木几来固定死者双足，便于穿鞋。

然后，把尸体搬到另一床，开始为死者洁身，即沐浴。《礼记·坊记》："浴于中霤，饭于牖下。"《说文·雨部》："霤，屋下流也。"本指屋檐下的流水，借指房屋。沐浴，其实沐是洗发，浴是洗身，《说文·水部》："沐，濯发也。""浴，洒身也。"

上述之事完毕，要"铭旌"。《说文·金部》："铭，记也。"本义为在器物上铸刻、记下文字。铭旌也称作"明旌"，即旧时竖在灵柩前标有死者官衔和姓名的旗幡。多用绛帛粉书。

沿袭古代习俗，吊唁时，亲友们要带一些礼品，一般要赠送死者衣物，但死者不一定都穿上，这称作"禭礼"，《说文·衣部》："禭，衣死人也。"或作"裞"，《说文·衣部》："裞，赠终者衣被。"或者前来吊唁的人送一些玉石之类的礼物。

除了含、禭之外，还有赗礼和赙礼，《说文·贝部》新附："赗，赠死者，从贝从冒，冒者，衣衾覆冒之意。抚凤切。"而"赙，助也。"可见，赗和赙的本义都是以财物帮助别人办理丧事。

死者在中霤之床经过洁身整容后，又要迁到含床，准备进行饭含之礼。饭含的目的是孝子为了向亲人尽孝而设的。饭含包括两项内容：饭和含。饭，实之以谷、粱、黍、稷之类，填塞死者口中，让死者吃得饱，口中不空；含，亦作"唅"、"琀"，实以珠、玉、贝等。《说文·口部》："唅，唵也。"本义为东西放在嘴里，不咀嚼。又《说文·玉部》："琀，送死口中玉也。"本义为古代塞在死者嘴里的珠玉，古人认为玉可以保护尸体，有防止腐烂的作用。

据《礼仪·士丧礼》记载，在死者沐浴之后，入殓之前，还要对尸体进行整理，包括插笄、掩瑱、袭、设冒、设掩、瑱、幎目及握等，然后还要设重、设燎等一系列仪式。

笄，《说文·竹部》："笄，簪也。"本义为古代盘头发或别住帽子用的簪。《礼仪·士丧礼》载："鬠笄用桑。"古代沐浴后，要为死者整理发髻，但不戴冠，所以要用笄把头发固定，男人死后用桑笄，女人则不用。死后也要整理梳理发髻犹如生前一样，这反映出事死如生，事亡如存的丧葬观念。

迁尸于袭床，袭，《说文·衣部》："袭，左衽袍也。"本义为死者穿的衣服，衣襟在左边。袭是为死者穿上新衣，穿衣时要换床，于是称换衣的床为袭床。在袭床上为死者穿好新衣服之后，要用帛巾将头裹起来，以代替帽子，即"掩"。再用一种小型的玉器塞耳，称之为"瑱"。《说文·玉部》："瑱，似玉充耳也。从玉，真声。

此外，死者双手也不能空着，要进行设握，也叫握手，《说文·手部》释为："握，搤持也。"本义为攥在手里，执持。另外，还要用一块黑色布，覆盖在死者脸上，四角有带，可以系结，称为"幎目"。《说文·巾部》解曰："幎，幔也。"也作"幂"，本义为覆盖。"幎目"的目的让人死时心里无牵挂。

接着要"设冒"。"冒"是用来套尸的布，设冒，也分等级，《礼记·丧大记》："君锦冒……大夫玄冒……士缁冒。"冒后又要用衾覆盖死者全身，《说文·衣部》："衾，大被。从衣今声。去音切。"本义为被子，也指尸体入殓时盖尸之物。

袭礼过后，对尸体的处理便告一段落，此时要设重、设燎。设重是在堂前庭中设置一块木牌，暂代后来正式的神主灵牌。而设燎是晚上在堂上和庭中点燃火把用以终夜照明，为亡者守灵，同时还要设烛，来照亮祭品，便于亡灵享用。

以上程序办妥，就开始入殓。殓分大殓、小殓。《说文·攴部》："敛，收也。"本义为收藏。殓是将死者整理仪容、穿好衣服之后装入棺中；关于入殓的地方和时间，也有具体的规定。小敛在屋内进行，而大殓则在室外堂上的台阶。《礼记·檀弓》曰："小敛于户内，大殓于阼。"《说文·阜部》："阼，主阶也。"至于时间，一般小敛在死后三日举行。

大殓之后，要将尸体迁入棺内，所以要事先准备好棺椁。《说文·木部》："棺，关也，所以掩尸。"这是用声训的训释方法说明用棺的目的在于掩护尸体，延缓其腐烂。"椁，葬有木郭也。"在棺的外边又套上的棺称为椁，繁体作"槨"。"槨"字从郭，郭的本义是外城，《说文》："槨，度也，民所度居也。从回，象城之重，两亭相对也。或但从口。"正因为郭表示外城，所以从郭之字多有"外边""外缘"的意义特征。

尸体入棺后，称为柩。《说文·匚部》："柩，棺也。"本义为装有尸体的棺材。《尔雅》："虚者为棺，实者为柩。"

在棺柩下葬之前，需要将柩放在某地方停留一段时间这称之为"殡"。《说文·歹部》："殡，死在棺，将迁葬柩，宾遇之。"本义为停柩待葬。殡时每天要"朝奠"于"日出"，"夕奠"于"逮日"（日落），用"醴"，即甜酒（《说文·酉部》："醴，酒一宿孰也。"）酒、醢（即肉酱）来祭奠死者。在停殡期间，逢朔日，也就是每月农历的初一，要进行"朔月奠"；或有新出的新鲜果物、五谷时，也要进行"荐新奠"，对死者祭奠。

至殡礼之后，整个迁尸之礼便告完成。

（2）殡葬之礼

殡葬之礼是指棺柩从停放到入土安葬的过程。将灵柩运往墓地下葬，称为"出殡"。"殡"字从歹、宾声。"殡"亦通"宾"，《说文·歹部》："殡，死在棺，将迁葬柩，宾遇之。从歹从宾，宾亦声。"以宾客之礼去对待停柩待葬之事，就是"殡"。

经占卜定下出殡日期后，要在前一天晚上将棺柩迁入祖庙，放置一夜，下葬前先于祖考庙辞行，此称为殡庙之礼。行殡庙之礼后，第二天便正式下葬。

朝庙之后，然后行大遣奠，将大遣奠的祭品预先陈设在大门外。大遣奠是为安葬遗体而设的，所以又称葬奠。这是最后一次为死者举行奠祭。《礼记·檀弓下》："陈鼎五于门外。"郑注："羊，豕，鱼，腊，鲜兽各一鼎也。"

即将起殡之前，另有读赗的仪节，即是宣读送葬之物的单子。目的是向死者一一报告宾客们所赠之礼，使死者知道。

将棺柩放上柩车后，并进行装饰。《礼记·丧大记》云："饰棺，君龙帷，三池，振容，黼荒，火三列，黼三列，素锦褚，加帷荒，……士布帷，布荒，一池。"这段文献里记述了许多棺饰，但最主要的有三种：褚、帷荒、池。

等级不同，其棺的装饰也有所不同，死者的身份不同，棺饰也不同。身份越尊贵，棺饰就越华丽；反之，棺饰也随之简陋。

殡时，送丧者执绋前导，称为"发引"，又叫"执引"。即出殡时用大绳将棺柩固定于輴车之上，留下长长的绳尾，供送葬的亲友能挽牵引灵车的绳索而行，故称执绋，绋或作绥，《玉篇》曰："同绋。"《说文·糸部》："绋，乱丝也。"本义为绳索。也就是说送葬的人用绳子拉灵车。

灵车出发之前，要奏乐，执绋前行的人还要唱挽歌。挽歌，又作"輓歌"，是执绋者所唱的哀悼死者的歌。这是春秋时期，送葬时的风俗，上古无挽歌。

亲友僚属在灵柩经过的沿途，用谷物祭奠，谓之路祭。《周礼·春官·小祝》："及葬，设道赍之奠。"本义为古代供祭祀用的谷物。

灵车到达墓地后，柩车至墓后，要先将棺饰脱下。柩车至墓圹后，为了便于下棺，要先除掉棺饰，然后利用棺束悬棺下葬。

从灵车抬下棺柩，称作"窆"，《说文·穴部》："窆，葬下棺也。"为了防潮，先在墓穴底下铺上称作"茵"的席子，慢慢用绳索把棺柩放入墓穴中，这个过程称为"封"棺柩下葬之后，丧主要捧着死者牌位回家，举行反哭之礼。《礼记》："既葬而反哭。"

此外，殡葬时，伴随着死者的棺柩埋入地下的，还有许多的陪葬品。一般的陪葬品都是死者生前用过或喜欢的器物，以及一些贵重的物品，甚至用人来陪葬，即"人殉"，这也是受到"视死如生"的思想影响。

殉葬可分为人祭、人殉两种。人祭也称"人牲"，就是把人也当作牛、羊、猪、狗一样，都是祭品，杀之以供祭祖先、神灵。它是远古时期食人习俗的遗风。而所谓人殉，就是为拥有特权而死去的人从死殉葬，其起源和产生于父系氏族的确立和私有制的出现。最初的人殉多为女人为男人从殉，幼儿、孩童为成人从葬。

商代，是杀殉最鼎盛的时期，人殉制度十分普遍，据安阳殷墟小屯侯家庄1001号墓发掘报告，总计人殉"约有400人左右"，可想而知，当时杀殉的数量是多么惊人。汉字中的"伐"、"烄"、"豆殳"等，就反映了这种野蛮而惨无人道的人祭习俗。

"伐"是个会意字，从人从戈，甲骨文字形象用戈砍人头，《说文·人部》："伐，击也。从人持戈。"本义就是砍杀。"伐"是商代使用最多的一种人祭方式。

"烄"，是商代求雨仪式中，用火烧人，以作祭品的一种人祭方式。此字甲骨文写作"㚥𠂔"，像一人被捆绑放在火上烧之形。

"豆殳",《说文·殳部》:"繇击也。"其义为宰割,用刀宰杀奴隶以作祭品。

2. 居丧的服饰、言行举止

(1) 言行举止

在整个治丧期间,什么时候可以哭,什么时候不可以哭,都有一定的限制与规定。分为小敛之前的哭、小敛之后的哭和反哭,最后是卒哭。在反哭后,要举行安抚死者灵魂的虞祭(详见 3. 祭名),虞祭后即是卒哭之礼。卒哭的意思就是止哭,也就是在丧礼中,以卒哭为界,从卒哭以后所举行的祭祀,都是吉祭了,不必再哭。

其次是踊,踊就是跳跃,许慎在《说文·足部》解说:"踊,跳也。"这是亲人对亡者表现极度哀伤的一种发泄方式,跳跃的动作也分成:"绝于地"和"不绝地",就是说双足跳跃时离开或不离开地面。"绝于地"之踊要比"不绝地"之踊更为强烈。

再者,在小敛时,主人要袒而踊之,即脱上衣露出左臂,而妇人不适宜袒,但要做出抚胸的动作,以之代袒,以示极度悲伤。

另外,居丧期间也不可聘娶、不言乐。《礼记·杂记下》:"父有服,宫中子不与于乐……小功至,不绝乐。"可见,服丧的级别越高,相应的忌讳就越多。不过,到了东汉,"不言乐"这项禁忌就不再流行了,反而以音乐来答谢送殡宾客,比如奏乐、吹鼓、唱挽歌等。还有,居丧期间不能访友,不近女色,不言不相关之事等多种禁忌。

(2) 服饰衣着

在整个丧礼中,活人为死者服丧也是按等级、血缘来规定,即丧服制度。据《仪礼·丧服》记载,丧服的规格是由重至轻,分为斩衰、齐衰、大功、小功、缌麻五个等级,称为"五服"。

斩衰,(读 zhan cui),亦作"斩縗",在五服中最重的一种,服期三年。《说文·糸部》:"縗,丧服衣。"《段注》曰:"丧服也。按縗,经典多段借衰为之。"本义为丧服。

其次是齐衰(读 zhai cui),丧期以一年为主。但因亲疏名分不同而略有增减,且有持杖与不持杖的区别。按照服丧期限的长短,依次分为齐衰三年、齐衰杖期、齐衰不杖期和齐衰三月等。

大功,次于齐衰,比齐衰稍细,比小功又粗一些,故称大功。

小功，又次于大功一等，服期五个月。

缌麻，是五服中最轻的一级丧服，服期三个月。

另外，倘若遭逢两个大丧同时发生，不能完全同时为两人服同一等的丧服，而需要全面考虑在服制上有所减杀而已，即降低一等丧服的规格，称为"降服"。

（3）饮食与居住处所

《礼记·问丧》："亲始死，……三日不举火，故乡里为之糜粥以饮食之。"大意是说，在居丧期间，朝臣以及其家属三天之内不能在自家生火做饭，三天之后，也只能吃粥，称为"纳财"。小祥之后可吃菜果，大祥之后可吃肉。另外还规定："齐衰之丧疏食，不食菜果；大功之丧不食醯、酱；小功、缌麻不饮醴酒。"

《礼记·间传》："父母之丧，居倚庐，寝苫枕块，……此哀之发于居处者也。"《说文·艸部》："苫，盖也，失廉切。"本义应为草垫，许慎所释为引申义，用席子、草垫铺盖之意。《礼记·疏》为："苫为蒲苹，为席，剪头为之，不编纳其头而藏于内也。"就是说铺设不纳头的蒲草席；从以上经文，可以看出，父母死后，儿子要住在临时搭建的简陋棚子里守孝，晚上睡草荐，枕土块，睡觉时不脱绖带。待到除服之后，才可以恢复正常的起居生活。

3. 祭名

当死者的棺柩下葬之后，要举行虞祭。虞祭的意义就是虞于寝，祔于祖庙。行虞祭时要用桑木为死者神灵做一个灵位，称为"主"。虞祭分初虞、再虞和三虞。虞祭之后是小祥，小祥也称为"练"，当死者的丧期满一周年的时候，要举行练祭，而死者的灵牌改为用栗木做成，这时候要埋桑主，而以练主藏于庙，其礼又称为"祔"。祔是指将新死者的神位附于在宗庙内先祖旁而祭祀，享受子孙们的定期供奉。《说文·示部》："祔，后死者合食于先祖。"

在丧期满两周年时，具体时间在死者死后的第二十五个月，要大祥之祭，《仪礼·士虞礼》："又朞而大祥，曰荐此祥事。"大祥过后，又经过一个月，到了第二十七个月，又要举行禫祭，《说文·示部》："禫，除服祭也。从示覃声。徒感切。"本义为除去孝服时举行的祭祀。禫祭后，随即除去丧服，恢复正常的生活。禫祭之后，以每年逢忌日这一天来纪念，忌日即是死者死亡的那一天，之所以有忌日是因为《礼记·祭义》所言："君子有终身之丧，忌日之谓也。"

二　现今越南人的丧葬礼俗

1. 现今越南人丧葬礼俗的状况

越南丧礼的程序和礼节与中国古代丧礼大同小异，越南人的丧礼过程，也有初终之礼、殡葬之礼、服丧之礼等。

现今越南人的丧礼，除了与古礼相同之处，还添加了很多现代化的仪式和成分，以符合新时代的发展和需求。

首先，在招魂仪式后，确定死者已绝气，就会在死者的腹部摆放一把香蕉，此举的目的是让死者体内的胀气能够在入殓前完全被香蕉吸收并排出体外。

再看服丧的礼仪，如今越南人的丧礼中，还在首绖的中间点上不同颜色的点，代表着不同身份，例如：孙为祖父母守丧，其首绖上点绿色为内孙、点红色为外孙；点黄色是曾孙为曾祖父母守丧。

时代发展，如今报丧还可以在报纸和电视上登讣告，让亲戚朋友得知。同时一些大户人家，举行丧礼时，不需要亲友在金钱和物质上的帮助，便在讣告上和灵前写明"免赙吊"（Miễn phúng điếu）。

丧礼的乐队也分为：西乐队、中乐队、民族乐队等，应有尽有，只求满足丧家的要求。

至于灵车，也有多种选择，按照古礼，把灵车装饰得很辉煌，有池、有帷、有荒等，也有的按西方丧礼，灵车只是一辆简单的黑色车。

此外，一些丧家在出殡时，还请一些人扮演"齐天大圣孙悟空"，为死者开路，走在道士、法师或和尚之前，目的是将妖魔鬼怪斩除，不让孤魂野鬼、路上亡魂欺负刚死去的亲人的亡魂（新鬼），这是佛教文化传入越南之后才有的产物。

丧家除了按古礼以音乐和设宴答谢亲戚朋友来吊唁之外，如今的越南人，在办好丧事之后，还在报纸和电视上登鸣谢启事，答谢亲友在举丧期间的帮忙和安慰，如有不周之处，敬请恕罪。

可见，如今越南人的丧礼，总体看来，其根本并没改变，都是为了体现生者对死者的一种悲哀、缅怀、尊重和孝道。

2. 现今越南人与越南华人的丧葬礼俗之对比

自17世纪起，华人已和当地的越南人混居。经过长时间的文化交流，京族（越南人）与华人的丧礼有相同之处，同时也各自带有本民族的特色。

例如在停柩期间，华人和越南人都会用白布遮掩家中的镜子，或用粉末涂抹镜子，使它不能光亮、照射，此举目的是避免镜中返照出多幅棺木，一来不吉利，寓意家中会丧事连连，二来到处都能看见棺木，令丧家增添悲伤。

另外，在派人去报丧时，华人常给亲戚朋友两个"桔子"，因为"桔"与"吉"谐音，图个好彩头、吉利的意思，希望不吉利的事，不会发生在亲友的身上。而越南人在报丧时，没有此俗。

在将死者的尸体放入棺材之前，华人常要举行"祭棺"仪式，即将花果、灯烛、冥钱放置在棺内，进行祭奠。祭奠过后，才将已殁的尸体放入棺内。而越南人则举行"伐木"之礼（Lễ phạt mộc），按一清在《乡村例规》中写道："法师一手烧香、口念咒、一手拿斧砍几下棺木，驱除躲藏在棺木中的精灵。"虽在形式上和名称上有所不同，但其根源是来自万物有灵的观念，相信树木也会有精灵存在，此举目的是要驱赶躲藏在棺木中、木头里的精灵，让"他"不能侵害死者的尸首、不能欺压死者的灵魂。

为死者穿衣服的时候，越南华人会将衣服上的口袋、纽扣剪去，原因是"袋"与"带"、"代"同音，"扣"与"抠门"的"抠"同音，寓意死者不带走任何东西，而留福荫给后代，不抠门，那么后代子孙才有所享。越南人虽不剪口袋，但也将死者所穿的衣服的纽扣剪去，把纽扣剪去，是让死者的魂魄不受束缚、死者不抠门。除此之外，给死者身上所穿的衣服，忌用动物的皮毛所制，不然下一辈亲人会投胎成畜生[4]。

华人丧俗中，儿子还要"担幡买水"。"买水"仪式在大殓那天举行，死者的儿子要拿着钵，沿街痛哭，行至有水的地方（河流、水井），将铜钱扔至水中，然后用钵盛水，回家用此水在遗体旁擦三次以洁净亡灵。"担幡"仪式，在出殡当日举行，由死者的嫡长子或长孙负责，当日手拿树枝，绑上白布条随风飘扬，引领亡灵，希望亡灵早日升天，得以超脱。越南人则没见此俗。

出殡的情景、灵车、出殡的队伍等，两个民族的风俗一致。只有下穴之前，华人添加了撒五谷的仪式。所谓"撒五谷"，是在灵柩下葬之前，先在墓穴撒上五谷的种子，越南人未见此俗。

祔祭之后，将死者的神主牌位附在祖先旁边一起供奉，华人只在神主牌位上写上死者的姓名、谥号，而不会在牌位上摆放死者的照片，而越南人则摆放死者的照片在神台上供奉。

此外,越南人把生的香蕉放在死者的腹部上。华人的丧俗中则未见此俗。

通过以上的对比,可以看出,越南人和越南华人的丧葬礼俗中也有很多相同之处,都保存了古礼中的仪礼、程序,另外,添加了一些当地或自己民族的传统特色,以符合时代的发展、自然环境、社会背景,其目的都出于让死者有一个庄重的丧礼,都体现了子女对亲人的孝道,体现了"事死如事生"的观念。

三 中越丧葬礼俗之对比

经过历朝历代的演变,由于地理环境、社会背景等因素,中越两国的丧葬礼俗也有自己本民族的特色及与众不同的特点,具体如下:

第一,越南人在亲人临终时,会询问亲人的意愿,想起一个怎么样的谥号,确定谥号后,并向土地神和祖先禀报。而在中国,谥号是在人死之后,根据他们生前的事迹和功过、品德修养,给予评价的一个称号。

第二,停殡时,对灵柩的摆放,两国也有不同之处。越南人的丧礼中,停殡之处也是堂上之中央,但有规定,若家中还有比死者更高的辈分尚健在,那么灵柩得往西边移,不能摆在正中央的位置,这体现了宗法尊卑等级之分。

第三,关于铭旌,同样是标志死者的官职、姓名、谥号的旗幡,中国多用绛帛粉书,另用纸书写死者姓名贴于旌下。而越南人则用红帛或白帛,再用黑纸剪字贴上,而不用粉书;越南华人则添加一对白灯笼挂在门外,灯笼上用黑字书写死者的姓名和岁数。

第四,越南丧礼中,若家中人丁单薄,则出钱雇用一些人来充当死者的亲属,在死者的灵堂痛哭,每当亲友来吊唁,这些"临时子孙"也叩拜答谢宾客,犹如死者的亲属一样,越南语称作"khóc thuê"(租哭),免得死者在泉下觉得冷清。

第五,出殡时,死者为严父,长子则手持圆形,用空心竹制成的哭丧棒,走在灵柩之后,表示尊重死者在家中最崇高的地位;死者为慈母时,长子则手持方形,用实心竹制成的哭丧棒,走在灵柩之前,表示没有娘的儿女会很凄凉,不愿也舍不得母亲离开,此俗越南语称作"cha đưa mẹ đón"(送父迎母)。中国的丧礼中父或母离世,长子手持哭丧棒都走在灵柩之后。

第六,越南人无论是长辈离世或者晚辈英年早逝,都互为守丧、戴孝,但长辈不为晚辈送葬。而中国的丧礼，规定"父不拜子"，长辈为晚辈守丧和戴孝的礼仪也不同。

第七，始死时，越南人有在死者的腹部摆放一把生香蕉的习俗，而中国丧葬礼俗中则没有。

第八，小殓时，为死者穿衣服之前，越南人把衣服上的纽扣剪去；而中国丧葬礼俗中没有此俗。

第九，出殡之前，除了在本族的宗庙进行朝拜之外，若在出殡的路上，经过亭、祠、庙、观等，也要将死者的灵柩在祠、庙门口转一圈或停一下，表示向祠、庙中的神灵朝拜，以示尊敬并给予放行。中国丧葬礼俗中未见此俗。

第十，越南有些地方，尤其是北部（包括首都河内），盛行改葬，亲人下葬三年之后，一般要为亲人改葬。而中国人，因受到"入土为安"的观念影响，一般不会去惊动死者的陵墓。

第十一，若死者为晚辈，长辈尚健在，本身还没报答双亲养育之恩就撒手人寰了，视为不孝。在为死者入殓时，先在死者的头上绑上首绖，以示在阴间也应为长辈尽孝。中国丧葬礼俗中则未见此俗。

第十二，越南的丧俗中，有"伐木"之礼（Lễ phạt mộc），中国的丧俗中未见。

经过对比，可见越南人的丧葬礼俗仍保留着很多中国的古礼，同时，也有自己的别具民族特色的风俗。总体看来，两国的丧礼文化，虽礼俗上大同小异，但其核心也是围绕着"孝"和"礼"而展开。

四　结语

（1）丧礼是表现"孝"和"礼"的方式

丧礼中的一系列繁琐的礼仪，大部分都出于孝道的观念，早期的孝道观念，尊祖和敬宗的成分多一些。随着宗法制度的完善，逐步把对祖先的"慎终追远"的一部分，转移到父母的身上，做人应当敬事生而慎事死。

丧礼和祭祀祖先之礼，形成了子孙行孝于父母、追念祖先宗族的礼制。丧祭之礼中，处处体现子孙对祖先、父母的孝道，子孙不忘祖先、父母的养育之恩。使人伦关系、宗法等级、社会秩序再一次得到认可和强化。"孝道"和"礼"便成了界定宗族等级、人际关系、社会等级的法则。丧祭之礼亦体现了中华民族重礼仪、尚孝道的价值取向。

（2）传统文化的传承是必然的

丧葬礼仪被看作传统文化中的重要内容，而此礼仪至今还继续得以传承，因为其道德观念得到人们的认可和赞同。传统文化无时无刻在影响着人们的思维和行为，人们既要保存着传统文化，也在更新着传统文化，这才使得传统文化得以延续流传。可见，传统文化不但没有阻碍现代的发展，而在某一程度上，传统文化还可以推动社会的进步。

礼仪和传统文化对整个社会都有深远的影响，中国古代社会因此才成为礼制社会而得"礼仪之邦"的美名。时至如今，礼仪和传统文化在现代社会生活当中仍有着密切的关系，虽然今天的礼仪和文化已经与古时的有所差别，但亲亲尊尊、尊老爱幼、父慈子孝、礼貌待人等美好的传统仍有其价值。这些都是中华民族的美德，也是东方文化的财富。

参考文献

中文工具书

[东汉]许慎《说文解字》，中华书局，1963。
[清]段玉裁《说文解字注》，上海古籍出版社，1988。
[清]桂馥《说文解字义证》，中华书局，1987。
陈戍国《周礼·仪礼·礼记》，岳麓书社，2006。
胡奇光　方环海《〈尔雅〉译注》，上海古籍出版社，2004。
孔颖达《礼记正义》，十三经注疏，中华书局，1980。
李如森《汉代丧葬礼俗》，沈阳出版社，2003。
王贵元《汉字与文化》，中国人民大学出版社，2005。
徐吉军　贺云翱《中国丧葬礼俗》，浙江人民出版社，1991。
徐吉军《中国丧葬史》，江西高校出版社，1998，P433。
于省吾等《甲骨文字诂林》，中华书局，1999。
赵诚《甲骨文简明词典》，中华书局，1988。

中文期刊、论文

丁鼎，试论中国古代丧服制度的形成与确立，《社会科学战线》，2002，第1期。
李清恒，《说文解字》与中国古代丧葬文化，《文化研究》2003.8。
吕胜男，从汉字看古人丧葬观念的变化，《辽宁工程技术大学学报》，2008，第1期。
马兰，从古汉字透视古代丧葬习俗，《华夏文化》，2008，第2期。

王立军，汉字与古代祭祀文化，《中国教师》，2008，1 月。
许蓓蓓 王立军，汉字与古代丧葬文化，《中国教师》，2009，8 月。
张焰红，汉代丧葬礼俗探析，《青海师范大学硕士学位论文》，2009。

中文网页

百度网：www.baidu.com
汉典网：www.zdic.net
中国国学网：www.guoxuecn.com

越文工具书

Hồ Gia Tân, Thọ Mai Gia lễ, Nhà xuất bản Hà Nội, 2009.
Ngô Bạch, Hỏi đáp về nghi thức Tang lễ theo Thọ Mai Gia Lễ, Nhà xuất bản Thời Đại, 2010.
Nguyễn Đăng Duy, Văn hóa tâm linh, NXB Hà Nội,1996.
Th.S Nguyễn Mạnh Linh, Thọ Mai sinh tử, Nhà xuất bản Văn hóa – Thông tin, 2009.
Nhất Thanh, Đất lề quê thói, NXB Thành phố Hồ Chí Minh, 1992.
GS. Trần Ngọc Thêm. Cơ sở Văn hóa Việt Nam, NXB Giáo dục, 1995.

越文论文

Dương Thị Hương Trà, Phong tục tập quán của người Hoa tại TPHCM qua nghi lễ tang ma, luận văn tốt nghiệp đại học ngành Trung Quốc học, khoa Đông Phương, trường ĐHKHXH&NV TPHCM, 2000.
Nguyễn Dư, Phong tục về tang ma.
Nguyễn Thành Đạo, Văn hóa tang lễ của người Việt TPHCM, Luận văn Thạc sĩ ngành Văn hóa học, Đại học Khoa học XHNV TPHCM, 2000.

The Study of Chinese Culture and the Traditional Funeral Etiquette and Customs Between China and Vietnam

Truong Gia Quyen / Vietnam

Deputy Director, Chinese Language Department, National University of Humanities and Social Sciences, Ho Chi Minh City

I. Funeral Etiquette in the *Origin of Chinese Characters*

1. Funeral etiquette

1.1 Etiquette when a person is just dead

When just dead, the corpse would be removed to under *You* " 牖 ". It is an associate compound, consisting of radicals like 片 , 戶 and 甫 , meaning window. Therefore, " 迁尸于牖下 " means moving the corpse to the north window in the main bedroom.

When someone is critically ill, the family should clean the house, remove the instrument and move the patient to a secluded place. Then put *Kuang* " 纩 "on the mouth and nose of the deceased to " 以俟绝气 ", which means to tell if the person died or not. If dead, they begin to call the soul for the dead. This ritual is called *Fu* " 复 ". According to the *Origin of Chinese Characters*, it has the same pronunciation with 彳复, and means return or come back, hoping that the soul can be attributed to the flesh, thus reviving. If that does not help, the family can start preparing the funerals.

First of all, we must set up 帏堂 and 奠 (ancestral halls). According to the *Origin of Chinese Characters*, 奠 comes from 酋 which means 酒 (alcohol). in the character 奠, the above part means alcohol and the under half means base for things. In the funeral ceremony, the sacrificial offerings on the ground, such as food and other offerings, are called 奠. The ancients collectively referred to the rituals from the beginning of death to the time of burial and burial as 奠. At the funeral of the modern society, the word 奠 is also written, which is the relic of the ancient customs.

After the evocation and confirmation of death, message should be sent to relatives so they would return home from afar. There is no 讣 in the *Origin of Chinese Characters*, only 赴, but according to many ancient books, 讣 has similar meaning with 赴 and 报, which means to inform the news of someone's death. It also indicates that 赴 means 趋. It has the meaning as 走 (walking), and got its pronunciation from 仆. The bad news must be quickly notified to relatives and friends. Later people realized that it can be informed by letters and words, so the radical changes and 赴 becomes 讣. The mourning customs of the Han Dynasty have continued to this day.

In addition, all those who are critically ill must live in the main room. The name of the main room is called 寝, that's where " 寿终正寝 " come from. According to the *Origin of Chinese Characters*, 寝 means the main room.

When the corpse was removed to the north window, his clothes should be took off and a horn would be inserted into the mouth of the deceased for 饭含. At the same time a 木几 will be used to fix the feet of the decease to make it easy to wear shoes.

Then, the corpse will be moved to another bed and be cleaned, which is called 沐浴. The *Book of Rites* writes " 浴于中霤, 饭于牖下 ". 霤 means the water under the eaves, referring to the house. In the word 沐浴 , 沐 means wash the hair and 浴 means wash the body.

After the completion of the above matters, it is necessary to "铭旌". According to the *Origin of Chinese Characters*, 铭 equals 记 , meaning casting on the artifacts or writing down the text. 铭旌 is also known as 明旌 , which is a flag that was originally marked with the title and name of the deceased in front of the coffin. Mostly use crimson silks powder.

In accordance with ancient customs, relatives and friends have to bring some gifts when they are condolences. Generally, the clothes of the deceased are to be presented, but the deceased may not always wear it. This is called "襚礼". According to the *Origin of Chinese Characters,* 襚 means put cloths on the deceased, sometimes writes as 祱 . Sometimes those to the condolences will bring gifts such as jade.

In addition to 含 and 襚 , there is also 赗 and 赙 , which means helping others with money for their funerals.

After cleaning comes 饭含 . This is established to show respect to parents. Rice contains two items: 饭 and 含 . In fact, 饭 means filling the mouth of the deceased with rice; 含 , also written as 唅、琀 , means putting jade, shellfish and so on in the mouth. The ancients believed that jade can protect the body and prevent it from rotting.

According to the *Book of Rites*, after the deceased was bathed, before en-coffining, the body was also sorted, including 插笄、掩籒、袭、设冒、设掩、籒、幎目 , 握 , 设重 , 设燎 , etc.

According to the *Origin of Chinese Characters* , 笄 means 簪 . In ancient times, it was used as a hairpin. After the deceased is bathed, it did not wear the a crown, but to use 笄 to fix the hair. When a man dies, he uses 桑笄 , while a woman could not. After death, we must also organize and comb our hair as if we were alive. This reflects the funeral concept that we should live up to the standard the same as before death.

"迁尸于袭床". According to the *Origin of Chinese Characters*, the original meaning is the clothes worn by the deceased person with its open side on the left. 袭 is to put on new clothes for the deceased and to change bed when dressing, so it is called 袭床. After wearing new clothes for the deceased in the bed, use 帛巾 (a towel) to wrap the head in place of the hat, that is 掩. Then put a small jade into the ear, that is "瑱". According to the *Origin of Chinese Characters*, 瑱 has get its meaning from 瑱 (jade) and its pronunciation from 真.

In addition, the deceased can not be empty hands and therefore there should be 设握, also known as 握手. The original meaning is holding something in his hands. Also, a black cloth should be used to cover the face of the deceased, that is called 幎目. According to the *Origin of Chinese Characters*, 幎目 makes people relieved and do not need worry about anything when they die.

Then 设冒. 冒 is the used to wrap a corpse of cloth, and also graded. After 冒, 衾 will be used to cover the whole body of the corpse. According to the *Origin of Chinese Characters*, 衾 means a big quilt, refers to the cloth cover the corpse when en-coffining.

After 袭, the treatment of the body will come to an end. Following this is 设重 and 设燎. 设重 refers to putting a wooden plate in the front court of the hall, temporarily used as the spiritual tablet. 设燎 means igniting torches in the hall and in the court to illuminate the night. They kept the spirits of the dead and also set candles to illuminate the offerings for the spirit to enjoy.

After the above procedures have been completed, they will begin to en-coffin after getting the deceased dressed. There are also specific rules about location and time.

A 棺椁 should be prepared in advance. According to the *Origin of Chinese Characters*, 棺 is 关, meaning to cover up the corpse. This is the use of sound training to illustrate that the purpose of coffin is to cover the body and delay its rot. 椁 is from 郭, and 郭's original meaning is "outside the city."

After the en-coffin, it is called 柩. According to the *Origin of Chinese Characters*, 柩 means 棺, with the original meaning being a coffin with a corpse.

Before the burial, you need to put 柩 in some place for a certain period of time, this is called 殡. According to the *Origin of Chinese Characters*, during 殡, it needs to make offerings, like 醴 (alcohol) and 醢 (meet) to the spirits of the dead at sunrise and sunset each day. Special sacrifice will be conducted on first day of each lunar month and when harvest.

After 殡, the entire ritual of the corpse is completed.

1.2 殡葬

To take a coffin to a cemetery for burial is called 出殡. The word 殡 gets its meaning from 歹 and its pronunciation from 宾, also written as 宾. According to the *Origin of Chinese Characters*, 殡 is a matter of treating the coffin as if it were laid to rest as a guest.

The coffin was to be carried to the ancestral temple the night before, after the date of 出殡 was fixed by divination. Before burial, a farewell should be made to the ancestral temple, which is called 殡庙. The funeral was followed by a formal burial the next day.

After the temple comes the 大遣奠, which is set up for the purpose of burial of bodies, also called 葬奠. The offerings were placed outside the gate in advance. This is the last 奠祭 held for the dead. According to the *Book of Rites*, sheep, pig, fish, bacon, fresh animal meat would be offered.

Before the process of 殡, they will read the list of gifts for the deceased, which is called 读赗. The purpose is to report the deceased the gifts presented by the guests and relatives.

The coffin is placed in a coffin carriage and decorated with what is often called 柳. There are many kinds of 柳 according to the *Book of Rites*, mainly three types: 褚, 帷荒 and 池.

If the rank and status are different, the decoration of the coffin will be different. The more noble the status, the more magnificent the coffin decoration will be.

During 殡, the person who sent the mourner took the lead and called it 发引, also called 执引. That is, with a large rope, the coffin is fixed on the hearse with a long rope and a long rope tail is left for the funeral friends and relatives to pull the ropes of the hearse. In other words, the mourners pulled the hearse with a rope.

Before the departure of the hearse, it is necessary to play music, and those who take the lead of the hearse should also sing 挽歌 (dirge), also called 軷歌. This is the custom for burial during the Spring and Autumn period. There is no dirge in ancient times.

The relatives and friends of the deceased will offer grain on the way along the route of the cemetery, called 路祭.

After the hearse arrives at the cemetery, to facilitate the burial, ornaments will be take off, and then to use a coffin bundle to hang the coffin and bury it.

According to the *Origin of Chinese Characters*, carrying the coffin from the hearse is called 窆. To prevent moisture, a mat called "茵" was placed under the tomb. Slowly placing the coffin into the grave with a rope is a process known as 封.

According to the *Book of Rites*, after the burial, the relative should bring home the deceased's tablet and hold a crying ceremony.

In addition, at the time of burial, there are many funerary objects accompanied by the death of the deceased. Ordinary funerary objects are artifacts used or liked by the deceased during his lifetime, as well as valuable items, and even people (called

人殉). This is also influenced by the idea of "seeing life like death."

殉葬 can be divided into two kinds: 人祭 and 人殉. 人祭 is also called 人牲. People are killed like cattle, sheep, pigs, and dogs for the sacrifice of ancestors and holy spirits. It is the legacy of cannibal customs in ancient times. 人殉 is the burial of people who have died for their privilege, and their origins are derived from the establishment of patrilineal clan and the emergence of private ownership. In most cases, women die for men and children die for adults.

The Shang Dynasty was the most prosperous period of the killing people for sacrifice. According to the report excavated at the tomb of No. 1001 Houjiazhuang, Xiaotun, Yinxu, Anyang, the total number of people killed for sacrifice was about 400. It can be imagined that how many people were killed at that time. 伐 , 焴 and 豆殳 in Chinese characters reflect this kind of savage and inhuman custom.

伐 is an associate compound, representing the most popular method of killing people for worship in the Shang Dynasty.

焴 is a way of sacrificing people by burning fire and offering sacrifices during the Shang Dynasty to pray for rain. In inscriptions on bones or tortoise shells of the Shang Dynasty, it is written as 🔥, which looks like a person being tied up and shaped on fire. 豆殳 means killing with knife and slaughtering the slaves to make sacrifices.

2. Dress and Behavior in the Funeral

2.1 Behavior

During the entire period of mourning, there are certain restrictions and rules as to when to cry and when not to cry. It is divided into crying before and after 小斂 , the anti-crying, and end of crying. Between anti-crying and end of crying, there is a 虞祭 .

Then is 踊 , which according to the *Origin of Chinese Characters* means jump. Moreover, in 小斂 , the host should take off his shirt, reveal his left arm and then dance. The woman is not suitable for doing this so she will put their hands on the chest to express her grief.

In addition, during the period of bereavement, marriage and music are not allowed. The higher the social status is, the stricter it will be. However, in the Eastern Han Dynasty, "no music" was no longer a taboo, but instead, music was used to thank and send guests, such as playing music, blowing drums, and singing elegiac songs. In addition, during the period of bereavement, there are other taboo like we cannot visit friends, cannot get close to women, and cannot talk too much about unrelated things, etc.

2.2 Clothing

Throughout the funeral ceremony, the living and mourning for the dead are also regulated by rank and blood, that is, the mourning system. The specifications of mourning garments are divided into five grades such as 斩衰、齐衰、大功、小功、缌麻.

斩衰, also known as 斩縗, is the heaviest type of service in five, with a service period of three years. According to the *Origin of Chinese Characters*, 縗 refers to mourning clothing.

Followed by 齐衰, the mourning period is mainly one year. However, there is a slight increase or decrease according to the closeness of their constipation, and there is a difference between holding a stick and not holding a stick. According to the length of the period of funeral, it is divided into three consecutive years of memorial, 齐衰 with stick, 齐衰 without stick and 齐衰 for three.

大功 is second only to 齐衰. 小功 is expected to serve for five months. 缌麻 is the lightest mourning suit of the five service classes and is served for three months.

In addition, if two major mourning events occur at the same time, they cannot serve the same mourning service for both of them at the same time, so they need to fully consider reducing the grade for one of them, calling 降服.

2.3 Eating and Living

According to the *Book of Rites*, during the bereavement period, the families of the deceased cannot cook in their own home for three days. After three days, they can only cook porridge. This is called 纳财. They can eat vegetables after 小祥 and meat after 大详.

It also stipulates that: "齐衰 should not eat vegetable or fruits; 大功 should not eat sauce and meat; 小功、缌麻 should not drinking."

According to the *Book of Rites*, after the parents died, the son has to live in a temporary shanty hut to keep his filial piety. At night, he sleeps with the grass and pillowed the soil. When he is sleeping he does not take off his cloths. Normal living can be resumed until the service is removed.

3. Name of the memorial ceremonies

After the deceased's burial, 虞祭 was held. 虞祭 means put the deceased in the ancestral temple. When making a 虞祭, it should use mulberry to make a tablet for the spirits of the deceased and call it 主. 虞祭 consist of first, second and third ceremony. After 虞祭 is 小祥, also called 练. At the one-year memorial of the death of the deceased, 练 is to be held, and the spiritual card of the deceased is made of chestnut wood to put it in the temple. The ceremony is also known as 祔, which is to put the spirit of the deceased in the ancestral temple and enjoy the regular worship of the children.

大祥 will be held at the 25th month after the death of the deceased, and 禫祭 at the 27th, after which people can remove the mourning clothes and resume normal life. After that, memorial will be held each year at the date of the death, which is the day when the dead died. According to the *Book of Rites*, the memorial and mourning for a gentleman should be lifelong.

II. Funeral Rituals of Vietnamese Today

1. Funeral rituals of Vietnamese today

The procedures and etiquette of the funeral ceremony in Vietnam are very similar to those in ancient China. The funeral process of Vietnamese people also includes the ceremony of 初终 , 殡葬 , 服丧 and so on.

Today's funerals of Vietnamese people, in addition to the same rituals as the ancient times, also add many modern ones to meet the development and needs of the new era.

First of all, after the ceremonial call of the soul and the death is confirmed, a bunch of bananas will be placed on the abdomen of the deceased, so that the flatulence of the deceased's body can be completely absorbed and exited by the banana before en-coffin.

In today's Vietnamese funerals, different colors in their clothes are used to represent different identities.

With the development of the times, death can also be reported on newspapers and television so that relatives and friends can learn about them. At the same time, for some large and rich families, they do not need money and material help from their relatives and friends in funerals, so they will write 免赠吊 "Miễn phúng điếu" on the death report.

There are all kinds of funeral band: Western band, Chinese band, national band, etc., to meet the requirements of the host family.

As for hearses, there are also many choices. According to ancient rituals, hearses are gloriously decorated with 池、帷、荒 . Some choose Western hearses, which are just simple black cars.

Sometimes, the host family will invite some people to play "Monkey King" to walk before the Taoist priests or monks, opening the way for the deceased. It aims at protecting the spirit of the deceased from the evil spirits. This is a product of Buddhist culture after it was introduced into Vietnam.

In addition to the music and banquets, today in Vietnam, people would publish acknowledgements in the newspapers and television to express appreciations for relatives and friends for their condolences.

In general, the funeral rites in Vietnam today does not change much, all to reflect the grief, remembrance, respect and filial piety of the living to the dead.

2. Comparison of Vietnamese and Chinese Funeral Etiquette

Since the 17th century, the Chinese have been mixed with local Vietnamese. After a long period of cultural exchanges, the funeral rituals of the Jing (Vietnamese) and Chinese have the same features, and they also have their own characteristics.

For example, when the coffin is staying home, both Chinese and Vietnamese use white cloth to cover the mirrors in their homes, or use powder to smear the mirror so that it cannot shine. This is to prevent the reflection of multiple coffins in the mirror, which may not be lucky. Also, it is done so in order not to add to the sadness of the mourners.

In addition, when sending the message of death, the Chinese often give relatives and friends two "oranges", because 桔 (orange) have a homonym with 吉 (lucky), which means they don't want anything unlucky to happen to friends and relatives. When the Vietnamese report deaths, they do not have such custom.

Before putting the bodies of the deceased in the coffins, the Chinese often held a "sacrificial ceremony" named 祭棺 , in which the flowers, lights, candles and money were placed in the chambers to pay homage. After the memorial service, the corpse will be placed in the coffin. The Vietnamese held a "lumber" ceremony (Lễ phạt mộc). According to the "Village Regulations", Yiqing wrote: "The wizard burns incense, speaks a curse, and takes an axe and cuts a few coffins to drive it away. The elf in the coffin." Although it differs in form and name, it is rooted in the concept of animism. It is believed that there will be spirits in the trees. The purpose of this move is to drive away from the wood and the wood. The elf is used so that "he" can not infringe the corpse of the dead and cannot oppress the soul of the dead.

When wearing clothes for the deceased, Vietnamese Chinese will cut their pockets and buttons on their clothes because the 袋 (pockets) are homophones with 带 (bring away) and 代 (instead of), and the 扣 (buttons) are homophones with 抠 (tightfisted). By doing this, they hope the deceased do not take anything away, but leave luck and happiness to future generations. Although the Vietnamese did not cut their pockets, they also cut the buttons of the clothes worn by the deceased to keep the souls of the deceased free from shackles. In addition, the clothes worn on the deceased shall not be made from animal skins, otherwise in his next life he will be transferred to animals.

In the funeral of the Chinese, the son also has to "buy water", which called " 担幡买水 ". The "buy water" ceremony took place on the day of 大殓 . The son of the deceased took an earthen bowl while crying along the street to a place where there was water (a river, a well). He threw copper coins into the water, and then he used water to go home and use the water to rub three times beside the remains to cleanse the dead. This ceremony will be held on the day of 出殡 . The eldest son or the eldest grandson of the deceased person was responsible for the matter. On that day, they held a branch and tied a white cloth strip to the wind and led the souls. They hoped that the soul would ascend to heaven. Vietnamese did not have this custom.

The customs, the hearses, and the out-of-town teams are the same. Before the burial, the Chinese added a ceremony to sprinkle the grain. The so-called "sprinkling of grain" was preceded by the burial of the cemetery and the seeds of grains were sprinkled on the tombs. The Vietnamese do not have this custom.

After 祔祭 , the main tablets of the deceased were enshrined beside the ancestors. The Chinese only wrote the names and posthumous names of the deceased on the main tablets, while the Vietnamese placed a photo of the deceased on it.

In addition, the Vietnamese placed raw bananas on the dead's abdomen. There is no such thing in Chinese funerals.

From the above comparison, it can be seen that there are many similarities in the funeral customs of Vietnamese and Vietnamese Chinese.

The ceremonies and procedures in ancient rites have been preserved and at the same time has been added with some traditional features of local ethnic groups to meet the development of the times, the natural environment, and the social background. Its purpose is to make the deceased have a solemn funeral, which reflects the children's filial piety to their loved ones and embodies the concept of "Treat the dead as if they were alive".

III. Comparison of Funeral Etiquette and Customs between China and Vietnam

Due to the evolution of dynasties, geographical environment, social background and other factors, the funeral rites of China and Vietnam also have their own national characteristics as follows:

First, the Vietnamese, when their loved ones are about to die, will ask them to determine their own posthumous title and then report to the land gods and ancestors. In China, the posthumous title will be given after the death of a man according to their deeds and merits and moral integrity.

Second, there are differences between two countries in how to put the coffin in the hall. For Vietnamese, if there are elder in the family, the coffin will be put a little bit westward, not in the center to show respect.

Thirdly, 铭旌, the flag with the title, name and posthumous of the deceased, is different. Chinese people often use red silk powder, and the names of the dead are pasted on paper. The Vietnamese, on the other hand, use red or white silk, and then black paper to cut the word affixed. Vietnamese Chinese will hang a white lantern outside the door with the name and age of the deceased written in black.

Fourth, in the funeral of Vietnam, if the family members are few, they will pay some people to serve as relatives of the deceased. They these "temporary descendants" cry in the mourning hall when relatives and friends come to mourn, also bow down to thank guests, which is called "khóc thuê" (租哭) so that the deceased will not feel lonely.

Fifthly, at a funeral, if the deceased was the father, the eldest son would walk behind the coffin, holding a round, hollow bamboo mourning stick, to show respect for the highest status of the deceased in the family. If the dead was the mother, the eldest son would hold a square, solid bamboo mourning stick and walk before the coffin, showing they do not want their mother left. In Vietnam, it is called "cha đưa. m. ẹ đon". In Chinese funerals, whether the father or mother dies, the eldest son should walk behind the coffin.

Sixth, Vietnamese people are mourning and wearing filial piety whether their elders or younger generations died. However, the elders need not to attend the burial ceremony of the younger. The funeral in China stipulates that "the father does not worship the son" and that the etiquette is different.

Seventh, at the time of death, the Vietnamese have the custom of placing a raw banana on the abdomen of the deceased, but not in the Chinese funeral customs.

Eighth, during 小殓, the Vietnamese cut the buttons on the clothes before dressing the deceased; there is no such funeral custom in China.

Ninth, in addition to worshipping in the family's temple, the coffin must stop or make a round at the gate if it walks by a temple on the road to show respect. There is no such custom in China.

Tenth, in some parts of Vietnam, especially in the north (including Hanoi, the capital), the location of the tomb will be changed after three years of burial. While in China, affected by the concept of "rest in peace after the burial", people do not disturb the dead.

Eleventh, if the deceased is a younger generation and the elders are still alive, they are regarded as having not repaid their parents for parenting. They will tie a strip of cloth at the head of the deceased to show his filial piety. There is no such custom in China.

Twelfth, in Vietnam, there is a " 伐木 " 之礼（Lễ phạt mộc）, which is not seen in Chinese funerals.

After comparison, it can be seen that the funeral rituals of the Vietnamese still retain many features of ancient Chinese rites. At the same time, they also have their own ethnic characteristics and unique customs. On the whole, the funeral cultures in the two countries are similar in etiquette and customs, but their core is also centered on "filial piety" and "courtesy".

IV. Conclusion

1. Funeral is the way to show filial piety and courtesy

In the funeral ceremony, most of the tedious etiquette are based on the concept of filial piety. The early concept of filial piety is focused more on the respect for the ancestors. With the improvement of the patriarchal system, it is focused more on respect for the parents. We should respect life and death.

Funeral rites and sacrifice ceremonies for the ancestors formed a system of filial piety for the children to honor their parents and their ancestors. In the funeral rites, the filial piety towards the ancestors and parents is everywhere reflected so that human relations, patriarchal hierarchy and social order are once again recognized and strengthened. "Filial piety" and "courtesy" have become the rules to define clan hierarchy, interpersonal relationship and social hierarchy. The funeral ceremony also reflects the value orientation of the Chinese nation, which emphasizes etiquette and filial piety.

2. The inheritance of traditional culture is inevitable

Funeral etiquette is regarded as an important part of traditional culture, and it continues to be passed down, because its moral concept has been recognized and approved by people. Traditional culture affects people's thinking and behavior all the time. People should not only preserve but also renew traditional culture, which makes traditional culture continue to spread. It can be seen that traditional culture has not hindered the development of modern society, but to a certain extent, it can also promote the progress of society.

Etiquette and traditional culture have a profound influence on the whole society, which makes the ancient Chinese society become a courtesy society, and hence the reputation of "the state of rites". Up to now, the etiquette and the traditional culture in modern society life still have a close relationship, though today's etiquette and culture has is different from that of the old, but fine tradition like respecting the elders, being polite and so on still has its value. These are the virtues of the Chinese nation and the wealth of the eastern culture.

从外国人的角度对中国文化色彩词语初探

——以《现代汉语词典》中含"气"、"道"、"德"、"阴"和"阳"等汉字的语词为例

约万诺维奇·安娜 【塞尔维亚】
贝尔格莱德大学语言学院东方语言系中文专业讲师

根据本人的自身经历以及多年的教学经验,笔者认为对于一名外国的汉语学习者来说,最有意思但同时也最让学习者感到困难的莫过于那些带有中国文化特色的词语和表达方式。这类语词不仅包括汉语特有的成语、俗语、歇后语等,也包括那些带有浓厚的中国文化色彩的语素而构成的复合词。本文试图通过阐述文化对语言,尤其是对词汇产生的影响,介绍笔者对带有中国文化色彩的特殊词语的初步研究和考察,并探讨此类研究在对外汉语教学领域中的作用。本文第一部分重点介绍其他学者对文化和语言间关系的认识和观点;第二部分先简单介绍本人对中国文化中的几个特殊概念(如"气""道""德""阴"和"阳")的理解和认识,然后介绍笔者对含有这些语素的语词及其表达所进行的初步研究和取得的成果;第三部分讨论如何在对外汉语教学中解释这些语词的语义引申过程,以及笔者对如何将文化内容与词汇教学结合起来的初步思考;最后是本文的结论。

一 语言与文化的关系

早在 20 世纪 20 年代,著名语言学家叶斯柏森(Otto Jespersen)在论及人类

语言共同点时说，不同语言之间之所以会显示共同或者相同之处，是因为使用它的人从其本质到其思维方式来讲就有许多共同点。20世纪80年代后开始兴起的认知语言学对概念化方式的研究将语言间的相异性提升为语言学家关注的焦点。据认知语言学家（Lakoff 1990, Lakoff & Johnson 1980, 1999, Yu 1998, 2009 等）的论述，基于人类共有体验的认知的概念化方式往往显示出不少相同之处，而这些认知层面上的相同点有时也会在语言层面上表现为有某种程度相似的具体表达。另一方面，基于特定文化模式的概念化方式是语言特异性的渊源。在其他语言学家研究的基础上，谢里夫（Sharifian, 2011）展开了对所谓"文化概念化方式 (cultural conceptualization)"以及"文化认知模型的形成（emergent cultural cognition）"的论述。他说，"文化概念化方式"，包括具有文化特色的图式和范畴（cultural schemas 和 cultural categories），是一个文化群体的产物，即在长期以来文化群体成员间的交往过程中产生的一种概念体系。此外，他还应用沃德罗普（Waldrop）的术语，把长期以来在一个文化群体成员之间的交往过程中通用的认知模型解释为由许多个别的复杂体系构成的"复杂适应体系（complex adaptive system）"。谢里夫（2011）还强调，"概念化和语言是文化认知的组成部分"，并且把语言视为"储存及传达文化概念化的首要机制之一"。

根据以往不同学者对文化词语的解释和分类，吕海飞对"文化词语"下了如下定义："是带有文化标记性的词语，表征词义特点，反映民特色，习俗民情，跟社会制度变革密切相关，是折射社会生活的词语"，并把文化词语根据众多学者所接受的文化的"四个层面"说分为"物态文化词语""制度文化词语""行为文化词语"以及"心态文化词语"四类。孟祥英更具体地把文化词语分成四个大类，即"表现中国独有的物质文化的词语""表现中国独有的制度、宗教的词语""表现中国独有的精神文化的词语"和"反映中国独特的风俗习惯的词语"。同时，她还强调，具有文化特色词语的教学以及其文化内涵的详细解释在中国学生语文课教学中的作用在于"可以深化学生对词义的理解，窥测到中国文化的堂奥，加深对民族的思维方式、文化心理结构、社会制度和生活习俗等的认识"。

二 几个具有中国文化色彩的概念及其构成的语词分析

正如谢里夫（2011）所言，文化概念化在词汇层面上能得到最好的体现。我们出于这一原因，选择了下面几个富有浓烈文化色彩的概念（词）作为考察对象。本研究的主要语料来源为《现代汉语词典》(第6版)(下文简称《现汉6》)。本文里出现的所有词汇实例均取自该词典,因此来自该词典的词条及其语义解释,虽加了引号也不再在文中注明出处;而对于其他来源的词语解释则都会注明出处。本研究所采取的具体研究步骤如下:首先我们对在《现汉6》中出现的由"气""道""德""阴"和"阳"五个汉字构成的词语作了统计,然后把搜集到的词语根据上述五个汉字的不同义项做了分析归类,最后对哪些复合词语属于具有文化特色的词语范畴作初步确定。虽然我们在分析当中对上述五个汉字的每个义项的派生能力作了初步的研究,由于篇幅的原因,本文只谈及那些具有浓厚文化色彩的语义范畴以及属于该范畴的具体词汇实例。

我们对由"气""道""德""阴"和"阳"五个汉字构成的词语作了初步统计,发现《现汉6》中一共收入了866个词项,其中391个是由"气"构成的词语,278个是由"道"构成的,由"德""阴"和"阳"三个词构成的复合词或相关表达的数量分别为33、91和73。

上述五个汉字当中构词能力最强的是"气",对其构成的词语以及相关表达的初步研究发现,《现汉6》中一共收入了391个由此词构成的词项。《现汉6》把"气体"列为该词的头一个义项,正好符合《说文解字今释》对其给以的解释,即:"气,云气也。(...)云气的气,后来泛指一切气,如蒸汽、雾气"。谈到中国古代哲学和伦理思想对汉语构词过程所起的影响时,郭锦桴详细解释了"气"这一概念在哲学典籍中的用法以及语义发展,指出此概念在西周时期的时候已经出现,后来造出来的与此相关的表达皆有"元气哲学"的道理为其源泉。根据张文昊的解释,"气"之所以被赋予哲学概念的涵义是因为古代哲学家从古人的普遍思维方式,即具体观察自然界的现象,发展到思维的"比类取象的方式",把它与那些模糊不测的生命本源连接起来了。换句话说,原有的表示自然现象的概念被古代哲学家借用来表示具有文化色彩的、中国哲学及中医的"气"概念。《现汉6》所列出的该汉字的第13个义项(即"中医指人体内能使各器官正常发挥功能的原动力")和第14个义项(即"中医指某种病象"),以及从此义而构成的复合词无疑是由该汉字(语素)构成的词语当中带有最浓厚的文化标记的词。这些词语包括:补气、肝气、火气、精气、理气、气功、气脉、气血、生气、胎气、血气、血气方刚、益气、元气、运气、养气、正气(属于第13个义项)和犯节气、脚气、气虚、邪气等(属于第14个义项)。但是,我们认为,除了上述的两个语义范畴外，《现汉6》列出的第9和第10项引申义的"生气；发怒"及"使人生气"的词语也带有浓厚的中华文化色彩，如：沉住气、出气、出气筒、垂头丧气、动气、斗气、赌气、发脾气、负气、夹板气、解气、可气、没脾气、闷气、闹脾气、闹气、闹意气、怒气、怄气、气冲冲、气冲牛斗、气愤、气鼓鼓、气哼哼、气呼呼、气话、气恼、气头上、惹气、生气、窝气、压气、消气、闲气、怨气等，同样也值得我们特别的关注。再次，虽然《现汉6》并未把"人的性格、性情、气概"列入该词条的语义范畴内，"气"这一概念往往会出现于表示这些意义的词语中，而这些词语，正如前引郭氏所言，归根结底，也是有其特殊文化的含义，例如，胆气、鼓气、骨气、脾气、心气等。总而言之，据我们对"气"及其相关表达的初步认识认为，凡是不属于"气"头几个语义范畴的（即"气体""特指空气""气息""自然界冷热阴晴等现象"和"气味"的）或多或少都带有一定的特殊文化色彩，因而，在对外汉语教学当中应当受到我们的关注。

《现代汉语词典（第6版）》收入的由"道"构成的词语共为278条。该词典分别列出了三个同形同音的词项，即"道¹"（共有12个义项），"道²"（共有2个义项）以及"道³"（共有4个义项）。与此不同，王朝忠主编的《汉字形义演释字典》（2006）谈论汉字"道"的形体演变以及语义引申过程时，详细解释由该汉字基本义派生出的共为20个不同义项。据其所给的解释，该字的本义为"道路"，由此本义直接或间接派生出所有其他的义项。至于本文所关注的，文化色彩较为浓厚、由"道"发展出来的义项，我们认为是王氏所列出来的"道"字"途经、方法"之义派生出来的"主张、思想、学说"，以及由"主张、思想、学说"进而引申出的"道家"的两个义项。因此，在分析由"道"构成的复合词时，需要特别重视由这两个义项而派生的词项。这些词项同时也是教学当中需要特别注意的对象。据我们对上述278个词项所进行的分析发现，由"道"的该义项造出的词语共为31个，其中25个词项直接跟中国文化有关。这些包括：传道、道场、道姑、道观、道家、道教、道门、道袍、道人、道士、道统、道学、道院、道藏、火居道士、孔孟之道、老道、离经叛道、仁道、天道、外道、文以载道、五斗米道、悟道、穴道等。属于同一个引申义的，但不限于表示具有中国文化特色的还有：布道、行道、修道、修道院、左道旁门（旁门左道）、卫道，共为6个词。由于其用法目前不限于表示具有中国文化特色的现象，我们觉得，这些词语暂时可以不纳入我们上边列出的范畴中。当然，由于语义引申过程一般来讲较为复杂，是个应用不同引申机制的过程,我们在属于其他引申义项的词汇当中也能找出带有中国文化特色的词项,有时候某个具体的复合词作为整体就会引申出文化色彩较浓厚的语义作为其比喻义项。类似的词语包括:道高一尺,魔高一丈、人道1(第3个义项)、一人得道,鸡犬升天、孝道(我们认为皆属于"道"字的"道德"引申义项)、大道(第3个义项,即"古代指政治上最高理想")、中道(第2个义项,即"中庸之道")等。后两个复合词我们认为本是由"道"字的"道路"义项派生出来的,因此该词的其他义项不带特殊文化色彩,但此处列出的义项却有这种含义。

《现汉6》中共有33个由"德"字构成的词语。"德"字本身共有4个义项,但由于第4项其实是一个中国人的姓氏,没有派生新词的能力,我们把它排在分析框架之外。换而言之,3个具有派生能力的义项当中,以"道德;品行;政治品质"为最强,由此义引申出的"恩惠"这一义项次之,由"道德"义引申出的"心意"再次之。由于"道德"一直以来为中华文化最高理想,我们认为,属于"道德;品行;政治品质"和"恩惠"语义范畴的由"德"字构成的复合词语或多或少都带有一定程度上的中国文化色彩,但在我们看来,那些如"医德""德行"等类似的词语在其他语言和文化当中具有相应的表达,并不专门属于中国文化的特殊概念。因此,根据这个标准,由"德"构成的属于中国文化中特殊的概念不外于"德治"及"功德"(第2个义项:"指佛教徒行善、诵经念佛、为死者作佛事及道士打醮等活动")两个。

据《现汉6》所给的解释"阴"字共有13个引申义(最后一项为中国人的姓氏,因此排在我们分析框架之外)。据我们的统计,由"阴"字所构成的复合词共为91个。值得一提的是,《现汉6》把"我国古代哲学认为存在于宇宙间的一切事物的两大对立面之一(跟'阳'相对)"列为该字的头一个义项,使我们(尤其是外国学习者)觉得,这是该字的本义。其实不然。王朝忠主编的《汉字形义演释字典》解释该字语义演变过程时指出,其本义为"天色阴暗。天空云层密布,没有日光",是"古代哲学概念,与阳相对"的义项来源。换句话说,表示"天色阴暗"的词是被借来表示有特殊文化意义的作为哲学概念的"阴"。此外,对比两部词典时我们还发现,其间也存在引申义项数量上的差别,即《现汉6》共分别出来了13个而《汉字形义演释字典》一共分出来了该字的6个不同义项。由于篇幅的原因,我们暂时不谈及产生这种差别的可能原因。对该词所构成的复合词作统计分析时,我们的依据还是《现汉6》分别出来的引申义项,因此认为最有文化特色的当然是那些属于第一个义项的词语，即属于"我国古代哲学认为存在于宇宙间的一切事物中的两大对立面之一（跟'阳'相对）"的语义范畴的词，如：阴柔、阴盛阳衰、阴阳、阴阳生（阴阳先生）、阴阳水等。此外，具有浓厚的文化色彩还有那些属于第2个义项的词，即"指太阴，即月亮"，包括如下词语：太阴、太阴历、阴历、阴历年、阴阳历等。

在《现汉6》出现的，由"阳"构成的复合词的词数为73，该词典所列出的"阳"的8个义项（第9个为中国人的姓氏）在这些复合词里得其体现。与上述的"阴"字情况相似，《现汉6》仍把"我国古代哲学认为存在于宇宙间的一切事物中的两大对立面之一（跟'阴'相对）"排列第一，给我们错误的感觉这本是该字的原义。与此相反，《汉字形义演释字典》解释，该字的本义就是"阳光"，此义进而引申出"太阳"之义，而"太阳"就是其他引申义的直接来源。此字还被借用来指"古代哲学概念"。我们对这些词语进行初步分析表明，《现汉6》收入的属于该义项的，也就是具有浓厚的中国古代哲学或中医色彩的词语包括：太阳穴、阳刚、壮阳三个。

三　对外汉语教学中的具有浓厚文化色彩词语的教学思考

上述由"气""道""德""阴"和"阳"五个字构成的、具有浓厚文化色彩的词语在对外汉语教学中应该受到重视。例如，作为外国人，笔者也是在进行此项研究时才准确理解了一些由"道""气"等字构成词语的语义来源。因此，我认为，了解词的语义演变过程，包括了解该词在其构成的词语中以什么义项出现，这是提高词汇教学效率不可或缺的手段。

正如上文所言，"气""道""德""阴"和"阳"皆有好几项引申义，有的（如"气""道"和"阴"）甚至具有十来个不同的语义，涉及不同的但却有关联的语义范畴。其实，上述五个词的全部语义可以用"辐射性范畴"这一概念来解释，即"辐射性的语义范畴 [是] 具有几个核心的引申义 [的范畴]，而这些核心引申义再引申出新的意义"。由该词构成的复合词或固定表达的语义肯定是由其中的某个义项派生出来的，因此在进行上述词语教学时，我们可以采用以下的几个步骤：首先，可以给学生解释"气""道""德""阴"和"阳"的基本义并且列出由此本义派生出来的相关语义及其表达。其次，可以简单地给学生介绍该词的语义引申过程，并且给每项语义举几个具体词汇实例来说明。对于那些具有显著的文化色彩的义项，可以在简单地介绍这些被借用来指示特殊概念的词语在古代哲学和中医学的具体意义后，再举具体实例来加以说明。笔者认为，如果对这些词语进行类似的系统性解释，词汇教学一定会取得更好的效果。

本人完全同意上文提到过的孟祥英（2007）对文化词语教学在语文教学中的重要作用的观点，认为熟悉基本的文化词语及其相关的表达同样是对外汉语教学中重要任务之一。这种教学对于外国的汉语学习者也许更重要，因为力求不断提高汉语水平就必须了解语言所承载的文化知识。来自汉字圈之外国家的学生更有必要在学习汉语的过程中熟悉中华文化特有的概念体系以便了解中国人的世界观和思维方式，因为只有这样来自另外语系的汉语学习者才能够突破自己母语的思维方式约束，流畅地用汉语表达。

四　结语

本文在其他学者关于文化与语言间关系所提出论断的基础上，以前人对汉语文化词语的研究作为本研究的启发，初步分析了《现汉6》中出现的具有浓厚文化色彩的"气""道""德""阴"和"阳"五个汉字所构成的复合词及其相关表达。笔者的研究目的是：通过分析这些复合词及固定表达的具体语义范畴，从而加深对这五个概念语义派生过程的了解。本文认为，这种研究也会帮助提高对外词汇教学的效果。同时，深入理解具有浓厚文化色彩词的语义衍生过程是对外汉语教师的重要任务之一，因为只有老师熟悉了这些词语的语义和用法，学生才会加深对该类词语的理解。遗憾的是，由于本研究仍处于初级阶段，本文所掌握的语料及相关的文献很有限，因此不免有许多不妥之处，请专家同行们多提宝贵意见。本文打算把其他重点词典和辞书所搜集的由上述五个汉字构成的带有文化色彩的词语都纳入本文将来的研究当中，以便将研究成果用于教学实践中。

A Preliminary Study on Chinese Cultural Terms from the Perspective of Foreigners

Ana Jovanović / Serbia

Docent at the Department of Oriental Languages, Literature and Cultures, Faculty of Philology, University of Belgrade

According to my own experience and years of teaching experience, I think the most interesting, and at the same time, the most difficult thing for a foreigner learning Chinese is to learn the words and expressions with Chinese cultural characteristics. These words and phrases not only include the idioms, proverbs and two-part allegorical sayings that are specific to Chinese, but they include the compound words combined by morphemes with strong Chinese cultural characteristics. This article attempts to introduce my preliminary study and investigation of special words with Chinese cultural characteristics by explaining the influence of culture on language, especially on the production of vocabulary, and to explore the role of this kind of study in the field of teaching Chinese as a foreign language. This article is divided into three parts: the first part focuses on the recognitions and viewpoints of other scholars on the relationship between culture and language. The second part briefly introduces my understanding and recognition of some special concepts, such as, "气 (Qi)", "道 (Tao)", "德 (Virtue)",

"阴 (Yin)" and "阳 (Yang)" in Chinese culture, and then introduces our preliminary study and achievements of the words and expressions that contain these morphemes. The third part introduces the process of semantic extension on how we should explain these words in teaching Chinese as a foreign language, and the preliminary thought on how to combine cultural content with vocabulary teaching. The fourth part is the conclusion.

I. The Relationship between Language and Culture

As early as the 1920s, the famous linguist Otto Jespersen, when speaking of the similarities of human languages, said that different languages show something in common because the language users have a lot in common from their nature to their way of thinking.[1] The study of conceptualization in cognitive linguistics since the 1980s has promoted the diversity of languages to the focus of linguists. According to cognitive linguists (Lakoff 1990, Lakoff & Johnson 1980, 1999, Yu 1998, 2009 et al), the conceptualization of cognition based on the common experience of human beings often shows many similarities, and these similarities at the cognitive level are sometimes manifested as the concrete expression of a certain degree of similarity at the language level. On the other hand, conceptualization based on specific cultural patterns is the source of language specificity.[2] Sheriff (Sharifian, 2011), based on the work of other linguists, discussed the so-called "cultural conceptualization" and "emergent cultural cognition". He said that "cultural conceptualization", including cultural schemas and cultural categories, is a product of a cultural group, that is, a conceptual system produced in the process of communication among the members of a cultural group over a long period of time[3]. In addition, he used Waldrop (1992)'s terms to explain the common cognitive model that has long been used in the process of communication among the members of a cultural group for a long time as a

---

1 Otto Jespersen. *Mankind, Nation, and Individual from a Linguistic Point of View. An Introduction by Ren Shaozeng*. Beijing: World Book Inc., Beijing Company, 2010: 169-171, 174, 181.
2 Please refer to the works of Lakoff (1990), Lakoff & Johnson (1980, 1999), Yu (1998, 2009) listed in the references for the detailed explanation of the influence of experiential cognition and cultural pattern on conceptualization and languages.
3 Sharifian, F. *Cultural conceptualisations and language: theoretical framework and applications*. Amsterdam/Philadelphia: John Benjamins Publishing Company, 2011: 5.

"complex adaptive system"¹, which is made up of many other complex systems. Sheriff (2011) also stressed, "(......) conceptualization and language are constituent parts of cultural cognition"², and he regarded language as "one of the primary mechanisms for storing and conveying cultural conceptualization"³.

According to the explanation and classification of cultural words by different scholars of the past, Lv Haifei has defined "cultural words" as follows: "[......] is a word with cultural markers that represents the characteristics of word meaning, reflects the features and customs of people, and is closely related to the social institutional reform, so it is a word to reflect social life"⁴. He has also divided the cultural words into "physical cultural words", "institutional cultural words", "behavioral cultural words" and "mental cultural words"⁵ according to the "four levels" theory of culture that has been accepted by many scholars. Meng Xiangying more concretely divided the cultural words into four major categories, namely, "words that represent the unique material culture of China", "words that represent the unique institutions and religion of China", "words that represent the unique spiritual culture of China" and "words that reflect the unique customs and habits of China"⁶. At the same time, she also stressed that the teaching of words with cultural characteristics and the detailed interpretation of these words' cultural connotations in Chinese students' Chinese language teaching can "deepen students' understanding of the meaning of the words, understand the essence of Chinese culture, and deepen

---

1 Sharifian, F. *Cultural conceptualisations and language: theoretical framework and applications.* Amsterdam/Philadelphia: John Benjamins Publishing Company, 2011: 23.
2 "(...) conceptualization and language as two integral aspects of cultural cognition" . Sharifian, F. *Cultural conceptualisations and language: theoretical framework and applications.* Amsterdam/Philadelphia: John Benjamins Publishing Company, 2011: 24.
3 "[In this sense] language can be viewed as one of the primary mechanisms which stores and communicates cultural conceptualisations" . Sharifian, F. *Cultural conceptualisations and language: theoretical framework and applications.* Amsterdam/Philadelphia: John Benjamins Publishing Company, 2011: 39.
4 Lv Haifei, Summary of the Study of Cultural Words, Jin Tian (Li Zhi), 2012 (11): 226.
5 Ditto
6 Meng Xiangying, Cultural Implication and Teaching Reflection of Chinese Words, *Journal of Shandong Education Institute*, 2007 (4): 1.

the cognition of the way of thinking, the cultural-psychological structure, the social institutions and living customs of the nation (......) "[1]

II. Analysis of Several Concepts with Chinese Cultural Characteristics and Words and Phrases Made up of These Concepts

As Sheriff (2011) said, cultural conceptualization can be best expressed at the lexical level[2]. For this reason, we have chosen the following concepts (words) with strong cultural characteristics as the subject of study. The corpus of this study is mainly derived from the Modern Chinese Dictionary (Version 6), hereinafter referred to as Modern Chinese 6. All the lexical instances in this article are taken from this dictionary, so the source of the entries and their semantic interpretation from the dictionary are no longer given in the text although they have quotation marks; however, the source should be given for the explanation of words from other sources. The specific steps taken in this study are as follows: First, we make a statistical analysis of words made up of the five Chinese characters " 气 (Qi)", " 道 (Tao)", " 德 (Virtue)", " 阴 (Yin)" and " 阳 (Yang)", then we analyze and classify the collected words and phrases according to different semantic items of the above five Chinese characters, and finally we preliminarily determine which compound words are words with cultural characteristics. Although we have preliminarily studied the derivational ability of each semantic item in the above five Chinese characters in the analysis, this article only talks about the semantic category with strong cultural characteristics and the specific lexical instances in this category due to the length of the article.

According to preliminary estimates on the words made up of the five Chinese characters " 气 (Qi)", " 道 (Tao)", " 德 (Virtue)", " 阴 (Yin)" and " 阳 (Yang)", we find that there are 866 lexical items in Modern Chinese 6, of which 391 are made up of " 气 (Qi)", and 278 are composed of " 道 (Tao)". The number of compound

---

1 Ditto: 1.
2 Sharifian, F. Cultural conceptualisations and language: theoretical framework and applications. Amsterdam/Philadelphia: John Benjamins Publishing Company, 2011: 48.

words or related expressions made up of "德 (Virtue)", "阴 (Yin)" and "阳 (Yang)" is 33, 91 and 73 respectively.

"气 (Qi)" has the most powerful ability for word-formation of the above five Chinese characters. Through the preliminary study of words and related expressions made up of "气 (Qi)", we find that there are 391 lexical items in Modern Chinese 6. In Modern Chinese 6, "气体 (gas)" is listed as the first meaning of the word, which is exactly consistent with the explanation given in *Modern Explanation of Shuo Wen Jie Zi*, namely, "气 (Qi) refers to floating gas. (…) the word gas in floating gas later generally refers to all gases, such as steam and mist (…)"[1]. When speaking of the influence of ancient Chinese philosophy and ethical thought on the process of Chinese word formation, Guo Jinfu (1992) has explained in detail the usage and semantic development of the concept "气 (Qi)" in philosophical classics, and pointed out that this concept had appeared in the Western Zhou Dynasty, and the subsequent expressions related to "气 (Qi)" are all derived from the "vitality philosophy".[2] Zhang Wenhao has explained that, "气 (Qi)" is given the meaning of philosophical concept because ancient philosophers developed their way of thinking from the universal way of thinking, that is, from concretely observing the natural phenomena, to the "comparative state method" of thinking, and connect it with those obscure life origins[3]. In other words, the original concept of natural phenomena is used by ancient philosophers to represent the concept "气 (Qi)" with cultural characteristics in Chinese philosophy and traditional Chinese medicine. The 13th semantic item ("the motive power that enables the normal function of internal organs in the human body in traditional Chinese medicine") and the 14th semantic

---

1   Xu Shen, *Modern Explanation of Shuo Wen Jie Zi*, compiled by Tang Kejing, Yue Lu Book Company, 2001: 58.
2   Guo Jinfu, Chinese Word Creation and Traditional Philosophical and Ethical View, *Journal of Renmin University of China*, 1992 (1): 77, 76.
3   Zhang Wenhao, A Brief Analysis of the Generation of the Concept "气 (Qi)" in Traditional Chinese Medicine from the Linguistic Perspective, *Journal of Yunnan University of Traditional Chinese Medicine*, 2010, Volume 33, No.3:8.

item ("a kind of symptom of a disease in traditional Chinese medicine")[1] of "气 (Qi)" listed in Modern Chinese 6, and the compound words made up of these two semantic items of "气 (Qi)" are undoubtedly the words with the strongest cultural markers of all of the words made up of the Chinese character (morpheme). These words include 补气 (tonifying qi), 肝气 (liver qi), 火气 (internal heat), 精气 (essence qi), 理气 (regulating qi), 气功 (qigong, a system of deep breathing exercises), 气脉 (qi channel), 气血 (qi and blood), 生气 (anger2), 胎气 (pregnancy edema), 血气 (sap), 血气方刚 (energetic), 益气 (benefiting qi), 元气 (primordial qi), 运气 (yunqi, directing one's strength, through concentration, to a part of the body), 养气 (cultivating qi), 正气 (healthy qi) (the 13th semantic item) and 犯节气 (have an attack of a seasonal illness), 脚气 (beriberi), 气虚 (qi deficiency), 邪气 (pathogenic qi) and so on (the 14th semantic item).[2] However, we

---

1 When going into details about different semantics of "气 (Qi)" in traditional Chinese medicine, Zhang Wenhao said that: "气 (Qi)" has derived rich meanings in the field of traditional Chinese medicine and pharmacy, and formed the semantic category peculiar to this field: (1) generally refers to substances that constitute the universe; (2) the basic substances that run through the human body and maintain the various organs of the human body; (3) the function of internal organs; (4) triggering the factors that cause illness; (5) performance and the effect of medicine; (6) disease location or stage of warm disease dialectics; (7) "needling sensation" in science of acupuncture and moxibustion (Zhang Wenhao, A Brief Analysis of the Generation of the Concept "气 (Qi)" in Traditional Chinese Medicine from the Linguistic Perspective, *Journal of Yunnan University of Traditional Chinese Medicine*, 2010, Volume 33, No.3: 7-8)." Because of the article length, we classify the lexical items that are included in Modern Chinese 6 and that belong to this semantic category based on the method of summary in TCM category instead of this classification method.

2 Unlike the classification method, Guo Jinfu classifies "气 (Qi)" based on the semantic category that is made up of "气 (Qi)" as a word creation morpheme, and that reflects ancient Chinese philosophical views, that is: "describe the constitution of the celestial body and the earth" (including concrete words like "weather (天气)" and "soil vapor (地气)"), "describe the motive power of the function of the human body" (including concrete expressions like "primordial qi (元气)", "essence qi (精气)" and "strength (力气)"), "describe symptoms of human physiological functions" (including "complexion (气色)", "qi deficiency (气虚)", "liver qi (肝气)", "pregnancy edema (胎气)" and so on), "describe mental state of people" (such as "ambition (志气)", "tolerance (气量)", "courage (勇气)" and "bravery (胆气)"), "describe the character and emotions of people" (such as "temper (脾气)", "anger (生气)", "indignation (气愤)", "furious (气冲冲, 气呼呼)", "rage (怒气)", "petulancy (闹气)", "get in a rage (赌气)" and so on) and "describe morality of people" (including concrete words like "moral integrity (气节)", "noble spirit (浩气)") (Gu Jinfu, Chinese Word Creation and Traditional Philosophical and Ethical Views, *Journal of Renmin University of China*, 1992(1): 76,77). Obviously, the semantic category listed by Guo is different from that in Modern Chinese 6, and in this article, the words made up of "气 (Qi)" are classified based on the semantic category in Modern Chinese 6.

believe that, besides the above two semantic categories, the words that represent "get angry, lose one's temper" and "displease sb." listed in the 9th and 10th items of Modern Chinese 6 also have strong Chinese cultural characteristics[1], like: 沉住气 (keep calm), 出气 (vent one's anger), 出气筒 (punching bag), 垂头丧气 (lose one's spirits), 动气 (lose one's temper), 斗气 (quarrel to vent one's spleen), 赌气 (get in a rage), 发脾气 (get angry), 负气 (in a fit of pique), 夹板气 (criticized by both sides), 解气 (vent one's spleen), 可气 (annoying), 没脾气 (tiny temper), 闷气 (sulky), 闹脾气 (lose one's temper), 闹气 (petulance), 闹意气 (sulk), 怒气 (rage), 怄气 (sulky), 气冲牛斗 (in a towering rage), 气冲冲 / 气鼓鼓 / 气哼哼 / 气呼呼 (furious), 气话 (angry words), 气头上 (in a fit of anger), 气愤 / 气恼 / 惹气 / 生气 (get angry) , 窝气 (feel injured and resentful), 压气 (calm one's anger), 消气 (cool down), 闲气 (anger about trifles), 怨气 (resentment) and so on, these also deserve our special attention. Moreover, although the semantic category of this entry in Modern Chinese 6 does not include the meaning "man's character, temperament and spirit", the concept of " 气 (Qi)" often appears in words that show these meanings, which, as Guo (1992) said, also has its special cultural meaning. For example, bravery (胆气), morale enhancement (鼓气), moral integrity (骨气), temper (脾气), ambition(心气) and so on. In a word, according to our preliminary understanding of " 气 (Qi)" and its related expressions, the words that are not in the semantic category of the first few meanings ("gas", "particularly air", "breath", "natural phenomena like cold, hot, rainy and shiny" and "odor") more or less have certain special cultural characteristics. Therefore, we should pay attention to them in teaching Chinese as a foreign language.

There are 278 words made up of " 道 (Tao)" in Modern Chinese 6, where three lexical items of homonyms are listed, that is, " 道 1(Tao)" (12 semantic items), " 道 2(Tao)" (2 semantic items) and " 道 3(Tao)" (4 semantic items). Unlike this, Wang Chaozhong has explained in detail the 20 different semantic items extended

---

1 See Yu (1998). According to Yu (1998: 54), the Chinese character "Qi(气)" is used in the words whose meaning is "angry" or "rage" , this is due to the conceptual metaphor of "ANGER IS THE HOT GAS IN A CONTAINER" in the Chinese nation. Please refer to Jovanović, 2009: 101, 102.

from the original meaning of "道 (Tao)" when he talked about the structural evolution and the process of semantic extension of "道 (Tao)" in the Dictionary of the Explanation of the Form and Meaning of Chinese Characters (2006) under his general editorship[1]. According to his explanation, the original meaning of "道 (Tao)" is "road"[2], from which all the other semantic items are directly or indirectly derived. As for the semantic items extended from "道 (Tao)" with strong cultural characteristics in this article, we believe that they are the "proposal, thought and theory" derived from "way, method", and two semantic items of the "Taoist school" extended from "proposal, thought and theory".[3] Therefore, when analyzing the compound words made up of "道 (Tao)", we should pay special attention to the lexical items derived from these two semantic items. These lexical items also require special attention in teaching. After analyzing the above-mentioned 278 lexical items, we have found that 31 words are created from these two semantic items, of which 25 words are directly related to Chinese culture, including: 传道 (preach), 道场 (Taoist rites), 道姑 (Taoist nun), 道观 (Taoist temple), 道家 (Taoist school), 道教 (Taoism), 道门 (religious sect), 道袍 (priest frock), 道人 (holy man), 道士 (Taoist priest), 道统 (orthodoxy), 道学 (Taoism), 道院 (monastery), 道藏 (collected Taoist scriptures), 火居道士 (folk Taoist religion), 孔孟之道 (the doctrine of Confucius and Mencius), 老道 (seasoned), 离经叛道 (rebel against orthodoxy), 仁道 (benevolence), 天道 (natural law), 外道 (heretic), 文艺载道 (literature and art are for conveying truth), 五斗米道 (way of the five pecks of rice), 悟道 (realize the truth or philosophic theory), 穴道 (acupoint) and so on. There are

---

1   We will not temporarily say more about the relations between characters and words and that how to judge whether two homonyms are two different lexical items, because they are not directly related to the theme of this article. The explanation of Wang (2006) is applied in this article, see Wang (2006): 1140.
2   Wang Chaozhong (editor-in-chief), *Dictionary of the Explanation of the Form and Meaning of Chinese Characters*, Chengdu: Sichuan Publishing Group: Sichuan Lexicographical Publishing House, 2006, 11: 1138.
3   The explanation of the semantic change and extension process of "道 (Tao)" is quoted from Wang Chaozhong (editor-in-chief), *Dictionary of the Explanation of the Form and Meaning of Chinese Characters*, Chengdu: Sichuan Publishing Group: Sichuan Lexicographical Publishing House, 2006: 1139, 1141.

also 6 words that belong to the same extended meaning but are not only for things with Chinese cultural characteristics: 布道 (preach), 行道 (aisle), 修道 (cultivate oneself according to a religious doctrine), 修道院 (monastery), 左道旁门 / 旁门左道 (heretical sect), 卫道 (defend traditional moral principles). Because their usage is not limited to show phenomena with Chinese cultural characteristics, we think that these words may temporarily not be included in the category mentioned above. Of course, the process of semantic extension is generally complex, and it needs a different mechanism of extension, so we can also find lexical items with Chinese cultural characteristics in words that belong to other extended semantic items, sometimes a certain specific compound word as a whole can extend meaning with strong cultural characteristics as its metaphorical semantic item. Similar words include: 道高一尺，魔高一丈 (While the priest climbs a post, the devil climbs ten), 人道 (humanity) (the 3rd semantic item), 一人得道，鸡犬升天 (When a man gets to the top, all his friends and relations get there with him), 孝道 (filial piety) (all semantic items extended from "morality", the semantic items of " 道 (Tao)" that we think), 大道 (great Tao) (the 3rd semantic item, that is "the supreme idea politically in ancient times"), 中道 (golden mean) (the 2nd semantic item). We think that the latter two compound words are derived from "road", one of the semantic items of " 道 (Tao)", so the other semantic items of " 道 (Tao)" have no specific cultural characteristics, but the semantic items listed here have this characteristic.

There are 33 words made up of " 德 (Virtue)" in Modern Chinese 6. " 德 (Virtue)" has 4 semantic items, but the 4th one is a Chinese surname, from which no new words can be derived, so we do not analyze it. In other words, among the other 3 semantic items that can derive new words, the most important ones are "virtue (道德), behavior (品行), political quality (政治品意)", from which the second semantic item "favor (恩 惠)"[1] is derived, and then "regard (心 意)"[2]. Because

---

1　Wang Chaozhong (editor-in-chief), The *Dictionary of the Explanation of the Form and Meaning of Chinese Characters*, Chengdu: Sichuan Publishing Group: Sichuan Lexicographical Publishing House, 2006, 11: 1228.

2　Ditto: 1229.

"virtue (道德)" is always the highest ideal in Chinese culture, we think that those compound words that are made up of " 德 (Virtue)" and that belong to the semantic categories of "virtue (道德), behavior (品行), political quality (政治品意)" and "favor (恩惠)" have Chinese cultural characteristics more or less. However, in our opinion, the words like "medical ethics (医德)" and "moral integrity (德行)" can be expressed in other languages and cultures instead of being a special concept of Chinese culture. Therefore, according to this standard, "rule of virtue (德治)" and "merits and virtues (功德)" (the 2nd semantic item: "refers to activities including doing good works, chanting sutras, praying to Buddha, carrying out a Buddhist ceremony for the dead and the Taoists' saying Mass for the departed souls") are two special concepts made up of " 德 (Virtue)" in Chinese culture.

According to the explanation in Modern Chinese 6, the Chinese character " 阴 (Yin)" has 13 extended meanings (the last one is the Chinese surname, so it is not included in the framework for our research). According to our statistics, there are 91 compound words composed of " 阴 (Yin)". It is worth mentioning that in Modern Chinese 6, the first semantic item of " 阴 (Yin)" is "one of the two opposites of all things that exist in the universe that ancient Chinese philosophy holds (opposite to ' 阳 (Yang)')", which makes us (especially foreign learners) think that this is the original meaning of " 阴 (Yin)". In fact, that is not the case. The Dictionary of the Explanation of Chinese Character Form and Meaning, chiefly edited by Wang Chaozhong, explains the semantic evolution of the word, pointing out that its original meaning is "dark and cloudy sky without sunlight"[1], which is the source of the meaning of "ancient philosophical concept, relative to 阳 (Yang)"[2]. In other words, the word "dark sky" is borrowed to express " 阴 (Yin)", which is a philosophical concept with special cultural significance[3]. In addition, when comparing these two dictionaries, we have found that the number of extended

---

1 Ditto: 420.
2 Ditto: 421.
3 Wang Chaozhong (editor-in-chief), The *Dictionary of the Explanation of the Form and Meaning of Chinese Characters*, Chengdu: Sichuan Publishing Group: Sichuan Lexicographical Publishing House, 2006, 11: 421.

meanings is also different, that is, there are 13 different semantic items of "阴 (Yin)" in Modern Chinese 6, and 6 in the Dictionary of the Explanation of the Form and Meaning of Chinese Characters. Due to the length of this article, we do not temporarily talk about the possible reasons for this difference. When making a statistical analysis of the compound words made up of "阴 (Yin)", we still base that analysis on the extended semantic items in Modern Chinese 6, so the words with the most cultural characteristics are of course the words of the first semantic item, that is, "one of the two opposites of all things that exist in the universe that ancient Chinese philosophy holds (opposite to '阳 (Yang)')", such as 阴柔 (gentle), 阴盛阳衰 (excessive yin causing yang deficiency), 阴阳 (yin and yang), 阴阳生 / 阴阳先生 (astrologer), 阴阳水 (well water and river water), and 滋阴 (nourishing yin). In addition, the words of the second meaning "lunar, namely moon" also have strong cultural characteristics, including: 太阴 (lunar), 太阴历 /(lunar calendar), 阴历年 (lunar year), 阴阳历 (lunisolar calendar) and so on.

There are 73 compound words made up of "阳 (Yang)" in Modern Chinese 6, and 8 semantic items (the 9th semantic item is a Chinese surname) of "阳 (Yang)" are reflected in these compound words. Similar to "阴 (Yin)" mentioned above, the first semantic item of "阳 (Yang)" is "one of the two opposites of all things that exist in the universe that ancient Chinese philosophy holds (opposite to '阴 (Yin)')", which gives us a false impression that this is the original meaning of "阳 (Yang)". On the contrary, according to the Dictionary of the Explanation of the Form and Meaning of Chinese Characters, the original meaning of "阳 (Yang)" is "sunshine", which then extends the meaning "sun", and "sun" is the direct source of other extended meanings.[1] "阳 (Yang)" is also used to refer to "the concept of ancient philosophy".[2] After preliminarily analyzing these words, we find that there are not many words that belong to this semantic item in Modern Chinese 6, that

---

[1] Wang Chaozhong (editor-in-chief), *Dictionary of the Explanation of the Form and Meaning of Chinese Characters*, Chengdu: Sichuan Publishing Group: Sichuan Lexicographical Publishing House, 2006, 11: 421.

[2] Ditto: 420.

is, the words that have strong characteristics from ancient Chinese philosophy or traditional Chinese medicine, including: 太阳穴 (temple), 阳刚 (masculine), 壮阳 (tonifying yang).

III. The Way of Thinking for the Teaching of Words with Strong Cultural Characteristics in Teaching Chinese as a Foreign Language

The above words that are made up of "气 (Qi)", "道 (Tao)", "德 (Virtue)", "阴 (Yin)" and "阳 (Yang)", and that have strong cultural characteristics should be taken seriously in teaching Chinese as a foreign language. For example, I, as a foreigner, did not accurately understand the semantic origin of words made up of "道 (Tao)" and "气 (Qi)" until I carried out this study. We believe that understanding the process of semantic evolution, including the semantic item of the character in the word that is constituted, is an indispensable means for improving the efficiency of teaching vocabulary.

As mentioned above, there are several extended meanings of "气 (Qi)", "道 (Tao)", "德 (Virtue)", "阴 (Yin)" and "阳 (Yang)". Some (such as "气 (Qi)", "道 (Tao)" and "阴 (Yin)") even have more than 10 semantic meanings, which involve different but related semantic categories. In fact, the whole semantics of the above five words can be explained by the concept of the "category of radioactivity"[1], that is, "the semantic category of radioactivity [is] [a category with] has several extended core meanings, from which new meanings are also extended"[2]. The meaning of compound words or fixed expressions made from this word is definitely derived from a certain semantic item, so we think the following steps can be used when teaching the above words: first of all, we can explain the basic meaning of "气 (Qi)", "道 (Tao)", "德 (Virtue)", "阴 (Yin)" and "阳 (Yang)" and list the related semantics and expressions derived from this meaning. Second, we can briefly introduce the process of semantic extension of the word to students, and give certain

---

1　According to the explanation of Lakoff (1990) about this category
2　Jovanovic Ana, The Study of the Conceptual Metaphor Theory and Chinese Human Body Vocabulary and Related Expressions—Role of the "Human Body" in the Conceptualization Process, Graduate School of Beijing Normal University (unpublished doctoral thesis), 2009: 63.

specific examples for each semantic extension. For those with significant cultural characteristics, we can simply introduce the specific meaning of these words used to indicate special concepts in ancient philosophy and traditional Chinese medicine, and then give specific examples to illustrate them[1]. We believe that vocabulary teaching will achieve better results if we make similar systematic explanations of these words.

I fully agree with Meng Xiangying's (2007) viewpoint regarding the important role of teaching cultural words in the teaching of Chinese, believing that knowing cultural words and their related expressions well is also one of the important tasks in teaching Chinese as a foreign language. This kind of teaching may be more important for foreign learners of Chinese, because people who strive to improve their level of Chinese must understand the cultural knowledge that language carries. In the process of learning Chinese, it is more necessary for students from a non-Chinese character circle to familiarize themselves with the system of Chinese cultural concepts in order to understand the world outlook and way of thinking of the Chinese, because only in this way can they break through the restrictions of the way of thinking of their native language and express themselves in Chinese.

IV. Conclusion

On the basis of other scholars' arguments on the relation between culture and language, and inspired by a former study of the Chinese cultural words, we have preliminarily analyzed the compound words and related expressions made up of the five Chinese characters "气 (Qi)", "道 (Tao)", "德 (Virtue)", "阴 (Yin)" and "阳 (Yang)" with strong cultural characteristics in Modern Chinese 6. The purpose of our study is to deepen the understanding of the process of the semantic derivation of these five concepts by analyzing the specific semantic categories of these compound words and fixed expressions. We believe that the study will also help to improve the effectiveness of teaching foreigners vocabulary. At the same time, it is one of

---

1   For example, similar word explanations appear in the Influence of Taoism Culture on Chinese Vocabulary (2013) written by Jiao Yuqin.

the important tasks for teachers of Chinese to foreigners to understand the process of the semantic derivation of the words with strong cultural characteristics, because only when teachers are familiar with the semantics and usage of these words can students deepen their understanding of the words. Unfortunately, this study is still in the primary stage, the materials and related literature we have mastered are very limited, so there are inevitably many inadequacies, experts are requested to give more valuable advice. We intend to incorporate the cultural words made up of the above five Chinese characters from other key dictionaries and lexicographical works in our future study so that the results can be used in teaching practices.

References

Mankind, Nation, and Individual from a Linguistic Point of View, 2010. Originally published in 1925.
Lakoff, G. Women, *Fire and Dangerous Things-What Categories Reveal about the Mind* (paperback edition). Chicago and London: The University of Chicago Press, 1990.
Lakoff, G. & Johnson M. *Metaphors We Live By*. Chicago and London: The University of Chicago Press, 1980/81.
Lakoff, G. & Johnson, M. *Philosophy in the flesh: the embodied mind and its challenge to western thought*. New York: Basic Books, 1999.
Sharifian, F. *Cultural conceptualisations and language: theoretical framework and applications*. Amsterdam/Philadelphia: John Benjamins Publishing Company, 2011.
Yu, Ning. *The Contemporary Theory of Metaphor - A perspective from Chinese*. Amsterdam/ Philadelphia: John Benjamins Publishing Company, 1998.
Yu, N. *From Body to Meaning in Culture*, Amsterdam/Philadelphia: John Benjamins Publishing Company, 2009.

汉语"一定、肯定、当然、绝对"与泰语"แน่นอน"的语义辨析

陈昌旭 【泰国】

泰国皇太后大学汉语教师

一 引言

在对泰汉语教学中,"一定、肯定、当然、绝对"是学习者难以掌握的一组词,因为它们不仅在意义上有共同点,即都可以表示确定无疑之义,翻译成泰语也都能与泰语的"แน่นอน"对应,但又不能完全译成"แน่นอน",如:

(1) 这部作品要是改编成电影,一定好看。(งานเขียนชิ้นนี้หากถ่ายทำเป็นภาพยนตร์ต้องน่าดูแน่นอน)

(2) 香喷喷的,肯定好吃。(หอมฉุยเลย อร่อยแน่นอน)

(3) 你这么说当然是不对的。(คุณพูดแบบนี้มันไม่ถูกแน่นอน)

(4) 我们保证绝对好卖。(เรารับรองว่าขายดีแน่นอน)

(5) 在山上走路一定要注意安全。(เดินทางในป่าต้องระวังความปลอดภัยให้ดี)

(6) 她语气很肯定。(น้ำเสียงของเขาแน่ใจมาก)

(7) 王林直率地说:"那是当然的。"(หวังหลินพูดตรงๆ ว่า มันแน่นอนอยู่แล้ว)

(8) 世界上并没有绝对的安全。(ในโลกนี้ไม่มีความปลอดภัยแบบโดยสิ้นเชิงหรอก)

从以上的例句,我们可以看出,例(1)-(4)句子中的"一定、肯定、当然、绝对"都能对应泰语的"แน่นอน",并且有的句子四者之间还可以互换,比如,例(1)(2)和(3)的"一定""肯定"和"绝对"都可以替换,而例(4)不能用

"当然"来替换。这样，当学习者造句或进行泰—汉翻译选词时非常有困难。此外，例（5）-（8）的情况又是另外一个问题，由上可见只有例（7）中的"当然"能对应"แน่นอน"，其余的有无对应的，也有与别的词对应的，即例（5）中的"一定"没有对应词，例（6）中"肯定"的对应词是"แน่ใจ"，例（8）中"绝对"的对应词是"โดยสิ้นเชิง"。上面这些问题主要是因为这几个词的语义有交叉，另外是因为与泰语对应的复杂性，所以本文将对"一定、肯定、当然、绝对"四个词进行深度考察它们的语义功能，并与泰语的对应词"แน่นอน"对比和辨析，找出它们之间的异同，为汉泰语学习者铲除学习和使用这些词的困惑。

二 "一定""肯定""当然""绝对"与"แน่นอน"的语义分析

（一）"一定""肯定""当然""绝对"的语义分析

1. "一定"的语义分析

"一定"的语义可分为作形容词的语义和作副词的语义，如下：

1.1 作为形容词：

总结《现代汉语八百词》、《现代汉语词典》、《商务馆学汉语词典》及王还（2005）对"一定"作为形容词能表示的义项如下：

A. 表示确定；明确的，如：

（1）最后谁赢谁输，还不一定。

（2）信息越封锁，国家越落后，这是一定的。

B. 表示相当程度的；不太高的，如：

（3）他的演奏具有一定的水平。

（4）投资这个项目有一定的风险。

C. 表示必然的，如：

（5）农作物的生长和土壤、水分、日光等都有一定的关系。

（6）见识、成就与身材、相貌没有一定的关系。

D. 表示特定的；某些或某个特别的，如：

（7）气温降到一定程度，空气中的水蒸气就会变成雪。

（8）这种药对一定的人有效。

E. 表示固定的，如：

（9）市场份额是一定的，别人进来，我们就少了。

（10）农民承包耕地的面积是一定的，按耕地面积征收。

1.2 作为副词：

杨寄洲、贾永芬（2013）指出"一定"作为副词表示：A. 态度坚决，B. 估计、推断和判断的确定无疑。

A. 表示态度坚决，如：

（11）我一定要把这件事情做好。

（12）我一定要实现自己当翻译或外交官的理想。

B. 表示估计、推断和判断的确定无疑，如：

（13）他一定是又起晚了。

（14）这个西瓜一定甜，不信我们切开尝尝。

2."肯定"的语义分析

《现代汉语词典》与《应用汉语词典》指出"肯定"1）作为动词表示事物的存在或事物的真实性（跟"否定"相对）；2）作为形容词表示：A. 承认的或正面的（跟"否定"相对），B. 确定的、明确的；3）作为副词表示无疑问、必定，如：

2.1 作为动词：表示事物的存在或事物的真实性（跟"否定"相对），如：

（15）应该肯定他们的工作。

（16）肯定一切和否定一切都是错误的。

2.2 作为形容词：表示承认的；正面的（跟"否定"相对）、确定或明确的。

A. 表示承认的；正面的（跟"否定"相对），如：

（17）我问他赞成不赞成，他的回答是肯定的。

（18）这件事应不应该立即去办呢？答案是肯定的。

B. 表示确定的、明确的，如：

（19）请给我一个肯定的答复。

（20）他的语气十分肯定。

2.3 作为副词：表示无疑问或必定，如：

（21）他肯定会同意的。

（22）你肯定记错了。

3. "当然"的语义分析

3.1 作为形容词：

《现代汉语词典》与《应用汉语词典》指出"当然"作为形容词表示应当如此的，如：

（23）取得这么好的成绩，心理高兴是当然的。

（24）邻里间有事互相关照也是当然的事。

3.2 作为副词：

《商务馆学汉语近义词词典》《商务馆学汉语词典》指出"当然"作为副词表示：A.没有疑问，B.对前边说的有所补充。

A. 表示没有疑问，如：

（25）人家帮了你的忙，你当然应该谢谢人家。

（26）这么难得的演出，门票当然贵了。

B. 表示对前边说的有所补充，如：

（27）出了问题，我们就要重视，当然，这只是个别人的问题。

（28）我们取得了很大的成绩，当然也存在着一些缺点。

4. "绝对"的语义分析

《现代汉语八百词》指出"绝对"1）作为形容词表示无条件的、不受任何限制的（跟"相对"的意思相反）；2）作为副词表示肯定、坚信。

4.1 作为形容词：表示无条件的、不受任何限制的（跟"相对"的意思相反），如：

（29）他说人都活不了一百岁，这也太绝对了吧。

（30）话说得过于绝对，恐怕不太好。

4.2 作为副词：表示肯定、坚信，如：

（31）他既然说来，绝对会来。

（32）这绝对是个误会。

表1　　　"一定""肯定""当然""绝对"的语义对照

词	词性与语义		
	形	副	动
一定	1. 表示确定的；明确的 2. 表示相当程度的；不太高的 3. 表示必然的 4. 表示特定的；某些或某个特别的 5. 表示固定的	1. 表示态度坚决 2. 确定无疑	-
肯定	1. 表示承认的，正面的 2. 表示确定的；明确的	1. 表示无疑问或必定	1. 表示事物的存在或事物的真实性
当然	1. 表示应当如此的	1. 表示没有疑问 2. 表示对前边说的有所补充	-
绝对	1. 表示无条件的，不受任何限制的	1. 表示肯定，坚信	-

从上表可看出，作为形容词"一定"和"肯定"有相同的义项，即表示"确定的；明确的"。作为副词，我们认为"一定""肯定""当然"及"绝对"具有相同的一个义项，即表示确定无疑之义。

三 "แน่นอน"的语义分析

由于《泰语规范词典》对"แน่นอน"标注的释义只有表示"เที่ยงแท้ จริงแท้（正确、真实）"之义。其次，《泰汉词典》[1]对"แน่นอน"的释义也只提供了两个义项：（1）表示必定、一定、肯定。（2）表示当然、自然。释义方式仅提供了对应词，缺乏其他解说或例句。可见，以上工具书的信息远不能满足于本研究的借鉴，所以笔者根据泰国朱拉隆功大学的国家泰语语料库[2]检索提取了含有"แน่นอน"及符合本研究范围的五百个例句，进行分析"แน่นอน"所能表示的意义，结果如下：

1. 作为形容词："แน่นอน"表示确定或明确的；承认的或正面的；应当如此的；正确的；稳定的；固定的。

A. 表示确定的；明确的，与汉语的"一定""确定""明确"及"肯定"相对应，如：

1　广州外国语学院编：《泰汉词典》，商务印书馆2001年版。
2　国家泰语语料库：是泰国朱拉隆功大学建设的泰语语料库，语料来源于新闻、报刊、杂志、小说、法律刊物。

（33）เขาจะเข้าร่วมการแข่งขันหรือไม่ ยังไม่แน่นอน（他能不能参加比赛还不一定。）

（34）อนาคตเป็นสิ่งที่ไม่แน่นอน（未来是不确定的。）

（35）ตอนนี้ยังไม่ได้แจ้งเวลาที่แน่นอน（现在还没有通知明确的时间。）

（36）คุณจะให้คำตอบที่แน่นอนได้เมื่อไหร่（什么时候才能给一个肯定的答复？）

B. 表示承认的、正面的，与汉语的"肯定"相对应，如：

（37）ซ้อมให้ดีๆ แล้วเอาเหรียญทองมาแลกคะแนนของฉันนะ แน่นอน! ผมรับคำด้วยรอยยิ้ม

好好地练，拿个冠军来抵我这门课的成绩。肯定的！我笑着回复。

（38）ที่แน่นอนคือ ไม่มีทางที่ผู้หญิงแบบนี้จะมั่นคงต่อเขาคนเดียว

这个女人不会只对他一个人一心一意，那是肯定的。

C. 表示应当如此的，与汉语的"当然"相对应，如：

（39）อกหักแล้วเสีย มันเป็นเรื่องแน่นอนอยู่แล้ว（失恋而感到伤心，那是当然的。）

（40）A: ถ้าจะออกไปแกต้องพิมพ์รายงานฉันให้เรียบร้อยก่อน（要出去的话你得先把我的报告做好。）

B: นั่นมันแน่นอนอยู่แล้ว เอามาเถอะ（那是当然的，拿来吧！）

D. 表示正确的，与汉语的"正确"相对应，如：

（41）ตรวจสอบได้ด้วยวิธีที่แน่นอน（能用正确的方法检测。）

（42）การวินิจฉัยที่แน่นอนควรได้รับการตรวจจากแพทย์（正确的诊断应由医生进行操作。）

E. 表示稳定的，与汉语的"稳定"相对应，如：

（43）อารมณ์ของเขาไม่แน่นอน（她的情绪很不稳定。）

（44）บริษัทนี้ผลิตชาผู่เอ๋อที่ได้คุณภาพแน่นอน（这家公司生产的普洱茶质量稳定。）

F. 表示固定的，与汉语的"一定"、"固定"相对应，如：

（45）ผู้สูงอายุส่วนใหญ่ไม่มีรายได้ที่แน่นอน（大部分老年人没有一定/固定的收入。）

（46）ไม่มีใครรู้ที่อยู่ที่แน่นอนของเขา（没有人知道他固定的住址。）

2. 作为副词，"แน่นอน"表示：A. 确定无疑，B. 对前边说的有所补充。

A. 表示确定无疑，与汉语的"一定"、"肯定"、"当然"和"绝对"相对应，如：

（47）แดดดีขนาดนี้ ฝนไม่ตกแน่นอน（太阳那么大，一定/肯定/当然/绝对不会下雨。）

（48）ความรู้นั้นไม่มีวันเรียนหมดแน่นอน（知识一定/肯定/当然/绝对是学不完的。）

B. 表示对前边说的有所补充，与汉语的"当然"相对应，如：

（49）เขารู้เรื่องประเทศจีนมากมาย แต่แน่นอนว่าไม่ใช่ทุกเรื่อง

（他对中国了解得非常多，当然，不是所有都了解。）

（50）มีคนได้คะแนนเต็มสามคน ซึ่งแน่นอนว่าหนึ่งในสามก็คือเธอ

（有三个人得满分，当然，其中之一就是你。）

表2　　　　　　　　　　"แน่นอน"的语义明细表

词性	义项与对应词	
	"แน่นอน"的义项	汉语对应词
形	1. 表示确定或明确的 2. 表示承认的或正面的 3. 表示应当如此的 4. 表示正确的 5. 表示稳定的 6. 表示固定的	1. 一定、确定、明确、肯定 2. 肯定 3. 当然 4. 正确 5. 稳定 6. 一定、固定
副	1. 表示确定无疑 2. 表示对前边说的有所补充	1. 一定、肯定、当然、绝对 2. 当然

四 "一定"、"肯定"、"当然"、"绝对"的语义对比

（一）相同之处

1. "一定"和"肯定"作为形容词，都具有"确定的；明确的"之义，如：

（51）最终我不会放过他，这是一定（肯定）的。

（52）这次考试能不能通过，还不一定（*肯定）。

（53）做父母的总是会担心孩子，那是肯定（一定）的。

（54）他回答得很肯定（*一定）。

根据以上的例子，我们发现"一定"和"肯定"表示"确定的；明确"时，两者在句中有时能互换，有时不能。比如以上例（51）、（53）的"一定"和"肯定"是可以互替的，而例（52）、（54）中的"一定"和"肯定"是不能替换的。

2. "一定""肯定""当然""绝对"作为副词，都可以表示确定无疑，在句子中作状语时一般可以互换，如：

（55）明天我一定/肯定/当然/绝对来。

（56）他学习这么好，一定/肯定/当然/绝对能考上名牌大学。

（二）不同之处

1. "一定""肯定""当然""绝对"作为形容词时，在语义上只有"一定"和"肯定"表示"确定的；明确的"时具有共性，此外，四者在语义上都没有共性，即"一

定"有5个义项（表示确定的、相当程度的、必然的、特定的、固定的）;"肯定"有2个义项（表示承认或正面的、确定的）;"当然"有1个义项（表示应当如此的）;"绝对"有1个义项（表示无条件或不受限制的）。

2."一定"作副词，可以表示态度坚决，常与助动词"要、得"等共现。"肯定、当然、绝对"不表示该意义，所以在句子中不能互换，如：

（57）你一定（*肯定/*当然/*绝对）得找到这个人。

3."肯定"具备动词性，表示事物的存在或事物的真实性，"一定、当然、绝对"不具备该词性及语义功能，所以都不能与"肯定"互换，如：

（58）大家一致肯定（*一定/*当然/*绝对）了这个建议。

4."当然"作副词表示对前边说的有所补充之义，是它独有的意义，是"一定"、"肯定"和"绝对"不具备的，所以三者在句中是不能与"当然"互换的，如：

（59）你的汉语说得很好，当然，还有一些小问题。

*你的汉语说得很好，一定，还有一些小问题。

*你的汉语说得很好，肯定，还有一些小问题。

*你的汉语说得很好，绝对，还有一些小问题。

以上例子，可以看出，"一定""肯定"和"绝对"因为没有"表示对前边说的有所补充"的用法，所以将它们与"当然"替换后的句子都说不通，均属病句。

表3　　　　　"一定""肯定""当然""绝对"的语义异同表

词性	形								副		
词汇	确定的;明确的	相当程度的	必然的	特定的	固定的	正面的	应当如此的	不受限制的	态度坚决	确定无疑	对前边说的有所补充
一定	+	+	+	+	+	-	-	-	+	+	-
肯定	+	-	-	-	-	+	-	-	-	+	-
当然	-	-	-	-	-	-	+	-	-	+	+
绝对	-	-	-	-	-	-	-	+	-	+	-

根据表3，我们可以看出"一定""肯定""当然""绝对"作为形容词时，在语义上只有"一定"和"肯定"表示"确定的;明确的"时具有共性，此外，四

者在语义上都没有共性。作为副词,"一定""肯定""当然""绝对"具有一个相同的义项,即都具有表示确定无疑之义。另外,作为副词表示对前边说的有所补充之义,是"当然"独有的义项。

五 "一定、肯定、当然、绝对"与"แน่นอน"的语义对比

(一) 相同之处

1. "一定"和"แน่นอน"作为形容词时都具有表示"确定的;明确的"和"固定的"之义。

1.1 表示确定的;明确的,如:

(60) 苦与乐,没有<u>一定</u>的分界线。(สุขกับทุกข์ไม่มีเส้นแบ่งที่แน่นอน)

(61) แน่นอนที่สุด หลังแต่งงานเราจะไปฮันนีมูนกัน (婚后我们要去度蜜月,那是<u>一定/肯定</u>的。)

(62) ตอนนี้เรายังไม่มีตารางเวลาที่แน่นอน (我们目前还没有<u>确定/明确</u>的时间表。)

根据以上的例句,可以看出"一定"和"แน่นอน"作为形容词表示"确定的;明确的"时,它们的对应情况属于一对多,即"แน่นอน"一词对应汉语的多个词,包括"一定""肯定""确定"和"明确"。

1.2 表示固定的,如:

(63) 心脏以<u>一定</u>的节奏搏动着。(หัวใจเต้นตามจังหวะที่แน่นอน)

(64) รายการโทรทัศน์นี้มีกลุ่มผู้ชมที่แน่นอน (这个电视节目有<u>固定</u>的收视群。)

2. "肯定"和"แน่นอน"作为形容词时都具有表示"确定的;明确的"和"正面的"之义。

2.1 表示"确定的;明确的",如:

(65) 现在很难做出<u>肯定</u>的回答。(ตอนนี้ยากที่จะสรุปคำตอบที่แน่นอน)

(66) 我很<u>肯定</u>,他今天一定不会来。(ฉันแน่ใจมากว่าวันนี้เขาไม่มาแน่นอน)

(67) เราได้บทสรุปที่แน่นอนแล้ว 我们已经得出了<u>肯定</u>的结论。

(68) ปีนี้ยังไม่มีแผนธุรกิจที่แน่นอน 今年还没有<u>确定</u>的营业计划。

(69) เขาไม่มีเป้าหมายชีวิตที่แน่นอน 他没有<u>明确</u>的人生目标。

根据以上例句,可以看出"肯定"与"แน่นอน"表示"确定的;明确的"时,两者的对应情况是多对多,即"肯定"的泰语对应有两个(แน่นอน 和 แน่ใจ),"แน่นอน"的汉语对应词有三个(肯定、确定、明确)。

2.2 表示"正面的"时,"肯定"与"แน่นอน"的对应情况是一对一,即"肯定"

的泰语译词是"แน่นอน","แน่นอน"的汉语译词是"肯定",如:

（70）我对这个问题的回答是肯定的。สำหรับฉัน คำตอบของคำถามนี้คือ แน่นอน

（71）ประเด็นนี้แน่นอน เราทุกคนเห็นด้วย（这一点是肯定的，我们大家都认同。）

3."当然"与"แน่นอน"作为形容词时，都可以表示应当如此的。在此义项中"当然"译成泰语时，它的对应词"แน่นอน"一般会与语气副词"อยู่แล้ว"共现，如:

（72）群众有不同的意见是当然的。（คนเรามีความคิดเห็นต่างกัน เป็นสิ่งที่แน่นอนอยู่แล้ว）

（73）ผู้ชายชอบผู้หญิงสวย นั่นมันแน่นอนอยู่แล้ว（男人喜欢漂亮的女人是当然的。）

4."当然"与"แน่นอน"作为副词时，都可以表示对前边说的有所补充，如:

（74）这对你来说是个好机会，当然，对我们也是个好机会。

（นี่เป็นโอกาสที่ดีของคุณ และแน่นอนว่าเป็นโอกาสดีของเราเช่นกัน）

（75）ภาษาไทยอีสานกับภาษาลาวคล้ายกันมาก แต่แน่นอนว่ามีความต่างอยู่ไม่น้อยเช่นกัน

（泰国东北方言跟老挝话很接近，当然，不一样的地方也挺多的。）

5."一定""肯定""绝对"与"แน่นอน"作为副词都可以表示确定无疑，并且一般可以互换，如:

（76）明天我们<u>一定 / 肯定 / 当然 / 绝对</u>会过去。（พรุ่งนี้พวกเราไปแน่นอน）

（77）报考的人这么多，明年的学生<u>一定 / 肯定 / 当然 / 绝对</u>会更多。

（เราคาดว่า ปีหน้าจำนวนนักเรียนเพิ่มขึ้นแน่นอน）

（78）ของขวัญที่เธอให้ เขาชอบแน่นอน（你送的礼物，她一定 / 肯定 / 当然 / 绝对喜欢。）

（79）ถ้าเธอชวน เขาไปแน่นอน（要是你约，他一定 / 肯定 / 当然 / 绝对会去。）

（二）不同之处

1."一定"和"แน่นอน"作为形容词的不同处有以下几点:

1.1 "一定"作为形容词，有表示"必然的"之义，但"แน่นอน"没有，如:

（80）文章的深浅跟篇幅的长短，并没有<u>一定</u>的关系。

（ความลึกซึ้งกับความสั้นยาวของบทความนั้นไม่มีความสัมพันธ์เชิงตายตัว）

（81）事物的发展有其<u>一定</u>的规律。

（พัฒนาการของสรรพสิ่งนั้นมีกฎที่ตายตัวของมัน）

以上例句中的"一定"表示的都是"必然"的意思，译成泰语的对应词是"ตายตัว"而不是"แน่นอน"，因为"แน่นอน"没有表示必然之义的用法。

1.2 "一定"作为形容词，有表示"相当程度的"之义，但"แน่นอน"没有，如:

（82）他这种想法也有<u>一定</u>的理由。

（วิธีคิดของเขาก็มีเหตุผลพอสมควร/อยู่เหมือนกัน）

（83）干这事需要一定的知识。

（ทำงานนี้ต้องมีความรู้ประมาณหนึ่ง/พอสมควร/พอประมาณ/อยู่เหมือนกัน）

以上例句中的"一定"都表示"相当程度的"的意思，而"แน่นอน"因为没有此语义功能，所以译成泰语后句中的对应词都不是它，而是"ประมาณหนึ่ง"、"พอสมควร"、"พอประมาณ"，以及短语"อยู่เหมือนกัน"。

1.3 "一定"作为形容词，有表示"特定的；某些或某个特别的"之义，但"แน่นอน"没有，如：

（84）考勤、考察和考试，都有一定的制度。
（การเช็คชื่อ การสังเกตุการณ์ และการสอบ ต่างมีระเบียบเฉพาะทั้งนั้น）

（85）大凡女性，到了一定的年龄便是渴望做母亲。
（ผู้หญิงพอถึงอายุประมาณหนึ่ง/ระดับหนึ่งก็อยากเป็นแม่กันทั้งนั้น）

以上例句中的"一定"都表示"特定的"的意思，而"แน่นอน"因为没有此语义功能，所以译成泰语后句中的词语对应不是"แน่นอน"，而是"เฉพาะ"、"ประมาณหนึ่ง"、"ระดับหนึ่ง"。

2. "绝对"作为形容词，有表示"不受限制的"之义，但"แน่นอน"没有，如：

（86）这个人说话做事太绝对了。（คนคนนี้พูดจาและการกระทำสุดขั้วมาก）

（87）我们有绝对的优势打败他们。（พวกเรามีความได้เปรียบโดยสิ้นเชิงที่จะเอาชนะพวกเขา）

以上例句中的"绝对"表示"不受限制"的意思，而"แน่นอน"因为没有此语义功能，所以译成泰语后句中的对应词不是"แน่นอน"，而是"สุดขั้ว"、"โดยสิ้นเชิง"。

3. "一定"作为副词，有表示"态度坚决"之义，但"แน่นอน"没有，如：

（88）你一定得找个人来帮忙才行。（เธอต้องหาคนมาช่วยแล้วหละ）

（89）我一定要考第一名。（ฉันต้องสอบให้ได้ที่หนึ่ง）

（90）这次机会一定不能再错过。（โอกาสครั้งนี้ต้องห้ามพลาดอีกนะ）

（91）你一定不能让他知道。（เธอต้องห้ามไม่ให้เขารู้เรื่องนะ）

根据以上的例句，我们发现"一定"在此语义功能上比较特殊。与泰语的词语对应时，有时是无对应词，有时能与"ต้อง"（要）对应。例（88）（89）属于无对应词，例（90）、（91）中有对应词，即"ต้อง"（要）。在此，值得一提的是，其实例（88）（89）中的泰语译文是有"ต้อง"的，但是此处的"ต้อง"对应的是句中的"得"和"要"，而不是"一定"，所以这两个句子中的"一定"是没有对应词的。

4."肯定"可以作动词，表示事物的存在或事物的真实性，"แน่นอน"不具备该词性及语义功能，如：

（92）我们都肯定了他的看法是对的。（พวกเรายอมรับทรรศนะของเขาแล้วว่าถูกต้อง）

（93）他们的试验结论，专家已经肯定了。（ผลการทดลองของพวกเขา ผู้เชี่ยวชาญได้รับรองแล้ว）

根据以上例句的泰语译文，我们可以看出"肯定"在句中作为动词表达的意义是无法用"แน่นอน"来表述的，只能采用与"肯定"作为动词相对应的词"ยอมรับ"（接受）或"รับรอง"（承认）进行表述。

5."แน่นอน"作为形容词具有表示"正确的"、"稳定的"和"固定的"的意义，其中表示"固定的"跟"一定"有共性，另外两个义项是"一定"不具备的。至于"肯定"、"当然"和"绝对"，三个义项都不是它们具有的，如：

（94）ผมคิดว่าน่าจะให้แพทย์ตรวจสักครั้ง เพื่อการวินิจฉัยที่แน่นอน（正确的）

（为了正确（* 一定 /* 肯定 /* 当然 /* 绝对）的医疗诊断，我认为应该让医生检查看看。）

（95）เขามีรายได้ที่แน่นอนทุกเดือน（固定的）

（他每个月都有一定的收入（* 肯定 /* 当然 /* 绝对）。

（96）อารมณ์ของเขาไม่แน่นอนสักเท่าไหร่（稳定的）

（他的情绪不怎么稳定（* 一定 /* 肯定 /* 当然 /* 绝对）。

表4 　　"一定、肯定、当然、绝对"与"แน่นอน"的语义异同表

词性	形									副			动
词汇	确定的；明确的	相当程度的	必然的	特定的	正面的	应当如此的	不受限制的	正确的	稳定的	固定的	态度坚决	确定；无疑	对前边说的有所补充	事物的真实性
一定	+	+	+	+	-	-	-	-	-	+	+	+	-	-
肯定	+	-	-	-	+	-	-	-	-	-	+	+	-	+
当然	-	-	-	-	-	+	-	-	-	-	-	-	+	-
绝对	-	-	-	-	-	-	+	-	-	-	+	-	-	-
แน่นอน	+	-	-	-	+	+	-	+	+	-	-	+	-	-

从表 4 中，可以看出"一定"、"肯定"、"当然"、"绝对"与"แน่นอน"作为形容词，它们的相同之处在于"一定"、"肯定"和"แน่นอน"都可以表示"确定的；明确的"，"肯定"和"แน่นอน"可以表示"正面的"，"一定"和"แน่นอน"可以表示"固定的"。作为副词，它们的相同之处是五者都可以表示"确定；无疑"，"当然"和"แน่นอน"可以表示"对前边说的有所补充"。五者的不同之处在于，作为形容词"一定"可以表示"相对程度的"、"必然的"、"特定的"，而"肯定"、"当然"、"绝对"与"แน่นอน"不能。"แน่นอน"可以表示"正确的"、"稳定的"，"一定"、"肯定"、"当然"和"绝对"不能。作为副词"一定"有表示"态度坚决"之义，而"肯定"、"当然"、"绝对"与"แน่นอน"没有。还有，"肯定"可以作为动词表示"事物的真实性"，而"一定"、"当然"、"绝对"与"แน่นอน"不能。

六　结论

"แน่นอน"与"一定"、"肯定"、"当然"、"绝对"在语义上既有共性，又有异性。它们的异同可分别展示如下：

1）五者之间的相同之处是，作为副词它们都具有"确定；无疑"之义。词语对应情况属于一对多，即泰语的"แน่นอน"一词能对应汉语的"一定"、"肯定"、"当然"、"绝对"四个词。

2）"แน่นอน"与"一定"、"肯定"、"当然"、"绝对"之间的不同之处是"แน่นอน"可以表示"正确的"和"稳定的"，而"一定"、"肯定"、"当然"、"绝对"不能。

3）"แน่นอน"与"一定"的相同之处是作为形容词，两者都具有"确定的；明确的"和"固定的"之义。词语对应情况属于一对多，即"แน่นอน"表示"确定的；明确的"时，与汉语的"一定"、"确定"、"明确"和"肯定"相对应。表示"固定的"时，对应汉语的"一定"和"固定"。

"แน่นอน"与"一定"的不同之处是"一定"作为形容词具有"相对程度的"、"必然的"和"特定的"之义，而"แน่นอน"没有。"一定"表示"相对程度的"时，泰语的对应词是"ประมาณหนึ่ง"、"พอสมควร"、"พอประมาณ"、"อยู่เหมือนกัน"。表示"必然的"，对应的是泰语的"ตายตัว"或是"ตายตัวแน่นอน"。表示"特定的"，与泰语的"เฉพาะ"、"ประมาณหนึ่ง"、"ระดับหนึ่ง"。此外，"一定"作为副词，可以表示"态度坚决"，而"แน่นอน"不能。"一定"表示"态度坚决"时，泰语中对应情况有两种，即一是与"要"对应，二是无对应词。

4）"แน่นอน"与"肯定"的三个义项全部相同，包括作为形容词的"确定的；明确的"和"正面的"之义，以及作为副词的"确定；无疑"之义。但是在词语对应方面是多对多，即"肯定"的泰语对应词有两个（แน่นอน 和 แน่ใจ），"แน่นอน"的汉语对应词有三个（肯定、确定、明确）。

5）"แน่นอน"与"当然"的三个义项也全部相同，包括作为形容词的"应当如此"之义，以及作为副词的"确定；无疑"和"对前边说的有所补充"之义。

6）"แน่นอน"与"绝对"相同之处是作为副词，两者都具有"确定的；明确的"之义。

不同之处在于作为形容词，"绝对"具有"不受限制"之义，而"แน่นอน"没有。在表示"不受限制"时，泰语的对应词是"สุดขั้ว"和"โดยสิ้นเชิง"。

附注：

1. 汉语例句摘自北京大学 CCL 语料库、《现代汉语词典》第 6 版、《商务馆学汉语词典》、《商务馆学汉语近义词词典》、HSK 汉语 8000 词词典。

2. 泰语例句摘自朱拉隆功大学泰国国家泰语语料库（TNC）及部分自编的。

参考文献

丁萍：《"一定"与"肯定"作状语时的比较》，《西南民族大学学报》2008 年。
广州外国语学院：《泰汉词典》，商务印书馆 2001 年版。
卢福波：《对外汉语常用词语对比例释》，北京语言大学出版社 2003 年版。
杨寄洲：《汉语 800 虚词用法词典》，北京语言大学出版社 2013 年版。
王还：《汉语近义词词典》，北京语言大学出版社 2005 年版。
芜崧：《"当然"的表义功用》，《三峡大学学报》，2010 年。
张谊生：《"绝对 X"的功能扩展与错位兼容》，杭州师范大学学报 2009 年。
เธียรชัย เอี่ยมวรเมธ (2553). พจนานุกรมจีนไทยฉบับพิมพ์หนังสือตัวย่อ .กรุงเทพมหานคร: รวมสาส์น
ราชบัณฑิตยสถาน(2546). พจนานุกรมฉบับราชบัณฑิตยสถาน พ.ศ.2542.กรุงเทพมหานคร: นานมีบุ๊คส์

The Semantics Analysis of "Yiding, Kending, Dangran, Juedui" in Chinese and "Naenon" in Thai

Teeraparp Predeepoch / Thailand

Chinese Teacher of Mae Fah Luang University, Thailand

I. Introduction

"Yiding", "Kending", "Dangran" and "Juedui" are difficult for Chinese language learners in Thailand. These four words share similarities as they all mean "undoubtedly". They can be translated as "แน่นอน" in some cases. Here are examples:

(1) If this work is adapted into a movie, it surely (Yiding) will be a good one. (งานเขียนชิ้นนี้หากถ่ายทำเป็นภาพยนตร์ต้องน่าดูแน่นอน)

(2) It is certainly (Kending) delicious as it smells good. (หอมฉุยเลย อร่อยแน่นอน)

(3) You are undoubtedly (Dangran) wrong. (คุณพูดแบบนี้มันไม่ถูกแน่นอน)

(4) We guarantee that it absolutely (Juedui) sells well. (เรารับรองว่าขายดีแน่นอน)

(5) It is necessary (Yiding) to be careful when walking on a mountain path. (เดินทางในป่าต้องระวังความปลอดภัยให้ดี)

(6) Her tone was affirmative (Kending). (น้ำเสียงของเขาแน่ใจมาก)

(7) Wang Lin said frankly: "That is understandable (Dangran)." (หวังหลินพูดตรงๆ ว่ามันแน่นอนอยู่แล้ว)

(8) There is no absolute (Juedui) security in the world. (ในโลกนี้ไม่มีความปลอดภัยแบบโดยสิ้นเชิงหรอก)

As is shown in the examples, "Yiding", "Kending", "Dangran" and "Juedui" in the first four sentences correspond to the Thai "แน่นอน", and they are interchangeable. For example, "Yiding", "Kending" and "Juedui" in example (1), (2) and (3) are interchangeable, while "Dangran" cannot be a substitute in example (4). Therefore, it is very difficult for learners to choose appropriate words in making sentences in Chinese or translating from Thai to Chinese. In the last four sentences, only "Dangran" in example (7) corresponds to "แน่นอน". There are either no equivalent or equivalents other than "แน่นอน" in the other three sentences. "Yiding" in example (5) has no equivalent. The equivalent of "Kending" in example (6) is "แน่ใจ". The equivalent of "Juedui" in example (8) is "โดยสิ้นเชิง". This is because these words share some meanings. Because of the complexity associated with the Thai equivalents, this paper will examine the semantic functions of "Yiding", "Kending", "Dangran" and "Juedui" and compare them with the Thai "แน่นอน" to find out the similarities and differences, which helps remove the confusion of learning and using these words for Chinese and Thai language learners.

II. Semantic Analysis of "Yiding", "Kending", "Dangran", "Juedui" and "แน่นอน"

A. Semantic analysis of "Yiding", "Kending", "Dangran" and "Juedui"

a. Semantic analysis of "Yiding"

"Yiding" has semantic meanings both as an adjective and an adverb.

1. As an adjective

Eight Hundred Words of Modern Chinese, Contemporary Chinese Dictionary,

The Commercial Press Learner's Dictionary of Contemporary Chinese and Wang Hai (2005) define the adjective "Yiding" as follows:

a) It means "sure and definite". Here are examples:

(1) Who is going to win or lose is not sure.

(2) It is sure that information blackout leads to the backwardness of a country.

b) It means "certain". Here are examples:

(3) His performance has a certain level.

(4) There are certain risks in investing in this project.

c) It means "necessary". Here are examples:

(5) The growth of crops has a necessary link with soil, water and sunlight.

(6) Knowledge and achievements do not have a necessary relationship with figure and appearance.

d) It means "specific" or "particular". Here are examples:

(7) When the temperature drops to a specific level, the water vapor in the air will turn into snow.

(8) The medicine is effective for a particular group of people.

e) It means "fixed". Here are examples.

(9) The market share is fixed. Others will take up our share.

(10) The area of arable land contracted by farmers is fixed and tax will be levied on the area of arable land.

2. As an adverb

Yang Jizhou & Jia Yongfen (2013) pointed out that as an adverb, "Yiding" means

a) "definitely" and b) "undoubtedly".

a) It means "definitely". Here are examples:

(11) I definitely have to do this well.

(12) I will definitely realize my dream of becoming a translator or diplomat.

b) It means "undoubtedly". Here are examples:

(13) He undoubtedly got up late.

(14) The watermelon is undoubtedly sweet. Let's have it.

b. Semantic analysis of "Kending"

Contemporary Chinese Dictionary and *Application Chinese Dictionary* point out that "Kending" means 1) "affirm" as a verb (its antonym: deny); 2) a) "affirmative" (its antonym: negative) and b) "sure and definite" as an adjective; 3) "undoubtedly" as an adverb. Here are examples:

1. As a verb, it means "affirm" (its antonym: deny). Here are examples:

(15) Their work should be affirmed.

(16) It is wrong to affirm everything or deny everything.

2. As an adjective, it means "affirmative" (its antonym: negative).

a) It means "affirmative" (its antonym: negative). Here are examples:

(17) I asked him whether he was in favor of it. His gave an affirmative answer.

(18) Should this be done immediately? The answer is affirmative.

b) It means "sure and definite". Here are examples.

(19) Please give me a definite reply.

(20) His tone was definite.

3. As an adverb, it means "undoubtedly" or "certainly". Here are examples:

(21) He will certainly agree.

(22) You certainly do not remember correctly.

c. Semantic analysis of "Dangran"

1. As an adjective

Contemporary Chinese Dictionary and *Application Chinese Dictionary* point out that "Dangran" means "understandable" as an adjective. Here are examples:

(23) It is understandable to be happy for this excellent performance.

(24) It is understandable that neighbors help each other.

2. As an adverb

The Commercial Press Guide to Chinese Synonyms and *The Commercial Press Learner's Dictionary of Contemporary Chinese* point out that "Dangran" means a) "undoubtedly" and b) "undeniably" as an adverb.

a) It means "undoubtedly". Here are examples:

(25) You undoubtedly should thank those who help you.

(26) The tickets are undoubtedly expensive as it is such a rare performance.

b) It means "undeniably". Here are examples.:

(27) We should pay attention to the problems. Undeniably, they are just individual problems.

(28) We have made great progress. Undeniably, there are also some shortcomings.

d. Semantic analysis of "Juedui"

Eight Hundred Words of Modern Chinese indicates that "Juedui" means 1) "absolute" (its antonym: relative) as an adjective; 2) "definitely" as an adverb.

1. As an adjective, it means "absolute" (its antonym: relative). Here are examples:

(29) He said that people can't live to 100 years old. It's too absolute.

(30) It is probably not good to say it absolutely.

2. As an adverb, it means "definitely". Here are examples:

(31) He will definitely come as he promised.

(32) This is definitely a misunderstanding.

Table 1   Semantic comparison of "Yiding", "Kending", "Dangran" and "Juedui"

Word	Parts of speech and semantic meanings		
	Adjective	Adverb	Verb
Yiding	1. sure and definite 2. certain 3. necessary 4. specific or particular 5. fixed	1. definitely 2. undoubtedly	-
Kending	1. affirmative 2. sure and definite	1. undoubtedly or certainly	1. affirm
Dangran	1. understandable	1. undoubtedly 2. undeniably	-
Juedui	1. absolute	1. definitely	-

As is shown in Table 1, "Yiding" and "Kending" share the same meaning as adjectives, which is "sure". It is believed that "Yiding", "Kending", "Dangran", and "Juedui" have one same meaning of "undoubtedly" as adverbs.

B. Semantic analysis of "แน่นอน"

The Standard Thai Dictionary defines "แน่นอน" as "เที่ยงแท้ จริงแท้ (correct)". *The*

Thai-Chinese Dictionary offers two meanings for "แน่นอน": (1) "surely" and (2) "certainly". Only equivalents are provided with no other explanations or example sentences. The above information in the reference books is far from enough for this study to refer to. Therefore, example sentences incorporating "แน่นอน" and other words suitable for this study have been retrieved and collected according to Thai National Corpus of Chulalongkorn University to analyze the meanings of "แน่นอน". Here are the meanings.

1. As an adjective, "แน่นอน" means "sure and definite", "affirmative", "understandable", "correct", "stable" and "fixed".

a) It means "sure and definite", "Yiding" "Queding" "Mingque" and "Kending" in Chinese. Here are examples:

(33) เขาจะเข้าร่วมการแข่งขันหรือไม่ ยังไม่แน่นอน (It is not sure whether he can participate in the competition or not.)

(34) อนาคตเป็นสิ่งที่ไม่แน่นอน (The future is not sure.)

(35) ตอนนี้ยังไม่ได้แจ้งเวลาที่แน่นอน (No definite time has yet been notified.)

(36) คุณจะให้คำตอบที่แน่นอนได้เมื่อไหร่ (When is a definite reply available?)

b) It means "affirmative", "Kending" in Chinese. Here are examples:

(37) ซ้อมให้ดีๆ แล้วเอาเหรียญทองมาแลกคะแนนของฉันนะ แน่นอน! ผมรับคำด้วยรอยยิ้ม

Practice and win a championship as a substitute for may class. I affirmed with smile.

(38) ที่แน่นอนคือ ไม่มีทางที่ผู้หญิงแบบนี้จะมันคงต่อเขาคนเดียว

It is affirmative that the woman will not treat him wholeheartedly.

c) It means "understandable", "Dangran" in Chinese. Here are examples.

(39) อกหักแล้วเสีย มันเป็นเรื่องแน่นอนอยู่แล้ว (It is understandable to be sad out of

disappointed love.)

(40) A: ถ้าจะออกไปแกต้องพิมพ์รายงานฉันให้เรียบร้อยก่อน (You have to get my report done before you get out.)

B: นั่นมันแน่นอนอยู่แล้ว เอามาเถอะ (That is understandable. Bring it to me.)

d) It means "correct", "Zhengque" in Chinese. Here are examples:

(41) ตรวจสอบได้ด้วยวิธีที่แน่นอน (Correct methods are used to detect.)

(42) การวินิจฉัยที่แน่นอนควรได้รับการตรวจจากแพทย์ (Correct diagnosis should be made by the doctor.)

e) It means "stable", "Wending" in Chinese. Here are examples:

(43) อารมณ์ของเขาไม่แน่นอน (Her mood is not stable.)

(44) บริษัทนี้ผลิตชาผู่เอ๋อที่ได้คุณภาพแน่นอน (The company produces Pu'er tea of stable quality.)

f) It means "fixed", "Yiding" and "Guding" in Chinese. Here are examples:

(45) ผู้สูงอายุส่วนใหญ่ไม่มีรายได้ที่แน่นอน (Most older people do not have a fixed income.)

(46) ไม่มีใครรู้ที่อยู่ที่แน่นอนของเขา (No one knows his fixed address.)

2. As an adverb, "แน่นอน" means a) "undoubtedly" and b) "undeniably".

a) It means "undoubtedly", "Yiding" "Kending" "Dangran" and "Juedui" in Chinese. Here are examples:

(47) แดดดีขนาดนี้ ฝนไม่ตกแน่นอน (The sun is bright. It undoubtedly is not going to rain.)

(48) ความรู้นั้นไม่มีวันเรียนหมดแน่นอน (We undoubtedly cannot learn all knowledge.)

b) It means "undeniably", "Dangran" in Chinese. Here are examples.

(49) เขารู้เรื่องประเทศจีนมากมาย แต่แน่นอนว่าไม่ใช่ทุกเรื่อง

(He knows a lot about China. Undeniably, he does not know everything about China.)

(50) มีคนได้คะแนนเต็มสามคน ซึ่งแน่นอนว่าหนึ่งในสามก็คือเธอ

(Three persons have got full credit. Undeniably, you are one of them.)

Table 2　　　　　　Semantic meanings of "แน่นอน"

Parts of speech	Semantic meanings and Chinese equivalents	
	Semantic meanings of "แน่นอน"	Chinese equivalents
Adjective	1. sure and definite 2. affirmative 3. understandable 4. correct 5. stable 6. fixed	1. Yiding, Queding, Mingque and Kending 2. Kending 3. Dangran 4. Zhengque 5. Wending 6. Yiding and Guding
Adverb	1. undoubtedly 2. undeniably	1. Yiding, Kending, Dangran and Juedui 2. Dangran

III. Semantic Comparison of "Yiding", "Kending", "Dangran" and "Juedui"

A. Similarities

1. As adjectives, "Yiding" and "Kending" share the same semantic meaning of "sure and definite". Here are examples:

(51) In the end, I will not let him go. This is definite (Yiding).

(52) It is not sure (*Kending) whether he will pass this exam.

(53) Parents are definitely (Yiding or Kending) always worried about their children.

(54) He gave a definite (*Yiding) answer.

It is noticed from the examples that "Yiding" and "Kending" are sometimes interchangeable in terms of the meaning "sure and definite". For example, they are interchangeable in example (51) and (53). But in example (52) and (54), they are not interchangeable.

2. "Yinding", "Kending", "Dangran" and "Juedui" all mean "undoubtedly" as adverbs. They are interchangeable as they serve as an adverbial in a sentence. Here are examples.:

(55) I underbtedly will come tomorrow.

(56) He studies so well, so he undoubtedly can be admitted to a prestigious university.

B. Differences

1. "Yiding", "Kending", "Dangran" and "Juedui" can all act as adjectives. Only "Yiding" and "Kending" share the meaning of "sure and definite". Beyond that, the four words have nothing in common in semantic meanings. "Yiding" has five meanings ("sure and definite", "certain", "necessary", "specific" and "fixed"); "Kending" has two meanings ("affirmative" and "sure and definite"); "Dangran" has one meaning ("understandable"); "Juedui" has one meaning ("absolute").

2. "Yiding" means "definitely" as an adverb and appears together with "Yao (want to)" and "Dei (should)". "Kending", "Dangran" and "Juedui" do not have this meaning, so they cannot serve as substitutes for "Yiding". Here are examples:

(57) You definitely (*Kending/*Dangran/*Juedui) have to find this person.

3. "Kending" can act as a verb, meaning "affirm". But "Yiding", "Dangran" and "Juedui" do not bear this semantic meaning. So "Kending" should not be replaced with these three words. Here are examples:

(58) Everyone affirmed (*Yiding/*Dangran/*Juedui) this suggestion.

4. "Dangran" means "undeniably" as an adverb exclusively. "Yiding", "Kending" and "Juedui" do not have this meaning, so they cannot act as substitutes for "Dangran". Here are examples:

(59) You speak Chinese well. Undeniably (Dangran), there are some minor problems.

*You speak Chinese well. Yiding, there are some minor problems.

*You speak Chinese well. Kending, there are some minor problems.

*You speak Chinese well. Juedui, there are some minor problems.

The examples show that "Yiding", "Kending" and "Juedui" do not bear the meaning of "undeniably", so the last three sentences are grammatically wrong.

Table 3　　Semantic comparison of "Yiding", "Kending", "Dangran" and "Juedui"

Parts of speech	Adjective								Adverb		
Semantic meanings											
Word	Sure and definite	certain	necessary	specific	fixed	affirmative	understandable	absolute	definitely	undoubtedly	undeniably
Yiding	+	+	+	+	+	-	-	-	+	+	-
Kending	+	-	-	-	-	+	-	-	-	+	-
Dangran	-	-	-	-	-	-	+	-	-	+	+
Juedui	-	-	-	-	-	-	-	+	-	+	-

According to Table 3, only "Yiding" and "Kending" share the semantic meaning of "sure and definite" as adjectives. "Yiding", "Kending", "Dangran" and "Juedui" all have the meaning of "undoubtedly" as adverbs. "Dangran" bears an exclusive meaning of "undeniably" as an adverb.

IV. Semantic Comparison between "Yiding" "Kending" "Dangran" "Juedui" and "แน่นอน"

A. Similarities

1. "Yiding" and "แน่นอน" have the same meanings of "sure and definite" and "fixed" as adjectives.

1.1 They share the meaning of "sure and definite". Here are examples:

(60) There is no definite dividing line between bitterness and happiness. (สุขกับทุกข์ไม่มีเส้นแบ่งที่แน่นอน)

(61) แน่นอนที่สุด หลังแต่งงานเราจะไปฮันนีมูนกัน (It is sure that we will go on a honeymoon after we get married.)

(62) ตอนนี้เรายังไม่มีตารางเวลาที่แน่นอน (We have not yet got a definite timetable.)

It is clear that referring to the meaning "sure and definite", "แน่นอน" has several equivalents in Chinese including "Yiding", "Kending", "Queding" and "Mingque".

1.2 They mean "fixed". Here are examples:

(63) The heart beats at a fixed pace. (หัวใจเต้นตามจังหวะที่แน่นอน)

(64) รายการโทรทัศน์นี้มีกลุ่มผู้ชมที่แน่นอน (This TV program has a fixed audience group.)

2. "Kending" and "แน่นอน" have the meanings of "sure and definite" and "affirmative" as adjectives.

2.1 They mean "sure and definite". Here are examples:

(65) It is hard to give a definite answer. (ตอนนี้ยากที่จะสรุปคำตอบที่แน่นอน)

(66) I am sure that he will not come today. (ฉันแน่ใจมากว่าวันนี้เขาไม่มาแน่นอน)

(67) เราได้บทสรุปที่แน่นอนแล้ว We have made a definite conclusion.

(68) ปีนี้ยังไม่มีแผนธุรกิจที่แน่นอน There are no definite business plans for this year.

(69) เขาไม่มีเป้าหมายชีวิตที่แน่นอน He does not have a definite goal in life.

According to the examples, "Kending" and "แน่นอน" have the meaning of "sure and definite". "Kending" has two Thai equivalents ("แน่นอน" and "แน่ใจ") and "แน่นอน" has three Chinese equivalents ("Kending", "Queding" and "Mingque").

2.2 "Kending" has the only Thai equivalent of "แน่นอน" as they share the meaning of "affirmative", and vice versa. Here are examples:

(70) My answer to this question is affirmative. สำหรับฉัน คำตอบของคำถามนี้คือ แน่นอน

(71) ประเด็นนี้แน่นอน เราทุกคนเห็นด้วย (This is affirmative. We all agree on it.)

3. "Dangran" and "แน่นอน" mean "understandable" as adjectives. But "แน่นอน" usually appears together with the modal adverb "อยู่แล้ว". Here are examples:

(72) It is understandable that people have different opinions. (คนเรามีความคิดเห็นต่างกันเป็นสิ่งที่แน่นอนอยู่แล้ว)

(73) ผู้ชายชอบผู้หญิงสวย นั่นมันแน่นอนอยู่แล้ว (It is understandable that men like beautiful women.)

4. "Dangran" and "แน่นอน" share the meaning of "undeniably" as adverbs. Here are examples:

(74) This is a good opportunity for you. Undeniably, this is a good opportunity for us. (นี่เป็นโอกาสที่ดีของคุณ และแน่นอนว่าเป็นโอกาสดีของเราเช่นกัน)

(75) ภาษาไทยอีสานกับภาษาลาวคล้ายกันมาก แต่แน่นอนว่ามีความต่างอยู่ไม่น้อยเช่นกัน (The Northeastern Thai dialect is very similar to Lao. Undeniably, they have many differences.)

5. "Yiding", "Kending", "Juedui" and "แน่นอน" mean "undoubtedly" as adverbs and they are interchangeable. Here are examples:

(76) We undoubtedly will come tomorrow. (พรุ่งนี้พวกเราไปแน่นอน)

(77) So many people sign up for the exam. There will undoubtedly be more

examinees next year. (เราคาดว่า ปีหน้าจำนวนนักเรียนเพิ่มขึ้นแน่นอน)

(78) ของขวัญที่เธอให้ เขาชอบแน่นอน (She will <u>undoubtedly</u> love the gift you give her.)

(79) ถ้าเธอชวน เขาไปแน่นอน (He will <u>undoubtedly</u> keep your appointment.)

B. Differences

1. The differences between "Yiding" and "แน่นอน" as adjectives are as follows.

1.1 "Yiding" has the meaning of "necessary" as an adjective, but "แน่นอน" does not have this meaning. Here are examples:

(80) The depth of the article does not have a <u>necessary</u> link with its length.

(ความลึกซึ้งกับความสั้นยาวของบทความนั้นไม่มีความสัมพันธ์เชิงตายตัว)

(81) The development of things has <u>necessary</u> laws.

(พัฒนาการของสรรพสิ่งนั้นมีกฎที่ตายตัวของมัน)

"Yiding" in the examples means "necessary". The Thai equivalent is "ตายตัว" rather than "แน่นอน", as "แน่นอน" does not have the meaning of "necessary".

1.2 "Yiding" means "certain" as an adjective, but "แน่นอน" does not have this meaning. Here are examples:

(82) There is also a <u>certain</u> reason for his idea.

(วิธีคิดของเขาก็มีเหตุผลพอสมควร/อยู่เหมือนกัน)

(83) Doing this requires <u>certain</u> knowledge.

(ทำงานนี้ต้องมีความรู้ประมาณหนึ่ง/พอสมควร/พอประมาณ/อยู่เหมือนกัน)

"Yiding" in the examples means "certain", but "แน่นอน" does not bear this semantic function. So the Thai equivalents are "ประมาณหนึ่ง", "พอสมควร", "พอประมาณ" and "อยู่เหมือนกัน".

1.3 "Yiding" has the meaning of "specific or particular" as an adjective, but "แน่นอน" does not have this meaning. Here are examples.

(84) There are specific systems for attendance, inspection and examination.

(การเช็คชื่อ การสังเกตุการณ์ และการสอบ ต่างมีระเบียบเฉพาะทั้งนั้น)

(85) Most women are eager to be mothers when they are at a particular age.

(ผู้หญิงพอถึงอายุประมาณหนึ่ง/ระดับหนึ่งก็อยากเป็นแม่กันทั้งนั้น)

"Yiding" in the examples means "specific". But "แน่นอน" does not have this meaning. So the Thai equivalent is not "แน่นอน" but "เฉพาะ" "ประมาณหนึ่ง" and "ระดับหนึ่ง".

2."Juedui" means "absolute" as an adjective, but "แน่นอน" does not have this meaning. Here are examples:

(86) The person says and does things so absolutely. (คนคนนี้ทั้งวาจาและการกระทำสุดขั้วมาก)

(87) We have the absolute advantage to beat them. (พวกเรามีความได้เปรียบโดยสิ้นเชิงที่จะเอาชนะพวกเขา)

"Juedui" in the examples means "absolute". But "แน่นอน" does not have this meaning. So the Thai equivalent is not "แน่นอน" but "สุดขั้ว" and "โดยสิ้นเชิง".

3. "Yiding" means "definitely" as an adverb, but "แน่นอน" does not have this meaning. Here are examples:

(88) You definitely need help. (เธอต้องหาคนมาช่วยแล้วหละ)

(89) I definitely should come top in the exam. (ฉันต้องสอบให้ได้ที่หนึ่ง)

(90) You definitely should not let the opportunity go. (โอกาสครั้งนี้ต้องห้ามพลาดอีกนะ)

(91) You definitely should not tell him. (เธอต้องห้ามไม่ให้เขารู้เรื่องนะ)

According to the examples, "Yiding" has special semantic functions. It sometimes has no Thai equivalent and sometimes has the equivalent "ต้อง" (should). It has no equivalent in example (88) and (89). It has the equivalent "ต้อง" in example

(90) and (91). It is worth mentioning that the Thai translations in examples (88) and (89) include the word "ต้อง", but here ""ต้อง" corresponds to "Dei (should)" and "Yao (want to)" rather than "Yiding". So "Yiding" has no equivalent in these two sentences.

4. "Kending" means "affirm" as a verb, but "แน่นอน" does not bear this meaning as it is not a verb. Here are examples.

(92) We all affirmed that he was right. (พวกเรายอมรับทรรศนะของเขาแล้วว่าถูกต้อง)

(93) The conclusion of their experiment was affirmed by experts. (ผลการทดลองของพวกเขา ผู้เชี่ยวชาญได้รับรองแล้ว)

According to the Thai translation of the sentences, "Keding" does not correspond to "แน่นอน" as a verb. Its Thai equivalent can be "ยอมรับ" (accept) or "รับรอง" (admit).

5. "แน่นอน" has the meanings of "correct", "stable" and "fixed" as adjectives. It shares the meaning of "fixed" with "Yiding". But "Yiding" does not have the other two meanings. "Kending", "Dangran" and "Juedui" do not have these three meanings. Here are examples.

(94) ผมคิดว่าน่าจะให้แพทย์ตรวจสักครั้ง เพื่อการวินิจฉัยที่แน่นอน (correct)

(To get correct (*Yiding/*Kending/*Dangran/*Juedui) diagnosis, I think we should ask the doctor to check it out.)

(95) เขามีรายได้ที่แน่นอนทุกเดือน (fixed)

(He has a fixed monthly income (*Kending/*Dangran/*Juedui).

(96) อารมณ์ของเขาไม่แน่นอนสักเท่าไหร่ (stable)

(His mood is not stable (* Yiding / * Kending/ * Dangran / * Juedui).

Table 4   Semantic meanings of "Yiding", "Kending", "Dangran", "Juedui" and "แน่นอน"

Parts of speech	Adjective										Adverb			Verb
Word	Sure and definite	certain	necessary	specific	affirmative	understandable	absolute	correct	stable	fixed	definitely	undoubtedly	undeniably	affirm
Yiding	+	+	+	+	-	-	-	-	-	+	+	+	-	-
Kending	+	-	-	-	+	-	-	-	-	-	-	+	-	+
Dangran	-	-	-	-	+	-	-	-	-	-	-	+	+	-
Juedui	-	-	-	-	-	-	+	-	-	-	-	+	-	-
แน่นอน	+	-	-	-	+	+	-	+	+	+	-	+	+	-

Table 4 shows that "Yiding", "Kending", "Dangran", "Juedui" and "แน่นอน" can be adjectives. They have similarities. "Yiding", "Kending" and "แน่นอน" can all indicate "sure and definite". "Kending" and "แน่นอน" can mean "affirmative". "Yiding" and "แน่นอน" can refer to "fixed". As adverbs, the five words can all mean "undoubtedly". "Dangran" and "แน่นอน" share the meaning of "undeniably". Here are the differences of the five words. As an adjective, "Yiding" means "certain", "necessary" and "specific". "Kending", "Dangran", "Juedui" and "แน่นอน" do not bear this meaning. "แน่นอน" can mean "correct" and "stable", while "Yiding", "Kending", "Dangran" and "Juedui" cannot. As an adverb, "Yiding" bears the meaning of "definitely", but "Kending", "Dangran", "Juedui" and "แน่นอน" do not have this meaning. In addition, "Kending" can be a verb, meaning "affirm". But "Yiding", "Dangran", "Juedui" and "แน่นอน" do not have this meaning.

V. Conclusion

"แน่นอน" and "Yiding", "Kending", "Dangran" and "Juedui" share similarities and differences in semantic meanings. Here are the similarities and differences.

1) In terms of similarities, they have the same meaning of "undoubtedly" as adverbs. The Thai "แน่นอน" has four Chinese equivalents including "Yiding", "Kending", "Dangran" and "Juedui".

2) As for differences, "แน่นอน" means "correct" and "stable", while "Yiding", "Kending", "Dangran" and "Juedui" do not have this meaning.

3) "แน่นอน" and "Yiding" share the meanings of "sure and definite" and "fixed" as adjectives. "แน่นอน" has the Chinese equivalents of "Yiding", "Queding", "Mingque" and "Kending" as they refer to "sure and definite". It has the Chinese equivalents of "Yiding" and "Guding" as they refer to "fixed".

The difference between "แน่นอน" and "Yinding" is that "Yinding" has the meanings of "certain", "necessary" and "specific" as an adjective. "Yiding" has the Thai equivalents of "ประมาณหนึ่ง", "พอสมควร", "พอประมาณ" and "อยู่เหมือนกัน" as they refer to "certain". It has the Thai equivalent of "ตายตัว" or "ตายตัวแน่นอน", as they mean "necessary". It has the Thai equivalents of "เฉพาะ" "ประมาณหนึ่ง" "ระดับหนึ่ง", as they indicate "specific". Besides, "Yiding" may serve as an adverb, meaning "definitely". But "แน่นอน" does not have this meaning. When referring to "definitely", "Yiding" either corresponds to "want to" or simply has no equivalent.

4) "แน่นอน" and "Kending" share three meanings. As adjectives, they mean "sure and definite" and "affirmative". As adverbs, they mean "undoubtedly". "Kending" has two Thai equivalents ("แน่นอน" and "แน่ใจ"). "แน่นอน" has three Chinese equivalents ("Kending", "Queding" and "Mingque").

5) "แน่นอน" shares three meanings with "Dangran" including "understandable" as adjectives as well as "undoubtedly" and "undeniably" as adverbs.

6) "แน่นอน" and "Juedui" both mean "sure and definite". The difference is "Juedui" has the meaning of "absolute", but "แน่นอน" does not have this meaning. "Juedui" has the Thai equivalents of "สุดขั้ว" and "โดยสิ้นเชิง" as they indicate "absolute".

对外古汉语教学的重要性和方法探索

吴淑铃 【美国】
美国南伊利诺大学

一 引言

随着中国近年来对传统文化的日益重视，文史哲的研究、国学的学习和倡导以及古文物的保护方面，都取得了重大的进展。古代汉语作为中国悠久的历史文化的主要传递媒介，经代代相传，至今仍处处反映在现代人的语言文字和思想行为之中，融入我们的沟通交际。以习近平主席近年来的谈话为例，2013年习主席在博鳌亚洲论坛年会上引用桓宽《盐铁论》里的名句"明者因时而变，知者随事而制"来强调亚洲地区应适时改变经济发展方式，适当调整经济结构；2012年习总书记在中央政治局的讲话引用苏轼《范增论》"物必先腐，而后虫生"来告诫党员当腐败问题越演越烈，最终必然会亡党亡国。不仅政治人物在讲话时引经据典，我们日常生活中常听到的成语也多半源于古文诗词，如"温故知新"出自《论语·为政》、"扑朔迷离"出自东汉《乐府·木兰诗》。援引古文不但能突出古今思想一脉相承、言简意赅地传递说话者想表达的信息，同时表现出更高雅的语言修养或更强烈的情感力度。

虽然古代汉语在当下华人的语言生活和母语语文教育中都受到重视，但在对外汉语教学领域里，教授古代汉语的学校仍属少数。根据全美教师协会2012年对美国216所大学所做的调查，仅有33%的大学教授古代汉语，其中六成的学校用中文教授，四成的学校用英语教授，用英语教授的学校多以翻译的英语文本为主。造成此现象的主要原因,一是教师普遍认为学习古代汉语难度较高,又没有适用的对外古代汉语教材,而偏重选择教授当代文学;二是一些大学中文课程没有中文专业,因而只提供有限的中文课,自然排除需要一定中文基础才能进阶的古代汉语课。不重视古代汉语教学导致许多学习中文多年的学生,在语言精进上出现瓶颈而难以突破,在文化理解时产生障碍而让学习无以为继,甚至在毕业时仍然不知道李白、杜甫是谁。相较于大学里学习其他语种的学生,学习汉语的毕业生对中国古典文学的认识更显得不足。朱瑞平明确指出有必要为以汉语为专业的留学生开设古代汉语课程,以提升其使用书面语的能力。

二 学习古代汉语的重要性

以下具体分析学习古汉语在对外汉语教学里的实质作用:

1. 强化对汉字本体的认识

当前对外汉语教学在教授词汇时沿用西方的语言观,以"词本位"为主(参见史方园,2013),如"学校"是"school"的意思,学生在学习新词汇时将"学校"视为一个语义单位,并不分析"学"是什么意思,"校"是什么意思。这样学习的优点是方便和英语对应,容易标注词汇的意思,缺点是忽略对单个汉字的理解,无法充分利用汉字的延展性来学习新词汇。以"学"为例,如果学生知道"学"本身的意思是"学习",那么"学科(学习的科目)""学历(学习的历程)"等词汇就不难理解其组词的方式了。反之,在"学"一系列延展出的词汇中,要是每个都将其视为单个没有关联的生词,只记忆个别生词的意思是"subject"、"record of schooling",不但在记忆上费时费力,学习效果更是事倍功半。相对的,古代汉语的教学是以单个汉字为主来作注解,如"物必先腐"一句,会为"物""必""腐"等字标注英文翻译。在汉语双音节化以前,古代汉语以"字本位"为主来表意,学习古代汉语,可以帮助学生回归对单个汉字语义的重视,学生一旦充分了解单个汉字的字义,就能够轻易地掌握两个已学过的汉字相结合所产生的新词汇,如"必学"科目里的"必学"一词,在知道"必"和"学"的字义以后就不再是新生词,而仅仅是两个已经熟悉的汉字相结合的产物。另外,对具备高级汉语水平的学生来说,分辨如何正确使用近义词,如"保持、保留(maintain)""保护、保卫(protect)",是显著的难点之一。这些词汇在用英语标注其意时,往往都是一样的,因此让学生以为两者为同义词,没有用法上的区别。回归"字本位"教学,可以有效地借此区辩近义词里的单个汉字来帮助学生掌握这些词汇的差异之处。在阅读和听力理解上，辨析同音词如"公式、公事、攻势"也需要学生借助对汉字的敏锐度和迅速反应来做正确的语义辨析。了解汉语"字本位"的特性并学习以"字本位"为主的古代汉语，才能有效地扩展汉语的词汇量。

2. 透过经典文学作品强化对文史哲的理解

古代汉语是文史哲不分家的，《史记》里的篇章不但记录史实、呈现细致的人物描写，同时囊括诸子百家的思想。学习历代经典作品如《论语》、《老子》以及王维诗等，可以帮助学生了解中国传统文化里儒释道三家的核心思想。中国当代社会的尊长孝亲和修己安人的观念源自儒家思想，顺应自然的智慧来自道家，明心见性的静心法则出于禅宗。学习历代集合文史哲思想的篇章是了解中国文化最直接的途径。在了解作品和作者的时代背景后，直接研读古代文本，仔细咀嚼语言文字的使用手法和理据思维，比抽象地描述或总结中国文史哲样貌对学习者来说更容易产生具体的印象。唯有了解中国传统文史哲思想才能帮助学生深入理解中国人的政治思维、外交模式、世界观等当代课题。

3. 提升高级汉语以及书面语的使用能力

现代汉语尤其是书面语仍用到许多古代汉语里使用的词汇，以《论语：述而篇》为例："子曰：三人行，必有我师焉。择其善者而从之，其不善者而改之"，虚词如"其（代词，指前文提到的"三人"）"、"者（后缀，接在名词、动词、形容词后，用来指人、指事或指物）"、"而（连词，表并列或转折关系）"等，都是书面语或是正式发言中经常出现的。习主席在2013年同各界优秀青年代表座谈里谈到"生活从不眷顾因循守旧、满足现状者，从不等待不思进取、坐享其成者，而是将更多机遇留给善于和勇于创新的人们"。在这一小段话里"者""其""而"三个虚字都用到了。此外，现今广泛使用的成语也多半来自古代作品。透过古文词汇语法的讲解，内容含义的领会，这些常用虚字和成语就可以扎扎实实地介绍给学生，从而提升学习高级汉语学生的遣词用字能力。

4. 培养阅读古代汉语的能力，奠定汉学研究的基础

王力指出学习古代汉语是为了帮助学习者阅读古代文献，以便研究、继承、检视中华文化遗产。对国外的汉学家来说，能否阅读古代汉语标志着其是否具有不依赖翻译文本，直接研究第一手文献资料的能力，也预示着是否能最终达到更精深、独到的学术水平。在对外汉语教学中提供学生学习古代汉语的机会，也就

是在培育海外青年汉学家的幼苗，引领学生迈出汉学文史哲研究的第一步，持续深化全球对中国历代文献和遗址的研究。

三 教授古代汉语的方法

本文接下来针对古代汉语教学在选文和练习活动设计方面提出具体的建议：

1. 选文的标准

在学生初次学习古代汉语时，应选择篇幅在300字以内的文本，以控制每一课的词汇量和难度，帮助学生适应古代汉语和现代汉语的差别。同时在教学上强调古代汉语和现代汉语的近似和传承之处，让学生在学习古文的同时能提高现代汉语的使用能力，提高学习动力。蔡蓉芝分析美国常见的六套文言文教材发现，这几套教材选文的特性包括：选文跨越各时代、体裁文体丰富，同时以名家作品和主流思想为重。按朝代顺序跨朝代选文可以建立学生的文学史观，而兼选各类文体则可以凸显不同朝代的文体特色，在散文、语录、诗歌的转换间，增加学习古代汉语的趣味性。此外，儒释道的主流思想贯穿历代文学作品，应当在课程初期就介绍给学生，再透过随后的文本分析，反复领略儒释道思想的精神内涵。

2. 练习活动的设计

古汉语教学的练习活动设计可以侧重古文字词、内容讨论和虚字及语法句型练习，并注重古代语言形式在现代汉语里的实际运用。在字词练习方面，可以标注古文单个汉字的字义在现代汉语里的双音节形式，如"学而时习之"的"时"已经延展为"时常、时时""习"变成"温习、复习"，如此一来，既可解释古文字义，又可以练习当代的用法，可有效帮助学生辨析现代汉语中大量存在的同音词和近义词。在内容讨论上，可以设计讨论内容的问题，如"作者怎么描写？""哪几句话跟……有关？"等，帮助学生掌握文本内容。另外，还可以加入修辞分析、开放性意见问题、白话文翻译等，让学生在课堂上分组讨论，报告讨论的结果。重要的虚字和语法点则可以选用更多的古文例句和运用该虚字的现代汉语例句让学生做翻译、填空或造句练习。在教材设计上，还可以加入与古文文本有关的现代汉语短篇阅读文章或听力练习，引入现代人对作者或文本的评价和赏析，透过循环复习、环环相扣的设计方式来降低学习古代汉语的难度、增进学生对古文文本的理解，并且与现代汉语的学习相互融会贯通。

四 结语

目前国内外在对外汉语教学领域里对教授古代汉语的重视程度仍有待加强。学习古代汉语可以强化对汉字本体的认识、增进对文史哲的理解、提升高级汉语以及书面语的使用能力、建立阅读古代汉语的能力，从而奠定汉学研究的基础。在实际教学上，选文应从一般中国人熟悉的历代经典名篇中选录，消弭第二语言学习者和母语人士之间的语言文化隔阂，强调古代汉语和现代汉语的共同特征和实际运用，使中文作为第二语言专业的学生得以体会完整的中华文化精髓，为培育未来的青年汉学家打好基础。

Exploration of the Importance and Methods of Ancient Chinese Teaching

Shu-ling Wu / United States of America

Chinese Assistant Professor and China Program Leader, Southern Illinois University in Carbondale

I. Introduction

With the increasing attention to traditional culture in China in recent years, great progress has been made in the study of literature, history and philosophy, the study and advocacy of Chinese classics, and the protection of ancient relics. As a main medium of the long Chinese history and culture, ancient Chinese, passed on from generation to generation, is still reflected in the languages and ideological behaviors of modern people and is integrated into our communication. Taking President Xi Jinping's recent talk as an example, President Xi, at the Boao Forum for Asia (BFA) Annual Conference 2013, quoted the famous line "Smart people change their strategies and methods according to the differences of period, and people of great wisdom make their management methods according to the difference of developmental direction" from *Discourses on Salt and Iron* written by Huan Kuan to emphasize that the economic developmental mode should be opportunely changed and the economic structure should be properly adjusted in Asia. In 2012, General Secretary Xi, in an address at the Political Bureau of the Central Committee of the CPC, quoted "Objects must be rotten first, then worms parasitize on them" from *Fan Zeng Lun* written by Su Shi to warn Party members that the increasingly serious corruption problems will eventually lead to the perishing of the Party and of the state. Not only does the politician quote the classics, but most of the idioms we often hear in our daily life are derived from ancient poetry, such as "gaining new insights through restudying the old material" from Chapter Two of *The Analects of Confucius*, and "confusing the eye (unable to distinguish whether one is a male or a female)" from *Eastern Han Yuefu: The Song of Mulan*. Quoting ancient Chinese prose, we can not only highlight the same origin of ancient and modern ideas and concisely convey the information we want to express, but we can also show the cultivation of more elegant language or stronger emotional strength.

Although ancient Chinese has received attention in current life of language and native language education of the ethnic Chinese, only a few universities teach ancient Chinese in the field of teaching Chinese as a foreign language. Of the 216 universities surveyed by the National Teachers Association in 2012 (Li, Wen, & Xie, 2014), only 33% taught ancient Chinese, of which 60% taught in Chinese and 40% taught in English, and most of the universities teaching ancient Chinese in English were mainly based on English translations. The first main reason for this phenomenon is that teachers generally think that learning ancient Chinese is more difficult for students and there are not any applicable teaching materials of ancient Chinese, so they prefer to teach contemporary literature. The second reason is that there are no Chinese majors in some university Chinese courses, so only limited Chinese courses are provided, and the ancient Chinese courses that require a certain Chinese basis to take advanced courses have been eliminated. The University's not attaching importance to the ancient Chinese teaching has made it so that many students who have learned Chinese for many years are unable to make breakthroughs in language progress. They have obstacles in cultural understanding, which causes them to fail to continue their study. They even do not know who Li Bai is and who Du Fu is when they graduate. Compared with those who learn other languages at the university, Chinese graduates are less aware of Chinese classical literature. Zhu Ruiping (2001) has clearly pointed out that it is necessary to set up ancient Chinese courses for foreign students majoring in Chinese, so as to improve their ability to use the written language.

II. The Importance of Learning Ancient Chinese

First, this article will analyze the substantial role of learning ancient Chinese in teaching Chinese as a foreign language:

1. Strengthening the understanding of the Chinese characters

For the current teaching of Chinese as a foreign language, the Western view of language, "word-oriented" (see Shi Fangyuan, 2013), is adopted in the teaching of vocabulary. For example, "学校" means "school". Students see "学校" as a semantic unit rather than analyzing what "学" means and what "校" means when learning new vocabulary. The advantage is that it is convenient to correspond to the English expression and write down the English meaning of the word, but the understanding of a single Chinese character may be ignored, and students are unable to make full use of the malleability of Chinese characters to learn new words. Taking "学" as an example, if students know "学" means "learning", then it will not be difficult to understand the ways of making up the words "学科 (subject of learning)", "学历 (process of learning)" and other words. On the contrary, when learning a series of extended words, if we see them as a single unrelated word and only memorize the meaning of certain new words such as "subject" and "record of schooling", it is not only time-consuming and laborious for the memory, but it is also less effective in learning. In contrast, in ancient Chinese teaching, we mainly use single Chinese characters to annotate them. For example, when annotating "物必先腐", we will write down the English meaning of "物", "必" and "腐". Before two-syllables occur in the Chinese language, ancient Chinese was character-oriented. Learning ancient Chinese could help students pay attention to the meaning of single Chinese characters. Once students fully understand the meaning of single Chinese characters, they can easily grasp the new word combined by two Chinese characters they have learned, such as "必学" in "必学" subject. The word "必学" is no longer a new word after students know the meaning of "必" and "学", but only the outcome of combining two familiar Chinese characters. In addition, it is one of the prominent difficulties for students with an advanced level of Chinese to understand how to correctly use the synonyms, such as "保持, 保留 (maintain)", "保护, 保卫 (protect)". The meaning of these words is often marked with the same English expression, which causes students to think that the words are synonyms and there is no difference in usage. The "character-oriented" teaching can effectively help students master the differences between these words by distinguishing a single Chinese character in the synonyms. In reading and listening comprehension, when discriminating homonyms such as "公式 (formula), 公事 (public affairs) and 攻势 (offensive)", students also need to make a correct semantic discrimination with the help of their acuity and rapid response to Chinese characters. We must understand the characteristics of "character-oriented" and learn the character-oriented ancient Chinese, so that we can effectively expand the Chinese vocabulary.

2. Strengthening the understanding of literature, history and philosophy through classic literature

In ancient Chinese, the literature, history and philosophy are related to each other. Historical facts, detailed descriptions of characters as well as a hundred schools of thoughts are all included in the chapters of *Records of the Historian*. Learning classical works of past ages, such as *The Analects of Confucius*, *Laozi* and Wang Wei's poems, can help students understand the core ideas of Confucianism, Buddhism and Taoism in Chinese traditional culture. The concept of respecting elders, filial piety, self-discipline and stabilizing others in contemporary Chinese society originates from Confucianism, the wisdom of conforming to nature comes from Taoism, and the meditation law of clearing one's mind and disclosing nature is derived from Zen. The most direct way to understand Chinese culture is to learn chapters of past ages which contain the thoughts of literature, history and philosophy. After understanding the historical background of the works and authors, learners can directly read ancient texts, and ruminate on the use of language and thought, which are more likely to create a specific impression on learners than abstractly describing or summarizing the features of Chinese literature, history and philosophy. Only by understanding the traditional Chinese literary, historical and philosophical thought can we help students understand the contemporary topics like Chinese political ideas, diplomatic manner and world outlook.

3. Improving the ability to use advanced Chinese and the written language

Many words used in ancient Chinese are still used in modern Chinese, especially in the written language. Taking Chapter Seven of *The Analects of Confucius* as an example: "The Master said: When I walk along with two others, they may serve me as my teachers. I will select their good qualities and follow them, their bad qualities and avoid them." The function words " 其 (pronoun, means I and two others above)", " 者 (suffix, after the noun, verb or adjective, refers to a person, thing or object)", " 而 (conjunction, shows coordinative or adversative relation)" and so on often appear in the written language or in a formal statement. In 2013, President Xi, with outstanding youth representatives from all walks of life, talked of "Life never favors people who are conservative and satisfied with the status quo, and never waits for people who make no attempt to make progress and reap the rewards, but gives more opportunities to people who are good at and brave in innovation" [1]. In this short paragraph, all the three function words " 者 ", " 其 " and " 而 " are used. In addition, the idioms widely used nowadays are mostly from ancient works. Through the explanation of the words and grammar of the ancient prose and the comprehension of the meaning of the content, these commonly-used function words and idioms can be introduced to students solidly, so that advanced Chinese students can improve their ability to choose and use the words.

4. Fostering the ability to read ancient Chinese and laying the foundation for the study of sinology

Wang Li (1997) has pointed out that the purpose of learning ancient Chinese is to help learners read ancient documents, so that they can study, inherit and inspect Chinese cultural heritage. For foreign sinologists, whether they can read the ancient Chinese shows whether they have the ability to directly study the first-hand literature without dependence on the translated texts, and it also indicates whether they can eventually reach a more profound and original academic level. In the teaching of Chinese as a foreign language, to provide the opportunity of learning ancient Chinese for students is to nurture young overseas sinologists, to lead students to take the first step in the study of the literature, history and philosophy of sinology, and to keep deepening the global study of Chinese literature and historic sites of past ages.

III. The Methods of Teaching Ancient Chinese

Next, this article will make specific suggestions for the text-selection and design of practice activities of teaching ancient Chinese:

1. The standards of text-selection

When students learn ancient Chinese for the first time, the teacher should choose a text with a limit of 300 words so as to control the amount of the vocabulary and the difficulty of each lesson, and help students adapt to the differences between ancient Chinese and modern Chinese. At the same time, the teacher should emphasize the similarity and inheritance of ancient Chinese and modern Chinese in teaching, so that students can also improve their ability to use modern Chinese as well as improve their learning motivation while learning ancient Chinese prose. Cai Rongzhi (2015), when analyzing six common teaching materials of classical Chinese in the United States, has found that the characteristics of these selected texts include: the selected texts of all ages, with rich style and genre, and mainly the famous works and mainstream ideology. The students' perspective of literary history can be set up through the cross-dynasty text selection in dynasty sequence, stylistic features of different dynasties can be highlighted through the selection of various styles, and the interest of learning ancient Chinese can be increased through the transformation of prose, quotations and poems. In addition, the mainstream ideology of Confucianism, Buddhism and Taoism runs through the literary works of past ages, which should be introduced to students at the beginning of the curriculum, and then students can comprehend once again the spiritual connotation of Confucianism, Buddhism and Taoism through the later text analysis.

2. The design of practice activities

The design of practice activities of ancient Chinese teaching can focus on the discussion of ancient Chinese words and content, the practice of function words, grammar and sentence patterns, and the practical use of the ancient language form in modern Chinese. In terms of word practice, we can use the double syllable form of words in modern Chinese to mark the meaning of single Chinese characters in ancient Chinese. For example, "时" in "学而时习之 (Isn't it a pleasure to study and practice what you have learned?)" has been extended to "时常, 时时 (frequently, often)" and "习" to "温习, 复习 (review)". In this way, the meaning of ancient Chinese characters can be explained and the contemporary usage of words can be practiced, which can effectively help students distinguish homonyms and synonyms in modern Chinese. In the discussion of content, we can design the questions of the discussed content such as "How does the author describe it?", "Which sentences are related to…?" to help the student to master the content of the text. In addition, rhetorical analysis, open-ended questions and vernacular translation can also be included, and then students can have group discussions in class before reporting the results of the discussion. For important function words and grammar points, more ancient Chinese example sentences and modern Chinese example sentences where the function words are used can be selected for students to translate, fill in the blanks or make sentences. In designing teaching material, we can also add short articles in modern Chinese or listening practice related to texts of ancient scripts, and introduce modern people's evaluation and appreciation of the author or texts, and through cyclic review and interlinked design methods, we can reduce the difficulty of learning ancient Chinese, enhance students' understanding of ancient texts, and combine the learning of modern Chinese.

IV. Conclusion

At present, people both at home and abroad should attach more importance to the teaching of ancient Chinese in the field of teaching Chinese as a foreign language. Learning ancient Chinese can strengthen the understanding of the Chinese characters, enhance the comprehension of literature, history and philosophy, improve the ability to use advanced Chinese and the written language, and establish the ability to read ancient Chinese, thus laying the foundation for the study of sinology. In actual teaching, the texts should be excerpts from the classics of past ages that are familiar to the Chinese people, eliminate the language cultural barriers between the second language learners and the native speakers, and emphasize the common features and practical use of ancient and modern Chinese, so that students whose second language major is Chinese can understand the complete essence of Chinese culture and lay a solid foundation for fostering young sinologists of the future.

论现当代文学在对外汉语教学中的作用

丹妮 【印度】
都安大学助理教授

随着中国的经济崛起，中文变成了热门语言。学习中文的热潮席卷了印度。学习中文不但给学生打开一个充满着机会的世界，也会帮助他们更好地理解我们的邻国——中国。目前在印度至少有七、八所大学正式建立了中文系，开设中文课程。这些大学中文系有的提供短期形式的证书课程，但现在越来越多的大学开设了本科与硕士课程。本科和硕士课程设置需要很精细、全面的研究，不但要包括语言成分，还应包括文化、历史、文学和翻译课。我们必须要考虑本科生或者硕士生毕业以后应该拥有什么样的能力，要为社会发挥什么样的作用。笔者认为一个以中文为专业的本科生、硕士生，应该对中国有全面的了解。要达到这个目标，当下的本科课程不但注意提高学生的语言能力，也要注重文化、历史、文学课。

对外汉语教学包括语言技能教学与文化教学两部分。对一个教印度学生中文的老师来说，应该用什么样的教材激发学生们的兴趣。笔者认为文学作为语言交际的工具，也是带着深厚的文化成分的文体，对教汉语的过程中会有很大的帮助。

过去语言教学理论把重点放在语言能力上，但近几十年，文化交际能力在外语教学中有了越来越重要的地位。在这种情况下，很多学者再次关注文学作品与文学在对外语教学中的作用。语言与文学有密不可分的关系，这是不争的事实。很多学者（Brumfit and Carter, Duff and Maley, Lazar, Hadaway 等）认同文学在语言教学中的作用。他们认为文学作品对学习语言有很大的帮助，文学作品可以把语言放在一个实际情况内，让学生们清晰地理解语言的实际运用。不同文体也带着不同的社会现象，政治意义，哲学含义，也能成为学生们学习的内容。

一 对外汉语教学中现当代文学的重要性

文学是文化的一部分，各个时代的文学作品都在一定程度上反映了其时代生活的面貌。开设现当代文学课，学习现当代文学作品，在提高留学生汉语语言水平的同时，也是较好地了解和掌握中国文化的一个重要渠道。

笔者认为把汉语作为外语的学生来说，通过文学课的学习，能更多地领略中国文学语言之美、更多了解新时代、新思潮。中国现当代文学作品可以帮助学生了解今天的中国，尤其是现代中国一个世纪以来所经历过的风雨变迁，而且如何从传统社会变为现代化社会的。现当代文学作品在对外汉语教学中有以下几个方面的作用：

1. 提高语言技能

学者认为学习外语的主要目的是提高语言交际能力。"留学生学习中文的一个主要目的是'使用'。""对外汉语留学生教学终究是以语言教学为主体，即便是文化课，也不能完全脱离语言教学之根本"，笔者同意这个观点，对一个学习汉语的印度学生来说，提高汉语水平是最重要的，那么要达到这个目的，笔者认为用现当代文学作品最合适。现当代文学作品语言通俗易懂，充满着文化色彩，描写的也是现代，当代的中国。"从语言上看，当代文学的语言最为鲜活，最多使用，也是留学生最感兴趣和最容易接受的。"

2. 培养跨文化交际技能

目前语言理论界最为关心的是要提高学生的跨文化交际技能（Intercultural Competence）。迈克·拜拉姆（Michael Byram）和其他学者提倡语言教学中加强文化教学的部分。他把语言教学看成一种教育而不是教语言技能而已。巴尔德斯（Valdes）说，"教一种外语的时候不能忽略文化。"他们认为文化是语言的一部分，语言本身也带着文化成分。所以语言教师有责任把文化也教给学生，培养拥有跨文化交际技能的人才。拥有跨文化交际技能的人才就说明，一个学习外语的学生应该了解目标文化，应该尊重目标文化，这样对母文化也会有更深的理解。

对培养学生的跨文化交际技能，现当代文学作品可以发挥很重要的作用。中国素有"文以载道"的文化与教育传统。文学作品就在一个特殊的时代，一个特殊的空间写成的，所以也带着本时代的历史，社会，文化印象。现代文学开始于五四运动。"五四运动"不但在中国文学，而且在中国历史很重要。五四时期的文学主要描写当时的混乱与黑暗的社会，提出当时的青年知识分子所倡导的个人主义，科学和民主，反对传统思想的观念。我们在当时的作品中可以欣赏当时的社会面貌与中国传统文化的印象。当代文学作品更好地能给学生展示出现在的中国，就是已经现代化的，全球化的经济大国。当代作品也能给学生介绍"主流文化"就是随着中国的经济发展，市场经济影响下的"大众商业文化"。这对学生们了解今天的中国有很大的帮助。

3. 欣赏文学之美

文学作品运用的语言有书面语也有口语。经典文学作品语言审美，多用比喻修辞，拟人，形容词等手法，描写地方或人。读文学作品可以帮助学生了解到文学中的修辞手法，能欣赏文学之美。文学本来是被作家虚构的世界，所以读者可以从自己的角度去理解作品中的概念，这样文学作品看重读者。尤其是诗歌，诗歌一般隐含着深层意义，读者从中可以进行不同的解释。

二 选用文学作品的方法

确立文学作品在对外汉语教学中的作用后，主要考虑的问题是：用什么样的文学作品呢？这主要要考虑文学作品的难度和学生们的接受能力。可以用不同时代的，不同风格的作家作品组成多样的内容和形式。这样也可以充实对外汉语教学的跨文化交流内容。

选文的标准主要有两个：文学作品和学生。笔者认为要选故事性强，语言通俗，主题有趣的作品。在此基础上可选取教学内容丰富的经典作品，有反映时代特色的现当代作品，既有小说、散文、也有诗歌、话剧。文学作品众多，教师选用作品的时候有很大的责任，应该注意学生的接受能力。根据学生的汉语能力，文学知识水平，学生的兴趣，实际要求，"以学生为中心"的教学方法来选择作品。比如，为印度学生选取中国文学作品时要考虑他们会喜欢看什么样的作品，而且也要考虑他们应该看什么样的作品。笔者认为一个以中文为专业的硕士生应该对中国现代和当代文学的文学现象，文学思潮，文学理论与作家作品有基础的了解。所以应该从现当代文学的名家名篇入手。鲁迅、巴金、老舍、矛盾等现代作家的代表作品要介绍给学生们，当代的王蒙、余华、莫言和贾平凹等也不能不提。我们探讨中国妇女文学也很重要，学生要全面了解中国，也必须要了解中国社会上妇女的地位。所以文学教材也要包括女作家如丁玲、张爱玲、张洁、谌容和池莉等女作家的作品。选取作品时也考虑选能代表一个时代的作品，探讨一个重要主题的作品。所以可以选取五四时期的鲁迅，矛盾的作品，或者毛泽东时代的社会主义文学作品，或者描写经济发展给中国社会带来的是什么影响的当代文学作品。比如巴金的《家》会让学生体会到五四运动时期青年参加革命的现实，也能理解到中国的家庭观念，张洁的《方舟》描写的是一个男权主义的社会里女人对自由空间的向往，谌容的《人到中年》介绍知识分子的困境，余华的《活着》系统地描写一个农民在中国20世纪的政治变化中艰难地生活。这些作品都从不同的角度，在不同的历史环境里，在不同的程度上描绘中国社会，中国人的人生观、思维方式、道德观念、哲学思想，等等。选取文学作品时可以选长篇、短篇或中篇小说，也可以选散文、诗歌或话剧。可以选郭沫若的爱国主义诗歌，也可以选北岛、舒婷的"朦胧诗"。

笔者认为文学作品中选取小说比较合适，因为小说篇幅有长也有短的，主题很明显，故事情节强，人物描绘丰富，而且教学小说的时候也可以随手讨论小说的历史，社会，政治背景，运用的创作方法和文学思潮。"文学作品尤其是小说，因其所富有的故事性和趣味性，更容易激发留学生的阅读兴趣。有了兴趣，自然就有了克服语言障碍的决心，这是文学无法取代的优势和魅力。"

三 文学在对外教汉语中的用法：以《骆驼祥子》为例

本文已经讨论对外汉语教学中为什么要用文学作品，应该用什么样的作品做教材，应该考虑哪些因素等问题。笔者现在试想选用语言大师老舍先生的现代文学名作《骆驼祥子》进行词汇归类、语法归类，文化重点作为高级教学的素材。本文主要考虑高级学生，即硕士生的汉语水平，阅读能力，需求，选取小说的最精彩的部分，结合印度学生的学习需要进行教材准备。笔者试想用《骆驼祥子》小说的例子来指明文学作品怎样可以用来进行语言教学和文化教学。

笔者选用老舍的《骆驼祥子》主要有两个原因，第一是老舍是中国现代文学史上的一位优秀的作家，而且这部是他的代表作，讲的是20世纪30年代的北京。第二个原因是"在语言上，老舍小说是充分口语化的，这不但在于他用了大量北京地区的方言，土语，使得小说有着深厚的地方风味，而且在于他的语言非常富有表现力。"

文学作品可以帮助学生提高语言的四种能力：读，写，听，说，也可以介绍文化内容。本论下面从词汇，语法，文化，翻译这四个方面介绍文学作品在中文教材中的作用。

1. 词汇/成语

文学作品的词汇很丰富，多种多样，有的平时用，有的只有在一些具体的情况下可以用。文学作品可以帮学生提高他们的词汇。文学作品经常用文学形式的语言，用很多成语或四个词组。中国人一般说话的时候用成语，报纸上也可以看到成语。如果要提高学生的写作能力，多把握好成语很重要。下面提《骆驼祥子》中的一些例子：

一）随手儿：顺便的意思；车口：放洋车的地方；不在乎，碰巧，出风头等等。可以学这些词应该怎么用，在什么情况下用。比如'车口'这个词现在不用了。

二）成语/四字词组：年轻力壮，腿脚灵活，抄近绕远，贪嘴恶舌，与众不同，立竿见影，连车带人等。

2. 语法

文学作品中的句子可以用来解释汉语的语法。下面提几个例子：

一）什么时候……都……

"爱什么时候出车与收车都有自由。"

二）像……

"像自己的手脚的那么一辆车。"

三）非……不可……

"他对自己起下了誓，一年半的功夫，他—祥子——非打成自己的车不可！"

四）既……又……

"他似乎既是个成人，又是个孩子，非常有趣。"

五）对得起/程度补语/反问句

"跑得不快，怎么能对得起自己呢，怎么能对得起那辆车呢？"

六）越……越……

"他越想着过去便越恨那些兵们了。"

七）不但……而且……

"他不但恨那些兵，而且恨世上的一切了。"

3. 文化

文化渗入到文学之中，文学与文化不能分开而看，该放在一起解读。文学作品中的文化色彩很丰富。《骆驼祥子》中的文化内容也很丰富。比如作品里把北京写成北平，学生要知道在20世纪初的中国，北京就是北平。作品里很多地方提到一些北京特殊的食品如热烧饼夹爆羊肉，臭豆腐等，学生可以体会到中国的素食文化。文学也提到中国的三大传统节日，举办生日晚会的场面，祥子与虎妞的婚礼等都充满着文化意义。

北京在这部作品里扮演很重要的角色，老舍把北京的四个季节时的面貌描绘得很精彩，也描写北京的地点，文明古迹，都是故事的一部分。老舍的作品的故事一般都发生在北京，所以他的作品多用北京的地方语言，可以加深学生的语言能力。

除了文化部分，我们通过这本小说也可以了解到20世纪30年代的中国。当时社会混乱，政府腐败，到处乱战，在这种政治环境里，生活在底层的一个车夫没有多大希望。笔者认为教师可以用对比法来进行母文化与目的文化之间的交流。中国和印度作为亚洲国家，文化上有很多共同点，可以对比。比如印度二十世纪初很多城市也有人力车和车夫。虽然现在学生不容易相信，但是人力车在印度也是事实，而且文学和电影里也提到过像人力车夫这样的下等平民面临的艰辛生活。对待妇女这方面也可以对比印度与中国社会，也有相似性。用对比法来进行文学作品中文化的解读会激发学生的兴趣。教师可以随时提有关的思考题，让学生讨论他们对作品中提出的一些重点的看法。比如：他们怎么评价祥子不断改善自己的精神？虎妞真的是个坏女人吗？祥子最后失败的原因是什么？等。

4. 翻译

笔者认为文学作品也可以用作翻译教材。在不同的文化之间，有时候很难找到相对应的词汇，有时候同一个词语承载的文化意义不相同。虽然翻译文学作品的难度比较高，但学生更喜欢。印度是一个多语言的国家，学生一般会三种语言，母语，印地语和英语。在这种特殊的情况下，教师可以让学生把文学作品的某一段翻译成英文，也翻译成印地语。把汉语翻译成英语和印地语时可以对比翻译后的句子与原句的差别。每种语言有自己的限制性，有些词可能在目标语中找不到相对应的词，面对这种问题的时候应该把词解释清楚。比如《骆驼祥子》中"炕"这个字英语或印地语没有相对应的词，所以可以把词的含义介绍清楚，不然的话会导致误解。再举个例子，"随手儿"这个词英语有"conveniently"的意思，但在印地语可以直接翻译成"लगे हाथ"跟中文词的意思更接近。

四　结论

目前在对外汉语教学领域越来越注重文学教材的选用。文学作品不但会帮助学生提高语言能力（读写，听说），而且也会提高他们的跨文化交际技能。本文探讨现当代文学作品在对外汉语教学中的作用。教师选取作品方面应该注重文学作品的难度和趣味性，也要考虑学生的接受能力。本文用老舍的代表作品《骆驼祥子》来指明文学作品怎样可以用来教词汇，语法，文化和翻译。文学作品的运用会帮我们培养出知识全面，有语言交际能力，也有文化交际技能的优秀人才。

On the Role of Modern and Contemporary Literature in Teaching Chinese as A Foreign Language

Tanvi Negi Malla / India

Assistant Professor of Doon University

With the rise of China's economy, Chinese has become a hot language. The trend of learning Chinese has swept across India. Learning Chinese not only opens a world of opportunities for students, but it also helps them better understand our neighboring country—China. At present, at least seven or eight universities in India have formally established the department of Chinese language and literature, offering Chinese language courses. Some of these departments have proposed short-term certificate courses, but more and more universities are now beginning to offer undergraduate and master's courses. The undergraduate-master curriculum setting requires very detailed and comprehensive research. It should not only include language components, but also include culture, history, literature and translation. We must consider these questions: What kind of ability should an undergraduate or postgraduate student have after graduation? What kind of role should the student play in the society? The author believes that an undergraduate or master student majoring in Chinese should have a comprehensive understanding of China. To achieve this goal, the current undergraduate courses should not only pay attention to improving students' language skills, but it should also pay attention to culture, history and literature.

That teaching Chinese as a foreign language contains two parts – the teaching of language skills and the teaching of cultural aspects. For a teacher who teaches Indian students Chinese, what kind of textbooks should he use to inspire students' interests? The author thinks that literature, being the tool for language communication, is also a literary form with profound cultural elements, and is of great help in the process of teaching Chinese.

In the past, the language teaching theory put stress on language competence. However, for the past several decades, cultural communicative competence is playing an increasingly important role in foreign language teaching. In such a case, many scholars have returned to paying attention again to the role of literary works and literature in foreign language teaching. It is an indisputable fact that language and literature are inseparable one from the other. Many scholars (Brumfit and Carter, Duff and Maley, Lazar, Hadaway, et al) acknowledge the role of literature in language teaching, and they believe literary works are helpful in learning a language. Because literary works can put language into a real situation, allowing students to clearly understand the practical application of language. Furthermore, different literary styles go with different social phenomena, political significance, and philosophical meanings, which could be appreciated by students.[1]

I. Significance of Modern and Contemporary Literature in Teaching Chinese as a Foreign Language

Literature is a part of culture. The literary works of all times reflect the life of each era to some extent. The establishment of modern and contemporary literature courses and learning modern and contemporary literary works are also important channels for better understanding and mastering the Chinese culture while

---

[1] Babaee, Yahya. Significance of Literature in Foreign Language Teaching.

improving overseas students' level of the Chinese language.[1]

The author believes that for students who take Chinese as a foreign language, they can appreciate more about the beauty of Chinese literary language and learn more about the new era and new trends of thought through the study of literature courses. Modern and contemporary Chinese literary works can help students to understand today's China, especially the hardships and vicissitudes that have taken place in modern China during the past century, and how it has changed from a traditional society to a modern one. Modern and contemporary literary works have the following functions in teaching Chinese as a foreign language:

1. The improvement of language skills

Scholars consider that the primary purpose of learning foreign languages is to enhance communicative competence in the language. "One of the main purposes for overseas students learning Chinese is to 'use' it."[2] "After all, teaching overseas students Chinese as a foreign language takes language teaching as the main body, and even the cultural courses could not completely break away from the basis of language teaching."[3] I agree with this opinion. For an Indian student learning Chinese, the most important thing is to improve one's proficiency in the Chinese language.. And to achieve this goal, the author believes that the most appropriate textbooks should be modern and contemporary literature. This is because these works are characterized by a simple language and filled with the color of culture; they describe a modern and contemporary China. "From a linguistic point of view, the language of contemporary literature is the most lively and most used, and it is also the most interesting and acceptable language for foreign students."[4]

---

1 Li Li. Contemporary Literature and Cultural Teaching of Chinese as a Foreign Language.
2 Wang Hai. Reading Chinese Literature or Reading China - Also on the Cross-cultural Theme Reading Method in Teaching Chinese as a Foreign Language.
3 Li Li. Contemporary Literature and Cultural Teaching of Chinese as a Foreign Language.
4 Li Li. Contemporary Literature and Cultural Teaching of Chinese as a Foreign Language.

2. The cultivation of intercultural competence

What concerns language theoretical circles the most right now is to enhance the students' intercultural competence. Michael Byram and other scholars advocate strengthening the role of cultural teaching in language teaching. He sees language teaching as a kind of education instead of merely teaching language skills. Valdes said, "When teaching a foreign language, the culture shouldn't be neglected." They think that culture is a part of language, and language itself carries cultural elements. Therefore, language teachers have the responsibility to teach students culture as well, so as to cultivate talents with intercultural competence. This emphasizes the fact that a student who learns a foreign language should understand the target (language) culture, and should respect the target culture. In this way, the mother (language) culture will also receive a deeper understanding.

Modern and contemporary literary works can play an important role in cultivating students' intercultural competence. "China has always had a cultural and educational tradition of 'morals expressed in words'."[1] Literary works are written in a special era and space, so they also bear the historical, social, and cultural impressions of that era. Modern literature began with the May Fourth Movement, which is not only important for Chinese literature but also for Chinese history. The literature in the period of the May Fourth Movement mainly describes the chaotic and dark society at that time, and proposes individualism, science and democracy advocated by young intellectuals then, opposing the concept of traditional thought. We can appreciate the social image of the time and the impression of traditional Chinese culture in the works of that time. Contemporary literary works can better show students the present China, namely the modernized and globalized economic giant. Contemporary works can also introduce students to "mainstream culture", i.e., the "mass business culture" under the influence of a market economy with the economic development of China, which is very helpful for students in understanding today's

---

[1] Wang Hai. Reading Chinese Literature or Reading China: Also on the Cross-cultural Theme Reading Method in Teaching Chinese as a Foreign Language.

China.

3. An appreciation of literary beauty

The language used in literary works is both written and spoken. The language aesthetics of classical literary works mostly uses metaphors, rhetoric, personification, adjectives and other techniques to describe places or people. Reading literary works can help students understand the rhetorical devices in literature and appreciate the beauty of literature. Literature is originally a fictional world created by writers, so readers can understand the concepts in the works from their own perspectives. Such literary works also value readers. Especially the poetry, which generally contains deep implications, so readers can make different interpretations according to their own experience.

II. Methods for the Selection of Literary Works

After determining the role of literary works in teaching Chinese as a foreign language, the next major question is: What literary works should be used? This decision depends mainly on considering the difficulty of literary works and the receptivity of students. It will be acceptable to use the writers' works of different eras and styles to form a variety of content and forms, which will also enrich the content of cross-cultural communication for teaching Chinese as a foreign language.

There are two main criteria for the selection of texts: literary works and students. The author believes that it is necessary to select works with strong stories, popular language, and interesting themes. On this basis, classical works with a rich teaching content can be selected, modern and contemporary works reflecting the characteristics of times can also be chosen, including novels, prose, poetry, drama, etc. There are so many literary works, which is why teachers have a great responsibility when choosing them, and they should pay attention to students' receptivity. They should select the works with the "student-centered" teaching methods according to the students' Chinese language proficiency, their level of literary knowledge, their interests, and what they actually need. For instance, when selecting Chinese literary works for Indian students, what kind of works they like and what kind of works they should read need to be considered. The author believes that a master student majoring in Chinese should have a basic understanding of the literary phenomena, literary trends, literary theories, writers and their works of modern and contemporary Chinese literature. Therefore, we should start with the famous masterpieces of modern and contemporary literature. Representative works of modern writers such as Lu Xun, Ba Jin, Lao She, and Mao Dun can be introduced to students, and contemporary writers like Wang Meng, Yu Hua, Mo Yan, and Jia Pingwa must also appear on the list. In addition, it is also important to explore Chinese women's literature. If the students intend to fully understand China, they must know the status of women in Chinese society. Therefore, literary textbooks should also include works by female writers such as Ding Ling, Zhang Ailing, Zhang Jie, Chen Rong, Chi Li, and so on. The choice of works should consider the ones that best represent an era and that discuss an important topic. Therefore, we can choose the works of Lu Xun and Mao Dun in the May Fourth period, or the socialist literary works in the Mao (Zedong) era, or the contemporary literary works that describe what kind of influence has been brought to Chinese society by economic development. For example, the *Home* by Ba Jin enables students to experience the reality of youth participating in the revolution during the May Fourth Movement, helping them understand the concept of family in China; the *Ark* by Zhang Jie describes the yearning of women for freedom in a male-dominated society; the *Men of A Certain Age* by Chen Rong introduces the plight of intellectuals; and the *To Live* by Yu Hua systematically describes a peasant's difficult life in the political changes of China in the 20th century. These works depict the Chinese society, Chinese people's outlook on life, their ways of thinking, moral concepts, philosophical thoughts, etc. from different perspectives, in different historical contexts, and to varying degrees. When selecting literary works, it is acceptable to choose long stories, short stories, or novelettes, or you may choose essays, poems or plays; patriotic poems by Guo Moruo could be selected, and you can also choose the "misty poetry" by Bei Dao and Shu Ting.

The author believes that selecting novels from literary works is more appropriate, as novels are usually short or long, and the subject is obvious, with a strong plot and abundant character depictions.. Moreover, the historical, social and political background of the novel could be discussed at any time during the process of teaching, as well as the applied creative methods and literary ideological trends. "Literary works, especially novels, are more likely to inspire overseas students' interests in reading because of their rich history and interesting contents. Regarding interest, there is naturally a determination to overcome language barriers, which is an advantage and charm that only literature has."[1]

III. Using Literature in Teaching Chinese as a Foreign Language: a Case Study of the *Rickshaw Boy*

The paper has discussed why literary works should be used in teaching Chinese as a foreign language, what kind of works should be used as teaching materials, and what factors should be considered. The author now chooses the *Rickshaw Boy*, a modern literary masterpiece by the language master Lao She, for vocabulary and grammar classification, with culture being the material for advanced teaching. This article mainly considers an advanced level of Chinese, reading ability and needs of students, that is, the master students, and selects the most exciting part of the novel, making preparations for the teaching materials in combination with the learning needs of Indian students. The author's objective is to try to indicate how literary works can be used for language teaching and cultural teaching with the example of the novel *Rickshaw Boy*.

There are two main reasons for the author to select the *Rickshaw Boy* by Lao She. First, Lao She is an excellent writer on the history of modern Chinese literature. The *Rickshaw Boy* is his masterpiece, and its setting is Beijing in the 1930s. Second, "In the language, Lao She's novels are fully colloquial, which is not

---

1 Li Li. Contemporary Literature and Cultural Teaching of Chinese as a Foreign Language.

only because he used a large number of dialects and local languages of the Beijing area, endowing the novel with a deep local flavor, but also because his language is very expressive."[1]

Literary works can help students improve the four language abilities: reading, writing, listening, and speaking. They can also introduce cultural contents to students. This paper is going to introduce the role of literary works in Chinese textbooks from the four aspects of vocabulary, grammar, culture, and translation.

1. Vocabulary/Idiom

The vocabulary of literary works is extremely rich and varied. Some words are used at ordinary times, while some are only used in specific situations. Literary works can help students improve their vocabulary, and they often use words of literary forms, using many idioms or four-character words. Chinese people generally use idioms when they speak, and idioms can also be seen in newspapers. If you want to improve a student's writing skills, it is very important to teach him to use idioms properly. The following are some examples from the *Rickshaw Boy*:

i) 随手儿: meaning conveniently; 车口: place where the rickshaw is put; 不在乎 (indifferent to), 碰巧 (by coincidence), 出风头 (push oneself forward), etc. Students can learn how these words are used and under what circumstances. For example, the word " 车口 " is no longer used now.

ii) Idioms/Four-character words: 年轻力壮 (young and strong), 腿脚灵活 (flexible and swift), 抄近绕远 (to take a shortcut or make a detour), 贪嘴恶舌 (garrulous and mean), 与众不同 (out of the ordinary), 立竿见影 (get instant results), 连车带人 (take away together), etc.

2. Grammar

Sentences in literary works can be used for the explanation of grammar. Here are

---

1 Zhou Siyuan. Outline of the History of 20th Century Chinese Literature, p.246.

some examples:

i) 什么时候…都… (Whenever...)

"I would like to start working whenever I like."

ii) 像… (Like...)

"A rickshaw like my own hands and feet."

iii) 非…不可… (Must…)

"He took an oath to himself. After a year and a half of work, he - Xiangzi – must have his own car!"

iv) 既…又… (Both... and...)

"He seemed to be both an adult and a child. It's very interesting."

v) 对得起 (Not let yourself down)/Degree complement/Rhetorical question

"How can you not let yourself down if you don't work hard? How will you be worthy of owning that rickshaw?"

vi) 越…越… (The more... the more...)

"The more he thought about the past, the more he hated those soldiers."

vii) 不但…而且… (Not only… but also...)

"He not only hated those soldiers but he also hated everything in the world."

3. Culture

Literature is permeated with culture, and the two cannot be viewed separately; instead, they should be interpreted together. The cultural colors in literary works are very rich. Like the *Rickshaw Boy*, it is also rich in cultural content. For example, in the story, Beijing was written as Peiping. To understand this, students need to know that in the early 20th century in China, Beijing was actually referred to Peiping. Besides, some of Beijing's special foods such as mutton in baked sesame-seed cake, stinky tofu, etc. were mentioned in many parts of the story, from which the students can find out about Chinese vegetarian culture. The novel also mentions the three major traditional festivals in China. The scene of hosting a birthday party, the wedding ceremony of Xiangzi and Huniu, and other scenes are all full of cultural significance.

Beijing plays an important role in this work. Lao She described a brilliant picture of Beijing in all four of the seasons, and he also described the locations and civilization and historical sites of Beijing, which were parts of the story. Because the stories in Lao She's works are generally set in Beijing, his works mostly use the local languages of Beijing, which could deepen students' language competence.

In addition to the cultural part, we can also learn about China in the 1930s through this novel. At that time, the society was chaotic, the government was corrupt, and civil war was everywhere. In such a political environment, there was not much hope for a rickshaw puller who was living at the bottom of society. The author thinks that teachers can use the comparing and contrasting method to achieve communication between the students' mother culture and the target culture. As Asian countries, China and India have many common grounds in culture that can be compared. For example, in the early 20th century, many cities in India also had rickshaws and rickshaw pullers. Although students now are less likely to believe it, the rickshaw is also a fact in India, and literature and movies have also encountered a hard life faced by inferior civilians such as rickshaw pullers. With respect to the attitude towards women, the Indian and Chinese society could also be compared to each other as they have some similarities. Applying the comparing and contrasting method to interpret cultures in literary works will inspire students' interests. Teachers can put forward relevant thinking questions at any time and ask students to discuss their views on some of the key points raised in the work. For example: How do they evaluate Xiangzi's spirit of continuously improving himself? Is Huniu really a bad woman? What was the reason for Xiangzi's final failure? And so on.

4. Translation

The author believes that literary works can also be used as translation texts. Sometimes it is very difficult to find the actual corresponding vocabulary between two different cultures, and sometimes the same word carries a different cultural meaning according to the culture it is used in. Although it is more difficult to translate literary works, students prefer it. India is a multilingual country, and each student usually speaks three languages: his/her mother tongue, Hindi and English. Under this special condition, teachers can request students to translate a certain piece of Chinese literary works into English and Hindi. During the translation, students can compare the difference between the translated sentences and the original ones. Every language has its own limitations, and some words may not find corresponding words in the target language. In such a case, the words should be clearly explained. For example, the word "炕 (a heatable brick bed in Northern China)" in the *Rickshaw Boy* does not have a corresponding word in English or Hindi. Therefore, it requires a clear explanation of the meaning of the word, otherwise it will lead to misunderstandings. For another example, the word "随手儿" has the meaning of "conveniently" in English, but it can be directly translated into "लगे हाथ" in Hindi, which is more similar to the meaning of the Chinese word.

IV. Conclusion

At present, in the field of teaching Chinese as a foreign language, more and more attention is being paid to the selection of literary texts. Literary works not only help students improve their language ability (reading, writing, listening, and speaking), but also enhance their intercultural competence. This paper explored the role of modern and contemporary literary works in teaching Chinese as a foreign language. When selecting works as texts, teachers should focus on the difficulty and interesting content of the literary works, as well as considering the receptivity of students. Taking Lao She's representative work *Rickshaw Boy* as an example, the paper illustrated how literary works can be used to teach vocabulary, grammar, culture and translation. Applying literary works to the teaching of Chinese as a foreign language can help us develop talents with comprehensive knowledge, communicative competence, as well as cultural communication skills.

对词块教学法中文化教学问题的思考
——以西班牙大学为例

赵婧萱 【西班牙】
西班牙格拉纳达大学教师

一 引言

欧洲对外汉语教学的兴趣产生于16世纪，来自西班牙的德拉达（1533—1578）以及万方济各（1627—1678）等传教士。可以说，最早的欧洲汉语学家是西班牙人。但是，因为历史、经济、政治方面的各种因素和原因，西班牙没能够保持住对外汉语教学的先锋位置。最近十几年，想学习汉语的西班牙学生愈来愈多，但是最常用的对外汉语教学法，即综合教学法，已不能满足他们的学习要求。

近两年，西班牙格拉纳达大学通过实验词块教学法提高对外汉语教学水平，成果显著。但是，研究还没完成，我们还有一些地方需要完善，如中国文化的教学。本学校翻译系、现代语言与文化系都有汉语专业。选择汉语专业的学生，除了汉语课还有中国概论课、中国哲学课、中国历史课、中国艺术课、中国古代和当代文学课等；这些课的内容都属于所谓大文化知识，而小文化只能通过汉语语言课来学习。但是汉语语言课一个星期只有四节课，时间很有限，所以如何让学生在上语言课的过程中理解中国的小文化点是一个相对紧迫的问题。本报告的目标就是从格拉纳达大学使用的词块儿教学方法的角度来看如何通过汉语语言课解释小文化。

二 词块教学法

1. 原始的词块教学法理论

所谓古典交际教学法是在20世纪70年代出现的，到90年代语言教育已经比较普及。那时教学法家注意到，交际教学法实际上无法满足学生通过语言交流的要求。那时的古典交际教学法正面临危机，危机的出现也促成了新理论的诞生，如道格玛教学法、后方法、词块教学法等新的教学方法。这些都属于所谓的当代交际教学法。

原始的词汇词块教学法理论的创始人是英国语言学家迈克尔·刘易斯。他的理论受到了不少专家和其他理论的影响，最明显的有弗恩的固定搭配和有限语言理论、辛克莱的料库语言学理论、鲍莱和西德尔的认知语言学词语块儿理论、施密特的注意推测、克拉申的自然教学法、威多森的教育交际教学法等。

词汇词块教学法的主要理论是：词汇是语言的核心，而不是语法。原始的词汇词块儿教学法的主要内容可以这么总结：

- 词汇是语言中最重要的因素，语法的重要性不能与词汇相提并论。
- 学习语言就要认出并背诵语法词块儿；只有这样学生才能达到一定的准确度和流利度。
- 课文、词汇、词汇环境是学习语言的主要单位。
- 学生要习得词汇，不能仅仅是学习词汇。
- 语言输入最好要是口头的、自然的。

对刘易斯来说，学习语言必须从注意词块或固定搭配开始。之后，通过在文本中再现上述内容，学生会自己发现并决定那些词可以一起用。刘易斯把这种教法叫作教育词块法（pedagogical chunking）。因为最常用的词汇搭配也是最常出现的，老师不需要告诉学生答案，养成观察及分析语言的习惯，然后自己决定哪些词可以形成固定搭配。

2. 原始词块教学法的发展

虽然词块教学法的发展比不上任务教学法等比较有名的教学法，刘易斯的理论也对外国的诸多专家有所启发。在西班牙格拉纳达大学的汉语课上，我们设计了一种以当代词块教学法为基础的具体教学法。本设计不仅包括原始词块教学法的理论，也包括当代词块儿学家的理论和建议。格拉纳达大学教学法的要点如下：

1. 词块是语言的基本单位。词块一般是以一起出现的词构成，如固定搭配等。

2. 词块同样也是学习语言的主要单位。最主要的词块儿有两种：第一，是生活中学生最可能要碰到的词块；第二，书上、课堂的材料中最常出现的词块。老师的任务之一是注意维持教材中真正的和改变的输入间的平衡。

3. 这一方法必须做到提前预习课文；面对新的课文学生要提前对新的词块有一定的熟悉程度。

4. 举例和提问题是课堂学习的重要方法。老师要通过这两个策略吸引学生的注意力。

5. 本教学法拒绝所谓演示，操练，成果的 3P（presentation, practice, production）教学法，而要用观察，假设，实验（observation, hypothesis, experimentation）教学法，让学生注意汉字结构、生词含义和用法以及语法规律。学生首先要注意语言的意思、形式、声音，通过自动化练习来练习语言，最后做自由表达练习。学习周期的最后一步是语言重复、语言回收和语言程序回收。

6. 词块儿教学法可以应用于所有的教材，但老师需仔细分析课本的内容。因为每一课的练习要涉及并平衡所有方面的锻炼。不能满足上述要求，老师则要自己准备补充材料。

7. 老师和学生在这一过程都"各司其职"。他们应该互相尊重，承认学习一门语言需要付出努力，不是一蹴而就的。学生的任务就是努力学习，老师的任务则是帮助学生学有成效。

8. 教学过程有六个步骤：第一，了解意思；第二，看口头和书面例子，例子必须有语境；第三，语音练习；第四，观察语言的特点和组合方式；第五，使用语言做练习；第六，经过一段时间之后，在不同的语言情况下再次重复第一至第五步骤。

本教学法已经过三个学期的实践，但由于还处于研究过程中，因而有些部分还需完善，如文化教学部分。考虑词块教学法如何面对文化教学首先要明确什么叫文化，再者要分析格拉纳达大学使用的教材涉及文化、如何教授这部分文化。特别是对于大学一年级的学生，因为他们一般对中国文化没有任何概念，所以疑问也相对多一些。

三 语言与文化的关系

按联合国教科文组织1998年斯德哥尔摩会议报告，"从最广泛的意义讲，文化现在可以看成是一个由社会或社会集团的精神、物质、理智和感情等特点构成的综合整体，它不仅包括艺术和文学，也包括生活方式、人类的基本权利、价值体系、传统和信仰……"也就是说，文化不仅包括历史、文学、建筑等比较具体的方面，同样也包括迷信、礼仪、颜面等抽象和不易描述的因素。第一组一般被称为大文化，第二组则是小文化。

在课堂上，怎么让学生理解这些比较抽象的文化概念是最难的，原因有二：第一，小文化的话题课本上很少会出现，出现的话练习当中也不会涉及。第二，这些因素都和个人的经验密切相关，很难掌握。举个例子来讲，课堂上老师讲"面子"是什么，学生可以明白也可以记住，但是不一定真正明白"丢面子"的含义，只有真正在生活中体会到才能理解。但在实际生活中，应用小文化因素远比大文化重要。因为使用频率高，所以出错的可能性大，误用的后果也更明显。再举个例子：如果一个学生说话时有语法错误或者发音不正确，对方还勉强可以明白他的意思；可是如果学生按西班牙的习惯在告别之前跟朋友一遍遍地说"再见"，他的中国朋友会觉得很奇怪；反过来，如果他的一个中国朋友走之前只说一句"我先走了"，学生会觉得他的中国朋友生气了。

每个人所处的文化环境像一副眼镜，我们通过我们文化的眼镜解释我们的世界。这副眼镜是不能摘掉的，因为它们帮我们"解读"背景、分析在自己的文化中什么是对的，什么是错的、怎么跟别人交流等。想学会别的文化首先要摘掉自己文化的眼镜。只有从客观角度看自己和对方的文化才能真实地找得到跨文化的视域。所谓跨文化可以说是一种"向不同文化学习"的态度，通过文化协作和文化交换获得经验交流。可是，在了解别的文化之前要了解自己的文化，只有这样才可以更深刻地明白每一种文化的特色、接受每一种文化的不同并承认在描述自己和对方的文化因素时不能用"对"和"错"的概念，世界上的文化只有不同没有对错。

课上，为了帮学生学会如何摘掉自己的"文化眼镜"，老师会准备一些简单的文化比较练习，通过照片、视频等帮学生考虑自己文化和对方文化的区别和共同点。比如，在中国可以用拇指和小指表达"六"的意思，但是同样的手势在西班牙是"我给你打电话"的意思；再举个例子，过生日时，西班牙人和中国人过生日时会请朋友吃饭，但是在西班牙朋友不会让过生日的人请客，中国过生日的人一定会请朋友们一顿饭。再比如颜色的意思也有区别：西班牙的葬礼颜色是黑色的，但在中国是白色的。这样的例子很多，最重要的是谈这些话题的时候老师要引导学生首先和自己的文化比较，这样对学生来说会更容易发现自身文化和对方文化的意义。

1. 从词块教学法看《新实用汉语》文化知识

格拉纳达大学翻译系和当代语言系的大一学生用的教材是《新实用汉语》。这本书每一单元都有一个叫"文化知识"的文化模块。"文化知识"中会谈论各种各样的题目，包括中国普通话、中国古代词典、简体字和繁体字的历史和区别、京剧、中药等。这些题目很有趣，也会引发学生的好奇心，但是对学生的小文化知识帮助不是很大，尽管课文里面学生要处理遇到的这些小文化的问题。

"举例"是老师的"得力助手"，所以，我们通过具体的例子来分析如何在《新实用汉语》这本书可以用词块教学法讲小文化。

第二课的对话中的一个人物在跟别人打招呼时说的是"你忙吗"。但西班牙文化中没有这样打招呼的方式，甚至可以说西班牙人很少问别人这样的问题。由于课本上没有什么解释，所以学生在遇到这句话时会百思不得其解。为了避免学生不理解，讲生词时老师会顺便讲其他的在西班牙语中不存在的打招呼词块，如"吃饭了吗？"等，这样学生的语境会逐渐丰富，也会帮助他们思考中国和西班牙打招呼方式的异同。

第四课也有一个类似的例子。课文里面有"您贵姓"和"你姓什么"，这是两个询问个人信息的不同问法。西班牙文化和中国文化在询问他人姓名时礼貌程度很相似，学生可以很容易发现这两句话用法的区别在于正式的程度。但即使相似，也不能说两种文化在所有的情况下都可以互换，注意帮学生区分文化之间的差异。在第四课，老师可以准备一些角色扮演游戏，通过扮演不同年龄和社会地位的人，学生不仅要学会如何询问不同人的个人信息，而且要了解和中国人交流，注意社会等级有多重要。

第六课也有两个例子：第一篇课文是学习如何邀请别人参加活动。中国和西班牙人在邀请别人时正式程度也很类似，问题是，课文的对话里一个学生给自己的老师打电话邀请他去打球。中国学生和他们老师的关系比西班牙的要紧密得多，西班牙学生一般没有老师的电话号码，下课后老师和学生也没有任何联系，所以西班牙学生很难理解课文中的学生如何能邀请老师出去。老师在带学生学习课文前可以先给学生解释中国和西班牙大学生活的区别，用图片或视频向他们展示中国校园的生活和活动。在熟悉情况后，学生可以放心地阅读课文，并能在课文中找到与"邀请"有关的词块儿进行语言练习。

第二个例子也和业余活动有关：课文里的两个学生在谈京剧。虽然京剧在中国文化的重要性无可厚非，但中国年轻人很少去看京剧，所以课文的选材角度不太实际。阅读课文时，西班牙学生会感到很意外，因为在西班牙也有类似京剧的表演形式，但是习惯看这样表演的一般都是老人，所以他们会觉得中国年轻人的爱好很奇怪。其实，这种情况可以避免，用同样的课文，老师可以把京剧换成某个流行的电视节目或某个明星歌手的音乐会，这样西班牙学生在学习课文时就不会觉得奇怪，会把注意力更多地放到语法和词汇点上。学完课文之后，如果有机会，老师可以对京剧文化做讲解和补充。

综上，我们提到的例子都是可改善的设计点，但是教材中也有直接可以用的课文。比如，在第九课的课文中一个留学生和一个中国学生在准备一个朋友的生日晚会，他们很自然地谈论到中国的生日习惯，其中课文语法、词汇和文化自然串联起来，老师可以通过课文直接培养学生的文化比较意识。

相似的例子还有很多，但是上述已经足能显示出词汇教学法的文化角色和教法。

四　结论

文化教学在语言课中很重要，但是文化不仅是一系列具体准确的知识，也是交流中一项需要掌握的实用的且具有社会语言性质的知识。因此，语言课老师不能忽视小文化因素。在词块教学法的课堂上，小文化和词块有很紧密的关系，学生在学习过程中不仅要学会查找、分析语言词块儿，还要考虑这些语言词块和小文化的联系。反思、比较分析是在词块教学法中最重要的学习文化的方式。

On Culture Teaching in the Teaching Method of Word Chunks

Isabel Maria Balsas Urena / Spain

Lecturer, University of Granada

I. Introduction

The interest in Europe for teaching Chinese as a foreign language originated in the 16th century, from Spanish missionaries such as Martin De Rada (1533-1578) or Francisco Varo (1627-1678). It can be said that the earliest European Chinese linguists were Spanish. However, because of historical, economic and political factors and reasons, Spain has not been able to maintain its pioneering position in teaching Chinese as a foreign language. In recent decades, there have been more and more Spanish students wanting to learn Chinese, but the most commonly used method of teaching Chinese as a foreign language, namely the comprehensive teaching method, cannot satisfy their learning requirements.

In the past two years, the University of Granada has improved its teaching of Chinese as a foreign language through the experiment of the Lexical Chunk Approach, and impressive results have been achieved. However, the study has not yet been completed. There are still some aspects that need to be perfected, such as the teaching of Chinese culture. In our university, both the Department of Translation and the Department of Modern Languages and Culture are set up with a Chinese major. Students who choose a Chinese major will have Chinese language courses; in addition, other courses such as Introduction to China, Chinese Philosophy, Chinese History, Chinese Art, Ancient and Contemporary Chinese Literature, etc. are also included; the contents of these courses belong to the so-called big cultural knowledge, and the small cultures can only be learned through Chinese language courses. However, the Chinese language course only has four classes a week, with limited time, thus a relatively urgent problem has become how to allow students to understand small Chinese cultural points in the process of taking language classes. The aim of this report is to explain how to present small cultural elements within Chinese language classes from the perspective of the Lexical Chunk Approach used by the University of Granada.

II. Lexical Chunk Approach

1. The theory of the original Lexical Chunk Approach

The so-called classical communicative teaching method emerged in the 1970s, then in the 1990s, language education became rather popular. The experts on teaching methodology noticed that the communicative teaching method was not able to meet the students' requirements for language communication in practice. At that time, the classical communicative teaching method was facing a crisis, and the emergence of the crisis also led to the birth of new teaching theories, such as the Dogme Approach, Postmethod, and the Lexical Chunk Approach. These all belong to the so-called contemporary communicative teaching methods.

The founder of the original theory of the Lexical Chunk Approach was the British linguist Michael Lewis. His theory was influenced by many experts and other theories, with the most obvious ones being Firth's fixed collocation and limited language theory, Sinclair's corpus linguistics theory, Pawley & Syder and Nattinger & Decarrico's cognitive linguistics lexical chunk theory, Schmidt's attention speculation, Krashen's natural teaching method, Widdowson's communicative teaching method, etc.

The main theory of the vocabulary Lexical Chunk Approach is: vocabulary is the core of language, not grammar. The main contents of the original vocabulary Lexical Chunk Approach can be summarized as follows:

- Vocabulary is the most important factor in a language, and the importance of grammar is not comparable to vocabulary.
- Learning a language requires recognizing and memorizing grammatical lexical chunks; only in this way can students achieve a certain degree of accuracy and fluency.
- Text, vocabulary and vocabulary environment are the main units for language learning.
- Students must acquire vocabulary, not just learn vocabulary.
- The best is that language input should be verbal and natural.

According to Lewis, the process of language learning must begin with the attention to lexical chunks or fixed collocations. Later, by reproducing the above content in the text, students will find out by themselves and decide which words can be used together. Lewis referred to this teaching method as pedagogical chunking. Because the most common vocabulary collocations are also the ones that are most often encountered, teachers do not need to tell students the answers, allowing them to develop the habit of observing and analyzing language, and then learning by themselves which words can form fixed collocations.

2. Development of the original Lexical Chunk Approach

Although the development of the Lexical Chunk Approach is not comparable to the famous teaching methods such as the Task-based Approach, Lewis' theory also inspired many foreign experts. In the Chinese class at the University of Granada, we designed a specific teaching method based on the contemporary Lexical Chunk Approach. The design includes not only the theory of the original Lexical Chunk

Approach, but it also includes theories and recommendations of contemporary lexical chunk experts. The key points of the teaching method at the University of Granada are as follows:

1. The lexical chunk is the basic unit of a language. Lexical chunks usually appear in combination, such as fixed collocations and so on.

2. The lexical chunk is also the main unit for language learning. There are mainly two types of lexical chunks: first, the lexical chunks most frequently encountered by students in their daily lives; second, the lexical chunks most commonly used in books and classroom materials. One of the teacher's tasks is to try to maintain the balance between real language input and changed input in the textbook.

3. For this method, students must view the text in advance; when learning a new lesson, students should familiarize themselves with new words in advance.

4. Giving examples and questions are important ways of learning in a class. Teachers must use these two strategies to attract the students' attention.

5. The so-called 3P (presentation, practice, and production) teaching methods are rejected; instead, there is a need for using observations, hypotheses, and experimentations to make students pay attention to the structure of Chinese characters, the meaning and usage of new words, and grammatical rules. Students should first pay attention to the meaning, form, and sound of the language, practice the language through mnemonic exercises, and finally perform activities using free expression. The final step for the learning cycle is language repetition, language recovery, and recovery of the language program.

6. The Lexical Chunk Approach can be applied to all teaching materials, but the teacher should carefully analyze the content of the textbook, because exercises in each lesson should involve and balance all aspects of training. If the textbook does not meet the above requirements, the teacher will have to prepare supplementary materials by himself/herself.

7. Both teachers and students should "perform their own functions" in this process. They should respect each other and acknowledge that learning a language requires effort, and it cannot be accomplished in one step. The mission for students is to study hard, while the mission for teachers is to help students learn effectively.

8. There are six steps in the teaching process: first, to understand the meaning; second, to analyze verbal and written examples, and the examples must be considered in contexts; third, the phonetic exercise; fourth, to observe the characteristics and combination patterns of the language; fifth, to use the language to practice; and sixth, to repeat the steps from the first one to the fifth one again in different language situations after a period of time.

This teaching method was practiced for three semesters, but as it is still in the process of research, some parts still need to be perfected, such as the cultural teaching part. When considering how the Lexical Chunk Approach confronts the teaching of culture, the first necessary step is to clarify what culture is. Then it is necessary to analyze the culture involved in the materials used by the University of Granada as well as how to teach culture. Especially for first-year university students, as they generally have no concept of the Chinese culture, they would have quite a few more questions.

III. The Relationship between Language and Culture

According to the report of the UNESCO Stockholm Conference in 1998, "in the broadest sense, culture can now be seen as a comprehensive whole consisting of the spiritual, material, intellectual, and emotional characteristics of a society or social group. It includes not only art and literature, but also lifestyles, basic human rights, value systems, traditions and beliefs...". In other words, culture includes not only specific aspects such as history, literature, and architecture, but also abstract and non-descriptive factors such as superstition, etiquette, and decency. The first group is generally called big culture, and the second group is called small culture.

In a class, the most difficult part lies in how to make students understand these abstract cultural concepts; there are two reasons: first, the topic of small cultures in textbooks rarely appears. Even if it does appear, it will not be involved in practice. Second, these factors are closely related to personal experience and are difficult to master. For example, in a class, when the teacher explains what "face" is, students can understand and remember it, but they may not necessarily understand the meaning of "losing face". Only when they experience it in life can they really understand its meaning. However, in practical life, it is more important to apply small cultural factors than big culture. Because of the high frequency of use, there is a high possibility of error and the consequences of misuse are even more obvious. Here is another example: If a student makes grammatical errors or has an incorrect pronunciation when he speaks, people can still roughly understand what he is talking about; but if the student follows his Spanish habit of saying goodbye to his friends over and over again before his farewell, his Chinese friend would feel strange; in return, if one of his Chinese friends just says "I'm leaving" for once before he left, the student would feel that his Chinese friend was angry.

The cultural environment of different people is like a pair of glasses. We explain our world through the glasses of our culture. This pair of glasses cannot be removed because it helps us "interpret" the background, analyze what is right, what is wrong, how to communicate with others, etc. in our own culture. If we want to learn other cultures, we must first remove the glasses of our own culture. Only when we view our own culture and other cultures from an objective angle can we find the cross-cultural vision. The so-called cross-culture can be said to be a kind of attitude which "learns from different cultures"; exchanges of experiences are gained through cultural collaboration and cultural exchange. However, before understanding other cultures, we must understand our own culture. Only in this way can we understand the characteristics of each culture more deeply, accept the uniqueness of each culture , and confess that we cannot use the concept of "right" and "wrong" to describe cultural factors of our own or others'. There are only different cultures in this world, not right or wrong cultures.

In a class, in order to help students learn how to remove their "cultural glasses", the teacher will prepare some simple cultural comparison exercises, helping them to consider the differences and common grounds between their own culture and other cultures through photos, videos, etc. For example, in China, the meaning of "six" can be expressed with the thumb and the little finger, but the same gesture means "I'll call you" in Spain; another example, when celebrating a birthday, both Spaniards and Chinese have meals with friends; in Spain, friends do not ask the birthday person to treat them; while in China, the birthday person treats his friends with a meal. Another example is the difference in color: Spain's funeral is black, but in China it is white. There are many other examples of this kind. The most important thing is that when discussing these topics, teachers should guide students to compare the topic with their own culture. This will make it easier for students to discover the meaning of their own culture and other cultures.

1. Analysis of the cultural knowledge in *New Practical Chinese* from the perspective of the Lexical Chunk Approach

Freshmen from the Department of Translation and the Department of Contemporary Language at the University of Granada use the *New Practical Chinese* as the textbook. Each unit of this book has a cultural module called "Cultural Knowledge". "Cultural Knowledge" requires students to discuss various topics, including Chinese Mandarin, the Chinese ancient dictionary, the history and distinction of simplified and traditional Chinese characters, Beijing Opera, traditional Chinese medicine, etc. These topics are very interesting and may also inspire students' curiosity, but they are of little help with students' small cultural knowledge, even though students have to deal with these small cultural problems encountered in the textbooks.

The technique of "giving examples" is the "helpful assistant" of the teacher. Therefore, we will analyze how to use the Lexical Chunk Approach to teach small culture in the book *New Practical Chinese* through concrete examples.

One of the characters in the conversation of Lesson 2 is greeting others with "Are you busy?", but there is no such way of greetings in Spanish culture. It can even be said that Spaniards rarely ask such questions. As there is no explanation in the textbook, students will feel puzzled when they encounter this sentence. In order to avoid the misunderstanding of students, when explaining new words, the teacher should nonchalantly introduce other greeting lexical chunks that do not exist in Spanish, such as "have you eaten?", etc., so that the students' context will be gradually enriched. They will be inspired to think about the similarities and differences between Chinese and Spanish greeting methods.

There is also a similar example in Lesson 4. The textbook contains the expression "What is your dignified last name?" and "What is your last name?", which are two different ways of asking for personal information. Spanish culture and Chinese culture are similar in their level of courtesy in asking others' names. Students can easily find that the difference between the usage of these two sentences lies in the degree of formality. However, even if they are similar, it cannot be said that the two cultures can be interchanged under all circumstances. Attention should be paid to help students distinguish among cultural differences. In Lesson 4, teachers can prepare role-playing games. By playing people of different ages and social status, students will need not only to learn how to ask different people for personal information, but also to understand the importance of social levels when communicating with the Chinese.

There are also two examples in Lesson 6: The first passage deals with learning how to invite others to participate in activities. China and Spain are similar in formality when inviting others, but the problem is that in the dialogue of the text, a student is calling his teacher to invite him to play a ball game. The relationship between Chinese students and their teachers is much closer than that in Spain. Spanish students generally do not have their teachers' telephone numbers, and there is no communication between teachers and students after class. Therefore, it is difficult for Spanish students to understand how students in the text can invite teachers to go out. Teachers can explain the difference between Chinese and Spanish university life before introducing the texts, and use pictures or videos to show them the life and activities of a Chinese campus. After familiarizing with the situation, students can read the text with confidence, and can find words related to "invitation" in the text for language practice.

The second example is also related to amateur activities: Two students in the text are talking about the Beijing Opera. Although the Beijing Opera is of great importance in Chinese culture, young Chinese people rarely watch the Beijing Opera nowadays, so the selection of materials is not practical. When reading the texts, the Spanish students may feel surprised because there are also similar performing forms in Spain, which, however, are usually watched by elderly people, then they will think that the young Chinese people's hobbies are very strange. In fact, this situation can be avoided. With the same text, the teacher can replace the Beijing Opera with a popular TV show or a concert of a star singer. In this way, Spanish students will not be surprised when reading and studying the text and will pay more attention to grammar and vocabulary. After finishing the text, if there is an opportunity, the teacher can explain the Beijing Opera culture as a supplement.

In summary, the examples mentioned here are all design points that can be improved, but there are also texts that can be used directly in the textbooks. For instance, in the text of Lesson 9, an international student and a Chinese student are preparing a birthday party for a friend, and they naturally begin to talk about the birthday habits in China. Grammar, vocabulary, and culture are naturally intertwined with each other in the text, and teachers can cultivate the students' awareness of cultural comparisons directly through the text.

There are many similar examples, but the above are plenty enough to show the cultural role and teaching method of the lexical approach.

IV. Conclusion

Cultural teaching is very important in language classes, but culture is not only a series of specific and accurate knowledge, but also a practical and social-linguistic knowledge that needs to be mastered in communication. Therefore, language teachers cannot ignore the factors of the small cultures In the class of the Lexical Chunk Approach, there is a close relationship between small culture and lexical chunks. Students must not only learn to find and analyze language lexical chunks in the learning process, but also consider the connection between these chunks and small culture. Reflection and comparative analysis are the most important ways to learn culture in the Lexical Chunk Approach.

"青年汉学家研修计划"研修成果

蔼孙那檀 【美国】
北卡罗来纳州立大学副教授

一 青年汉学家研修计划介绍

2017年9月9日至30日,我有幸参加了在中国北京举办的青年汉学家研修计划。在为期三周的学术研讨会期间,中国著名的知识分子和政界人物李国强、金灿荣、葛剑雄等作了讲座。讲座涵盖了中国历史上的很多重要话题,但主要聚焦于中国在"一带一路"上的新进展。由亚洲基础设施投资银行提供资金的"一带一路"倡议,可以被看作基础设施融资、建设项目和过去三十年间在中国内地建立的经济特区的延伸。这些项目旨在建立高铁连接、航运港口、采掘工业、科技研究和贸易中心等。"一带一路"倡议最终将通过铁路连接北京和西欧的马德里,并已开始在非洲大陆建立主要铁路项目。正如葛剑雄所强调的,这一倡议标志着中国在全球事务中从被动变为主动,苏联解体后,中国的经济崛起使其跻身全球大国行列,尤其是在东亚。"一带一路"倡议本质上是经济性的,旨在促进市场经济的发展和东南亚、中亚、中东、非洲和欧洲各民族国家间的贸易。

承担推动"一带一路"倡议的政策制定者和知识分子认识到,历史上在汉代就出现的丝绸之路这一基于陆地和海洋的贸易网络,不是由中国政策建立或管理的,因为它们运作在安德森式民族国家的范围之外,这些历史贸易模式被视为当前经济项目的一个模型。也就是说,"一带一路"倡议的依据之一是这个可以追溯到几千年前的庞大全球贸易网络,尤其是中国大陆、东南亚、中亚邻国内陆生产者间陶瓷、丝绸、香料和白银的流通。同时"一带一路"倡议强调经济发展，它们也认识到中国在世界舞台上的地位上升，因为中国肩负着维持地区稳定的任务，也在专注人工智能开发的第四次工业革命中发挥愈加重要的作用。

青年汉学家研修计划可以在许多方面被视为"一带一路"倡议的文化和学术分支，目的是让学者和文化团体熟悉中国人文和社会科学领域的状况。这个计划汇聚了众多领域的学者、青年学者、国际关系领导人，以及来自非洲、南亚、东南亚、欧洲和美洲的27个国家的思想家。这一青年汉学家研修计划标志着英语术语"汉学家"的意义发生了改变，最初它指传教者，其翻译工作的目的是劝他人改变宗教信仰，后来指研究中国古典文献学和哲学的学者，二战后则与地域研究有关。汉学在很多方面都关乎外界对中国的认识，也可能迎合各国的国家安全考量。在日本，汉学的发展在很大程度上也出于帝国利益的考量。像"一带一路"这样的项目，其中一个不言自明的目的是让中国在知识产业中发挥更积极的作用，定义生成关于中国的知识主题和术语。

我住在北京国家图书馆，是北京语言大学语言文学组的成员之一。黄卓越教授和他的中国汉学研究所的同事们另外安排了一系列关于中国语言和文明丰富历史的精彩讲座。这些讲座包括进一步说明汉学的历史和意义，全球文化交流中中国面临的挑战，以及孔子学院在促进中国语言文化教学、促进汉语研究和汉学在汉语研究资金不足或受忽视的国家教学起到的作用。我们还参观了他们最先进的翻译实验室，学生们在高级翻译学院接受翻译和口译培训。最后，东道主北京语言大学还向我们介绍了中国外文局副局长兼中国翻译研究院执行院长王刚毅。在访问中国外文局的过程中，我们看到了外文局精彩的翻译出版史，了解到他们将中国领导人的作品翻译成各国语言的辉煌历史，最近的出版物则是有关习近平思想的。

在京期间，我们应邀参加了中国文化翻译和世界研究中心承办的2017年"翻译和汉学历史"国际会议，该会议在北京国家图书馆和北京语言大学校园的西郊宾馆举办。这次国际会议有以跨国视角介绍汉学历史的学者，还有来自中国、东亚、俄罗斯、日本、韩国的杰出汉学家和汉学历史学家，以及东南亚华人。

东道主还请我们参观了江西，包括景德镇的窑炉和周围环境，让人大开眼界。在江西，我们有幸参观了许多名胜古迹，了解了当地的经济、历史和文化贡献。我们还参观了著名的道教圣地三清山、农村和簧岭的梯田。

二 研究成果

我主要的学术研究目标是对中国科幻小说历史的持续考察，以及现代中国各种媒体对科学的普及。尽管目前对中国科幻小说的研究集中在刘慈欣、韩松、陈楸帆、王瑶和郝景芳等人身上，我认为中国科幻小说的历史，不管是作为全球形式的一部分，还是社会主义现实主义历史这一特定本土的一部分，都未能充分理论化。因此，我的研究旨在扩大科幻小说的定义，从而同时涵盖 1949 年以后的中文乌托邦和科普写作。

三 研究出版

2017 年 3 月我在法国杂志《华人世界》上发表了一篇题为《新时代的科学机构和乌托邦之旅》的短文，我认为对科幻小说类型和皇室设想可能是同谋的认识以及使用该类型进行反叙事的渴望是中国科幻小说出现的前提。当中国从世界霸主沦落成一潭死水，晚清的人们寻求调停。晚清的知识分子在如何调和西化、现代化，采用外国技术与中国的认识论框架之间苦苦思索。早在对东方主义的批评流行并成为后殖民研究的基石之前，碧荷官主人的《新时代》和萧然郁生的《乌托邦游记》就隐晦地表示，东方主义曾深刻地影响 20 世纪早期的地缘政治。该短文侧重于晚清科幻小说的一个方面：在科幻小说关注"科学"的概念或关注实际的科学发现，而不是复仇幻想的时候，晚清知识分子却常常将科学描绘成博物馆、博览会、图书馆等机构，或其他用以展示国家成就的教育场所的产物。

四 正在进行的研究

2018 年的夏天，我将以学者身份做客北卡罗莱纳国家人文中心，致力于研究 1949 年后中国的公共卫生运动与大众文化之间的关系。这个研究项目的成果已经被安排在明年的《奥西里斯》杂志上发表。这个项目考查各种科普类型之间的关系，包括科学相声、科学诗、科学童话和公共卫生运动的关系。我尤其想考察流行文化在促进"灭四害"运动中所起的作用。期刊将主要考察作为全球类型之一的科幻小说，科幻小说作为一种文学模型的各种迭代之间的关系，以及更广泛层面上科学和科学教育的历史。

五 研究展示和会议

2018年5月，我在中国香港进行两场研究展示。在香港举行的这两场会议后，将会出版会议资料中关于中国科幻小说和翻译的篇章。《戴上美国人的眼镜来阅读韩松；戴上世界史的眼镜来阅读韩松》安排在2018年5月28至30日、由香港科技大学主办的题为"汉语世界的科幻小说及其变体"的会议上展示。在这次会议之后，2018年6月1日至2日我在香港中文大学主办的中国科幻小说翻译会议上发表题为《中国科幻小说翻译中的一些问题》的论文。这两个国际会议将汇聚许多杰出的作家和汉语科幻小说领域及广义实验文学领域的学者。这些会议的文件将会收录进会议资料，在之后的几个月里出版。

六 翻译成果

我翻译了一篇关于科幻小说和20世纪早期中国学者贾立元（飞氘）的科普报道的文章，已经被学术期刊《科幻小说研究》出版了。文章《追魂砂：新纪元中的时间与战争》研究了当地媒体报道中的当代科学发现如何被用作晚清中欧战争故事中的叙述手段，以及历法系统竞争如何导致这种假想中的20世纪初的冲突。我正在等待韩松三个短篇小说的翻译，李广益、王瑶（夏笳）的两篇学术文章，以及我为着眼中国科幻小说的《中国今日文学》特刊写的章节介绍，该特刊尤其关注了韩松。为了该特刊，我翻译了李广益的文章《诡异的寓言/预言——韩松科幻小说评析》和夏笳的《进化抑或轮回？——韩松科幻作品中的时空迷思》。最后，我还翻译了1980年电影《珊瑚岛上的死光》的字幕，该电影于2017年8月在纽约现代艺术博物馆作为全球科幻电影系列的一部分展出。

七 对汉学的贡献

过去的一年里，我在教学、科研和大学服务方面取得了一些成果。我曾担任过"帕尔格雷夫·麦克米伦出版社全球科幻小说"的外部评审员，并担任杰米·毕肖普科幻奖学金竞赛的中文作品评委。这个奖项已经开始吸引中文参赛选手，我也评判了半决赛的参赛作品。最后，我还参与了北卡莱罗纳州立大学亚洲研究和世界文学委员会的课程开发，并在北卡莱罗纳州立大学孔子学院咨询委员会任职。同北卡莱罗纳州立大学孔子学院一道，我正努力创建一个由南京师范大学主办的第一年调查项目。这个为期两周的年度计划，将向美国新生介绍汉学、中国历史和文学研究领域，同时也向他们介绍中国南京的丰富文化历史和地标。

2018年5月，我带领一群来自杜克大学福库商学院工商管理专业的学生，前往中国的三个城市——北京、黄山和上海，进行一次全球学术体验旅行。我们将前往一些具有重大文化和历史意义的地点，并访问上海和北京的各种企业。此次黄山之行，直接受到了精彩的青年汉学家研修项目的启发，我们将访问景德镇一天，参观景德镇陶瓷博物馆和古窑址。学生们做了大量阅读，了解了景德镇在历史上是瓷器生产中心，并在近年转变成联合国认可的世界遗产地。我希望与我的MBA学生们分享对中国丝绸之路与国际贸易的历史联系以及现代全球贸易模式与消费之间的历史联系的理解。

接下来的一年里，我希望继续开发和拓展中国语言和文化研究课程。我希望在近期出版三篇文章和四篇译文：包括上面提到的会议卷以及《奥西里斯》期刊上的一篇文章。我将继续与那些致力于推动促进国际研究和亚洲研究的北卡罗来纳州的组织和委员会合作。

Research Accomplishments of the Visiting Program for Young Sinologists

Nathaniel Isaacson / United States of America

Associate Professor of North Carolina State University

I. Introduction: Visiting Program For Young Sinologists

From September 9-30, 2017, I had the honor to attend The Visiting Program for Young Sinologists in Beijing, China. This three-week long academic seminar featured a number of lectures from prominent Chinese intellectuals and political leaders, such as Li Guoqiang, Jin Canrong, and Ge Jianxiong. These lectures covered a wide range of important topics in Chinese history, but focused particularly on China's recent advances in the One Belt, One Road Initiative. The One Belt One Road Initiative, with funding from the Asian Infrastructure Investment Bank (AIIB), can be seen as an extension of the infrastructure funding and construction projects, and special economic zones, established in Mainland China over the last thirty years. These projects aim to establish high-speed rail connections, shipping ports, extractive industries, science and technology research and trade hubs, and a number of other projects. The project will eventually connect Beijing to Madrid in Western Europe via rail, and has already begun establishment of major rail projects in the

African continent. As Ge Jianxiong emphasized, this project signifies China's move from a reactive to a proactive role in global affairs, recognizing that in the wake of the collapse of the Soviet Union, China's economic rise has put it in the position of a major global power, especially in East Asia. OBOR development projects are intended to be economic in nature, promoting development of market economies, and trade between nation-states throughout Southeast Asia, Central Asia, the Middle East, Africa, and Europe.

While the policy makers and public intellectuals tasked with promoting the project recognize that the historical Silk Routes–land based and oceanic trade networks dating as far back as the Han Dynasty–were neither managed nor established by a Sinitic polity, as they both pre-dated and largely functioned outside of the purview of an Andersonian nation-state, these historical trade patterns are seen as a model in the current economic project. That is to say, OBOR projects look to evidence of a vast network of global trade that can be dated back for millennia, especially the circulation of ceramics, silk, spices, and silver, between inland producers in Mainland China, and their neighbors in Southeast and Central Asia. At the same time as OBOR policies emphasize economic development, the also recognize a shifting position for China on the world stage as the nation is tasked with maintaining regional stability, and an increased role for the People's Republic of China in the development of a fourth industrial revolution, focused on the development of Artificial Intelligence.

The Visiting Program for Young Sinologists may in many ways be understood as a cultural and scholastic arm of this economic development project, one that aims to familiarize scholars and cultural attaches with the state of the field in Chinese Humanities and Social Sciences. The program featured academics in a number of fields, young scholars, leaders in international relations, and other thought-influencers from a total of 27 countries, from Africa, South and Southeast Asia, Europe and the Americas. The Visiting Program for Young Sinologists signals a shift in the meaning of the English term, "Sinologist". Originally referring to missionary workers whose translation projects were aimed at proselytization, later referring to scholars of classical Chinese philology and philosophy, and in the post-WWII era being tied to the concerns of area studies, Sinology has in many respects been a question of knowledge produced about China, from outside of China, and potentially to suit foreign national security concerns. In Japan as well, the history of *kangaku* (漢学) owes its development in no small part to imperial interests. A clear, if unspoken aim of programs like this one is for China to play a more active role in the knowledge industry, defining the subjects and the terms by which knowledge about the country is produced.

Housed at the Beijing National Library, I was part of the Language and Literature cohort, which was hosted by Beijing Language and Culture University. Professor Huang Zhuoyue and his colleagues in the Institute of Sinology, arranged yet another series of exciting lectures on the rich history of China's language and civilization. These lectures included further edification in the history and significance of Sinology, the challenges China faces in global cultural engagement, and the role of Confucius Institutes in promoting the teaching of Chinese language and culture and promoting the establishment and development of departments of Chinese Studies and Sinology in nations where Chinese studies has traditionally been underfunded or otherwise neglected. We were also introduced to the various support units for language training and translation that Beijing Language and Culture University is connected to. We were also treated to a tour of their state of the art translation laboratory, where students are trained in translation and interpretation at the School of Translation and Interpreting. Finally, our hosts at Beijing Language and Culture University also introduced us to Wang Gangyi, Deputy Director of China International Publishing, and Executive President of the China Academy of translation. During our visit to the offices of China International Publishing, we were treated to a fascinating display of the bureau's history of translated publication, and learned of their illustrious history translating works of China's leadership into various world languages, most recently publications concerning Xi Jinping thought.

During our stay in Beijing, we were also invited to observe the 2017 International Conference of "Translation and the History of Sinology," hosted by the Research Center for Chinese Culture Translation and Studies Worldwide, at the campus of the Beijing National Library, and the Xijiao Hotel on the Campus of Beijing Language and Culture University. This international conference featured papers on this history of sinology from a transnational perspective, and featured prominent Sinologists and historians of Sinology from China and East Asia, Russia, Japan, Korea, and the Chinese diaspora in Southeast Asia.

Our hosts also treated us to an eye-opening tour of Jiangxi, where we visited the kilns at Jingdezhen and surrounding environs. While in Jiangxi, where we had the pleasure to see a number of historical sites and to learn about local economy, history, and cultural contributions. We also visited the renowned sacred Daoist site, Mount Sanqing, and the peasant villages and rice terraces at Huangling.

II. Accomplishments in Research

The main thrust of my academic research involves a continuing examination of the history of Chinese science fiction, and popularization of science through various media in modern China. While much current research on Chinese science fiction focuses on contemporary authors like Liu Cixin, Han Song, Chen Qiufan, Wang Yao and Hao Jingfang, I argue that the history of Chinese science fiction is inadequately theorized both as part of a global form, and within the specific local context of the history of socialist realism. Thus, my research aims both to expand the definition of science fiction in a manner that accommodates Chinese-language utopian and popular science writing from 1949 onward.

III. Research Publications

I published a short article in the French journal *Monde Chinois,* which was printed in March of this year. The article, "Science as Institutional Formation in *The New Era and Journey to Utopia,*" argues that, "the emergence of science fiction in China was conditioned by an awareness of the potential complicity of the genre with the imperial imagination, and a desire to use the genre as a means of creating counter narratives. Late Qing audiences sought mediation as their nation was transformed from hegemon into a crumbling backwater. Late Qing intellectuals agonized over how to reconcile westernization, modernization, and the adoption of foreign technologies with a Chinese epistemological framework. Long before critiques of Orientalism had gained traction as a cornerstone of postcolonial studies, Biheguan Zhuren's （碧荷官主人）*The New Era* （新纪元，1908), and Xiaoran Yusheng's （萧然郁生）*Journey to Utopia* (乌托邦游记，1906), expressed an implicit understanding that Orientalism profoundly conditioned early 20th century geopolitics." The paper focuses on a a particular aspect of late Qing science fiction: insofar as SF addressed notions of "science," or was focused on practical scientific discoveries, rather than revanchist fantasy, it was often the case that late Qing intellectuals depicted science as the product of institutional formations like museums, expositions, libraries, and other educational venues dedicated to displaying national achievements.

IV. Ongoing Research

During the summer of 2018, I will be a scholar in residence at the National Humanities Center, in North Carolina, working on a project investigating the relationship between public health campaigns and popular culture in post-1949 China. This research project has already been slated for publication in the journal *Osiris* in the coming year. This project examines the relationship between various popular science genres – among them the *kexue xiangsheng* (科学相声)*, kexue shi* (科学诗), and *kexue tonghua* (科学童话) – and public health campaigns. In particular, I intend to examine the role that popular culture played in promoting the campaign to "eliminate the four pests." The journal issue in general will be an examination of science fiction as a global genre, and the relationship between various iterations of SF as a literary mode, and the history of science and scientific education more broadly.

V. Presentations and Research Conferences

May, 2018, I will give two research presentations in Hong Kong China. The two conferences in Hong Kong will lead to publication of chapters in conference volumes on Chinese science fiction and translation. "Viewing Han Song through an American Lens; Viewing Han Song Through the Lens of World History", at a conference titled "Science Fiction and Its Variations in the Sinophone World," hosted by Hong Kong University of Science and Technology, on May 28-30, 2018. Following this conference, I will deliver a paper entitled, "Some Issues in Translating Chinese Science Fiction" at the Conference on Chinese Science Fiction Translation, hosted by the Chinese University of Hong Kong on June 1-2, 2018. Both of these international conferences will feature a number of prominent authors and academics working on the field of Sinophone Science Fiction, and experimental literature more broadly. The papers presented at each of these conferences will be collected into conference volumes for publication in the months to follow.

VI. Accomplishments in Translation

My translation of an article on science fiction and early 20th century science reportage in the popular press by Chinese scholar Jia Liyuan (Fei Dao) has been printed by the academic journal *Science Fiction Studies*. The article, *"Soul-stealing Sand": War and Time in Xin jiyuan [The New Era],"* examines the ways in which contemporary scientific discoveries, reported in local newspapers, were incorporated as narrative devices in a late Qing dynasty story of war between China and Europe, and also examines the role that various competing calendrical systems play in leading to this imagined early-20th century conflict. I am currently awaiting publication of the translations of three short stories by author Han Song, and two scholarly articles by Li Guangyi and Wang Yao (Xia Jia 夏笳), as well as section introductions I myself wrote for a special issue of *Chinese Literature Today* on Chinese science fiction, with a particular focus on Han Song. For this special issue, I translated Li Guangyi's article. "Eerie Parables and Prophecies – An Analysis of Han Song's Science Fiction" and Xia Jia's piece, "Evolution or Samsara? Spatio-temporal Myth in Han Song's Science Fiction". Finally, I also translated the subtitles for a screening of the 1980 film, "Death Ray on a Coral Island", which was shown at the Museum of Modern Art (MOMA), NYC in August of 2017 as part of a series on global science fiction cinema.

VII. Service to the Field of Sinology

Over the past year, I have made a number of accomplishments in teaching, research and university service. I served as an outside reviewer for a volume on global science fiction for Palgrave Macmillan Press, and as a judge for Chinese-language entries in the Jamie Bishop Science Fiction Scholarship Award contest. This award has begun to attract Chinese-language entrants, and I judged the semi-final round of essay submissions. Finally, I have been engaged in development of curriculum with the NCSU Asian Studies and World Literature Committees, and served on the advisory board of the NCSU Confucius Institute. In conjunction with the NCSU Confucius Institute, I am working to create a First-Year-Inquiry program to be hosted by Nanjing Normal University. This two-week annual program, will introduce American freshmen to the field of Sinology and Chinese historical and literary studies, while also introducing them to the rich cultural history and landmarks of Nanjing, China.

In May of 2018, I will lead a group of MBA students from Duke University's Fuqua School of business on a Global Academic Travel Experience (GATE) trip to three cities in the People's Republic of China – Beijing, Huangshan, and Shanghai. This trip will include visits to a number of sites of cultural and historic significance, as well as visits to various businesses in Shanghai and Beijing. The trip to Huangshan, directly inspired by my wonderful experience with the Young Sinologists program, will feature a day trip to the city of Jingdezhen to visit the Jingdezhen Ceramics Museum, and historical kiln cites. Students have done extensive reading in the history of Jingdezhen as a center of porcelain production and its transformation in recent years to a UN-recognized world heritage site. It is my hope to share the experience of understanding the historical connections between China's Silk Road and international trade and modern patterns of global trade and consumption with my MBA students.

In the coming year, I hope to continue development and expansion of Chinese language and cultural studies course offerings. I expect three articles and four translations to move towards publication in the coming year: the above-mentioned conference volumes and an article in *Osiris*. I will continue to work with those organizations and committees at NC State that are dedicated to developing and promoting International Studies and Asian Studies.

经验、记忆与写作的叙事：马原1987年短篇小说《错误》的叙事学分析

高伟林　【澳大利亚】
澳大利亚布里斯班昆士兰大学语言及文化学系中文翻译讲师

马原（1953—）是中国20世纪80年代一位重要的先锋派作家，被许多批评家视为中国首位元小说家。在中国文坛匿迹20多年后，他于2012年出版小说《牛鬼蛇神》，再次点燃了大众对这位极具吸引力、引人深思的作家的兴趣。马原的作品中，最著名、被分析次数最多的两部为1986年出版的《虚构》和1985年出版的《冈底斯的诱惑》。《虚构》尤其被认为是马原的"代表作"，其高度复杂费解的自反手法，使之无愧于众多评论的关注。而《冈底斯的诱惑》是马原一部以西藏为背景的著作，将后现代自反手法和西藏神话巧妙地结合起来。虽然这两部著作是不折不扣的"马原风"代表作品，马原的大部分作品相对来说鲜有人知，如《错误》，其受到的评论和关注度远低于马原其他更著名的作品。因此，对马原的理解只停留在少数其他代表作上，而这些作品可以说仅占其总文学产出极小的一部分。另外，许多批评方法探讨的是一系列作品在主题或结构上的共同点，而非对特定文本的单独具体分析。因此，现今解读马原，在广度和深度上还远远不够，而且他的大部分作品仍未引起任何批评家关注。因其最近重返文坛，出版小说，对马原的学术研究不能仅限于《牛鬼蛇神》和近期出版的《纠缠》，而要从马原上世纪八十年代的创作高度重新评价他已有的作品。

《错误》是马原典型的一部还未进行过任何重要文本分析的作品。但这部作

品非常值得评析，因为它超出了两大主要研究领域的范围，既不是一部明显的自反小说，主题也和西藏无关。在《虚构》中，自反这一主题达到了很高的高度，而《冈底斯的诱惑》可以说是他有关西藏的最优秀的作品。除此之外，马原还创作了大量其他的作品，如《旧死》和《上下都很平坦》。这两部作品一点都没有涉及到西藏，而在自反叙述这一方面可以说是更加细致入微。很少有人认为这些作品是马原元小说的代表作，也很少有人用其来证明马原是位元小说作家。尽管如此，很多这类较不出名的作品反而内容更为丰富，也能给人更多收获，因为比起《虚构》这样公认的元小说，这些作品的自反叙述更加微妙。《错误》是一部优秀的元小说，绝对值得我们长期对其进行评论研究。分析如《错误》这类文本能够加深我们对马原全部作品的理解，更重要的是还能探索出更加具体的方法来研究马原作品中的自反叙述。

一　方法论

分析马原的元小说时需要结合20世纪80年代中国先锋运动这一知识背景。此外，我们有必要运用几种叙事学方法来梳理作者复杂的叙事结构。阅读马原的任何作品，基本上都要考虑到文本的叙事结构，尤其还要考虑到作者运用自反叙述时的动态变化，否则很容易把非现实主义文本误读为现实主义文本。因此，本文对小说《错误》的文本分析分为两部分。首先，本文将解构分析文本的叙事结构和自反元素；其次，本文将通过其结构和元叙述手法进行文本解读。此次分析将广泛运用元小说理论，尤其是温卡·奥门森1993年作品《元小说》。这部作品巩固并发展了帕特莎·渥厄的分析方法。该方法认为，元叙述并不只是一种体裁，而且还是一种复杂的文学写作手法。其次，马原的元叙述小说常有复杂的叙述机构，需要叙述"聚焦"等关键叙事学手法，才能解构《错误》中的结构元素，进而揭示文本中自反的构建。马原的自反小说本质上复杂难解，所以只有理清《错误》中的结构元素，才可得出有关诠释该文本的可靠结论。如上所述，本文分析了《错误》的叙述结构，展示了文本元叙述的技巧，最后得出结论，提出如何在本次结构分析的指导下解读《错误》。

二　《错误》的叙事结构

乍看之下《错误》的叙述结构似乎远没有马原《虚构》和《冈底斯的诱惑》

这类"多变"的"碎片化"小说复杂。尤其是《错误》的叙述聚焦通篇一致，全文都用全知的第一人称叙述，没有明显地"转向"其他的叙述聚焦者或外部的"全知式"叙述。第一人称叙述视角贯穿全文，自反小说意味着这一叙述者是作者本人讲述过去的事情。尽管叙述人称全文一致，叙述结构仍旧十分复杂。从本质上讲，小说《错误》的叙述聚焦有三种主要形式：

第一类聚焦：第一人称内聚焦叙述者向"读者"叙述。

第二类聚焦：第一人称内聚焦叙述，直接引用对话，没有目标"读者"。

第三类聚焦：第一人称内聚焦叙述，没有目标读者，和第二类聚焦的时空背景不同，和第一类聚焦的时空背景相同。

小说的自反性通过第一类聚焦得到强化，而其非元叙述通过第二类聚焦来实现。这就使得"作者"这一小说人物和叙述本身之间区分开来了。这种区分在许多马原小说中极其相似。通常，自反叙述者和真正"现实"中的叙述者之间的差别通过"叙事"和"次叙事"之间的关系变得更加明显，因而读者更容易分辨"作者"和"文本"分别处在哪个叙述层面上。比如在《旧死》中，叙述很明显被分成了两个层面，一个代表作者形象，另一个代表作者过去的自己，这两个不同的时空背景区别很明显。在《错误》中，尽管作者这个"我"和小说中的"我"明显不同，但读者不能立马确定它们是否各自对应两个不同的时空。实际上，《错误》中有些地方并没有区分这两种聚焦者：

"现在想起来我仍然说不清道理，我为什么突然来了气恼，气不打一处来，我恶狠狠叫大家'都他妈的滚开'。马上又都滚开了，好像同伴的好心真的成了一场自找的没趣。只有二狗仍然蹲在我跟前。这正好。"

第一类聚焦代表"讨论"如何描写或叙述过去亲身经历的作者形象，而第二类聚焦代表作品中历事的叙述者"我"，而这个"我"对他所处世界的未来一无所知，只是不自知地经历这些在现实生活中"确实发生过的"往事。这就是小说中作者现在的自己（即"作者"）和叙述者过去的自己（即"主人公"）之间的区别。在上文的引用部分，第一人称叙述者很明显处于他所代表的世界，但是其时空背景却改变了。这是第三类聚焦一个很好的例证。在运用第三类聚焦叙述时，作者常常使用像"后来"或"现在"这类词，正如前例所示。在这些例子中，"历事的"第二类聚焦者对叙述者所讲述的事情毫不知情，因为这一时空的事件对第二类聚焦来说是未来事件。此外，这种类型的叙述者会用"我记不清"这类表达来表示叙述者对往事的回忆可能不是很可靠，以增加文章的可信度。因此，从本质上来说，这三种聚焦形式微妙地促进了三种不同的叙述形式，即创造或"创作"一段叙述的叙述、回忆往事的叙述以及经历往事的叙述。这三类第一人称叙述者之间最主要的区别就是时间，更确切地说，是叙述者所处的两个不同的时空背景。反过来这些不同的背景在文本中建立了两个不同的叙述层面，最主要的"叙述"呈现了叙述者现在的自己（第一和第三类聚焦者），而"次叙述"呈现了叙述者过去的自己（第二类叙述者）。从某种程度上讲，第一类和第三类叙述者极为相像，然而在主要的叙述层面所表现出来的不同自反程度意味着他们可以相互独立，以保证"回忆"往事的叙述者和"讨论"文本写作的叙述者可以在文本中被划分为两个独立的实体。

尽管上述叙述结构展示了文本中独立聚焦者的逻辑差异，这一差异本身常常十分模糊，因为叙述本来就会在不同叙述者和叙述层面之间"跳跃"。尤其是第二、三类叙述和第一、三类叙述常常融合在一起，而"我"这一称呼却一直未变，使人难以分辨叙述者。然而，用这种方式理解《错误》中完全独立的叙述结构元素极其重要，因为这一结构强化了文本的自反性，以及描写叙述者所处世界的即时性和真实性，使得文本能够同时被"记住"、"书写"和"经历"，并且隐瞒叙述中的信息，尤其是"错误"背后的事实，以及对作者"过去的自己"的误解。

三 死亡、出生和遗失的帽子：《错误》中的主要叙述

《错误》的开篇第一句有力地表明，主要的叙述焦点将会是两个婴孩的诞生：
"这俩孩子一个有妈没爸，一个没妈没爸。"
在《旧死》的开篇中，叙述者声明叙述围绕着早亡朋友的"旧死"。类似地，《错误》也在开头就突出了叙述焦点。还有一点和《旧死》相似的地方就是，自反叙述者/作者形象通过下列篇章建立该"文本"起始点以后的主要事实。
"我翻动这些旧事无非是想写一篇小说什么的，这些事情已经过了十几年，所谓恍若隔世。俩孩子是同一个夜里出现的。"
因此叙述者明确要描写两个孩子的诞生。然而，就在小说第一章，叙述者接着很快又转移了这一叙述焦点：
"那个夜里还发生了另外一件事。我的军帽不见了，丢了，丢得真

是又迅速又蹊跷。"

尤其是在小说的前半部分，在叙述遗失的军帽时带着很强的讽刺口吻。《错误》中有很多感染力很强的悲剧性叙述元素，然而这些元素都体现在看似无足轻重的事情上。其实，当第一人称叙述者把小说第一章的重点转向和"两个孩子的故事"最不相关的方面时，对两个孩子的叙述几乎立刻就停止了。尽管如此，军帽在《错误》的叙述者眼中是最主要的关注点，也是全文主要的"认知任务"。正如《错误》轻描淡写了两个孩子的出生，这一首要的主题可以说也只占用了第一人称叙述聚焦者（第二类聚焦者）的一点点精力而已。因此，从小说的开始，在对应世界里不同事件之间重要性的对比有着很明显的讽刺意味。这奠定了该文本叙述者的角色，使他成为一个在他所代表的过往世界里主观的、带有瑕疵的"视角"，而非一个被动的、"客观的"媒介，通过他来忠实地呈现事物。

王璞对《错误》的分析认为该文本主要的叙述线索就是两个孩子的出生，以及四位主要的人物：二狗、赵老屁、黑枣和江梅。有趣的是，王璞认为这些叙述本身的"内容"相对缺少趣味，有点陈腐，里面的故事"已经被'新时代'的小说家写烂了"。很多故事讲述了中国偏远地区"下乡青年"的坎坷人生，充斥着有关死亡、暴力和私生子的描述，而这类描写对读者，或者至少对批评家来说已是少见多怪。但王璞也注意到《错误》的叙述结构使主题焕然一新（但未作具体解释）。《错误》有一个很突出的方面，即叙述线索的重要性和表面上看起来不一致。尽管一项看似无足轻重的军帽和文本真正悲剧性的元素并列很讽刺，叙述者还是屡次试图强调他的认知任务的重要性：

"关于帽子我还想再啰嗦几句。我的帽子一年前是崭新的，我拿到帽子的当时就下决心与它共存亡，我咬破右手食指用血在帽里写上我的名字。这一年时间我几乎帽不离头，谁都知道这顶帽子是我的命，相信整个农场都知道我为这顶帽子会毫不犹豫地跟人玩刀子玩命。戴了一年可以想见它已经不那么新了。"

叙述者在这里不厌其烦地想要强调这顶帽子的重要性。然而，本文有一点很明显，即读者被迫质问叙述者的判断。事实上，本文叙述者甚至明确说明，军帽的叙述要比最开始两个孩子的出生更加重要：

"那时候抢军帽成风，你经常可以听到诸如为了抢军帽而杀人的传闻。不是马路消息。我军帽就这么丢了。丢得轻轻巧巧。而且那天晚上有了那两个孩子。人们因为这两个新奇的尤物马上把我的悲痛淡忘了。"

很明显这一任务在叙述者所在世界并不重要，因此这里叙述者就更加缺乏判断力。当叙述者执意要叫醒所有人，检查他们的私人物品中是否有帽子时，文中的气氛很紧张。从象征意义和结构上来说，军帽是《错误》中叙述的主要推动力，至少在小说初始的几个章节肯定是这样，尽管从主题上来说是无足轻重的元素。当自反叙述者"我"试图"写"两个孩子出生的故事时，小说中历事的叙述者"我"在小说世界正面临着帽子的丢失。两个叙述者之间有着明显的时空差异，这就意味着他们对事实有着不同的认知，并且做出不同的判断。当故事中的"我"说，帽子非常重要，因为"它还是一个小伙子可否在社会上站得住脚的象征"，这一叙述者的不可靠性和真实性就同时增加了。从这种意义上来说，叙述者似乎很天真，因为读者可以"信任"对事件的陈述，但是不一定会信任叙述者的价值体系及信仰。

叙述者执意要找回帽子，表明他有种不成熟的欲望，想要和同性竞争，而这正是缺乏作为男性的安全感所致，同时也表明他情商很低。故事中的"我"是真实作者十九岁时的自己。他有一个认知任务，就是重新找回他的军帽，但是自反叙述者却想要写两个孩子出生的故事。前者是小说世界（亦即过去的世界）的逻辑，而后者是作者现在的自己所关注的事。《错误》中还有一些更加重要的叙述，而这顶帽子也就成了这些叙述的主要推动力，因为它和第四章几乎所有的主要元素都结合在了一起。在叙述者被黑枣殴打之后，二狗把孩子放在被叙述者鲜血浸润的帽子里带到了营地。这一举动有着很强的象征性，尤其是因为叙述者自己的血迹浸透了他的帽子，盖住了他（写在帽子里面）的名字。当叙述进行到这里，看似错误的认知任务结束了，或者至少可以说是被最重要的叙述元素取代了，即叙述者误以为江梅生的孩子是赵老屁的。叙述者缺少安全感，目光短浅，使得他找帽子几乎到了荒唐的地步，还把气无端地撒在了江梅身上，怪她怀了孩子。

"我想江梅生孩子这件事也许没人比我更沮丧了。我和大家都眼看着她肚子慢慢鼓起来，日复一日，但我没有充分的精神准备面对怀孕可能导致的结果。我只是想，她被人干了，肚子干大了，她不是叫我干的。如此而已。"

营地里其他的男性成员都很喜欢这个新生婴孩，而叙述者却暗自嫉妒，生着江梅甚至孩子的闷气，总是叫孩子"小杂种"。在描写江梅的篇幅里，叙述者表现出一种不和谐、占有欲强且好斗的男性气质,把江梅怀孕看成是件龌龊的事情。

在《错误》中,江梅孩子的出生时发生了三次激烈的暴力行为。第一次是黑枣殴打叙述者,第二次是叙述者打二狗,最后是黑枣打自己,作为第一次伤人的补偿。《错误》中的暴力源于冲动,场面血腥,对身体伤害的描写非常细致,但是对伤者痛苦的描写却相对较少,没能很好地打动读者。此外,尽管找帽子这一任务是通过故事中的叙述者"我"来呈现的,叙述者承受的伤害却是通过他"现在的自己"(即第三类聚焦者)被叙述出来的:

"他看来心平气和,一点急的样子都看不出来。他慢慢摇动钉头,钉子被他拔出来了。接着他利用门槛退下了锹头。我知道好戏就要开场了。我记不住细节,因为时间已经过去太久。结果我的脚踝被木锹把扫成粉碎性骨折,我成了终生跛脚。"

尽管对帽子的叙述被放在了过去的时空背景,以使事件随着叙述"展开",引文中暴力情节的一波三折却因叙述者回忆的不完全而被弱化了。事实上,文章的不同叙述视角之间有着一种奇特的张力——小说中"历事的"叙述者"我"具有即时性,而"现在的自己"这一叙述者有时置身事外,冷静地叙事。

"这个江梅后来死了,我也是听说。我先回锦州了,她留在农场,听说她终于自杀了。又是后话,后话不提。"

因此,一方面叙述有一个认知任务,由叙述者在过去的时空背景来叙述。但另一方面,叙述者现在的自己将信息放置在一个赤裸裸的真实背景下,如上述引文。这便突显了一点,即看似都是一致的第一人称聚焦,背后却有着复杂而细微的差别,在不同时空背景之间,在"历事"的、"忆事"的、自反的叙述者之间不停地转换。找帽子的任务结束后,随着叙述在三个不同的叙述视角之间频繁"跳跃",文章的时间结构变得越来越复杂。结果,叙述焦点变得越来越模糊,叙述的时间顺序在以下事件中接连转换:江梅怀了孩子;叙述者以为是赵老屁的;叙述者从黑枣那里得知,孩子是田会计的;张兰生了赵老屁的孩子,自己却死了;二狗在目睹张兰死后,用叙述者的帽子把这个孩子带回营地;二狗死于癌症;最后江梅自杀。相比叙述中对帽子的关注度,这一连串的悲剧性事件从各种不同的时空视角被叙述出来,视角转化的速度让人晕头转向。当下置身事外的叙述者"我"所回忆的事情有时候时空跨度很大:

"江梅的死讯就是他告诉我的,江梅对我来说早就不存在了。我后来像许多正常人一样恋爱，结婚，生孩子，江梅已经过分遥远了。那是前不久他来市里卖活鸡，碰上我就一定要拉我喝啤酒，酒到半酣他讲起了江梅，讲江梅一直不嫁人可是肚子又大了，后来就投井死了，死得很惨，身子泡得像水缸一样粗。"

引文中，之前用来找帽子的时间长得几近荒诞，因为从叙述意义上讲，江梅的价值很小。江梅自杀是《错误》中最悲剧的事件之一。但是奇怪的是它的影响被它的叙述方式弱化。同样，二狗的死几乎也是一笔带过：

"'二狗，你早该说。早就该说了。'

'你别哭。男儿掉泪让人受不了。我求求你了，别哭吧。'

他死的时候我一直守在旁边。癌症真是不得了，他本来个子矮小，现在只剩一把干枯的骨头了。他火化，他妈留了骨灰。"

和描述江梅的死不同，叙述者在描写二狗的死时虽然也很简短，但之前有一大段直接引述的对话，以表达此次事件对叙述者感情的影响。二狗在死之前讲述了整件事情的来龙去脉，包括张兰在生孩子的时候去世，张兰怀上赵老屁的孩子，他用叙述者的帽子把孩子带回营地，让江梅代管。从本质上讲，尽管小说全篇都是"错误"和误解，二狗在死之前补上了缺失的信息，使叙述者理解了当时他所不能理解的一切。他的死成为了叙述本身残忍而悲剧的开篇，因为如果没有他所提供的信息，叙述者不可能知道"错误"的存在。

总之，《错误》包含了各种不同的线索，从看似无关的帽子到十分悲剧性的死亡和自杀，而所有的这些线索之间都有着某种联系。叙述聚焦频繁地不同时空背景之间转化，而叙述者的可信度也急剧变化，使得本来已经很复杂的、相互关联的叙述更加复杂。结果，叙述者在现实和过去的自己之间（或者说叙述和次叙述之间）不停转化，尽管读者掌握了被隐瞒的真实世界的确切信息，叙述仍旧使人晕头转向。

四 《错误》中的"错误"

一本小说的题目经常对文本本身有很深的影响。虽然没有特定的重要理论来解释题目的作用，但题目有核心的结构逻辑，即题目在本质上是叙述以外的元素，并和文本内的叙述元素产生逻辑联系，这种联系和主要叙述、次叙述之间的联系非常相似。这些叙述以外的元素处于叙述逻辑之外，通过"隐含作者"这一概念，这些元素就很好理解了，因为它们暗示了更高层次的"作者的"存在及其对叙述的评述和赋名。从马原的其他作品中，我们可以发现，有的题目常常是文章的焦点或者是主要概念的关键词，在表述上通常隐晦模糊。《虚构》是个很好的例子，因为"虚构"这一概念在此短篇小说内直接被提及，通过虚构主要的叙述将主导结构合法化，尽管这同时也表明叙述本身就是"虚构"的。或许在题目和文本的关系上和《错误》最为相似的是《旧死》。用"旧死"作题目就是在暗示，文章中最重要的叙事就是"旧死"。然而，对旧死的叙述在最后一章才出现，使得最悲剧的元素成为悬念，一直持续到文末，营造出一种持续的紧张。"错误"这一概念是《错误》中一个非常重要的方面，在文中多次被提及。和"旧死"一样，"错误"这个题目表明"错误"可能就是一个关键的叙述事件。"错误"这一概念首次出现在"寻帽"的叙述里：

"我想问一下，是不是有人拿错了？拿错了没关系，现在拿回来还不晚。谁拿错了？有人拿错了吗？"

因此帽子就成了文中第一个"错误"。然而，随着这一认知任务慢慢涣散，读者只能自己去寻找《错误》中的错误。叙述到此，"错误"这一概念很可能不只是一个可鉴别的叙述"事件"，它还可以被拓宽到更广的含义，即不可靠性和误解。作者在文中多处都有伏笔，比如"假如我没记错，那是在六月"表明，文中的"错误"可以表示叙述中的误解。事实上，叙述者在文中多次用到"我记不清"、"我闹不懂的是"、"我不懂"以及"我没想到"，以表明其回忆和对小说世界的理解是残缺的。但最后尽管叙述者的理解错误不计其数，最清晰可辨的"错误"在文末才得以揭示：

"直到这时我开始知道全都错了。

二狗死的当天上午还是清醒的，我到时他说他本来昨天前天就应该死了，但他说他死不了，死了也闭不上眼睛，因为我没有来。他说他早知道我会来，他就一直等到我来了他说了那些话以后再安心去死。"

根据文中事件的时间顺序，二狗在两个孩子出生五年后去世，而叙述者现在的自己在二狗死后十七年讲述整件事情。直到孩子出生五年后二狗揭露孩子出生的来龙去脉，叙述者才最终意识到过去的"错误"。从这个意义上说，事件之间的联系令人痛心，因为悲剧性死亡的同时也正是错误的"产生"。叙述聚焦的时间结构非常琐碎，以致叙述者过去的自己经历了《错误》中的"错误"却毫不知情，而现在的自己却回忆起这些错误，并由自反叙述者来调解（尤其体现在第四章，叙述者十分苦恼，因为他完全不知道该如何充分地叙述二狗的死，也不确定到底要不要写他的死）。叙述者想让读者一直保留悬念，等到最晚才揭示错误，以达到非常讽刺的效果，就像在《旧死》文末才揭示"旧死"一样。因此，《错误》中的"错误"既是关键事件也是关键术语。关键事件是终极叙述焦点，而关键术语含义更广，暗示了更为抽象的概念，如叙述的不可靠性和主观性。

五 开篇引用

　　文本的题目有时点明一个叙述焦点，有时揭示主要的叙述主题，同样地，叙述开头的引语往往也揭示了"作者"（即我们所说的"隐含作者"）对后文本质的理解，此外还提供了一种互文合法化的形式。在叙述主体之前开篇引用是马原常用的一种建构叙述的手法。如果我们用1994年出版的《虚构》作品集中的作品当作例子，除了一篇文章，其余的全都用了和《错误》一样的开篇引用。然而，马原的引语运用往往是有问题的，《虚构》作品集中许多作品中的开篇引用都出自贝尔托·布莱希特、巴尔特、萨默塞特·毛姆和但丁，但马原也常引用自己说的话、他自己出版的作品、自己创作的其他实时文本中的虚构文本，或者干脆不标明出处，如《错误》的开篇引用。

　　　　"玻璃弹子有许多种玩法，最简单又最不容易的一种，是使弹子途
　　中毫不耽搁，下洞。——题记"

　　这一引用下面的出处只写了"题记"二字，继而产生了一种有趣的互文形式，因为该引用的出处模糊不定，很可能是作者自己虚构的。虽然这一引用的出处让人质疑，但其内容本身所蕴含的意象却很有趣。首先，此处意象并没有在文中直接或间接地出现，所以，如果要在这两种叙述元素之间建立逻辑联系，就需要把引用的语句当作隐喻来理解。比如打弹珠的方法从逻辑上可以和第一类聚焦者构建和描写次叙述文本的方法联系起来，这样弹珠游戏就是写作的隐喻。这就表明，打弹珠代表了写作这件事，而玩家就是作者，"直接"方法就代表了对"直接"叙述风格某一形式的评论。如果真是这样，那么赞扬"直接"叙述的隐含作者和完全不采用直接叙述且令人迷惑的作者之间自然就形成了强烈的讽刺。如果我们从第二类聚焦者的视角阅读弹珠的隐喻，那么直截了当地深入游戏这一简单直接但却危险的策略就和小说中历事的叙述者"我"寻找帽子这一认知任务之间就有了

相似的特点。内聚焦者为了一个非常具体的认知目的，将读者直接塞进了叙述中心。但是，当真实世界开始变得真正复杂的时候，这个策略很快就失效了。

六 《错误》中的自反手法

和马原其他的一些更明显的自反小说（如《虚构》）相比，《错误》中运用到了一系列相对微妙的元叙述手法。这些手法不但没有破坏现实世界的真实性，还使得"作者"形象与他的文本之间形成了一个平行结构，这在马原的许多作品中都可见一二。正如上文所强调的那样，第一类人称叙述聚焦中包含的三层时间结构意味着自反叙述者可以"讨论"他的叙述以及他正在创作的"文本"，却不打破小说中历事的叙述者"我"作为"作者"形象过去自己的模仿完整性。

从这个意义上来说，叙述者的自反性没有破坏次叙述的真实性，反而还说明，在当下这个时空背景下，作为"作者"形象的叙述者正试着将他的过去"叙述化"。因此，时间就成了《错误》中一个至关重要的促进因素，因为时间刻画了叙述者"我"的各种"角色"，继而使得这些角色能够共存，互相之间却没有明显的矛盾。

《错误》中自反的"我"多次参与文本和叙述的自反活动，因为它突出了一个"文本"的创作和一个"故事"的叙述，如下引文：

"我实在不想用倒叙的方法，我干吗非得在我的小说的开始先来一句——那时候？我不知道那件事的因由结果，我甚至不知道这俩男孩是不是活下来了。"

在这里，叙述者公开宣布他没有用到上帝视角，不知道现实世界中所发生的事，同时他也不确定该如何"书写"这部小说。这种叙述的不可靠性通过主题化的"作者"形象呈现出来，是元叙述文本中一种常用的技巧。尽管第一人称叙述者没有直白地将自己称作文本的"作者"，在下面一段自反性很强的段落中，"读者"的出现展示了一个主题化的、"作者"到"文本"再到"读者"的动态变化。

"这个故事比较更残酷的一面我留在后边，我首先想的是这样可以吊吊读者的胃口；其次我也在犹豫，我不知道我讲了是否不太合适。我说了它比较更残酷一些，我无法从原罪或道德的角度对这个事件作出恰如其分的评价。

讲不讲？怎样讲？

这都是我在后面要遇到的难题。我相信船到桥头自然直。我暂且不去过多地伤脑筋。我说要挑黑枣大筋是以后的事，当时我瘫在门前地上，这天夜里的故事似乎完结了。

　　细心的读者马上会说没完。说我在开篇时讲过有两个男孩。是的，没完。那个男孩没出现。他就要出现了。

　　但是首先出现的是我这个故事中另外一个没出现的角色，二狗。"

"读者"和该引文中真正"认真的读者"突显了文本的自反性。每当叙述中有一个"作者"形象对一个"读者"形象发话，讲一个"故事"的叙述或叙述中"文本"创作，该文本就不再是代表现实的小说世界，而是叙述者的叙述。更确切地说，该文本代表了代表的代表，即小说世界的代表——叙述者。因此，当这个叙述者"讨论"他叙述的"创作"方法时，主题化的作者就在对一位主题化了的"读者"谈论一个主题化了的"文本"。主题化"作者"向读者发话是马原元叙述小说一个重要的特征。在《错误》中，这一叙述技巧是文章的基本结构，而文本的自反性在此结构之上建立起来。文本中还有一些相对微妙的自反现象，比如，小说中"历事"的叙述者"我"问"早有结果有什么不好？"。这和自反叙述者想要把有关"错误"的重要信息留到文末的决定形成了强烈的讽刺。除此以外，该文本的自反性主要建立在上述两个带有明显自反性的段落之上，还包括"读者"的出现、文本中暗含的"作者"、以及第一人称叙述者的三个独立"角色"的建立。

　　总之，《错误》包含了一个叙述—次叙述的叙述结构，通过这个结构，一个主题化作者（或叙述聚焦者）在主要的叙述层面向一位读者讲述有关叙述的事，而作者"过去的自己"在次叙述层面经历着代表作者过去的小说世界。这一结构使得文本不仅是被陈述的叙述，而且还是对该叙述的叙述，从而强化了文本的自反性。尽管通过叙述聚焦之间的清楚差异，叙述和次叙述之间的逻辑差异得以建立，但是叙述在聚焦的不同形式之间频繁转换淡化了各类聚焦者所在的不同叙述层面和时空背景之间的界线。因此，这一自反结构使得"错误"同时代表了作者当下正在"叙述"的自己、作者当下正在"创作"的自己、以及作者之前"历事"的自己，但同时也淡化了这三种不同视角之间的叙事学界线。

七　叙述的不可靠性、全知性和易错性

　　《错误》中的叙述聚焦者有一个重要的特征，即缺少全知性，并带有不同程

度的不可靠性。具体来说，不可靠性根据詹姆斯·费伦可以分成三种不同的形式，分别处于事实（或事件）、价值（或判断）、和知识（或认知）这三条轴线。比如该文本的最后一句强调了一个事实，即叙述者对现实世界没有全知性的认识，只对其经历有一系列的印象或回忆：

"我想赵老屁那个夜里一定是因为听说江梅生孩子想到了他的小寡妇张兰，张兰死了他又到什么地方去了呢？"

在这里，主要叙述层面的第一人称叙述聚焦者并不完全了解次叙述中的事件，也不确定该如何将这些事件叙述化。叙述者在叙述中屡次声明自己的认知有限，并对文本中的外部聚焦叙述没有全知性。这就表明叙述总是保留了不可靠性和公开承认的"易错性"。尽管第一、三类聚焦者在知识或事实轴上显示出不可靠性，次叙述者却在该轴上表现出可靠性，同时在价值或判断轴表现出极度不可靠性。这从叙述者最初的"寻帽任务"中便得以突显。因此，《错误》中有两种不可靠的聚焦类型，一种是知识或事实轴上公开阐明的不可靠性，另一种是价值或判断轴上作者未承认的不可靠性。《错误》中的叙述不可靠性和文本的叙述结构密切相关。这一叙述结构使得处于不同时空背景的各类叙述聚焦者在两个叙述层面展开叙述。但这两个叙述层面的叙述者都不完全可靠。然而，因为这两个层面和文本紧密相连，不可靠性的各种形式和叙述者自反性的各个层面其实都相互抵消了——无知的次叙述者经历着过去的事件，做出了有瑕疵的判断，对事件的意识有局限、理解不透彻，被基本叙述层面上的自反、自觉的叙述者抵消。在叙述聚焦结构中运用不同的时空背景有效地促进了不同层面的文本的不可靠性。比如，读者可以真正理解一个事实，即在次叙述层面历事的叙述者"我"正经历着现实世界的过去，而过去就像"发生在当下"一样，尽管在基本叙述层面的叙述者称"这个故事比较更残酷的一面我留在后边"。因此，处于高叙述层面的叙述者的所知对于低叙述层面的叙述者来说就是不可知的，因为在有着不同层面的不可靠性和自反性的不同时空背景下，该文本结构可以容纳不同的叙述聚焦者。同样，第二类聚焦者一直寻找帽子，荒诞不经，且他明显误解了代表过去的小说世界，但通过第一、三类聚焦者较为成熟的视角，这些行为和误解也就说得通了。因此，不可靠性的多种转变形式增加了不同时空背景下叙述者的真实性，而聚焦者是否真实可信是文本叙述结构的一个重要的元素。

八　诠释《错误》

下乡青年的真实内心其实是许许多多中国某一代作家选择的主题，所以可以理解为什么一些批评家认为这类高度政治化的文学形式已经没有更多解读的余地了。然而，《错误》用独特的表述方式表达熟悉的内容，它远不只是一部"简单的""寻根"文学作品或有关"下乡青年"的文学作品。在毛泽东以后的文学作品中都明显含有"宣泄"的思想，而《错误》中却没有。《错误》通过其独特的结构，使得大部分心酸和煽情的叙述元素都消解于误解和误读。叙述聚焦的不可靠性、自反性、以及全知式外聚焦叙述的缺失将文本中大部分悲剧性元素边缘化了，因为这些元素不是叙述者所亲身经历的，所以也就处于叙述之外了。然而与此同时，叙述中看似无关的方面被赋予了相当高的重要性，如寻找作者的帽子（《错误》中的第一次"错误"）。文中对江梅和二狗离世的轻描淡写，对叙述者的帽子却大染笔墨，这两者之间的张力以一种重要的方式突出了叙述者的不可靠性，即在《错误》中，不可靠性、自反性和主观性紧密相连，叙述者永远也不可能突破叙述者"我"的认知局限而进入一个全知的"客观"结构。

这样，该叙述并不缺少思考深度，相反还极其重视叙述聚焦在不同时空背景之间不停变化的主观性的真实度：历事的"我"代表过去的自己，他天真无知，感情不成熟；而叙述者当下的自己能够做出可靠的判断，但是也公开承认带有一定的易错性。结果，小说世界中发生的事件只能随着历事的实体的变化而变化，因为叙述者没有"叙述"文本的悲剧性元素，而是"重新呈现"了直接引用的对话，通过这些话语，小说世界里的叙述者才知道这些事情，而这便是他历事的限度。所以，要体会《错误》中的心酸苦楚，"读者"不能通过经历外部叙述的悲剧，而是要经历悲剧中叙述者真实经历过的事情、记忆和创作过程。因为叙述者具有不可靠性，读者总能"看到"叙述聚焦者的叙述之外，来体会比历事的"我"的叙述更加充分、多样和苦楚的小说世界，继而意识到，这些对叙述者现在的情感仍有影响的往事没有被完全揭露。从某种程度上来说，《错误》呈现的不是一段普通的"下乡青年"的故事，而是与之相关的叙述，而读者实际上却接触不到"下乡青年"的文本本身。在《错误》中，读者知道叙述者怎样经历和回忆过去，也知悉叙述者是如何书写过去的，但是读者却读不到一个全知的叙述，无法看到往事的细枝末节都被"客观地"呈现出来，并以一种"可靠的"方式被"重新经历"。

《错误》中，过去的错误通过对当下的误解叙述出来。主流现实主义叙述根据时间和重要性来安排事件的叙述顺序，但已经被一种高度主观的内聚焦叙述取代，这种新的叙述并没有标榜其"往事"具有真实性，而是强调"从往至今一直在发生的事情"。叙述者下乡的青春也就成了一段激荡的、暴力的、伤痕累累的过往，而叙述者在经历这段往事时，天真无知，感情上还未成熟：如果这段经历缺少不可靠性和主观性，那就不像是真人真事了。因此叙述中允许有易错性，满是"错误"便也无碍。时光流逝允许主观性发生改变，马原以此来叙述过去的"错误"，把自己的下乡青春经过部分取舍后，再在小说中经历、忆起和记述，而不是将其完整地"重现"。马原没有重写主要的叙述，而是叙述了缺失、不完整和未解决的事情。和那些过时的主题相比，这或许是《错误》中最重要的一方面。

马原作品的一个最明显的特征就是他不信任全知叙述的"客观性"。比如，《虚构》提醒读者"虚构"具有欺骗性，从叙述意义上来说权力就是通过虚构而建立的。在《冈底斯的诱惑》中，叙述来自多种声音，读者无法分辨谁"正在说话"，"谁"又是说话的对象，从而不得不怀疑该叙述是否可以被"相信"和"信任"。然而在《虚构》中，马原拒绝用毛泽东以后现实主义文学中的陈词滥调来"客观地"重写过去。相反，马原给文章赋予了他主观性、他的身份以及他的"错误"。这样，马原在述说生与死、痛与殇情的同时，也正是在述说那顶遗失的军帽。

The Narrative of Experience, Memory and Writing: A Narratological Analysis of Ma Yuan's 1987 Short Story *Mistakes*

William Gatherer / Australia

Lecturer in Chinese Translation, School of Languages and Cultures, University of Queensland, Brisbane, Australia

Ma Yuan (马原 1953 -) is highly regarded as one of the most important authors of the Chinese "avant-garde movement" (先锋派 *xianfengpai*) of the 1980s and is seen by many critics as being China's first author of metafiction[1]. After a prolonged absence from the Chinese literary scene for over 20 years, the publication of the novel *Niuguisheshen*[2](牛鬼蛇神) in 2012 has reignited interest in one of China's most compelling and provocative authors. Ma Yuan's two most famous and most frequently analysed works are "Xugou" (虚构) published in 1986 and "Gangdisi de

---

1 Metafiction here refers to the post-modern concept of metafiction as a specific genre. This is to say Ma Yuan is certainly not the first author in China's history to have employed self-reflexive literary techniques which can be found in all manner of pre-modern texts. On this issue for example Henry Zhao states that "looking back to the Chinese philosophical tradition, one can see that meta-sensibility has been perceived and discussed since ancient times, especially in Taoism and Buddhism" Zhao, Henry. 1992. "The rise of metafiction in China." *Bulletin of the School of Oriental and African Studies, University of London* LV (1): p.95.

2 Ma, Yuan. 2012. *NiuguiSheshen*. Shanghai: Shanghai Art and Literature Publishing House.

youhuo" (冈底斯的诱惑) published in 1985[1]. "Xugou" in particular has become established as the author's "representative work"[2] and has deservedly received a high volume of critical attention due to its dazzlingly complex and disorientating self-reflexivity. Likewise, the fascinating mixture of post-modern self-reflexivity and Tibetan mysticism in "Gangdisi de youhuo" has established this text as one of the most famous of the author's works set in Tibet. Whilst these two superb works are certainly excellent examples of works of fiction that are unmistakably "Ma Yuan" texts, the vast majority of the author's works have gone relatively unnoticed with "Cuowu" for example, having received vastly less critical attention than the author's more famous works. Critical understanding of the author therefore has been largely based upon an incredibly limited number of the author's other "representative" texts which arguably only represent an extremely limited sample of the author's entire literary output. Furthermore many of these critical approaches have attempted to identify thematic or structural commonalities from arrange of texts[3] rather than engage in the detailed textual analysis of specific individual texts. As a result, there are significant gaps in the contemporary understanding of Ma Yuan both in terms of the scope and depth of analysis and the majority of the author's works have received no critical attention at all. Considering the author's recent return to publishing novels therefore, scholarship on Ma Yuan urgently needs further attention paid not only to the author's new works such as *Niuguisheshen* and the recently published

---

1   "Xugou" was first published in the May edition of *China Culture* (*Shouhuo* 收获) in 1986 whilst "Gangdisi de youhuo" was first published in 1985 in the February edition of *Shanghai Literature* (*Shanghai Wenxue* 上海文学).

2   There is a distinct trend within Chinese scholarship on Ma Yuan towards identifying the most "representative" texts by the author and providing broad summaries of the author's most unique features. "Xugou" is by far the most commonly analysed work by Ma Yuan, Xiao Yingying for example states of "Xugou" that "not only is "Xugou" Ma Yuan's representative work, it is also the clearest display of the core literary concept of the author, this being that fiction is fabrication" Xiao, Yingying. "Ma Yuan 'Xugou' de shenceng yiyun." *Literature Education*, no. 10 (2008): p. 121.

3   By far the most nuanced and insightful of these broader stylistic and thematic overviews is Zhao, Henry. 1995. "Ma Yuan the Chinese Fabricator." *World Literature Today* (University of Oklahoma) 69 (2): 312-316. Zhao's introduction to Ma Yuan is still one of the best single pieces of analysis on Ma Yuan and it avoids many of the problem areas of Chinese scholarship on the author which can often be excessively politicised and often lack an adequate grounding in literary theory, metafiction theory and narratology.

Jiuchan (纠缠), but also to reassessing the author's existing body of work from the height of his creative output during the 1980s.

"Cuowu" is an excellent example of one of the vast majority of texts by Ma Yuan that have not been subjected to any significant textual analysis. It is also a text that is particularly deserving of critical attention because it falls outside of the two main points of focus for critics, namely works that are highly self-reflexive, and works that are thematically focused on Tibet[1]. In addition to reaching the height of his self-reflexivity in "Xugou" and creating arguably the finest of all his works on Tibet[2], "Gangdisi de youhuo", the author wrote a sizable number of other texts such as "Jiusi" (旧死) and "Shangxiadou hen pingtan" (上下都很平坦) for example, that do not involve Tibet in any way and furthermore display an arguably more subtle and intricate form of self-reflexivity. Whilst these works are rarely identified as representative Ma Yuan metafictions and are rarely used as "evidence" to prove that Ma Yuan is an author of metafiction, in many ways many of these less famous texts are more rich and rewarding because their self-reflexivity is arguably more subtle than more obviously metafictional pieces such as "Xugou". "Cuowu" is an excellent work of metafiction that is certainly deserving of long-overdue critical attention. Analysing texts such as "Cuowu" will not only widen the understanding of Ma Yuan's entire body of works but more importantly will develop a more nuanced approach to the author's self-reflexivity.

---

1 There is a risk that within the English speaking world Ma Yuan is becoming understood primarily as a Chinese writer of Tibet, rather than a Chinese author of metafictions: For example, the entry on the author in *China's New Cultural Scene: A Handbook of Changes* by Marie Claire Huot (p.10) underplays the author's self-reflexivity and also states that "His short stories all take place in Tibet, where he was assigned to work as a journalist in 1982. Tibet overwhelmed him, but also bored him". This statement is simply not true when judging the author's entire literary output from the 1980s and is even less relevant now after Ma Yuan's recent return to publishing novels. In addition, the only two dedicated collections of the author's works published in English translation are Herbert Batt's *Ballad of the Himalayas: Stories of Tibet* and Tony Blishen's *No Sail on the Western Sea*, both of which exclusively focus on works set in Tibet.
2 When looking at the chronology of Ma Yuan's literary output between 1982 and 1992 it is certainly not the case that the author had any particular "phases" in which any defining stylistic or thematic tendencies can be identified. The author's self-reflexivity in particular is a constant and fluctuating presence which first appeared within the first 2 years of the author's literary career.

I. Methodology

Analysing Ma Yuan's works of metafiction requires a contextualised understanding of metafiction in China in the intellectual climate of the 1980s "avant-garde movement"[1]. Furthermore, several key narratological tools are also essential to be able to navigate the author's often complex narrative structuring. Essentially, any reading of the author's works must take into account the narrative structure of the texts and in particular the dynamics of the author's use of self-reflexivity, otherwise there is a strong risk of imposing essentially realist readings on non-realist texts. This article therefore will provide a two-stage textual analysis of "Cuowu": firstly, the text's narrative structure and self-reflexive elements will be deconstructed and analysed, and secondly the text will be interpreted through its structure and metafictional devices. This analysis will employ a broad understanding of metafiction theory drawing, in particular, on Wenche Ommundsen's excellent 1993 work *Metafictions?*[2] which reinforces and develops the analytical approach

---

1 Key texts to be referred to in historicising and contextualising the "avant-garde movement" in China include Widmer, Ellen, and Dewei Wang, eds. 1993. *From May fourth to June fourth: fiction and film in twentieth-century China*. Harvard University Press and Wang, Jing. *High culture fever: Politics, aesthetics, and ideology in Deng's China*. Univ of California Press, 1996. These highly influential works situate China's avant-garde within a wider cultural context and also contextualise the (realist) writing forms that avant-garde fiction was attempting to deconstruct, problematise and surpass. As Ma Yuan was one of the leading figures within this "avant-garde movement", the author's self-reflexive writings must be situated within this cultural framework and in doing so, the naturalised and standardised narrative conventions that the author's metafictions were destabilising are inherently linked to the post-Maoist literary landscape of the 1980s.

2 Ommundsen, Wenche. 1993. *Metafictions?* Carlton: University of Melbourne Press. In *Metafictions?* Ommundsen argues that literary self-reflexivity can be understood in three ways: as a genre, as a tendency inherent in all fiction, and as a form of reading. Whilst Ommundsen is in no way suggesting that these three understandings are independent from each other, I would argue that metafictions must be understood as an amalgamation of all three of these theories: metafiction as a "genre" can only exist if metafictions have particular qualities that identify them as "metafictions"; as a part of this process, metafictions are inherently reliant upon naturalised narrative conventions so that the reader is somehow aware that metafictions function in a different way to "standard" fiction; In turn, this difference, which defines what is and what is not a metafiction, is literary self-reflexivity. The genre, reading response, and literary trend therefore, are entirely reliant upon each other.

established by Patricia Waugh[1] through which metafictions are not just understood as a genre but rather as a complex literary device. Secondly, as Ma Yuan's metafictions often contain complex narrative structures, key narratological tools such as narrative "focalization"[2] are required to be able deconstruct the structural elements of "Cuowu" which in turn will reveal how the self-reflexivity has been established within the text. Given the complex and intricate nature of Ma Yuan's self-reflexive writings, it is only through a careful navigation of the structural elements of "Cuowu" that any firm conclusions about the possible interpretations of the text can then be made. As such, this article analyses the narrative structure of "Cuowu", demonstrates how the text is metafictional, and then finally proposes conclusions about how the text can be interpreted in light of this structural analysis.

II. "Cuowu"'s Narrative Structure

On first inspection, "Cuowu" appears to have a significantly less complex narrative structure in comparison to Ma Yuan's more "kaleidoscopic" and "fragmented" narratives[3] such as "Xugou" and "Gangdisi de youhuo". In particular,

---

1　Perhaps the most important early text on metafiction theory is Waugh, Patricia. 1984. *Metafiction: the theory and practice of self-conscious fiction*. London: Methuen. Within this ground-breaking early piece of analysis, Waugh identifies literary self-reflexivity as being a trend inherent in all novels rather than a specific literary genre. Subsequently, Brian Mc Hale's more recent work on postmodernism such as McHale, Brian. 1992. *Constructing postmodernism*. Routledge, and McHale, Brian. 2004. *Postmodernist fiction*. Routledge, are extremely important texts in the understanding of metafictions as part of the wider socio-cultural phenomenon of "postmodernism".

2　The concept of narrative "focalization" was formulated by the influential narratologist Mieke Bal. "Focalization" essentially formalises the concept of narrative "perspective" or "point of view". For a full overview of this concept see Bal, Mieke. *Narratology: Introduction to the Theory of Narrative*. Toronto: University of Toronto Press, 1985: p.142.

3　The metaphor of "fragmentation" is an extremely commonly used concept within scholarship on Ma yuan. Xiao, Li. "Yuanxiaoshuo "cuipianhua" xiezuo: dianfuchuantongxushu de zhengtixing." *Journal of Fujian Normal University (Philosophy and Social Sciences Edition)* 3, no. 150 (2008): 54-59 for example argues that metafiction is a form of "fragmented" writing, and specifically uses "Gangdisi de youhuo" as an example of metafictions' effort to compromise and break the structures and therefore the logic of the fictional narrative process. The fact that any text can be referred to as "fragmented" or "broken" is somewhat problematic as it presupposes that a more "complete" and "logical" version of the text somehow exists and presents metafictions as a kind of literary aberration which is inherently in a subservient position to "standard" fiction.

the narrative focalization appears to remain consistent throughout, with an omnipresent "I" narrator and no obvious "shifts" to other narrative focalizers or external "omniscient" narration. The identity of the first person narrator appears to be consistent throughout the text and the self-reflexive passages imply that this narrator is an "author/narrator" figure recounting past events. In spite of this consistency however, the narrative structure is surprisingly complex:In essence there are three distinct forms of narrative focalization within the text:

Focalization one: first person internally focused narrator narrates to "reader" addressee.

Focalization two: first person internally focalized narrative, direct reported speech, no "reader" addressee.

Focalization three: first person internally focused narrative, no addressee, different spatio-temporal context to focalization two, same spatio-temporal context as focalization one.

The text's self-reflexivity is facilitated through narrative focalization one, whilst the non-metafictional elements of the text are narrated through focalization two. This creates a divide between a represented "author" figure and the narrative itself which is an extremely common feature of many of Ma Yuan's novels. Usually, this split between a self-reflexive narrator and an essentially "realist" narrator is also strengthened through a relationship between a diegesis and a hypo-diegesis through which the "author" and the "text" can be clearly split across two distinct narrative levels. In "Jiusi" for example, the narrative is clearly split into two narrative levels, one representing an author figure and another representing the author's past self with a clear divide between these two separate spatio-temporal contexts. Within "Cuowu", although there is a clear split between the "author" "I" and the "experiencing" "I" narrators, it is not immediately obvious whether there are two distinct represented worlds in two separate spatio-temporal contexts. In fact there often appears to be no divide between these two focalizers in some parts of the text:

"Now that I am thinking about it I still can't explain why I suddenly got so angry, I angrily shouted at everyone "Piss off all of you!". And so everyone pissed off as it seemed that their friendly concern wasn't doing any good. Only Er Gou was left by my side which was exactly what I had wanted."[1]

Focalization one is a representation of an author figure "discussing" the writing or narration of past events experienced firsthand and focalization two is the experiencing "I" narrator figure who is represented as encountering these past events "as they happen" without displaying any specific knowledge of the future outcomes of the represented world. This essentially is the represented distinction between the "author's" current self as "writer" and the narrator's past self as "protagonist". Within this quotation above the first person narrator is clearly operating within the represented world but from a different spatio-temporal context, and this is a good example of focalization three which often occurs where the narrator uses terms like "afterwards" or "now" as in the example above. In these instances the narrator often refers to events that the "experiencing" focalizer two could not have had any perception of (events which in this spatio-temporal context would constitute future events). Furthermore, this form of focalizer facilitates passages in which the narrator's memory of past events may be unreliable through phrases such as "I can't remember clearly". In essence therefore these three forms of focalization subtly facilitate three different forms of narrative: the narrator creating or "writing" a narrative, the narrator recollecting a past event, and the narrator experiencing a past event. The key differentiator between these internal first person focalizers is time, or to be more specific the two distinct spatio-temporal contexts within which the focalizers are operating. In turn these separate contexts establish two distinct narrative levels within the text: the primary diegesis presents the narrator's present self (focalizers one and three), whilst the hypo-diegesis presents the narrator's past self (focalizer two). In a way focalizers one and three are incredibly similar,

---

1 All English translations provided here are by William Gatherer.

however the different degrees of self-reflexivity displayed on the primary diegetic level means that they can be separated to ensure that the narrator that is "recalling" past events and the narrator that is "discussing" the writing of the text can be compartmentalised as two separate entities within the text.

Whilst the narrative structure above demonstrates the logical divide between separate narrative focalizers within the text, this divide itself is often extremely unclear as the narrative essentially "jumps" between the different focalizers and narrative levels. In particular, focalizations two and three and focalizations one and three are often heavily intertwined and the consistency of the "I" narrator often renders the shifts between them hard to detect. However, understanding the distinctly separate elements of the narrative structure of "Cuowu" in this way is extremely important as this structure facilitates the text's self-reflexivity, heightens the immediacy and verisimilitude of the represented world, enables the text to be "remembered", "written" and "experienced" simultaneously, and facilitates the withholding of information within the narrative, in particular, the facts behind the "mistakes", misconceptions and misunderstandings of the author's past self.

III. Death, Birth and a Lost Hat: The Main Narratives Within "Cuowu"

The opening sentence of "Cuowu" strongly suggests that the main focus of the narrative will be the two births within the text:

> "There were these two kids, one had a mother but no father, and the other had neither a mother nor a father."

Similar to the opening passages of "Jiusi" in which the narrator states that the narrative revolves around an "old death" of a friend who had died young, "Cuowu" appears to foreground the focal point of the narrative right from the start. Also in a similar way to "Jiusi", the self-reflexive narrator/author figure establishes the basic facts behind the point of inception of this "text" through the subsequent passage:

"No doubt I'm going over these details simply because I want to write something, this all happened over ten years ago, what you might call a lifetime ago. These two kids appeared on the very same night."

The stated purpose of the narrator therefore is to write the narrative of the births of two children, however within the opening chapter the narrator figure quickly proceeds to shift this focus:

"That evening something else happened: My hat went missing. All of a sudden, and in very strange circumstances, it was lost."

Throughout the first half of the text in particular, there is a strong ironic tension created by the narrative of the lost army hat. "Cuowu" has many highly tragic and emotive narrative elements, however they are all juxtaposed against a seemingly inconsequential event. Indeed, the narratives of the two children are almost instantly abandoned as the first person narrator focuses the initial chapters of the text on what appears to be the least relevant aspect of this "story about two children". Despite this, however, the army hat is established by the narrator as the primary focus within "Cuowu" and functions as the text's primary "epistemological quest"[1]. As much as "Cuowu" may be "about" the birth of two children, this overarching subject arguably occupies relatively little of the first person narrative focalizer's

---

1   Within his ground-breaking work on postmodernist fiction (McHale, Brian. *Constructing postmodernism*. Routledge, 1992) Bryan McHale analyses a huge range of stylistic and thematic features of modernist texts that postmodernist texts are somehow references and destabilising. One such feature of modernist texts that appear within self-reflexive postmodernist texts is the "epistemological quest" acted out by a "cognitive hero" which will often "revolve around problems of the accessibility and circulation of knowledge, the individual mind's grappling with an elusive or occluded reality" (McHale 1992: p.147). The epistemological quest is the driving force behind the narratives of many modernist texts whose "plot is organised as a quest for a missing or hidden item of knowledge" (McHale 1992: p.147). According to McHale, one of the key features of the shift from modernism to postmodernism is the move from the epistemological to the ontological: whilst a modernist epistemological quest searches for knowledge, for truth, for causality, a postmodernist epistemological quest will do the same whilst simultaneously foregrounding its own "ontological status", or in other words, the postmodernist epistemological quest is a self-reflexive epistemological quest. Within "Cuowu" there is a clear epistemological quest, however the status of this quest is destabilised by the narrative unreliability and self-reflexivity.

(focalizertwo) attention. From the start of the text therefore there is a clear ironic tension between the relative statuses of the narrative events within the represented world, which foregrounds the narrator's role within the text not as a passive and "objective" medium through which to faithfully represent, but rather a subjective and flawed "perspective" within a represented world of past events.

Wong Pok's analysis of "Cuowu" identifies the text's main narrative threads as being those of the two births, and also the narratives of the four main characters namely Er Gou, Zhao Laopi, Hei Zao and Jiang Mei. Interestingly, Wong suggests that the "content" of these narratives themselves is relatively lacking in interest and somewhat clichéd, stating of "Cuowu" that "the stories that it is telling have already been written to death by the 'new era' novelists"[1]. Readers (or at least critics) may have become inured to the vicissitudes of "rusticated youth" narratives about death, violence and illegitimate births set in China's remote regions, however Wong also notes that the structure of the text somehow reinvigorates this subject matter (without necessarily explaining how it does so). One instantly noticeable aspect of "Cuowu" is that the relevant statuses of the narrative threads do not appear to be aligned with their apparent significance. Despite the ironic juxtaposition of the seemingly inconsequential army hat narrative against the genuinely tragic elements of the text, the narrator repeatedly attempts to highlight the seriousness of his epistemological quest:

> "I want to just say a few more words about my hat though. The year before it had been brand new and when I got it I vowed to wear it for the rest of my life. I had bitten my finger and signed my name in blood inside the hat. Within this year my hat almost never left my head, everybody knew that this hat was my life. I didn't believe that anyone within the camp would doubt that I would fight anyone to the death for my hat. You can imagine how old it looked after I had worn it for a whole year."

---

1 Wong Pok 1995. "Jiegou de moshu – Ma Yuan de xiaoshuo "Cuowu" de fenxi" (Structural magic – An analysis of Ma Yuan's novel "Cuowu"). *Bulletin of Chinese Studies*.1995:2. P.54.

The narrator here seems to go to excessive lengths to stress the importance of the hat, however, what is certainly clear from this passage is that the reader is being forced to question the narrator's judgement. Indeed the narrator even makes it clear that the narrative of the hat should take on more importance than the two births which are signposted at the start of the narrative:

> "At that time army hats were very fashionable, you would often hear stories of people being killed for their army hats. These weren't just wild rumours either. This was how my army hat was lost, it was simply gone. However those two kids were born on the evening of that same day. As soon as these two strange miracles appeared everybody forgot about my grief."

Here the narrator's lack of judgement is reinforced by the fact that this quest is clearly not considered as being important within the represented world. There is a clear tension within the text when the narrator insists on waking everyone up to look through their personal belongings to find the hat. Whilst thematically, the hat is an inconsequential element of "Cuowu", symbolically and structurally it is one of the main driving forces of the narrative, certainly within the initial chapters. As the self-reflexive "I" narrator is attempting to "write" the story of two births, the experiencing "I" narrator within the represented world is experiencing the loss of a hat. There is a clear spatio-temporal division between these two narrators which means that they operate with a different perception of facts and sets of judgements. When the experiencing "I" states that his hat is so important because "it is a symbol of whether a man can hold his own in society" (Ma 2009: p.286), both the unreliability and verisimilitude of this narrator are increased simultaneously. In this sense, the narrator appears to be a naïve narrator as the reader can "trust" the narrator's representation of events but can not necessarily trust the narrator's value system and beliefs.

The narrator's fixation on his hat is presented as an immature desire to compete on a homosocial level suggesting an insecure form of masculinity coupled with a lack of emotional intelligence. The experiencing "I", as the narrator's 19 year old past self, is on an epistemological quest to regain his hat whilst the self-reflexive narrator attempts to write the story of the two births: the former is the logic of the represented (past) world whilst the latter is the focus of the narrator's present self.

The hat therefore is a key driving force and facilitator of the text's other more important narratives in that it intersects almost all the other major elements of the text in chapter four. After the narrator has been attacked by Hei Zao, Er Gou brings a baby wrapped in the narrator's blood soaked hat into the camp. There is an extremely strong symbolism in the baby being carried in the now blood soaked hat, especially considering that the blood has now soaked through the hat so that the narrator's name (written in his own blood inside the hat) is no longer visible. At this point in the narrative the seemingly misguided epistemological quest ends, or at least is replaced by what is arguably the most important element of the narrative, namely the narrator's mistaken belief that Jiang Mei has given birth to Zhao Laopi's child. The narrator's insecure and somewhat myopic masculinity which drove him to look for his hat in an almost absurd manner now seems to have become a misplaced anger directed at Jiang Mei for becoming pregnant.

> "I doubt anyone felt more depressed than I about Jiang Mei having a baby. I watched her belly swell up along with everyone else, day after day, yet I still wasn't mentally prepared to deal with the consequences of her being pregnant. All I could think was that someone had screwed her, someone had screwed a baby into her and it wasn't me. That was all I thought about."

Whilst all the other male members of the camp fawn over the new baby, the narrator becomes obsessed with a thinly veiled jealous rage projected onto Jiang Mei and even the child itself, repeatedly referring to it as a "little bastard" (*xiaozazhong*). The narrator displays an uncomfortable, possessive and at times aggressive masculinity within the passages about Jiang Mei and interprets her pregnancy in a highly sexualised way.

The birth of Jiang Mei's child is intersected by three quite gruesome acts of violence within "Cuowu": firstly Hei Zao's violence against the narrator, then the narrator against Er Gou, and then finally Hei Zao onto himself to make up for the first incident. The violence within "Cuowu" is portrayed in a visceral and gruesome way with detailed descriptions of the physical injuries but with relatively little emotive text describing the experiencing of the pain from these injuries. Furthermore, whilst the quest for the hat is narrated through the "experiencing" "I" narrator, the injuries the narrator receives are represented through the narrator's "current self" of focalizer three:

> "He seemed quite calm and not at all rushed. He moved the head of the nail back and forth until it came out and then pressing against the door step he pulled the head of the spade off.
>
> I knew something was about to happen. I can't remember the details as this happened a long time ago. The result was that my ankle was smashed to pieces by the handle of the spade and I was left lame for the rest of my life."

Whilst the seemingly irrelevant hat narrative is narrated within a past spatio-temporal context so that the events appear to "unfold" as they are being narrated, in the passage above the vicissitudes of violence are muted by the fact that they are represented through an act of partial recollection. Indeed there is an odd tension between the different narrative perspectives within the text as the immediacy of the "experiencing" "I" narrator is juxtaposed against the sometimes distanced and dispassionate "present self" narrator:

> "I heard that afterwards Jiang Mei died. I had gone back to Jinzhou and she had stayed on at the farm, I heard that she killed herself. But this will come later, I won't mention it here."

On the one hand therefore, the narrative contains an epistemological quest which is narrated from the spatio-temporal context of the narrator's past self, but on the other hand the narrator's current self introduces contextualised information in an almost cruelly factual way such as in the instance above. This highlights the subtle complexities below the surface of the seemingly uniform first person focalization which is constantly shifting between different spatio-temporal contexts, and amongst an "experiencing", a "recollecting" and a self-reflexive narrator. After the quest for the hat ends the time structure of the text becomes increasingly complicated as the narrative frequently "jumps" back and forth between the three different narrative perspectives. The result of this is that the focus of the narrative becomes increasingly unclear and the narration shifts between the following chronological sequence of events: Jiang Mei has a baby, the narrator believes it is Zhao Laopi's, the narrator finds out from Hei Zao that it is Tian the accountant's, Zhang Lan dies giving birth to Zhao Laopi's child, Er Gou brings this child back to the camp in the narrator's hat after watching Zhang Lan die, Er Gou dies of cancer, and finally Jiang Mei commits suicide. In contrast to the amount of attention paid to the hat within the narrative, this almost absurdly tragic chain of events above is narrated at a disorientating speed from various different spatio-temporal perspectives. At times the distanced present day "I" narrator recalling past events, narrates across a vast spatio-temporal range:

> "I heard about Jiang Mei's death from him, but as far as I was concerned Jiang Mei had long ceased to exist. Afterwards I fell in love, got married and had kids just like many normal people, and Jiang Mei was already a distant memory. Not long before I had bumped into him when he came in to town to sell chickens and of course he took me out drinking. When we had been drinking to our hearts' content he started to talk about Jiang Mei, saying that she had never married but had gotten pregnant again, she had drowned herself, a horrible death, her body was swollen up like a water vat."

In the narrative above for example the amount of time previously devoted to finding the hat is rendered almost cruelly absurd considering how little worth Jiang Mei has in a narrative sense. Jiang Mei's suicide is one of the most tragic events within "Cuowu", however its impact is strangely muted by how it is narrated. In the same way, Er Gou's death is narrated in an almost alarmingly minimal fashion:

> "Er Gou, you should have said earlier, you really should.
> "Don't cry, it's not right for a man to cry, I'm begging you please don't cry."
> "I was by his side when he died. There really is no going back from cancer, he was quite short to start with and now all that was left of him was just withered bone. He was cremated, his mother kept the ashes."

In contrast to the descriptions of Jiang Mei's death however, before the narrator describes Er Gou's death in an equally stark manner, there is an extensive dialogue in direct reported speech which illustrates the emotional impact of this event on the narrator. Before his death, Er Gou recounts how Zhang Lan had died during child birth, how the baby was Zhao Laopi's and how he had brought the baby back to the camp in the narrator's hat and asked Jiang Mei to look after it. In essence, in a text full of "mistakes" and misunderstandings, Er Gou provides the missing pieces of information as his last act before he dies to enable the narrator to make sense of all the narratives he had failed to understand at the time. This death therefore becomes the cruel and tragic point of inception of the narrative itself because without this information the narrator could not have known that a "mistake" had been made.

In conclusion, "Cuowu" contains various different narrative threads which vary from the seemingly irrelevant hat narrative to highly tragic narratives of death and suicide all of which are somehow interconnected. To further complicate this intricate web of interconnected narratives, the narrative focalization frequently shifts between different spatio-temporal contexts and in turn the reliability of the narrator fluctuates wildly. The result is a disorientating narrative in which the narrator shifts between represented present and past selves (or the primary diegesis and hypo-diegesis), whilst the reader has key factual information about the represented world withheld.

IV. "Mistakes" within "Cuowu"

The title of a work of fiction often has a complex influence over the text itself.

Whilst there is no specific overarching theory to explain the role of titles in general, the core structural logic of titles is that they are essentially extra-diegetic elements that have a logical connection to the diegetic elements of the text (much in the same way that a primary diegesis has a logical connection to the hypo-diegesis). Extra-diegetic elements such as these fall outside of the diegetic logic of the narrative itself and can be broadly understood through the concept of the "implied author"[1] in that they hint at a higher "authorial" presence that is commenting on and naming the narrative. We can see from Ma Yuan's other works that some of the author's titles often present focal points of the text or overarching concepts in an often vague and sometimes ambiguous way: "Xugou" is a perfect example of this as the concept of "fabrication" is directly referenced within the novella itself in terms of the legitimisation of hegemonic structures through the "fabrication" of master narratives whilst simultaneously suggesting that the narrative itself is a "fabrication"[2]. Perhaps the most similar title to "Cuowu" in terms of the relationship it has with the text itself is "Jiusi" (旧死) in which the "old death" referenced in the title signifies the most significant narrative event within the text. This death however is only narrated within the last chapter so that the most tragic element within the narrative is suspended over the text creating a constant sense of tension. The concept of "mistakes" is an extremely important aspect of "Cuowu" and is repeatedly referenced throughout the text and in a similar way to "Jiusi", this title suggests that a "mistake" may be a key narrative event. The first such occasion where the concept of a "mistake" is referenced in the text occurs when the narrative is initially focused on the hat quest:

---

1 This theory was first formalised by Wayne Booth in 1961 in *The rhetoric of fiction* (re-issued in 1983 as Booth, Wayne C. *The rhetoric of fiction*. University of Chicago Press, 1983). For a exploration of the reception of Booth's concept of the implied author within China see Shen, Dan. "Booth's The Rhetoric of Fiction and China's Critical Context" *Narrative* (The Ohio State University Press) 15, no. 2 (May 2007): p. 176.

2 The opening quotation of "Xugou" explains the term used in the title as being a process through which narratives become legitimised and hegemonies are established. This warning, or "caveat lector" however is in itself a fabrication in that it is a Borgesian quote from a fictional text from within another of Ma Yuan's texts.

> "Can I ask, has anyone taken it by mistake? If it was a mistake then it doesn't matter, it's not too late to give it back to me. Who took it by mistake? Did anyone take it by mistake?"

The hat therefore becomes the first "mistake" within the text. However as this epistemological quest dissipates, the reader is left trying to identify where the mistake lies within "Cuowu". At this point in the narrative, the concept of "mistakes" can potentially broaden out to not necessarily be one identifiable narrative "event" but a wider sense of unreliability, misinterpretation and misunderstanding. This is foreshadowed within the text in statements such as "This was in June if I'm not mistaken" (Ma 2009: p.290) which suggest that "mistakes" within the text can take on the form of misunderstandings within the narrative. Indeed the narrator frequently uses phrases such as "I can't remember clearly", "I can't understand", and "I didn't realise" throughout the text suggesting an incomplete recollection and understanding of the represented world. Ultimately however, despite the numerous misunderstandings and misconceptions on the part of the narrator, the most clearly identifiable "mistake" within "Cuowu" is revealed at the end of the narrative:

> "It was only at this point that I started to realise that everything had been a mistake.
>
> Er Gou was still awake on the morning of the day he died, when I arrived he said he should have died yesterday or the day before but he couldn't die, there was no way he would die until I came to see him. He said that he knew that I would come, he had been waiting for me to come all this time and after he said all those things to me he could die in peace."

According to the timeline of events presented within the narrative, Er Gou dies five years after the night on which the two children are born, and the narrator's current self is narrating 17 years after his death. It is not until 5 years after the fact, when Er Gou reveals the full details about the events surrounding the births of the two children, that the narrator is finally aware of the "mistake" that had been made.

In this sense, there is a cruel correlation of events as the "creation" of the mistake coincides with a tragic death. The fragmented time structuring of the narrative focalization is such that the "mistake" within "Cuowu" is being naively experienced by the narrator's past self, recollected by the narrator's current self, and is also being reconciled by the self-reflexive narrator (in particular, for example, in chapter 4 when the narrator agonises over how to adequately narrate Er Gou's death or whether to narrate it at all). There is also a cruel irony in the narrator keeping the reader in suspense and waiting as late as possible to finally reveal the mistake, just as with the "old death" in "Jiusi". The "mistakes" within "Cuowu", therefore, should be interpreted both as a specific reference to a key narrative event which acts as the ultimate focal point of the narrative, and as a more broad overarching term which hints at more abstract concepts such as narrative unreliability and subjectivity.

V. The Opening Quotation

Much in the same way that the text's title often suggests either a focal point or overarching theme of the narrative, quotations at the start of narratives will often give an "authorial" (by which we mean the "implied author") insight into the nature of the text that follows it and furthermore offer a form of intertextual legitimisation. The strategy of having an opening quotation before the main body of the narrative begins is a form of narrative framing device frequently used by Ma Yuan. If we take the works within the "Xugou" collection published in 1994 as examples, all but one has an opening quotation in the same manner as "Cuowu". Ma Yuan's usage of quotations however is often somewhat problematic, for whilst many quotations within the "Xugou" collection come from "legitimate" sources such as those from the works of Brecht, Barth, Somerset Maugham, and Dante, in other opening quotations Ma Yuan often quotes, his own works, himself, fictional texts found within other real texts by Ma Yuan, or leaves quotes unattributed to any particular source as is the case with the opening quotation of "Cuowu":

> "There are many different ways to play marbles, the easiest one also happens to be the hardest, which is making the marble go straight into the

hole without any deflections - inscription."

The fact that this quotation is merely attributed as an "inscription" creates an interesting form of intertextuality in that the source of this quote is vague, indeterminate and potentially fictional. Despite the questionable provenance of the quotation however, the content of the quotation itself is certainly intriguing in its imagery. Firstly, as the specific imagery used is not directly or indirectly referenced within the narrative itself, creating a logical connection between these two narrative elements suggests reading the quotation along metaphorical lines. The methodology of playing marbles for example could be logically associated with narrative focalizer one's discussion of how to structure and write the hypo-diegetic text so that the game of marbles is a metaphor for writing. This would suggest that playing marbles represents writing, the player is therefore the author, and the "direct" method is a commentary on some form of "direct" narrative style. If this is indeed the case then there is certainly an ironic tension between the implied author extolling the virtues of "direct" narrative and the disorientating and far from direct narrative itself. If we read the marble metaphor against focalizer two's narrative however, the direct, uncomplicated, but perilous strategy of driving straight into the heart of the game situation has interesting parallels with the epistemological quest for the experiencing "I" narrator's hat. The internally focalized narrator thrusts the reader right into the heart of the narrative for a very specific epistemological purpose but this strategy quickly falls apart when the true complexity of the represented world starts to reveal itself.

VI. Self-reflexive Devices within "Cuowu"

In comparison to many of Ma Yuan's other more "overtly" self-reflexive works such as "Xugou" for example, "Cuowu" contains a range of relatively subtle metafictional devices. These devices do not destroy the verisimilitude of the represented world, but rather, as with many of Ma Yuan's works, create a parallel structure of an "author" figure and his "text". As highlighted above, the three-tiered time structure within the first person narrative focalization means that a self-reflexive narrator can "discuss" his narrative and the "text" that he is writing, without breaking the mimetic integrity of the experiencing "I" narrator as the past self of the "author" figure. In this sense the narrator's self-reflexivity does not destroy the verisimilitude of the hypo-diegesis, but rather it creates the impression that a narrator as "author" figure within a contemporary spatio-temporal context is trying to "narrativise" his past self. Time, therefore, becomes a crucial facilitator of the self-reflexivity of "Cuowu" as it delineates the distinct "roles" of the "I" narrator thereby allowing them to coexist without apparent contradiction.

The self-reflexive "I" within "Cuowu" frequently engages in both textual and narrative self-reflexivity as it foregrounds both the narrating of a "story" and the writing of a "text" as is the case within the following passage:

> "I really don't want to use flashbacks, why should I start my novel with an "at that time"? I don't know how all this came to be and I even don't know if those two kids are even still alive today."

Here, the narrator is openly declaring his lack of omniscience in terms of his knowledge of the events within the represented world and is also presenting a lack of certainty about how to "write" this novel. This representation of narrative unreliability functions through a thematised "author" figure which is a commonly used technique within metafictional texts. Whilst the first person narrator does not overtly refer to himself as the "author" of the text, the presence of the "reader" in the next clearly self-reflexive passage within the text suggests a thematised "author"/"text"/"reader" dynamic.

> "I am leaving the cruellest part of this story until the end. Initially I thought of doing this to keep the reader in suspense, but then I also hesitated because I don't know if it's appropriate of me to tell this part of the story. As I've said it is quite cruel and I've no way of judging it from and kind of moralistic perspective.
>
> Should I go on, and if so how?

These are difficulties though that I'll come to later, I'm confident that I'll be able to cross that bridge when I come to it but I'm not going to worry too much about it now.

When I said that I was going to cut Hei Zao's leg open that was after the fact, at the time I was spread out in front of the door so the story of that night seems to have ended.

Careful readers though will instantly say no it hasn't finished and that at the start I said there were these two kids. Well that is true, it hasn't finished. That boy hasn't appeared yet, he's about to appear though.

But before that there will be another character within this story who hasn't appeared yet, Er Gou."

The appearance of both the "reader", and indeed the "careful readers" within this passage clearly foregrounds the text's self-reflexivity. Wherever an "author" figure addresses a "reader" figure about the narration of a "story" or the writing of a "text" within a narrative, the text is no longer a realist representation of a represented world but rather a representation of a narrator narrating, or to be more precise a representation of a representation being represented. When the narrator above therefore "discusses" how he is going to "write" his narrative, it is of course a representation of a thematised author figure addressing a thematised "reader" addressee about a thematised "text". The presence of a thematised "author" addressing a "reader" addressee is one of the key features of many of Ma Yuan's most metafictional texts and within "Cuowu" this narrative device is the fundamental structure upon which the text's self-reflexivity is established. Elsewhere within the text there are other relatively subtle instances of self-reflexivity such as when the "experiencing I" narrator asks "could this not have been resolved earlier? (Ma 2009: p.297)" which creates a clear ironic tension with the self-reflexive narrator's decision to leave the crucial information about "Cuowu" until the end. Otherwise the text's self-reflexivity is primarily established through the two most significantly self-reflexive passages above, the presence of the "reader" and by implication the "author" within the text, and furthermore the establishment of the three separate narrative "roles" of the first person narrator.

In summary, "Cuowu" contains a diegesis/hypo-diegesis narrative structure through which a thematised author/narrator focalizer addresses a "reader" narratee about the narrative on a primary diegetic level, whilst the author's "past self" experiences the represented world of the author's past on the hypo-diegetic level. This structure facilitates the text's self-reflexivity through enabling the text to act not just as a representation being represented, but as a representation of a representation being represented. Whilst the divide between the diegetic and hypo-diegetic is logically established through the clear difference in narrative focalizations, the fact that the narrative frequently shifts between different forms of focalization means that the delineation between the different narrative levels and spatio-temporal contexts in which the various focalizers operate is de-emphasised. This self-reflexive structure therefore allows "Cuowu" to simultaneously represent the author's current "narrating" self, the author's current "writing" self, and the author's previous "experiencing" self, whilst deemphasising the narratological boundaries between these three distinct perspectives.

VII. Narrative Unreliability, Omniscience, and Fallibility

One of the most significant features of the narrative focalizerswithin "Cuowu" is their lack of omniscience and their different levels of unreliability. To be specific, unreliability can be broken down into three different forms according to James Phelan's identification of unreliability falling along the axis of facts/events, values/judgements, and finally knowledge/perception[1]. The final sentence of the text for example foregrounds the fact that the narrator does not have omniscient knowledge about the represented world, but rather a set of impressions or memories of his experiencing of that world:

---

1 For an explanation of these three forms of unreliability see Phelan, James and Martin, Mary, "The Lessons of 'Weymouth': Homodiegesis, unreliability, Ethics, and *The Remains of the Day*". In *Narratologies*, edited by David Herman, 88-109. Columbus: Ohio State University Press, 1999.

"I thought that Zhao Laopi must have thought of his widow Zhang Lan when he heard that Jiang Mei had given birth, but after Zhang Lan died where could he have gone to?"

Here, the first person narrative focalizer on the primary diegetic level displays an uncertainty about the events within the hypo-diegesis and also an uncertainty about how to narrativise those events. The narrator's frequent statements about the limits of his perception throughout the narrative and the absence of omniscient externally focalized narrative within the text mean that the narrative always retains a constant degree of unreliability and openly acknowledged "fallibility". Whilst focalizers one and three display an unreliability on the axis of knowledge/facts, the hypo-diegetic narrator on the other hand is reliable on the axis of facts/knowledge but extremely unreliable on the axis of values/judgement, which is clearly foregrounded by this narrator's initial quest to recover his hat. There are therefore two types of unreliable focalization within "Cuowu": One type of focalization displays an openly declared unreliability on the axis of knowledge/facts, whilst another type displays an unreliability on the axis of values/judgement which is not itself acknowledged by the narrator.

The narrative unreliability within "Cuowu" is closely linked to the text's narrative structure which enables different narrative focalizers from different spatio-temporal contexts to narrate on two narrative levels. Neither of these narrative levels contain completely reliable narrators. However, because these two levels are heavily intertwined within the text, the different forms of unreliability and levels of self-reflexivity displayed by the different focalizerseffectively cancel each other out: the naïve hypo-diegetic narrator, experiencing past events with flawed judgement, incomplete understanding and limited awareness, is balanced by the self-reflexive and self-aware narrator on the primary diegetic level. The usage of different spatio-temporal contexts within the narrative focalization structure plays a crucial role in facilitating the differing levels of unreliability within the text. For example, the reader can realistically rationalise the fact that the experiencing "I" narrator on the hypo-diegetic level is experiencing the represented world of the past "as it happens" despite the fact that the narrator on the primary diegetic level states that "I am leaving the cruellest part of this story until the end". (Ma 2009: p.292) The knowledge held by the narrator on the higher narrative level, therefore, is clearly not "available" to the narrator on the narrative below because of the structure of the text which accommodates different narrative focalizers in different spatio-temporal contexts with different levels of unreliability and self-reflexivity. Likewise, focalizer two's absurd quest for his hat and his clear misinterpretations of the represented world of the past can be rationalised alongside the less naïve and immature perspectives of focalizers one and three. The shifting forms of unreliability therefore strengthen the verisimilitude of the focalizers operating within different spatio-temporal contexts which is a crucial element of the text's narrative structure.

VIII. Interpreting "Cuowu"

The visceral realities of rusticated youth have indeed served as subject matter for numerous writers of a certain generation within China and so it is understandable that some critics believed that the interpretive possibilities of this form of highly politicised literature had been entirely exhausted. However the unique delivery method for this familiar content means that "Cuowu" is far from being a "simple" piece of "Roots seeking" or "rusticated youth" literature. In particular, the idea of "catharsis" which features so prominently in many works of post-Mao literature is notably absent within "Cuowu" which is structured in such a way that the most poignant and emotive elements of the narrative are lost amongst misunderstandings and misinterpretations. The unreliability and self-reflexivity of the narrative focalization and the lack of omniscient externally focalized narrative marginalises many of the text's most tragic elements because they fall outside of the narrator's first-hand experience and therefore fall outside of the narrative. At the same time however, the seemingly irrelevant aspects of the narrative, such as the quest for the author's hat (the first "mistake" within "Cuowu"), are given an absurdly high level of importance. The cruel tension between the sparse narratives of Jiang Mei's and

Er Gou's deaths and the elaborate detail with which the narrator's hat is described highlights the unreliability of the narrator in an extremely significant way: within "Cuowu", unreliability, self-reflexivity, and subjectivity are heavily intertwined and the narrative is never able to escape out of the limits of perception of the "I" narrator into an omniscient and "objective" structure.

In this way the narrative is not poorly mediated, but rather places a great deal of importance on the verisimilitude of the changing subjectivities of the narrative focalization as it shifts between different spatio-temporal contexts: the experiencing "I" as past self is naïve and emotionally immature, whilst the narrator's current self is more reliable in terms of judgement but has an openly declared level of fallibility. The result is that the events of the represented world can only exist as a function of an experiencing entity – the narrator does not "narrate" the tragic elements of the text but instead "re-presents" the direct reported speech through which the narrator became aware of these events within the represented world (which is the extent of his experience of these events). The poignancy of "Cuowu" therefore is not elicited through how the "reader" experiences externally narrated tragedy but rather how the reader experiences the narrator's experience, memory and writing of such tragedy. Given the narrator's unreliability, the reader is always able to "look beyond" the narrative focalizer's representations to sense that the represented world is clearly more rich, diverse and painful than the experiencing "I"'s narrative, and that the emotional impact these past events still have on the narrator's current self is not being fully disclosed. In a way, "Cuowu" does not offer a typical "rusticated youth" narrative but instead it presents the narratives surrounding a "rusticated youth" text in which the reader is, in effect, given everything but the text itself: within "Cuowu" the reader is shown how the narrator experienced the past, how the narrator remembers the past, and how the narrator is trying to write the past, but what is absent is an omniscient narrative through which the full details of past events can be "objectively" represented and "re-experienced" in a "reliable" way.

Within "Cuowu", the mistakes of the past are narrated through the misunderstandings of the present. The realist master narrative that orders events according to chronology and importance has been abandoned for a highly subjective internally focalized narrative that does not privilege the verisimilitude of "what happened" but rather emphasises "what was and what still is being experienced". The narrator's rusticated youth therefore was a turbulent and sometimes violent and traumatic past that was experienced in a naïve and emotionally immature way: removing the unreliability, and subjectivity of this experience risks dehumanising it, and so instead the narrative is allowed to be fallible and full of "mistakes". In narrating the "mistakes" of the past therefore through the shifting subjectivities allowed by the passage of time, Ma Yuan is empowering his rusticated youth to be partially experienced, remembered, and written, rather than "re-presented" intact. Rather than attempt to re-write the master narrative, Ma Yuan provides the narrative of absence, the narrative of incompletion, the narrative of the unresolved – this perhaps, given the clichéd subject matter, is the most significant aspect of "Cuowu".

One of the most distinctive features of Ma Yuan's writing is his clear distrust of the "objectivity" of narrative omniscience. "Xugou" for example warns the reader about the deceptive "fabrications" through which power is established in a narrative sense; "Gangdisi de youhuo" offers a polyvocal narrative in which it is impossible to tell who is "speaking" and to "whom", which forces the reader to question whether the narrative can be not only "believed" but "trusted". Within "Cuowu" however, Ma Yuan refuses to "objectively" re-write the past using the damaged lexicon of post-Maoist realist literature that he had inherited. Instead Ma Yuan sacrifices his text for the sake of his subjectivity, his identity, and his "mistakes" so that his narrative of birth and death, of pain and lost love, also becomes the narrative of a lost hat.

中国传统文化

Chinese Traditional Culture

论古琴美学思想与儒道家修身养性的作用

菲李普 【意大利】
乌比诺大学副教授

一 引言

这篇文章旨在分析古代音乐的修身养性作用,特别要强调古琴艺术的重要地位及其价值。

古琴是中华民族最古老最崇高的弹拨乐器。也可以说,古琴是中华民族传统文化的象征之一。在三千多年的发展过程中,古琴与儒、释、道教修身养性方法一直有着密切关系。古琴之所以可以修身养性,主要原因有二:一方面,由于音乐在儒家教育中的核心作用;另一方面,在所有的中国民族乐器中,古琴最能体现文人的智慧和优雅高贵的灵魂。古琴艺术对文人的道德情操、美学思想发展等起到深远的影响。

本文着重要分析古琴美学思想与儒家、道家修身养性方法的密切关系。第一部分,分析先秦音乐思想,特别呈现了传统儒家与老庄音乐思想的不同概念和理论。第二部分,分析琴乐对先秦思想的影响。先秦主要理论一方面特别影响古琴美学思想,另一方面分析古琴艺术与修身养性方法的密切关系。

二 古代音乐与修身养性的密切关系

音乐在古代中国社会中的作用一直是至关重要的,李泽厚认为最主要的原因是在古代中国音乐和祭祀之间的密切连接。古乐有沟通鬼神、天地、人心的作用。

古代中国重要的例子就是在商代社会祭乐的价值作用：殷人叫尚声就是"乐感天人"的意识。[1]

后来儒家传统文化充分承继音乐的重要性，儒家坚信音乐对个人道德修养、人心和安、天人情感交流的主要作用。在不同的先秦儒家经典显示了音乐对和谐、平安、秩序社会的作用。《左传·昭公元年》中说："先王之乐所以节百事也，故有五节，迟速、本末以相及。中声以降，五降之后不容弹矣。于是有烦手淫声，慆堙心耳，乃忘平和，君子弗听也"。还说："君子之近琴瑟以仪节也，非以慆心也。"[2]

孔子自己多次表达了音乐对社会形成的重要性。《论语·子罕》中写道："吾自卫反鲁，然后乐正，《雅》《颂》各得其所"。[3]尤其是在孔子思想里音乐对个人道德修养有主要作用。

《论语·泰伯》中写道："兴于诗，立于礼，成于乐。"[4]孔子认为对音乐的学习是在君子养成过程中最后且最重要的阶段。《论语·阳货》中写道："礼云礼云，玉帛云乎哉？乐云乐云，钟鼓云乎哉？"[5]就是音乐主要意义并不在于一般人所感受到的欢乐，君子感受的是音乐深刻的精神和道德。《论语·八佾》中写道："人而不仁，如礼何？人而不仁，如乐何？"[6]就是说没有"仁"这种道德概念，乐就失去其存在的意义；音乐与个人道德修养一定有密切的关系。

后来的荀子也承继并且发展了上面提出的音乐价值。荀子坚信音乐是文明的强大媒介，《荀子·乐论》："乐者，圣人之所乐也，而可以善民心，其感人深，其移风易俗，故先王导之以礼乐而民和睦。"[7]音乐也是修养的强大媒介："夫乐者，乐也，人情之所必不免也，故人不能无乐。乐则必发于声，形于动静，而人之道声间动静，性术之变尽足矣，故人不能不乐，乐则不能无形，形而不为道，则不能无乱。先王恶其乱也，故制雅颂之声以道之，使其声足以乐而不流，使其文足以纶而不息，使其曲直繁声廉肉节奏，足以感动人之善心，使夫邪污之气无由得

1　Li Zehou (2010) *The Chinese Aesthetic Tradition*, translated by Maija Bell Samei. Honolulu: Hawaii University Press.
2　《左传·昭公元年》卷四十一。
3　杨伯俊编注 (2006)《论语译注》。中华书局，第 105 页。
4　同上书，第 93 页。
5　同上书，第 209 页。
6　同上书，第 25 页。
7　《荀子·乐论》转引自张娣 (2011) 中国古代琴道思想研究。博士学位论文，武汉大学。第 41 页。

接焉,是先王立乐之方也。"¹ 又说:"君子乐得其道,小人乐得其欲。以道制欲,则乐而不乱;以欲忘道,则惑而不乐"。² 上面荀子提出了音乐与快乐情感的关系,"乐"(yue)和"乐"(le)不能分开,因为音乐是人之快乐情感的真实表达和体验。³ 另外,也对比了君子与小人对待音乐态度的极大差异:君子看重音乐内在的正心的价值和作用,就是音乐制欲的能力;小人只有对音乐外表欢乐比较感兴趣。

在战国末期和秦汉时期之间音乐道德能力和作用已经达到成熟的形式。从战国末期的《吕氏春秋》到汉代的《乐记》《淮南子》,还有董仲舒都显示音乐文明强大媒介。《吕氏春秋·大乐》里写道:"乐之所由来远矣,生于度量,本于太一。太一出两仪,两仪出阴阳。阴阳变化,一上一下,合而成章……和适先王定乐,由此而生。天下太平,万物安宁。皆化其上,乐乃可成。"⁴ 董仲舒的《举贤良对策》:"王者功成作乐者,乐其德也。乐者,所以变民风,化民俗也。其变民也易,其化人也著。"⁵

除了上面提出的音乐道德能力以外,秦汉经典开始展现音乐基于宇宙与大自然的声音;还分析音乐和声音的精神和本原。秦汉音乐理论与价值受到儒家竞争对手的极大影响。这里特别要强调老子和庄子对音乐论和美学思想伟大贡献。借用高罗佩先生的说法,由于老子和庄子的这些贡献,音乐开始作为一种修身和智慧的手段将被发展。⁶ 老子和庄子都批评儒家有限音乐论:真正的音乐是纯粹的,没有明确的类别,乐源于道。《老子》中最有名的"大音稀声"的概念要代表最大的、最美的音乐就是"稀声"之乐,"稀声"就是五官感觉不到的深刻经验。《老子》第十四章:"视之不见名曰夷,听之不闻名曰希,搏之不得名曰微,此三者不可致诘,故混而为一。"⁷ 修海林先生说明"稀"概念属于"道"自然本性,而"道"的存在方式,就是自然而然的存在。⁸ 庄子承继又发展《老子》里的思想。首先提

---

1 《荀子·乐论》转引自张娣:中国古代琴道思想研究,武汉大学 2011 博士学位论文,第 41 页。
2 《荀子·乐论》转引自修海林《中国古代音乐美学》,福建教育出版社 2004 年版,第 193 页。
3 参见同上。
4 《吕氏春秋·大乐》转引自修海林《中国古代音乐美学》,福建教育出版社 2004 年版,第 199 页。
5 《举贤良对策》转引自同上,第 231 页。
6 参见 Van Gulik, R.H. (1969) *Lore of the Chinese Lute An Essay in Ch'in Ideology*. Monumenta Nipponica, no.3. Tokyo: Sophia University Press/Charles E. Tuttle Company. 第 49 页。
7 陈鼓应:《老子今注今译》,商务印书馆 2009 年版,第 126 页。
8 修海林:《中国古代音乐美学》,福建教育出版社 2004 年版,第 165 页。

出了"天地有大美而不言"¹的美学思想："大美"就是"不言"，与老子提出的"稀声"有直接关系。其次还有讲了"天乐"和"天籁"主要概念。真正的音乐就是大自然的音乐，"天乐"就使万物与天地相沟通。《庄子·天道》："以虚静推于天地，通于万物，此之谓天乐。"²同文又说："与人和者，谓之人乐；与天和者，谓之天乐。"³通过感知真正的音乐可以体验"道"，不是通过听的感性体验，这是老子和庄子的本义。《庄子·天地》："视乎冥冥，听乎无声，冥冥之中，独见晓焉；无声之中，独闻和焉。"⁴老子的"稀声"和庄子的"无声"都需要一种超越感性的深刻体验，就是说音乐的经验具有把握"道"存在的能力变成内省的有力手段。

三 古琴艺术与修身养性的作用

在中国传统音乐的历史上，古琴艺术是最体验和代表文人的智慧、优雅而高贵的灵魂。古琴艺术对文人的道德情操、美学思想发展等起到深远的影响。借用De Woskin的说法，古琴地位和价值首先是由于它的古老起源；其次是古琴物理特性和音质比其他乐器有儒家理想音乐形式的仪器更好。这些因素使古琴艺术与传统文化和经典的密切关系。⁵

关于认识到古琴与修身养性的作用，战国末期秦汉代之间是最关键的时间。在西周春秋时期古琴艺术还有祈天地、祭鬼神的作用；《左传》卷四一是表达与修身养性关系的第一个经典之一："君子之近琴瑟，以仪节也，非以慆心也。"琴瑟音乐有自我修养的重要作用不是耽于游戏，玩物丧志的。战国末期的《吕氏春秋》为我们留下了很主要的记录，就是很有名的伯牙鼓琴："伯牙鼓琴，钟子期听之．方鼓琴而志在太山，钟子期曰：'善哉乎鼓琴，巍巍乎若太山。'少选之间，而志在流水，钟子期又曰：'善哉乎鼓琴，汤汤乎若流水。'钟子期死，伯牙破琴绝弦，终身不复鼓琴，以为世无足复为鼓琴者。非独琴若此也，贤者亦然。虽有贤者，而无礼以接之，贤奚由尽忠？犹御之不善，骥不自千里也"。（《吕氏春秋·孝行览·本

---

1 陈鼓应：《庄子今注今译》，中华书局2010年版，第601页。
2 同上书，第364页。
3 同上。
4 同上书，第325页。
5 De Woskin, K. J. (1982) A Song for One or Two. Music and the Concept of Art in Early China. Michigan: Ann Arbor Center for Chinese Studies. 第112页。

味篇》)¹

　　这一记载说明古琴艺术的特别，还有古琴艺术的高要求，借用李祥霆先生的说法："并不是随便什么人都能从音乐中理解演奏者的艺术表现，钟子期能从伯牙的精彩演奏中听出其音乐的精神和意境，说明演奏者和听者双方都居于同一高水平的音乐修养。"²

　　汉代时期是古琴的修身养性作用发展最快的成熟时期。在古琴作为修身养性手段的定义中，两个基本概念是中心的：第一个与儒家思想理论有直接关系，就是说古琴是自我控制和正心的工具，它的美德可以解决激情，恢复心灵的平和。第二个受到了老庄思想的影响，就是说古琴艺术的大需求是模仿大自然，达到"道"的目的，通过古琴的修养可以进入一种深刻、微妙、无象的境界。琴乐最深感受并不依靠五官感觉的现实，最终目的是把握它的原则。这个概念变成一种很主要的内省手段。

四　儒家"琴—禁"思想对修身养性的作用

　　古琴与"禁"关系的理论发生于汉代。"禁"的意思就是"禁止邪淫"，因而与孔子和先秦儒家乐教理论有直接关系。汉代时这一概念的影响比较大，比如许慎《说文解字》称："琴，禁也。神农所作，洞越。练朱五弦，周时加二弦。象形。"³ 就是说在汉代时期"禁"作为"琴"之本性的规定。受到这种概念影响的汉代经典比较多：东汉桓谭在其《新论·琴道》中提到了"琴之言禁也，君子守以自禁也。"⁴ 就是古琴是君子用以自守自禁之器。还有汉代《白虎通·礼乐》中提出："琴者，禁也，所以禁止淫邪，正人心也。"⁵ 琴乐正人心能力的手段直接受到先秦儒家的乐教理论，但在所有中国民族乐器中"琴"代表自守自禁能力的第一个原因是古琴的音量。桓谭提出："大声不震哗而流漫，细声不湮灭而不闻。八音广博，琴德最优，古者圣贤玩琴以养心。"⁶ 古者圣贤抚琴以养心，是因为琴音的音量大小适中，所以琴是节人情最合适的乐器。同一时期的《风俗通义》也有说明"以为琴

1　《吕氏春秋·孝行览·本味篇》李祥霆《古琴综议》，中国人民大学出版社2012年版，第40—41页。
2　参见李祥霆《古琴综议》，中国人民大学出版社2012年版，第40—41页。
3　[汉]许慎撰，清段玉裁注：《说文解字注》，浙江古籍出版社2006年版，第633页。
4　[汉]桓谭著《新论》，上海人民出版社1977年版，第64页。
5　[东汉]班固等撰《白虎通》，上海商务印书馆（1936），第63页。
6　[汉]桓谭著《新论》，上海人民出版社1977年版，第64页。

之大小得中而声音和，大声不喧哗而流漫，小声不湮灭而不闻。"¹ 这种说法与上面显示的《左传》有明显的关系。《左传》说的"琴瑟以仪节"与"琴德最优，古者圣贤玩琴以养心"有共同意义。还有《白虎通·礼乐》中提出："雅者，古正也，所以远郑声也。孔子曰'郑声淫'何郑国土地民人山居谷浴，男女错杂，为郑声以相诱悦怪。故邪僻声皆淫色之声也。……琴者，禁也，所以禁止淫邪，正人心也。"² "禁"就是要禁淫邪之声，而存雅正之音，"雅正之音"是最能修养正心的音，古琴就是代表"雅正之音"的乐器之一。

这种古琴价值和意义的影响到后来时期，唐代薛易简的《琴诀》重申："鼓琴之士志静气静，则听者易分心乱神浊，则听者难辨矣。常人但见用指轻利，取声温润，音韵不绝，句度流美，俱赏为能，殊不知志士弹之，声韵皆有所主也。……盖其声正而不乱，足以禁邪止淫也。"³ 宋代司马承正《素琴传》说："琴者禁也，以禁邪僻之情而存雅正之志，修身理性，返其天真"⁴还有朱熹作诗《紫阳琴铭》"养君中和之正性，禁尔忿欲之邪心，乾坤无言物有则，我独与子钩其深。"⁵ 例子都显示弹琴禁邪僻之情，禁忿欲之邪心，养中和之正性，因此弹琴超越简单的音乐活动达到修身养性的作用；弹琴还懂琴就让人修身理性返其天真，古琴是一种完美修养的手段，是对先秦儒家乐教继承与发展。

五　从老庄音乐思想到琴乐的修身养性作用

琴乐养人"中和"和返其天真的作用，无疑也受到老庄思想的影响。老庄音乐思想强调克服五官感觉的现实和强调"道"原则的必要性。就是说音乐的体验超过简单的欢乐作用进入一种深刻的现实。关于对古琴艺术的道教影响，魏晋南北朝是最主要的时期。其中，最主要的人物是"竹林七贤"之一的嵇康。嵇康的音乐思想直接受到老庄的影响，也发展为对儒家乐教的批评。嵇康反对音乐作为政治功利、自我控制手段的儒家传统思想。他认为音乐是客观存在的，其体自若而不变。音乐不能固有地体现主观的情感，同时情感不能影响到音乐。人情与音

1　《风俗通义》转引自张娣中国古代琴道思想研究，武汉大学2011博士学位论文，第53页。
2　[东汉] 班固等撰、王云五主编《白虎通》，上海商务印书馆，第63页。
3　[唐] 薛易简著《琴诀》转引自蔡仲德注译《中国音乐美学史资料注译》，人民音乐出版社2004年版，第555页。
4　[明] 蒋克谦编《琴书人全》转引白文化部文学艺术研究院音乐研究所、北京古琴研究会编《琴曲集成》第5册，中华书局，第324页。
5　《晦庵先生朱文公文集》，北京图书出版社2006年版，第45页。

乐没有直接的关系和影响。在他著名的《声无哀乐论》中提到:"夫喜、怒、哀、乐、爱、憎、惭、惧,凡此八者,生民所以接物传情,区别有属,而不可溢者也。""声音自当以善恶为主,则无关于哀乐;哀乐自当以情感,则无系于声音。"[1] 嵇康认为音乐形式是没有确定的哀或乐的情感在内的,而音乐引起人的不同情感是人听到音乐后所产生的不同感受。

虽然嵇康基本上否定音乐控制人情能力的儒家乐论,但在他的音乐思想中"和"的儒家概念的地位和价值还是最高的:"然声音和比,感人之最深者也。……夫哀心藏于苦心内,遇和声而后发。和声无象,而哀心有主。夫以有主之哀心,因乎无象之和声,其所觉悟,唯哀而已。"[2] 借用 Middendorf 的说法,嵇康的"和"是"音乐的美学本质"[3]。嵇康以"和"为形而上的概念,就是音乐的无变本体。因此音乐主要目的在于使人心"和"。因此尽管嵇康音乐的目的不在政治社会的那种和谐,但在能达到心的和谐,只有保有了其"和"之本体的声音,才能最深地感动人心。

嵇康在《琴赋》中提出:"可以导养神气,宣和情志,处穷独而不闷者,莫近于音声也。"[4] 就是说音乐的最高目的是涵养人之"和"的心境,音乐可以"导养神气,宣和情志";借用张娣的认知:"移风易俗,使人们安乐于自足的生活,因此,在这样的意义上,乐的形式之音声就变得不重要了,其关键还在于如何去领悟乐之'和'的本体。"[5] 这里嵇康受到老庄美学思想的影响;音乐还有音乐家最高目的是达到"和"的完美体验。但这里的"和"与儒家的"和"不同,是一种自然而然的"和",万物的本体。就是说能顺应自然而然、养人心之"和"是音乐最高的形式。《琴赋》又说:"然非夫旷远者。不能与之嬉游。非夫渊静者。不能与之闲止。非夫放达者。不能与之无隙。非夫至精者。不能与之析理也。"[6] 嵇康认为只有"至精者"会有真正的音乐体验,因为只有君子能达到析"理"的体验。

关于琴乐,嵇康强调古琴的高尚地位和价值,他认为只有最优秀的人能把握

---

1 修海林《中国古代音乐美学》,福建教育出版社 2004 年版,第 267 页。
2 同上书,第 268 页。
3 参见 Middendorf, U. (2005) Music without emotions. Xi Kang meets Hanslick. In Power Beauty and Meaning, eight studies on Chinese music. Galliano, L (ed.). Leo S. Olshki Editore. 第 50 页。
4 [魏] 嵇康著《嵇康集校注》转引自修海林《中国古代音乐美学》,福建教育出版社(2004)年版,第 294 页。
5 张娣:《中国古代琴道思想研究》,武汉大学 2011 博士学位论文,第 70 页。
6 修海林:《中国古代音乐美学》,福建教育出版社 2004 年版,第 294 页。

古琴音乐:"愔愔琴德,不可测兮;体清心远,邈难极兮;良质美手,遇今世兮;纷纶翕响,冠众艺兮;识音者希,孰能珍兮;能尽雅琴,唯至人兮!"[1] 嵇康认为古琴的品质深不可测,它的影响力对人是深刻而强劲的,所以是一种能力大的修身养性手段。又说:"众器之中,琴德最优"[2],在各种乐器中,古琴具有最优异的品德,最适宜君子作为修身养性的手段:"性洁静以端理,含至德之和平。诚可以感荡心志,而发泄幽情矣!"[3] 古琴是最能代表形而上的、自然而然的、一直无变的"和",琴音包含了琴德的平和,因而琴的品德就是静人心,发泄内在的幽情。

最后,在同一个方向和背景,我们可以了解后来陶渊明的著名"无弦琴"说法。在《晋书·陶潜传》"陶潜……性不解音,而畜素琴一张,弦徽不具,每朋之会,则抚而和之,曰'但识琴中趣,何劳弦上声'。"[4] 琴乐最终的需求是超越不同的感官经验,要达到它本体的了解和感受。唐代士人张随在《无弦琴赋》来讲:"《幽兰》无声,媚庭际之芬馥;《绿水》不奏,流舍后之潺湲。以为心和即乐畅,性静则音全,和由中出,静非外传。若穷乐于求和,即乐流而和丧;扣音以征静,则音溺而静捐。"[5] 这就是说,人不是通过乐外在的声音来获得《幽兰》和《绿水》美好的审美感受,而是通过人的内在心性去感受乐的内在蕴涵。张随的说法和主张与上面显示的嵇康就很近,音乐深刻意义和真正感受不在外面出现的声音,而在"无象""稀声"的审美感受。能把握其深刻意义的人并不需要事实上听到《幽兰》或《绿水》的有名琴曲,而音乐的最大意义在于以其"和"的本体来感人,与外在音声相分离。借用张娣的了解:"琴曲不作,却能引人无限之遐想。"[6] 嵇康所说的"和",陶渊明"无弦琴"的说法都代表老庄思想的发展:音乐最终目的不在于外在的音,而在于内心本能所感受到的声音,它的本体就是"无象""稀声""和谐"的,与宇宙万物同一;所以通过音乐本体的把握可以进入一种深刻、微妙、无象的境界,让人心安静和平的。嵇康还说乐器之中,古琴是最优秀的,因而是最适宜君子作为修身养性的手段;琴音是最能反映平和、安静、深刻的音。陶渊明"无弦琴"的说法也是用古琴艺术来代表音乐最终目的,和嵇康有同样的想法。

---

1 同上第 293 页。
2 同上第 293 页。
3 李祥霆:《古琴综议》,中国人民大学出版社 2013 年版,第 87 页。
4 张娣:《中国古代琴道思想研究》,武汉大学 2011 博士学位论文,第 71 页。
5 参见同上,第 75 页。
6 参见同上,第 73 页。

六 结论

本文作者分析了音乐与儒家、道家修身养性的作用，特别强调了琴乐的作用。

文章第一部分分析了古代和先秦音乐思想，特别展现了传统儒家与老庄音乐思想的不同概念和理论。第二部分析了在这两种传统思想的影响下，特别在修身养性的过程中对古琴艺术及其价值的理解。首先，展现了汉代儒家坚信古琴的控制人情正心的能力。这种看法受到孔子和先秦儒家音乐思想的极大影响。汉代儒家从"禁"字来讲古琴的作用和能力，"禁"就是"存雅正之志，修身理性，返其天真"。其次，分析老庄道教音乐思想的影响。显示了"竹林七贤"之一的嵇康深受老庄乐论的影响。嵇康认为音乐是最能超越五官感觉的人类活动，能顺应自然而然的万物本体的，有让人接近"道"的能力。他还认为琴乐是最高远、最深刻的音乐，也是最难掌握的；古琴的品质深不可测，它对人的影响力都是深刻而强劲的。

最后，嵇康的看法影响到后来的音乐家和琴家，作者提到了陶渊明的"无弦琴"主要影响的例子。"无弦琴"代表琴乐最终的需求而超越不同的感官经验，要达到它本体的了解和感受。这种说法对后来琴家的影响比较大。结论，本文显示了古琴对修身养性的作用基本上具有两种不同的源头：第一强调琴与"禁"的关系和作用；第二强调琴乐研究宇宙万物本体的能力；即使它们属于不同的传统，它们共享相同的看法：琴乐是一种正心静情的有力手段。借用高罗佩先生的引文来综合，"Playing the lute purifies one's nature by banishing low passions, therefore it is a sort of meditation, a means for communicating directly with tao [dao]. Its rarefied notes reproduce the 'sounds of emptiness', and so the music of the lute tunes the soul of the player in harmony with tao [dao]."[1]

1　Van Gulik, R.H. (1969) Lore of the Chinese Lute An Essay in Ch'in Ideology. Monumenta Nipponica, no.3. Tokyo: Sophia University Press/Charles E. Tuttle Company. 第 46 页。

On the Aesthetic Thought of Guqin and the Role of Confucianism and Taoist in Self-Cultivation

Fillippo Costantini / Italy

Associate Professor, University of Urbino

I. Introduction

This paper aims to analyze the self-cultivation functions of ancient music, with stress on the important status and values of Guqin art.

Guqin is the most ancient and noble plucked musical instrument of the Chinese nation. It is fair to say that Guqin is one of the symbols of traditional Chinese culture. In the course of development of more than 3,000 years, Guqin has been closely related to Confucian, Buddhist, and Taoist methods of self-cultivation. There are two main reasons why Guqin can help one's self-cultivation. On the one hand, music plays a core role in Confucian education. On the other hand, among all Chinese folk instruments, Guqin can best reflect the literati's wisdom and their noble soul. Guqin art has profound influence on the literati's moral sentiment and the development of aesthetic thought.

This paper has attached importance to the analysis of the close relationship between Guqin aesthetics and Confucian and Taoist methods of self-cultivation. The first part analyzes the musical thoughts during the pre-Qin period, with a special presentation on different concepts and theories of traditional Confucian and musical thoughts of Laozi and Zhuangzi. The second part analyzes the influence of Qin music on the thoughts of the pre-Qin period. On the one hand, the main theories during the pre-Qin period have special influence on Guqin aesthetics; on the other hand, it represents the close relationship between Guqin art and the methods of self-cultivation.

II. Close Relationship between Ancient Music and Self-cultivation

Music always played a vital role in ancient Chinese communities. Mr. Li Zehou holds that the main reason lies in the close relationship between ancient Chinese music and sacrifice. Ancient music was used to connect the gods and monsters, heaven and earth, and among human beings, and it also played a crucial role in social sacrifice music in the Shang Dynasty of China. Shang note of Yin people represents that music may touch the heaven and earth, and people.

Later on, the importance of music was partially carried out in traditional Confucian culture. According to Confucianism, music benefits individual moral cultivation, peace of mind, and communication between the heaven and earth and among people. The benefits music provided for harmony, peace and social orders are manifested in various pre-Qin Confucian classics. As is written in *the First Year of Zhaogong in Zuo Zhuan*, the former emperor's music is used to tell people to do things with restraint, so there is a five-note rhythm. If the speed of the five sounds is connected with the sound properly, a harmonious music will be played. At the end of the song, all five sounds turn silent, and no one can play any music at this time. The tactics will be messy and mixed in case of any further play, and you may play the decadent music. Any man of noble characters will not listen to such music. A gentleman who is close to any lady must follow the etiquettes, never being seduced by the beauty of them.

Confucius stressed the importance of music to the formation of society. As is written in *Zihan of The Analects of Confucius*, "When I returned from State of Wei to State of Lu, I have been sorting out the musical tones of the poems so that Ya (Festival Odes) and Song (Sacrificial Songs)" can be appropriately placed. Music plays a crucial role in individual moral cultivation especially in Confucianism. It has been written in *Zihan of The Analects of Confucius* that human beings' cultivation starts from poems, gets independent from etiquettes and completes with music. Confucius holds that the learning of music plays the ultimate and paramount role in the self-cultivation process of a man of noble characters. It is written in *Yanghuo of The Analects of Confucius* that the significance of music does not lie in the pleasure that the common can understand but in the spirits and morality comprehended by men of noble characters. As is written in *Bayi of The Analects of Confucius*: "What is the meaning of etiquette when one does not have the heart of love? What is the meaning of etiquette when one does not have a heart of love?" In other words, music shall lose its significance of existence without benevolence, and there is a close relationship between music and individual moral cultivation.

Later on, Xunzi carried on and developed the musical values as stated above. Xunzi believed that music served as a strong medium of civilization. It is written in *On Music of Xuncius* that saints like music, which can be used to make the people kind-hearted and change the old customs. Therefore, the former emperors resorted to the rites and music to guide people, with people keeping a harmonious relationship with others. Music also acted as a strong medium of self-cultivation. Joy is indispensable in human temperament. Joy must be expressed by voice and expressed by action. This is human nature. Voices and movements represent the changes in people's inner thoughts and emotions, all of which are expressed exhaustively. Therefore, people cannot be without joy. "Joy has to be manifested, while any improper manifestation may make it confusing. The former emperors abominated the evil, so they created the songs of Ya (Festival Odes) and Song (Sacrificial Songs) to guide their fellows to be joyful but never indulged, to make the rises and falls, level and oblique tones, complexity and simplicity, subtlety, resonance and rhythm of the songs inspire people's good intentions and prevent themselves from being affected by the evil. This is the purpose that former emperors created the music." "Men of noble characters enjoy music improving their moral cultivation, while mean persons enjoy music satisfying their personal desires. One will feel joyful rather than confused if he resorts to morality to control their desires." Joy and music can never be separated from each other as mentioned in the relationship by Xunzi, since music serves as the real expression and experience of human beings' joyful emotions. Besides, the greatly different attitudes that men of noble characters and mean persons show toward music have been compared. Men of noble characters lay emphasis on the values and functions of music, that is, the function of desire restraints, while mean persons are just interested in the superficial joy that music brings to people.

The moral abilities and functions of music became mature in the late Warring States period and the ensuing Qin and Han period. The strong media functions of music can be seen in *Spring and Autumn Annals of Lv Buwei* in the late Warring States period, *The Book of Music* and *Huai Nan Zi* in the Han Dynasty, and works by Dong Zhongshu. As is written in *Great Joy of Spring and Autumn Annals of Lv Buwei*, the origin of music starts from long time ago, and arises from the increase and decrease of the degree of musicality with nature as the origin. Taoism produces the heaven and earth, which generate Yin and Yang. Changes happen to Yin and Yang, one coming up as another down, while the meeting generates grace. Formers emperors created music in the principle of harmony and moderation. The entire world keeps peaceful with everything silent and people obedient to their emperors. Therefore, music is born from harmony. As is said in *The Strategy of Suggesting Talents* by Dong Zhongshu, the emperors create music after they succeed in fame and causes, extolling his achievements by the means of music. Music can be used to change the folk customs and improve folkways, making it effective in improving people.

Apart from the musical functions in mortality mentioned above, the classics of the Qin and Han dynasties also expressed the voices of the universe and nature and analyzed the spirits and origin of music and voice. The rivals of Confucianism had a great impact on the music theories and values of Qin and Han. Hereby, special attention shall be paid to the great contribution of Laozi and Zhuangzi to musical theories and aesthetics. As Robert Hans van Gulik says, music starts to be developed as a method of self-cultivation and wisdom due to the great contribution of Laozi and Zhuangzi. Both Laozi and Zhuangzi criticized the limited musical theories of Confucianism: True music is pure without absolute classification and originates from Tao. According to *Laozi*, the loudest and greatest music is "voice-free" music, profound experience not touched by the five sense organs. According to The Fourteenth Chapter of *Laozi*, anything that cannot be seen is called "intangible", anything that cannot be heard is called "silent", and anything that cannot be touched is called "subtle". The three are integrated, making it too difficult to distinguish. Mr. Xiu Hailin said that "silent" serves as the nature of "Tao", while the existence manner of "Tao" remains natural. Zhuangzi carried on and developed the opinions of *Laozi*. First of all, he proposed the aesthetic idea that we cannot express the great beauty in words. The "great beauty" means "silent", which has a direct relationship with the "silent" by Laozi. Besides, he proposed "natural music" and "sound of nature". True music means music of nature, and "natural music" makes it possible for human beings to communicate with the universe and the heaven and earth. As is said in *Tao of Heaven in Zhuangzi*, the tranquility of the void that is transferred to the heaven and earth and spreads to everything is called natural music. As is said in the same paper, being harmony with people is called music, and being harmony with the heaven is called natural music. One can experience the "Tao" by means of true music instead of experience by hearing. That is the original idea of Laozi and Zhuangzi. As is said in *The heaven and Earth of Zhuangzi*, Tao looks so dark and deep and sounds so silent. However, in the darkness and depth, it is possible to see the light of the true traces and hear the sympathy out of silence. Both the "silent" by Laozi and "non-voice" by Zhuangzi require a kind of profound experience exceeding sensibility, that is, music helps one understand the existence of "Tao" to change it into an effective manner of self-cultivation.

III. Guqin Art and Roles of Self-cultivation

In Chinese history of traditional music, Guqin art can express and represent the wisdom and elegant and noble characters of literati to the most. Guqin art has profound influence on the literati's moral sentiment and the development of aesthetic ideas. De Woskin holds that Guqin's status and values are matters in its ancient origin; then, the physical characteristics and sound quality of Guqin are better than those of other musical instruments used to express Confucian ideals. These factors make the close relationship between Guqin art and traditional culture and classics.

The late Warring States period and Qin and the Han Dynasty marked the supreme periods for the roles of Guqin in self-cultivation. During the Western Zhou Dynasty and the Spring and Autumn period, Guqin art was used to praying for heaven and earth and worshiping ghosts and gods. *Zuo Zhuan* of the Spring and Autumn period and the Warring States period is one of the classics that state the relationship between Guqin and self-cultivation, which is "A gentleman who is close to any lady must follow the etiquettes, never being seduced by the beauty of them." The importance of the music for self-cultivation is not to be indulged in playing. At the end of the Warring States period, *The Spring and Autumn Annals of Lv Buwei* left us with a very important record about Boya playing Guqin.

Boya played the Guqin while his friend Zhong Ziqi enjoyed it on the side. Boya began to express his aspirations as great as the Mount Tai, while Ziqi could not help but sigh and said, "That's so great! It's exciting and as high as the mountain." After a while, Boya expressed his intention as gentle as the flow, and Ziqi said, "It's so great that I feel it like running river." Unfortunately, Ziqi passed away, and Boya broke his Guqin, tore the strings and stopped playing since then. Because he held that nobody deserved his playing except for Ziqi. Not only the Guqin but also the sage is like this. If you did not treat the talented with courtesy, how could they be loyal to you? If you were not good at riding horse, it could not play its abilities to the best. (Extracted from *Benwei Chapter of Xiaoxing Overview in The Spring and Autumn Annals of Lv Buwei*)

This record suggests that Guqin art is of special features and high demands. As Mr. Li Xiangting says, not everyone can understand the art performance of the players from music. Zhong Ziqi can comprehend the musical spirits and contexts from Boya's music, suggesting that both the listener and performer are at the same level of musical cultivation.

Han Dynasty was the period when the function of self-cultivation of Guqin came into play in the fastest and most mature way. Among the definitions of Guqin as a means of self-cultivation, two basic concepts play a core role. Firstly, there is a direct relationship with Confucianism, that is, Guqin serves as a tool for self-control and righteousness, and its virtues may help press the zeal and restore the peace of mind. Secondly, it is influenced by the idea of Laozi, that is, the greater demand of Guqin art is to imitate nature to realize the purpose of "Tao". One may enter a profound, subtle and avatar realm. The best manner to experience Guqin music is not to rely on five sense organs but to grasp its principles. Such a concept becomes a main introspective manner.

IV. Effects of Confucian "Qin-prohibition" Thought on Self-cultivation

The theory of relationship between Guqin and "prohibition" appeared in the Han Dynasty. "Prohibition" means "forbid any prostitution", having a direct relationship with the Confucius' thoughts and the Confucian music education theory of the pre-Qin Dynasty. This concept of the Han Dynasty had a profound effect. For example, as is written in *Analytical Dictionary of Chinese Characters* by Mr. Xu Zhen, "Guqin is a great tool used to settle the soul and prohibit evil thoughts. It is said to be a musical instrument invented by Shennong. There is a sound outlet at the bottom of Guqin. Five strings are made of vermilion tiffany, and another two strings are added in the Zhou Dynasty. The character pattern of Guqin is like the shape of musical instrument." That means "ban" determined the nature of "Guqin" in the Han Dynasty. There were many classics of the Han Dynasty that were influenced by such a concept. Huan Tuan of the East Han Dynasty wrote in his *Guqin Theory of New Interpretation*, which goes as "Guqin means prohibition, and men of noble characters will take it for self-control." That means men of noble characters using Guqin as a tool for self-control. As is written in the *Rites and Music of Baihutong*, "Guiqin serves as a tool to help prohibit prostitution and develop self-cultivation." The abilities that Quqin can help develop self-cultivation were related to the music education theory of pre-Qin Confucianism. However, the prime reason that "Guqin" can represent the abilities of self-control lies in the volume of Guqin among various traditional Chinese musical instruments. As Huang Tan proposed, "One may not feel too noisy even if the sound of Guqin is too loud; one may not feel inaudible even though the sound of Guqin is too thin. Only Guqin is of the most virtues among various musical instruments. Men of noble characters in ancient times played the Guqin to help develop self-cultivation." Men of noble characters in ancient times played Guqin to help develop self-cultivation because of the proper volume of Guqin. As is stated in *Comprehensive Meaning of Customs and Habits*, "Guqin makes harmony due to its proper volume. One may not feel too noisy even if the sound of Guqin is too loud; one may not feel inaudible even though the sound of Guqin is too thin." Such an idea has an apparent relationship with that of *Zuo Zhuan* as shown above. "You have to get to close to a lady with etiquette", and "Guqin can represent the abilities of self-control because of the volume so that men of noble characters in ancient times used it to help develop self-cultivation". This carried on the similar significance. As is written in the *Rites and Music of Baihutong*, "Why do we need stay away from Zheng Di due to his voice? Because his voice is too attractive. Confucians have to avoid any excessively attractive voice, for it may indulge people. Guqin is used as a tool, so it can help prohibit the prostitution and develop self-cultivation." "Prohibition" means prohibiting the sound of any prostitution to remain the positive sound. "Positive sound" refers to the sound that is helpful in developing self-cultivation, and Guqin is one of the representatives of "positive sound".

The values and significance of Guqin lasted for a long period of time. Xue Yijian of the Tang Dynasty claimed in his *Qin Jue*: "one literati playing the Guqin keeps silent and positive, making it clear for the listener. The average can only see that the performer plays the Guqin in a gentle manner with proper and attractive voice, while not knowing that it is played by the literati regulating the rhythm well. Its sound is so positive that it can be used to prohibit the prostitution." As is written in *Su Qin Zhuan* by Sima Chengzhen of the Song Dynasty, "Guqin is used to prohibit the prostitution to remain the positive and help one develop self-cultivation to stay true." Zhu Xi wrote in his poem *Ziyang Su Ming*, "Men of noble characters develop self-cultivation and prevent themselves from prostitution. Everything in the world is being with laws." All the cases show that playing the Guqin has a function of driving away prostitution and helping develop self-cultivation. Therefore, the significance of playing the Guqin is beyond the average musical activities, helping realize the purpose of self-cultivation. Anyone who plays the Guqin and can understand it shall help himself develop self-cultivation and stay true to his nature. Guqin is a great manner to help self-cultivation and facilitates the development of pre-Qin music education.

V. From Musical Thoughts of Laozi & Zhuangzi to the Function of Self-cultivation of Guqin Music

Guqin music develops men and help them stay true to their nature, which is undoubtedly influenced by the thoughts of Laozi. Musical thoughts of Laozi stress the necessity to conquer the reality of five sense organs and the principles of "Taoism", that is, the musical experience can help one exceed simple joy to enter a profound reality. Wei, Jin, Northern and Southern Dynasties were the important periods when Guqin art had the most influence on Taoism. Ji Kang, one of Seven Sages of the Bamboo Grove was the most important figure. Laozi and Zhuangzi had a direct influence on the musical thoughts of Ji Kang, which developed into criticism on music education of Confucianism. Ji Kang opposed the idea that music served as a fashion to control traditional Confucianism thought for the sake of political rights and self-control. He believed that music is an objective existence, of which the nature remains unchanged. Music cannot express the subjective emotions in a fixed manner, nor can emotions affect music. There is no direct relationship between human emotions and music, both of which do not affect each other. As is mentioned in *The Theory of Music without Emotion* by Ji Kang, "The eight principles of happiness, anger, sadness, joy, love, hatred, guilty, and fear are used to contact with the outside world and convey emotions, and distinguish people from others, which cannot be applied at random. In fact, there is only good and bad sound, which are unrelated with sadness and joy." Ji Kang held that the forms of music had no apparent inner emotions of sadness or joy, while different emotions caused by music were determined by different feelings of people after their listening to music.

Ji Kang almost opposed the Confucian music theory that music was used to control one's emotions, but he appreciated the greater status and values of the Confucian thought of "harmony" in the music thought. "Voices combined together in a harmony manner shall make people moved. The working men express their sufferings by the means of songs, and the joyful people dance to express their happiness. Anyone who feels sad may tell some sad words, which are combined together to form poems to generate music. People gather for singing and listening, their inner world touched. They are affected by the sad lyrics and wear tears before the sign ends. People hide their sadness in their inner part and express it in case of any proper sound. As proper sound is intangible, one's sadness is regulated. The regulated inner part can be expressed by the virtue of intangible and proper sound. What one feels is only the sadness." Middendorf said that the "harmony" of Ji Kang is "aesthetic nature of music" and the "harmony" by Ji Kang is a metaphysics concept, that is, unchanged ontology. Therefore, the main purpose of music is to help achieve inner "harmony" instead of the harmony of political society. Only the "harmony" nature of music would remain as it can make people touched to the most.

As is said in *Ode to Guqin*, "Music is beneficial to one's sentiment and manners, help regulate their emotions and distract one from their adversities." That suggests the purpose of music is to help cultivate one's sentiment and express his emotions. Zhang Di said, "Music can help change the customs, making it possible for people to live a self-sufficiency life. Therefore, the forms of music are no longer too important, while the key lies in how to comprehend the nature of harmony." Hereby, Ji Kang was affected by aesthetic thoughts of Laozi and Zhuangzi. The purposes of music and musician were to gain the prefect experience of "harmony". However, it is different from the "harmony" of Confucianism, stressing the ontology of all. That is to say the best form of music is to follow the nature and develop self-cultivation. As is written in *Ode to Guqin*, those who are not broad-minded cannot take Guqin as a tool for pleasure; those who are not composed cannot enjoy Guqin; those who are not bold and unconstrained cannot experience the everlasting joy of Guqin; and those who are not skilled cannot analyze the theory of Guqin." Ji Kang held that only those who had exquisite skills can get the true musical experience, because only men of noble characters were able to obtain the experience of Guqin by analyzing its theory.

Ji Kang laid emphasis on the status and values of Guqin, believing only the most excellent people can grasp the Guqin music. Ji Kang wrote in his *Ode on Guqin*, "The composed features of Guqin are too difficult to understand. The pure body makes it possible for the sound of Guqin to spread afar and help one be elegant. If a Guqin of fine quality is combined with a skilled performer, it can be called "destiny". He can play the Guqin exquisitely and show his outstanding skills. Unfortunately, few can really comprehend the sound of Guqin. Who can treasure and love Guqin? Who can play the merits of Guqin to the most? Only those who have exquisite skills and are concentrated can do it! Ji Kang believed that the quality of Guqin was too unfathomable, with a strong influence on people, so it was a great method to help develop self-cultivation. He also held that Guqin was of the best quality among all the musical instruments, suitable to be used as a method of self-cultivation. Guqin is of pure characters and with placid sound. Being honest serves as a method to agitate one's will, so one can express their inner voice by the means of Guqin. "Guqin can represent the metaphysical, natural and unchanged 'harmony'." The sound of Guqin includes the placidity of Guqin's characters, helping one calm down and express his inner voice.

In the end, we can get to the idea of "string-free Guqin" by Tao Yuanming in the same direction and context. As is written in *Autobiography of Tao Yuanming in Jin Shu*, "Tao Qian is not an expert in music but holds a Guqin without strings. Once he takes drinks with his friends, he would like to touch his Guqin and say, 'If one knows the true significance of Guqin, how is it necessary to resort to it for any sound?'". The ultimate goal of Guqin music is to exceed different experience of sense organs to obtain the understanding of Guqin itself. As is written in *Ode on String-free Guqin* by Zhang Sui, a scholar official in the Tang Dynasty, "People do not gain the great aesthetical experience of *You Lan* and *Lv Shui* from outer sound, but from inner emotion." The ideas and proposition of Zhang Sui were close to that of Ji Kang. The profound significance of music and true feeling do not lie in outer sound but in the "intangible" and "silent" aesthetical experience. Anyone who can understand the true meaning of *You Lan* or *Lv Shui* do not need to hear physically, while the most significance of music is to touch people by its "harmony" and isolate itself from other music. Zhang Di said: "Guqin music can give the listeners great imagination without any physical sound." Both the "harmony" by Ji Kang and "string-free Guqin" of Tao Yuanming represented the development of the thoughts of Laozi and Zhuangzi. What matters to music is not the outer sound but the inner voice, and its ontology is "intangible", "silent" and "harmonious" and in line with the universe. One may enter a profound, subtle and intangible realm by the understanding of music ontology, making one peaceful and placid. Ji Kang also held that Guqin was of the most excellent characters among all the musical instruments, because it was the most suitable method for men of noble characters to develop self-cultivation. The sound of Guqin can reflect the peaceful, silent and profound sound to the most. The idea of "string-free Guqin" by Tao Yuanming represented the ultimate goal of music, which was the same as Ji Kang.

VI. Conclusion

In this paper, the author analyzes the functions of music and self-cultivation of Confucianism, with special stress laid on the functions of Guqin music. In the first part, the music thoughts in ancient times and the pre-Qin Dynasty are analyzed, with a special representation of various concepts and theories of Confucianism and Laozi as well as Zhuangzi's music thoughts. In the second part, the understanding and values of Guqin art are analyzed under the influence of these two traditional thoughts and especially in the course of self-cultivation. First of all, Confucianism in the Han Dynasty held that Guqin can affect one's sentiment, which was influenced greatly by the musical thoughts of Confucius and pre-Qin Confucians. The Confucians in the Han Dynasty stated the functions and abilities of Guqin from the Chinese character of "prohibition", which means driving away the evil and remaining the positive, helping developing self-cultivation and staying true to one's original will. Then, the influence of musical thoughts of Laozi and Zhuangzi are analyzed. It is suggested that Ji Kang, one of the Seven Sages of Bamboo Grove, is influenced by the music theories of Laozi and Zhuangzi. Ji Kang held that music was the activity that can surpass the feeling of five sense organs and the ontology that can be in line with everything and help one get close to "Tao". He also believed that Guqin music was the most profound music, making it the most difficult to comprehend. The characters of Guqin was too unfathomable, with a profound and strong influence on people.

In the end, Ji Kang's idea influenced the following musicians, and the author of this paper also mentions "string-free Guqin" of Tao Yuanming. The ultimate goal of "string-free Guqin" can exceed various experience of sense organs so that the listener can comprehend and experience the ontology of Guqin music. This thought has profound influence on the following Guqin artists. A conclusion is reached that Guqin has the functions of self-cultivation due to two reasons. For the first one, the relationship between Guqin and "prohibition" and their functions are stressed; for the second, an emphasis is laid on Guqin music for the purpose of studying the ontology of the universe. Even though they belong to different traditions, they are of the same idea. Guqin music serves as a method to develop self-cultivation. A summary can be made by words of Robert Hans van Gulik: "Playing the lute purifies one's nature by banishing low passions, therefore it is a sort of meditation, a means for communicating directly with tao [dao]. Its rarefied notes reproduce the 'sounds of emptiness', and so the music of the lute tunes the soul of the player in harmony with tao [dao]."

中国古代先秦音乐和乐器研究

宋镇烈 【韩国】
庆星大学中文博士在读

本文提到的研究是为了探索中国古典《诗经》里出现的先秦音乐和乐器。研究方法是通过分析音律和度量衡之间的关系来完成。研究结果表明：中国古代社会的音乐是与自然现象密切相关的。

在中国古代，乐器的长度（管类乐器）是用小米来测量的。这是一种测量黄钟的基本方法。分隔音阶的方法是三分损益法（减一添三的方法），然后（通过这一方法）构成其他音阶，宫、商、角、徵、羽。

中国古代宴请宾客时使用音乐，举行宗教庆典和仪式。但是不能认为礼（仪）和（音）乐是各自分离的。古人用礼乐来表现赞美和欣赏。虽然礼是（帝王）统治的手段，即使没有乐的辅助，礼依旧可以保留。乐在其中可以达到同质感。从这一传统来看，乐律会受自然秩序制约，也会成为人类和谐的一种手段。研究员想要探究在《诗经》中，古代中国人是如何使用音乐和乐器的。同时，也将探讨中国古代音乐哲学。

一 序文

观察大自然，感知大自然，并产生疑问之后，人类一直被这样一个问题所困扰——人到底是谁。文学作品是展示人类思考的载体，人类以文学的形式探寻人与世界的存在论问题。文学作品不仅会影响当代人，也会影响后代。文学是通过抽象的文字来表现作者的思想和情感，进而反映社会的，可分为抒情诗（韵律和节奏的形式）和叙事诗（小说）。

研究者想探索"礼"和"乐"在中国古代经典中是如何表达"中国中心主义"的。古代中国社会的"礼"包括规则、法律、制度和社会秩序。孔子是阐释"礼"和"乐"关系的伟大学者之一。研究者试图在《诗经》中找到音乐和乐器的使用。《诗经》是孔子编订的一本书。我们可以看到很多诗中都有音乐和乐器的使用。因此，研究者想要通过这些诗，了解古代中国人使用音乐的很多形式，如宴会、仪式和娱乐，探索《诗经》中音乐和乐器的使用以及其哲学意义。

二 礼乐为核心看中和思想

最基础的概念是"中和"，即"中"与"和"。"中"指的既不是超过也不是缺乏的一个状态。在音乐中，种类繁多的乐器各不相同，它们是如何能够实现和谐的呢？这个问题非常重要，阐述了人类和谐的本质。中和思想的关键就在于"和"。因为自然之声是和谐的，那么人类和谐的音乐就能在自然中有所反映。和谐的音乐与自然宇宙有着千丝万缕的关系，因为它是从自然发展而来，比如小米和度量衡。通过本质和谐的音乐，人类能够实现和谐。在大宇宙，人类和宇宙发展，天道运行的和谐中，我们能够看见古代中国的美和音乐特点。这就使人类的发展能够实现和谐。音乐是可以表达人类心灵的一种方式。音乐是一种可以通过强弱高低，长度和音色的运用来表达人类思想的一种艺术。

儒家思想中的政治可以被定义为"以礼治国"。它同样也强调了"礼"能够被音乐完美地表现出来。人类最完美的事物就是由音乐表达出来的。以礼治国应该和音乐联系起来，那么礼与音乐就能达到和谐。鉴于礼乐结合的"和"的思想，礼乐即是完美。礼是一种人应该遵守的法律法规和对皇帝所表示的尊敬。在法律法规下，皇帝是一国之主。如果有人违反了"礼"的规定，他就被惩罚。但是如果社会一味地强调"礼"，这将会变得过于严苛。这就是统治者强调和谐的原因，也是孔子推崇的。人们要通过学习诗歌来实现修身。

人们也要学习音乐，这样他们就可以达到完美。古代人简要地作了总结，即修身，治国，齐家，平天下。君子修身是第一条，包括了学习和音乐的帮助下达到完美。假如君子修身，并没有学习礼乐，他就不是一个完美的人。这就解释了孔子的成于乐，和人要通过学习音乐来实现完美的思想。

孔子强调人要通过音乐培养自己的个性。从这个层面来说，音乐就是一种教化人的方式。孔子在音乐上有很大的兴趣和天赋。孔子说，听过韶（由古代皇帝舜所制作）之后，"三月不知肉味"，即，没想到音乐能有这样的力量。他把诗歌和音乐紧密地结合起来，使人身心愉悦，使人处于和谐之中。当诗歌加入其中，并被歌颂的时候，宴席变得更加隆重。孔子在《论语·阳货篇》里也讨论了诗歌的有效性。

子曰：诗，可以兴，可以观，可以群，可以怨。

显而易见，诗是可以使人们身心愉悦的一种形式。如果人们把诗歌结合到音乐中来，就可以使人更加愉悦。音乐是非常神秘的，因为它是看不见摸不着的。即使是相同的音乐，它也可能因表演者和地点和气氛，展现不同的内涵。礼乐的文化可以追溯到周和春秋战国时代。

三 古代中国乐器的历史

中国人从新石器时代开始就制作道具，用陶器制作能够演奏音乐的彩色鼓。在河南发现了8000—9000年前中国最古老的乐器——骨笛。

1987年5月，在河南省舞阳县发掘的新石器时代的遗址出土了25个骨制的笛。这些骨笛大部分是用鹤的腿骨做成的，分别有5、6、7个指孔。其中有一个原形保存相对完整，大概20厘米长，身上有7个大小相同的指孔。特别的是，骨笛末端的最后一个指孔旁边还有一个小孔。经实验得出，这个小孔能对音高进行细微的调节。

从大汶口文化时期开始，用土器制作鼓。在6300—4600年前，中国人制作乐器，用皮革挂着进行演奏。以世界四大文明发祥地之一黄河为中心，就可以看到中国文化的发达。

图一 盆

上图的盆具有约5000多年的历史，内壁画了3组舞蹈演员。每一组由5名舞者构成，他们相互牵着手跳舞。并且舞者的脑后部戴着类似装饰物的东西，或者把头发绑了起来。身体下边挂着如尾巴模样的物体，这可能是鸟或者动物的装饰。

在中国，这个陶瓷盆上的画是与舞蹈有关的最久远的记录。盆上画的舞者以5人一组，都做着同样的动作，这可能跳的是团体或者小组形式的舞蹈。

公元前21世纪中国进入奴隶社会，最先建立的国家是夏朝（公元前21世纪——公元前16世纪）。夏朝音乐的文献资料和出土遗物很少，除了石磬和陶瓷中的陶钟、埙、鼓以及陶铃等几种乐器可以考证，很难知道具体的音乐形式。

商代有用角做的号角，战争时会吹号角。电影《孔子》中也有在战斗中吹号角的场面。

青铜器时代的周朝或春秋战国时期制作了钟或编钟。钟是用手抓着进行演奏，但是编钟是固定在木质框架里的。编钟上下挂着多个钟进行演奏，音阶不同产生不同的音高。

进入周代，在国家的祭祀或宴会上使用很多青铜乐器。制作乐器的材料被称为"8音"，即金、石、土、革、丝、木、匏、竹。

早在西周时期，古人便创造出了世界上最早的乐器分类法，即"八音"分类法。"八音"是指金、石、土、木、丝、竹、匏、革这八种类型。"八音"分类法是以制作乐器的材质来进行分类的乐器分类法。同时，它还具有音色归类的作用，以及音色选择的导向作用。在七千年前，我们的祖先就已经创造了骨笛、骨哨，但在"八音"中却没有"骨"这种材质，这说明我们的祖先在材质选择及音色选择上是有着一定审美规范的。像瑟和扬琴，如果用"八音"分类法来分乐器，那么瑟和扬琴则归属弦乐器类，而这两种乐器从音色、音乐的角度来看应是更接近于弦乐器。[1]

周代为了维持建国的正统性，维持严格的身份制度和阶级，音乐的演奏规模根据身份等级来规定。编钟是用青铜做的乐器，编磬是用石头做的乐器。他们用编钟和编磬来规定身份等级。

乐队的规模有四种：王宫县、诸侯轩县、卿大夫判县、士特县。当时的雅乐分为堂上官和堂下官，堂上官主要是布置与瑟相似的弦乐器。

---

[1] 张金娣：《中国器乐——中国国粹艺术读本》，中国文联出版社2010年版，第2页。

四　乐律和度量衡的规则

我们常说语言是有规则的，音乐当然也有规则。音乐的语言称为"乐律"（rhythm），与大自然有着密切的关系。作曲者利用乐律调节时间和速度，完成和声，如同多种乐器演奏出的交响乐一般，表达人的情感。

中国和日本的音乐以 2 拍子为标准，韩国音乐以 3 拍子为标准，西方音乐则以 4 拍子为标准。以三分损益计算法确定的一个八度音阶，是黄钟将原有长度 3 等分再减去其一份，确定标准音，接着将三分之二中的三分之一，加上四分之三，定振动数，以此方法确定十二音律。音乐是解决东方三角文化的重要因素。从黄帝开始，到文王、武王，一即位就重新制作音乐。在东方，制作音乐的意义是确定八度音阶中十二个半音的标准音——黄钟。

音乐的美妙之处在于和谐，不管是中国人还是古代雅典人都是这样的。但是雅典人和谐的根源，不是风，而是从水中找到的。风和水分别代表中国和西方文化的特征。当然，这并不意味着中国人在制作音程的时候，忽略了数学，或者说只制作出了像风一样模糊的感觉。

中国的十二音体系确立后，又有三分损益法，包涵了对数学原理的理解。在中国的乐律，数学也占非常重要的位置。在中国，最初的乐律确立者，正是在管鲍之交伟大友情故事中被人们熟知的管仲。他比毕达哥拉斯约早出生 140 年，而当时中国已经形成了用"三分损益法"确定的"宫商角徵羽"五音音程。

所谓三分损益法，是三分损一，三分益一的意思。古代中国音律的数字与完全数 9 有关联。雅典学者毕达哥拉斯以 1 为标准，重视比例，相反，古代中国的全部标准音，成为宫音的数字是完全数 9 的平方得到 81。依照三分损益法，接着，宫音数值的 81 加上其三等分值 27，得到 108，由此确定徵音数值。然后从 108 去掉其三等分值 36，得到 72，即商音数值。72 加上其三等分值 24，得到 96，成为羽音数值。96 去掉其三等分值 32，得到 64，即角音数值。当然弦的长度越长，音越低。依照三分损益法确定的黄钟基本音，按照低音顺序排列，即 108，96，81，72，64。但有趣的是，标准音"宫音"在五音的中间。

这样的三分损益法是最容易被人接受的寻找自然音阶的过程；也可以看作是通过宫商角徵羽的音，寻找绝对音——天上之音的过程。这种音律的计算是我们从自然获得的食物——黍的数字来确定的物理过程，但也包含了寻找天上之音的精神过程。这种寻找人间好音乐，可以称为"弘益音"。希腊哲学是寻求人类完美音乐的过程，而中国的目标是寻找"绝对音"。毕达哥拉斯把一切都定义为数字。

在东方，一个八度音阶被制作成12个半音，基本音由黄钟来定。中国音乐最基本的黄钟的振动数是怎么决定的呢？黄钟的振动数或者说音高，是由管子的长度决定的。按黄钟的音调制作律管，黄钟律管的管长为1尺。黄钟成为基本音质律管的标准音，以此为标准，制作了其他11个半音。

黄钟的尺长度，用在现实生活的度量衡里。黄钟1尺，成为现实生活中度量衡的基础。音乐是由律和自然材料构成的，是与大自然和谐的象征。音乐的基本音黄钟，以摆放黍米谷粒的数量作为尺度，制作出管乐器。以音质为基础的律管标准用在实际生活度量衡里的原理，说明了东亚民族顺应大自然的天人合一思想。乐器的长度和度量衡的标准都是从大自然来的，表现了古代中国人的艺术观和自然观。如乐，秩序是从大自然来的。从大自然定标准——黍（小米）摆放10粒的长度，视为1寸，再把90寸、100寸的长度，视为一尺，制作律管，定黄钟的尺度或者金管的长度。人类用自然中收获的黍米来定基本音和度量衡，当乐器演奏这种音乐时，人类生活就有了秩序。度量衡是人类的生活秩序，其媒介就是音乐。

古代天子即位，必先制定数，用黍米作黄钟尺度，以此制作度量衡，治理国家。一国建立，统一国家的度量衡才能保持秩序，可见统治秩序是从大自然来的。

黄钟的长度是根据中国的气候和饮食决定的。南方出产丰富的大米，而满洲地区以黍米为主食。现今出土的8、9千年前碳化的黍米证明了黍米定乐律规则的事实。确定音乐规则——音律时，是按照摆放黍米的长度来决定律管长度的。同样，度量衡的制定规则也是与音律的规则在一个思维体系里的。

音乐是根据自然现象制定规则的，而它的标准用在人类社会度量衡的统一上。这说明音乐的规则和度量衡是一脉相承的。

音乐是受政治、宗教、思想、战乱、和平等多种影响的，而且，影响音律形成哲学的、天人合一的理念，形成人的礼仪，达到共鸣。从《诗经》可以看出，它不仅包括贵族、王室等上层人的艺术，还包括民歌等俗文学，是被当时人广泛歌唱的。

天子在建立国家时，为了标榜家族和王族的正当性而制定音乐，并在制度上设立掌管音乐的官吏和官厅。音乐实际上不仅是区分阶级的手段，还是宫中宴会、宗庙、祭乐中不可或缺的必要因素。因此，这样的研究是需要仔细观察宫中文庙活动或祭祀礼乐内容的领域。

作曲家通过节拍调节时间和速度，用技巧调节音速，诱发紧张气氛，营造出与听众融为一体的氛围。三分损益法是针对振动数来确定标准音，而带着跟随音，即派生音编故事。黄钟律管的主音确定后，作曲是把材料的音调形象化。

作曲有对位法或和声学，把有同感的两个以上的音调放到一起。作曲是一种视觉化的看法，把声音转到音乐里去的就是节奏。通过对位法，多个单声部合并成多声部。

所谓律，是音乐中使用的黄钟、大吕、太簇、夹钟、高选、仲吕、蕤宾、林钟、夷则、南吕、诬逆、应钟等12音律。度是指分、寸、尺、丈、引等长度单位。量是指龠、合、升、斗、斛等容量单位。还有衡，是指铢、两、斤、钧、石等重量单位。律管以一定数量的黍米谷粒为基础，表示长度（度）、表示容量（量）、表示重量（衡）。通过这种标准确定的律，与季节、日月时间的规律一样，是在自然现象为根源成立的。

通过发音，将作品塑造成形象的"共鸣艺术"，是一种"时间艺术"。艺术可以利用时空和感觉，容纳音乐的美感。乐曲失去了旋律则不能成为乐曲。音律影响人的感性，带着两个以上同质感的音，化成美妙的旋律。

作曲家以五音阶为基础作出旋律，表达自己的情感，与人共享。音乐通过风，通过振动，传到人的耳朵里，影响人的情绪，作曲家就达到自己的创作意图。

五　关雎和音乐

诗歌有长短高低，当它和旋律结合在一起，就能够唱出来。诗歌是通过乐器的帮助使歌唱者表达感情的一种形式。人类具有向同伴表达自己情感的欲望，音乐的产生很可能是与人类历史的开始同步的。社会和文化的主要目的就是教化人类意识，通过音乐来提升人性。社会文化发展的动因通常由人类所创造的音乐所表现的。音乐家是他所处的社会或集团所必需的存在。音乐家在民族统一中发挥了重要作用，也参加了集团群舞或典礼。中国古代人把自然融入自己的文化里，再把它升华为适合他们心性的东西。演奏自然八音的乐器，就可以建立与自然的亲密关系，就能在演奏音乐时悟出人生哲学。

诗经是一本经典。我们可以从中找到许多中国古代音乐和乐器。诗经是可以唱出来的。皇室贵族用诗来描写礼仪盛典和皇帝和贵族的庄严。比如说，在第一章《关雎》中，一个贵族男子追求一个美丽的女子。他很高兴见到这个女子，他用音乐来表达他的喜悦并传达给这个女子。他开了一场宴会，钟鼓齐鸣。

《诗经·关雎》

关关雎鸠，在河之洲。

窈窕淑女，君子好逑。

参差荇菜，左右流之。

窈窕淑女，寤寐求之。

求之不得，寤寐思服。

悠哉悠哉，辗转反侧。

参差荇菜，左右采之。

窈窕淑女，琴瑟友之。

参差荇菜，左右芼之。

窈窕淑女，钟鼓乐之。

正如我们在第三章我看见的，这名君子遇到这位美丽的女子，为她表演琴和瑟。琴是一种中国古人使用的弦乐器，是由梧桐制成的共鸣板和七根弦组成。它的共鸣板是空心的，拨动七根真丝弦，声音会十分清脆。

这里的"友"字有亲近融合之意。历来的解释都是说琴瑟相配最为和谐，所以优秀的男子（君子）与俊美的女子（淑女）相爱，最为理想、最为和谐。但应看到这一句诗应该还有另一层意思，则是"友"作为动词，君子以琴瑟表达自己的爱慕之心，弹琴瑟以亲近淑女，以"友"淑女，用琴瑟来打动淑女。[1]

另一方面，瑟有25根弦，它的声音非常柔和高雅。当琴的清脆和瑟的柔和交织在一起的时候，就会奏响和谐的乐章。

第二、三章则从男主人公"君子"方面落笔，先说他在未得到"淑女"时饱受思念之苦，以致食不甘味，夜不能寐；然后再说他幻想如何千方百计地与淑女鱼水和谐，用琴、瑟、钟、鼓使她心情欢愉舒畅。如果说第二章近于现实主义的描写，那么第三章便带有浪漫主义情调，主人公虽未获得成功的爱情，但却为想象的美好情节所陶醉。[2]

---

[1] 李祥霆：《古琴综议》，中国人民大学出版社2013年版，第24页。
[2] 赵会生、王旭：《图说中国音乐》，吉林人民出版社2010年版，第18页。

中国古代乐器的文章跟反映人类价值的礼乐有关。琴就像一名男子，瑟则像一名女子。它表现了中国传统哲学中阴阳和谐的理论。在中国古代，琴瑟和鸣意味着夫妻生活和谐。

琴也为贵胄的重要社会交往、政治联络而起着加强影响、深化关系、提高地位的作用："我有嘉宾，鼓琴鼓瑟，和乐且湛"，"鼓钟钦钦，鼓琴鼓瑟，笙磬同音，以雅以南，以籥不僭"。而《小雅》中的《车舝》则是贵族之家婚宴时的燕乐，是在上层社会人们的心情表达时引琴以为喻："六辔如琴"。[1]

在第四章，君子奏响钟鼓庆祝宴会，取悦美丽的女子。这意味着只有君子才能用钟鼓，即乐器也是社会地位的象征。在这首诗歌中，音乐和乐器可以使人产生情感的共鸣。

"鍾"的聲音必須適合大小。大或者小声达到"和"，使人感受美感。《关雎》里演奏的音乐（琴、瑟、钟鼓），余音袅袅，沁人心脾。君子的礼是感动人心的。关雎的琴瑟和鸣，就意味着夫妻生活的和谐。礼就是在乐的帮助下变得更完美，而且这诗里包含了孔子的礼乐思想。音乐使人愉悦，使人心情安定，指导"仁"。通过音乐，我们可以看到中国人的美学观念。中国人的美学观是美指导"善"。"礼"指社会秩序，"乐"给人们带来快乐和幸福。所以，让"善"乐把僵化的礼变得更完美一些，使人们体会"乐"后，有同质感。

六　那和音乐

《那》是一首描写古代仪式的音乐诗歌，我们从中可以窥视商代社会的一面。诗中，我们看到所展现的礼乐和对祖先的祭祀。

猗与那与！
置我鞉鼓。
奏鼓简简，
衎我烈祖。

当商朝后裔对汤王举行仪式时，子孙们做三次礼乐祭祀他。这首诗也是一首用鼓进行配乐的歌曲。

汤孙奏假，

---

[1] 李祥霆：《古琴综议》，中国人民大学出版社2013-10年版，第27—28页。

绥我思成。

鞉鼓渊渊，

嘒嘒管声。

既和且平。

依我磬声。

于赫汤孙！

穆穆厥声。

汤王的后裔为汤王主持祭祀，希望祖先赐福自己。他们一边演奏音乐，一边祭祀，希望祖先显灵赐福他们。

庸鼓有斁，

万舞有奕。

我有嘉客，

亦不夷怿。

自古在昔，

先民有作。

温恭朝夕，

执事有恪，

顾予烝尝，

汤孙之将。

庸是由小鼓、大鼓和长笛组成的在礼堂表演的乐器。在礼堂，编磬也被演奏。子孙演奏乐器来纪念汤王。

对这首诗，毛、韩认为是祭祀汤之乐词。魏源、王先谦等皆认为是宋国人追纪祖先而作。杨公兖从诗的内容着眼，提出祭祀开始以歌舞娱祖先神：鞉鼓、击磬、吹管、口钟，商族子弟唱歌跳舞，最后才献上祭品牺牲。

宗庙祭礼时匕鬯不惊。祭祀给天上，神秘的鍾聲感动天。天听到自然乐器之聲表示回报给人，这是所谓天人合一思想。通过宗庙祭礼，天赐下福气，国际安宁，达到礼的政治。礼的最好例子就是祭礼，祭礼加上乐成为人类和谐的一种手段。所以，在乐的帮助下礼变得更完美。

宗庙祭礼是音乐家可以演奏编钟的国家级仪式。从这首诗，我们可以看到，作为一种国家级仪式，音乐是一种展现权威的方式。"乐"确实是与"礼"紧密相连的。

七 结论

在中国古代，音乐在宗庙祭祀中扮演了重要的角色。在《诗经》中，诗和音乐被运用在许多场合，如战争、宴会和国家祭祀上。从周朝到春秋时期，礼乐制度被建立起来。音乐是陶冶情操的工具，在激励善行方面有一定作用。许多中国古人知道礼乐的重要性。孔子（公元前551—479）就知道音乐劝善的功能，并关注了它的艺术性和教化性。他建立了统治者要以"礼乐"作为治国手段的理念。[1]

正如我们在《关雎》和《那》所看到的，音乐是陶冶人的情感，使人产生共鸣的一种纽带。这一古代传统传承下来，在中国社会有着长远的影响。

总而言之，音乐可以培养美好品德，中国古代的礼乐是值得分享的人文遗产。

---

[1] 韩兴燮：《韩国古代音乐思想》，首尔艺文书院2007年版，第18页。

A Study on the Music and Musical Instruments in the Ancient Qin Dynasty

Jinyeul Song / Republic of Korea

Doctoral Candidate of Chinese Department, Kyungsung

This research explores the music and musical instruments in the Pre-Qin Period that appeared in *The Book of Songs*. The research method is analyzing the relationship between temperament and weights and measures. The research shows that in ancient China, music was closely related to natural phenomena.

In ancient China, the length of musical instruments (wind instruments) was measured with millet which was a basic method of measuring the bronze bell. The Method of Subtracting and Adding Thirds was applied to divide scales, and the five tones of the five-tone scale were formed, namely Gong, Shang, Jue, Zhi, and Yu.

In ancient China, music was used for entertaining guests and holding religious ceremonies and rituals. However, the rites and music were not separate. The ancients used rites and music to express praise and appreciation. Rites were the means of rule, which could be preserved even without the aid of music. Music could achieve a sense of sympathy in it. This tradition revealed that temperament was constrained by the natural order, showing human harmony. The researcher wants to explore how the ancient Chinese used music and musical instruments in *The Book of Songs* and ancient Chinese music philosophy.

I. Introduction

After observing and perceiving nature as well as generating doubts, mankind has been plagued by such a question as who the man is. Literary works are the carrier for human thinking, through which humanity explores the ontological issues of man and the world. Literary works will affect not only contemporary people but also future generations. Literature expresses the author's thoughts and emotions through abstract words, and further reflects society. Literature can be divided into lyrics (the form of rhyme and rhythm) and narrative poems (fictions).

The research aims to explore how "rites" and "music" expressed "Chinese centralism" in ancient Chinese classics. The "rites" in ancient Chinese society included rules, laws, systems and social order. Confucius was one of the great scholars who explained the relationship between "rites" and "music". The researcher has tried to find the use of music and musical instruments in *The Book of Songs*. *The Book of Songs* was compiled by Confucius, in which many poems used music and musical instruments. Therefore, the researcher aims to understand such occasions of using music in ancient China as banquets, ceremonies and entertainment through these poems and to explore the use of music and musical instruments in *The Book of Songs* and their philosophical significance.

II. Neutralization Centered on Rites and Music

The fundamental idea "neutralization" means "moderation" and "harmony". "Moderation" refers to a state that is neither excess nor lack. In music, musical instruments are different. How can they achieve harmony? This question is very important as it reveals the essence of human harmony. The key to neutralization is "harmony". As the sound of nature is harmonious, the harmonious human music can be reflected in nature. Harmony music is inextricably linked to the universe because it evolves from nature such as millet and weights and measures. Human beings can achieve harmony through harmonious music. In the great universe, the harmonious development of human and the universe demonstrates the beauty and musical characteristics of ancient China. This helps enable human development to achieve harmony. Music is a way to express emotions. Music is an art that can express human thoughts through the use of pitch, sound length and tone.

The politics in Confucianism can be defined as "ruling the country with rites", which emphasizes that "rites" can be perfectly represented by music. The most perfect thing for human beings is expressed by music. To govern a country with rites should be linked with music, then rites and music can live in harmony. Rites and music are perfectly connected due to "harmony". Rites are a kind of laws and regulations that people should abide by and a sort of respect for the Emperor. Under the laws and regulations, the Emperor is the owner of a country. If someone violated the "rites", he would be punished. However, if a society focuses exclusively on "rites", it will become too harsh. This is why the ruler emphasizes harmony, which is also advocated by Confucius. People want to achieve self-cultivation by learning poetry.

People learn music so that they can achieve perfection. Ancient people made a brief summary, that is, cultivating the self, regulating the family, governing the state and harmonizing the world. The gentleman's self-cultivation comes first, meaning to achieve perfection through learning and music. If a gentleman is self-cultivated without rites and music, he is not a perfect person. This explains why Confucius believed that success came out of music and that people must learn music to achieve perfection.

Confucius noted that people should cultivate their own personality through music. From this perspective, music is a way to educate people. Confucius had great interest and a gift in music. After listening to the music Shao (made by the ancient Emperor Shun), Confucius said, "For three months, I did not know the taste of flesh." This means he did not expect that music had such power. He closely combined poetry and music to make people feel happy in harmony. When the poems were included in music and chanted, the feast became more grand. Confucius also discussed the validity of poetry in "Yang Huo" of Confucian Analects.

The Master said, "The Odes serve to stimulate the mind. They may be used for purposes of self-contemplation. They teach the art of sociability. They show how to regulate feelings of resentment."

Obviously, poetry can make people happy. One combined with music, it can make people more enjoyable. Music is very mysterious because it is invisible. Even the same music may show different connotations due to the player, occasion and atmosphere. The culture of rites and music can be traced back to the Zhou Dynasty and the Spring and Autumn and the Warring States periods.

III. The History of Ancient Chinese Musical Instruments

The Chinese started making props from the Neolithic Age and used pottery clay to make colored drums that can play music. In Henan Province, the bone flute made 8,000 or 9000 years ago, the earliest Chinese musical instrument, was discovered.

In May 1987, 25 bone flutes were unearthed in the Neolithic site excavated in Wuyang County, Henan Province. Most of these bone flutes are made of crane's leg bones, featuring 5, 6, or 7 finger holes respectively. One of the flutes owns relatively intact prototype, which is about 20 cm long and has 7 finger holes of the same size. In particular, there is a small hole next to the last finger hole at the end of the bone flute. Experiments revealed that this small hole could finely adjust the pitch.

Starting from Dawenkou Culture, clay was used to make drums. From 6300 BC to 4600 BC, the Chinese made musical instruments and played with the instrument hanging on leather. Centering on the Yellow River, one of the birthplaces of the world's four major civilizations, it shows the developed Chinese culture.

This pot has a history of about 5,000 years. Three groups of dancers were painted in the inner wall of the pot. Each group consisted of five dancers who danced hand in hand. And the dancers wore some ornaments on the head or tied their hair. Underneath the body were objects like small tails. This may be the decoration shaped like a bird or other animals.

In China, the painting on this ceramic pot is the oldest record related to dance. The dancers on the pot were in groups of five and all performed the same movement. This may be a group dance.

In the 21st century BC, China entered the slave society. The first state founded was the Xia Dynasty (21st century - 16th century BC). The literature and unearthed relics of the Xia Dynasty music are few. Except for the stone bells, Xun (an ancient earthen, egg-shaped wind instrument), drums, and pottery bells in stone pottery and ceramics, it is difficult to know the specific musical forms.

The Shang Dynasty people blew horns during the war. There is also such kind of scene in the movie Confucius.

In the Bronze Age of the Zhou Dynasty or the Spring and Autumn and the Warring States periods, bells or chimes were produced. The bell was played by hand, but the chime was fixed in the wooden frame. There were several bells on the top and bottom of the chime which produced different pitches.

In the Zhou Dynasty, bronze instruments appeared mostly at the country's ceremonies or banquets. The materials used to make musical instruments were divided into eight categories, including metal, stone, clay, leather, silk, wood, gourd and bamboo.

As early as the Western Zhou Dynasty, the ancients created the world's earliest musical instrument classification according to the eight categories including metal, stone, clay, leather, silk, wood, gourd and bamboo. The classification was in line with the materials of the musical instruments. At the same time, it also played a role in tone classification and selection. 7,000 years ago, our ancestors created bone flute and bone whistle. However, bone was not included in the eight categories, which exemplified that our ancestors had a certain degree of aesthetic standard in material selection and tone selection. According to this classification, Se and dulcimer belong to stringed instruments, and the two instruments should be closer to stringed instruments in terms of their tone and music.

The performance of music in the Zhou Dynasty was regulated according to the hierarchy of status to maintain the legitimacy of the state and a strict identity system and class. The chimes were musical instruments made of bronze and the stone-chime was made of stone. Chimes and stone-chime were used to define the hierarchy of status.

There were four bands in terms of scale. The nobility hung musical instruments on four walls, vassals on three walls, high officials on two walls and scholars on one wall. At that time, officials higher than senior third rank and lower-ranking officials enjoyed different Ya music. Officials higher than senior third rank mainly enjoyed stringed instruments similar to Se.

IV. Rules of Rhythm and Weights and Measures

It is often said that language has rules, so does music. The language of music is called rhythm, which has a close relationship with nature. The composer adjusts time and speed via temperament to complete the harmony. It is like a symphony played by a variety of musical instruments to express emotions.

Music in China and Japan is based on 2 beats, Korean music 3 beats, and Western music 4 beats. The Method of Subtracting and Adding Thirds determined an octave. It meant subtracting 1/3 of the bronze bell to identify the standard pitch and adding 3/4 to 1/3 of the remaining. The vibration was then determined. The 12 tone equal temperament was completed. Music was an important factor in solving the eastern triangle culture. The Yellow Emperor, Emperor Wen of the Zhou Dynasty and Emperor Wu of the Zhou Dynasty formulated music as soon as they ascended the throne. In the East, music was designed to determine the standard pitch of the 12 semitones in the octave - bronze bell.

For Chinese and ancient Athenians, the beauty of music lies in harmony. But the roots of Athenian harmony are not the wind but the water. Wind and water represent the characteristics of Chinese and Western cultures respectively. Of course, this does not mean that the Chinese neglected mathematics when producing intervals, or that they only produced the feeling of being as vague as wind.

After the 12-tone system was established, Chinese created the Method of Subtracting and Adding Thirds, which included an understanding of the principles of mathematics. Mathematics also occupied a very important place in Chinese music. In China, the earliest maker of temperament was the well-known Guan Zhong who was a close friend of Bao Shuya. Guan Zhong was born about 140 years earlier than Pythagoras. At that time, China had already formed a five-note interval of Gong, Shang, Jue, Zhi and Yu via the Method of Subtracting and Adding Thirds.

The Method of Subtracting and Adding Thirds meant subtracting or adding 1/3 of the original length. The number of ancient Chinese temperament was related to 9. Pythagoras, an Athenian scholar, regarded 1 as the standard, and paid attention to the proportion. On the contrary, for all the standard pitches in ancient China that became the Gong sound, the number was 81 which was 9 squared. According to the Method of Subtracting and Adding Thirds, 1/3 of the Gong sound was 27. 27 adding 81 equaled 108, which was the number of Zhi sound. Subtracting its trisection 36 from 108 would be 72, the number of Shang sound. 72 adding its trisection 24 was 96, the number of Yu sound. Subtracting its trisection 32 from 96 was 64, the number is Jue sound. Of course, the longer the string, the lower the sound. The fundamental tone of bronze bell was determined in this order: 108, 96, 81, 72 and 64. But the interesting thing was that the standard pitch Gong was in the middle.

The Method of Subtracting and Adding Thirds was the most easily accepted process of finding the natural scale. It can also be seen as the process of finding the absolute tone through the tone of Gong, Shang, Jue, Zhi and Yu. This calculation of temperament was a physical process determined by millet we obtain from the nature, and it also included the spiritual process of finding the sound of heaven. The search for good music on the earth could be called "Hongyi sound". Greek philosophy sought perfect music, while China's goal was to find "absolute sound". Pythagoras defined everything as numbers.

In the East, an octave was made into 12 semitones. The basic tone was determined by the bronze bell. How did the most basic bronze bell vibration of Chinese music be determined? The vibration of the bronze bell or pitch depended on the length of the pipe. The pitch pipe was made according to the tone of the bronze bell. The length of the pitch pipe was 1 foot. Bronze bell became the standard pitch of the pitch pipe with basic sound quality. Based on this, the other 11 semitones were made.

The length of bronze bell was weights and measures in real life. The basic unit was 1 foot. Music was made up of temperament and natural materials, symbolizing harmony with nature. The basic tone of music was bronze bell. The millet was used as a scale to make wind instruments. The application of the pitch pipe standard based on sound quality in the weights and measures in real life illustrated the harmony between man and nature in East Asia. The length of the musical instrument and the standard of weights and measures were all from nature, showing Chinese ancients' outlook on art and nature. Like music, order came from nature. The length of 10 grains of millet was taken as 1 inch, and 90 inches or 100 inches was taken as 1 foot to make pitch pipe. The scale of the bronze bell or the length of the gold pipe was then determined. People used millet harvested in nature to determine basic tone and weights and measures. When musical instruments played this kind of music, human life had an order. Weights and measures were the order of human life, and the medium was music.

When the ancient Emperor ascended the throne, he must first define measurement by using millet as scale of the bronze bell. This served as the weights and measures to govern the state. A state with unified weights and measures could maintain order. It was clear that the order of reign came from nature.

The length of bronze bell was based on China's climate and diet. The south produced abundant rice, while the north fed on millet. The unearthed millet 8,000 or 9,000 years ago proved the fact that millet determined temperament. In terms of temperament, the length of pipe was determined by the length of grains of millet. The rule of weights and measures was also of similar thinking with that of temperament.

The rules of music were formulated according to natural phenomena, and the standards were applied to weights and measures in society. This accounted for the consistency of the rules of music and the rule of weights and measures.

Music was influenced by politics, religion, ideology, war and peace. Moreover, the philosophy of harmony between nature and man, which influenced the formation of temperament, formed human rites and achieved resonance. *The Book of Songs* not only included the arts of nobles, royal family and other people of the upper class, but also popular literature such as folk songs, which was widely sung at that time.

During the founding of a state, the Emperor formulated music for the purpose of proclaiming the legitimacy of the family and the royal family, established a bureaucratic office and appointed officials in charge of music. In fact, music was not only a means of distinguishing classes, but also an indispensable element in banquets, ancestral temples and worship music. Therefore, this kind of research requires careful observation of temple activities in the court or music for sacrifice.

The composer adjusts time and speed by beats and adjusts the speed of sound with skills to create tension that integrates with the listener. The Method of Subtracting and Adding Thirds determined the standard pitch by vibration and along with the derived sound came the story. The main tone of bronze bell determined, composition was to visualize the tone of the material.

Composition incorporates counterpoint or harmonics, putting together two or more sympathetic tones. Composing is visualized, and it is temperament that transfers sound to music. Counterpoint allows several pieces of monophony to be merged into polyphony.

The 12 tone equal temperament included bronze bell, the great bell in the Zhou Dynasty, Taicu, clip clock, Gaoxuan, Zhonglv, Ruibin, Linzhong, Yize, Nanlv, Wuni and Yingzhong. The units of length referred to fen, inch, foot, zhang and yin. The units of volume included yue, ge, liter, dou and hu. There were such weight units as zhu, liang, jin, jun and dan. The pitch pipe was based on a certain number of grains of millet to measure length, volume and weight. This was similar to the laws of the season and the time of day and month, which were all natural phenomena.

The sound creates the "resonance art" which is a kind of "time art". Art utilizes time and space to accommodate the beauty of music. Music cannot do without melody. Temperament influences the sensibility of the person with beautiful melody out of two or more sympathetic tones.

Composers make melody based on pentatonic scale to express their emotions and share them with others. Music is heard through wind and vibration. Composers achieve their creative intentions by affecting people's emotions.

V. Crying Ospreys and Music

A poem is either long or short. When combined with melody, it can be sung. The singer's emotion can be expressed with the help of musical instruments. Human beings have the desire to express their emotions to their peers, and music was likely to appear at the beginning of human history. The main purpose of society and culture is to cultivate human consciousness and to enhance humanity through music. The social and cultural development is usually represented by the music created by mankind. Musicians are necessary in the society or group they belong to. Musicians play an important role in national unity, who also participates in group dances or ceremonies. Ancient Chinese people integrated nature into their own culture and turned it into something that suited their nature. Playing the natural eight categories of musical instrument in ancient orchestra helped establish a close relationship with nature and realize the philosophy of life.

The Book of Songs is a classic. A lot of Chinese ancient music and musical instruments can be found in it. *The Book of Songs* can be sung. The royal family used poems to describe the ceremony and the solemnity of the Emperor and the nobility. For example, in Chapter 1 of Crying Ospreys, a noble man pursued a beautiful woman. He was very pleased to see this woman. He used music to express his joy and conveyed his intention to the woman. He organized a party with bells and drums.

Crying Ospreys

Pre-Qin Period　The Book of Songs

　　Merrily the ospreys cry,
　　On the islet in the stream.
　　Gentle and graceful is the girl,
　　A fit wife for the gentleman.
　　Short and long the floating water plants,
　　Left and right you may pluck them.
　　Gentle and graceful is the girl,
　　Awake he longs for her and in his dreams.
　　When the courtship has failed,
　　Awake he thinks of her and in his dreams.
　　Filled with sorrowful thoughts,
　　He tosses about unable to sleep.
　　Short and long the floating water plants,

Left and right you may gather them.

Gentle and graceful is the girl,

He'd like to wed her, the qin and se (1) playing.

Short and long the floating water plants,

Left and right you may collect them.

Gentle and graceful is the girl,

He'd like to marry her, bells and drums beating.

In Chapter 3, this gentleman met this beautiful woman and played Qin and Se for her. Qin is a stringed instrument used by Chinese ancients. It consists of a sound board made of sycamore and seven strings. The sound board is hollow, and the seven silk strings produce crisp sound.

The word "befriend (You)" here bears the meaning of intimacy. It was believed that the match of Qin and Se was the most harmonious, so the excellent man (gentleman) and the beautiful woman (lady) loving each other was the most ideal and most harmonious. But it should be noted that there was another meaning in this poem. "Befriend (You)" served as a verb. The gentleman expressed his love by Qin and Se, hoping to impress the lady.

On the other hand, Se has 25 strings and its voice is very soft and elegant. When the crisp sound of Qin is intertwined with the soft sound of Se, a harmonious movement will be played.

Chapter 2 and 3 were about the hero's characteristic as a "gentleman". First, he suffered from misses when he had not got the lady's love. He could not eat or sleep well. Then he imagined how to make every possible effort to harmonize with the lady and make her happy by Qin, Se, bell and drum. If Chapter 2 was realistic description, then Chapter 3 had romantic sentiment. Although the protagonist did not get the love, he was intoxicated with the beautiful scene of imagination.

The articles about ancient Chinese musical instruments were related to rites and music that reflected human values. Qin was like a man, and Se was like a woman. It represented the theory of yin and yang harmony in traditional Chinese philosophy. In ancient China, the harmony of Qin and Se symbolized the harmonious relations of husband and wife.

Qin also played a role in strengthening the influence, deepening relations, and enhancing the status for the important social contacts and political ties of the nobles. "I have here admirable guests. For whom are struck the lutes, large and small. The lutes, large and small, are struck. And our harmonious joy is long-continued." "His bells ring out qin-qin. His lutes, large and small, give their notes. The tones of his organs and sounding stones are in unison. They sing the Ya and the Nan, dancing to their flutes without error." "Chugging Axles" in Xiaoya was court banquet music of the nobility. People from the upper class quoted "The six reins like lute music I play" to express their emotions.

In Chapter 4, the gentleman played the bell and drum to celebrate the feast and please the beautiful woman. This meant that only the gentleman could use the bell and drum. The musical instrument was a symbol of social status. In this poem, music and musical instruments could produce emotional resonance.

The "bell" sound must fit in size. The high or low sound achieved "harmony" to present beauty. The music (Qin, Se, bell and drum) in Crying Ospreys was refreshing. The gentleman's rites were moving. The harmony of Qin and Se in Crying Ospreys implied the harmony of husband and wife. Rites became more perfect with the help of music, and this poem reflected Confucius thoughts on rites. Music made people happy and peaceful and influenced "benevolence". Music reflected the aesthetic concept of the Chinese people, that is, beauty guided "goodness". "Rites" regulated the social order and "music" brought happiness to people. Therefore, the "good" music enabled the rigid rites to be more perfect and allowed people to be sympathetic.

VI. *Na* and Music

Na is a musical poem depicting ancient rituals, reflecting the society of the Shang Dynasty. The poem showed rites and music in ancestral shrine sacrifice.

> How admirable! how complete!
> Here are set our hand-drums and drums.
> The drums resound harmonious and loud,
> To delight our meritorious ancestor.

When the Shang Dynasty descendants held a ceremony for Tang, they performed three rites and music to worship him. This poem was a song with a drum.

> The descendant of Tang invites him with this music,
> That he may soothe us with the realization of our thoughts.
> Deep is the sound of the hand-drums and drums;
> Shrilly sound the flutes;
> All harmonious and blending together,
> According to the notes of the sonorous gem.
> Oh! majestic is the descendant of Tang;
> Very admirable is his music.

The descendants of Tang worshipped Tang for blessing. They played music and worshipped their ancestor.

> The large bells and drums fill the ear;
> The various dances are grandly performed.
> We have admirable visitors,
> Who are pleased and delighted.
> From of old, before our time,
> The former men set us the example; -
> How to be mild and humble from morning to night,

And to be reverent in discharging the service.

May he regard our sacrifices in summer and autumn,

[Thus] offered by the descendant of Tang!

Yong is a musical instrument played in the auditorium which consisted of a snare drum, a bass drum and a flute. In the auditorium, stone-chime was also played. Children and grandchildren played musical instruments to commemorate Tang.

Mao and Han believed that this poem was the lyrics for worshiping Tang. Wei Yuan and Wang Xianqian considered it to be made by people in the State of Song to commemorate their ancestors. From the content of the poem, Yang Gonggui proposed that sacrifice began with singing and dancing to entertain the ancestors. The Shang descendants must play the drum, beat chime stone, blow the pipe, play the bell and sing and dance before providing offerings.

The ancestral shrine sacrifice was well-ordered. The mysterious bells could touch the heaven. Heaven heard the sound of natural instruments and would return to the people. This was the idea of harmony between man and nature. The ancestral shrine sacrifice brought about blessing and peace to the country so as to apply rites in politics. Rites were best exemplified by ancestral shrine sacrifice. Ancestral shrine sacrifice was combined with music to realize harmony for humanity. Therefore, rites became more perfect with the help of music.

Ancestral shrine sacrifice was a national ceremony where musicians could play chimes. This poem revealed that, as a national ceremony, music was a way to show authority. "Music" was indeed closely linked with "rites".

VII. Conclusion

In ancient China, music played an important role in the ancestral shrine sacrifice. In *The Book of Songs*, poetry and music were used in many occasions, such as wars, banquets, and national sacrifices. From the Zhou Dynasty to the Spring and Autumn Period, the system of rites and music was established. Music was a tool for cultivating sentiment and it had a role in encouraging good deeds. Many ancient Chinese knew the importance of rites and music. Confucius (551-479 BC) knew that music could encourage good deeds and paid attention to its artistry and educational function. He put forward the idea that the ruler should use "rites and music" to govern the country.

As is seen in Crying Ospreys and Na, music was a kind of bond that resonated with people's emotions. This tradition has been passed down to exert long-term influence on Chinese society.

In conclusion, music can cultivate moral standing. Ancient Chinese rites and music are humanistic heritage that worth sharing.

中国20世纪20—30年代摄影理论研究

罗飞 【意大利】
巴塞罗那自治大学客座讲师

　　本文是笔者未来几年一系列新研究的开端，主题是第二次世界大战之前中国的摄影理论发展。笔者将研究20世纪20—30年代这一艺术和视觉文化创作的非凡时期。

　　本文是历史性的导论，为笔者未来的研究奠定了基础。第一部分介绍了业余摄影团体以及他们对媒介的研究，这产生了第一个重要的理论摄影方法。接下来讨论摄影的发展，直到以纪实视角重现抗战的摄影师的出现。

　　结论部分包含了未来研究的起点。笔者提出了一些对这一时期在中国摄影领域占主导地位的"画意摄影"的批判性观点。这些观点也是对第二次世界大战前中国主要摄影风格进行评析的基础。

一 民国时期的摄影

　　1911年，1644年建立的最后一个封建王朝——清政府的统治被推翻。次年，中华民国成立，孙中山（1866—1925）宣布就任临时总统。

　　这是中国新纪元的开始，中国的摄影工具对于国家走上这条新道路的记录非常重要。有政治抱负的两兄弟：高剑父（1879—1951）和高奇峰（1889—1933），是岭南画派的创始人，也是将现实元素引入新绘画的捍卫者，创办了《真相画报》杂志（1912—1913），这是中国第一本拍摄杂志。

艺术领域出现的现实主义不仅归因于欧洲潮流，而且得益于摄影工具的传播。正如 Francesca dal Lago（2009）所说："在欧洲，学术现实主义是现代主义的反对极，在中国则呈现出一种语言的激进价值，可以在原有传统中实现突破。"

尽管出现了现实主义，但20年代的第一批美术摄影作品受到了国际画意摄影主义的启发，主要是景观、静物和裸体的复制。一方面需要认定摄影是艺术，我们将会看到，这暗示着对中国绘画传统的引用：

"因此，尽管摄影的发明背景是科学发展和渴望捕捉到欧洲的绝对现实，但在传入中国时，这种现代主义的野心大都丧失了。早期的摄影实践主要用于熟知的中国视觉表达的情景中，与绘画一样[……]。结果，早期的摄影实践主要是为了装饰、崇拜、美学表达、社会性、广告和宣传。尽管当时拍摄的照片现在被认为具有文献价值，但对记录历史和代表现实（无论是科学的还是社会的）的关注却微不足道。"

另一方面是技术动机，因为更便宜的相机具有最高速度的快门，在运动中获得高质量的图像变得很复杂。结果，描绘的物体主要是风景和静物。

与此同时，20年代初出现了"五四运动"，即1919年签署《凡尔赛条约》之后的示威运动，这是一次对中国文化进行大规模改造的运动。这次运动影响了每一个艺术领域，自然也影响了摄影作品。

尽管摄影通过连年增加的研究以及杂志不断传播，成本高昂的摄影设备却无法触及大部分人群。至少直到20年代，少量业余摄影师才出现。

在这些摄影师里，陈万里（1892—1969）和黄振玉（1895—1978）相识，于1919年决定在北大校园组织摄影展。之后，他们决定在1923年创建北京大学艺术写真学会。随着刘半农（1891—1934）和老焱若（1883—1966）等新成员的加入，学会改名为光社，基本目的是肯定"美术摄影"工具的艺术价值。1924年6月14至15日，他们在北京的中央公园（现中山公园）举办了一场展览，近3000人协助举办，其中包括艺术家和知识分子。

社团的成功促成了全国各地摄影协会的成立：1922年，广州摄影工会成立；1926年，潘达微（1880—1929）和傅秉常（1896—1965）在广州成立了景社；1928年，张篷舟和金满城在南京创办了美社；1925年，林泽苍（1903—1961）在上海创办了第一个全国社团——中国摄影学会（E. K. Lai，2000年，第32页）。

1927年，光社成员、中国摄影理论先驱刘半农出版了摄影专著《半农谈影》。

他巧妙地使用术语来指出中国的审美传统，旨在确认摄影不仅仅是一个简单的记录现实的工具，而是能够通过作者的内心世界再现现实（Kent，2013），目的是实现画意摄影。关于刘半农在形式方面的现实意义，爱德文（Edwin K. Lai，2000）指出：

"为此，摄影师必须美化他们拍摄的照片。不仅需要选择美丽的事物作为主题，还需要在照片中精美地呈现这些主题。他敦促摄影师特别注意拍摄对象的形式和照明条件，并遵守构图规则或章法。"

实际上，这些理论体现了国外画意摄影趋势的强烈影响。在具体案例中，这些作者试图参考中国传统绘画的构图和典型元素。

30年代，上海成为中国新的文化中心，这不仅有利于摄影作品创作，也有助于中国现代主义灵感艺术的发展。这个时期在上海工作的最重要的摄影师是郎静山（1892—1995年），他与胡伯祥（1896—1989）、黄伯惠（1894—1981年）以及上文提到的陈万里和黄振玉创办了中华摄影学社，简称"华社"。

郎静山的摄影作品有关中国山水画传统，通过有趣的实验室技术来实现。图片产生于印在不同底片上的各种元素，然后共同创造出一种现实中不存在的风景。这与中国绘画传统类似，中国传统绘画的风景不是对现实的精确呈现，而是作者对被观察者的"印象"。

郎静山受到了欧洲摄影流派"高级美术摄影"设计的"合版印刷"摄影技术的启发，奥斯卡（Oscar Gustave Rejlander，1813—1875）和亨利（Henry Peach Robinson，1830—1901）也属于该流派（Su, Lin, Liu, & Zhou，2009，第55页）。关于这项技术，郎静山写道：

"发现一棵多余的树或一块岩石毁坏了好风景，只能按原样拍摄，或者根本不能拍，我们常常很失望；但随着合成图片的出现，这种失望最终可以得到补救。我们现在可以消除不需要的东西，并添加缺乏的东西：现在我们可以把各种单个照片制作成理想的照片，而不会失去照片所必需的任何效果或品质。俗话说，自然常常是不完美的，现在我们有能力使其完美。"

在郎静山30年代的作品中，可以找到上海、鸟瞰和现代建筑的照片，这受到了一种新的现代主义摄影方法的影响。

为了参加国际展览，郎静山与两位同事黄仲长（1900年—？）和徐祖荫（生卒不详）一起创立了三友影会。其目标是提升中国的海外形象，因为中国在境外的大部分照片都呈现出一个负面形象，即一个落后的欠发达国家。

另一个与中国摄影发展息息相关的社团是上海的黑白影社。黑白影社创办于1931年，创始人包括卢施福医生、外企销售经理丁升保以及棉花企业经理聂光地（Gauffre & Willaume，1984年，第16页）。创始人的不同职业使社团具有业余性质，因此被认为是最不优秀的社团。该社团有约168个成员，是成员遍及全国的少数几个社团之一。

每个社团都有自己的出版物，用于宣传其成员或者其展出并出版的作品。这类出版物通常得益于爱克发、柯达等大品牌的广告（Gauffre & Willaume，1984年，第16页）。同时也出现了一些专门的摄影杂志：《摄影杂志》（1922/23），《中华摄影杂志》（1933/35）[图4]，《晨风》（1933/35）和《飞鹰》（1936/37）。

30年代的上海不仅有摄影出版物，还有其他几个经常使用摄影的杂志。最著名的是《良友》（1926/46），内容广泛，包括时尚、文学、艺术、新闻等。在当时的上海，《良友》是新兴城市流行文化的象征出版物。

讽刺杂志，如《上海漫画》（1928/30）和《时代漫画》（1934/37），提供了广泛的摄影内容。在这些杂志中，我们可以找到蒙太奇的例子以及摄影媒介的具体用途。

30年代的摄影不仅有风景和静物，许多摄影师受俄罗斯建构主义的启发，试图为摄影实践找到一种更现代的方法。使用新的方式来构图或选择诸如上海现代建筑的主题，采用黑白对比，表现出强烈的实验愿望。许多照片都占据了《时代画报》、《中华月刊》或《方舟》等杂志的封面。

二 抗战时期的摄影

1937年，日本侵占了中国大部分领土，这是所有艺术领域的决定性转折点。上海被占领之前，一系列猛烈轰炸破坏了许多文化制作和推广中心，包括之前几十年创办的许多杂志印刷厂、电影制作中心、艺术学校和艺术家工作室等等。许多艺术家失去了工作室和里面的作品，或者当他们决定离开这座城市时，永远失去了工作。只有少量的艺术品、绘画、电影和照片被保存了下来，奇迹般地在战争的破坏中留存下来。研究这个特定时期的艺术史学家面临着复杂的工作。

受战争的影响，摄影出版物停止出版，摄影协会也停止活动。我们可以看到摄影和其他艺术领域在抗战中的不同反应。这种复杂情况是由于中国领土被分为了三部分：日本侵占了东北，中华民国政府和国民党控制了西南，共产党根据地在西北。

在每一个地区，我们都可以找到使用摄影媒介的不同形式。在日军占领区，一方面，摄影者对情境漠不关心，或者继续进行美术摄影；另一方面，有一些人默默地抵制，拍摄的照片隐喻地唤起爱国主义精神（Willaume，1984，第46页）。

在国民党控制的地区，继续创作美术摄影的摄影师和其他人试图通过摄影来帮助抗日。

最后，在共产党占据的地区，吴印咸、沙飞、徐肖冰（1916-2009年）等摄影师推动了纪实摄影的发展。沙飞在1939年编辑的吴印咸所著《摄影常识》一书中，就摄影器械的使用做了一些介绍：

"[……] 首先，它能以最真实的程度反映现实，因此它可以给人们最真实的感受和最深刻的印象，最容易被人们接受和欢迎。其次，它能够以最快的速度反映现实，并能以最快的速度广泛传播它反映的现实的图像。因此，这无疑是宣传的工具，是斗争的有力武器，肩负着新闻报道的重要政治责任。"

延安根据地制定了宣传摄影原则，后来中华人民共和国成立时沿用了这些原则。

意识到摄影图像的实力不仅为国内使用而且为海外中国形象考虑，便创办了《晋察冀画报》（1942/47），用于在共产党领导的自由领土上进行政治宣传。

这一时期的著名战争照片是沙飞跟随解放军拍摄的作品，还有吴印咸、徐肖冰创作的毛泽东和中国共产党主要领导人的肖像画。

应特别注意的是1938至1940年间创作的、1940年9月刊登于《良友》杂志的一部摄影作品：西康省庄学本（1909—1984年）开展的民族志研究。西康省是中华民国在与西藏接壤的地方建立的，很多不同的民族在这里聚居。最近才重新发现，庄学本的摄影作品是对这些人群的习惯和习俗的全面记录。他认为"文明"社会的成员研究"原始"人口。正如Mo（2013）所说："强调文明中的观察者与被观察者之间的距离类似于西方和日本殖民者所写的旅行叙事"。他的照片除了是这些人群习惯的重要证据外，还是摄影媒介专业实践的结果，其特点是采用120毫米格式的优雅黑白相间的照片。

三　郎静山摄影作品与"画意摄影"运动评析

我们看到，刘半农、郎静山等摄影作者和理论家试图用摄影媒介来保持中国绘画传统的连续性。在他们的文本和照片中，提到了几个世纪以来一直影响中国绘画的"文人艺术"的角度和概念。

这些作者使用摄影媒介为图像传统连续性服务。他们反复提及传统绘画理论方面的正式构图和主题。

在这里，笔者想分析一下这种特殊的艺术方法，笔者认为这是对媒体内在特征的背叛。许多学者认为郎静山的作品是完全概念化的，并将其与达达主义的蒙太奇照相技术或最近的数码摄影相比较。

郎静山拍摄的一些照片，起点是在不同时刻拍摄的各种底片。他的视觉构造颇具独创性，因为这些现实片段之间没有关系，时间也不接近。我们会认为这种构造是概念性的，但结果远不是概念性的。郎静山将自己的作品作为传统风景画的遗产展示，其中描绘的东西并不总是重现真实的地方，而是作者内在的视角。他的技术仅仅是用相机替代铅笔。这与同时期国际"画意摄影"运动的尝试并无差别。这是对媒介"本身"的背叛，其内在特征与绘画的内在特征相反。

最常讨论的也是最具象征性的一个特征（Barthes，1980年；Krauss，1977年；Dubois，1983年）就是指示性。照片不是也不能与拍摄对象分离，同时也不能与拍摄的精确时刻分离。如果我们牢记这个概念，郎静山的照片则是在不同时刻、不同地点拍摄的山、树和人，然后再统一成一个整体，以一种正式的方式使人想起传统的山水画。这些图片的每个元素都是特定的事物或特定的时刻，因此将它们放在一起并没有什么效果。因为观察它们，我们想更多地了解这个特定的地方或人物，以及拍摄照片的时刻。

摄影的另一个特点是分析性：照片只能代表现实，它是一个冷酷的"记录"。郎静山知道这一点，因为对他而言，拍摄"只能照原样拍摄"的风景是没有用的。在这一点上，创作者肯定希望使用相机创作理想的风景，并完善"自然"，这种将相机作为铅笔使用的方式很明显。但是相机是一台机器，可以自然而然地冷却和再现现实。尽管他想创造一个新的理想主义的现实，他也不得不面对与摄影的主题之间不可分割的联系。

这时，再来看郎静山一开始想给我们带来的风景，那就是中国传统绘画。虽然他创造了一幅理想化的景观，是创作者内在视角的结果，但有些方面似乎与他想要提及的传统有很大的距离。"文人"绘画的一个特征不是机械复制经典或自然，而是由于控制了铅笔的使用，其内化促成了原创作品和"真实"的自然肖像的实现。郎的照片是机械和计算过程的结果，它们是在摄影实验室产生的。中国传统绘画中笔画的自发性、直接性和自然性是通过画家手中流动的"气"来表现，可以表现自然和"理"的内部结构。郎静山的作品中没有这种自发性，却有机械质量。他的照片在形式和表面上体现了传统绘画，但未能恢复这一传统所特有的观念和哲学概念。在作品中，他放弃了中国绘画的哲学特征和摄影固有的特征，使得每一种艺术形式都是独一无二的。他的作品使绘画领域与摄影领域之间没有了界限。

四 结论

第二次世界大战前中国的艺术发展这一主题很有吸引力，许多学者都进行了这方面研究。我们对这个视觉世界只有部分的了解，因为这个时期的许多艺术作品已经被摧毁，并且经历了列强或时代的"自然"选择。在摄影中，我们面临着同样的问题，因为我们可用的材料很少。

笔者研究的第一步作为导论，目的是分析第二次世界大战前的几十年间，中国的摄影理论和概念特征。为了归纳这个亚洲国家的主要摄影发展，我将分析书籍中或者专门介绍该媒介的众多杂志上发表的理论文章。

其中一个目标是找出并理解为什么"画意摄影"和"纪实摄影"是这一时期中国摄影作品的主要趋势。当需要肯定或重申自己的传统或需要记录正在改变国家的事件时，历史时势无疑是对这种二元论的解释。但是这些动机并没有阻止受欧洲先锋启发的艺术发展，特别是在上海。因此，可以说这些实验趋势也以某种方式进入了摄影领域。

分析来自其他国家的影响十分重要，这些影响对于大都会上海的艺术偏好发展以及有机会出国留学的人们至关重要。可以说，来自日本的影响远比来自"西方"的影响重要得多。这个"日出之国"和中国一样，有两个类别的摄影作品，即"画意摄影"和"纪实摄影"。但也有例外，例如摄影家安井仲治（1903—1942年），或者诸如野岛康三（1889—1964年）和小石清（1908—1957年）等作家的作品。最后这几位摄影家在中国有对应的例子。

在此，笔者要感谢"青年汉学家研修计划"的主办方，使我有机会2017年9

月在北京进行短期研修。我还要感谢我的导师、中国艺术研究院王保国教授,他帮助我提高了对中国摄影的认识。也正是因为他,我结识了陈申教授。陈教授耐心地给我介绍了中国第一批业余摄影师的情况,并向我展示了一些他的私人收藏。

An Introduction to Theoretical Aspects of Photography in China During the '20 and '30

Roberto Figliulo / Italy

Guest Lecturer of the Autonomous University of Barcelona

This paper is the beginning of a new line of research that I will realize in the course of the following years: the subject are the theoretical developments of photography produced in China during the years previous to the Second World War. I will look into the '20 and the '30, as a period of remarkable production in the arts and visual culture.

This paper is a historic introduction that allows me to lay the groundwork for the future research. In the first part I present the amateur photographic groups and their researches on the medium, which represent the first serious theoretical approach to photography. In the continuation I talk about the developments until the appearance of those photographers that started reproducing the beginning of the war with Japan using a documental point of view.

In my conclusions, there is also a starting point for my future research, I present some critical ideas of the "pictorialist" photography, which dominate the photographic sphere in China during this period. These ideas are also the basis for a future widespread critical view on the predominant photographic styles in the Country before the Second World War.

I. Photography during the Republican Period

1911 was marked by the fall of the last imperial dynasty, the Qing, that ruled the country since 1644. The following year the Republic of China was founded and Sun Yat-Sen (1866-1925) was proclaimed as temporary president.

This is the beginning of a new era for China, where the photographic instrument becomes very important for the documentation of this new path taken by the country. The highly politicized brothers Gao Jianfu (1879-1951) and Gao Qifeng (1889-1933), founders of the *Lingnan* painting school (*Lingnan huapai*) and defenders of the introduction of realistic elements into the new Chinese painting, created the magazine "*The True Records*" (*Zhenxiang huabao*, 1912-1913), which is probably the first magazine published in China that used photographs.

The emergence of realism in the art world it is due not only to the arrival of European trends, but also to major diffusion of the photographic instrument. As Francesca dal Lago (2009) asserts: "the same Academic Realism that in Europe was the antinomic pole to the emergence of Modernism, in China took on the radical value of a language that could allow for a breakthrough with the pre-existing tradition" (p.852).

Despite the emergence of realism, the first examples of art photography during the twenties are inspired by international pictorialism, mostly with the reproductions of landscapes, still life and nudes. On the one hand there was the need to accredit photography as art, which implied, as we will see, references to the Chinese painting tradition:

"Thus, even though photography was invented against a background of scientific fever and an urge to capture the absolute reality in Europe, this modernist ambition was mostly lost when it was introduced to China. Most of its early adopters framed its use in the familiar context of Chinese visual expression, on the same continuum with painting.[…] Consequently, early photographic practices were mostly for the purposes of decoration, worship, aesthetic expression, sociality, advertising and propaganda. Recording history and representing reality (either scientific or social) were marginal concerns, even though pictures taken then are now considered to have documentary value." (Wu & Yun, 2007, p.32).

On the other hand, there was also a technical motivation, since the economically more accessible cameras had a maximum speed of the shutter and it was thus complicated to get good quality of pictures in movement. As a consequence, objects depicted were mostly landscapes and still life.

Meanwhile, in the beginning of the twenties the "4th May Movement" appears, the name of which refers to the demonstrations following the Treaty of Versailles in 1919, and that consists in a huge movement of renovation of Chinese culture. This movement influenced every artistic field and naturally also the photographic production.

Despite the diffusion of photography through studies that had been increasing year after year and its presence in magazines, the high cost of photographic equipment did not allow its diffusion among a large part of the population. At least until the twenties, when small groups of amateur photographers emerged.

In one of this groups of photographers Chen Wanli (1892-1969) and Huang Zhenyu (1895-1978) met each other and in 1919 decided to organize a photographic exhibition in the Beijing University Campus[1]. After this experience they decided to create the *Beijing daxue yishu xiezhen shehui* (Beijing University's Research

---

1   In those days the director of the Beijing University was professor Cai Yuanpei 蔡元培 (1868-1940), who converted the educative center into one of the principal cores of cultural production of the country. For Cai, art is of fundamental relevance. In regard to this, see Cai, Y. (1996). Replacing Religion with Aesthetic Education. In K. A. Denton, *Modern Chinese Literary Thought: Writings on Literature 1893-1945*, (pp.182-189). Stanford: Stanford University Press.

Association for Art Photography) in 1923. With the arrival of some new members, such as Liu Bannong (1891-1934) and Lao Yanruo (1883-1966), the association changed its name to *Guangshe* (the Light Society). Its fundamental aim was to affirm the artistic value of the instrument, of the "artistic photography" (in chinese *Meishu sheying*). Between the 14 and 15 June 1924 they organized an exhibition in the Zhongyang Park (now Zhongshan Park) in Beijing, assisted by almost three thousand people, among which artists and intellectuals.

The success of the society led to the creation of various photographic association throughout the country: the *Guangzhou Sheying gonghui* (the Guangzhou's Syndicate of Photography), founded in 1922; in 1926, also in Guangzhou, the *Jing she* (the Lanscape Association) was founded, with Pan Dawei (1880-1929) and Fu Bingchang (1896-1965)[1] among its founders; the *Mei she* 美社 (the Beauty Society) founded by Zhang Penzhou and Jing Mancheng, in Nanjing in 1928; in 1925 Lin Zecong (1903-1961) founded the first national society in Shanghai, the "*Zhongguo Sheying Xuehui*" (Photographic Society of China) (E. K. Lai, 2000, p.32).

In 1927 Liu Bannong, one of the members of the *Guangshe* Society and a pioneer of theory of photography in China, published a treatise dedicated to photography, titled "*Bannong tanying*" (Bannong's Comments on Photography). Liu skilfully uses terminology that reminds of the Chinese aesthetic tradition, when he wants to affirm that photography is not just a simple instrument of recording the reality as it is, but is capable of reproducing it through the internal world of the author (Kent, 2013)[2].

---

1 Fu Binchang covers various diplomatic assignements, among others the one of ambassador in the Soviet Union (1943-1949) for the ROC government. His photographs are of high quality and included personal pictures or portraits of personalities, for example of the Nationalist Party leader Chang Kai-shek (Meccarelli & Flamminii, 2011).

2 An opinion that is not shared by one of the advocates of the painting tradition, in response to the arrival of new techniques from abroad, Chen Hengque 陳衡恪 (or Chen Hengke or Chen Shizheng 陈师曾, 1876-1923) affirms: "[if literati painting] were 'mechanical' and 'simplistic', it would be exactly like photographs, undifferentiated and repetitive, and what could be precious about it then? How can it be important as art? How can it be valuable as art? What is precious about art lies in its ability to nurture the spirit, express individualism, and reflect feelings" (as cited in Wong, 2000, p.306)

The aim was to create an artistic photography. In regard to the relevance of the formal aspects for Liu, Edwin K. Lai (2000) states:

"to do this the photographers must beautify the pictures they made. Not only did they need to select beautiful matters as their subjects, they also needed to present these subjects beautifully in the photographs. He urged the photographers to take special notice of the forms of the subjects and the lighting conditions, and observe the rules of composition, or 'zhangfa'" (p.39).

In practice, these theories reflected a strong influence of the pictorialist trend coming from abroad. In the specific case of these authors, they were trying to refer to the formal compositions and typical elements of the Chinese traditional painting.

During the thirties, Shanghai became the new cultural nerve centre of the country, not only for the photographic production, but also for the art of modernist inspiration that began to be produced in China.

The most relevant photographer of this period working in Shanghai is Lang Jingshan (Long Chin-san,1892-1995), who, together with Hu Boxiang (1896-1989)[1], Huang Bohui (1894-1981)[2] and the already mentioned Chen Wanli and Huang Zhenyu, founded the *"Zhonghua sheying xueshe"* (the China Photographic Study Society), known under the abbreviated name *"Huashe"*.

Lang's photographs, which refer to the Chinese landscape painting tradition, are realized with an interesting laboratory technique. Pictures are the result of the printing of various elements belonging to different negatives, which then together create a landscape that does not exist in reality, similar to the Chinese painting

---

1 In addition to photography, he was one of the most sophisticated makers of British American Tobacco advertising pictures, in the well-known format of calendars (*Yuefenpai* 月份牌). Regarding his work in advertising, see Johnston Laing, E. (2004) *Selling happiness: calendar posters and visual culture in early twentieth-century Shanghai*. Honolulu: University of Hawaii Press.
2 Owner of the *Eastern Times* magazine, where many of the photographers of the society found their space. In the magazine's building several photographic exhibitions were held as well (Roberts, 2013, p.83).

tradition, where the landscape was not the result of an exact representation of reality, but of an author's "impression" of the observed.

Lang Jingshan is inspired by the photographic technique of "combination printing" devised by the European photographic trend "High Art Photography", which Oscar Gustave Rejlander (1813-1875) and Henry Peach Robinson (1830-1901) were members of, among others (Su, Lin, Liu, & Zhou, 2009, p.55). Regarding this technique Lang writes:

"We are often disappointed to find a good piece of scenery spoiled by an unneeded tree, or ruined by an excrescent bit of rock, which can only be photographed as it is, or not at all; but with the advent of composite pictures, such disappointment can at last be remedied. We can now eliminate what is not wanted and add in what is lacking: we can now make up an ideal picture out of various individual photographs without losing any of the effects or qualities that are necessary to a photograph. Nature is often imperfect, as the saying goes, and now it is within our power to perfect her." (Long, 2004, p.154).

In his work of the thirties it is possible to find examples of pictures of Shanghai, aerial views and modern buildings, result of the influence of a new modernist approach to photography.

In order to participate in international exhibitions, Lang Jingshan, together with two colleagues Huang Zhongchang (1900-?) and Xu Zuyin (without dates), founded a new society that was named "*San you yinghui*" (Three Names Photographic Society). The goal of this new society was to improve the image of China abroad, given that most of the photographs representing China outside of its territory were presenting a negative image of a backward looking and underdeveloped country (Willaume, 1984, p.42).

Another society of remarkable relevance for the further development of photography in China, also established in Shanghai, is *Heibai yingshe* (the Black and White Society). Founded in 1931 by Lu Shifu, a doctor, Ding Shengbao, a sales manager of a foreign enterprise, and Nie Guangdi, a manager in a cotton enterprise (Gauffre & Willaume, 1984, p.16). The different professions exercised by the founders allow us to understand the amateur character of this society that is inter alia distinguished to be the least elitist. It would appear to have about 168 members and was one of the few societies that spread over the rest of China (Su et al., 2009, p.49)[1].

Every society had its own publication that promoted its members or where the works, shown in exhibitions held by the same society, were published. These publications were often financed thanks to the advertisement of big brands such as Agfa, Kodak, etc. (Gauffre & Willaume, 1984, p.16). Simultaneously, however, several magazines devoted exclusively to photography existed as well: the "*Sheying Zazhi*" (the Photography Review, 1922/23), the "*Zhonghua Sheying Zazhi*" (The Chinese Journal of Photography, 1933/35), "*Chenfeng*" (Dawn Wind, 1933/35) and "*Feiying*" (Flying Eagle, 1936/37).

In Shanghai of the thirties we do not only find publications dedicated to photography. There were also several other magazines that used photography frequently. The most well-known was probably the "*Young Companion*" (*Liangyou*, 1926/46), a magazine with diverse content, spreading from fashion to literature, from art to news, etc. It was an emblematic publication of emerging urban popular culture in Shanghai of that period.

Satirical magazines, such as "*Shanghai Manhua*" (Shanghai Sketch, 1928/30) and "*Shidai Manhua*" (Modern Sketch, 1934/37) offered a broad photographic content. In these magazines we can find examples of photomontage and also of a specific use of the photographic medium.

Photography of the thirties does not only represent landscapes and still lives,

---

1 Among their members we find Sha Fei 沙飞 (1912—1950) and Wu Yinxian 吴印咸 (1900—1994), that we will talk about in the following pages.

many photographers were, inspired by trends like the Russian constructivism[1], trying to find a more modern approach to their photographic practice. The uses of new ways of framing the picture or the choice of subjects such as modern architectures of Shanghai, made with contrasted blacks and whites, synonyms of a strong desire of experimentation. Many of these pictures occupied covers of magazines such as *"Shidai huabao"* (Modern Miscellany), *"Zhonghua yuebao"* (The Central China Monthly) or *"Fangzhou"* (The Ark).

II. Photography in War Time

Japanese invasion of a great part of the Chinese territory in 1937 is a decisive inflexion in all the art fields. Before the Shanghai occupation and after a series of strong bombardments, numerous cultural production and promotion centers were destroyed: print shops of many magazines created in the previous decades, cinematographic production centers, art schools, artists' studios, etc. Many artists lost their studios with their works still inside, or lost their work for good when they decided to leave the city. The few works of art, paintings, movies and photographs that are still preserved, miraculously survived the destruction of war. This makes the work of art historians who want to study this specific period very complicated.

As a consequence of the war, photographic publications stop being edited and the photographic societies quit their activities. In photography, as well as in other artistic fields, we can observe different reactions to the war with the Japanese. This complex situation is due to the division of Chinese territory into three parts: the one occupied by the Japanese in the North-East of the country, the one under the control of the government of the Republic and of the Guomingdang in the South-West, and the communist bases in the North-West.

In each of these areas we can find different modalities of using the photographic medium. In the part occupied by the Japanese there are on the one hand photographers

---

1 Regarding the "Progressive Movement" in China see Minnick, S., & Ping, J. (1990). *Chinese Graphic Design in the Twentieth Century*. London: Thames & Hudson.

either indifferent to the situation or favourable to the occupation who continue producing artistic photography, and on the other hand there are a few who silently resist, taking pictures that metaphorically recall the patriotic spirit (Willaume, 1984, p.46).

In the areas under the control of the Guomingdang, photographers that prefer to continue creating artistic photography are present and others that try to use the photography to help in the war against the Japanese.

Finally, within the territories occupied by the communists, photographers such as Wu Yinxian, Sha Fei and Xu Xiaobing (1916-2009) promote documentary photography. In the introduction to Wu Yinxian's book *"Sheying Changshi"* (The Common Sense of Photography), edited in 1939, Sha Fei writes in regard to the use of the photographic instrument:

"[…] first, it can reflect reality in the most truthful degree, therefore it can give the people the most truthful feelings and the most substantial and profound impressions, which become most easily accepted and welcomed by the people. Second, it can reflect reality in the fastest speed, and can widely disseminate the images of reality it reflects in the fastest speed. Therefore undoubtedly, it is a tool of propaganda and a powerful weapon for struggle which shoulders the important political responsibility of news reportage." (as cited in E. K. Lai, 2000, p.48).

The principles of propaganda photography that will be utilized with the foundation of the PRC were established in the Yan'an[1] base.

Aware of the strength of the photographic image, not only for the domestic use but also for the image of China abroad, the magazine *"Jin-Cha-Ji huabao"* (Three Province, 1942/47) was founded for promotion of the politics executed in the free territories under the communist control.

Well-known war photographs of this period are the ones by Sha Fei following the

---

1 In Yan'an the "Forum on literature and art" was held in May 1942, in which the opening and closing discourse realized by Mao Zedong will be the guide line for the cultural production in the communist China.

People's Liberation Army, or portraits of Mao Zedong and the principal leaders of the Chinese Communist Party made by Wu Yinxian and Xu Xiaobin.

Special attention should be given to a particular photographic work realized between 1938 and 1940 and published in the September of 1940 edition of the *Liangyou* magazine: an ethnographic research carried out by Zhang Xueben (1909-1984) in the province of Xikang. This region was created by the Republic in an area on the border with Tibet that was inhabited by a great number of different ethnic groups. Zhang's photographic work, only recently rediscovered, is a thorough documentation of the habits and customs of these populations. His point of view is the one of a member of a "civilized" society studying "primitive" populations. As Mo (2013) states: "This emphasis on the distance between the observer and the observed in the scale of civilization bears a resemblance to travel narratives penned by western and Japanese colonial travelers" (p.128). His photographs are, in addition to being an important testimony of habits of these populations, also the result of a professional practice of the photographic medium, characterized by the use of an elegant black and white in 120 mm format.

III. Critical Analysis of Lang Jingshan Photographic Work and the "Pictorialist" Movement

As we have seen, authors and theoreticians of photography, such as as Liu Bannong and Lang Jingshan, tried to use the photographic medium to maintain continuity with their country's painting tradition. In their texts as well as in their photographs they referred to the aspects and concepts, typical of the "literati art", that have been influencing the Chinese painting for centuries.

Those authors conceived the use of the photographic medium as an instrument at the service of the continuity of the pictorial tradition. They repeat formal constructions and subjects that refer to theoretical aspects of the traditional painting.

Here I want to analyse this particular artistic methodology, which I consider to be a betrayal of the intrinsic characteristics of the medium. Many scholars consider

Lang's work as thoroughly conceptual and compare it to the Dadaist technique of photomontage or with the recent digital photography.

In some of Lang's photographs, the starting point are various negatives taken at different moments in time. His visual construction is quite original, since these fragments of reality have no relation between them and also no temporal proximity. This could lead us to think that the construction is conceptual, but the result is far from being conceptual. Lang presents his work as a legacy of the traditional landscape painting, where what was portrayed not always reproduced a real place, but an internalized vision of the author. Lang's technique is merely a substitution of the pencil with the camera[1]. This is not very different from what the international "pictorialist" movement was trying to do everywhere else at approximately the same time. This is a profound betrayal of the medium "per se", whose intrinsic characteristics are opposed to those of the painting.

One of these characteristics, the most discussed (Barthes, 1980; Krauss, 1977; Dubois, 1983; etc.) and the most emblematic one, is the indicality. A photograph is not and can not be separated from its referent, from the object photographed, and at the same time from the precise moment in time in which it was taken. If we keep this concept in mind, Lang pictures are reduced to a pastiche of mountains, trees and people that have been photographed in different moments and different places, then reunited into a whole that reminds of the traditional landscape painting only in a formal way. Every element of these pictures refers to a specific thing or particular moment, so the intention to put them together is ineffective. Because observing them we want to know more about this particular place or person, and about the moment when the photographs was made.

The other characteristic of photography is analytical: photographs can only represent reality as it is, it is a cold "document". Lang is aware of this aspect, since for him it is useless to shoot a landscape "which can only be photographed as it

---

[1] We can consider it the "Chinese" chapter of a larger discussion on the relationship between painting and photography.

is". At this point the author affirms the wish to use the camera in order to create an ideal landscape and to perfect "nature". This is a clear way of using the camera as a pencil, but the camera is a machine and can as such reproduce reality coldly and automatically. As much as he wanted to create a new and idealistic reality, he had to face this indissoluble connection relation with the subject represented photographically.

At this point it could be interesting to move to the terrain to which Lang wanted to bring us since the beginning, that is the Chinese traditional painting. Although he achieved to create a picture of an idealized landscape, the result of an internalized vision of the author, there are some aspects that seem to substantially distance him from the tradition to which he wanted to refer. One of the characteristics of the "literati" painting was not the mechanical copy of the classics or of the nature, but their internalization that, thanks to the control of the use of the pencil, resulted in the realization of an original work and a "real" portrait of nature. Lang's photographs are the result of a mechanical and calculated process, keeping in mind that they were produced in a photographic laboratory. The spontaneity, immediacy and naturalness of the stroke in Chinese traditional painting was the expression of a flowing "*qi*" (氣) through the hand of the painter, who could accomplish to represent the nature and its internal structure the "*li*" (理). This spontaneity disappears in Lang's works, which are characterized by their mechanical quality. The result of Lang's pictures are photographs that could in a formal and superficial level remind of a traditional painting, but they fail to recover all the ideas and philosophical concepts that are characteristic of this tradition. In his work, Lang forsakes both the philosophical characteristics of Chinese painting and the characteristics inherent in photography that made each of these art forms unique and inimitable. His works are lost in kind of a limbo between the realm of painting and the world of photography.

IV. Conclusions

The artistic developments in China during the years before the Second World War is a fascinating subject that moves numerous scholars dedicated their research to it.

We only have a partial insight into this visual world, because many artistic works from this period have been destroyed and have undergone the "natural" selection of hegemonic groups or trends. In photography we are faced with the same problems, since the material available to us is scarce.

This first step of my research serves as an introduction: my intention is to analyse the theoretical and conceptual characteristics of photography produced in China during the decades before the Second World War. I will analyse theoretical texts published in books or in the numerous magazines dedicated to the medium, in order to synthesize the principal photographic developments of this Asiatic country.

One of the objectives will be to find and comprehend the reasons why the "pictorialist" and the "documentarist" trends were the main ones in the Chinese photographic productions of this period. The historical conjuncture, when there was the need to affirm or reaffirm the own tradition or the need to document the events that were changing the country, is without a doubt an explanation of this dualism. But these motivations did not prevent the development, especially in Shanghai, of an art inspired by the European vanguards. Therefore, we can suppose that these experimental trends somehow arrived to the photographic sphere as well.

It will be crucial to analyse the aspect of the influences coming from other countries, that were essential for the development of artistic preferences in the cosmopolitan Shanghai of this period and for those who had the chance to study abroad. We can suppose that influences coming from the close Japan were far more important than those coming from the "West". In the "Land of the Rising Sun" we can also identify two categories in the photographic production, the "pictorialist" and the "documentarist", the same as in China. But we can also find exceptions, for example photographer Nakaji Yasui (1903-1942), or in the work of authors such as Yasuzō Nojima (1889-1964) or Kiyoshi Koishi (1908-1957). These last examples could have their equivalents in China.

At this point I should say thank you to the organizers of the "Visiting Program for Young Sinologist" for giving me the chance to have a short period of research in Beijing in September 2017. I should also mention my tutor from the "Chinese National Academy of Arts" professor Wang Baoguo, who helped me to increase my knowledge of Chinese photography. Thanks to him I could meet professor Chen Shen, who taught me with a lot of patience about the first amateur photographers in China and showed me a part of his private collection.

References

Barthes, R. (1980). *La chambre claire: Notes sur la photographie*. Paris: Gallimard.
Cai, Y. (1996). Replacing Religion with Aesthetic Education. In Kirk A. Denton (Ed.), *Modern Chinese Literary Thought: Writings on Literature 1893-1945*, (pp.182-189). Stanford: Stanford University Press.
Chen, S., (1990). *Lang Jingshan ji "Jijin sheying"* 郎静山及"集锦摄影". (Self-published article, courtesy of the author).
Dal Lago, F. (2009). Realism as a Tool of National Modernization in the Reformist Discourse of Late 19th and Early 20th China. In *Crossing Cultures: Conflict, Migration & Convergence. Proceedings of the 32nd International Committee of the History of Art (CIHA) Conference, Melbourne, 13-18 January 2008* (pp.852-856). Melbourne: Ed. Jaynie Anderson.
Dubois, P. (1983). *L'Acte photographique*. Paris-Bruxelles: Nathan-Labor.
Gauffre, D., & Willaume, J. (1984). Shanghai années 30: la société « Noir et Blanc »: Entretien avec le photographe Wu Yinbo. In J. Boissier & J. Willaume (Eds.) *30 Ans de photographie chinoise (1930-1960)*, (pp.16-21). Paris: Presses de l'Université de Vincennes.
Johnston Laing, E. (2004) *Selling happiness: calendar posters and visual culture in early twentieth-century Shanghai*. Honolulu: University of Hawaii Press.
Kent, K. R. (2013). Early Twentieth-Century Art Photography in China: Adopting, Domesticating, and Embracing the Foreign. *Trans Asia Photography Review*, *3* (2). Retrieved from http://quod.lib.umich.edu/t/tap/7977573.0003.204/--early-twentieth-century-art-photography-in-china-adopting?rgn=main;view=fulltext.
Krauss, R. (1977). Notes on the Index: Seventies Art in America. *October*, *3* (Spring), 68-81.
Lai, E. K. (2000). *The life and art photography of Lang Jingshan (1892-1995)* (Doctoral Dissertations). Retrieved from http://hub.hku.hk/bitstream/10722/31239/11/Bibliography.pdf?accept=1 (Last accessed 11 July 2016).
Long, C. S. (2004). Composite Pictures and Chinese Art. In J. B. Danzker, K. Lun, S. Zheng

(Eds.), *Shanghai Modern: 1919-1945*, (pp.154-158). Ostfildern-Ruit: Hatje Cantz.

Meccarelli, M., & Flamminii, A. (2011). *Storia della fotografia in Cina: Le opere di artisti cinesi e occidentali*. Aprilia: Novalogos.

Minnick, S., & Ping, J. (1990). *Chinese Graphic Design in the Twentieth Century*. London: Thames & Hudson.

Mo Y. (2013). The New Frontier, Zhuang Xueben and Xikang Province. In Y. Du & J. Kyong-McClain (Eds.), *Chinese History in Geographical Perspective,* (pp.121-139). Lanham, Maryland: Lexington Books.

Roberts, C. (2013). *Photography and China*. London: Reaktion Books.

Si, S. (2012). *Sha Fei he tade zhanyoumen* 沙飞和他的战友们. Beijing: Xinhua chunbanshe.

Su, Z., Lin, L., Liu, N., & Zhou, J. (2009). *Zhongguo sheying shilue* 中国摄影史略. Beijing: Zhongguo wenlian chubanshe.

Willaume, J. (1984). «Le tigre de cuir»: Une introduction à l'histoire de la photographie chinoise. In J. Boissier & J. Willaume (Eds.) *30 Ans de photographie chinoise (1930-1960)*, (pp.28-55). Paris: Presses de l'Université de Vincennes.

Wong, A. (2000). A New Life for Literati Painting in the Early Twentieth Century: Eastern Art and Modernity, a Transcultural Narrative?. *Artibus Asiae, 60* (2), 297-326.

Wu, J., & Yun, G. (2007). Beyond Propaganda, Aestheticism and Commercialism: The Coming of age of Documentary Photography in China. *Javnost-The Public, 14* (3), 31-48.

中国与世界

China and the World

中国与南非经济关系（1990—2010）

布拉西马·迪亚凯特 【科特迪瓦】
费利克斯乌弗埃博瓦尼大学讲师、研究员

引言

21世纪初以来，中国一直在改善和巩固其在非洲的影响力，而传统上非洲是西方大国的领地。在外交、商业、经济、工业和政治方面，中国建立并加强与非洲国家的合作，特别是南非。本文以收集到的相关资料为基础，重点关注中国在南非的实际影响力。之所以选择南非作为中非关系宏观背景下的一个案例，是因为南非与中国之间的联系越来越紧密。尽管在1990年因为"两个中国"问题，中国和南非的关系动荡不安，但自2010年以来，中国与南非的关系越来越成熟，已发展成全球性的全面战略伙伴关系。2010年，中国成为南非的主要贸易伙伴。现在，在与南非的贸易合作方面，中国领先于像德国和美国这样与南非有着悠久贸易历史的国家。我们不禁要问：从1990年到2010年，中国与南非的关系何以进展显著？

本文旨在回答这一问题，其主要辅助文件是已公开发表的文章和各种口头资料。

口头资料包括对南非国际关系与合作部顾问的采访，为回顾1990-2010年间中国与南非的关系提供了有用的信息。它们不仅突出了两国关系的开始和发展过程，也强调了两国之间的差距。第一手资料主要由南非驻科特迪瓦大使馆提供，包括关于中国和南非实施全球战略伙伴关系的《北京宣言》的资料。这些资料让人们了解了决定双方在相关领域关系的机制。至于描述"中华人民共和国概况"的文件，则主要强调了中国这一亚洲巨人的政治和经济状况。浏览双方的协议也很有用。

其他书籍也有关联，特别是涉及新兴国家宏伟蓝图的书籍，包括南非和中国在国际体系的改革和中国在非洲日益增长的影响力方面的利害关系。事实证明，所有这些书都有利于优质信息的收集，它们构成了本文的基础。本文围绕以下三条主线展开：

1. "两个中国"问题中断关系：1990—1997 年；
2. 关系正式化且活跃：1998—2004 年；
3. 合作关系增强：2004—2010 年。

一 "两个中国"问题中断关系：1990—1997 年

从 1990 年起，南非与中华人民共和国开始在各方面对彼此开放，这奠定了官方承认中华人民共和国的基础，但官方的承认却在 1994 年中止了。

1. 官方承认中华人民共和国的开始

南非与中国之间的联系可以追溯至 17 世纪，当时第一批中国移民迁至开普敦（曾为殖民地）。但是，当 1949 年中华人民共和国建立时，台湾仍未统一。当时在种族隔离制度支配下的南非也陷入了危急的境地。一方面，南非被认为在非正式、秘密地与中国（中华人民共和国支持世界上受压迫人民的斗争，反对种族隔离制度）往来，却又从 1976 年开始与台湾建立官方联系。然而，1990 年这一种族隔离制度的结束引发了"两个中国"的困境，这一困境源自于南非在与台湾建立官方关系的同时，也承认了中华人民共和国。中方争论的焦点是中国认为台湾是其领土不可分割的一部分，并拒绝同任何与台湾有官方联系的国家建立外交关系，并且无论南非与该国关系的开放性还是随之而来的商业增长，都不会改变中方的立场。因此，南非必须在保持与台湾的关系和转而承认中华人民共和国为中国唯一合法代表之间作出选择。这看似简单却很难抉择。南非外交当局、利益集团和权力集团花了至少两年的时间来讨论与这一转变有关的选择。其中一方支持选择台湾，另一方则支持选择中华人民共和国。

而之后中国支票簿的影响力又加剧了不同观点和意见间的差异。

2. 支票簿的影响力

为了吸引他们的南非伙伴，台湾地区的官员提出了支票簿外交。克里斯·奥尔登（Chris Alden）和加斯·谢尔顿（Garth Shelton）注意到，在这方面，台湾地区允许来自南非政治和社会领域的200多名国会议员和其他高级官员访问台湾，而台湾当局则给予了他们出差津贴。此外，20世纪90年代初，台湾地区大幅增加了在南非的投资，还承诺承担价值超过10亿兰特的重建和发展计划。中华人民共和国并没有忽视台湾在南非的强大经济影响力。为了弥补损失的时间，增强中国在南非的影响力，中国北京方面宣布，中国将在南非投资180亿美元。作为回应，台湾当时也宣布为一合资项目投资35亿美元。但因差距过大，南非的意向不出所料地倾向了中华人民共和国。

这样的经济优势给了中国吸引南非当局的关注并抓住他们兴趣的有利条件。而考虑到与台湾地区的关系，南非当局试图说服中国允许其同时承认中国和台湾，但这一尝试失败了，因为北京坚决拒绝了这一想法。因此，经济是影响南非与中国、台湾地区关系的决定性因素。值得一提的是，在那个时候，南非迫切需要资金进行国家重建。这在一定程度上解释了为什么南非最终选择了中华人民共和国。虽然台湾地区所做的经济投资并非微不足道，但中国确实提供了一个更好的选择，其稳健的未来项目投资组合的价值不低于180亿美元。在南非当局看来，中国提供的条件无疑最好。此外，中国即将加入世界贸易组织也是一个加分项。最重要的是，它将允许外资进入中国的巨大市场，而南非当局希望与中国的和解能够帮助他们进入这个新兴市场。

另一方面，南非官员意识到，鉴于中华人民共和国不仅是联合国安理会常任理事国，而且是77国集团成员，站在中国这边对他们会有很大帮助。除了前面说到的经济原因，南非官员选择中华人民共和国是因为南非希望增强其在地区和国际层面的领导力，这在南非前总统纳尔逊·曼德拉于1996年11月发表的演讲中可以看出："维持和台湾的关系与南非在非盟和联合国等国际组织日益增长的影响力并不兼容"。

在这方面，自1997年12月以来，中国和南非的关系受到青睐，而台湾和南非的关系则受到损害，可能出现并影响中国和南非关系的困难也就随之瓦解了。

二 关系正式化且活跃：1998—2004 年

这些制度框架旨在使两个主体之间的关系正式化，并允许他们定期讨论关于合作的事项。为此，在进行了一系列正式访问之后，两国于 2001 年成立了双边委员会。

1. 和解中的核心制度框架

南非和中华人民共和国现在可以发展并维持正式而活跃的关系，这一关系一方面得益于南非在非洲不断增强的领导力，另一方面得益于中国在非洲大陆日益增长的影响力。因此，1998 年 1 月 1 日，双方签署了一项协议，宣布中国与南非正式建立外交关系。

中国和南非的和解首先受到南非当局的推动，因为他们认为这是"彩虹之国"发展的重要机遇。但值得一提的是，中国也是受到经济利益的驱使，因为中国需要原材料和大宗商品来促进国内发展和全球扩张，而南非拥有异常丰富的矿产资源和大约 5000 万消费者的活跃市场。

吸引中华人民共和国的不仅是南非，还有整个非洲大陆。为了在非洲扩大交往，中国需要依靠南非的援助与合作。实际上，南非是非洲大陆的主要参与者，是大陆组织（非洲统一组织）和区域组织（南部非洲发展共同体、南部非洲关税联盟）中的领导者。此外，南非在亚欧海上航线上的战略位置，也是中国感兴趣的重要资源，因为从中国到欧洲的船只可以在抵达目的地之前停靠南非的港口。最后也是很重要的一点，南非占了非洲铁路网络的四分之一，而且是通往内陆（南部和中部非洲）进行贸易的必经之路。

因此，中国与南非互动的方式有时被认为是中国的非洲政策。在很多方面，南非都是中国的首要目标。随着时间的推移，两国都加强了双边关系。在进行了一系列正式访问之后，两国于 2001 年成立了双边委员会。这一官方框架允许他们定期讨论关于合作的事项。2001 年 12 月在北京举行第一次会议之后，双方就四项议题设立了四个专题委员会：外交事务、贸易交易、科学技术和国防。设立这些委员会是为了让两国在部级层面上讨论与合作相关的事项。更具体地说，这些委员会的任务是"促进和加速缔结贸易协定和投资，并就国际外交的重大问题进行磋商和讨论"。

换句话说，保持两国之间活跃的经济和外交关系无疑是理想的目标，他们也很快实现了这一目标。

2. 经济关系增强

从1990年到1997年，双边贸易额从1400万美元增长到15亿美元。随着正式外交关系的建立，贸易额也进一步上升，从1998年到2004年，这一数字急剧上升至50亿美元。因此，中国成为南非第五大贸易伙伴，而南非成为中国在非洲最大的合作伙伴，中国和南非的贸易额占中国和非洲贸易总额的20%左右。南非出口到中国的主要产品是铁、锰、金、铜、铝和汽车零部件，而南非从中国进口的商品则是补给品、电视机、电子设备和服装等。

除了贸易，双边投资也大幅增长。2004年，中国在南非的外商直接投资约为5亿兰特，而南非在中国的外商直接投资约为40亿兰特。中国和南非的企业在农业、纺织、电子、采矿、银行、交通和通信等多个领域投资合作。但是，与中国在南非的投资相比，南非在中国的投资要多得多。

2002年，中国就已授予南非"被批准的旅游目的地国家"称号。南非官员认为这有利于促进旅游业和其他相关部门和行业。2003年，来自中国内地的33000多名游客访问了南非，中国成为游客访问南非人数增加最快的国家之一。2004年，尽管欧洲和美国反对，南非政府仍授予中国"市场经济"的地位。事实上，这一承认源自两国建立战略伙伴关系所产生的政治动机（超越了商业动机）。

战略伙伴关系，在词源意义上是一个经济短语，基本是指两个伙伴达成协议以实现一个或多个战略目标。对合作伙伴来说，战略伙伴关系包括拓展市场的可能性、获得所缺乏的新技术和知识的途径，以便通过引进建立自身品牌的新规则或新标准更好地构建市场。

2004年6月，在双边委员会第二次会议之后，南非和中国参与了这一倡议，双方都承诺推进双边关系。

随着两国经济和政治合作的发展，两国关系（在大约6年时间里）迅速升温，让世界各地的许多观察家惊叹不已。双方无意半途而废，自从建立战略伙伴关系以来，加强合作仍然是一项重大关切。

三 合作增强：2004—2010年

中国—南非关系的不平衡确实有利于中国，因此南非当局要求调整关系，以促进两国的共同发展，而不仅仅是中国的发展。

1. 促进两国的共同发展

调整中非关系以促进两国的共同发展是双方设立的新目标。

双方都致力于推动建立公平的全球经济体系，还同意支持南非谋求联合国安全理事会常任理事国的席位。事实是，在改革国际金融机构和联合国安理会以及让发展中国家在全球安全理事会中发挥更大作用方面，双方有着相同的看法。为此，南非和中国在基础四国和金砖四国等论坛上愈加活跃，这也一直在影响着决策。南非主动加入基础四国，其加入金砖四国受到中国和俄罗斯的支持。基础四国和金砖四国是多边论坛，会就许多国际问题进行磋商，并协调新兴国家在这些问题上的行动。

但除了这些国际性的宏伟蓝图，从2009年起，南非外交和经济利益之间联系更加紧密，这成为了合作加强的关键。

2. 调整关系

外交政策基本被定义为国家政策的延伸。换句话说，就是在外国领土上追求某一特定国家的价值观和利益。中国和南非之间的经济关系在某种程度上让后者重新思考其经济模式，并取得相对强劲的经济增长，因为它不再只关注与欧洲和美国的关系。然而，需要指出的是，这一经济增长并没有对南非的社会和产业发展产生真正有益的影响，主要是因为中国和南非的关系是不平衡的（中国在2009年成为南非第一大全球贸易伙伴）。在这种合作框架内，南非被限制在出口原材料和低附加值商品的传统角色内。此外，由于中国企业日益增多，越来越多的南非本土企业在当地的市场竞争中遇到了困难。南非本土纺织企业因面临中国企业的竞争而急剧削弱，这更加切实地证明了在面对来自中国的竞争日益激烈的行业，南非经济实体无法生存。南非工会公布的数据表明，南非当地企业正在变弱。非洲人国民大会的辅助机构南非工会大会表示，不少于800家的中小型企业关闭，导致大约60000个工作岗位流失。

这种情况促使南非当局要求调整与中国的关系，以促进两国的共同发展。他们敦促中国采取措施改变合作结构，以缓解失衡。事实上，这一敦促的目的是支持南非的工业政策，发展产业项目，以遏制当地急剧上升的失业率。南非人还要求中国通过合资企业（半国营的承包商）的形式，增加对矿业和建筑业的投资。投资金融和电信行业比投资矿业和建筑业更利于快速发展，但投资矿业和建筑业在创造就业和提升技能方面更有优势。

这些调整是在 2010 年 8 月 23 日至 26 日举行的全球战略对话框架下协商的，最终双方签署了全球战略伙伴关系。这一伙伴关系加强了双方在非洲和世界舞台上的合作。南非愿与中方共同努力，加强中非合作，推动国际关系民主化。中国承诺从南非进口更多制成品和加工产品，并鼓励在南非经营的中国企业增加在南非的投资。

因此，在一份共同意向声明中，双方宣布了一系列连接中国和南非集团的合资企业，特别是在矿业和能源领域。中国煤炭科工集团将与林波波走廊矿业资源公司（Limpopo Corridor Mining Resources Company）合作，将林波波省变成"煤炭之都"，并在 2014 年之前创造 3 万个就业岗位。中国的冀东发展集团有限公司和中非发展基金提供了另一笔 2.17 亿美元的投资，与南非威普霍尔公司（Wiphol）和大陆水泥公司（Continental Cement）一起合作建设水泥厂，其中两个投资者方将共同持有 51% 的股份。

除了创造就业机会，这样的合资企业对南非还有两个好处。第一个是拓展勘探开采的领域，南非的产品不只出口到中国，也出口到欧洲、日本和韩国。第二，大多数合资企业创造了附加值，这是南非当局在与中国讨论时十分重视的一个问题。

能源领域则受益于 2010 年 11 月签署的一项为南非能源产业提供 200 亿美元信贷额度的协议。为了实现可持续的经济增长，最根本的目标是发展核能和可再生能源技术。因此，能源部门需要当地缺乏的大规模投资。

此外，一家市值 4.35 亿美元的合资公司也非常重视能源的发展，建立了一家太阳能组件生产工厂。南非支持解决气候变化问题是这类经济交易背后的主要原因。所有这些投资都显示了中国在南非的经济参与。中国似乎准备为南非的发展做出让步。由于这些让步，后者对两国经济关系的发展仍持乐观态度。

结论

随着南非放弃与台湾建交，转而在官方和外交层面上承认北京的地位，南非政府显然已决定让中华人民共和国参与其经济发展和维护其国际领导地位的斗争。中国重新关注非洲，尤其是南非，符合其战略意图。中国不仅希望阻止台湾在非洲国家获得地位和认可，也希望发展和维护强有力的经济关系，支持其出口导向型市场经济。

因此，南非和中国当局的合作是基于他们的国际抱负和扩大的贸易，贸易的迅速发展也促进了南非的经济增长。然而，南非产业部门的不稳定和不平衡的贸易关系正危及南非的发展。南非当局已经意识到这些风险，正努力调整和平衡和中国的关系，而他们的中国伙伴似乎愿意做出让步。

The China-South Africa Economic Relations (1990-2010)

Brahima Diakite / Cote d'Ivoire

Teacher & Researcher of Felix Houphouet-Boigny University, Cote d'Ivoire

I. Introduction

Since the early 2000s, China has been improving and consolidating its presence in Africa, which is traditionally Western powers' preserve. In either diplomatic, commercial, economic industrial or politic terms, China establishes and strengthens its cooperation with african countries, notably with South Africa. This paper is based on relevant materials gathered and which highlight the realities of the Chinese presence in South Africa. The reason behind the choice of South Africa as a case study in the largest context of the China-Africa relations is that the relationship between South Africa and the Asian nation is growing ever stronger. The China-South Africa relationship has now matured into a global and comprehensive strategic partnership since 2010, while in 1990 it was a very disturbed one, because of the "Two Chinas" issue. In 2010, indeed, China has become the principal trading partner of South Africa. China now stands ahead of countries like Germany and United States which have a long history of trading with South Africa. This inevitably begs the question: what explains the remarkable progress of the China-South Africa relations from 1990 to 2010?

To address this concern, the supporting documentation of this research is mostly composed of published articles and various oral sources.

Oral sources, including the interview with the Counsellor in charge of International Relations and Cooperation with South Africa (DIRCO) provided useful inputs for the review of the relationship between China and South Africa for the period 1990-2010.They not only highlight the very beginning and the progress of the relationship between the two countries, but also focus on its gaps. Among the first hand sources which were mainly provided by the South African Embassy in Côte d'Ivoire are materials related to "The Beijing Declaration" on the implementation of a global strategic partnership between China and South Africa. These materials allowed the gathering of information on institutional mechanisms that govern the relationship between the parties in relevant fields. As for documents describing "The Profile of the People's Republic of China", they mainly highlight the political and economical situation of the Asian giant. Looking at Agreements between the two sides proved useful too.

Other sets of books were relevant too, particularly books dealing with the ambitions of emerging countries, including South Africa and China in regards with the reform of the international system and the stakes of China's ever growing presence in Africa. All these books have proved useful in gathering quality information; they form the basis of the present paper which evolves around three main axes:

A Relationship Disrupted by the "Two Chinas" Issue : (1990-1997).
Formal and Dynamic Relations (1998-2004).
Cooperation Strengthening (2004-2010).

II. A Relationship Disrupted by the "Two Chinas" Issue: (1990-1997)

The beginnings of open relations with the People's Republic of China, on all fronts, starting from 1990, has laid down the foundations for an official recognition which however failed in 1994.

1. The Very Beginnings of an Official Recognition of the People's Republic of China

The links between South Africa and China date back to the 17th century, as the first Chinese migrants arrived in Cap (once a colony). But on one side since the People's Republic of China (PRC) established in 1949 the Island of Taiwan was still seperated; on the other side, South Africa, then in the grip of the segregationist apartheid system, found herself in a critical situation. On one hand, the South African nation was perceived as being in an informal and clandestine situation vis-à-vis the RPC, (The PRC was supportive of the struggles of the oppressed masses over the world and hostile to the apartheid system), while it started building official linkages with Taiwan from 1976. However, the end of this segregationist system in 1990 raises the issue of the "two Chinas" dilemma which emanated from South Africa's will to recognize the PRC while having official ties with Taiwan. The bone of contention the PRC had in regard to that was that it considers the Taiwan as an integral part of its territory, and refuses to establish diplomatic ties with any state that maintains official relations with that island. And neither the open character of their relationships[1] nor the commercial growth[2] that results from this relationship does change anything. South Africa therefore had to make a choice between keeping ties with Taiwan or shifting to the official recognition of the PRC as the sole legitimate representative of China. Simple in appearance but obviously difficult to apply. It took a least two full years for South African diplomatic authorities and interest and power groups to discuss options related to that shift. There were pro-

---

1 With the lifting of the ban of the ANC (African National Congress) and the Communist Party in February 1990, followed with the abolition of apartheid legislation the following year, these trade and political ties could be addressed publicly.
2 Between 1990 and 1994, bilateral trade increased by 225% (although it should be mentioned that in ante-1990 statistics trade was not mentioned), see Chris ALDEN and Gareth SHELTON, *Camarades : parias et hommes d'affaires : Mise en perspective des relations entre l'Afrique du Sud et la Chine, Politique africaine,* No. 76, pp.19-29.

Taiwan advocates on one side and on the other side those who were in favor of the choice of the PRC.

These conflicting perspectives and divergent viewpoints were exacerbated by the power of the Chinese checkbooks.

2. The Power of the Checkbooks

In order to seduce their South African counterparts, officials from Taiwan and China have put forward the diplomacy of the checkbooks[1]. In that respect, more than two hundreds members of parliament and other top officials from both political and social arenas in South Africa were allowed to visit China and were granted meaningful per diem by Taiwan authorities as noticed by Chris Alden et Garth Shelton (C. ALDEN et SHELTON. G 2012. p23.,). In addition, in the early 1990s Taipei increased substantially its investments in South Africa[2]. Moreover, Taiwan committed to undertake reconstruction and development programs valued at over 1 billion Rand[3]. The People's Republic of China did not ignore Taiwan's strong economic presence in South Africa, where it has also been active, but to a lesser extent. To make up for lost time and boot PRC's presence in South Africa, declared PRC would invest about 18 billion USD in South Africa (C. ALDEN et SHELTON G., 2012 p24). In response, Taiwan Prime Minister announced an investment of 3.5 billion USD in a joint-venture arrangement (C. ALDEN et SHELTON G 2012, p.24), but the gap was substantial, so the balance went, with no surprise, in favor of the People's Republic of China.

---

1 Consists in using economic weight as a political instrument. Either cultivate the favor of specific rich countries or contribute to world diplomacy in a certain way.
2 According to MILLS (GREG), « Afrique du sud et Afrique Australe » ,Courier Afrique Caraïbes Pacifique - Union Européenne, N.153 ,Octobre 1995, pp.59-62, the Taiwan Raildays awarded a contract of R 420 million to the union of South African wagon carriers, the Taiwan Industry Association bought 300 thousand tons of maize before April 1995 valued at 122.5 million rand, while Taiwan Power Company increased the purchase of 0.5 million tons of coal and 140 million rand in vocational training under the reconstruction and development program. It also notes loans to South African companies ESKOM, MACSTELL and the Southern Africa Development Bank valued at R $ 105 million, R 70 million, and US $ 15.5 million respectively.
3 MILLS (GREG), Idem P23.

With such an economic advantage, the PRC was best positonned to get South African authorities' attention and capture their interest. But considering their ties with Taiwan, South African authorities had sought to convince the PRC of dual recognition (of both PRC and Taiwan), but failed, as Beijing[1] firmly rejected that idea. Thus, the economic argument has been a determining factor in the decision of South Africa in regards with the changing of relations with the two Chinas. It is important to mention that at that time, there was an urgent need for national reconstruction in South Africa, which also required important cash-flow. This partly explained why South Africa ended up opting for the PRC. While the economic investments made by Taiwan were not insignificant, the PRC did propose a better choice with a robust portfolio of prospective projects worth not less than US 18 billions. In the eyes of South African authorities, there could be no doubt that the PRC has the best offer. In addition, the forthcoming PRC integration to the World Trade Organisation (WTO) was a plus. It would, above all, allow foreign investment in the large Chinese market. And, South African authorities hoped that the rapprochment with China will help them tap into this new market too.

On the other hand, South Africa officials realised that being with the PRC will help them a lot, given the fact that the PRC is not only a permanent member of the UN Security Council but belongs to the G77[2]. Beyond the economic reason

---

1 For example, in July 1989, the State of Grenada (micro-Caribbean State) recognized both the People's Republic of China and Taiwan by establishing diplomatic ties with Taipei while having diplomatic relations with Beijing a few years earlier. Although Taiwan has accepted this model, the People's Republic of China has expressed serious discontent and severed its formal ties with Grenada. In February of this year, Burkina Faso also tried this option, which to its disappointment was immediately rejected by Beijing. It has been said that this action could serve as an example for other States, particularly those with a certain political and economic weight, to pursue a similar strategy.

2 Convened for the first time in 1964 in Geneva at the United Nations Conference on Trade and Development (UNCTAD), the G77 is an intergovernmental group now composed of 132 countries instead of 77 precursors of the movement, overwhelmingly developing countries (DCs), but also from China. The main objective was to promote "south-south" cooperation in order to fight against international poverty

expressed earlier, the choice of the PRC by South African officials is justified by the fact that South Africa wanted to bolster its claim to leadership at regional and international levels as evidenced in this excerpt of a speech by former South African President Nelson Mandela delivered in November 1996: "Maintaining relationship with Taiwan is incompatible with the growing presence of Pretoria within international organisations such as AU and UN"[1].

In that respect, the Beijing-Pretoria axis has been favoured to the detriment of the Taiwan-Pretoria axis, since December 1997. Then the difficulties that might have risen and affect the relationship between Beijing and Pretoria were done away with.

III. Formal and Dynamic Relations : 1998-2004

These institutional frameworks aim at formalising the relations between the two actors and allowing them to discuss matters relevant to their cooperation on a regular basis. To that end, a bi-national commission was set up in 2001, following a bunch of official visits in the two countries.

1. The Institutional Frameworks at the Heart of the Rapprochement

South Africa and the PRC could now develop and maintain formal and dynamic relations; relations that are nurtured by South Africa growing feeling leadership in Africa on one hand, and on the other hand, by China ever growing presence on the continent. Thus, on January 1st, 1998, the two parties signed an agreement announcing the establishment of official diplomatic relations between China and South Africa.

The rapprochement of China and South Africa was first spurred by South African authorities as they saw it as an important opportunity for the growth of the rainbow nation. It is however important to mention that China also was guided by economic interests as it needed raw materials and commodities for a domestic development

---

1 Chris Alden et Gareth Shelton, Op.cit, p24.

and for global expansion. South Africa, in fact, is a country with exceptional abundant mineral resources[1] and dynamic market of about fifty millions inhabitants.

But beyond the South African state, it is the whole african continent that attracts the People's Republic of China. In order to expand all over Africa, the PRC counts on the assistance and the cooperation with South Africa. Indeed, South Africa is a major player on the African continent; it holds firsthand positions in continental (OAU[2]) and regional organisations (SADC[3], SACU[4]). In addition, South Africa's strategic positioning on the Asia-Europe maritime route is a key asset that interests China, as ships leaving China to Europe could call at South African ports before reaching their final destination. Last but not the least, South Africa accounts for the quarter of all the African railroad network and is an obligatory pathway to reach the hinterland (Southern and Central Africa) for trade. (diplomatie internationale) (F. LAFARGUE, 2012, pp.11-28).

Thus, China's approach of South Africa is sometimes considered as China's policy in Africa. South Africa is, in more ways than one, a prime target for China

---

[1] Its subsoil contains a large part of the planetary reserves of titanium (30%, 1st worldwide), gold (40%, 1st worldwide), chromium (54%, 1st worldwide), platinum (70%, 1st in the world), vanadium (45%, 1st in the world), diamonds (24%, 2nd in the world), or manganese (82%, 1st in the world), as well as a multitude of other products more or less rare and precious (uranium, iron, lead, zinc, coal, silver, tin, zirconium, vermiculite, etc.) which give it a strategic importance and constitute a considerable asset on the economic level: : MERVEILLEUX (G), *Afrique du Sud : l'émergence d'une puissance africaine*, La revue Géopolitique en ligne, Avril 2009 : http://www.diploweb.com/Afrique-du-Sud-emergence-d-une.html./

[2] Organization of African Unity (OAU), an inter-African organization founded in 1963 to promote the unity and solidarity of African States, to harmonize political, economic, cultural, medical, scientific and military policies, to defend the independence and the territorial integrity of the Member States and eliminate colonialism in Africa. In 2002, the OAU was dissolved and replaced by a new structure, the African Union (AU).

[3] SADC: Southern African Development Community. It is an organization that aims to promote the economic development of Southern Africa. Created on 17 August 1992 to replace the Southern Africa Development Coordination Conference founded on 1 April 1980. The founding Member States are: Angola, Botswana, Lesotho, Malawi, Mozambique, Swaziland, Tanzania, Zambia and Zimbabwe. South Africa adheres to it on August 30, 1994.

[4] SACU: Customs Union of Southern Africa created in 1969, includes South Africa, Botswana, Lesotho, Namibia, Swaziland. It was created in 1990 under the name Custom Union Agreement.

and both strengthen their relations as time goes by. The two parties set up a binational commission in 2001, following a bunch of official visits in the two countries. This official framework allows them to discuss matters relevant to their cooperation on a regular basis. In the aftermath of their first meeting in December 2001 in Beijing, they established four thematic committees on the range of four issues: Foreign Affairs; Trade and Exchanges; Science and Technologies; National Defense. These committees were set up to allow the two countries to discuss matters relevant to their cooperation at an inter-ministerial level. More specifically, the mission of these committees is to "facilitate and speed the conclusion of trade agreements and investments and to allow a consultation and discussions of major issues of international diplomacy."[1](F. LAFARGUE, 2012, p.25.)

In other words, maintaining dynamic economic and diplomatic relations between the two countries was without any doubt the desire objective; and objective they quickly achieved.

2. Growing Economic relations

From 1990 to 1997, the volume of bilateral trade increased from 14 million $ to 1.5 billion $. But the establishment of official diplomatic relations takes the volume of that trade a step higher. Since, it has increased dramatically to reach about 5 billion $ between 1998 and 2004[2]. As a result, China becomes South Africa's fifth largest trading partner, while South Africa becomes China's largest partner in Africa with about 20% of the total volume of the China-South Africa trade[3]. Iron, manganese, gold, copper, aluminum and car spares represent the bulk of total merchanse export in China. While South Africa imports from China manifactured goods such as supplies, TV sets, electronic devices and clothing.

Beyond trade, bilateral investment has also risen sharply. In 2004, Chinese Foreign Direct Investment (FDI) in South Africa amounted to around R500 million,

---

1 François LAFARGUE, Idem, p.25.
2 Idem., p.467.
3 Ibidem., p.467.

while South African FDI in China was around R4 billion[1]. Chinese and South African industries operate in various and diverse fields such as agriculture, textiles, electronics, mining, banking, transportation and communication. But, South African investments in China are much larger compare to China investment in South Africa.

Since 2002, China has granted the status of "Approved destination" to South Africa. South African officials see this as an advantage to boost the sector of tourism and other related sectors and industries. More than 33,000 tourists from mainland China visited South Africa in 2003[2]. The increase in visits by Chinese nationals is one of the fastest of the different groups of visitors to the country. The South African State, for its part, conferred the title of "Market Economy" to China, in 2004, notwithstanding the opposition of Europe and the United States. This recognition in fact, emanates from (beyond a commercial motivation) a political motivation resulting from the establishment of a strategic partnership between the two countries.

The strategic partnership, by its etymologically meaning, is an economic phrase which basically designates an agreement between two companies by which they agree to work together to achieve one or more strategic objectives. It includes, for the partners, the possibility of developing their territorial hold, to access to new technologies and know-how they lack, so as to better structure a market by introducing new rules or new standards to build their brand[3].

In June 2004, the South African and Chinese parties engaged in such an initiative in the aftermath of the second edition of the bi-national commission meeting. The

---

1 Naidu (S). Op.cit., p. 471. However, these numbers remain highly controversial as they vary from author to author. On the issue, see Stephen GELB, Foreign direct investment links between South Africa and China, The EDGE Institute, Johannesburg, 2010.
2 Ibid., p.472.
3 Manufacturing Terms, Definition at a click:www.manufacturingterms.com/French/Strategic-Partnership.html, consulted on March 24, 2014.

commitments of both parties were focused on the development of their linkages[1].

The rapid growth of China-South Africa relations (in about six years), as the result of economic and political cooperation of the two actors amazes and impresses a lot many observers all over the world. The parties do not intend to stop off on the way. The strengthening of their cooperation remains a significant concern since the creation of the strategic partnership.

IV. Cooperation Strengthening (2004-2010)

The unequal character of the China-South Africa relationship which indeed favors China is the main reason why South African authorities are demanding for an adjustment of this relationship in order to promote the two countries and not China only.

1. Promoting Mutual Development of the Two Countries

Adjusting the China-Africa relationship so as to promote mutual development within the two countries : this is the new goal set by the parties.

Both partners committed to embark in a common struggle for the promotion of a fair global economic system. They also agreed to support the South Africa's quest for a seat as a permanent member of the United Nations Security Council. The fact is that they share the same view on the need to transform the international financial institutions and the United Nations Security Council, as well as the need

---

1 In short, they commit to:
Promote peace, stability and development in Africa through the Addis Ababa Action Plan and the China-Africa Cooperation Forum;
Mutually support the New Partnership for Africa's Development (NEPAD);
Launch trade negotiations between the Southern African Customs Union (SACU) and China;
Recognize China's market economy status;
Defend multilateralism and equality in the treatment and resolution of international problems such as WTO reform, the war on terror;
Confirm their position in the quest for a new international order based on peace, stability and equality;
Strengthen South-South cooperation;
Engage in the politics of one China.

for developing countries to play a greater role in the global security council. To this end, South Africa and China have become more and more present and active in forums like BASIC[1] and BRICS[2] where they have been influencing decisions. If South Africa joined BASIC on its own initiative, its membership in the BRICS was sponsored by China, supported by Russia. BASIC and BRICS are multilateral forums for consultation on many international issues and for the coordination of emerging countries' actions on these issues.

But, beyond these international ambitions, the closer articulation between South African diplomacy and economic interests, from 2009[3] is central to the strengthening of the cooperation.

2. Adjusting the relationship

Basically, foreign policy is defined as the extension of national policies. In other words, it is the pursuit of the values and interests of a given state in foreign territories. The economic relations between China and South Africa have, in some ways, allowed the latter to rethink its economic patterns and score relatively strong economic growth[4], as it was no longer focus on its relations with Europe and US only. However, it is important to point out that this growth did not have a real impact on the social and industrial development of the country, mainly because the China-South Africa relationship was unbalanced (China became South Africa's first global trade partner in 2009). In the framework of this cooperation, South Africa is confined in its traditional role of exporting raw materials and commodities with low

---

1 The BASIC Forum (Brazil, South Africa, India, China), created in 2009 on the occasion of the Copenhagen summit on climate change, focuses on environmental issues.
2 The BRICS Group (Brazil, Russia, India, China) is a political forum, created in 2008 by Brazil, Russia, India and China, allowing member countries to share the same vision on multilateral issues and issues. such as the reform of the IMF or the UN Security Council
3 After the presidential election of May 2009, Jacob Zuma, head of the South African state, is elected on a domestic agenda (fight against unemployment, reduction of inequalities, public services). The new officials soon announced that foreign policy would be considered as a tool for the economic development of the country. And the priorities of this diplomatic orientation are the emerging economies while maintaining trade links with older partners.
4 the economic growth rate of South Africa since 2000 is 3.1%.

added value. In addition, an increasing number of South African local companies are having trouble competing in the local market place due to the growing presence of Chinese companies. The sharp weakening of local South African textile companies' as they face Chinese competitors is a more tangible evidence of South African economic entities' inability to survive in sectors where Chinese competition is significantly increasing. The figures put forward by South Africa Trade Unions speak for themselves in regard to the weakening of local companies. According to COSATUS, an ally of the ANC (African National Congress), not less than 800 small and medium enterprises closed their doors and as a result some 60,000 jobs were lost. (V, Darracq, 1994; p31).

Such a scenario, has prompted South African authorities to request an adjustment of the relations with China, in order to promote the joint development of the two countries. They are urging their Chinese counterparts to take some measures to transform the structure of their cooperation so as to reduce the imbalances. In fact, The idea behind this push is to support the South African industrial policy that intends to develop industrial activities in order to help curb local skyrocketing unemployment. This move also leads South Africans to ask for an increase of Chinese investments in the mining and construction sectors, based on joint ventures (with parastatal contractors). Investments in mining and construction sectors are less beneficial in terms of faster growth than investments in the financial and telecommunications sectors, but they proved to be more advantageous in terms of job creation and skills upgrading.

These adjustments have been negotiated in the framework of a global strategic dialogue held from August 23rd to 26th, 2010 which ended up with the signing of a global strategic partnership between the two parties. This partnership strengthens their cooperation on both the African and world stage. South Africa is willing to work with China to strengthen the China-Africa cooperation and to democratize international relations. China, on its side, is committed to importing more manufactured and processed products from South Africa and encouraging Chinese companies operating in South Africa to increase their investment in their host country.

Thus, in a joint declaration of intent, the two parties announced a series of joint-ventures connecting different Chinese and South African groups, particularly in mining and energy sectors. The Coal Technology Enginering Group is expected to partner with Limpopo Corridor Mining Resources Company to transform Limpopo into a "coal capital" and create 30,000 new jobs by 2014 (Alden.C, 2012, p207). Another 217 million US $ investment was made by Chinese company Jidong Development Group and CAD Fund, in collaboration with South African companies Wiphol and Continental Cement, to build a cement plant in which the two investors will hold 51% of shares (Alden.C, 2012, p168).

In addition to job creation, such joint-ventures have two advantages for South Africa. The first advantage is the expansion of the exploitation field and the production is not exported to China only, but also to Europe, Japan and Korea. The second one is that most of these joint-ventures create added value; an issue that South Africa authorities hold dear while discussing with the Chinese counterparts.

As for the energy sector, it benefited from an agreement signed in November 2010 for the allocation of a 20 billion $ credit line to the South African energy industry (C.Alden, 2012 p.168). The most essential goal, for a sustainable economic growth, is to develop nuclear and renewable energy technology. The energy sector therefore requires large investments that do not exist locally.

The focus on energy was also supported by a 435 million $ joint-venture to build a solar module production plant (Alden, 2012 p.168). South Africa supports on the issue of climate change would have been the main reason behind such economic transactions. All these inputs show China's economic involvement in South Africa. The Asian nation seems to be ready to make concessions for the development of the South African state. The latter, thanks to these concessions, remains optimistic about the evolution of economic relations between the two countries.

V. Conclusion

With the shift from the official and diplomatic recognition of Taipei to the recognition of Beijing, the South African government has clearly decided to involve The People's Republic of China in its economic development and its struggle in asserting its international leadership. China's renewed focus on Africa, and especially its particular emphasis on South Africa, is in line with its strategy that consists, not only, in countering Taiwan's efforts to achieve status and gain recognition among african states but which also aims at developing and maintaining strong economic ties that support its export-oriented market economy.

South African and Chinese authorities have therefore based their cooperation on their international ambitions and the expansion of their trade that developed rapidly and nurtured South Africa's economic growth. However, the risks of destabilization of the South African industrial sector and the creation of an unequal relationship are jeopardising the development of South Africa. South African authorities have identified these risks and are working hard to adjust and balance the relationship between China and South Africa, a request that their Chinese counterparts seem to want to concede to them.

References

-Oral Sources

-M. QOMOY, Advisor of the Department of International Relations and Cooperation of South Africa (DIRCO), Abidjan; June 26, 2013, Interpreter Miss DOSSO, Political Secretary at the Embassy of South Africa in Ivory Coast.

-Printed Sources
-Département des Relations Internationales et de la Coopération de l'Afrique du sud (DIRCO), Déclaration de Beijing sur la mise en place d'un partenariat stratégique compréhensive entre la République d'Afrique du Sud et la République Populaire de Chine. DIRCO, p.6.
- Department of International Relations and Cooperation of South Africa (DIRCO)

- *République Populaire de Chine. Profil du pays et document d'information, DIRCO*, p.22.

Alden C. « Relations entre la Chine et l'Afrique du sud », in S/D de GABAS J.J et CHAPONNIERE J.R, *Le temps de la Chine en Afrique: Enjeux et réalité au sud du Sahara*, Gemdev-Kartala, Paris, July 2012, pp.157-173

Alden C. andShelton G., *Camarades: parias et hommes d'affaires: Mise en perspective des relations entre l'Afrique du Sud et la Chine, Politique africaine*, N°76, pp.19-29.

Darracq V., « l'un plus égal que l'autre? La relation économique entre la chine et l'Afrique du Sud depuis 1994 » in programme Afrique saharienne juillet et 2013: www.ifri.org/downloads/notedelifriafriquevdarracq, visited on June 25, 2013.

Merveilleux G. « Afrique du Sud: l'émergence d'une puissance africaine », La revue Géopolitique en ligne: http:www.diploweb.com/Afrique-du-Sud-emregence-d-une.html.

Mills G. « Afrique du Sud et Afrique australe», Courrier Afrique caraïbes pacifique-Union Européenne, no153, October 1995, pp.59-62

Naidu S. "South Africa's relation with People's Republic of China: mutual opportunities or hidden threats" in HSRC, State of Nation2005-2006, HSZRC Press, Pretoria, 2006, pp.457-48

Toure A., « LA SADCC: dix ans de coopération régionale « *Marchés tropicaux et méditerranéens,* no23904, October 1991, pp.2403-2408.

有中国特色的负责任核主权国

麦克斯韦尔·莱纳德·乔纳森·多曼　【英国】
英美安全信息委员会、上议院

　　在 2015 年召开的《不扩散核武器条约》(NPT) 审议大会上，中国代表团宣布"中国始终保持负责任的态度，积极参与防扩散合作"，中国在国际关系中勇于承担责任的形象不断提升。那么中国认为负责任的核行为到底是什么呢？

　　本文旨在评估中国的核责任观，希望对建立"负责任的核主权"框架有所裨益。中国在考虑负责任的核行为方面起着十分重要的作用。中国是五核国成员，是朝核危机中关键的利益攸关方，与另外三个核武器国家接壤，并越来越多地参与和影响全球治理，包括未来的全球核秩序。

　　本文首先广泛讨论了有关核武器的"责任"以及中国对国际关系的参与。随后，评估了中国在威慑、裁军、军备控制和防扩散方面采取的措施。在关注当代中国认识的同时，也有必要借鉴中国的历史参与。不过，本文并没有提供中国参与全球核秩序的历史，也没有对中国的核武库进行技术性分析。

　　笔者认为，中国采取以"工具主义"的方式来承担责任，其根本出发点在于维护中国国家利益。中国对其核责任的认识具有层级性：首先是威慑责任，中国拥有核武器的唯一目的是为了捍卫自己，而绝非是为了任何攻击性行动；其次，中国的不扩散责任是平衡其对抗核扩散的承诺和对国家安全需求的理解；第三是中国的裁军和军备控制责任。中国特色的裁军路线图，强调国家核态势和宣示性政策的重要性，以及美国和俄罗斯在领导裁军和军备控制方面的"特殊责任"。

虽然这些责任以某些方式相互补充和抵触，但都希望创建一个更加多极化的世界，以便主权国家能参与到合作安全中，这对中国明显是有利的。与这种对其核责任的现实政治理解相反，它表现了世界主义伦理学家所倡导的多种行为，包括受限制的核态势和对裁军的承诺。因此，中国的经验有助于传达核武器国家的"负责任的核主权"概念，弥合核责任的世界主义伦理和古典现实主义观点——负责任的中国特色核主权。

一　国际关系中的责任

考虑到中国对核秩序的参与，责任是一个重要的概念。根本来讲，责任与"应该"而不是"就是"这个伦理问题有关，即国家所设想的全球核秩序应该是什么样的。它与"责任，权力，主权和目的"有关，解决谁有权塑造目标以及为什么塑造这样的目标的问题。

在英国国际关系学院，这场辩论分为与世界主义相关的社会连带主义原则以及多元主义原则。正如安德鲁·赫瑞尔（Andrew Hurrell）所说，在全球秩序中，"治理世界的社会连带主义和世界主义概念跟旧的多元秩序共存，这往往是非常不幸的"。世界主义者认为，责任超越国家，并认为国家"有责任考虑特定行动的因果影响以及与国家交流的方式，并引导他们走向正确的目标"。他们都指出了正确的行动，并认为全球安全的责任应以此出发，并以"他们的行动与他们影响其他国家安全的权力"为出发点。对于多元主义者来说，责任植根于国家。虽然各国可以基于共同利益和共同价值观进行合作，但这种合作存在于国家社会中。在加强国际社会责任和国家责任的竞争压力之间产生了维持国际秩序的责任。

最近，学者们试图弥合这一鸿沟。2010年，沃克（Walker）提出了负责任的核主权来弥合现实主义伦理和更多世界主义关切的"中间立场"，同时指出了达成国家协议的困难。这个想法后来发展成对责任意义的探索性讨论。圆桌会议商讨之后，"基础四国"提出了负责任的核主权愿景，即"负责任地采取行动，并符合在战略层面上增强全球安全的国际法律和准则"。

那么如何评估何种行动有益于增强全球安全？尼古拉·霍斯堡（Nicola Horsburgh）认为，全球核秩序包括核威慑，军备控制，不扩散和裁军。这些要素具备战略稳定的共同目标，但由于实现这些目标的策略可能有所不同，因此它们可能相互补充甚至彼此破坏。虽然核威慑，军备控制和不扩散往往会有利于改进现状，但霍斯堡认为，裁军可以是一把"双刃剑"，一方面增强了当前核秩序的合法性，另一方面也通过"非核秩序的转变性要求"起了破坏作用。本文建议通过研究国家行为如何支持或破坏这一秩序，阐明各国认为的核秩序的应有之义，并了解负责任行为的概念。

二 中国的国际关系责任观

许多学者研究了与国际关系和全球核秩序相关的责任观。自20世纪90年代末和21世纪以来，中国的崛起已经被描述为责任。尤其是2005年，美国国务卿罗伯特·佐利克（Robert Zoellick）呼吁中国成为"国际事务中负责任的利益攸关方"。中国似乎比较接受这样一个标签，因为这有助于缓解"中国威胁论"，并暗示作为利益相关者，中国有塑造全球秩序的权利。随后，中国也在全球秩序中承担责任，并指出需要"使国际秩序更加公平合理"。中国已经将自己定位为"负责任的大国"。在此期间，中国强调国际合作并融入包括不扩散体制在内的国际机构中。学者们常认为，中国承担了"深化中国全球化，减少对中国力量的恐惧，并积极参与现有世界秩序"的责任。

中国参与全球秩序的同时，对责任的意义也有着自己特色的见解。一些人强调中国的责任观为"对不干涉主义和自治的儒家思想倾向"。责任是对国家的唯一保护，并且这种全球责任将被划分为每个国家的国际责任。这会使得中国不愿意接受约束、限制它的国际责任。正如斯科特（Scott）所称，中国是一个负责任的"务实的工具主义者"，维护国家利益时参与其他事务，并将此视为不对全球秩序构成挑战的"合理"行为。

中国负责任的行为是否仅仅是为了维护其国家利益呢？如果是，那么中国外交政策的连续性就会让人失望。中国在国际关系中的根本驱动因素仍然是保护其主权和领土完整、经济发展以及与其权力相称的国际尊重和国际地位的需求。同样，王缉思注意到中国外交政策的三个指导性准则：中国共产党的长存，维护中国主权以及中国的经济和社会发展。与此一致的是，中国呼吁建立一个更加公平和多极的世界秩序。虽然中国会接受促进多边全球治理的多元主义责任观，但对"社会连带主义议程"日益谨慎。罗斯玛丽·福特（Rosemary Foot）指出，中国在主权平等和不干涉的基础上开始接受国际社会责任，而西方国家开始倡导一种社会连带主义的责任模式。

与批评相反，中国的外交政策在很大程度上具有连续性。虽然中国越来越适应全球秩序，但在要求改变与其地位相称的歧视性因素和需求影响方面更加坚定。张建认为，习近平的外交政策不是对责任的拒绝，而主要是对胡锦涛时代负责任的利益相关者主义的延续，但更强调互惠和更大的决心，以反映国家利益。由于这些是中国责任观的关键，因此这些概念依然非常重要。

那么，中国如何看待参与全球核秩序的责任？这一部分将分析中国认为的对核威慑、裁军、军备控制和不扩散负责任的做法。人们认为，中国已经对全球核秩序采取了工具主义和分层次的方法，从国家利益的角度考虑中国的责任。中国的主要责任是捍卫主权和领土完整，并将此与中国特色裁军路线图紧密联系在一起，该路线与其受限制的核态势有根深蒂固的关系。因此，中国认为威慑和裁军是互补的而不是相互矛盾的。虽然中国接受了参与军备控制和不扩散的责任，但这些都与美国和俄罗斯裁军的特殊责任、促进其国家安全的更大责任以及反对国际秩序中的歧视性因素相平衡。

三 中国的核威慑：受限制的态势

安全一直是中国核行动的最大动力，反映了中国的主要责任，即保护其主权和领土完整。在朝鲜战争和台湾海峡危机期间，中国一直是美国核高压的对象，俄罗斯的威胁在中国的核战略中也尤为突出。事实上，正是1969年的中苏战争和俄罗斯潜在的核打击促使中国寻求最低限度的可信威慑，而不是美国的威胁。安全问题与中国对1839—1949年长达一个世纪的屈辱史有关，这使得中国对主权和不干涉问题高度敏感，并且有意识地不在技术方面落后于西方，以免自己被利用。结果，中国已经接受核武器，但通过其一贯执行的"不首先使用"的承诺（NFU）来限制其使用范围，并通过消极安全保证（NSA）永不对无核国家使用核武器。

中国对美国核武器战略思想持批评态度。主要是中国反对核讹诈或核强制。中国担心核武器的"强大威胁效应"，拒绝威慑作为一种强制性行为，认为这是不负责任的行为。在战略层面，中国认为美国的威慑与强制之间几乎没有区别。但是，尽管如此，中国军方（中国人民解放军）已经在理论上接受了威慑。中国批评美国的核武库和推动其扩张的逻辑。中国认为，美国不断扩大自己的军武库并为新的情况培养新的能力。美国的核态势旨在发挥战略主导地位，针对战争和升级动态，这被认为是不负责任的表现。

相比之下，中国认为其最低限度的可信威慑的立场，仅仅是为了以负责任的态势确保第二次打击。中国2006年的《国防白皮书》指出，中国核战略的根本目的是"阻止其他国家对中国使用或威胁使用核武器……中国在发展核力量方面表现出极大的克制，从未涉足也绝不会跟其他任何国家参与核军备竞赛。"

杰弗里·刘易斯（Jeffrey Lewis）将中国的威慑力量描述为"最低限度的报复性手段"———一种以牺牲进攻能力来换取政治控制和最大限度降低经济成本的核威慑力量，这种想法反映在中国对其"精简且高效的武器库"的描述中，旨在阻止核攻击。这被认为是负责任的表现，原因有很多：首先，它阻止了对中国的核攻击，保护中国的切身利益；其次，它的目的不是为了对任何核国家构成攻击性威胁，而是保障其主权；第三，它最大限度地减少了其他国家的扩散动机。

然而，中国有限的武库引出了透明度为负责任的表现的概念。吴日强指出，由于依赖陆基导弹，中国很难保持透明度，如果系统受到打击，透明度可能会削弱其第二次打击能力。因此，尽管对于中国而言，透露核武器的位置、范围和准确性是不负责任的表现，但可以很容易地揭示其数量和意图。中国强调意图的透明度而不是能力的透明度，但由于美国核武库的规模和安全性，美国更有责任将其意图透明化。呼吁提高透明度对美国的发展构成越来越大的挑战，美国的发展有损中国的威慑力。具体而言，中国反对美国弹道导弹防御的发展，认为这是针对中国并消除中国的威慑。发展被视为对中国主权的直接挑战，有可能使台湾更有信心采取行动。吴日强很快指出美国的态势，认为弹道导弹防御、核讹诈和次战略核武器都是不负责任的表现。

尽管如此，美国的发展已经对中国传统的核思想提出了挑战，许多西方学者担忧中国现代化。反对者认为，中国正在对其核武库进行现代化改造，以反映在此战略情景下可用于核战争的反作用力态势，因此背离了中国传统的态势。一位资深学者担心，中国传统的克制可能会受到接受西方思想的挑战，也担心中国将探索其批评的内容，例如发出警戒和启用次战略武器。虽然学者审查中国的核能力是对的，但有人认为中国现代化的目的完全是为了对抗美国的弹道导弹防御，而中国并没有寻求从根本上扩大核武库。霍斯堡指出："中国的核力量现代化表明，不会出现严重偏离报复战略的倾向。"许多人认为中国的现代化是负责任的表现；一位资深学者认为中国的现代化增强了战略稳定性，另一位学者认为中国有责任跟上时代变化，提升自身战略稳定性"，只要这些能力能在传统战略中得以运用。

中国的核武库及其对此的责任保持相对稳定。中国认为"精简而高效"的军备是负责任的表现,自己的责任首先是保护自己,其次是确保这一武器库不会威胁到其他任何国家。由于规模、能力、姿势和战略的原因,超出这个范围的武器被视为严重不负责任的表现。然而,有人指出,一个稳定的武库本身"并不会促进全球裁军和不扩散"。因此,为了扩大霍斯堡的类比,中国的威慑责任可能会削弱其裁军的责任。

四 宣示性政策:中国特色裁军与军控路线图

中国的宣示性政策是其威慑的直接延伸,并与中国特色的裁军路线图密不可分。中国自1964年10月16日进行第一次核试验以来,一直承诺永不首先使用核武器,并且决不对无核国家使用核武器。这两个声明支撑了中国的核武器完全用于自卫且决不强迫他国的观点。中国强调宣示性政策是负责任的表现,这种观点具有唯一性,因为不首先使用核武并不被其他核武器国家普遍接受,并且威慑和裁军也通常被视为是相互破坏的。

相反,不首先使用核武代表了中国的裁军路线图。中国已经呼吁建立基于互信、互利、平等和合作的安全秩序,其中核裁军应该有利于促进"全球战略平衡和稳定,且不有损所有国家的安全"。如果所有核武器国家放弃核威胁,那么他们在国际关系中的显著作用将大大减弱,实际上就成了毛泽东所说的"纸老虎"。事实上,中国已经呼吁达成不首先使用核武的全球协议。1994年谈判失败后,达成了俄中双边不首先使用核武的协议,后来与美国的谈判失败后,达成了保留面子而不设定目标的协议。中国的国家利益是通过以国际不首先使用核武协议为条件进行裁军而实现的。霍斯堡指出:"通过采用这种方式,中国可能正设法提升其负责任的国家形象,并满足更广泛的共产主义和不结盟利益。"潘振强指出不首先使用核武器使中国在裁军谈判中具有"高度的道德基础"。

如一位资深学者所言,"中国不首先使用核武政策是否可信,对于不首先使用核武承诺以及它反映的军事态势来说并不重要。"不首先使用核武是中国拒绝西方威慑的关键,因为西方的威慑是不负责任的行为。同样,它也可以解释中国如何批评别人的现代化计划,但称自己的现代化是负责任的行为。正如潘振强所说,"在不首先使用核武的前提下",现代化是可以接受的。

除了中国的路线图，中国政府强调美国和俄罗斯在裁军方面具有特殊责任。中国在2008年的《白皮书》中指出："两个国家拥有最大核武库，对核裁军负有特殊和主要责任。他们应认真遵守已经缔结的有关协定，以可证实且不可逆转的方式进一步大幅度削减其核武库，为其他核武器国家参与核裁军创造必要条件。"

除非产生这样的进程，否则中国将很难核裁军。例如，虽然中国表示支持《禁止核武器条约》的构想，但由于安全考虑，必须保持战略稳定。

因此，尽管中国有核裁军路线图，但核裁军在短期内不大可能，并且这也是美国和俄罗斯的首要责任。一位资深学者指出："作为一个较小的核武器国家，中国不可能在短期内完全放弃其核武器"，而且"核武器是中国最终安全的保证"。一位资深学者认为中国不再希望领导不首先使用核武进程，因为它不想"捣乱"；现在看起来，五核国家的团结对推动裁军进程更重要。的确，中国拒绝印度的双边不首先使用核武协议，因为这将使印度成为核武器国家合法化。

与中国声称美国和俄罗斯有解除武装"特殊责任"相关，中国强调其领导军控的责任。这反映了工具主义的责任观；通过对其他国家的批评在国际上提高中国的负责任形象。中国强调纵向和横向扩散的危险，呼吁关注反对横向核扩散到无核国家的虚伪行为，却通过现代化和扩大其核武库来进行纵向扩散。核军备竞赛代表对霸权的追求这一看法，渲染了纵向扩散的不负责任本质。中国坚持称"不会参与任何核军备竞赛"，并且将现代化视为诱使中国参与军备竞赛的伎俩。中国的现代化是有理由的，是对美国危险的反应。与美国和俄罗斯相比，中国对核武器的投入极少，自邓小平提出"四个现代化"以来，国防支出一直服从经济发展。但是中国积极参与军备控制一直都是褒贬参半。中国一直认为，只有当美国和俄罗斯大幅度减少核武器数量，中国才会加入军备控制进程，实现不首先使用核武承诺，并摆脱"不稳定因素（如弹道导弹防御和威胁中国的体系）"。

但是，中国利用军控谈判提升其作为新兴力量和负责任的中等规模核大国的形象。在《中程导弹条约》谈判期间，中国坚持认为，"中小国家有权维持必要的国防力量。裁军进程绝不应有损任何国家的独立、主权和安全。"中国担心俄罗斯中程导弹转移到亚洲。同样，中国更倾向于在多边和共识论坛中进行军备控制谈判。

因此，中国认为裁军和军控责任主要与美国和俄罗斯有关。这些进程中的国别责任牢牢扎根于中国政府及其负责任的宣示性政策。如果反对中国的路线图，这种被动的责任观并不会给中国领导层带来多大希望，但是也没有迹象表明中国反对这些进程。

五　不扩散：平衡承诺

中国认识到不扩散体制的价值，并于1992年正式加入《不扩散核武器条约》（NPT）。中国的责任又有所帮助，因为总的来说不扩散符合中国利益。中国的不扩散责任往往受到更广泛的相关责任的挑战，包括在面对歧视性国际惯例时保护国家主权，促进经济发展以及改善区域安全等。

中国并不总是支持不扩散。实际上，1964年中国的扩散促成了全球对于需要制止核扩散的共识。人们通常认为，毛泽东著名的"纸老虎"表述反映了中国对核武器显著作用的相信是有限的，它实际上促进了核武器的扩散。周恩来指出："如果所有国家都拥有核武器，核战争的可能性就会减少。"霍思堡阐明了这是如何引出中国20世纪60年代的"社会主义扩散"理论的。中国宣称其扩散是为了"热爱和平的中立不结盟国家"的利益。从历史上看，中国已将扩散的责任与促进全球裁军的责任联系起来，并将此与帝国主义不负责任的行为进行对比。

此后，中国已经接受了不扩散体制的责任。在20世纪90年代和21世纪，关于中国是否是一个负责任的利益相关方的讨论往往以中国融入体制为中心。事实上，中国在1980年加入了裁军谈判会议和国际原子能机构（IAEA），1992年加入了《不扩散核武器条约》（NPT），1996年加入了《全面禁止核试验条约》（CTBT），2002年加入了核供应国集团（NSG）。然而，中国的扩散纪录也受到批评，原因有很多：首先，由于通过卡迪尔·汗（AQ Khan）帮助巴基斯坦的核扩散受到谴责；其次，美国指责中国没有对朝鲜采取足够强硬的行动；最后是与伊朗弹道导弹计划的联系。尽管本文并不是要判断中国在这些情况下的作用，但有必要从这些角度考虑责任。

中国试图平衡不扩散和其他责任。以巴基斯坦为例，由于美国支持印度，中国被指责支持巴基斯坦的核计划，特别是2005年的民用核合作协议，针对印度的核计划合法化，中国被批评为"不负责任"。在朝鲜，虽然中国反对扩散，但它也突出了对朝鲜政府的安全的担忧。中国对把制裁作为防止扩散工具持怀疑态度。同样在伊朗，中国一直对制裁持怀疑态度，对这些行为侵犯了主权表示担忧。赵洪指出，在伊朗，中国被迫平衡相互竞争的责任观：让伊朗参与并融入全球经济的责任，以及防止扩散和促进中东安全的责任。

一位资深学者认为，中国对扩散不负责任，称中国"向印度施压，向巴基斯坦提供核武器并向朝鲜施压"。他认为，中国的防扩散责任受到其安全利益的影响，"不扩散不应该是纯粹的国家安全利益工具。相反，它必须被视为一项原则，不屈服于与之相抵触的安全利益。"沈丁立认为美国的行为非常不负责任，但同样也批评中国。学者们指出了中国平衡行为的困难。在朝核危机中，中国对中国人民、对区域安全和不扩散负责。

如果中国只是为了国家利益而参与不扩散，那么中国领导人有着多重责任感，不扩散便是其中之一。中国对扩散问题有更全面的看法。郭小兵认为，尽管西方优先考虑扩散的主观因素，即扩散国家的安全，经济和政治考量，但中国更强调客观因素，即《不扩散核武器条约》的歧视性质和国际安全环境。中国对扩散问题有着更加不可知论的观点，如果国际体系中不平等的基本因素得不到解决，那么就只能说中国不是完全不负责任的。与此同时，这种不可知论却被中国的一些行为所掩盖。例如，中国拒绝与印度达成不首先使用核武协议，因为这可能使印度成为核武器国家合法化。尽管支持《不扩散核武器条约》表面上是负责任的行为，但实际上这削弱了中国的一个最基本的责任，即不首先使用核武。这种行为表明权力政治和区域安全问题的说服力以及中国核行为责任错综复杂的相互作用。

中国负责任地参与不扩散体制被拥有可靠的威慑责任所渲染。例如，中国对《全面禁止核试验条约》（CTBT）和暂停核试验的支持都反映了中国的责任感。与其他核大国相比，由于"生存能力、安全、能力、数据和经验方面的差距"，该条约对中国的歧视性更大。然而，中国认为威慑是不太敏感的变化，这就意味着中国能够参与，而其他核武器国家在类似的立场上可能不会参与。

六 负责任的中国特色核主权

总之，中国的核责任观与其世界观以及建立多极世界秩序有着内在联系。这些责任可能在层次结构中被概念化。最根本的是，中国的责任是保护其主权和领土完整，因此需要核武器。一个负责任的核态势只限于捍卫其公民。正如中国反对国际责任的统一原则一样，如果保护核武器并不损害国家主权，那么核武器就是合法的、负责任的。虽然中国接受裁军和军控，但这又跟一直强调的国家主权意识和不干预原则有根深蒂固的关系；其裁军进程由不首先使用核武承诺和对此表示认可的各国证实。中国很快注意到其他俄罗斯和美国的不负责任行为以及他们领导军控和裁军进程的特殊责任。这再一次强调了国别国际责任。最后，尽管中国已经接受了不扩散责任，并且这已成为负责任地参与国际关系的象征，但这往往涉及更大的责任，即平衡国家安全问题，保护国家主权和创造一个更公平的世界秩序。中国的责任反映了一个应该更加多极化和更具代表性的世界观。因此，中国已经自诩为特别的核大国，不参与美国和俄罗斯的"不负责任"的行为。

国际关系的一个长期存在的问题是：中国的不断崛起将如何影响全球秩序，特别是核秩序？相比于游戏规则改变者，中国更像是一个游戏玩家。虽然中国不可能在未来积极推进横向或纵向扩散，但也不可能领导一个转型的裁军进程。中国已经表现出了明显的克制，但仍然认为其拥有核武器是负责任的表现。正如一位资深学者所言，中国的首要任务是"不捣乱"。同样，沈丁立认为，中国作为现实主义者将继续拥有核武器，并且只要稳定，就没有理由参与破坏稳定的行为。中国的行为在反应迅速，正如中国持续强调美国和俄罗斯的特殊责任一样。

那么，中国的责任观能如何有助于我们提出负责任的核主权概念呢？中国倡导主权国家之间应互信、互利、平等和合作，共同利益要与共同理解相协调。这一愿景表现出可信的联系，以及威慑与裁军进程，而威慑与裁军通常被认为是相互破坏的。最后，中国的责任观可以让各国保护其国家责任，并参与到减少扩散诱因的裁军进程中。然而，必须面对其他核武器国家的反对和战略模糊性的问题。无论如何，负责任的中国特色核主权概念值得深入探讨。

Responsible Nuclear Sovereignty with Chinese Characteristics

Maxwell Leonard Jonason Downman / United Kingdom of Great Britain and Northern Ireland

British American Security Information Council, House of Lords

At the 2015 Non-proliferation Treaty Review Conference (NPT RevCon), the Chinese delegation declared "China has always taken a responsible approach in actively engaging in engaging with non-proliferation cooperation,"[1] and China has increasingly sought to be seen as a responsible actor in international relations. So what does China see as responsible nuclear behaviour?

This paper seeks to assess China's conceptions of its nuclear responsibilities and hopes to contribute to developing a framework of "responsible nuclear sovereignty." China is important in thinking about responsible nuclear behaviour. It is a P5 nuclear weapons state, is a key stakeholder in the North Korean crisis, shares borders with

---

1 Chinese delegation to 2015 NPT Review Conference, *Statement by the Chinese Delegation at the Main Committee II of the NPT 2015 Review Conference on the Non-Proliferation of Nuclear Weapons and the Establishment of a Middle East Zone Free of Nuclear Weapons and all other Weapons of Mass Destruction*, New York, 4 May 2015, http://www.un.org/en/conf/npt/2015/statements/pdf/main2_china.pdf

three other nuclear weapons states and is increasingly engaging and shaping global governance, including the future of the global nuclear order.

This paper begins with a broad discussion of "responsibility" in relation to nuclear weapons and Chinese engagement in international relations. Subsequently, it assesses how China perceives its nuclear responsibilities in terms of its approach to *deterrence, disarmament, arms control* and *non-proliferation*. While focusing on contemporary Chinese understandings, it is necessary to draw on China's historical engagement. This report, however, does not seek to provide a history of China's engagement with the global nuclear order or give a technical analysis of China's nuclear arsenal.

I argue that China takes an "instrumentalist" approach to responsibility that is firmly rooted in advancing the Chinese national interest. China has a hierarchical understanding of its nuclear responsibilities: first and foremost are its deterrence responsibilities, to possess nuclear weapons for the sole purpose of defending China but never for any offensive action; second, are its non-proliferation responsibilities of balancing its commitment against the spread of nuclear weapons with an understanding of state's security needs; third, are China's disarmament and arms control responsibilities, it's unique roadmap for disarmament that emphasises the importance of states nuclear postures and declaratory policies as well as US and Russian "special responsibility" to lead disarmament and arms control. While these responsibilities complement and contradict each other in certain ways, they are all underpinned by a desire to create a more multipolar world in which sovereign states engage in cooperative security, to the obvious benefit of China. Contrary to this real politik understanding of its nuclear responsibilities, it has exhibited many of the sorts of behaviours a cosmopolitan ethicist would advocate, including a restrained nuclear posture and commitment to disarmament. Therefore, China's experience could help inform a concept of "responsible nuclear sovereignty" that is appealing to the language of nuclear weapon states, bridge a cosmopolitan ethics of nuclear responsibility and classical realist view—Responsible Nuclear Sovereignty with

Chinese Characteristics

I. Responsibility in International Relations

Responsibility is an important concept for considering China's engagement with the nuclear order. At its most basic, responsibility relates to the ethical questions "on the *ought* rather than the *is*"—what do states envisage the global nuclear order should be?[1] It links with "questions of duties, power, sovereignty, and ends", dealing with who has the power to shape their ends and why they shape them as such.

In the English School of International Relations, this debate has divided between *solidarist,* linked with cosmopolitan, and *pluralist* principles. As Andrew Hurrell notes, the global order is "a world in which solidarity and cosmopolitan conceptions of governance coexist, often rather unhappily, with many aspects of the old pluralist order."[2] Cosmopolitans argue that responsibilities extend beyond the state and that states have a "responsibility to consider the causal impact of particular actions and the ways they will interact with others and, guide them towards the right ends."[3] They both identify right action and argue that responsibility in global security eminates from this and "from the *consequences* of their actions and their powers to affect the security of others."[4] For pluralists responsibilities are rooted in the state. While states can cooperate based on shared interests and common values, this cooperation exists within a society of states. Competing pressures between responsibilities to strengthen international society and states national responsibilities create a responsibility to maintain order internationally.[5]

Recently, scholars have attempted to bridge the divide. In 2010 Walker articulated

---

1 Anthony Burke, David Norman, and Nicholas J. Wheeler, Scoping Paper: Nuclear Ethics and Responsible Nuclear Sovereignty, 2016: 2. (available from author on request).
2 Nicola Horsburgh, *China and Global Nuclear Order: From Estrangement to Active Engagement,* (Oxford: Oxford University Press, 2015): 3.
3 Burke et. al., Scoping Paper, 3.
4 *Ibid,* 84.
5 Rosemary Foot, 2001, Chinese Power and the Idea of a Responsible State, *The China Journal,* p.45 (2001): 3.

the idea of *responsible nuclear sovereignty* as an "intermediate position" that bridged a realist ethic and more cosmopolitan concerns, but noted the difficulty of state agreement[1]. This is developed into an exploratory discussion into what responsibility could mean.[2] Following a roundtable discussion, BASIC articulated a vision of Responsible Nuclear Sovereignty as, "acting responsibly and in accordance with international laws and norms that strengthen global security for all at a strategic level."

So how can one assess what action strengthens global security? Nicola Horsburgh argues that global nuclear order consists of, *nuclear deterrence, arms-control, non-proliferation* and *disarmament*. These elements share the common goal of strategic stability, but because the strategies for attaining these may differ they can both complement or undermine each other. While deterrence, arms control and non-proliferation often bolster the status quo, for Horsburgh, disarmament can be a "double-edged sword"; it both lends the current order legitimacy but also undermines it through "the transformational imperative of a non-nuclear order". This paper suggests that by looking at how states action supports or undermine this order we can illuminate what states think the order *ought* to be, and understand conceptions of responsible behaviour.

II. China's View of Responsibility in International Relations

Many scholars have studied the idea of responsibility in international relations with and its engagement with the global nuclear order. Since the late 1990s and 2000s China's Rise has been described in terms of responsibility. Most notably in 2005, US Secretary of State Robert Zoellick called on China to be a "responsible stakeholder in international affairs."[3] China seemingly embraced such a label as it helped alleviate the China threat thesis and implied that, as a stakeholder, China

---

1 William Walker, The UK, threshold status and responsible nuclear sovereignty, *International Affairs*, 86: 2 (2010): 450.
2 Burke et. al., Scoping Paper.
3 Robert B. Zoellick, Whither China: From Membership to Responsibility, *National Committee on US-China Relations* (2005), https://2001-2009.state.gov/s/d/former/zoellick/rem/53682.htm.

had rights to shape the global order. Subsequently, as well as taking responsibilities in the global order, China noted the need to "make the international order fairer and more equitable"[1]. China has presented itself as a "responsible great power" (*fuzeren de dagou*). In this period China emphasised international cooperation and integration into the international institutions, including the non-proliferation regime. Scholars have often argued that China embraced responsibility to "deepen China's globalization, reduce fear of Chinese power, and steer active participation in the existing world order"[2].

While Chinese has engaged in the global order it has unique ideas of what responsibility means. Some highlight China's conception of responsibility as "confucian dispositions towards non-interventionism and self-governance". Responsibility is the sole preserve of the state, and as such global responsibilities would be divided up into states individual responsibilities.[3] This can make China reluctant to embrace international responsibilities that bind and constrain it. As Scott argues China is a "pragmatic instrumentalist" with responsibility, engaging when in the national interest and otherwise presenting responsibility as the "reasonableness" of not challenging this global order.[4]

So is Chinese responsible action merely that which promotes its national interest? If so, there is surprising degree of continuity in Chinese foreign policy. The underlying drivers of China in international relations continue to be the protection of its sovereignty and territorial integrity, economic development and the demand for respect and status commensurate with its power.[5] Similarly, Wang Jisi observes three guiding norms in China's foreign policy: the survival of the CPC, the

---

1 Hu Jintao at APEC Business Summit, 7th September 2007, http://www.fmprc.gov.cn/mfa_eng/wjdt_665385/zyjh_665391/t360596.shtml
2 Yong Deng, China: The Post-Responsible Power, *Washington Quarterly*, 37:4 (2014): 121.
3 Shih Chih-Yu and Huang Chiung-Chiu, "Preaching Self-Responsibility:the Chinese style of global governance," Journal of Contemporary China, 22:80 (2013): 354.
4 David Scott, China and the "Responsibilities" of a "Responsible" Power—The Uncertainties of Appropriate Power Rise Language, Asia-Pacific Review, 17:1 (2010): 75.
5 Evan S. Medeiros, *China's international Behaviour* (Santa Monica: RAND, 2009): 13.

maintenance of China's sovereignty and China's economic and social development.¹ Consistent with this is China's call for a more equitable and multipolar world order. While China would accept a pluralist conception of responsibility that promotes multilateral global governance it is increasingly wary of a "solidarist agenda". Rosemary Foot notes how just as China began to accept its responsibility to international society based on sovereign equality and non-interference, western states started to advocate for a solidarist model of responsibility.²

In more recent years, scholars have begun to debate whether China still accepts the notion of responsibility under Xi Jinping. Deng argues that China has turned its back on responsibility and has begun to "justify their national objectives in the name of global responsibilities."³ Responsibility is about abiding by "the rules of the game", where states exercise self-restraint, emphasise mutual obligations and manage interdependence for the public good.⁴ A more assertive China is a rejection of responsibility.

Yet contrary to this critique, there is large degree of continuity in Chinese foreign policy. While China is increasingly comfortable with the global order, it has become more assertive in its demands to change discriminatory elements and demand influence commensurate with its stature. Jian Zhang argues that, rather than a rejection of responsibility, Xi Jinping's foreign policy is largely a continuation of the Hu Jintao era of responsible stakeholder-ism, yet with greater emphasis on reciprocity and greater determination for order to reflect the national interest. As these are key Chinese conceptions of responsibility, this would suggest the concepts continuing importance.

So how does China see as responsible engagement with the global nuclear order. This section analyses China sees as a responsible approach to nuclear deterrence,

---

1   Wang Jisi, China's Search for Grand Strategy: A Rising Great Power Finding its Way, *Foreign Affairs, 90*:2, (2011): 7.
2   Rosemary Foot, Chinese Power and the Idea of a Responsible State.
3   Yong Deng, China: The Post-Responsible Power, 124.
4   *Ibid,* 129.

disarmament, arms control and non-proliferation.[1] It argues that China have taken an instrumentalist and hierarchical approach to the global nuclear order that conceives of China's responsibilities in terms of national interest. China's primary responsibility is to defend its sovereignty and territorial integrity and linked to this is China's unique road map for disarmament rooted in its restrained nuclear posture. Thus China views deterrence and disarmament as complementary rather than contradictory. While China also accepts the responsibility to engage in arms control and non-proliferation, these are balanced with the United States and Russia's special responsibilities to disarm and wider responsibilities to promote its national security and oppose discriminatory elements of the international order.

III. China's Nuclear Deterrent: A Restrained Posture

Security has been the largest driving force in Chinese nuclear action, reflecting China's primary responsibility to protect its sovereignty and territorial integrity. China has a history of being the subject of US nuclear coercion during the Korean War and Taiwan Straits crisis, and the threat of Russia has also loomed large in Chinese nuclear strategy. Indeed, it was the 1969 Sino-Soviet War and the possibility of a Russian nuclear strike that prompted China to seek a minimum credible deterrent, not the threat of the United States. Security concerns have combined with China's memory of the century of humiliation from 1839 to 1949. This has instilled China with a hyper-sensitivity to the issue of sovereignty and non-interference and a sense of duty to not lag behind the west technologically, lest China be taken advantage of. Resultantly, China has embraced nuclear weapons but limited the scope of their use through its consistent No-First Use pledge (NFU) never to use nuclear weapons first, and Negative Security Assurances (NSAs) to never use nuclear weapons against non-nuclear weapons states.

China is critical of US strategic thinking on nuclear weapons. Primarily China objects to nuclear blackmail or nuclear coercion. China worries about the "strong

---

1 This use of conceptualisation is indebted to Horsburgh, *China and Global Nuclear Order: From Estrangement to Active Engagement.*

intimidation effect" of nuclear weapons and rejects deterrence as a form of coercive, and thus irresponsible, behaviour.¹ On a strategic level, China sees little difference between US deterrence and compellence. Despite this critique, however, the Chinese military (PLA) have accepted deterrence at a *doctrinal* level. China criticises US nuclear arsenal and logic driving its expansion. China observes that the United States continually expands its arsenal and builds new capabilities for new scenarios. The US nuclear posture intends to project strategic dominance and designs for warfighting and escalation dynamics is deemed as irresponsible.²

In contrast, China see its position of a minimum credible deterrent designed for the sole purpose of delivering a secure second strike as a responsible posture. China's 2006 White Paper on Defence states, the fundamental purpose of China's nuclear strategy is,

> "to deter other countries from using or threatening to use nuclear weapons against China... China exercises great restraint in developing its nuclear force. It has never entered into and will never enter into a nuclear arms race with any other country."³

Jeffrey Lewis has described China's deterrent as "'the minimum means of reprisal'—a nuclear deterrent that sacrifices offensive capability in exchange for political control and minimising economic cost," and this thinking is reflected in Chinese descriptions of their "lean but effective arsenal" designed to only deter nuclear attack.⁴ This is seen as responsible for a number of reasons: first, it deters a nuclear attack on China protecting China's vital interest; second, it is not designed to be an offensive threat to any nuclear state, ensuring their sovereignty; and third, it

---

1 Li Bin, Differences Between Chinese and U.S. Nuclear Thinking and Their Origins, in Li Bin and Tong Zhao (eds.), *Understanding Chinese Nuclear Thinking* (Washington: Carnegie Endowment for International Peace, 2016): 9, and REDACTED.
2 REDACTED
3 Information Office of the State Council of the People's Republic of China, China's National Defense in 2006, December 29, 2006, http://www.fas.org/nuke/guide/china/ doctrine/wp2006.html
4 Jeffrey Lewis, Minimum Means of Reprisal, (London: MIT Press, 2007): 206.

minimises the incentives of others to proliferate.

However China's limited arsenal has led to conception of whether transparency is responsible. Wu Riqiang notes that China struggle to be transparent due a reliance on land-based missiles, transparency could undermine its second-strike capability, if systems became strikeable. Thus while it would be irresponsible for China to reveal the location, range and accuracy of its nuclear weapons, it can easily reveal the number and intent of them.[1] China emphasise transparency of *intent* rather than transparency of *capability*, but also see the United States as having a greater responsibility to be transparent, due to the size and security of its nuclear arsenal. The call for greater transparency is increasingly challenged US developments that are seen to undermine China's deterrent. Specifically, China oppose to the development of US BMD, arguing these could be aimed at China and neutralise its deterrent.[2] Developments are seen as directly challenging China's sovereignty by potentially giving Taiwan confidence in action. Wu Riqiang is quick to point to elements in the US posture, BMD, nuclear blackmail and sub-strategic nuclear weapons as irresponsible.

Nevertheless US developments have challenged traditional Chinese nuclear thinking, and many western scholars have expressed concerns over subsequent Chinese modernisation. Opponents argue that China is modernising its nuclear weapons arsenal to project a counterforce posture that could be used for nuclear warfighting in sub-strategic scenarios and therefore is a departure from China's traditional posture. A senior scholar worries that traditional Chinese restraint may be under challenge from an acceptance of western thinking and that China will explore elements it has critiqued such as launch on warning and sub-strategic weapons.[3] While scholars are right to scrutinise China's nuclear capabilities, there

---

[1] Wu Riqiang, How China Practices and Thinks About Nuclear Transparency, in *Understanding Chinese Nuclear Thinking,* 231-4.
[2] Sun Xiangli, China's Nuclear Strategy: Nature and Characteristics, *World Economic and Politics,* 9 (2006): 23-9.
[3] REDACTED.

is a convincing argument to be made that China's modernisation is designed solely to counter US BMD and China is not seeking to radically expand their nuclear arsenal. As Horsburgh notes, "China's nuclear force modernisation indicates no drastic deviation from a strategy of retaliation."[1] Many see Chinese modernisation as responsible; a senior scholar argues it enhances strategic stability and another argues that it is responsible to upgrade to keep pace with the changing times as long as these capabilities are exercised within traditional doctrine.[2]

China's nuclear arsenal and its responsibilities with this have remained relatively stable. China views a "lean and efficient" arsenal as responsible. First and foremost are China sees its responsibilities are to protect itself and second to ensure this arsenal does not threaten anyone else. An arsenal that goes beyond this, due to size, capabilities, posture and doctrine, is viewed as grossly irresponsible. However, some point out that a stable arsenal "doesn't promote global disarmament and non-proliferation" in itself.[3] Thus to expand Horsburgh analogy, China's responsibilities to deter could undermine its responsibilities to disarm.

IV. Declaratory Policy: China's Unique Roadmap for Disarmament and Arms Control

China's declaratory policy is a direct extension of its deterrent and is inextricably linked to China's unique roadmap for disarmament. China has maintained its pledge to never use nuclear weapons first and never use them against a non-nuclear weapon state since its conducted its first nuclear test on October 16, 1964. These two statements underpin China's argument that its nuclear weapons exist solely for self-defence, and never to coerce others. China's emphasis on declaratory policy as responsible is unique as NFU is not a universally accepted by other nuclear weapon states and the deterrence and disarmament are normally viewed as undermining each other.

---

1 Horsburgh, *China and Global Nuclear Order: From Estrangement to Active Engagement*, 131.
2 REDACTED.
3 Shen Dingli, Revitalising the Prague Agenda, *Washington Quarterly*, 36: 2 (2013).

Conversely NFU represents China's roadmap to disarmament. China has called for a security order based on mutual trust, mutual benefit, equality and cooperation, in which nuclear disarmament should promote "global strategic balance and stability and undiminished security for all."[1] If all nuclear weapons states renounce nuclear threats, then their saliency in international relations is vastly diminished - they in essence become Mao's "Paper Tigers". Indeed, China has called for a global NFU agreement. In 1994 failed negotiations led to a bilateral Russia-China No-First Use agreement and later failed negotiations with the United States led to a face-saving no targeting agreement.[2] China's national interest is served by making disarmament conditional on an international No-First Use agreement. As Horsburgh notes, "by adopting this approach China was perhaps seeking to promote the image of a responsible state and appease wider Communist and non-aligned interests."[3] And General Pan notes that No First Use give China the "high moral ground" in disarmament negotiations.[4]

As a senior scholar notes "the question of whether China's NFU policy is credible is of less importance to the signals that a NFU pledge send and the military posture it reflects."[5] NFU is a linchpin to Chinese rejections of western deterrence as irresponsible western behaviour. Similarly it can explain how China can critique the modernisation plans of others but call it's own responsible. As General Pan notes modernisation is admissible if "exercised under the premise of no-first-use."[6]

Beyond China's roadmap, Beijing emphasises that the United States and Russia

---

1 Hu Jintao, Unite as One and Work for a Bright Future (statement, UN General Assembly, New York, September 23, 2009), http://www.fmprc.gov.cn/eng/wjdt/zyjh/ t606276.htm and "Statement of Chinese delegation, the 3rd PrepCom for 2010 NPT Review Conference," New York, May 4—15, 2009 http://www.fmprc.gov.cn/chn/pds/ziliao/zyjh/ t575071.htm (in Chinese).
2 Hui Zhang, China's Perspective on a Nuclear-Free World, *The Washington Quarterly*, 33: 2 (2010): 145.
3 Nicola Horsburgh, *China and Global Nuclear Order*, 70.
4 Pan Zhenqiang, China's No First Use of Nuclear Weapons, in *Understanding Chinese Nuclear Thinking*, 61.
5 REDACTED.
6 Pan Zhenqiang, China's No First Use of Nuclear Weapons, 64.

have a special responsibility to disarm. In its 2008 White Paper, Beijing noted that,

> "The two countries possessing the largest nuclear arsenals bear special and primary responsibility for nuclear disarmament. They should earnestly comply with the relevant agreements already concluded, and further drastically reduce their nuclear arsenals in a verifiable and irreversible manner, so as to create the necessary conditions for the participation of other nuclear-weapon states in the process of nuclear disarmament."[1]

Unless such a process happens China will find it difficult to disarm. For example, while China said it supported the vision of the Ban Treaty it abstained due to security reasons and need to maintain strategic stability.[2]

Thus while China has a roadmap for disarmament, disarmament is unlikely in the near term and is the United States and Russia's initial responsibility. A senior scholar notes, "as a lesser nuclear weapon state, Beijing couldn't conceive of relinquishing its nuclear weapons entirely in the near term," and that "nuclear weapons are the guarantor of [China's] ultimate security."[3] A senior scholar argues that China no longer wants to lead a NFU process as it "doesn't want to rock the boat;" P5 solidarity now appears more important pushing its disarmament process.[4] Indeed, China rebuffed India's call for a bilateral NFU agreement, because this would legitimise India as a nuclear weapon state.[5]

Related to China's claim that the United States and Russia have a "special responsibility" to disarm is China's emphasis on their responsibility to lead arms control. This reflects an instrumentalist view of responsibility; it promotes a responsible image of China internationally through a critique of others. China highlights the dangers of both *vertical* and *horizontal* proliferation. China calls

---

1 China 2008 National Defense document, art. 16, http://www.gov.cn/english/official/ 2009- 01/20/content_1210227_16.htm ("Arms Control and Disarmament").
2 REDACTED.
3 REDACTED.
4 REDACTED.
5 REDACTED.

attention to the hypocrisy of opposing horizontal nuclear proliferation to non-nuclear weapon states, yet proliferating vertically through modernising and expanding their nuclear arsenals. The irresponsible nature of vertical proliferation is coloured by the belief that nuclear arms races represent a quest for hegemony.[1] China insists that it "would not engage in any [nuclear] arms race," and views modernisation as a trick to lure China into an arms race.[2] China's modernisation is justified as being responsive to US dangers.[3] Compared to the United States and Russia, China has devoted few resources to nuclear weapons and defence spending has been subordinated to economic development since Deng Xiaoping's Four Modernisations.[4] Yet Beijing's active participation in arms control has remained mixed. China has maintained it would only join the process of arms control when the United States and Russia drastically reduce their number of nuclear weapons, commit to a NFU pledge and get rid of destabilizing factors (such as BMD and systems that threaten China).[5]

China has, however, used arms control negotiations to raise its profile as a rising power and responsible middle-sized nuclear power. During the INF Treaty negotiations, China insisted that,

> "small and medium sized states are entitled to maintain their necessary forces for national defence. The disarmament process should in no way jeopardise the independence, sovereignty and security of any state."[6]

As it was concerned that Russian intermediate range missiles would be transferred to Asia. China preferred arms control negotiations in multilateral and consensual forums.[7]

---

1 Li Bin, Differences Between Chinese and U.S. Nuclear Thinking and Their Origins, 14.
2 Nicola Horsburgh, *China and Global Nuclear Order*, 123.
3 Li Bin, Differences Between Chinese and U.S. Nuclear Thinking and Their Origins, 14.
4 Nicola Horsburgh, *China and Global Nuclear Order*, 80.
5 Alexei Arbatov, Engaging China in Nuclear Arms Control, *Carnegie Moscow Center*, October 2014.
6 Quoted in J. Mohan Malik, China and the Intermediate Range Nuclear Forces Talk, *Arms Control*, 10:3, (1989): 248.
7 Nicola Horsburgh, *China and Global Nuclear Order*.

Thus Beijing views disarmament and arms control responsibilities lying primarily with the United States and Russia. Its individual responsibilities to these processes are firmly rooted in the Chinese state and its responsible declaratory policy. This passive view of responsibility does not hold much hope for Chinese leadership, given opposition to China's roadmap, but nor does it indicate Chinese opposition to these processes.

V. Non-proliferation: Balancing Commitments

China sees value in the non-proliferation regime, formally joining the NPT in 1992. Yet once again Beijing's responsibilities are instrumental, because non-proliferation generally serves China's interest. And Chinese non-proliferation responsibilities are often challenged by more wider relating responsibilities, including the protection of state sovereignty in the face of discriminatory international practice, the promotion of economic development, and the amelioration of regional security concerns.

China has not always supported non-proliferation. Indeed, China's proliferation in 1964 shaped the global consensus on the need to halt nuclear proliferation. Mao's famous "Paper Tiger" doctrine, commonly lauded as reflecting China's limited belief in the saliency of nuclear weapons, in fact promotes the proliferation of nuclear weapons. As Zhou Enlai noted, "If all countries have nuclear weapons, the possibility of nuclear wars would decrease."[1] Horsburgh highlights how this led to China's doctrine of "socialist proliferation" in the 1960s. Beijing asserted that its proliferation was for "peace-loving neutralist non-aligned countries".[2] Historically China have linked a responsibility to proliferate with a responsibility to promote universal disarmament and contrasted this against the irresponsibility of imperialistic behaviour.

Since then China has accepted responsibilities to the non-proliferation regime.

---

1   Quoted in Mingquan Zhu, The Evolution of China's Nuclear Non-Proliferation Policy, *The Nonproliferation Review*, 4:2, (1997).
2   Nicola Horsburgh, *China and Global Nuclear Order.*

In the 1990s and 2000s discussion of whether China was a responsible stakeholder often centred around China's integration into the regime. Indeed, China joined the Conference on Disarmament and IAEA in 1980, NPT in 1992, CTBT in 1996 and NSG in 2002. Yet China's proliferation record has also been critiqued for a number of reasons: first, due to accusations of helping nuclear proliferation in Pakistan through the AQ Khan network; second, the United States has accused it of not taking strong enough action on North Korea; and finally, for links to Iran's ballistic missile programme. While it is beyond the scope of this paper to pass judgement on China's role in these instances, it is necessary to think of these instances in terms of responsibility.

China has sought to balance non-proliferation and other responsibilities. In the case of Pakistan, China has been accused of supporting Pakistan's nuclear programme because of US support for India, notably the 2005 civilian nuclear cooperation deal which China criticised as "irresponsible" in legitmising India's nuclear programme. In North Korea, while China has opposed proliferation, it has also highlighted the security concerns of the North Korean Government. China has generally been more skeptical of sanctions as a tool for preventing proliferation. Similarly in Iran, China has been skeptical of sanctions, voicing concern that these impinge on sovereignty. Zhao Hong notes that in Iran, China id forced to balance competing ideas of responsibility: a responsibility to engage and integrate Iran into the global economy and a responsibility to prevent proliferation and promote a secure Middle East.[1]

A senior scholar argues that China has been irresponsible with proliferation, claiming China "pushed India, gave nukes to Pakistan and pushed North Korea."[2] He argues that China's non-proliferation responsibilities have been tempered by its security interests and that,

---

1 Zhao Hong, China's Dilemma on Iran: between energy security and a responsible rising power, *Journal of Contemporary China*, 23:87 (2014): 424.
2 REDACTED.

"nonproliferation [should] not be a mere tool of national security interest. Instead it has to be taken as a principle, unbending to competing security interests."[1]

Shen sees US action as grossly irresponsible, but critiques China equally. Scholars note China's difficult balancing act. In North Korean crisis, China is responsible to the Chinese people, for regional security and non-proliferation.[2]

It would be reductive to argue that China only engage in non-proliferation when it is in its national interest, rather Chinese leaders have a diverse sense of responsibilities of which non-proliferation is one of many. China has a more holistic view of proliferation. Guo Xiaobing argues that while the West prioritises subjective factors of proliferation, namely security, economic and political considerations of proliferating countries, China highlights the objective factors, the discriminatory nature of the NPT and international security environment. China has a more agnostic view of proliferation, seeing it as not wholly irresponsible if the underlying factors of inequality in the international system are not dealt with. Yet at the same time, this agnosticism is belied by some examples of Chinese action. For example China has refused a NFU agreement with India as this would legitimise India as a nuclear weapon state. While ostensibly responsible behaviour in supporting NPT, this undercuts one of China's most fundamental responsibilities - NFU. Such behaviour indicates the persuasiveness of power-politics and regional security concerns the complex interplay of responsibilities in China's nuclear behaviour.

China's idea of responsible engagement with the non-proliferation regime has been coloured by its responsibility to have a reliable deterrent. For example China's support for the CTBT and moratorium on nuclear testing reflects a sense of responsibility. Compared to other nuclear powers, this treaty was far more discriminatory towards China due "gaps in survivability, safety, capabilities, data and experience." Nevertheless, China's view that deterrence is insensitive change

---

1 Shen Dingli, Revitalising the Prague Agenda, 128.
2 REDACTED.

means that China was able to engage, whereas other nuclear weapon states in similar positions may not.

VI. Responsible Nuclear Sovereignty with Chinese Characteristics

To conclude, Chinese conceptions of its nuclear responsibilities are intrinsically linked to vision of itself in the world and the creation of a more multipolar world order. These responsibilities can be conceptualised in a hierarchy. At the most base level, China's responsibility is to protect its sovereignty and territorial integrity, for which nuclear weapons are needed. Thus a responsible nuclear posture is one that is restrained and limited to defending its citizens. Just as China opposes solidarist principles of international responsibility, nuclear weapons are legitimate and responsible if they protect and do not undermine state sovereignty. While China accepts a disarmament and arms control this is once again rooted in a heightened sense of state sovereignty and the principle of non-intervention; its disarmament process is exemplified by its NFU pledge and states agreeing to this. China is quick to note the irresponsible behaviour of other Russia and the United States and their special responsibility to lead arms control and disarmament processes. This once again emphasises states' individual responsibilities. Finally while China has accepted the responsibility of non-proliferation, and this has become emblematic of responsible engagement in international relations, this is often subsumed by greater responsibilities, namely to balance state security concerns, protect state sovereignty and create a less discriminatory world order. China's responsibilities reflect a vision of world that ought to be more multipolar and more representative, and thus China has self-identified as a special kind of nuclear power–one that does not engage in the "irresponsible" behaviours of the United States and Russia.

A perennial question of international relations is, as China's rise continues, how will it shape the global order, and in particular the nuclear order? China is more of a game-player than game-changer. While it is unlikely that China will actively promote horizontal or vertically proliferate in the future, it is unlikely that it will lead a transformative process of disarmament. Beijing has demonstrated remarkable restraint, but has continued to see its possession of nuclear weapons as responsible. As a senior scholar argues, China's priority is to "not rock the boat."[1] Similarly, Shen Dingli argues that China, as a realist, will continue to possess its nuclear weapons and, as long as stability remains, will have no reason to engage in destabilizing behaviour. China's behaviour is largely responsive, as reflected by China's continued emphasis on the United States and Russia's special responsibilities.

So how can China's conception of responsibility help us develop a concept of responsible nuclear sovereignty? China promotes a vision of mutual trust, mutual benefit, equality and cooperation between sovereign states in which shared interests harmonise towards shared understanding. And this vision presents credible links and a process between deterrence and disarmament, which are normally seen to undermine each other. Ultimately, Chinese views of responsibility could allow states to protect their national responsibilities and engage in a process of disarmament that reduces the drivers of proliferation. However questions relating to other nuclear weapons states opposition and strategic ambiguity must be confronted. Nevertheless, the concept of responsible nuclear sovereignty with Chinese characteristics is worth exploring.

---

1   REDACTED.

非洲重建：来自中国快速发展的经验

黑豹 【马拉维】
马拉维国家税务局专员

一 引言

一个明显的事实是，中国已从一个贫穷的国家发展成为世界上最富有的国家之一。自20世纪70年代末开始市场改革以来，中国已经使8亿多人口摆脱了贫困；根据世界银行最近的支出基准计算，中国贫困人口比例已从1981年的几乎90%锐减至不到2%。

统计数据表明，贫穷依然是人类的一个悲剧问题。世界银行的数据显示，世界上每10个人中，就有1个人每日生活费不足1.9美元，他们其中一半以上生活在非洲。撒哈拉以南非洲地区的极度贫困人口数量自1990年以来不断增长，并于2010年达到了3.99亿人的历史最高水平。在过去20年中，印度一半的人口生活在贫困之中。今天，印度依然是世界上贫困人口最多的国家。

二 中国是如何攻坚克难取得成功的

中国的减贫经验有时会被借鉴，事实上，中国在这方面有很多经验。但是，中国解决亿万人口贫困问题的成功故事是独一无二的，它在对的时间、对的地点采取了对的措施，这是因为中国抓住了全球化这一机会。

1. 发展中国家的工资水平、发达国家的基础设施

1978年，中国领导人邓小平启动了改革开放进程，首先解决长期以来低迷的

农业增长问题。他允许重新以家庭为单位进行农业生产。这一政策的实施显著地提高了农民的收入和存款,有助于为下一步的工业和城市化发展提供资金。

当企业开始将工厂从发达国家转移到发展中国家的时候,中国当时的工资水平还很低。即使到 2004 年,中国工人的小时工资也只有 64 美分,而墨西哥的这一数字是 2.48 美元。根据美国劳工统计局对 30 个国家的统计数据,中国工人的小时工资是其中最低的。但是,低工资水平本身并不一定会让中国与其他拥有大量低工资劳动力的国家相比更具吸引力。

20 世纪 80 年代,中国投入大量精力建造大坝、灌溉工程和公路。"劳动换食物"计划为工人提供免费食物,推进了在农村地区的公路建设。1994 至 2000 年,中国每年建设的农村公路里程达 4.2 万公里(2.61 万英里),这意味着每天有 1200 公里的公路建成(即使今天,印度每天建设的公路里程也仅 20 公里)。

Gaveka Drag-onomics 是一家以中国为研究重点的咨询公司。该公司创始合伙人 Arthur Koreber 在其 2016 年所著的《中国的经济》一书中写道:"中国到 21 世纪初已经形成了将发展中国家水平的低工资与良好的、几乎是富裕国家水平的基础设施相结合的一套独一无二并且可能是无法复制的体系。"中国工人的工资虽然较低,但是却接受过基本教育。1980 年,中国成年男子识字率约 80%,这一点吸引了外国在中国投资建厂并创造了数以百万计的就业机会。中国人均 GDP 从 1980 年的不足 200 美元(低于孟加拉国当时的水平)已经增加至 8000 多美元。

2. 货物运输的革命

中国为工厂从西方的转移做好了充分准备。但是如果没有在通讯和运输领域取得的成就,从而对广泛分布的供应链进行管理以促进全球贸易,那么工厂也不会涌向中国。这些变革的核心似乎只是一个相对简单的创新——海运集装箱。1956 年发明了海运集装箱,但是广泛使用却是在大约 20 年以后了。海运集装箱使得远洋货船可以更快、更多地装载货物,货船规模变得更大,运输成本变得更低。如《经济学人》所述,"集装箱对全球化的促进作用,比过去 50 年里所有贸易协定加在一起都要大。"集装箱发明 50 多年后的今天,使用它所带来的好处大部分或许都已实现了。

3. 消费电子产品的创新

个人电脑、随身听、手机,所有这些开创性的小家电在 20 世纪 80—90 年代开始改变消费者的生活方式,开辟了新的生产线。中国在这一时期出口的繁荣发展很大程度上是由电子和机械制造产品带来的。1992至2005年期间，中国出口的商品发生了显著的变化，从诸如纺织品和服装等农业和轻工产品转为诸如消费电子产品和家电等更高附加值的产品。由于对这些商品的需求井喷，向美国和欧洲这一世界最大市场出口的壁垒在减少，特别是2001年中国加入世界贸易组织之后。

2015年，中国在全球出口中的份额达到了13.8%，这一比例自美国50年前实现过以来，至今没有任何其他国家达到过。

三 经济发展带来了新的挑战

当然，中国的脱贫攻坚战尚未结束。截至2016年底，中国还有4300多万人仍然生活在年收入2300元贫困线以下（这一标准是按2010年购买力计算的由国家界定的贫困线）。中国称，其目标是到2020年扫除贫困，中国共产党宣布在2020年建党100周年之前，将在中国全面建成小康社会。

事实上中国的崛起毫无疑问是过去100年世界发展史上最重要的事件之一。

在中国的经济增长使得世界工业生产规模翻了一倍的同时，"中国价格"也随之降低了工业制成品的成本，能使所有人承受得起并极大地提高了全球生活水平。虽然这一过程可能会对那些与中国直接竞争的行业和国家造成负面影响，但是却不仅为之前提到的原材料供应国提供了大量机会，同时也为像德国这样的国家提供了大量机会——德国的先进设备和制造工具因此拥有了中国这样一个巨大市场，从而使得德国的失业率降至20年以来的最低水平。

同时，随着中国老百姓变得越来越富裕，他们也为西方领先企业的商品和服务提供了一个更大的市场——从快餐连锁店到消费品再到奢侈品。中国劳动力不仅组装苹果手机和平板电脑，而且渴望购买这些产品；中国已成为苹果产品全球第二大市场，丰厚的产品利润几乎全部流回到其位于美国的公司。2011年，通用汽车在中国销售的汽车比在美国还多，中国快速增长的市场成为这家标志性的美国企业生存的至关重要的因素。中国已成为麦当劳全球第三大市场，也是必胜客、塔可钟和肯德基这些品牌的美国母公司全球利润的主要引擎。

仅仅用了一代人多一点的时间就将一个有10亿农村人口的国家改变成为一个几乎有10亿城市人口的国家，这不是一件容易的事情。以这样惊人的速度发展工业和经济，必然会带来巨大的社会成本。

四 非洲与中国的贸易

根据世界银行负责非洲事务的副行长的说法，中国与非洲的贸易远在以投资为主的当前阶段以及伴随其的各种观点出现之前就已开始。比如，坦桑尼亚就曾出土过1000多年前中国宋代（960—1279）的钱币。中国的商船曾在14世纪抵达肯尼亚，留下了大量中国瓷器，同时将那里的长颈鹿带回了中国。

非洲经济自20世纪90年代中期以来经历了明显的好转。1995至2013年，实际GDP年均增长4.5%，五分之一的非洲国家实现了7%或更高的年均增长率。非洲的经济增长可与其他地区的发展中国家媲美；事实上，只有亚太地区的增长速度超过了非洲。这一时期，非洲的经济规模翻了一番（扣除物价因素）。最近对国民账户重新定基计算的结果显示，加纳的经济体量比之前认为的大60%，而尼日利亚则是之前的1.8倍。这说明非洲经济体量在这一时期的增长可能比之前认为的更高。

预测显示，2015年非洲的经济增长率为4.6%；得益于基础设施投资、农业产量增加和服务业领域扩大等因素，2017年的增长率将达5.1%。就外部因素而言，非洲的增长与大宗商品的繁荣密切联系在一起——中国的经济增长和中国作为非洲贸易和投资伙伴出现，以及跨境资金流动等。就内部因素而言，非洲在宏观经济管理上的完善和可持续发展使得通胀率更低、财政决算结果更好以及增长波动更低。危机波动大幅降低，因为本地区变得更不容易受到宏观经济灾难的影响。非洲大陆为经受住2008年金融危机所采取的方式很好地证明了非洲经济的复原力。此外，监管环境也得到了完善，这一点体现在不断向好的营商指数。

对非洲的这一经济增长现象也有一些警告：这一增长是基于要素积累，特别是在资金密集型领域；"贫困—增长"弹性非常低；创造的有质量的就业机会很少，导致收入增长不足；增长主要在资金密集型和低生产率领域；高生育率造成人均增长率低于其他发展中国家等等。非洲的这一要素积累模式将面临局限，因为我们现在已进入了一个低商品价格的时代。

1. 生产率

非洲实际GDP的稳步增长（在过去10年的年均增长率为5%）得益于通货膨胀、财政赤字和金融可持续性方面的强劲基本面支撑。这来自于要素积累，因为对自然资源和其他大宗商品的投资促进了劳动力的增长。正如这样的增长是积极的一样，事实上，要素积累贡献了 2.1% 的人均 GDP 实际增长。伴随这样增长的是生产率的提高，同时人口的高增长率也进一步限制了这样的增长。底线是，非洲的经济体必须应对生产率的挑战，从而取得可持续的、分享的增长并减少总体贫困。

　　制造业不是从出口自然资源向价值链上游移动的唯一途径。其他的可能途径还包括生产高附加值的农业产品，如尼日利亚的木薯粉、肯尼亚的鲜切花和马达加斯加的巧克力等。这些转变可以在某些方面提高农业生产力，而这正是非洲需要的。某些非洲国家已经在出口多元化方面取得了成功：卢旺达扩大了蔬菜和饮料的出口，而埃塞俄比亚则增加了皮革和园艺产品的出口。向制造业转型、向农业价值产业链上游移动和出口多元化这三种策略，可以促进非洲的经济体提高生产力和面对全球趋势的复原力。

　　关于非洲结构转变的因素和前提的辩论再次出现了。总的来说，以从低生产率活动到诸如制造业这样现代和高生产率领域的资源再次分配为特点的经济转型，在非洲的繁荣进程中是缺位的。这引发了辩论：可持续增长是需要向制造业转型；还是向质量阶梯的高端移动，这样可以利用和依靠现有的比较优势模式并保持增长。

2. 人力资本：教育

　　打造人力资源是中国崛起的一个主要手段。除了进行提高生产力的改革之外，中国还培育了大批高素质的人力资源。中国成年人平均受教育年限从 1950 年的 1.5 年增至 2010 年的 7.5 年，翻了 4 倍！显然，人力资源是中国实现惊人发展的众多有利因素之一。

　　如果以同一时期受教育年限这一简单标准衡量非洲的人力资源的话，非洲成人平均受教育年限从 1.3 年增至 5.2 年，也增长了 4 倍。但是，当我们考察受教育的质量时，会发现两者存在明显的差距。虽然没有直接比较中国各地与非洲各国的学习效果，但是两者之间确实存在真切的差距，所产生的相关影响也是深远的。

　　非洲需要熟练劳动力以便能够取得像中国一样的经济增长。与过去几十年的有限参与相比，世界银行和其他合作机构正在对高等教育给予姗姗来迟的重视，重点是针对学生进入职场和促进非洲增长和发展所需的大学课程内容和技能，尤其是科学和技术。掌握熟练技能的大学毕业生对非洲向价值链上游移动并显著地提高生产力水平是至关重要的。

3. 中国在非洲的几个项目

- 发电量为 2600 兆瓦的尼日利亚马比拉（Mambilla）水电站建设项目是本文所列的最大水电项目。项目的开工时间目前尚不确定。
- 目前已完成的最大电力项目是 1250 兆瓦的苏丹麦罗维（Merowe）大坝项目。
- 2008 年 11 月，深圳能源集团宣布，计划与尼日利亚第一银行合作在尼日利亚建立一个 3000 兆瓦的发电厂。该项目预计耗资 25 亿美元，计划于 2009 年初启动。尼日利亚总装机容量为 3500 兆瓦，但是由于电站老化、腐败和管理不善等原因，发电量有时仅为 1000 兆瓦，从而造成频繁断电。
- 2008 年 10 月，肯尼亚与中国水电建设集团签订了一项 6.5 亿美元的合同，在肯尼亚西部建造一个新的 20 兆瓦的水电站。这一名为"桑格罗水电站"的建设项目计划 3 年内完工。
- 2008 年 10 月，中国国际合作集团与莫桑比克签订了一项 4.5 亿美元的合同，在中部的马尼卡省（Manica）建设一个供水系统。该项目包括在 Chicamba 大坝建设一座新的水处理站以及建造 6 个储水罐。
- 2009 年 3 月，中国水电建设集团宣布将承建赞比亚卡里巴湖（Kariba）北岸的一个耗资 4 亿美元的发电厂项目。中国进出口银行为该项目提供 85% 的资金，南非发展银行提供剩余 15% 的资金。根据其 2030 年发展规划的愿景，赞比亚计划建设一系列的电力项目。
- 最后，中国水电建设集团承建加蓬 Poubara 水电站。该项目是耗资 30 亿美元的贝林加（Belinga）铁矿石项目的一部分。不过，尚不知晓中国对该项目的融资金额。

4. 聚焦《2063 年议程》：非洲的愿景

非洲联盟在《2063 年议程》中提出了 7 个愿景，包括：

1. 建立在包容性增长和可持续发展基础上的一个繁荣的非洲；
2. 一个政治上统一、建立在泛非主义理想和非洲复兴愿景基础上的一体化大陆；
3. 一个治理良好、民主、尊重人权、公正和法治的非洲；
4. 一个和平和安全的非洲；
5. 一个具有强烈文化认同、共同遗产、价值和道德标准的非洲；

6. 一个发展建立在以人为本基础上、发挥妇女和青年潜力的非洲；

7. 一个作为强大、统一和具有影响力的全球参与者和合作者的非洲。

非洲既在崛起，又有斗争。积极的一面是，非洲正在崛起成为全球经济的一个值得注意的参与者。这一地区的平均GDP增长率预计2016年和2017年分别增长4%和5%（世界银行，2015年）。非洲目前在外国直接投资增长上已经领跑世界其他地区（Fingar，2015年）。

尽管非洲对外国投资者的吸引力正在上升，但并非所有非洲国家都从中平等受益。某些国家获得了大部分的外国直接投资（如南非、尼日利亚、埃及、摩洛哥等），而另外的国家则没有赢得投资者的青睐（Ernest和Young，2014年）。

非洲是一个经济增长地区，跨国公司日益考虑在非洲投资。因此，对企业管理者而言，理解这一地区未来50年的路线图是非常重要的。《2063年议程》将可能为本地区带来积极影响和重要的制度性变革。

《2063年议程》旨在借鉴过去的经验教训，定位非洲未来50年的增长。最终的目标是确保3个理想的实现——所有非洲人民的统一、繁荣与和平。

《2063年议程》是一个全球性的战略滚动规划，包括短期（10年）、中期（10—15年）和长期（25—50年）规划。这一议程旨在使得非洲能够做得不同（以人为本），做得更好（权衡和审视），实现更好的治理，做出更好的成就，为人民带来更好的影响。

《2063年议程》重要的成功因素包括：多方利益团体在各个阶段的参与，具有量化目标、以结果为导向的路径，灌输与非洲复兴相一致的正确非洲价值观，实现态度、价值和心态的转变（非盟委员会，2015b；K. De-Ghetto et al，2016年）。

五 非洲发展的前景

更多的非洲人民现在享有了基本的政治权利；实现责任治理的努力取得了局部但却明显的进步，这为应对本地区发展经济和减少贫困的挑战提供了一个更好的平台。

冷战刚结束的时候，大多数非洲国家还是由单一政党、军人和其他个人强权政府组成的混合体所统治的。根据位于华盛顿的自由之家的统计，1989年非洲（撒哈拉以南地区，不包括袖珍岛国）只有3个"选举制的民主政体"，即博茨瓦纳、冈比亚和毛里求斯，总人口不到350万。根据这一数字计算，在当时的非洲，每100人中只有不到1人生活在达到最低自由和公平选举标准的国度。然而，2007年所做的最近评估显示情况发生了非常不同的变化。撒哈拉以南的民主国家已经壮大到20个，占该地区总人口的比例超过四分之一。

20年前，南非这个非洲经济和军事强国由白人少数政府统治，经常破坏邻国的稳定；而尼日利亚这个非洲人口最多的国家则接连不断的处于腐败军人政府的独裁统治之下。然而最近，同样是这两个国家，却站在了促进地区和平与发展的前沿。它们促成了一个新的非洲联盟的建立，其创立原则体现了政治领袖对"良好治理"日益增长的承诺。比如，去年晚些时候几内亚在其长期执政的总统去世后，发生了一场军事政变，随后该国的非盟成员国资格被立即暂停。

尽管出现了上述充满希望的趋势，但是过去20年发生的主要悲剧性灾难突出体现了存在于该地区的民主和发展面临的障碍。最大的不稳定因素也许就是20世纪90年代中期陡增的暴力冲突，尤其是中非大湖地区遭到了严重冲击。在卢旺达发生了种族灭绝恐怖行径之后，刚果民主共和国（前扎伊尔）出现了内战并蔓延至周边国家。根据国际救援委员会的调查，1998年以来，在冲突中直接和间接死亡的人数超过500万。根据某些统计结果，这一冲突是自第二次世界大战以来造成死亡人数最多的冲突。

与此同时，非洲死于艾滋病的人数也可与该地区战争导致的死亡人数相提并论。20世纪80年代末，这一传染病还处于传播初期。尽管统计数据还相当不确定，但是近年来非洲每年大约有150万人死于艾滋病。这意味着非洲每天死于艾滋病的人数比美国2001年9.11恐怖袭击事件中的死亡人数还多。

针对非洲面临的挑战，任何有价值的评估都必须考虑到该地区的活力和多样性。比如，国际社会的大量援助帮助刚果民主共和国走出了内战的阴霾。同时，针对艾滋病的公共政策得到了极大地完善，特别是在南非这个世界艾滋病毒感染者人数最多的国家。当津巴布韦自由落体式的崩溃——政府镇压加上恶性通货膨胀导致出现万亿面额的大钞——成为国际媒体头条新闻的时候，邻国博茨瓦纳却平稳地保持着世界最引人瞩目的可持续经济增长记录。

六 非洲的改革

虽然冷战结束后民主化浪潮的势头在非洲并未出现，但是20世纪80年代内部和外部的批评者已经开始就该地区独裁政府的执政提出了尖锐的问题。由于受到全球经济震荡和国内政治失败的拖累，该地区从20世纪70年代开始严重落后于世界其他地区的发展中国家。到20世纪80年代末，几乎每个非洲国家都与国际货币基金组织和世界银行签署了市场化改革的协定。对于缺乏资金的政府而言，这些协定提供了急需的资金援助，但是却规定了重要的附加条件。接受国被要求大幅减少预算赤字，贬值其货币，更大范围地减少国家对经济的干预。

不管这些颇受争议的改革方案会带来什么样的经济效益，它们却直接地动摇了非洲各国政府的政治基础。国际货币基金组织和世界银行希望削减的开支对维持政权的庇护者网络是至关重要的，而现行的政府干预模式则保护了核心政治团体在面对经济危机时不会完全束手无策。在国际金融组织的政策要求和国内政治生存需要两者的压力下，非洲国家政府的典型做法是通过不同程度的"部分改革"实现足够的政策改变，从而牵制外部资金提供机构，同时止步于最为敏感的政治领域。

从20世纪80年代末以来，大多数非洲国家政府保持了这一平衡，尽管这一做法使得它们遭到了来自双方越来越多的批评。尤其在工会组织强大的高度城市化国家，其削减公共部门就业机会和提高生活成本的政策遭到了强硬的国内政治反对。针对这一点，世界银行于1989年发布了一个标志性报告，认为"治理危机"是非洲经济问题的核心，呼吁进行制度性转变以便更加全面和有效地实施市场改革。

苏联的解体迅速扩大了非洲治理改革的议程范围。超级大国之间的竞争使得西方大国之前不愿意将双边的、政府对政府的援助与民主化挂钩。现在劳动分工出现了，国际货币基金组织和世界银行继续以"非政治化"政策和制度性改革为条件提供资金，而双边资金提供国，比如美国，则附加了后来被非正式地称为的"政治附加条件"。寻求保持外部资金援助的非洲国家政府面临着要求建立开放和竞争政权的日益强大的压力。这一背景鼓励了国内反对力量希望像他们的东欧同行一样，在"公民社会"的旗帜下大胆地发动力量，要求民主改革。

本地区之外发生的事件也是非洲民主化浪潮的一个关键催化剂。但是民主化推进的速度则反映了这一地区内部存在的紧张局势，这与独裁政府处理20世纪80年代经济困局的方式相关。

七 民主让非洲变得更好了吗？

非洲新的民主国家遭到的质疑并不少。许多分析家对这些国家的民主是否能够持续提出了质疑——如果不能持续，是否还能够为经济复苏和贫困扫除继续做出贡献？

其中一种质疑观点认为，现有民主国家缺乏结构上的"必要条件"。这里的一个关键前提是，民主化历史上就是更大范围社会转型的一个组成部分，涵盖诸如工业化、全民教育、一个更大规模的中产阶层的出现以及至少具备明显的国家认同感等进程。许多非洲国家目前的社会经济水平还很低，族群高度碎片化，这加大了对稳定民主所需的结构基础的忧虑。

另一种相关的质疑观点认为，非洲的政治转型是外部驱动的，不相信这些国家在后冷战时期与市场和民主的内在兼容性。20世纪80年代末非洲的紧张局势显示了更为棘手的现实情况。国内反对势力通常来自宣称市场改革已走得太远的那些团体，而世界银行关于"治理危机"的观点则认为改革进行得还不够。因此，民主化似乎可能一方面会使得市场政策的反对者获得权力，同时成功的市场改革需要仁爱的"发展性国家"，而不是民主政治短兵相接的肉搏战。

总而言之，怀疑者将非洲的民主浪潮解读为一个"历史偶然事件"，是狡猾的统治者对外部改革议程的回应，缺乏存在于非洲社会的制度性基础。正如非洲领导人在20世纪80年代设法摆脱了经济附加条件一样，他们现在正在设法规避政治附加条件的实质内容。通过定期举行大选，他们创造了民主合法性的表象，以保持援助资金的不断流入。但是即使在这样的表象得以维持的国家，民主所能带来的真正的发展收益似乎并不可能成为现实。

然而，非洲的民主国家却比最初期望的持续地更长，表现得更好。

国际因素在支持非洲民主方面发挥了重要作用。自冷战结束以来，全球形势使得非民主国家明显地感到不舒服，日益剥夺了其合法性和掌握的资源；非洲内部的趋势也强化了这一点。南非的政治转型使其成为本地区的主要大国，其理想目标和战略利益正在通过促进民主和人权得以实现。非洲联盟的成立和"非洲发展新型合作伙伴关系"倡议的通过（这一倡议将"良好治理"作为"可持续发展"的基本条件），体现了南非在地区政策方面的推动作用。虽然津巴布韦的危机明显地表明把一个精明老练和毫不妥协的独裁者赶下台是多么困难，但是民主规范在非洲的影响要远比 20 年前大得多。

同时，不断出现的证据似乎确认，在民主已经建立的那些非洲国家，国家倾向于作为经济发展的代理人做出更好的表现。这似乎得益于对领导人的自由决定权施加的制度性约束，而推翻未能改善人民福祉的政府的能力则支撑了这一点。与之形成对比的是，本地区最具灾难性的发展失败事件，包括津巴布韦当前的经济滑坡，都是由于宪法制约和平衡的缺失或打破而变得失控。民选政府对经济的政策观点是没有垄断的；但是在民主政体下，由于"坏的经济"最终会变成"坏的政治"，这使得政府有强烈的动力去做出改变。

考虑到非洲的多样性，任何对民主和发展前景的笼统概括都会产生误导。以下笔者将简要讨论一下特别值得在今后追踪的三个领头羊国家。

第一，刚果民主共和国是后冲突时代重建和平的一个重要案例。和之前的塞拉利昂和利比里亚一样，刚果民主共和国从联合国和地区组织获得了大量援助。2006 年举行的总统大选是可信但是在技术上有缺陷的，这加强了对内战的脆弱政治解决。该国目前政治派别复杂，基础设施十分脆弱，不能够满足选举民主的可接受标准（尽管其国名叫"民主共和国"）。即使非常有限的进步也会刺激地区发展，但是目前出现的相对和平的破裂可能再次使得中非地区陷入动荡。

第二，尼日利亚是 2007 年总统大选之后脱离选举民主俱乐部的国家，那次大选充满舞弊和暴力。在尼日利亚，这一被高度质疑的大选让国家管理体系面临无法承受的压力。作为该地区的主要大国，尼日利亚下一轮全国大选将被密切关注。

第三，南非年轻的民主体制面临的挑战有所不同。尽管该国民选政府的记录是具有榜样作用的，但是其最初的四次大选均是执政的非国大一次比一次赢得了更多的多数选票——其在 2004 年大选中赢得了 70% 的选票。该党在姆贝基总统任期结束前要求其辞职的决定造成了内部的分裂。

非洲的政变同时也导致了发展的停滞。非洲一些国家因为政变而出现经济滑坡。最近，津巴布韦正在经历一场有可能的动荡政变，目前局势处于停滞状态。

非洲需要向中国学习，放弃权力斗争，将重点放到确保非洲大陆向更好的方向前进。舶来的民主是否改变了非洲，还是给非洲带来了比期望的更多的问题，这一点是值得质疑的。非洲需要强有力的领导人确保国家上升到一个新的高度。非洲国家的政府需要向年轻人投资，特别是通过向他们提供高质量的教育这一方式。这是本地区发展的关键。

八 结论

非洲许多国家都可以学习中国。学习的核心要素是在所有领域保持纪律性，比如教育、金融、发展战略等。

腐败对本地区毫无益处，因为它使得非洲陷入瘫痪。中国已经通过在所有领域展现坚定的纪律性而赢得了消除贫困的斗争。非洲从目前的混乱中走出来，现在还为时不晚。需要一场伟大的革命，确保《2063年议程》的所有愿景目标得以实现。

我的祖国马拉维具有崛起的所有潜力要素。马拉维资源资源丰富，河流众多，但是灌溉并不被重视，人民不时死于饥饿。马拉维拥有足够的阳光可以开发为能源。马拉维拥有世界上最肥沃的土地，但是我们却仍在为了生存与饥饿做斗争。非洲借鉴中国的发展模式，现在正当其时——我们每个人都需要一个更加美好的非洲。

Re-constructing Chinese Model Into Africa: Experience from Chinese Rapid Development

Donasius Pathera / Malawi

Compliance &Business Analyst, Domestic Taxes, Malawi Revenue Authority

I. Introduction

The obvious fact is that China has changed dramatically from a poor nation to one of the richest countries in the world. Since China began its market reforms in the late 1970s, it has lifted more than 800 million people out of poverty, slashing the rate from nearly 90% in 1981 to under 2%, as measured by the World Bank's latest spending benchmark.

Statistics have shown that poverty remains a tragedy to humanity. World Bank data show that of the one in 10 people in the world still living on under $1.90 a day, more than half are in Africa. The ranks of the extremely poor in sub-Saharan Africa have expanded since 1990—peaking in 2010 at 399 million (pdf, p.38). India, for its part, halved the share of its population living in poverty in the past two decades. Still, the country remains home to the largest number of poor people anywhere.

II. How China has Defied Odds

China is sometimes looked to for lessons on how to reduce poverty—and there are definitely many to be had. However, the story of how China lifted its hundreds of millions is a particular story of implementing the right policies at the right time in the right place, as the country took advantage of the rise of globalization.

1. Developing-country wages amid well-developed infrastructure

In 1978, Deng Xiaoping began the "reform and opening-up". It allowed a return to family farming. That led to dramatic gains in agricultural incomes and savings, helping to provide funding for the industrial and urbanization coming next.

When companies first began to shift factories from the developed world, wages were low in China. Even by 2004, Chinese factory workers earned an estimated 64 cent per hour, as compared to 2.48$ in Mexico, the lowest hourly compensation among the 30 foreign countries measured by the US Bureau of Labor Statistics. But low wages alone may not have made China that much more attractive than other countries with large, low-paid labor forces.

In the 1980s, China launched major efforts to build dams, irrigation projects, and highways. The "Food-for-Work" program, which offered free meals to workers, promoted highway construction in rural areas. Between 1994 and 2000, some 42,000 kilometers (26,100 miles)—about 1,200 kilometers a day—of rural highways were built a year. (Even now, India manages just about 20 kilometers a day.)

Arthur Kroeber, founding partner at Gavekal Dragonomics, a China-focused research consultancy founder, in his 2016 book *China's Economy* wrote:

"By the early 2000s, China had a unique and probably unrepeatable combination of low, developing-country wages and good, almost-rich-country infrastructure. The combination of low-wage workers with a basic education—adult male literacy was about 80% in 1980—drew foreign investment in factories and created millions of jobs. China's per capita GDP went from being less than Bangladesh's in 1980—

under $200—to more than $8,000.

2. The revolution in cargo transport

China was well-prepared for the offshoring of factories from the West. Yet the factories wouldn't have headed to China without gains in telecommunications and transportation that made it possible to manage far-flung supply chains, boosting global trade. At the heart of those changes was what seemed a relatively simple innovation—the shipping container, invented in 1956, and not widely adopted until about two decades later. The container made it easier to load more on ships and do it more quickly—allowing for bigger ships and cheaper cargo costs. According to the Economist (paywall), "containers have boosted globalization more than all trade agreements in the past 50 years put together." Now, more than half a century after their appearance, most of the gains from its adoption may have already been made.

3. Innovation in consumer electronics

Personal computers. Walkmans. Mobile phones. All these ground-breaking gadgets started to change consumers' lives in the 1980s and 1990's—opening up new lines of manufacturing. China's export boom over that period was largely driven by electronics and machinery. Between 1992 and 2005, Chinese manufacturing exports shifted significantly from agriculture and soft goods, such as textiles and clothing, to higher-value items like consumer electronics and appliances. And as demand for these goods was about to explode, barriers to selling to the biggest markets—the US and Europe—were coming down, particularly after China entered the World Trade Organization in 2001.

China's share of global exports reached 13.8% in 2015, the highest share any country has enjoyed since the US almost 50 years ago.

III. Advancement Brings New Challenges

China's own battle against poverty isn't quite over, of course. By the end of 2016, there remained more than 43 million Chinese citizens still living below the nation's official poverty line of 2,300 yuan annual income (about 350$), measured in terms of 2010 purchasing power. China says it aims to wipe out poverty by 2020, with CPC vowing to build a "moderately prosperous society" ahead of the 100th anniversary.

To be frank, the rise of China surely ranks among the most important world developments of the last 100 years.

Meanwhile, as China's growth gradually doubles total world industrial production, the resulting "China price" reduces the cost of manufactured goods, making them much more easily affordable to everyone, and thereby greatly increases the global standard of living. While this process may negatively impact those particular industries and countries directly competing with China, it provides enormous opportunities as well, not merely to the aforementioned raw-material suppliers but also to countries like Germany, whose advanced equipment and machine tools have found a huge Chinese market, thereby helping to reduce German unemployment to the lowest level in 20 years.

Figure 1,2   1,250 MW Merowe Dam Hydropower project in Sudan

And as ordinary Chinese grow wealthier, they provide a larger market as well for the goods and services of leading Western companies, ranging from fast-food chains to consumer products to luxury goods. Chinese workers not only assemble Apple's iPhones and iPads, but are also very eager to purchase them, and China has now become that company's second largest market, with nearly all of the extravagant profit margins flowing back to its American owners and employees. In 2011 General Motors sold more cars in China than in the U.S., and that rapidly growing market became a crucial factor in the survival of an iconic American corporation. China has become the third largest market in the world for McDonald's, and the main driver of global profits for the American parent company of Pizza Hut, Taco Bell, and KFC.

Transforming a country in little more than a single generation from a land of nearly a billion peasants to one of nearly a billion city-dwellers is no easy task, and such a breakneck pace of industrial and economic development inevitably leads to substantial social costs.

IV. Africa and China Trade

According to Makhtar Diop, World Bank Vice President for the Africa, trade between China and Africa began long before this current phase of investments and the range of views that have accompanied it. For example, Chinese coins from the Song dynasty, more than one thousand years ago (960-1279), have been recovered in Tanzania. There were Chinese ships sailing on the coast of Kenya in the 1400s, leaving Chinese porcelain behind and taking giraffes back to China with them.

Africa has seen a remarkable turnaround in economic growth beginning in the mid-1990s. Real GDP growth has averaged 4.5 percent a year during 1995-2013, with nearly one-fifth of countries in the region growing at an average rate of 7 percent or better. The region's growth has been comparable to that of developing countries outside the region, and has been outperformed only by East Asia and the Pacific region. Overall, the size of the regional economy has more than doubled (in real terms) during this period. The results of recent rebasing of the national accounts— the size of Ghana's economy was 60 percent larger than previously thought and Nigeria's was around 80 percent larger—suggest that the increase in Africa's economic size during this period is likely to be even larger than previously thought.

Prospects were for Africa to grow by 4.6% in 2015, and reach a growth level of 5.1% in 2017, lifted by infrastructure investment, increased agricultural output, and an expanding services sector. On the external front, African growth has been closely linked to the commodities boom – growth in China and the emergence of China as one of Africa's main trade and investment partners – as well as the surge in cross-border financial flows. On the internal front, improved and sustained macroeconomic management in the Region has resulted in lower inflation, better fiscal outcomes, and lower growth volatility. Crisis volatility was sharply reduced as the Region became less susceptible to macroeconomic disasters. The way in which the African continent weathered the 2008 financial crisis is a good indication of African Economic Resilience. In addition, the regulatory environment has improved, as reflected in our rising Doing Business indicators.

All that said, there are some caveats to this African Growth: it has been based on factor accumulation, particularly in capital-intensive sectors; there has been a very low poverty-to-growth elasticity; there has been low creation of quality jobs, leading to insufficient income growth; growth has been more rapid in capital-intensive/low-productivity sectors; and per capita growth has been lower than in other developing countries due to the high fertility rate. This factor accumulation model in Africa will face limitations as we now move into a period of lower commodity prices.

1. Productivity

Africa's steady growth in real GDP – averaging 5% per year over the past decade, was possible thanks to strong underlying fundamentals in terms of inflation, fiscal deficits and financial sustainability. It resulted from factor accumulation as investments in extractives and other commodities helped to grow the labor force. As positive as such growth is, in fact it equates to 2.1% per capita real growth: it has not been accompanied by an increase in productivity, and has been further limited by high rates of population growth. The bottom line is this: African economies must address the challenges of productivity in order to achieve sustained, shared growth and reduce overall poverty.

Manufacturing is not the only way to move up the value chain from exports of extractives. There is also the possibility of producing higher-value agricultural products, such as cassava flour in Nigeria, cut flowers in Kenya, or chocolate in Madagascar. These shifts may deliver some of the agricultural productivity gains that Africa needs. Some African countries have demonstrated success in diversifying exports: Rwanda has expanded exports of vegetables and beverages, while Ethiopia has expanded leather exports as well as horticulture. All three of these strategies – shifting into manufacturing, moving up the agriculture value chain, and diversifying across exports – can help Africa's economies increase both productivity and resilience to global trends.

There has been a resurgence in the debate over the factors and prerequisites to structural transformation in Africa. Overall, economic transformation characterized by a reallocation of resources from low-productivity activities into modern, high-productivity sectors such as manufacturing has been lacking from Africa's boom. This has fueled a debate on whether sustainable growth in fact requires a shift in favor of manufacturing (as advocated by McMillan, Rodrik, Verduzco-Gallo); or moving up the quality ladder in sectors where countries can exploit and build on their current patterns of comparative advantage and sustain growth (as espoused by Hausmann and Hidalgo).

2. Human Capital: Education

Moulding human capital is one essential tool for the rise of China. Beyond reforms that increased productivity, China has nurtured a population with high levels of human capital. The average years of schooling for Chinese adults (ages 15 and up) rose from 1.5 in 1950 to more than 7.5 in 2010, a fivefold increase! Clearly human capital has been one of many enabling factors in China's meteoric growth.

When we look at human capital in Africa by the simple metric of years of schooling during the same period, average years of schooling rose from 1.3 to 5.2, a four-fold increase. The really stark differences arise, however, when we examine the quality of schooling. While there are no direct comparisons of learning outcomes in various regions of China versus individual countries in Africa, there is a very real disparity between learning outcomes – with profound related impacts – in Africa and China.

Africa needs a skilled labor force in order to experience growth like China's. After decades of limited engagement in post-secondary education, the World Bank Group and other partners are directing a long-overdue focus on higher education and, most importantly, on the content of university studies and the skills students need to enter the job market and contribute to Africa's growth and development – notably, science and technology. Skilled graduates are crucial for Africa to move up

Fugyre 3   Chinese funded 2 600 MW Mambilla power scheme in Nigeria

the value chain and achieve critical productivity increases (Makhtar Diop, World Bank Vice President for the Africa Region Beijing, China).

3. Some Chinese Projects in Africa

• The largest hydropower project on this list is the 2 600 MW Mambilla scheme in Nigeria, implementation of which is now uncertain.

• The largest power project completed to date is the massive 1 250 MW Merowe dam in Sudan

• **November 2008** China's Shenzhen Energy Group announced that it was planning to go into partnership with the First National Bank of Nigeria PLC, to build a 3000 MW power plant in Nigeria. The estimated cost of the project is 25 billion US$, with a commencement date for early in 2009. Nigeria's total installed capacity is 3500 MW but frequent power disruptions sees power generating capacity collapse to just 1000 MW on occasions due to poor maintenance its aged power stations, corruption and mismanagement.

• **October 2008** Kenya awarded a 65 million US$ contract to Sinohydro

Corporation to build a new 20MW hydroelectric power plant (HEP) in Western Kenya. The new HEP, Sangoro plant, will be located 5km downstream from Sondu Miriu HEP. The project is expected to be completed within three years.

• **October 2008** China's International Cooperation Group (CHIC O) has been awarded a 45 million US$ contract by Mozambique to construct a supply system in the central province of Manica. The project will include the construction of a new water treatment station at Chicamba Dam and six water storage tanks.

• **March 2009** it was announced that China's Sinohydro Corporation will undertake construction of a 400 million US$ power plant on the Kariba North Bank in Zambia. China's Export and Import Bank is providing 85 percent of the funding, while the Development Bank of South Africa (DBSA) is providing the remaining 15 percent. Zambia intends to develop a number of power projects in alignment with its vision for the 2030 development plan.

• Finally, the Poubara hydropower dam in Gabon is to be built by Sinohydro as part of the 3 billion US$ Belinga Iron Ore project; however, the amount of Chinese financing committed into the project is not known.

IV. Reflecting on Agenda 2063: Africa's Aspirations

African Union has seven aspirations for Agenda 2063. The aspirations are:

1. A prosperous Africa based on inclusive growth and sustainable development
2. An integrated continent, politically united and based on the ideals of Pan Africanism and the vision of Africa's renaissance
3. An Africa of good governance, democracy, respect for human rights, justice and the rule of law
4. A peaceful and secure Africa
5. An Africa with a strong cultural identity, common heritage, values and ethics
6. An Africa where development is people driven, unleashing the potential of its women and youth
7. Africa as a strong, united and influential global player and partner

Africa is both in a position of emergence and a position of struggle. On a positive note, Africa is emerging as a noteworthy player in the globe economy. The region's average gross domestic product (GDP) is expected to rise between 4% and 5% in the 2016 and 2017 (World Bank, 2015). Africa is currently outpacing other regions in terms of foreign direct invest (FDI)growth (Fingar, 2015).

Although Africa's attractiveness to foreign investors is on the rise, all countries are not benefitting equally. Certain countries receive a substantial share of FDI (i.e South Africa, Nigeria, Egypt, Morocco) while others fail to capture investors' attention (Ernest and Young 2014).

Africa is a growth region, and multinationals are increasingly considering investment. Thus, it is important for managers to understand the region's roadmap for the next 50 years. The Agenda will likely have positive impacts on the region and result in important institutional changes.

Agenda 2063 aims to position Africa for growth over the next 50 years, incorporating lessons and experiences from the past. The ultimate goal is to secure three ideals-unity, prosperity, and peace-for all its citizens.

It is a global strategic rolling plan with short (10 years), medium (10-25 years), and long term (25-50 years) perspectives. Agenda 2063 is aimed at getting Africa to do things differently (people centred), bigger (scaling and scoping up), and better governance, performance outcomes, impact on citizens, etc.

Critical success factors for Agenda 2063 include the participation of multiple stakcholder groups at all stages, a results-based approach with measurable objectives, and inculcating the right set of African values in line with the African Renaissance which suggests the transformation of attitudes, values, and mindsets (African Union Commission-AUC),2015b) K. DeGhetto et al, 2016).

V. Developmental Sights in Africa

Many more Africans now enjoy basic political rights, and a clear yet partial move toward accountable governance offers a better platform for tackling the region's steep challenges of economic development and poverty reduction.

When the Cold War ended, most of Africa was ruled by a mixed bag of single-party, military, and other personalized "big man" regimes. According to the Washington-based Freedom House, in 1989 the region (south of the Sahara and excluding island microstates) was home to only three "electoral democracies"—Botswana, Gambia, and Mauritius—with a combined population of less than 3.5 million. By this count, less than one in every hundred Africans lived in countries that met minimum standards of free and fair electoral competition. The most recent ratings, for 2007, paint a very different picture. The number of sub-Saharan democracies has swelled to 20, accounting for more than a quarter of the region's population.

Two decades ago, Africa's economic and military powerhouse—South Africa—was ruled by a white minority government that regularly destabilized its neighbors, while its most populous country—Nigeria—was suffering under a series of corrupt military dictatorships. More recently, these same two countries have been at the forefront of initiatives to promote regional peace and development. They helped launch a new African Union (AU), whose founding principles reflect growing commitment to "good governance" among political leaders. For example, when a military coup followed the death of Guinea's long-time president late last year, the country's AU membership was immediately suspended.

Despite these promising trends, major tragedies of the past 20 years have highlighted obstacles to democracy and development in the region. Perhaps most destabilizing was a sharp spike in violent conflict during the mid-1990s, with the Central African Great Lakes region especially hard hit. Following the horrors of the Rwandan genocide, a civil war in the Democratic Republic of Congo (formerly Zaire) spilled over the borders into neighboring countries. According to the International Rescue Committee, the conflict has directly and indirectly claimed more than five million lives since 1998. This by some reckonings makes it the deadliest international conflict since World War II.

Meanwhile, the death toll due to HIV/AIDS in Africa rivals that of the region's wars. The pandemic was still in its infancy in the late 1980s. Though estimates are subject to considerable uncertainty, in recent years it appears that the disease has been killing at a rate of approximately one and a half million annually in Africa. To put this figure in perspective, it means that more Africans are dying of HIV/AIDS every day than died in the September 11, 2001, attacks on the United States.

Any useful assessment of Africa's challenges must account for the dynamism and diversity of the region. For example, considerable international assistance has helped the Democratic Republic of Congo emerge from civil war. Meanwhile, public policy responses to HIV/AIDS have improved considerably, particularly in South Africa, which has the largest HIV-positive population in the world. And while crises like Zimbabwe's free-fall—combining state repression with inflation rates running into the trillions—grab international headlines, directly next door Botswana has quietly maintained one of the world's most impressive records of sustained economic growth.

VI. Any Reform in Africa

Though the wave of democratization in Africa did not gain momentum until after the Cold War ended, in the 1980s critics inside and out began asking tough questions about the performance of the region's authoritarian governments. Dragged down by global economic shocks and domestic policy failures, from the 1970s the region was falling sharply behind developing economies elsewhere. By the late 1980s, nearly every African country had formally adopted a market-oriented reform agreement with the International Monetary Fund (IMF) and the World Bank. For cash-strapped governments, these agreements unlocked much-needed financial assistance, but with major strings attached. Recipients were required to reduce budget deficits substantially, devalue their currencies, and more generally scale back state intervention in their economies.

Whatever the economic merits of these controversial reforms, they struck directly at the political foundations of African governments. Expenditures that the IMF and World Bank wanted cut were central to patronage networks that helped keep incumbents in power, while existing patterns of state intervention helped shield politically pivotal groups from the full brunt of the economic crisis. Squeezed between the policy demands of international financial institutions and the domestic imperatives of political survival, governments typically responded with varying degrees of partial reform—delivering enough policy change to keep external donors at bay, while dragging their feet on the most politically sensitive items.

Through the end of the 1980s, most governments maintained this balancing act, though doing so exposed them to mounting criticism from both sides. Highly urbanized countries with strong trade-union movements faced particularly stiff domestic political opposition to policies that scaled back public-sector employment and raised the cost of living. From its side, the World Bank released a landmark 1989 report arguing that a "crisis of governance" was at the heart of Africa's economic problems, calling for institutional changes to enable fuller and more effective implementation of market reforms.

The collapse of the Soviet Union quickly expanded the agenda of governance reform in Africa. Superpower rivalry had previously discouraged Western powers from linking bilateral, government-to-government aid to democratization. Now a division of labor emerged in which the IMF and World Bank continued to make their funds conditional on "apolitical" policy and institutional changes, while bilateral donors like the United States added what came to be known informally as "political conditionality". African governments seeking to maintain flows of external financial assistance confronted increasingly strong pressures toward establishing open and competitive political regimes. This environment emboldened domestic opposition groups who, like their Eastern European counterparts, mobilized behind the banner of "civil society" in demanding democratic reform.

Events outside the region were a crucial catalyst for Africa's wave of democratization. But the speed of the wave reflected existing tensions within the region, which were related to the ways authoritarian governments handled the economic difficulties of the 1980s.

VII. Has Democracy Made Africa Better

No shortage of skepticism greeted Africa's new democracies. Many analysts questioned whether they would last—and, if so, whether they would make any significant contribution to economic recovery and poverty reduction.

One set of doubts stemmed from the absence of structural "requisites" observed in established democracies. A key premise here was that democratization has historically been part of a broader social transformation—encompassing processes like industrialization, mass education, the ascendancy of a large middle class, and at least a clear sense of national identity. Many African countries remain at low levels of socioeconomic development and are highly ethnically fragmented, raising concerns about the structural bases for stable democracy.

A related set of doubts sprang from the perception that Africa's political transition was externally driven, while questioning post-Cold War faith in the inherent compatibility of markets and democracy. Tensions within Africa during the late 1980s revealed a messier reality. Domestic opposition typically emanated from groups who claimed that market reforms had gone too far, while the World Bank's own views about a "crisis of governance" implied that they had not gone far enough. In this view, democratization seemed likely to have the effect of empowering the opponents of market-oriented policies, while successful market reform would require benevolent "developmental states" insulated from the cut and thrust of democratic politics.

In general, skeptics have interpreted Africa's wave of democracy as almost a "historical accident"—the product of wily rulers' responses to an external reform agenda and lacking structural foundations in African societies. Just as African leaders managed to sidestep economic conditionality in the 1980s, they were now dodging the substance of political conditionality. By staging periodic elections, they created a facade of democratic legitimacy and kept donor funds flowing. But even where the facade was maintained, any genuine developmental benefits of democracy seemed unlikely to materialize.

International factors have played an important role in supporting African democracy. Since the end of the Cold War, the global climate has become decidedly more uncomfortable for nondemocratic governments, which are increasingly deprived of legitimacy and resources, and trends within Africa have reinforced this. South Africa's own political transition has given the region a dominant power whose ideals and strategic interests both are served by promoting democracy and human rights. The launch of the AU and its adoption of the New Partnership for Africa's Development (NEPAD)—an initiative that identifies "good governance" as an essential "condition for sustainable development"—embody the thrust of South Africa's regional policy. While the Zimbabwean crisis starkly illustrates how difficult it is to dislodge a skilful and intransigent dictator, democratic norms are much more influential in Africa than they were two decades ago.

Meanwhile, emerging evidence seems to confirm that, in African countries where democracy has been established, states have tended to perform better as agents of economic development. These effects seem to hinge on the benefits of imposing institutional checks on leaders' discretionary authority, backed by the ability to remove governments that fail to improve the well-being of their people. By contrast, the region's most catastrophic developmental failures—including Zimbabwe's current plunge—have only spun out of control when constitutional checks and balances have been absent or dismantled. Democratically elected governments have no monopoly on economic insight, but under democratic regimes "bad economics" eventually becomes "bad politics", giving government's strong incentives to change course.

In light of Africa's diversity, any sweeping generalization about prospects for democracy and development would be misleading. In conclusion, I briefly discuss Three bellwether countries that are particularly worth tracking in the coming months and years.

First, the Democratic Republic of Congo is a crucial case of post conflict peace building. Like Sierra Leone and Liberia before it, it has benefited from considerable assistance from the United Nations and regional organizations. Credible but technically flawed presidential elections in 2006 reinforced a fragile political settlement of civil war. The country is plagued by complex political divisions and extremely weak infrastructure and does not currently meet accepted standards of electoral democracy (despite its name). Even very modest progress would boost regional development, but a collapse of the relative peace now prevailing could again destabilize Central Africa.

Second, Nigeria is a country that slipped out of the club of electoral democracies following 2007 presidential elections plagued by massive fraud and violence. In Nigeria, a hotly contested election put the administrative machinery under strain it could not withstand. As one of the region's leading powers, Nigeria's next round of national elections will be closely scrutinized.

Third, South Africa faces a somewhat different challenge to its young democracy. Though the country's record of electoral administration has been exemplary, its first four general elections have seen the ruling African National Congress (ANC) win large and increasing majorities—its 2004 vote share approaching 70 percent. However, the party's decision to "recall" President Thabo Mbeki before the end of his term prompted an internal split (Rod Alence, The Journal of the International Institute, 2009).

The coups in Africa have also contributed to the development retardation. There are countries in Africa who have suffered coups resulting into "economic plunge". Recently, Zimbabwe is going through a tumultuous possible coup and things are at a standstill.

Africa needs to learn from China that instead of fighting for power, they need to be focused to ensure that the continent moves for the better. It's doubtful if the imported democracy into Africa has changed Africa, it has created more problems than what Africans anticipated. Africa needs strong leaders to ensure that their countries are taken to new heights. There is need for African Governments to invest in the youth especially by providing quality education, this is key to the development of the region.

VIII. Conclusion

There is a lot African countries can learn from China, and the core element is the discipline in all areas.

Corruption has not done good for the region as it has crippled the region. China has won the battle against poverty through the unwavering discipline in all sectors. It's not too late for Africa to recover itself from the mess it is going through. There is need for a great revolutionary to ensure that all aspirations on Agenda 2063 are realised.

The country, I come from, Malawi has all the potential to rise. Malawi is rich in natural resources, for example, a lot of rivers that run throughout the year. Yet irrigation is not being taken seriously and at times some people die of hunger. The country has enough sun light that can be cultivated for solar energy. We have one of the richest soils for Agriculture yet we still struggle to survive from hunger. It's high time for Africa to learn from the Chinese model of development—a better Africa will be necessary for us all.

References

http://www.un.org/africarenewal/web-features/why-infrastructure-development-africa-matters

https://www.ashurst.com/en/news-and-insights/insights/road-infrastructure-in-africa/

https://qz.com/983460/obor-an-extremely-simple-guide-to-understanding- chinas-one-belt-one-road-forum-for-its-new-silk-road/

http://www.hindustantimes.com/analysis/why-india-needs-to-take-china-s- one-belt-one-road-initiative-seriously/story-OpfzM34MJoEyGLE7z8GkSI. html

https://www.ashurst.com/en/news-and-insights/insights/road-infrastructure-in-africa/

https://www.alitravelstheworld.com/malawi/malawi_road_2.jpg

http://www.nyasatimes.com/wp-content/uploads/The-upgraded-Masau- ko-Chipembere-Highway-600x377.jpe

http://www.transport.gov.za/Portals/0/images/2015/Umgeni_2015.jpg

http://www.nationsencyclopedia.com/economies/Africa/Malawi-INFRA- STRUCTURE-POWER-AND-COMMUNICATIONS.html

https://www.nytimes.com/2017/02/07/world/africa/africa-china-train.html

http://globalriskinsights.com/2017/06/three-domestic-challenges-chi- nas-one-belt-one-road-initiative/

https://www.google.com/search?source=hp&ei=T9QTWpepIYWsU4X- AreAN&q=Analysing+the+seven+aspirations+of+the+Agenda+2063&o- q=Analysing+the+seven+aspirations+of+the+Agenda+2063&gs_l=p- sy-846.0.25328.51.45.0.0.0.0.1211.9059.2-1j3j4j5j2j1.17.0..
..0...1c.1.64. psy-ab..34.11.6349.0..0j33i22i29i30k1j33i160k1j33i21k1.617.UABKLzT3eO8

https://quod.lib.umich.edu/j/jii/4750978.0016.202/--democracy-and-development-in-africa?rgn=main;view=fulltext

http://hdl.handle.net/2027/spo.4750978.0016.202

从军事合作到经济外交：中国与安哥拉关系变化的研究

托科库·英纳森特·奥可可 【尼日利亚】
阿布贾大学历史外交研究讲师

一 引言

本文主要研究中国与安哥拉关系的一个方面，重点关注促使两国关系不断变化的历史、理念和促进因素。在这一背景下，本文开篇对可追溯至安哥拉独立前的中安关系发展进行概述。特别是从1961年安哥拉解放斗争期间开始，北京支持解放运动。本文讨论了中国主要盟友安哥拉民族解放阵线（简称"安解阵"）和争取安哥拉彻底独立全国联盟（简称"安盟"）夺取政权的失败如何影响中国重新检视其外交政策、与崛起的安哥拉人民解放运动（简称"安人运"）修好。这一转变为两国在后独立时代进一步发展双边关系奠定了基础。

二 中安关系发展概述

对非洲反殖民主义运动的历史研究认为，中国在许多非洲国家争取民族独立的斗争中都起到了关键作用，其中也包括安哥拉。中国与安哥拉的关系可追溯至1961年，当时安哥拉争取解放的斗争刚刚开始。安哥拉欢迎中国对其反抗殖民统治争取民族解放的运动提供军事和政治支持。在安哥拉处于萌芽阶段的各种解放运动力量中，中国最初支持其中夺取政权的三个主要力量；后来，在其中两个力量崛起并被非洲统一组织（简称"非统"）正式认可为合法力量后，中国调整了政策，开始对这两个力量提供支持。中国对安盟和安解阵的青睐在1963和1964

年变得十分明显；两个力量的领导人与共产党中国的领导人见面，双方在军事培训和援助一系列关键问题上意见一致。1963年，安解阵领导人奥尔登·罗贝托（Holden Roberto）在内罗毕会见了中国外长陈毅。同时，1964年，安盟领导人若纳斯·萨文比（Jonas Savimbi）在中国见到了毛泽东主席和周恩来总理；他在中国接受了军事培训并成为了毛泽东思想的忠实拥护者。

冷战政治在中国与非洲关系中起到了决定性作用。安哥拉是一个很好的案例，因为在寻求冷战盟友的过程中，中国（也包括美国和南非）主要支持安盟和安解阵，而苏联和古巴则倾向于安人运。安哥拉解放运动各种力量的不同政治立场在很多方面明显体现了北京与莫斯科的分裂，而且显然与控制资源的斗争相关。安哥拉拥有巨大的石油资源并于1968年开始在卡宾达省海岸的浅水水域进行石油开采。这对安哥拉国家统一和解放产生了巨大影响后果。

北京与安人运短暂的外交关系在20世纪70年代实现了缓和，双方通过谈判达成了一系列协议，主要为安人运夺取政权提供了所需的帮助。安人运的军官接受了中国提供的军事培训、武器和其他装备，北京的目的是平衡苏联对安人运的影响力。安人运夺取了政权，巩固了对安哥拉大部分领土的控制，并于1975年11月宣布国家独立。但是这并没有为安哥拉带来所期望的统一与和平。

中国与安哥拉于1983年1月12日正式建交，随后分别于1984年和1988年签订了贸易协定和建立了经商处。这些里程碑式的事件体现了两国外交关系缓和的趋势。20世纪90年代后期进行了高层互访并实现了贸易的迅速增长。科尔金（Corkin）指出，两国关系的正常化与执政的安人运政府体现了外交边缘博弈，这使得苏联支持的安人运和与苏联对抗的中国达成了共识。因此，为了不因为寻求海外目标而使得国家主权受到侵害，中国以对安人运的支持换取该党领导的政府对"一个中国"的承认。换句话说，台湾以金元外交的方式寻求与安哥拉建立外交关系的努力在中安关系实现缓和的形势面前彻底失败了。表面上，作为这一形势发展的具体体现，安哥拉于1993年在北京设立了大使馆，这也是台湾与安哥拉建立双边关系的梦想彻底的破灭了。之后，由于香港、澳门和上海在安哥拉不断增长的投资，安哥拉于2007至2008年在上述城市分别设立了总领馆。

内战结束之后，基础设施的重建成为了安哥拉的当务之急。长达四分之一个世纪的内战摧毁了国家大部分的基础设施，经济面临危机，社会政治问题随之而来，战争造成的其他后果层出不穷。本文重点讨论后内战时代安哥拉面临的复杂问题的一个方面，旨在理解安哥拉如何通过与中国的基础设施外交来应对社会经济重建的挑战。

三 中国—安哥拉"石油换基础设施"外交的基础

考虑到安哥拉在20世纪初期发展和稳定的势头，在重建经济、解决人道主义危机和国家重心转移到发展上的努力中，忽视国际和多边援助在现实上是不可能的。关于安哥拉内战的后果，维基百科认为，内战在安哥拉导致了灾难性的人道主义危机，使得占其总人口三分之一的423万人流离失所。联合国2003年的评估结果显示，80%的安哥拉人民缺乏基本医疗，60%缺乏用水，30%的儿童5岁之前会死亡，全国人均预期寿命不到40岁。为应对这些挑战以及其他问题，这个非洲国家采取了以发展为导向的政策战略，旨在通过建立和加强伙伴关系获得外部资金。这一趋势正如期望的那样符合战后危局的要求，因为需要利用必要的发展政策和资金刺激经济复苏并进而保持社会政治稳定。正是在这一背景下，中国与安哥拉的关系在2002年之后显著地体现了从军事合作到经济参与的转型，以此作为实现发展的手段。毫无疑问，安哥拉的资源，特别是原油资源，为促进并支撑这一转型提供了主要经济价值。

尽管某些西方国家（如美国、葡萄牙、西班牙等国）和东方国家（如日本、印度、韩国等国）在安哥拉的石油经济中享有既得利益，但是这与今天中国在安哥拉的利益相比毫无疑问是不可相提并论的。正如本文将要分析的一样，以下的事件使得这一点变得显而易见：2004年3月中国副总理曾培炎访问安哥拉期间，中国通过其进出口银行向安哥拉提供了一笔总金额为20亿美元、以石油为担保的贷款额度；2007年9月，安哥拉与中国进出口银行在罗安达签署了新增20亿美元贷款额度的协议，以帮助安哥拉开展战后基础设施重建。这只是中国提供的一系列贷款计划的一部分。与这些慷慨的贷款计划巧妙挂钩的是中国对自然和矿产资源永无止尽的胃口，中国需要这些资源以支撑其不断发展的经济，保持其社会稳定，并进而维持其人民接受一个非民主的共产主义政府的合法性。取得这些战略性目标（以及其他目标）对两国都是至关重要的并需要一个健康的双边关系。中安两国之间频繁的高层互访以及涉及外交、政治、社会文化和经济领域的多个协定的签署也进一步地体现了两国在双边合作方面取得的稳步进展。

表1　　　中国与安哥拉政府官员之间的双边互访（1983-2007）

曾访问过安哥拉的中国高层官员	曾访问过中国的安哥拉高层官员
外交部副部长宫达非（1983年5月）	总统 Jose Eduardo dos Santos（1988年10月、1998年10月）
外交部部长钱其琛（1989年8月）	国民议会议长 Fernando Jose de Franca Dias Van Dunem（1993年11月）
国务院副总理朱镕基（1995年8月）	外交部长 De Mora（1994年3月）
外交部副部长李肇星（1996年4月）	安人运总书记 Lopo do Nascimento（1998年9月）
外交部部长助理吉佩定（1997年9月）	国防部长 KundyPayama（2000年5月）
外交部部长唐家璇（2001年1月）	安人运总书记 Joao Lourenco（2000年5月）
中央政治局委员李铁映（2001年10月）	国民议会议长 Roberto de Almeida（2001年5月）
全国政协副主席王文元（2002年4月）	安哥拉国家石油公司（Sonangol）首席执行官 Manuel Vicente（2004年3月）
外交部副部长杨文昌（2002年7月）	总理 Fernando da Piedade dos Santos（2004年5月、2006年11月）
国务院副总理曾培炎（2004年3月、2005年2月）	外交部长 Joao Bernardo de Miranda（2004年5月）
中国进出口银行行长羊子林（2004年9月）	安哥拉武装力量总司令 AgostinhoNelumbaSanjar 将军（2005年6月）
外交部副部长吕新华（2005年7月）	商务部长 Joaquim lcuma Muafuma（2006年9月）
工信部副部长蒋耀平（2005年11月）	外交部副部长 Irene Neto（2006年9月）
国务院总理温家宝（2006年6月）	教育部长 Antonio Burity da Silva（2007年10月）
中国进出口银行行长李若谷（2007年9月）	

来源：《安哥拉与中国：实用主义的伙伴关系》

四　中国—安哥拉"石油换基础设施"外交的理念和意义

尽管对其理念和实施有多种解读，但是中国与安哥拉之间的"石油换基础设施"外交的确是建立在某些理念基础之上且具有深刻的社会经济、政治和外交意义。首先，这一外交体现了安哥拉针对西方的胜利。安哥拉之前希望从西方金融机构获得重建资金，而西方国家提供资金是有一整套附加条件的。与治理和人权相关的问题成为安哥拉与西方关系的痛点，也成为安哥拉从西方控制的金融机构获得资金的障碍。附加条件这一传统方式没有解决安哥拉基础设施融资的需求，而中国的出现则实现了这一点。

在安哥拉与国际货币基金组织还在就贷款谈判时，中国进出口银行向安哥拉慷慨地提供了20亿美元低息贷款，以换取其每日向中国提供4万桶原油。尽管这一信贷安排没有一连串的附加条件并且偿还期更长，但是批评者指出这让安哥拉政府逃避了责任，而且长远来讲，从根本上侵犯了安哥拉人民的经济、社会和文化权利。

安哥拉的主权被认为会因为西方坚持需要满足其提出的一整套条件而受到影响。这样，中国的方案就具有了吸引力。根本来讲，这反映了安哥拉行使主权与西方要求良好治理之间严重的冲突，双方都在争夺占据上峰。尽管两者都重要，但是修复安哥拉在内战中被摧毁的基础设施在其战后经济复苏议程中至关重要。正是满足了这一需求，中国的出现（以及它的基础设施优惠贷款）推动了这一关键议程的实施。

此外，两国外交为签署这样规模的一揽子协议铺平了道路，这体现了双边关系的显著改善。因此，外交边缘政策（这使得两国关系从1983年实现正常化）意味着双边关系缓和，为以"石油换基础设施"协议为代表的中方强劲参与提供了舞台。换句话说，不管历史上有多少政治分歧，这些协议体现了双边关系中的一个重要进步。

同样，中安"石油换基础设施"外交是以进一步提升中非之间新的关系为主要特点的，尽管其也是第三世界团结运动的一个组成部分——这一运动寻求挑战建立在帝国主义基础上的国际关系不对称本质。从20世纪中叶以来，亚非关系就是南方为抗衡北方帝国主义影响力的回应努力的一个组成部分。南方大部分地区均有被北方殖民和新殖民势力长期统治的历史，这导致了当代格局在政治、经济和社会上的某些不平衡。因此，鼓励南方团结、合作和互助就成为了可以帮助南方国家与北方霸权国家在更公平基础上谈判的策略。在本文案例中，中国在安哥拉的出现增加了安哥拉的选项，扩大了外国投资者在其经济发展中的竞争，并有望在安哥拉逐步实现消除新殖民主义趋势的诺言。

中安"石油换基础设施"外交同时也有某种经济上的意义。这个一揽子交易协议是经济互助的代表案例，两国均在其中利用了各自的比较优势。尽管中国已经实现经济的高增长率并崛起为具有全球重要性的超级大国，为其增长和发展进一步提供动力依然是中国的优先任务。同样，石油资源丰富的安哥拉也需要社会经济基础设施网络为其发展提供支持，但却缺乏技术并需要资本投入。正是在这一比较优势（也包括比较劣势）的背景下，两国谈判达成了"石油换基础设施"一揽子协议，以此作为实现各自需求的经济战略。本质上讲，这代表了解决问题的一种互助途径。

此外，"石油换基础设施"外交体现了针对令人诟病的"武器换石油"交易的结构性转变；这一交易加剧了安哥拉的动荡，却为法国和美国公司带来了好处，如道达尔—菲纳—埃尔夫、雪佛龙、德士古、菲利普斯石油公司、埃克森美孚以及英国石油公司等。Madsen 的分析显示，法国和美国公司与安哥拉腐败的领导层进行了阴暗的交易，这是这个非洲国家依然不发达的原因之一。与之形成对比的是，"石油换基础设施"安排为资源利用所带来的有质量的改变（尽管仍有其局限），改变了安哥拉的经济和基础设施面貌，甚至安哥拉人民生活水平也得到了显著提高。这一点是非常有意义的。

五　结论

本文对中国与安哥拉关系的历史和变化进程进行了大致介绍。从独立前初期的合作到安哥拉独立后的 10 年，这期间两国关系主要受中国与苏联冷战对抗的影响。随着两国于 1983 年正式建立外交关系，中安关系得以改善并发展强劲。1993 年，安哥拉在北京的大使馆正式开放，这为下一个 10 年的合作奠定了基调，也为长期的内战日益接近终结并最终在 2002 年新千年来临之时实现停战做出了贡献。

本文重点关注中安基础设施外交的基础、理念和意义，对经济外交在分别实现两国能源和战后重建目标方面发挥的作用进行了背景研究。本文的结论是，尽管有各种问题，两国共同发展的政策在巩固双边关系和提高人们生活水平方面很大程度上是成功的。这一政策正在不仅以非常独特的方式改变人民生活和惠及双方，而且代表了更宏伟承诺的可行基础。具体而言，本文的结论是，随着基础设施发展所取得的成功，长期投资项目已经确立，双边关系正在加强。这意味着，两国关系开始在其他重要经济领域实现具体的发展，这将得益于基础设施所提供的服务。

另一个重要结论是，两国寻求建立多样化国际合作关系的努力具有坚实的基础。这得益于西方不愿为安哥拉战后重建提供资金，也得益于中国对能源来源多元化的需求。这代表了中安这两个南方国家在建立可行关系上所取得另一个成功。这些趋势所带来的社会经济和外交价值，体现了针对经济上邪恶的武器换石油交易（至今仍是安哥拉石油经济的特点之一）的富有成效的转变，对两国和世界的发展产生了不容置疑的深刻意义。

From Military Cooperation to Economic Diplomacy: A Study of the Changing Relations Between China and Angola

Tochukwu Innocent Okeke / Nigeria

Lecturer of the Department of History and Diplomatic Studies, University of Abuja

I. Introduction

Essentially, this paper studies an aspect of Sino-Angolan relations with a deliberate emphasis on the history, philosophy and dynamics of their changing relations. To set the context, it begins with an overview of the development of Sino-Angola relations which dates back to Angola's pre-independence era. Specifically, it began in 1961 in the midst of Angola's liberation struggle as Beijing switched its support for the liberation movements. The paper discusses how the failure of China's main allies, i.e. *Frente Nacional para Libertacao de Angola* (FNLA) and *Uniao National para a Independencia Total de Angola* (UNITA), in their bid to capture power in Angola contributed to the review of China's diplomacy towards rapprochement with the ascendant *Movimento Popular de Libertacao de Angola* (MPLA). This prepared grounds for further bilateral relationships between both countries in the post-independence period.

Further, the next section examines the foundation and growth of Sino-Angola oil for infrastructure diplomacy. This was a strategic policy response to the post civil war challenges of socio-economic reconstruction in Angola. The desirability of this policy choice was also underscored by the reluctance of Western donors to fund post civil war reconstruction in the war torn African country. With China's groundbreaking offer of initial $2 billion in 2004 and subsequent deals that run into billions of dollars, both countries set off the work of infrastructural development in Angola cutting across various sectors of the economy.

In addition, the paper also explores the philosophy and significance that underlines this policy approach. It evaluates how the ideas that drove the economic diplomacy have, in spite of some concerns, continued to strengthen ties between Angola and China.

II. The Development of Sino-Angola Relations: an Overview

The historiography of Africa's anti-colonial movement recognizes that China played a pivotal role during the struggle for the independence of many African states, of which Angola is a part. China's relations with Angola dates back to 1961 when Angolan struggle for emancipation began. The struggle welcomed China's military and political support in their quest for liberation from colonial domination. Among the budding liberation movements in Angola, China initially supported the major three[1] that vied for power, and later adjusted its support for the emergent two, after they

---
1   According to Indira Campos and Alex Vines, "Angola and China; A Pragmatic Partnership" in Jennifer Cooke (ed.), *US and Chinese Engagement in Africa, Prospect for Improving U.S.-China-Africa Cooperation,* Center for Strategic and International Studies (CSIS), Washington DC, July 2008, p. 34, The three major liberation movements were *Movimento Popular de Libertacao de Angola* (MPLA),*Uniao National para a Independencia Total de Angola* (UNITA) *and Frente Nacional para Libertacao de Angola* (FNLA). A slightly different opinion by Tareq Y. Ishmael, "The People's Republic of China and Africa" in *The Journal of Modern African Studies*, Vol. 9, No. 4, Dec., 1971, pp. 517-518, holds that the Angolan groups that competed for power were two; M.P.L.A. and F.N.L.A., but added that the third, G.R.A.E. (Republic of Angola Government in Exile) was the political wing of F.N.L.A.

were officially recognized by the Organization of African Unity (OAU) as legitimate movements.[1] China's preference for UNITA and FNLA became significantly visible when in 1963 and 1964, the leaders of both movements met with the leaders of the communist China and they agreed on a number of issues central to which was military training and assistance. In recognition of this, Campos and Vines notes that In 1963, Holden Roberto of FNLA met with Foreign Minister Chen Yi in Nairobi. Likewise, in 1964, Jonas Savimbi of UNITA met with Chairman Mao Zedong and Premier Zhou En-lai in China, where he received military training and became a disciple of Maoism.[2]

It is very important to note that the Cold War politics played a divisive role in China's relations with African states. The Angolan case is a good example because while China (United States and South Africa) mainly stood with UNITA and FNLA, Soviet Union and Cuba gravitated towards MPLA in their search of Cold War allies. Evidently, the political divisions in Angola amongst the liberation movements were clearly, in many ways, a reflection of the split that had occurred between Beijing and Moscow,[3] and was clearly not unconnected with the struggle to control resources. Angola has enormous deposits of oil resources and production from her shallow waters started off the coast of Cabinda province in 1968.[4] These had immense consequences for the unity and liberation of the Angolan state.

Beijing's short-lived diplomacy with MPLA reached a *détente* when in the 1970s both negotiated some agreements which principally yielded the needed front to prosecute the MPLA's contest for power. MPLA rose to power, consolidated its control of most of Angola and declared the independence of the country in November, 1975.

---

1 Indira Campos and Alex Vines, Angola and China.
2 *Ibid,* for similar perspectives also see Tareq Y. Ismael, pp. 517-518.
3 Lucy Corkin, China's Interest in Angola's Construction and Infrastructure Sectors', in Dorothy-Grace Guerrero and FirozeManji, *China's New Role in Africa and the South; a search for new perspective,* Published by Fahamu, Oxford, 2008, pp. 160-161.
4 Indira Campos and Alex Vines, Angola and China; *ibid,* p. 32.

Official ties between China and Angola had come into effect on 12th January, 1983, and was followed by the signing of Trade Agreements and establishment of Economic/Trade Commissions in 1984 and 1988 respectively.[1] These land mark events signified trends of conciliatory diplomacy between Angola and China. Again, inconsistent with the accusations of the early 90s, the late 90s were characterized by incidences of high level diplomatic visits between the two countries, whose trade volumes had increased tremendously.[2] This was an indication of the diplomatic brinkmanship that enabled both the Soviet-supported MPLA and the Soviet-rivaled China to find a common ground. Among other factors, China's diplomatic switch in favor of MPLA-controlled government must have also derived from Angola's potential recognition of Taiwan whose overtures to Angola was intensely pursued in the early 1990s. Therefore, rather than erode its sovereignty at home while pursuing its other objectives abroad, China *traded* its support for UNITA to earn MPLA-led government's recognition of one China. In other words, Taipei's (unsuccessful) bid to negotiate diplomatic ties with Angola in the 1990s using its dollar diplomacy collapsed in the face of Sino-Angola rapprochement. Ostensibly, as a practical demonstration of this development, Angola opened its embassy in Beijing in 1993, perhaps signifying the final demise of Taiwan-Angola *bilateral* dreams. Subsequently, in 2007/2008, Angolan consulates were established in Hong Kong, Macau and Shanghai owing to their growing investments.[3]

In the wake of the civil war, the challenge of infrastructural reconstruction (among others) became a major part of Angola's immediate concern. This is because, the devastation that accompanied the two and a half-decade civil war left the country's infrastructure largely destroyed, and the economy in crisis, the concomitant socio-political problems and other consequences of the war notwithstanding. Deliberately,

---

1 Lucy Corkin, *ibid*., pp. 160-161.
2 While Chinese Deputy Minister of Economy, Trade and Cooperation, Yang Wesheng visited Angola in October 1997, Angolan President dos Santos visited China in October 1998, where he met Beijing's high ranking officials including Premier Zhu Rongji, seeking to expand China-Angola bilateral relationship. For more, see Indira Campos and Alex Vines, Angola and China, p. 35.
3 Indira Campos and Alex Vines, Angola and China.

this research focuses on an aspect of the complex problems that confronted post-civil war Angola in other to understand, how the country grappled with the challenges of socio-economic reconstructions through infrastructural diplomacy with China.

III. The Foundation of Sino-Angola Oil-for-infrastructure Diplomacy

Given its developing and stability status in the early 2000s, it was pragmatically impossible for Angola to ignore international and bilateral assistance in its efforts to rebuild Angola economically, fix its humanitarian crisis and focus the country on the path of development. In the aftermath of the civil war in Angola, Wikipedia notes that the civil war spawned a disastrous humanitarian crisis in Angola, internally displacing 4.28 million people – one-third of Angola's total population. The United Nations estimated in 2003 that 80% of Angolans lacked access to basic medical care, 60% lacked access to water, and 30% of Angolan children would die before the age of 5, with an overall national life expectancy of less than 40 years of age.[1] To address these and several other issues, the African country (among other strategies) pursued a development oriented policy strategy aimed at accessing external funds through building and strengthening partnerships. This trend was expectedly consistent with the post war exigencies which required necessary development policies and capitals that would stimulate economic recovery, and by extension socio-political stability in Angola. It is against this backdrop that Beijing's relations with Angola after 2002 remarkably reflected that of a transition from military cooperation to economic engagement as means towards development. Expectedly, Angola's resources, particularly crude oil, provided the main economic value that lubricates and sustains this transition.

Although some countries of the West (such as the United States, Portugal, Spain, etc.) and the East (such as Japan, India, South Korea, etc.) have vested interests in the oil economy of Angola, today, China's is undisputedly unparalleled. As will be analyzed in this study, this became evident when in March 2004, during

---

1 http://en.wikipedia.org/wiki/Angolan_Civil_War#Aftermath<date accessed 18 November, 2012>

the official visit of Vice Premier Zeng Peiyang to Angola, through her Export and Import Bank (Exim Bank), China pledged an initial sum of US$2 billion oil-backed credit line to Angola and by September 2007, a new credit line of additional US$2 billion loan was signed in Luanda between Angola and China's Exim bank, to aid Angola's post-war infrastructural reconstruction process. These, however, were in addition to other funding arrangements provided by China. Neatly tied to these generous funding arrangements is China's insatiable appetite for natural and mineral resources needed to sustain its growing economy, maintain social stability and by extension preserve the legitimacy or the people's acceptance of the *non-democratic* communist government. Achieving these very strategic (and other) objectives was for both countries very crucial and requires a healthy relationship. Further reflective of the steady progress that both countries have made in their bilateral co-operations were frequent high profile visits to both China and Angola, and the signing of several agreements ranging from diplomatic, political, socio-cultural to economic.

Table 1: Bilateral Visits of State Officials between China and Angola, 1983-2007

Senior Visitors to Angola from China	Senior Visitors to China from Angola
Gong Dafei, vice minister of foreign affairs (May 1983)	José Eduardo dos Santos, president (October 1988 and October 1998)
Qian Qichen, minister of foreign affairs (August 1989)	Fernando José de França Dias Van Dunem, speaker of the National Assembly (November 1993)
Zhu Rongji, deputy prime minister (August 1995)	De Mora, minister of foreign affairs (March 1994)
Li Zhaoxing, vice minister of foreign affairs (April 1996)	Lopo do Nascimento, general secretary of the MPLA (September 1998)
Ji Peiding, assistant minister of foreign affairs (September 1997)	Kundy Payama, defense minister (May 2000)
Tang Jiaxuan, minister of foreign affairs (January 2001)	João Lourenço, general secretary of the MPLA (May 2000)
Li Tieying, member, political bureau,	

Central Committee of the Communist Party (October 2001)	Roberto de Almeida, speaker of the National Assembly (May 2001)
Wang Wenyuan, vice president, Chinese People's Political Consultative (April 2002)	Manuel Vicente, CEO, Sonangol (March 2004)
Yang Wenchang, vice minister of foreign affairs (July 2002)	Fernando da Piedade dos Santos, prime minister (May 2004 and November 2006)
Zeng Peiyan, deputy prime minister (March 2004 and February 2005)	João Bernardo de Miranda, minister of foreign affairs (May 2004)
Yang Zilin, president, China EximBank (September 2004)	General Agostinho Nelumba Sanjar, commander of the Angolan Armed Forces (June 2005)
Lü Xinhua, vice minister foreign affairs (July 2005)	Joaquim Icuma Muafuma, minister of commerce (September 2006)
Jiang Yaoping, vice minister of information industry (November 2005)	Irene Neto, vice minister of foreign affairs (September 2006)
Wen Jiabao, prime minister (June 2006)	Antonio Burity da Silva, minister of education (October 2007)
Li Ruogu, president, China EximBank (September 2007)	

Source: Indira Campos and Alex Vines, *Angola and China: A Pragmatic Partnership*, Center for Strategic and International Studies, Washington, 2008.

IV. The Philosophy and Significance of the Sino-Angola Oil-for-Infrastructure Diplomacy

Although its conception and implementation had been a subject of various interpretations, the oil for infrastructure diplomacy between China and Angola was premised on some philosophical foundations with profound socio-economic, political and diplomatic significance. First, it represented Angola's triumph over Western set conditionality against its earlier desire to accessing reconstruction funds from Western financial institutions. Governance and human rights related issues had constituted a sore point in Angola's relation with the West. As a result, this remained a stumbling block for Angola's efforts at accessing funds from the Western controlled financial institutions. The traditional attachments of conditions did not help Angola's infrastructural financing needs either, rather the emergence of China did.

While Angola was still negotiating for loan with the International Monetary Fund (IMF), China's Exim Bank offered a generous low interest 2 billion $ loan to Angola in exchange for 40,000 barrels of crude oil per day.¹ Much as this credit facility had no conditional strings attached to it, plus longer repayment periods, critics have pointed out how it (potentially) allows Angolan government escape accountability, even as it inherently violates economic, social and cultural rights of the Angolan people on the long run.²

Priced Angola's sovereignty is perceived to be susceptible to the Western insistence on meeting its set of conditions, hence the attraction to the Chinese alternative. Essentially, the emerging picture reflects a serious conflict between (Angola's) exercise of sovereignty and (Western) demand for good governance each of which contends for supremacy. In spite of the importance of both, fixing Angola's war-torn infrastructure remained crucial in its post conflict economic recovery agenda. It is in meeting this need that China's emergence (with its soft infrastructure loans) set this crucial agenda in motion.

More so, Sino-Angola diplomacy which paved the way for a deal of that magnitude signifies a marked improvement in their bilateral relations. Therefore, the diplomatic brinkmanship that went into the normalization of their relation as from 1983 is indicative of a movement, setting the stage for robust engagements which the oil for infrastructure deals partly represent. In other words, the deals signify an important element of progress in the bilateral relationship between Angola and China irrespective of their history of political differences.

Likewise, Sino-Angola oil for infrastructure diplomacy characterizes a further boost in the emerging Sino-African relations even as it symbolizes a component

---

1 Ian Taylor, "Sino-African relations and the problem of human rights", *African Affairs*, 107/426, Oxford University Press, 2008, pp. 80-81, also see Alex Vines, Markus Weimer and Indira Campos, "Asian National Oil Companies in Angola", in Alex Vines et al, *Thirst for African Oil: Asian National Oil Companies in Nigeria and Angola,* Chatham House Report, Royal Institute of Int'l Affairs, UK, 2009, p. 47 here the authors hold that China Construction Bank (CCB) and China's Exim Bank jointly provided the 2 billion $ credit line.
2 Human Rights Watch, "Some transparency, no accountability: the use of oil revenue in Angola and its impacts on human rights" (Human Rights Watch, New York, NY, 2004), p. 1, quoted in Ian Taylor.

of the *Third World* solidarity which seeks to challenge the asymmetrical nature of international relations founded on imperialism. Afro-Asian ties as from the mid-20th century are part of the global South's response to counter the imperial influences of the global North. Much of global South had a long history of colonial and neo-colonial domination by the North, resulting in some contemporary structural imbalances politically, economically and socially.[1] Encouraging Southern solidarity, cooperation and interdependence were therefore chosen strategies that could help them to negotiate more fairly with the hegemonic North. In this case, the emergence of China in Angola increased Angola's choices, scaled up competition among foreign investors in its economy and holds the promise of gradually dismantling neo-imperial tendencies in the country.

The Sino-Angola oil for infrastructure also has some economic significance. Economically, the deals represent a case of economic interdependence in which both countries leverage their comparative advantages. Although China has achieved high growth rate and emerged as a super power of global significance, oiling its further growth and development remains its priority. So also, the oil-rich Angola requires a network of socio-economic infrastructures to support its development needs but lacks both the technology and the required capital investments. It is in the context of this comparative advantage (and disadvantage) that both countries negotiated the oil for infrastructure deals as an economic strategy to meet their needs. Intrinsically, this reveals an interdependent approach to problem solving.

Furthermore, oil-for-infrastructure diplomacy represents a constructive shift from the odious arms-for-oil deals that fuelled instability in Angola to the advantage of French and American oil companies such as Total-Fina-Elf, Chevron, Texaco, Philipps Petroleum, Exxon Mobil, and BP-Amoco. Madsen has shown how French and American complicity in the murky oil deals with the Angolan

---

1 Charles W. Kegley Jr., *World Politics: Trend and Transformation*, 11th edition, Peking University Press Beijing, 2007, pp. 128-149.

corrupt leadership contributed to the underdevelopment of the African country.[1] In contrast, the qualitative change in the resource use introduced by the oil-for-infrastructure engagements (in spite of its limitations) transforms Angola's economic and infrastructural landscape even as living standards of the people are lifted considerably. This is very significant.

V. Conclusion

This paper has presented a broad overview of the history and changing dynamics of China's relationship with Angola. From its early days of pre-independence cooperation up to the decade following Angola's independence period, relationship was mainly shaped by China's Cold War rivalry with USSR. Improved and robust bilateral relations found expression with the establishment of official ties in 1983. By 1993, Angolan embassy in Beijing was officially opened. These set the tone for another decade of cooperation that, perhaps, contributed in the decline of the long waging civil war till its cessation in 2002, the dawn of the new millennium.

With specific focus on the foundation, philosophy and significance of Sino-Angola infrastructure diplomacy, the paper contextualizes the roles of economic diplomacy in meeting their energy and post war reconstruction priorities respectively.The paper concludes that, associated problems notwithstanding, the mutual development policy is to a good extent a success in consolidating their relationships and improving living standards. It is not only transforming lives and benefitting both sides in very unique ways, but symbolizes a viable foundation for greater promise. In concrete terms, the paper concludes that with the successes recorded in infrastructural development, long term investments have been established and the intensification of bilateral exchanges ongoing. This means that the relationship is set to advance into concrete economic development in other critical sectors that will benefit from the support services of the infrastructural sector.

---

1 Wayne Madsen, Report Alleges US Role in Angola Arms-for-Oil Scandal, CorpWatch, 17 May 2002, http://www.corpwatch.org/article.php?id=2576<date accessed 19 November, 2012>

Another important conclusion is that both countries' drive to diversify international partnerships found a strong footing. This was aided by Western reluctance at funding Angola's post war reconstruction as well as by China's need for diversified energy sources. This exemplifies another success in building viable connections between two countries of the global South, while indirectly eroding the position of the hegemonic North in the economy of the South. Marking a productive change from the economically perverse arms-for-oil deals that hitherto characterized Angolan oil economy, the socio-economic and diplomatic values added by these trends have incontrovertible implications for the development of both countries and the world.

纵向重叠与实施差距：加拿大与中国的气候战略比较

米凯拉·彼得森-麦克纳布 【加拿大】

加拿大英属哥伦比亚大学硕士研究生

在 2017 年 5 月举行的七国集团峰会上，尽管受到来自其他成员国的重大压力，美国总统唐纳德·特朗普依然拒绝签署《巴黎气候变化协定》（以下简称"巴黎协定"）。2017 年 6 月 1 日，特朗普总统正式宣布启动美国退出《巴黎协定》的程序。由于美国是全球第二大温室气体排放国，美国的退出将可能严重影响其他缔约国履行承诺。巴黎谈判之前，中国作为全球最大温室气体排放国和新兴发达国家，始终反对在《巴黎协定》通过之前对气候变化实施国际监管治理，同时始终倡议减排义务应当由历史上对气候变化造成影响的国家承担。因此，美国的退出将尤其可能对中国履行其所做出的承诺带来消极影响。

然而，在 2017 年 1 月 19 日举行的世界经济论坛上，中国国家主席习近平说，"《巴黎协定》是气候治理历史上的一个里程碑。我们必须确保这一努力不会脱离正常运行的轨道。"此外，中国领导人还公开指出，美国外交政策的变化"将不会影响中国支持气候谈判和落实《巴黎协定》的承诺。"除了口头上的表态支持，中国还落实了一系列国际倡议和国内改革措施，以此应对人为气候变化，包括推出世界上最大的排放交易机制以及政府授权孵化可再生能源企业。

加拿大联邦政府通常被认为是美国最紧密的盟友（这一关系不仅通过正式协定而且也通过非正式的行为准则所体现），但这一次也对美国的退出提出了批评。2017 年 6 月 1 日，加拿大总理贾斯廷·特鲁多说，"对美国联邦政府退出《巴黎协定》的这一决定，我们深感失望。加拿大会毫不动摇地履行其应对气候变化和支持清洁经济增长的承诺。加拿大人民深知，我们需要采取坚决和共同的行动，应对不断变化的气候所带来的众多严峻现实问题。"近年来，加拿大和中国政府在一系列国际问题上立场日益一致，其中包括气候治理。鉴于加中两国政府均表示改善气候治理是两国的战略优先任务，同时加中两国都是全球十大二氧化碳和温室气体排放国之一（分别居于第9位和第1位），对两国采取的气候战略进行比较是有合理理由的。

　　本文将比较中国和加拿大现行的气候战略，以发现各自面对的挑战和机遇。笔者认为，加中两国均面临一个管辖权的问题：在加拿大，并行管理体制限制了联邦政府进一步完善减排规定的能力。联邦政府可以制定一项国家气候政策，但是《加拿大宪法》规定，能源和自然资源政策属于省级管辖权范围，因此对气候变化的监管并不能总是在加拿大全境统一地实施，这将在近期和长期延缓加拿大实现减排目标的进程。

　　与加拿大相比，中国的气候战略是在国家层面制定的，但却是在省级和其他地方层面落实的。各地在排放监管、报告和执行上的不一致，以及缺乏可信的行业碳排放统计，从长期来看，这将最终减缓中国改善气候治理的进程。这并不是说中国自2015年以来没有取得重大进展。事实上，与前些年相比，中国对空气污染的治理要有效得多，特别是在像北京这样的大城市。然而，中国目前的气候战略更有助于空气污染的治理，而不是气候治理，因为中国关注的是短期内减少地方污染，而不是监管执行和报告流程的协调一致。

　　本文将对加中两国气候战略的特点进行梳理并对两国中央政府面对的挑战和机遇进行比较。在加拿大，减排存在的最大障碍是省级和联邦政府职能的重叠，这造成了碳定价的不均衡、低效和无用。管辖权的重叠一直也是中国减排存在的一个主要障碍。中国决策者面对的最大挑战是国家战略和地方能力之间存在的差距。改善纵向层面的协调也应是中国未来气候改革的重点。

一　加拿大的气候战略

　　在加拿大，气候治理因为省级和联邦监管管辖权的重叠（并行监管）而变得复杂。《加拿大宪法》第32章将自然资源的管理和发展权赋予了各省；与此同时，各省负责辖区内与经济和能源安全相关的事务。然而，跨省污染的问题则在联邦管辖范围内，包括刑事司法权、征税权和其他任何被认为实现"和平、秩序和良好政府"所需要的权力，以及被认为涉及"国家利益"的环境问题。此外，所有没有明确规定为省级管辖的事务均为联邦层面的责任。虽然没有具体规定气候治理是由联邦还是省一级管辖，但是气候治理明显地与经济、自然资源、能源和总体国家利益重叠，因此即受省级监管也受联邦监管。这对排放监管是一个巨大挑战，本文将之后讨论这一问题。

在哈珀政府未能实现《京都议定书》规定的减排目标以及加拿大最终退出该协定后，加拿大在气候政策方面的行动就停滞了。加拿大联邦政府变得不愿接受国际压力，以降低二氧化碳和温室气体的排放。这在很大程度上是因为加拿大的经济依赖于能源开采行业的出口，特别是石油和天然气。由于不满于联邦政府缺乏气候治理和排放监管的领导力，特别是缺乏一套国家碳定价体系，多个省级政府在联邦行动之外，单独颁布了自己的气候政策。值得强调的是，2007 年，魁北克省开征碳税，这是在加拿大首次征收碳税。2013 年，魁北克省又针对这一税种增加了限额交易制度，该制度现在与业已存在的加州制度挂钩。

目前由贾斯廷·特鲁多领导的自由党政府因为在竞选纲领中承诺联邦政府将在包括气候治理等多个领域发挥更为积极和主动的作用而赢得大选。特鲁多 2016 年当选总理后，联邦政府就颁布命令，要求各省提交气候战略或接受联邦监管。同样，作为其《2017 年气候领导计划》的一部分，阿尔伯塔省颁布了更为激进的碳税政策，鼓励"阿尔伯塔省的居民减少私人汽车和家庭的碳污染"。这一省级政策尤其重要，因为阿尔伯塔省的国民生产总值几乎占全国的 16%，其石油和天然气产量几乎占全国的 80%，而石油和天然气是碳税征收的最大行业，到 2020 年将征收总计 10 亿美元的碳税。这一激进碳税政策的实施表明，某些省份已经采取了更为积极和坚决的措施开展气候治理，并得到了现任联邦政府的名义支持。

在巴黎气候谈判中，特鲁多政府承诺加拿大将实现前任哈珀政府在京都所承诺的国家减排目标，即到 2030 年，加拿大将在 2005 年水平的基础上减少 30% 的排放量。《巴黎协定》签署之后，2016 年 12 月，特鲁多总理宣布了《泛加拿大清洁增长和气候框架》，规定了在国家层面开展气候治理的七个领域：实施具有强制力的最低碳定价，"减排行动"（包括清洁电力倡议、新的建筑标准、绿色交通等等），建模和报告标准，清洁技术和创新，公园和环境保护区建设、适应和恢复措施（包括建造一座跨海大桥以应对海平面上升 1 米），以及成立一个气候委员会以促进各省、地区和联邦政府之间的沟通与协调。如果得以施行，这一框架将极大地改善目前加拿大气候政策所采用的"拼凑式"的模式，确保所有省份和地区实行同一最低标准。

然而，加拿大目前并未走上实现《巴黎协定》所规定的激进目标的轨道。截至 2017 年 12 月，加拿大向《联合国气候变化框架公约》提交的年终报告显示，加拿大离实现碳排放目标还有 66 吨的差距。联邦政府尚未回应如何实现加拿大所承诺的目标。联邦政府面对的一个重要挑战是，各省和地区实施的碳定价、排放标准和燃煤逐步淘汰计划是不平衡的。同样，联邦气候行动计划，如其当前所言，是一个庞大混乱的政策拼凑物，没有有效地针对任何一个问题领域。涉及各省管辖范围的不均衡的监管，限制了联邦政府协调和执行特鲁多政府在巴黎所承诺的国家减排行动的能力。

这些问题是由加拿大气候治理存在的内生限制因素所造成的，因为污染和气候治理是省级和联邦政府的共同责任，目前拼凑式的战略在监管行业和家庭排放方面低效而无用，特别是针对加拿大的能源行业。这些重叠的管辖权限常常导致多个标准的出现，鼓励地方省份在联邦法律出台之前制定宽松的标准，以避免将管辖权拱手让给联邦政府。即使新的泛加拿大框架成为法律或政策，这一问题也将继续存在。

二 中国的气候战略

无论国际还是国内层面，中国都是气候治理的相对后来者。在京都谈判中，中国积极反对国际强加的减排标准，而是倡议在满足国际承诺方面给予发展中国家更大的灵活性。在前国家主席胡锦涛的任期内，中国领导人始终主张工业化国家应当承担实现具有约束力的减排目标的义务，因为发达国家要为地球大气中的历史排放负责，而发展中国家不应承担上述义务，因而享有发展的权利（即在《京都议定书》中所规定的"共同但有区别责任"原则）。同样地，在 2009 年的哥本哈根谈判中，中国与其他几个发展中国家阻挠了一项具有约束力的国际协定的形成，而是倡议采取国家层面的途径，维护气候和环境政策的主权。

气候和环境保护在"十三五计划"中被提升为国家优先任务。这之后，中国在国际气候谈判中采取的方法在 2015 年发生了明显变化。时任美国总统贝拉克·奥巴马与中国国家主席习近平共同起草的《中美元首气候变化联合声明》体现了中国的这一新的参与姿态。联合声明涵盖了《巴黎协定》的大部分体系结构：中美两国同意"在有意义的减缓行动和具备实施透明度的背景下，发达国家承诺到2020年每年联合动员1000亿美元的目标，用以解决发展中国家的需要。该资金将来自各种不同来源，其中既有公共来源也有私营部门来源，既有双边来源也有多边来源，包括替代性资金来源。"这一表述体现了中国的一贯立场，即发展中国家应当享有实现目标的灵活性，同时保留发展和经济增长的权利。不过，这一声明同时也体现了中国致力于在国内和国际层面通过合作以减少排放和增强气候变化适应能力的这一新的雄心抱负。

在2015年的《巴黎协定》中，中国承诺2030年左右达到碳排放峰值并实现碳排放强度比2005年下降60%至65%的目标。中国同时承诺非化石燃料在其主要能源消费结构中的占比将提升至20%左右，并承诺森林蓄积量比2005年增加450万立方米。在国内层面，习主席承诺中央政府将"向污染宣战"，通过城市基础设施的现代化改造、加大对雾霾的治理、回收农业土地和自然空间等方式，解决中国一直以来存在的空气、水和土壤污染的问题。

中国已经为兑现其巴黎承诺而实施了多项国内改革措施：7个限额交易计划（包括5个市级和2个省级计划）已于2015年实施，并随后纳入了2017年底正式启动的世界规模最大的国家限额交易计划。同样在2017年，中国中央政府宣布在国内汽车制造领域建立行业级别的限额交易体系，并对所有汽车制造企业实行10%的低排放或零排放的汽车配额。习主席还引入了环保监察制度，地方政府官员不但要对经济业绩而且要对环保后果承担个人责任。比如，2017年8月，甘肃省100多位地方官员因批准了一系列对祁连山生态造成破坏的项目而受到公开问责——祁连山是新建立的自然保护区所在地，也是中国西部大部分地区的水源涵养地。追究个人责任和监督环保执法可以明显地改善针对国家政策的地方管理，尽管目前评估这些措施到底能产生多大效果还为时尚早。

在改善地方对国家规定的执行方面，根据地方媒体的报道，2017年四川省暂时关停了7000多家工厂。山东淄博一地在2017年就暂时关停了5000家化工企业。这些行动短期内改善了空气质量，但是长期来看，不太可能对中国的减排产生持续的影响作用。同样，个人问责制度和环境执法检查具有短期效果，但是也不太可能对日常执法和长期制度性转型产生长远和持续的作用。关停企业同时也带来了巨大的社会和经济成本，员工因为企业关停而下岗。因此，长期而言，这些政策有可能会损害国民对环保政策的支持。针对地方管理的个人问责制度、国家层面对地方能源市场的干预以及个别行业和企业的关停，是显示中央政府与地方政府之间缺乏协调的 3 个例证，这可能会从长期影响中国的减排努力。

不过，中央政府还是在降低排放强度、可再生能源产能以及逐步淘汰燃煤使用等方面取得了难以置信的跨越式进步。中国正在提前实现其在《巴黎协定》中所做的 2020 年承诺，而且中国的排放已在签署《巴黎协定》之前于 2014 年达到了峰值。然而，实现这些目标所取得的成功某种程度上被过去几年日益严重的几个重要的能力和执行挑战所冲淡。风能削减量从 2014 至 2016 年翻了一倍，太阳能削减量则在 2015 年和 2016 年增加了 50% 多。可再生能源产能（过剩产能）在中国持续增加，这很大程度上是因为中央和地方政府之间缺乏纵向协调和报告机制。中央政府不断地对地方能源市场实施政府干预，倾向于可再生能源发电而不是化石能源发电。这导致了地方削减其他能源的生产，而可再生能源产能和发电量则过剩。

三　执行差距和管辖权重叠

中国环境治理的很多问题，其根源都与加拿大环境治理面临的问题如出一辙，即中央和地方政府部门之间存在纵向重叠。不过，就气候治理而言，中国存在的最大障碍恰恰与加拿大相反：上级和下级政府命令之间存在执行差距，而不是管辖权重叠。中国目前的体制是以县市为管理单元，对县市领导实施绩效考核制度，针对个体企业自由裁量而不是实施连贯性的政策执行。特别是对官员的考核制度阻碍了长期的制度性变革，而政府对地方能源市场的干预则加大了政策与执行之间的差距。这一体制更有利于解决短期性、地方性的问题，如空气污染的治理，但是并不适合长期的气候治理（这需要一个完全不同的时间尺度）。因此，中国目前的气候计划对打赢习主席所说的"治理雾霾的斗争"可能是有效的，特别是在像北京这样的中心城市，但是排放监测、报告和执行体制的重要转变要求弥合政府命令之间的差距。良好的纵向协调对确保中国的排放降至 2℃ 全球温升阈值至关重要。

相反地，加拿大所提出的《泛加拿大框架》可能会极大地完善其目前气候治理"拼凑式"的模式，并从长远上改善各省与联邦政府之间的纵向协调。但是，加拿大的气候治理模式受到宪法规定的并行管理体制的内在制约。在许多方面，即使所有省份和地区都全面执行《泛加拿大框架》，宪法的不明确以及联邦政府与各省之间的责任分工，也将激发各省实施自己的规定以避免将管辖权拱手让给联邦政府。中国则能够避免这种管辖权上的重叠，因为气候治理已被提升为国家优先任务。因此，治理是以自上而下的方式而不是并行监管的方式进行的。中国面对的挑战是，弥合国家规定与地方管理之间的执行差距。

四 结论和建议

虽然中国的气候战略在长期上依然存在重大挑战，但是与加拿大相比，中国也面临一个重要机遇，因为现任加拿大自由党政府在2019年10月的下次联邦大选中是否能够赢得多数继续执政，这一点还不明确。特鲁多政府在其第一个任期内已花了一半以上的时间制定气候行动方案，且国会下议院目前尚未通过该方案，各省也未批准该方案。因此，提出的这一方案是否能够成为政策文件或法律，目前尚不明朗。同样，如果四年一届的新政府上台，省级气候行动方案也可能被废除。与之相比，中国的中央政府在其上一个五年计划中所做的通过长期战略逐步实现环境目标的规划，已取得了极大的成功。2017年10月召开的中国十九大宣布，环境治理是国家最优先的任务。鉴此，本文建议，中国可以充分利用其规划未来的能力这一优势（与加拿大议会政治选举制度相比而言），构建国家主导的碳排放数据搜集、监测和执行体系，以确保中央与地方政府之间有效的沟通。这将完善中国的长期环境战略，而现行的战略仅仅在短期层面针对空气污染防治。

加拿大和中国均面临取得重大减排目标的管辖权挑战。对加拿大而言，纵向协调受到《加拿大宪法》规定的并行监管体制的负面影响。即使《泛加拿大框架》得以实施，这一挑战也将很可能继续存在。对中国而言，挑战不在于管辖权的重叠，而在于国家政策与地方执行之间的差距，这将很可能需要通过重大的制度性改革加以克服。

Vertical Overlap and the Enforcement Gap: A Comparison of Canadian and Chinese National Climate Strategies

Michaela Celeste Pedersen-Macnab / Canada

Master Degree Candidate, University of British Columbia, Canada

At the G7 Summit in May 2017, American President Donald Trump refused to endorse the Paris Climate Agreement, despite significant pressure from the other G7 members, and on June 1 2017, President Trump officially announced the beginning of the American withdrawal process from the Paris Agreement.[1] As the United States is the second largest global emitter of greenhouse gases, it seemed likely that a US withdrawal would significantly impact the commitments of the other signatories.[2] Prior to the Paris negotiations, China, the largest greenhouse gas emitter and an emerging developed state, consistently opposed internationally regulated climate change governance prior to the Paris Agreement, and also consistently advocated that the burden of emission reduction should be on states that have historically contributed to climate change.[3] It therefore seemed likely that American withdrawal

---

1 Michael D. Shear, "Trump Will Withdraw U.S. From Paris Climate Agreement", *The New York Times* (New York, NY), June 1, 2017.
2 *Ibid.*
3 Resource Watch, "Country Profiles", *Climate Watch Data*. Last modified 2018. Accessed March 31, 2018. https://www.climatewatchdata.org.

would negatively impact China's commitment to the climate agreement in particular.

However, on January 19, 2017 at the World Economic Forum, President Xi Jinping stated, "The Paris Agreement is a milestone in the history of climate governance. We must ensure this endeavor is not derailed."[1] Further, Chinese leadership has since publicly stated that changes in the foreign policy of the United States "won't affect China's commitment to support climate negotiations and also the implementation of the Paris Agreement".[2] This rhetorical support was supplemented by a variety of international initiatives and domestic reforms since undertaken by China to combat anthropogenic climate change, including the world's largest emission trading scheme, and government-mandated incubation of renewable energy firms.[3]

The Canadian federal government, often thought of as America's closest ally (both through formal agreements and informal norms of conduct), also criticized American withdrawal: on June 1, 2017, Prime Minister Justin Trudeau stated "we are deeply disappointed that the United States federal government has decided to withdraw from the Paris Agreement. Canada is unwavering in our commitment to fight climate change and support clean economic growth. Canadians know we need to take decisive and collective action to tackle the many harsh realities of our changing climate."[4] In recent years, the Canadian and Chinese governments have become increasingly aligned on a number of international issues, including climate governance. Given that both the current Canadian government and the Chinese government have indicated that improved climate governance is a strategic priority

---

1 *China Daily*, "Quotes from President's Speech", January 20, 2017. Accessed March 27, 2017. http://usa.chinadaily.com.cn/epaper/2017-01/20/content_28010820.htm.
2 Isabel Hilton, "With Trump, China Emerges As Global Leader on Climate", *Climate Politics*. Last modified November 21, 2016. Accessed March 27, 2017. http://e360.yale.edu/features/with_trump_china_stands_along_as_global_climate_leader.
3 Debra Kahn, "China Is Preparing to Launch the World's Biggest Carbon Market", *Scientific American*, August 14, 2017.
4 Government of Canada, "Statement by the Prime Minister of Canada in response to the United States' decision to withdraw from the Paris Agreement", *Prime Minister of Canada*. Last modified June 1, 2017. Accessed March 31, 2018. https://pm.gc.ca/eng/news/2017/06/01/statement-prime-minister-canada-response-united-states-decision-withdraw-paris.

for both countries, and that both Canada and China are within the top 10 emitters of carbon dioxide and greenhouse gases (in the ninth and first position, respectively), a comparison of the climate strategies used by both countries is warranted.[1]

This paper will compare China's current climate strategy to Canada's current climate strategy to identify challenges and opportunities for each country. It will be argued that both Canada and China face a jurisdictional problem: in the case of Canada, concurrent regulation will constrain the federal government's ability to further improve emission reduction protocols. The federal government may mandate a national climate policy, but because the Canadian constitution requires that energy and natural resource policy are provincial jurisdictions, regulatory changes are not always applied consistently across Canada, which will slow Canada's progress towards nominal emission reduction in both the short and long term.[2]

In contrast to Canada, China's climate strategy is mandated at the national level, but implemented at the provincial and local levels.[3] Inconsistent mission monitoring, reporting, and enforcement by municipalities, coupled with a lack of credible carbon accounting by industry, will ultimately slow China's progress toward improving climate governance in the long term.[4] This is not to say that there have not been significant gains since 2015: air pollution in China is targeted much more effectively now than in previous years, particularly with respect to large urban centers like Beijing.[5] However, China's current climate strategy is more conducive to air pollution reduction than climate governance, as it focuses on short term local level pollution reduction, rather than coordination of regulatory enforcement and reporting processes.

This paper will outline key features of both the Canadian and Chinese climate

---

1 Resource Watch.
2 Jesse Snyder, "Canada Still on Pace to Fall Short of Paris Target, despite Ambitious Climate Policies: UN Filings", *Financial Post*, December 29, 2017.
3 Yixian Sun, "The Changing Role of China in Global Environmental Governance", *Rising Powers Quarterly* 1, no. 1 (September 2016): 45.
4 *Ibid*, 43.
5 Snyder.

strategies, and compare the opportunities and challenges for both national governments: in the Canadian case, the most significant obstacle to emission reduction are the overlapping roles of provincial and federal governments that have caused uneven, inefficient, and ineffectual carbon pricing. While jurisdictional overlap remains a significant obstacle for China's emission reduction as well, the most significant challenge facing Chinese decision-makers is an enforcement gap between the national strategy and local capacity. Improved vertical coordination should be focus of China's future climate reform.

I. Canada's Climate Strategy

In Canada, climate governance is complicated by overlapping provincial and federal regulatory jurisdictions (concurrent regulation).[1] Section 92 of the Constitution devolves authority and development over natural resources to the provinces, and likewise, provinces are responsible for energy matters relating to economic and energy security within their borders.[2] However, trans-boundary pollution falls under federal jurisdiction, as does criminal law power, taxation power, anything that can be construed as "peace, order and good government", as well as environmental concerns that are deemed in "the national interest".[3] Anything that is not expressly designated a provincial jurisdiction is also a federal responsibility.[4] Climate governance is not specifically delineated as either a federal or provincial jurisdiction, but climate governance overlaps significantly with economic, natural resource, energy, and the general national interest, and is thus concurrently regulated under both federal and provincial jurisdictions.[5] This

---

1 "Federal, Provincial and Territorial Energy Jurisdiction", *Government of Canada.* Accessed April 1, 2018. https://sencanada.ca/content/sen/committee/411/enev/dpk-energy/appendices/Appendix05-EN.pdf.
2 Brenda Heelan Powell,*Climate Change Legal Roadmap: A Snapshot of Alberta's Climate Change Law and Policy*, Environmental Law Centre (Alberta), 2016, 3. Accessed April 1, 2018.
3 *Ibid.*
4 *Ibid.*
5 Shawn McCarthy, "Harper Calls Climate Regulations on Oil and Gas Sector 'Crazy Economic Policy'", *Globe and Mail*, December 9, 2014. Accessed April 1, 2018. https://www.theglobeandmail.com/news/politics/harper-it-would-be-crazy-to-impose-climate-regulations-on-oil-industry/article22014508/.

represents a significant challenge for emission regulation, which will be returned to later in the paper.

After the Harper government's failure to achieve its emission reduction targets under the Kyoto Protocol, and Canada's eventual withdrawal from the accord, Canada's action on climate policy was stalled. The Canadian federal government appeared unreceptive to international pressures to reduce carbon and greenhouse gas emissions.[1] This was, in large part, because of Canada's economic reliance on the export of energy extraction industries, specifically oil and natural gas.[2] Unhappy with the federal government's lack of leadership on climate governance and emission regulation, specifically with respect to the lack of a national carbon price, several provincial governments enacted their own climate policies independently of federal action. Of note, the Quebec carbon tax (2007) was the first of its kind in Canada, and in 2013, Quebec supplemented this tax with the creation of its own cap-and-trade scheme that is now linked with the pre-existing California scheme.[3]

The current Liberal government, led by Justin Trudeau, campaigned and was successfully elected on a platform that promised a more active and engaged role for the federal government on several issue areas including climate governance. Upon Trudeau's election in 2016, the federal government mandated that provinces submit their own climate strategies, or be subject to federally imposed regulations.[4] Likewise, as part of its 2017 "Climate Leadership Plan", the province of Alberta enacted a progressive carbon tax to encourage "Albertans to reduce carbon pollution from their cars and homes.[5] "This provincial policy is particularly significant because Alberta represents almost 16% of Canada's total GDP, and almost 80% of

---

1 *Ibid*.
2 Government of Quebec, "The Québec Cap and Trade System for Greenhouse Gas Emissions Allowances", *Climate Change*. Accessed April 1, 2018. http://www.mddelcc.gouv.qc.ca/changements/carbone/Systeme-plafonnement-droits-GES-en.htm.
3 *Ibid*.
4 *CBC*, "Provinces Have until the End of 2018 to Submit Carbon Price Plans: McKenna", December 15, 2017. http://www.cbc.ca/news/politics/carbon-price-2018-mckenna-1.4450739
5 Government of Alberta, "Climate Leadership Plan", *Climate Change*. Accessed April 1, 2018. https://www.alberta.ca/climate-leadership-plan.aspx.

Canada's oil and gas production, which is the largest industry targeted by the carbon levy for a total of US$1 billion by 2020.[1] The implementation of a progressive carbon tax suggests a more proactive and assertive approach to climate governance by some of the provinces, with nominal support by the current federal government.

At the Paris climate negotiations, the Trudeau government committed Canada to the same national emission reduction targets as the previous Harper government did at Kyoto: 30% reduction in emissions from 2005 levels by 2030.[2] Following Paris, in December 2016, Prime Minister Trudeau also announced a "Pan-Canadian Framework on Clean Growth and Climate", which targets eight areas of climate governance at the national level: the implementation of a mandatory minimum carbon price, "actions to reduce emissions" (which includes clean electricity initiatives, new building codes, green transportation, etc.), modeling and reporting standards, clean technology/innovations, the creation of parks and protected environmental spaces, adaptation and resilience measures (including the construction of a maritime bridge to accommodate a one meter rise in sea level), and the establishment of a climate council to improve communication and cooperation between provinces, territories, and the federal government.[3] If enacted, a Pan-Canadian framework would significantly improve the existing "patchwork" approach to climate policy in Canada, and ensure that all provinces and territories are held to the same minimum standard.

However, Canada is currently not on track to meet its aggressive targets under the Paris Agreement: as of December 2017, Canada's year end report to the United Nations Framework Convention on Climate Change suggests that Canada is on pace to miss its goal by 66Mt of carbon.[4] The federal government has not yet responded

---

1 Chris Varcoe, "Carbon Tax Overhaul Will Cost Alberta's Big Industry $1.2B by 2020", *Calgary Herald*, December 6, 2017.
2 Snyder.
3 Government of Canada, "Canada's Action on Climate Change", *Climate Change*. Last modified February 22, 2018. Accessed April 1, 2018. https://www.canada.ca/en/services/environment/weather/climatechange/climate-action.html.
4 Snyder.

on how it expects to meet Canada's target. One of the main challenges facing the federal government is its uneven carbon pricing, emission standards, and coal phase-out programs across provinces and territories.[1] Likewise, the federal climate action plan, as it is currently articulated, is a sprawling patchwork of policies and therefore does not effectively target any one issue area. Uneven regulation across provincial jurisdictions limits the federal government's ability to coordinate and enforce the national emission reductions that the Trudeau government committed to at Paris.

These issues stem from an endogenous limit on Canadian climate governance: because pollution and climate governance are a shared responsibility between the provincial and federal governments, the current patchwork strategy is both inefficient and ineffectual at regulating industry and household emissions, particularly with respect to the Canadian energy industry. These overlapping jurisdictions often create more than one standard, and incentivize provinces to create lenient standards in advance of federal legislation to avoid surrendering jurisdictional power to the federal government. This problem will persist, even if the new Pan-Canadian framework is enacted as law or policy.

II. China's Climate Strategy

China is a relative newcomer to climate governance at both the international and domestic levels. In the Kyoto negotiations, China actively opposed internationally imposed emission reduction standards, and instead advocated for increased flexibility for developing countries to meet international commitments.[2] Under former President Hu Jintao, Chinese leadership consistently argued that industrialized countries should be held to binding emission reduction targets, as developed countries were responsible for historical emissions contained in the earth's atmosphere, while developing countries should not be held to binding targets,

---

1 *Ibid.*
2 Elena Gladun, and Dewan Ashan, "BRICs Countries' Political and Legal Participation in the Global Climate Change Agenda", *BRICS Law Journal* 3, no. 3 (2016): 13.

and should therefore be afforded the "right to develop" (known as the Common but Differentiated Responsibilities principle under the Kyoto Protocol).[1] Likewise, in 2009 at the Copenhagen negotiations, China, along with several other developing countries, obstructed the formulation of a binding international agreement, and instead advocated national-level approaches to maintain sovereignty over climate and environmental policy.[2]

China's approach to international climate negotiations changed dramatically in 2015 after climate and environmental protection were elevated to national priorities in the 13th Five Year Plan.[3] This newly engaged posture was reflected in the Joint Presidential Statements on Climate Change, drafted by then-American President Barack Obama and President Xi Jinping. The joint statement established much of the architecture of the Paris Climate Agreement: the two countries agreed that "in the context of meaningful mitigation actions and transparency on implementation, developed countries committed to a goal of mobilizing jointly 100 billion USD a year by 2020 to address the needs of developing countries and that this funding would come from a wide variety of sources, public and private, bilateral and multilateral, including alternative sources of finance."[4] This language reflects China's position that developing countries should be afforded flexibility to meet targets, while preserving the right to develop and to grow their economies. However, this announcement also indicated China's newfound ambition to work cooperatively to reduce emissions and improve climate adaptation capacity, both domestically and abroad.

Under the 2015 Paris Agreement, China committed to peaking its carbon

---

1   David G. Victor, *The Collapse of the Kyoto Protocol and the Struggle to Slow Global Warming*: Princeton University Press (2001) 33.
2   "China's Thing about Numbers", *The Economist*, December 30, 2009.
3   *The 13th Five-Year Plan for Economic and Development of the People's Republic of China*, Beijing: Central Committee of the Communist Party of China, 2015. Accessed April 1, 2018. http://en.ndrc.gov.cn/newsrelease/201612/P020161207645765233498.pdf.
4   "U.S.-China Joint Presidential Statement on Climate Change", *The White House*. Last modified September 25, 2015. Accessed April 1, 2018. https://obamawhitehouse.archives.gov/the-press-office/2015/09/25/us-china-joint-presidential-statement-climate-change.

emissions around 2030, and to lowering its carbon intensity by 60% to 65% from its 2005 levels.[1] China also committed to increasing the share of non-fossil fuels in primary energy consumption to around 20%, and to increasing its forest stock volume by around 4.5 billion cubic meters from its 2005 levels.[2] At the domestic level, President Xi committed the national government to a "war on pollution" to combat China's chronic air, water, and land pollution by modernizing urban infrastructure, tightening controls on smog, reclaiming agricultural lands and natural spaces.[3]

China has implemented several domestic reforms to meet its Paris targets: seven pilot capand trade programs (five city-wide and two provincial programs) were established in 2015, and later were fed into the world's largest national cap-and-trade program, officially launched at the end of 2017.[4] Also in 2017, the Chinese national government announced an industry-level cap-and-trade system in its domestic auto-manufacturing sector, as well as a 10% low/zero emission car quota for all auto manufacturers.[5] President Xi also introduced an environmental inspection system, under which local-level managers are personally responsible for economic performance as well as environmental protection outcomes: for example, in August 2017, more than 100 local level officials in Gansu province were publicly reprimanded and punished for approving projects that caused ecological harm to the Qilian mountains, which are the site of a newly established nature preserve, as well as the water basin for much of western China.[6] This devolution of personal responsibility and oversight over environmental protection enforcement may significantly improve local administration of national policies, although it is too soon to tell how great this impact will be.

1 Resource Watch.
2 *Ibid*.
3 Xiangwei Wang, "Xi Faces One of His Greatest Tests yet - China's Environment", *South China Morning Post,* August 27, 2017.
4 Kahn.
5 Norihiko Shirouzu, and Adam Jourdan, "China Sets 2019 Deadline for Automakers to Meet Green-Car Sales Targets", *Reuters*, September 28, 2017.
6 Wang.

In an attempt to improve local enforcement of national regulations, more than 7,000 factories were temporary closed in Sichuan province in 2017, according to local media.[1] Likewise, Zibo in Shandong province alone saw the temporary closure of 5,000 chemical companies closed this year.[2] Such actions improve air quality in the short term, but in the long term are unlikely to have a lasting impact on China's emission reduction. Likewise, the personal incentive structures and environmental enforcement inspections are likely to have short term impacts, but are unlikely to have a long lasting impact on day-to-day enforcement or on long term institutional transformation. The closure of these firms also represents a significant social and economic cost to workers and staff that were laid off as a result of the closures, and these policies are therefore likely to harm citizen support for environmental protection policies in the long term. The personal incentive structure for local-level management, the national level intervention in local energy markets, and the closure of individual industries and firms are three examples of a lack of coordination between the national government and local governments, which is likely to impact China's efforts to reduce emissions in the long term.

The national government has, however, made incredible strides with respect to emission intensity reduction, renewable energy capacity, and coal phase-out: China is currently on track to meet its commitments under the Paris Agreement well in advance of 2020.[3] It also appears that China's emissions had already peaked in 2014 prior to signing the Paris Agreement.[4] However, the success of meeting these goals is somewhat tempered by several significant capacity and enforcement challenges that have worsened over the last few years. Wind curtailment doubled from 2014 to 2016, while solar curtailment increased more than 50 percent in both 2015 and

---

1 Tom Hancock, "China Targets Pollution on Eve of Xi Jinping's Second Term", *Financial Times*, October 12, 2017.
2 *Ibid.*
3 "China-Climate Action Tracker", *Climate Action Tracker*. Last modified November 6, 2017. Accessed March 31, 2018. http://climateactiontracker.org/countries/china.html.
4 *Ibid.*

2016.¹ Renewable energy (over) capacity continues to grow in China, due in large part due to poor vertical coordination and reporting between national and local levels of government.² The national government continues to mandate government intervention in local energy markets which preferences renewable energy generation over fossil fuel-fired generation. This has led to local-level curtailment and excess capacity and generation.

III. Enforcement Gaps and Jurisdictional Overlap

Much of China's environmental governance problems stem from the same issues that plague Canadian environmental governance, that is, vertical overlap between national and local government agencies. However, with respect to climate governance in particular, China's greatest obstacle is the reverse from Canada: there exists an (enforcement) gap, rather than overlap, between higher and lower orders of government. China's current system is administered at the individual municipality level, uses personal incentives for municipal managers, and targets individual firms rather than consistent enforcement. In particular, the personal incentive prevents long term institutional changes, and government intervention in local energy markets widens the gap between policy and implementation. Such a system is more conducive to short term, localized problems like air pollution reduction, but is not well suited to long term climate governance (which deals in an altogether different time scale). Therefore, China's current climate plan will likely be effective at waging President Xi's "war on smog", particularly in large urban centers like Beijing, but a significant transformation of the emission monitoring, reporting, and enforcement system will be required to bridge the gap between orders of government. Improved vertical coordination will be essential to ensure that China reduces its emissions to below the 2℃ global warming threshold.³

Conversely, the proposed Pan-Canadian framework is likely to significantly

---

1　Kyle Mullin, "Can China Live up to Its Climate Fighting Promise?", *The Diplomat*, June 13, 2017.
2　*Ibid.*
3　Pu Wang, Lei Liu, and Tong Wu, "A Review of China's Climate Governance: State, Market and Civil Society", *Climate Policy*, 2017:670.

improve the current patchwork approach to climate governance in Canada, and will improve vertical coordination between provinces and the federal government in the long term. However, Canada's approach to climate governance is endogenously constrained by constitutionally mandated concurrent regulation. In many respects, even if the Pan-Canadian Framework is fully implemented by all provinces and territories, constitutional ambiguity, the division of responsibilities between the provinces and the federal government will incentivize provinces to impose their own regulations to avoid surrendering jurisdiction to the federal government. China will be able to avoid this jurisdictional overlap, as climate governance has been elevated to a national priority, and therefore governance is conducted through a "top-down" approach, rather than concurrent regulation. For China, the challenge will be to bridge enforcement gaps between national regulation and local administration.

IV. Conclusions and Recommendations

While substantial challenges remain for China's climate strategy in the long term, there is a significant opportunity for China in comparison to Canada: it is unclear whether the current Canadian Liberal government will remain in power, with a majority, in the next federal election in October of 2019. Given that the proposed climate action plan took more than half of the Trudeau government's first term in office to construct, and has not yet been passed in the House of Commons, or ratified by provinces, it is not clear whether the proposed plan will ever become policy or law. Likewise, provincial climate action plans can be repealed, should a new government come into power every four-year election cycle. In comparison, the Chinese national government has been extremely successful at continuous progress towards environmental goals through long-term strategies outlined in the last Five-Year Plan.[1] Given that environmental governance has been articulated as top priority at the most recent National Party Congress in October 2017, it is the recommendation of this paper that China takes full advantage of its ability to plan far into the future (in comparison to Canada's electoral parliamentary

---

1 *The 13th Five-Year Plan for Economic and Development of the People's Republic of China.*

political system) to construct a national-led carbon data collection, monitoring, and enforcement system that will allow for more effective communication between national and local levels of government. This will improve China's long term climate strategy, as opposed to its current strategy, which merely targets localized air pollution reduction on a short time scale.

Both Canada and China face jurisdictional challenges to achieve nominal emission reductions: for Canada, vertical coordination is negatively impacted by concurrent regulation mandated in the Canadian Constitution. This challenge will likely persist, even after the Pan-Canadian Framework is implemented. For China, the challenge is not a jurisdictional overlap, but a gap between national policy and local implementation, that will likely require significant institutional reform to overcome.

References

CBC. "Provinces Have until the End of 2018 to Submit Carbon Price Plans: McKenna." December 15, 2017. http://www.cbc.ca/news/politics/carbon-price-2018-mckenna-1.4450739
"China - Climate Action Tracker." *Climate Action Tracker*. Last modified November 6, 2017. Accessed March 31, 2018. http://climateactiontracker.org/countries/china.html.
China Daily. "Quotes from President's Speech." January 20, 2017. Accessed March 27, 2017. http://usa.chinadaily.com.cn/epaper/2017-01/20/content_28010820.htm.
The Economist. "China's Thing about Numbers." *The Economist*, December 30, 2009. *The 13th Five-Year Plan for Economic and Development of the People's Republic of China*. Beijing: Central Committee of the Communist Party of China, 2015. Accessed April 1, 2018. http://en.ndrc.gov.cn/newsrelease/201612/P020161207645765233498.pdf.
Gladun, Elena, and Dewan Ashan. "BRICs Countries' Political and Legal Participation in the Global Climate Change Agenda." *BRICS Law Journal* 3, no. 3 (2016): 8-42.
Government of Alberta. "Climate Leadership Plan." *Climate Change*. Accessed April 1, 2018. https://www.alberta.ca/climate-leadership-plan.aspx.
Government of Canada. "Canada's Action on Climate Change." *Climate Change*. Last modified February 22, 2018. Accessed April 1, 2018. https://www.canada.ca/en/services/environment/weather/climatechange/climate-action.html.
Government of Canada. "Federal, Provincial and Territorial Energy Jurisdiction." Accessed

April 1, 2018. https://sencanada.ca/content/sen/committee/411/enev/dpk-energy/appendices/Appendix05-EN.pdf.

Government of Canada. "Statement by the Prime Minister of Canada in response to the United States' decision to withdraw from the Paris Agreement." *Prime Minister of Canada*. Last modified June 1, 2017. Accessed March 31, 2018. https://pm.gc.ca/eng/news/2017/06/01/statement-prime-minister-canada-response-united-states-decision-withdraw-paris.

Government of Quebec. "The Québec Cap and Trade System for Greenhouse Gas Emissions Allowances." *Climate Change*. Accessed April 1, 2018. http://www.mddelcc.gouv.qc.ca/changements/carbone/Systeme-plafonnement-droits-GES-en.htm.

Hancock, Tom. "China Targets Pollution on Eve of Xi Jinping's Second Term." *Financial Times*, October 12, 2017.

Heelan Powell, Brenda. *Climate Change Legal Roadmap: A Snapshot of Alberta's Climate Change Law and Policy*. Environmental Law Centre (Alberta), 2016, 3. Accessed April 1, 2018.

Hilton, Isabel. "With Trump, China Emerges As Global Leader on Climate." *Climate Politics*. Last modified November 21, 2016. Accessed March 27, 2017. http://e360.yale.edu/features/with_trump_china_stands_along_as_global_climate_leader.

Kahn, Debra. "China Is Preparing to Launch the World's Biggest Carbon Market." *Scientific American*, August 14, 2017.

McCarthy, Shawn. "Harper Calls Climate Regulations on Oil and Gas Sector 'Crazy Economic Policy'." *Globe and Mail*, December 9, 2014. Accessed April 1, 2018. https://www.theglobeandmail.com/news/politics/harper-it-would-be-crazy-to-impose-climate-regulations-on-oil-industry/article22014508/.

Mullin, Kyle. "Can China Live up to Its Climate Fighting Promise?." *The Diplomat*, June 13, 2017.

Phippen, J. Weston. "Trump's Paris Climate Accord Indecision." *The Atlantic*, May 27, 2017. Accessed June 1, 2017. https://www.theatlantic.com/news/archive/2017/05/trumps-paris-climate-accord/528411/.

Resource Watch. "Country Profiles." *Climate Watch Data*. Last modified 2018. Accessed March 31, 2018. https://www.climatewatchdata.org.

Shear D., Michael. "Trump Will Withdraw U.S. From Paris Climate Agreement." *The New York Times* (New York, NY), June 1, 2017.

Shirouzu, Norihiko, and Adam Jourdan. "China Sets 2019 Deadline for Automakers to Meet Green-Car Sales Targets." *Reuters*, September 28, 2017.

Snyder, Jesse. "Canada Still on Pace to Fall Short of Paris Target, despite Ambitious Climate

Policies: UN Filings." *Financial Post*, December 29, 2017.

Sun, Yixian. "The Changing Role of China in Global Environmental Governance." Rising Powers Quarterly 1, no. 1 (September 2016): 43-53.

"U.S.-China Joint Presidential Statement on Climate Change." *The White House*. Last modified September 25, 2015. Accessed April 1, 2018. https://obamawhitehouse.archives.gov/the-press-office/2015/09/25/us-china-joint-presidential-statement-climate-change.

Varcoe, Chris. "Carbon Tax Overhaul Will Cost Alberta's Big Industry $1.2B by 2020." *Calgary Herald*, December 6, 2017.

Victor, David G. *The Collapse of the Kyoto Protocol and the Struggle to Slow Global Warming*: Princeton University Press, 2001.

Wang, Pu, Lei Liu, and Tong Wu. "A Review of China's Climate Governance: State, Market and Civil Society." *Climate Policy*, 2017:664–679.

Wang, Xiangwei. "Xi Faces One of His Greatest Tests yet - China's Environment." *South China Morning Post,* August 27, 2017.

中国国际关系理论的兴起：对西方其他国家范式的挑战？

保罗 【菲律宾】

菲律宾综合科技大学社会学系讲师

本文旨在针对关于中国国际关系理论学说创立的争论提出不同的观点。目前占据主导地位的观点认为，中国的国家体系、智库和学者正在与时间赛跑，看谁能够为中国目前在国际格局中的作为提供一个开创性的诠释。这一观点建立在西方现实主义和自由主义理论及其新学说的背景下，将中国的倡议行动视作机会或者挑战（这取决于使用这些理论的人们）。笔者认为，对西方概念和理论的机械应用，无助于理解在世界这个地方所发生的社会现象，因为这些概念和理论植根于不同的历史经验。笔者认为，中国国际关系理论学说的发展是学术热情的自然产物，而这正是由改革开放中发生的结构性变化所激发的。这些学术努力受到了中国历史经验中丰富的文化传统的启示，促使产生了能够更好理解在世界这个地方的现实细微差别的理论学说。这些学术努力不是对新的国际秩序进行理论化，而是可能带来一场新的科学革命，因为旧的理论框架已不再适应我们这个时代不断变化的现实。本文首先从所选择的优秀学者的专业经历的角度，对中国高校国际关系学科的出现进行历史梳理。其次，对中国国际关系理论的当前潮流趋势进行概括。第三，对中国意识这一国际关系研究的独特方法进行研究。最后，对中国国际关系理论学说的前景提出看法。

中国现在已是世界第二大经济体，而且很可能将超过美国，因为中国制定了"两个一百年"的奋斗目标，其中一个就是全面建成小康社会。中文正在成为世界领袖、商界人士和学者们的第二外语，因为学习中文打开了通向各个重要领域的大门，包括中国政治、经济、历史和商业机会等。由于中国在全球事务中有了更大的影响力，与此同时欧洲和美国的经济正在努力从此前的金融危机中缓慢复苏，世界现在期待中国发挥领导者的作用。在这一背景下，世界希望中国摈弃邓小平提出的"韬光养晦、决不当头"的格言，在国际政治中发挥更加积极的作用。

关于中国将如何参与国际事务和全球化问题，学者将中国的参与置于一个非常广泛的范围——从乐观地认为中国将领导现有国际和地区机制并捍卫法治，到悲观地将中国物质财富的增长及其针对与邻国争议所采取的行动看成是一个相对收益的问题；同时一个类似但是极端的看法是，中国将对西方和世界其他地区造成挑战，因为中国不愿放弃社会主义制度，不想照搬西方历史做法。正因为这些原因，中国为创立自己的国际关系理论学说所做的努力，被认为是企图改变现行国际秩序、为其成为霸权国家铺平道路的国家行为。

一 "中国的崛起"及其在西方引起的恐惧使中国国际关系理论学说的创立成为不可避免的事实？

国际关系学科领域的学者、理论和方法长期以来受到美国和欧洲地缘政治既得利益的支配和影响。因此，这些以欧洲和美国为中心的诠释所得出的分析是，中国创立自己的国际关系理论学说这一不断发展的计划旨在粉饰其霸权野心。克里斯滕森（Kristensen）和尼尔森（Nielsen）的文章反驳了目前流行的观点，即中国在其文化、哲学和历史传统基础上建立一套不同的国际关系理论学说，是因为需要弱化中国的崛起、不断增长的政治抱负以及对西方霸权的不满这些因素对其他国家的影响并使其他国家能够接受。中国认为，理论创新可以通过追求关注和卓越的知识分子的微观社会学透镜，而不是通过权力转移和反对霸权这样的宏观透镜，被世人理解。中国将其观点归纳如下：

"使得某些观点在学术界成为创新观点的原因是，这些观点在各自领域或主题范围内是新出现的和与众不同的。"

理论创新的引擎存在于学术活动的内部层面。我们希望外部层面仅具有间接的影响——或者通过促进学术争论或派系斗争（实质的转变），或者简单地在更大程度上放任学术界（叠加的程度）。

中国将在地位和声望的基础上在同行中选择学者，让他们成为与对手辩论的代表,从而表明学术地位与理论创建是相互联系的;中国的理论辩论是反对声音中的一支重要力量,这一点可以从其对第一代和第二代学者的划分上识别。第一代中的某些学者,通过对西方理论的翻译和介绍享有了突出的地位。但是在当前的背景下,第二代中的青年学者正在把时间花费在参与学术辩论和创建理论上以便为自己扬名立万,因为像老一代学者那样仅仅通过翻译和介绍西方理论不足以获得学术地位。这就是中国所认为的推动理论创立的内部层面。

外部层面包括中国在地缘政治层面的崛起、国内政治、叠加的消亡、经济增长、不断增强的物质基础、大学政治以及不断增加的职业机会。中国不断上升的政治实力拓展了外交政策利益,这需要国际关系学者的建议。一个崛起的经济大国可以在研究领域投入更多的资金。改革开放使得学术上的冲突和对立得以产生,因为国家为新的学术观点的互动打开了大门。学术互动以学术和学生交流、在大学建立教学和研究中心、政府不采纳学术界推动的智库所提出的观点等为代表特征。在中国经济快速增长时期,现有机构获得了更多资金,提高了研究人员的收入,从而鼓励学者和官员加入到以大学为基地的国际关系研究计划中。人员流动性的增加和经济繁荣使得国际关系研究成为有竞争力的职业,而绩效管理和能力竞争促使学术人员追求卓越。

充斥着美国和欧洲中心论偏见的宏观层面的诠释,将会导致对中国国际关系学者的学术生活内部和外部层面所激发的学术热情产生置疑。关于中国针对其世界地位的定位所推动的理论创建努力,如果我们赞同西方的分析,就可能落入理论上的"修昔底德陷阱"并做出过激反应。对过去几十年中国学术文化发生的变化进行定义,将有助于针对西方关于中国理论创立的主导观点提出不同的诠释。西方这一悲观论调是不可避免的,因为西方文化已渗透到全球的生活方式中,特别是在如何对中国的行为进行理论化诠释方面。

二 一个理论源自西方还是东方,并不重要,只要其对现实具有意义

科学带来的飞跃进步被认为是革命性的,而不是累积性和渐进性的;这一过程中,旧的模式被新的模式所推翻。阎学通反对革命的提法,认为目前的情况依然还存在问题,宣告西方国际关系理论的死亡还为时尚早,但是在当前的时代其确实面临经验和理论上的许多困惑。

关于东亚争端的国际政治问题给主流国际关系理论造成了困惑,如新现实主

义、新自由主义和社会建构主义。施耐德（Schneider）的文章对中国国际关系理论的当前潮流趋势进行了考察，并以中国南海主权争端为例，分析了中国国际关系学者提出的观点，证明这些观点如何创造性地重建了近代中国政治学理论，从而为国际关系学者看待世界提供了新的途径。他认为，非西方的理论创立是有价值的，因为其具有潜力，可以为一直被现有主流国际关系理论所歪曲的领域提供新的路线图。中国提供的概念框架借鉴了其丰富多样的文化传统，能够为国际政治的运行提供深刻见解。

施耐德（2014）指出，学者中盛行的关于中国国际关系理论创立的一个重要主题是，从当代的角度对历史进行评价，正如司马迁的《史记》或《春秋》的各种评注著作所采用的方式，这一点与西方对修昔底德的评价叙述相似，被冠以"现实主义"的写法。他同时指出，蒋庆采用了这一传统，他的方法旨在通过借鉴儒家精英统治体系和儒家社会关系，改善中国国内政治；而阎学通则从当代国际关系的角度，审视了近代中国政治思想。笔者关注了赵汀阳的"天下"观点，其旨在用乌托邦秩序替代民族国家的无政府体系——所有的关系，无论是在世界、国家还是家庭层面，都由同一个道德原则进行传导性管理。

施耐德（2014）强调了从石之瑜和秦亚青提出的中国角度对国际政治进行概念化的尝试努力。石之瑜认为，中国外交政策是复杂的角色形成和角色扮演过程的产物，这一过程受到了国内和国外参与者的双重影响。秦亚青的"程序建构主义"观点认为，中国社会的一个基本特征是关系导向，就是说，"关系"是社会生活最重要的内容，是所有社会活动的中枢。这一点与西方在思维模式和理论构建中的因果关系逻辑不同，并对集体性的参与者（如国家）不断变化的身份认同进行概念化。与主流国家关系理论形成对比的是，石之瑜和秦亚青适用在冲突问题上的理论框架抓住了问题的复杂性并为将来的讨论提供了前景。

通过借鉴中国博大精深的政治哲学传统，这些学者试图超越现有理论的已知局限，而强调现行国际关系理论未予足够重视的国际政治的三个相互关联的方面，如国内和跨国进程在国际政治中的重要性，关联过程和互动的相关性，以及集体认同和自我形象不断变化的情境性。通过类似的方式，秦亚青提出了理论创立的其他潜在来源，如中国的革命性思维与现代化愿望相结合，这一主题对知识界和老百姓而言，具有打破旧中国、建立新中国的目标。另一个来源是改革主义思维及其与国际体系的融合，在制度、社会和概念层面具有三个代表性变化。后者将在中国社会产生根本性的变化，正如本文开篇所述的中国知识界的发展所体现的变化一样。这一变革性的理念体系已经改变了中国的国际关系学科，因为所做的努力正在开花结果，这可以从"清华模式"这一案例中看到。

三 "百家争鸣，百花齐放"

正如本文开篇部分所述，在改革开放这一时期涌现出了致力于国际关系研究的机构；同时，随后出现的激励机制使得知识分子致力于理论学说的创立。张教授（2012）引用了普林斯顿大学出版社出版的阎学通所著《古代中国思想与现代中国权力》的英译本，指出中国国际问题研究出现了转折点。

笔者认为，"清华模式"具有理论上的抱负和政策上的动机；其所使用的方法表明，一个具有中国意识的国际关系研究的独特方法已经出现。张教授认为，这不仅仅是一种方法，而是一个成熟的"清华学派"。这一模式具有3个代表性特征：第一，其动机产生于丰富国际关系理论并为中国汲取政策教训的愿望；第二，其寻求通过借鉴中国春秋战国时期这一中国哲学黄金时代所产生的政治思想，实现上述愿望；第三，其将阎学通自己的科学方法应用于对古代中国思想的分析。

张教授认为，这一模式依然在方法论上存在需要解决的困境。他谈到了两个问题：第一，在研究分析古代文献时使用"字面意思"而未考虑其"实际含义"；第二，现代主义的问题。第二个问题是关于当代方法论假设的使用，比如使用"分析的层次"，对墨子和老子在天下层面的观点，管子和韩非子在国家层面的观点，孔子、孟子和荀子在个人层面的观点进行分析。"分析的层次"这一方法在当代的使用方面提出了深刻见解，但是却使得研究古代问题的某些具有中国特色的思考模式变得模糊不清。在所研究分析的文章中，除了此前真实性的问题，上述问题也被提了出来。因此，所获得经验教训会脱离其产生的背景，并将导致质疑的观点，而不是富有成果的理论学说。

这一模式真正的重要性在于使得中国的国际关系学科本土化，而不是依赖于从西方引入的概念和理论。中国学者正在有意识地丰富现有的理论或通过借鉴中国自身的概念和思想发展新的理论。这一模式的主要贡献是为将来的研究工作提供了理论方面的基本知识，因为阎学通也承认，系统性的理论尚未建立，这是未来的任务。

四　结论

中国在创立自己的国际关系理论学说所做的努力使得我们了解了植根于主流文化的当前的各种模式之间的联系。正是这些文化特征之间的互动使得我们了解了学者对世界的分析。我们深受西方学科的影响，我们的分析研究植根于古希腊的两分辩证法的传统；而中国人则以整体论的方法理解世界，这一点充分体现在以阴阳构成的象征主义。正是由于在这一点上对世界的不同看法，中国的国际关系理论创立试图借鉴中国的传统并体现一种不同的现实主义观点。由于对世界看法的不同分析，新的趋势是，亚洲特别是中国模式为世界其他地区提供了不同的选择，因为西方模式在解决国际体系中的全球性需求方面已经不够合格了。因此，随着中国在世界上的崛起，一场新的理论革命已经为期不远了。

历史课题在主流国际关系理论中并不常见，但是在英国学派中具有突出的地位。这也将会成为从历史中寻求国际关系理论创立源泉的一个先例。Wang 和 Buzan（2014 年）提出了对中国国际关系理论的未来具有启示性的观点。通过对英国学派的过往经历与中国国际关系理论创立的当前发展进行比较，两位学者预测，未来不仅会出现"中国学派"，而且有可能出现两个学派并立的情形，从而形成有助于进一步辩论和加强理论传统的学术环境。忽视中国知识界的学术热情和追求声望的学术竞争以及在中国出现的日益繁荣的学术文化，而仅仅依赖于地缘政治观点的诠释，这将为中国国际关系理论创立蒙上一层铁幕并将中伤其所提出的理论。

与产生了毛泽东思想的传统类似，混合模式也是可能的，比如产生了独特的毛泽东思想的"马克思主义中国化"的模式。"清华模式"将丰富现有理论。将西方理论置于中国背景下分析研究问题是基于丰富文化传统的复杂性，而这些传统产生过能够更好理解现实的理论。

The Rise of a Chinese International Relations Theory: Challenge to the West of a Paradigm for the Rest?[1]

Paulo Benedicto Villar / Philippines

Lecturer, Department of Sociology, University of Science and Technology, Philippines

The goal of this review article is to demonstrate an alternative perspective in the debate about the theorizing of a Chinese theory of International Relations. The dominant view places China's state hierarchy, think tanks, and scholars locked in a race against time as to who could pave the way for a pioneering explanation of China's current actions in the global landscape. This is situated in the backdrop of a dominant Western theoretical explanation of Realism and Liberalism, together with their neo-versions, elegantly placing China's initiatives as opportunities or a challenge depending on those who utilize these theories. I contend that the mechanical application of Western concepts

---

1 Peerenboom's normative claims in his book mentions that China is being held to double standards, globalization has led to an increase in inequality counter to what liberal democracy promises, democratization at low levels of wealth has failed to produce positive benefits claimed by democracy advocates. In the book, it also poses an idea that China can be a paradigm as existing western ideas have failed to address global issues. In Peerenboom, Randal. (2007) China Modernizes: threat to the west or model for the rest? Oxford University Press.

and theories will not help efforts of understanding the social phenomenon in this part of the world as such concepts and theories are rooted in a different historical experience. I argue that the development of a "Chinese International Relations Theory" is a natural product of the intellectual fervor stimulated by structural changes initiated during the Reform and Opening Up and these efforts are informed by the rich cultural traditions from Chinese historical experience producing theories better able to comprehend the nuances of reality in this part of the world. The implication would be that these efforts are not geared towards theorizing a new international order but possibly a new scientific revolution as old paradigms are unfit to contend with the changing realities of our time. The article would firstly, historicize the emergence of an international relations discipline in Chinese universities from the viewpoint of the careers of select scholars. Secondly, survey current streams of Chinese IR theorizing providing the trends and trajectories. Thirdly, examine the emergence of a distinctive approach to the study of IR with a particular type of Chinese consciousness. And lastly provide insights into the prospects of Chinese International Relations theorizing.

China is now the second largest economy in the world and is soon to overtake the United States as they set their sights on the first of the "two Centenary Goals", making China a moderately prosperous society. Chinese as second language is growing popular among world leaders, business people, and academics as taking classes opens the way to different important fields such as Chinese politics, economy, history, and business opportunity[1]. With a larger impact on global affairs, the world now looks to China for a leadership role as Europe and the United States' economy tries to recover from recent financial crisis. In this context it is expected of China to abandon Deng's dictum of "…bide our time, be good at maintaining a low profile, and never claim leadership"[2] and take up a more proactive role in

---

[1] Shao, Grace. (March 3, 2015). "Chinese as Second language growing in popularity". From: http://www.cctv-america.com/2015/03/03/chinese-as-a-second-language-growing-in-popularity

[2] Deng Xiaoping's "24-Character Strategy" in relating with the world. Originally: "Observe calmly; secure our position; cope with affairs; hide our capabilities and bide our time; be good at maintaining a low profile; and never claim leadership" .

international politics.

As to how China would participate in world affairs with globalized issues, scholars would situate China's participation in a very wide spectrum from optimistically stating that China would lead existing international and regional institutions and uphold the rule of law, pessimistically eyeing China's growth in material wealth as well as their actions regarding disputes with its neighbors as an issue of relative gains, and in a similar yet extreme notion that they pose a "threat to the West and the rest" in their reluctance to abandon socialism and follow suit in the trajectory of the history in embracing liberal democracy[1]. It is under these pretenses that China's effort in creating its own International Relations (IR) theory is seen as a national effort to revise the existing global order and to pave a way for establishing itself as a hegemon.

I. Was the "Rise of China", and the Fear that this Inspired in the West, that Made Chinese IR Theorizing Inevitable[2]?

Scholars, theories, and methodologies in the discipline of International Relations have been dominated[3] and informed by vested American and European geopolitical interests[4]. Hence, these Eurocentric and American-centric interpretations would point to the analysis that the growing project of China of creating their own IR theory is an effort to white wash their hegemonic ambitions. Kristensen and Nielsen's article[5] counters the prevailing notion that the Chinese drive to build a distinct IR theory with roots stemming from Chinese culture, philosophy, and history is driven by the need to soften the impact and reception of other states with

---

1 Fukuyama, Francis. (1989). "The End of History?" The National Interest. That the end point of mankind's ideological evolution and the universalization of Western liberal democracy.
2 Adapted from the original: "It was the rise of Athens, and the fear that this inspired in Sparta, that made war inevitable." In Thucydides' Peloponnesian War.
3 Kristensen & Nielsen, p.7.
4 Schneider, p.684.
5 Kristensen, Peter M. & Nielsen, Ras T. (2013). Constructing a Chinese International Relations Theory: A Sociological Approach to Intellectual Innovation. International Political Sociology 7, pp.19-40. The authors would conduct an in-depth qualitative interview with 27 Chinese IR scholars and a minor questionnaire distributed to 305 scholars at top universities with a 49% general response rate.

regards to "China's rise", growing political ambition, and discontent with Western hegemony. They argue that theoretical innovation should be understood through the micro-sociological lens of intellectuals seeking attention and prominence, rather than through the macro-lens of power transition and counter-hegemony. They would summarize their argument as:

> "..what makes certain ideas innovative among intellectuals is that they are new and distinctive in their own field or argument.
>
> The engine of theoretical innovation is found in the inner layer of intellectual life. We expect the external layers to be only indirectly influential, either by facilitating certain intellectual debates or factions (material shifts) or simply by leaving intellectuals alone to a greater extent (degree of overlay)."[1]

They would map Chinese scholars based on prominence as reputation among contemporary peers, situate them as representatives of rival debates indicating that prominence is related to theorizing, and that the Chinese theory debate is an important line of opposition. This opposition is seen in their categorization between the first-generation[2] and second generation[3] scholars. It is from this "first" generation that translation and introduction of Western theories made certain scholars prominent. But in the current context, these "young" scholars from the second generation are now occupying their time in creating a name for themselves by engaging in debates and theorizing as it is not enough to translate and introduce Western theories[4] to gain

---

1 Kristensen & Nielsen p.21
2 Kristensen & Nielsen would classify them as those in the 1980s scholars favoring a socialist theory of Chinese characteristics emphasizing Mao's "Three Worlds", "The Great triangle", and "Multipolarity". P. 24
3 Kristensen & Nielsen would classify them as those returned from the United States who favored American theories and social science methods and opponents of the politicized scientific practices related to "IR with Chinese characteristics" and as exponents of a value-neutral scientism. P.24
4 Kristensen & Nielsen would mention Qin Yaqing as China's leading constructivist, now becoming the main proponents of a Chinese School; Yan Xuetong as China's leading neorealist, is leading a team of researchers to theorize ancient Chinese thoughts in IR; and Ni Shixiong who built his reputation by introducing Western theories stating that it is inadequate to just introduce Western theories, but now to innovate. P. 25.

prominence as the older generation had done. This, as they argue, is the inner layer driving theorizing.

The external layers would comprise the geopolitical rise of China, domestic politics and the dissolution of overlay, economic growth and expanding material bases, and university politics and improving career opportunities. China's rising political power has expanded foreign policy interests and demands advice from IR scholars and a rising economic power has more money to spend in research[1]. The "reform and opening up" period enabled the intellectual dynamics of conflict and opposition to emerge as the country opened up interactions of new academic ideas exemplified by academic and student exchanges, the establishment of teaching and research centers at universities, and with the reluctance of the government to take advice from the academe prompted think tanks to be created. With existing institutions in place, at the time of China's economic growth, these institutions received more funding corresponding to increase in salaries urging the migration of scholars and officials toward university-based IR research programs. Increased mobility and economic prosperity made an IR intellectual a viable career and with the introduction of performance management and competition increased the drive for excellence among intellectuals.

Relying on the macro-level explanation riddled with American and Eurocentric bias would discredit the intellectual fervor being cultivated by the internal and external layers of the intellectual lives of these IR scholars in China. We tend to fall into this theoretical "Thucydides trap" and react in an aggressive manner when we subscribe to the western analysis for the drive of China to theorize about how its place in the world should be. Locating the changes in the Chinese intellectual culture across decades would benefit alternative explanations to the dominant western perception against Chinese theorizing. This pessimistic tendency is

---

1   Kristensen & Nielsen would disclaim that some money would go to universities but less to IR research and even less to theorizing. P.30. The reason for less funding for theorizing is that there is geared towards producing research projects and policy reports for the government, mainly in the "applied policy research" category for funding. pp.33-34.

inevitable as western culture has permeated global way of life and in particular, how we theorize China's actions.

II. It doesn't Matter whether a Theory is from the West or East as Long as it Makes Sense of Reality[1]

It is believed that the great leaps of progress made by science are not cumulative and continuous but rather revolutionary where an old paradigm is overthrown by a new one. Yan Xuetong[2] would forestall the call to revolution by stating that conditions are still problematic in that it is too early to claim the death of Western IR theory but recognizes that it faces many empirical and theoretical puzzles in current times.

It is in issues in international politics of disputes in East Asia that have arguably posed a puzzle for mainstream IR theories such as neorealism, neoliberalism, and social constructivism[3]. Schneider's article[4] examines current streams of Chinese IR theorizing and confronts them with the case of territorial disputes in the East China Sea subsequently, analyzing the arguments made by Chinese IR scholars showing how they creatively revive pre-modern Chinese political theory in attempts to

---

1. Adapted from the original: "It doesn't matter whether a cat is white or black, as long as it catches mice." Used by Deng Xiaoping explaining the adaptation of Marxism, Leninism, and Mao Zedong Thought to China's changing context.
2. Yan Xuetong (2011). Why is there no Chinese School of IR theory? In Ancient Chinese Thought, Modern Chinese Power. Princeton University Press.
3. Realist accounts would focus on the geopolitical concerns in the region stressing the disputed territories are potential sources for oil and gas as well as strategic relevance to project naval power which ignores the restraint that the various parties regularly displays and thus cannot fully capture the continuing rise and fall of conflict over the islands. Liberal authors would focus on the economic ties between the actors, arguing that trade relations have repeatedly fostered the de-escalation of Sino-Japanese conflict over maritime and territorial rights and believing that trade is too mutually advantageous to be held hostage to pieces of disputed rocks yet economic ties as a force for peace contradicts much of their own data and would these ties be sufficient to constrain further escalation of conflict. Social Constructivists posit that states are socialized by an already existing international culture that constructs their identities and interests but what happens in a region where there is no obvious structure of ideas. Schneider (2014), p 696.
4. Schneider, Florian (2014). Reconceptualising world order: Chinese political thought and its challenge to International Relations theory. Review of International Studies 40, 683-703

provide new ways in which IR scholars view the world. He adds that non-western theorizing is valuable because it has the potential to provide fresh roadmaps to a territory that has been misrepresented by the established maps of mainstream IR theories. Conceptual frameworks from China[1] draw from rich and diverse cultural traditions that can offer insights into the workings of international politics.

An overarching theme prevalent among scholars mentioned by Schneider (2014) in Chinese IR theorizing is to comment on the past from a contemporary position in the same tradition as Sima Qian's Records of the Historian or the various commentaries to the Spring and Autumn Annals similar to westerners viewing accounts of Thucydides and branding it as realist. He adds that Jiang Qing follows in this tradition as his approach is aimed specifically at improving Chinese domestic politics by reviewing the Confucian meritocratic system of rule and Confucian social relations while Yan Xuetong provides a survey of pre-modern Chinese political thought from a contemporary IR perspective[2]. Zhao Tingyang's usage of the idea "Tianxia" is given attention by the author as it aims to replace the anarchical system of nation-states with a utopian order in which all relations, whether at the level of the world, the state, or the family, are transitively governed by the same moral principle.

Schneider (2014) highlights attempts that conceptualize international politics from Chinese perspectives coming from Shih Chih-yu and Qin Yaqing. Shih argues that Chinese foreign policy is the outcome of complex role-making and role-taking processes that are influenced both by domestic actors as well as actors abroad. Qin's "procedural constructivism" asserts that one basic feature of Chinese society is its relational orientation, which means that "relations" are the most significant content of social life and the hub of all social activities. It differs from western logic of causation in its way of thinking and theoretical construction and conceptualizes

---

1 Schneider would discuss mainland China as well as Taiwan but for this review essay I would follow the policy of "One China" and include Taiwan in the imagining of "China" and situate Shih Chih-yu's role-taking and role-making theorizing as in line with the Chinese tradition.
2 Schneider (2014) mention's Yan's book entitle "Thoughts on World Leadership and Implications".

the changeable identity of group actors such as states. In contrast to mainstream IR theories, Shih and Qin's frameworks as applied in the disputes capture the complexities of the issue and provide prospects for further discussion.

Drawing from the rich Chinese tradition of political philosophy they attempt to overcome perceived limitations of existing theories to stress three related aspects of international politics that established IR theories underemphasize such as the importance that domestic and transnational processes play in the formation of international politics, the relevance of relational processes and interactions, and the changing situational nature of collective identities and self-images. In a similar fashion Qin Yaqing[1] points to other potential sources for theorizing, such as: China's revolutionary driven thinking married to modernization desires where this theme for intellectuals and masses alike has its goal being to break up the old China and set up a new one[2]; another source would be the reformist thinking and the integration into the international system having three characteristic changes in terms of institutional, social, and ideational[3]. The later would have fundamental changes in Chinese society as demonstrated by the developments of Chinese intellectual lives in the initial parts of this essay. This transformative mind set has now transformed China's IR discipline as efforts are now blooming and can be seen in the case of the Tsinghua approach.

---

1   Qin Yaqing. (2007). "Why is There No Chinese International Relations Theory?" International Relations of the Asia-Pacific, Vol. 7, No.3, pp.313-340.
2   Qin Yaqing cites that since the failure of reform in 1898, revolution has been dominant the dominant theme. Citing that May fourth movement culminated this thinking and a few decades later would lead to Deng's "learning from the West". In Why is there no Chinese International Relations Theory, p.43.
3   A similar mindset is demonstrated at how current reforms of the PRC against corruption has been undergone in the same framework of instituting institutional change, reforming the social aspects, and building a strong ideology promoting proper socialist values. In. Keliher, Macabe and Wu, Hsinchao. (2016). Corruption, Anticorruption, and the Transformation of Political Culture in Contemporary China. Journal of Asian Studies, 75 (1), 1-14.

III. One Hundred Schools of Thought Contend, one Flower Starts to Bloom[1]

As discussed in the initial parts of this essay, the Reform period brought about in the emergence of institutions devoted to the study of IR as well as the ensuing incentives to intellectuals devoting their time to theorizing. Zhang (2012) cites the translation to English of Yan Xuetong's "Ancient Chinese Thought, Modern Chinese Power" which was published by the Princeton University Press suggests a turning point in China's international studies[2].

The author argues that the "Tsinghua approach" has the theoretical ambitions and policy motivations animating the project which also has a method[3] implying the emergence of a distinctive approach to the study of IR with a particular type of Chinese consciousness. Zhang disclaims that it is still an approach and does not yet amount to a full-fledged "Tsinghua School". The approach has three characteristic features: Firstly, its motivation originates in a desire to enrich modern IR theory and draw policy lessons for China; Secondly, it seeks to do so by drawing on China's political thought from the golden age of Chinese philosophy in the Spring and Autumn and Warring States period (770-222BC); and Lastly, it applies Yan Xuetong's own brand of scientific method to the analysis of ancient Chinese thought.

Zhang contends that the approach still has methodological dilemma that needs to be addressed. He cites two problems: the usage of "literal meaning" without

---

1 Adapted from the original: "Let a hundred flowers bloom; let a hundred schools of thought contend" Mao Zedong used this to encourage the intellectuals enter into the discussion with bureaucrats.
2 Zhang's article aims to situate the book within the disciplinary context of Chinese IR to identify its promise as well as problems, and to suggest its implications for the development of Chinese IR, the emergence of Chinese theories in IR.
3 Exemplified by Yan Xuetong's book "Practical Methods of International Studies" as well as other publications from the Institute. Also annually conducting a methodological training workshop at Tsinghua University. Yan calls their method a "scientific method" influenced by a positivist understanding of social sciences. Zhang (2011) P.74

consideration to the "real meaning" in the analysis of ancient texts[1], and the problem of presentism[2]. Referring to the second problem, the usage of contemporary methodological assumptions such as the use of "levels of analyses" in the views of Mozi and Laozi on the level of the system, Guanzi and Hanfeizi on the level of the state, and those of Confucius, Mencius, and Xunxi on the level of the individual. The "levels of analysis" approach has yielded insights in contemporary usage, but it has obscured some distinctively Chinese modes of thinking on ancient issues. These problems are put forth aside from the initial question of authenticity in the texts being examined. Being said, lessons gained would be taken out of context and would generate questionable claims rather than fruitful theorizing.

Its true significance is the indigenization of China's IR discipline rather than relying on IR concepts and theories imported from the West. Chinese scholars are now consciously trying to enrich existing theories or develop new ones by drawing on Chinese concepts and thought. And its main contribution is that of raising certain rudiments of such theories for future work as Yan Xuetong acknowledges that no systematic theory has yet to be created and this sets the future task.

IV. Conclusion: prospects for Chinese IR theorizing

The Chinese attempts at creating a Chinese IR theory inform us about the link between our current paradigms which are rooted in our prevalent culture. It is in this interaction of cultural predispositions that inform our scholarly analysis of the world. Those of us who are heavily influenced by western disciplines, would all root our analysis to Greek dialectics of a dichotomy while the Chinese would embody how they understand the world in a holistic manner as exemplified by the symbolism of the yin and yang. It is from this different world view that Chinese IR

1　The "literal meaning" points to the thought contained in the text while the "real meaning" what was author of the text being examined was doing with his/her arguments in his/her historical, political, intellectual, and linguistic context. Zhang (2012), pp.82-83.

2　"Presentism" in application of Zhang (2012) was the 'contemporary assumptions are read back into classical authors instead of being opened up for reflection through the use of classical authors. Zhang (2012) p.83

theorizing tries to draw from and would produce a different sense of reality. From this opposition in analytical world view, there would be a tendency to see Asian and in particular Chinese paradigms as alternatives for the rest as the west has not been up to par in addressing the globalized needs of the international system. Hence, a scientific revolution would not be far along as China situates itself in the world.

Historical projects are not common in mainstream IR theory but have strong features in the English School. This would point to a precedent of looking to the past as sources of IR theorizing. An informative insight to the future of Chinese IR theory is mentioned by Wang & Buzan (2014)[1]. Basing on the current developments in Chinese IR theorizing in comparison to English School experience, they predict that not only would a "Chinese School" emerge; but there's a possibility of a plurality of Schools ushering in an environment conducive for further debates and strengthening of a theorizing tradition. Brushing aside the fervor and competition among intellectuals vying for prominence and the bourgeoning intellectual culture in China and relying on geopolitics' explanations would veil Chinese IR theorizing in an iron curtain and vilify any that would be created.

Similar to tradition that produced Maoism, hybrids are possible such as the "Sinification of Marxism"[2] producing a distinctive Mao Zedong Thought. As the Tsinghua approach would promote the enrichment of existing theories, placing western theories in a Chinese context would be informed by the complexities of the rich cultural traditions producing theories better able to comprehend reality.

References:

Fukuyama, Francis. (1989). "The End of History?" The National Interest. Summer of 1989.
Keliher, Macabe and Wu, Hsinchao. (2016). Corruption, Anticorruption, and the Transformation of Political Culture in Contemporary China. Journal of Asian Studies, 75 (1),

---

1 Wang, Jiangli and Buzan, Barry. (2014). The English and Chinese Schools of International Relations: Comparisons and Lessons. *The Chinese Journal of Politics*, Vol.7, No.1, 1-46.
2 Knight, Nick. (1983). "The Form of Mao Zedong's Sinification of Marxism". *The Australian Journal of Chinese Affairs*, 9, 17-33.

1-14.

Knight, Nick. (1983). "The Form of Mao Zedong's Sinification of Marxism". The Australian Journal of Chinese Affairs, 9, 17-33.

Peerenboom, Randal. (2007) China Modernizes: threat to the west or model for the rest? Oxford University Press.

Qin Yaqing. (2007). "Why is There No Chinese International Relations Theory?" International Relations of the Asia-Pacific, Vol. 7, No.3, pp.313-340.

Shao, Grace. (March 3, 2015). "Chinese as Second language growing in popularity". From: http://www.cctv-america.com/2015/03/03/chinese-as-a-second-language-growing-in-popularity

Wang, Jiangli and Buzan, Barry. (2014). The English and Chinese Schools of International Relations: Comparisons and Lessons. The Chinese Journal of Politics, Vol.7, No.1, 1-46.

Yan Xuetong (2011). Why is there no Chinese School of IR theory? In Ancient Chinese Thought, Modern Chinese Power. Princeton University Press.

中国在全球应对气候变化的作用：对其贡献的评估

李开 【加拿大】
加拿大亚太基金会中国研究伙伴关系项目专员

应对气候变化已成为21世纪的严峻挑战，并可能成为我们这个时代最大的全球公共政策挑战。但是，由于应对气候变化超出了任何国家政府的能力，因此在这个问题上采取有意义的行动需要各国和参与者的广泛参与。15至20个国家占了全球排放量的约75%，但没有一个国家的排放量超过26%。因此，减排需要全球努力。随着生态系统恶化超越国界，有效的环境保护必须要有区域和全球协议，以及参与者、国家和非国家之间的良好合作。然而，这样的国际谈判和协议难以实现。中国是世界上最大的经济体和最大的碳排放国，它参与全球应对气候变化的斗争至关重要，中国必须成为应对气候变化的任何国际协议的一部分。考虑到目前的排放量以及当前和未来的能源使用量，中国在这场斗争中确实变得越来越重要。

中国已成为世界主要大国，其行动和投入对应对全球气候变化十分必要。由于中国巨大的环境挑战具有全球意义，中国政府对气候变化的态度和环境政策将对世界环境的改善产生重大影响。事实上，中国的气候政策及承诺被视为气候变化制度成功的关键。虽然中国的经济增长和整体生活水平的提高令人瞩目，但是它在环境方面一直表现不佳。据世界银行统计，自21世纪初以来，中国的碳排放量增幅高于其他国家。中国的选择不仅影响中国人民的健康和幸福，也影响地球的未来。中国政府如何应对气候变化将是未来几十年的重要政策问题。

特别是美国退出《巴黎协定》后，全球气候政治方面出现空白，许多人猜测中国在应对全球气候变化中的作用。中国政府当然可以利用美国的不作为不履行承诺的借口，但这似乎并不是中国选择的道路。中国各级政府官员多次表示，中国希望在国际上承担更多的气候政策责任。例如，在2017年10月召开的中国共产党第十九次全国代表大会上，中国国家主席习近平表示，中国将在国际合作中担当重要角色，应对气候变化。最近，习主席还表示中国正在国内和国际应对气候变化方面展现领导力。事实上，中国政府表示愿意与欧盟等其他大国，小岛国和其他脆弱国家合作。许多最不发达国家将受到气候变化的破坏性影响，而中国表示愿意提供财政和技术支持。

有人认为，中国已成为全球应对气候变化斗争新的最大的支持者。在最近的一项全球调查中，当被问及"哪个国家在维持和平方面做得更多"时，中国以11%的支持率击败了美国。当被问及"谁在为解决环境问题做得更多"时，中国以6%的支持率击败了美国。

这些发展表明理解中国能源、气候变化和环境政策演变的重要性。本文旨在回顾中国的气候政策及其最近对气候谈判的态度，以评估中国作为"气候领导者"的潜在作用。这将有助于我们更好地了解中国在全球治理中的角色，并为我们提供一个窗口，观察其行为和未来意图。本文首先回顾全球气候变化问题并评估中国的责任，随后回顾中国的能源政策及其应对气候变化的行动，最后评估中国的承诺和行动。

一　什么是气候变化？

"气候变化"一词是指由于大气中二氧化碳、甲烷、一氧化二氮和其他气体（统称为"温室气体"）浓度水平的变化而导致的广泛的全球现象。这些现象包括全球变暖等温度升高趋势，也包括海平面上升等变化；格陵兰岛、南极洲、北极和高山冰川的冰层流失；花卉和植物开花的变化以及极端天气事件。

有明显的证据表明，自工业革命开始以来，大气中的二氧化碳含量一直在增多，所以解决气候变化问题最合理的方法是大幅减少温室气体排放。但是这项任务并不像表面上那么简单，因为各国的二氧化碳排放并不均匀。政府间气候变化专门委员会（IPCC）称，二氧化碳的第一个主要来源是燃烧化石燃料，因为全球80%的二氧化碳排放来自能源生产、工业过程和运输。由于工业和财富分配不均,这些排放并不是均匀分布在世界各地,而且发达国家在历史上的排放量远远超过发展中国家,因为自从18世纪后半叶的工业革命以来,发达国家一直在排放。但根据国际能源机构(IEA)的预测,即使这种历史性的碳负担很重要,情况却正在迅速变化。据估计,从2015年到2044年,全球将向大气中排放50万吨二氧化碳,与1750年至2015年间的排放量相同。这主要是因为中国、印度、南非、巴西等发展迅速的国家正以巨大的速度增加其温室气体排放。

二 全球环境治理和中国的气候变化政策

第二次世界大战后,全球经济复苏,越来越多有害污染的证据越来越明显。一些国际协议是在20世纪50年代和60年代签署的,主要是为了解决油轮泄漏和排放问题,但没有涉及任何环保措施。1968年,联合国大会同意于1972年召开联合国人类环境会议,成立了联合国环境规划署,许多国家的政府成立了环保部。由于排除了东德,苏联和其他华约组织成员国抵制会议,会议的成功受到限制。发达国家和发展中国家之间也出现分歧。中国代表团对美国谴责越南和世界各国的行为抱有敌意的立场,中国的立场也鼓励了其他发展中国家发表了针对美国的声明。

跨国污染日益成为全球关注的焦点。科学表明,一些环境问题在规模上真正地呈现出全球化发展趋势。1988年,联合国成立了政府间气候变化专门委员会(IPCC),授权其就气候变化科学知识,气候变化对社会和经济的影响以及可能的应对措施、战略和要素等问题编写全面的评论和建议。这有可能被纳入未来的国际气候公约。政府间气候变化专门委员会于1990年发布了第一份评估报告,其结论是人为温室气体在大气中持续积累将导致气候变化,其速度和规模可能对自然和人类产生重要影响。

除了提高认识外,冷战的结束还促成了第2次更有成效的联合国会议:联合国环境与发展会议(UNCED)。本次会议提出召开地球峰会/里约会议,同时签署了《联合国气候变化框架公约》(UNFCCC),开启了应对气候变化的国际合作。《联合国气候变化框架公约》是一个国际框架,通过限制全球平均温度上升和由此造成的气候变化来应对全球变暖。《联合国气候变化框架公约》确定了一个长期目标,即稳定大气中的温室气体浓度,以防止危及人类活动和干扰气候系统。获得足够多的国家批准后,《联合国气候变化框架公约》于1994年3月生效。

公约缔约方从1995年开始每年在缔约方会议（COP）上评估应对气候变化的进展。1995年在柏林召开的缔约方会议第一届会议启动了加强全球应对气候变化的谈判，1997年通过了《京都议定书》。发达国家的工业活动已经持续了150多年，发达国家应对目前高水平的温室气体排放负主要责任，因此，《京都议定书》根据"共同但有区别的责任"原则，给发达国家提出了更重的减排负担。

"共同但有区别的责任和各自能力"的概念是《联合国气候变化框架公约》的关键原则。这一概念意味着，尽管所有国家都必须为世界气候变化承担责任，但发达国家应立即承担责任，因为他们从工业化中受益，而工业化一般被认为是造成平均温度上升的过量二氧化碳的排放来源。《联合国气候变化框架公约》确实承认，不同国家的温室气体排放量不同，因此需要做出不同程度的努力来减少排放。例如，在20世纪90年代，美国人口仅占世界人口的4.5%，排放量却占全球总量的25%左右，而中国人口约占世界人口的20%，排放量占全球总量的14%。在谈判中形成了3个不同的国家集团。所有发达国家组成附件一国家，其余国家组成非附件一国家。当一些国家认为其经济处于转型期时，附件一随后被分为附件一和附件二。结果，最富裕的国家被列入附件二的附加类别，其余则列于附件一。

1995年，各国启动了全球应对气候变化的谈判，1997年12月在日本京都举行的缔约方会议第三届会议将谈判汇总。经过深入谈判后，通过了《京都议定书》。它概述了附件一国家的温室气体减排义务，以及后来被称为京都机制的措施，如排放交易、清洁发展机制和联合执行。大多数工业化国家和一些转型期的中欧经济体（均定义为附件二国家）同意在2008—2012年期间，即第一个排放量承诺期内，具有法定约束性的温室气体减排量比1990年平均低6%至8%。但《京都议定书》在发达国家和发展中国家之间划出了一条清晰的界线。例如，一方面，美国被要求其总排放量平均比1990年低7%。另一方面，在"共同但有区别的责任"原则下，包括中国在内的发展中国家不需要设定具有法律约束力的温室气体排放目标。

《京都议定书》的第一个承诺期（2008—2012）进一步延长至第二个时期，即2013年1月1日开始，2020年结束。根据责任区分原则，为发达国家制定了减排目标，而发展中国家，包括中国在内的新兴经济体根本不需要减排。这是为了平衡发达国家历史遗留的排放量，前提是发展中国家将加入2012年后协议。在第一个承诺期内,决定限制非附件国家排放看起来主要是一种战术行动,以延迟处理印度和中国等主要发展中国家排放限制的棘手问题。京都谈判明确了排除中国或印度的气候变化条约无法避免气候变化,但两国都不会接受限制其发展能力的排放限制。

2007年的缔约方会议第13届会议开启了2012年后的《后京都议定书》协议的谈判,制定了《巴厘路线图》。主要挑战是找到一种方法将发展中国家纳入减少温室气体排放的全球努力中。预计将在2009年哥本哈根缔约方会议第15届会议达成正式协议。虽然在某些领域取得了进展,哥本哈根会议未能达成备受期待的具有法律约束力的后京都时代条约。发达国家和发展中国家责任分化后的紧张局势在哥本哈根的谈判中达到高潮并变得明显。中国首次被指责拖延了国际气候谈判进程,之前一直是美国遭到这样的指责。例如,法国总统尼古拉·萨科齐公开声称中国在哥本哈根会议期间阻碍了会谈的进展。在这次会议筹备阶段,中国和印度与其他发展中国家合作,试图达成有利于自身的协议。如果中国得到印度和巴西的正式支持,人们认为之前的谈判对中国来说是战斗。

哥本哈根会议没有达成强有力的、具有法律约束力的全球协议,却至少使发达国家和发展中国家之间的责任区分变得模糊不清,标志着对未来框架主要内容达成共识的开端。在哥本哈根所取得的成就的基础上,接下来的坎昆会议和德班会议帮助讨论恢复正轨,在巴黎举行的缔约方会议第21届会议通过了2015年应当商定的气候协议时间表。

在2015年12月召开的巴黎气候大会上,195个国家通过了有史以来第一个具有法律约束力的全球气候协议。该协议提出了一项全球行动计划,使世界免遭危险的气候变化。协定制定了将全球变暖限制在2℃以下,特别是将温度增幅控制在1.5℃的目标,因为这将显著降低风险,减少气候变化的影响。《巴黎协定》是目前的政策与21世纪末以前的气候中立之间的桥梁。它承认世界需要尽快限制全球温室气体排放量的增加,但发展中国家需要更长的时间。

在巴黎气候大会之前和会议期间,各国提交了全面的《国家气候变化行动计划》(INDC)。这些还不足以使全球变暖保持在2℃以下,但协议探索了实现这一目标的方式。例如,《巴黎协定》寻求加速并增加可持续低碳未来所需的行动和投资。其核心目标是将21世纪全球升温与工业化前水平相比限制在远低于2℃,努力将温度升幅进一步限制在1.5℃以下,加强全球对气候变化威胁的响应,并加强各国应对气候变化影响的能力。《巴黎协定》被誉为是具有历史意义、持久和雄心勃勃的协议,甚至被称为世界上最伟大的外交成就。

今天人们对气候变化的认识令人难以置信。皮尤研究中心一项新的调查显示,全球各地的人们认为气候变化是国家安全第二大主要威胁,仅次于伊斯兰国(ISIS)。然而,唐纳德·特朗普领导下的美国退出了《巴黎协定》,引起了国际和国内的广泛谴责。中国批评美国的决定,并表示将坚持其对《巴黎协定》的承诺。随着中国在气候变化领域展示新兴领导力,本文下一节将回顾中国的气候变化政策评估,评价中国的承诺和行动。

三 中国的气候变化政策

大多数国家认为,中国在20世纪70年代开始更加重视环境问题。在此之前已经有了一些环境管理,但规模很小,环境保护只局限于控制空气污染和水污染。中国在1971年加入联合国后,于20世纪70年代后期更加正式地加入了全球环境运动,1978年邓小平启动改革后,重新对外开放。中国参加了各种环境会议并签署了许多国际条约。1972年,中国参加了联合国人类环境会议,该会议被公认为是推动环境保护的环境概念的开端。1989年,中国签署了《保护臭氧层维也纳公约》等国际条约。在国内,1973年,中国召开了第一次全国环境保护大会,并于1978年将环境问题纳入宪法。1972年中国发生的三次环境灾难重新唤起了环境意识,制定了其他环保法律。然而,气候变化在中国仍然是一个禁忌话题,因为它被视为西方生态帝国主义崛起的一部分。例如,在1972年的联合国人类环境会议上,中国代表团对这个问题持高度怀疑态度,并谴责西方企图干涉其外交。作为77国集团的领导成员,中国在引导发展中国家不为发达国家工业革命和高消费率付出代价方面发挥了重要作用。

气候变化是20世纪80年代后期进入中国的公共话语,当时为了协调气候变化相关研究,首次成立中国国家气候委员会。当时,气候变化只是一小部分高层决策者关心的问题;特别是在地方一级,气候变化成为经济发展的障碍。一些例子表明,当时一些中国人看到了将环境保护与经济发展结合起来的可能性,但仅在20—30年后,我们才看到措辞上的重大转变。的确,1978年推出的改革促进了中国崛起和经济快速增长。中国经济改革是20世纪最伟大的一次成功经验,但环保工作落后并被经济增长所取代。

经过几年的经济改革后，地方官员开始报告木材短缺，生态系统变化，土壤侵蚀，河床沉积，洪水和当地气候变化等。到了20世纪90年代，中国开始更加关注环保，更加积极主动地与其他发展中国家一道，参与1992年在里约热内卢地球峰会关于《联合国气候变化框架公约》的谈判。尽管中国的情况开始发生变化，自1972年联合国大会以来，中国的立场却始终没有改变。中国提出了环境保护五项基本原则，提出了其发展权和发达国家的责任。对许多观察员来说，中国在里约会议上是僵硬的阻挠者，联合发展中国家对抗先进的工业化国家，阻止达成气候变化国际协议。中国明确拒绝考虑限制其排放的任何目标或时间表，如1972年一样认为，作为一个新兴工业化国家，中国对气候变化问题承担的历史责任很小。中国在1997年京都通过的第一份联合国气候变化框架公约气候协议的谈判中保持了自己的立场。

中国参加里约会议引发了国内的一些变化。首先，中国制定了《环境与发展十项措施》，率先发布了《中国21世纪议程——中国人口、资源、环境白皮书》。官员们也开始将可持续发展纳入他们的规划过程。尽管环境议题提上了政治议程，但环境状况的恶化表明，中国领导人尚未准备弥补认识保护环境重要性和应对挑战之间的差距。

20世纪90年代中期，为了应对气候变化，谈判首次达成了限制温室气体排放的协议，中国坚定立场，提出了"共同但有区别的责任"原则。事实上，在1997年12月签署的《京都议定书》中，发达国家在法律上有义务减少其温室气体排放量，而发展中国家的排放量不受限制，只是鼓励其采取促进绿色增长的政策。《京都议定书》是具有里程碑意义的外交成就，注定要成功。条约生效后的头两年发布的报告表明，大多数参与者未能达到其排放目标。即使达到了目标，对环境的好处也不会太大，因为中国这个第二大温室气体排放国并未受到《京都议定书》的约束。美国、加拿大、俄罗斯和日本把缺乏中国这样的大型排放国的广泛参与作为他们放弃条约的理由。虽然条约没有达成，但它的一个主要价值是揭露了什么不起作用，即将世界分为两方：一方负责气候变化，另一方不负责。它还指出了下一份国际工作协议需要修正的问题。因此，在寻求后京都气候制度的谈判中，中国和其他排放量大的发达国家在承诺制定有约束力的减排目标时面临着巨大压力。

谈判期间，各国领导人同意将全球地表温度的上升幅度维持在高于工业化前水平2℃以下，为后京都条约奠定了基础。但是，由于发展中国家希望发达国家分担温室气体减排的大部分责任，谈判脱轨了。特别重要的是2009年哥本哈根会议期间中国与美国之间的僵局，各方由于对方缺乏行动而拒绝承诺有意义的削减目标。这被认为是峰会失败的原因之一。基于20世纪80年代和90年代的趋势，美国能源信息署估计，中国的温室气体排放量在2030年之前不会赶上美国的排放量，因为中国在1980年至2000年间国内生产总值翻了两番，能耗仅增加了一倍。但中国的能源使用量在2000年至2007年间激增。尽管与前几十年的增长率相似，但其在此期间的能源使用量增加了一倍多，中国于2007年成为世界最大的温室气体排放国。

直到哥本哈根会议失败之前，中国对国际气候谈判的态度一直与国内和国际环境的变化同步发展。虽然自气候谈判初期以来，中国一直非常积极地参与国际气候谈判，制定并开展国内气候减缓和适应措施，但其国内行动与国际上同时采取的行动之间存在差异。这也是中国领导层希望成为气候变化问题积极参与者的转折点。除了日益严峻的国际压力之外，中国数十年来忽视了环境和全球变暖的影响，开始意识到自身环境问题的可怕后果。随着中国近年来成为全球最大的二氧化碳排放国，人们日益认识到，应对全球变暖的趋势必须付出全球性努力，中国必须成为提供解决方案的一分子。2011年，中国空气污染特别严重的大城市令人震惊。由于雾霾导致飞机停飞、儿童住院，并且很明显中国不断壮大的中产阶级也迫切地想要得到解决方案。

中国政府应对气候变化的第一个重大转变是发布了"十二五"规划（2011—2015）。中国首次把绿色低碳发展作为生态文明建设定义的重要组成部分，认为其是加快转变经济发展方式，促进经济结构调整的重要机遇。2014年，中国启动了《国家应对气候变化规划》（2014—2020），提出到2020年应对气候变化的主要目标和任务。根据在利马举行的第19次缔约方会议的决定，中国还向联合国气候变化框架公约（UNFCCC）秘书处提交了国家自主贡献文件。中国国家自主贡献确定了若干目标，包括最晚于2030年左右达到二氧化碳排放峰值，并提出了确保实现目标的措施。在具体行动方面，中国已采取措施调整产业结构，节约能源，提高能源效率，优化能源结构，控制非能源相关的温室气体排放。中国首次承诺限制其碳排放量，并发出积极信号鼓励其余主要国家紧随其后，这为2015年在巴黎举行的缔约方会议提供了巨大的推动力。中国还在奥巴马执政后期积极与美国进行了讨论,美中都大力支持巴黎气候大会进程,通过无数多边和双边举措推动其早日获得批准。在巴黎气候大会上,习近平主席的讲话表明中国发挥了更为明显的作用,中国设定了雄心勃勃的减排目标,承诺到2030年达到排放峰值,并将单位国内生产总值二氧化碳排放量在2005年基础上削减60-65%。当唐纳德·特朗普将美国退出巴黎气候变化谈判进程时,中国政府立即表明了对这一进程的坚定承诺,从而将自己定位为整个联合国谈判进程的新兴领导者。习近平主席在2017年1月的达沃斯世界经济论坛上发表主旨演讲时,所有人的目光都集中在中国的全球领导力上,不仅在气候变化领域,而且在自由贸易和多边主义方面,中国都展现了领导力。几十年前,难以想象美国和中国的角色调换。现在,中国被要求在阻止全球变暖的斗争中发挥领导作用。据报道,在刚刚结束的波恩缔约方会议第23届会议上,中国再次在促进发达国家和发展中国家之间的合作方面发挥了积极作用。

四 结论

过去十年,中国在气候变化问题上的国际立场经历了巨大的变化。多年来,中国与其他发展中国家坚持认为,历史上,西方工业化国家应对全球变暖负责,他们应该付出代价,同时声称发展中经济体由于处于发展和工业化早期阶段,有权继续使用更多的化石燃料。哥本哈根会议一直是气候变化国际谈判中的一个低谷,也是中国领导层希望成为气候变化问题更积极参与者的转折点。除了不断增加的国际压力之外,中国经历了几十年的忽视环境和全球变暖的影响,开始意识到自身环境问题的可怕后果。随着中国近年来成为全球最大的二氧化碳排放国,人们日益认识到,应对全球变暖的趋势必须付出全球性的努力,中国不仅要成为提供解决方案的一分子,还必须成为这场全球斗争的主导力量。

目前关于中国作为全球气候变化领导者的潜在角色,有两种看法。第一种强调中国已经制定了有效的政策来治理国内的污染。例如,王长建和汪菲表示,经过几十年的低碳发展,中国能源相关碳排放量2015年首次下降了0.1%,2016年下降了0.7%。自2014年以来,煤炭消费量不断下降。中国在水电、风能和太阳能等可再生能源领域也一直处于领先地位。中国还计划形成一个全国范围的碳交易计划,这个计划的规模将比目前世界上最大的欧盟的碳交易体系更大。美国退出《巴黎协定》后,中国一直备受瞩目。

第二种看法承认中国在气候谈判方面的新的积极立场，但质疑其意图。例如，伊丽莎白·伊科诺米指出，中国仍然是世界上最大的二氧化碳排放国，并且在可预见的未来仍然如此。由三个国际研究机构发起的气候行动追踪组织显示，中国目前的减排目标与确保地球变暖保持在2℃以下并不一致。然而，人们更关心中国在国内采取的任何积极措施都并未在其国外行为中得到实施。中国是世界上最大的燃煤电厂金融和技术出口国。尽管习近平呼吁建立"一带一路"绿色发展国际联盟，但中国正在支持"一带一路"沿线国家100多个新的燃煤发电项目。除了中国在国内外气候政策的局限之外，至今没有迹象表明中国计划采取任何起领导作用的措施，例如联合其他国家制定另一轮更具雄心的温室气体减排目标，并推动限制甲烷等其他有害温室气体排放。

随着近年来中国的空气、土地、水和其他污染情况恶化，采取更平衡的发展方式的公众呼声不断增加，因此中国政府采取重大行动。在习近平的领导下，中国明确表示希望在全球舞台发挥更大的作用，包括在全球治理和多边合作中发挥领导作用。面对气候变化，世界要等待中国能否有效率先发挥作用。该研究表明，中国认真对待气候变化，但不会优先于其他的国家目标。事实上，如果中国能够使减缓气候变化与促进经济增长保持一致，中国会在应对气候变化方面采取行动，并有可能起领导作用。

China's Role in the Global Fight on Climate Change: An Assessment of its Contribution

Charles-Louis Labrecque / Canada

Project Specialist for the China Research Partnership, Asia Pacific Foundation of Canada

Tackling climate change has emerged as one of the defining challenges of the 21st century and possibly the greatest global public policy challenge of our time. But as addressing climate change goes beyond the capacity of any national governments, taking meaningful actions on this issue requires the participation of a wide range of countries and actors. Fifteen to twenty countries are responsible for roughly 75% of global emissions, but no one country accounts for more than about 26%. The efforts to cut emissions must therefore be global. And as the degradation of ecosystems transcends national boundaries, effective environmental protection must necessarily involve regional and global agreements and sound collaboration between a variety of actors, states and non-sates alike. Such international negotiation and agreements are however hard to achieve. As China is the largest economy in the world and the biggest carbon emitter, its participation in the global fight on climate change is essential and it must be part of any international agreements designed to tackle climate change. Due to its current emissions and its current and projected future energy use, China has indeed become increasingly important in this fight.

China has clearly become a major world power whose actions and input are necessary to fight global climate change. As China's huge environmental challenges are globally significant, Beijing's attitude to climate change and its environmental policies will have major implications for the health of the world's environment. Indeed, China's climate policies and its commitment are regarded as critical for the success of a climate change regime. If China's performance in terms of economic growth and the improvement of general living standards is spectacular, it has constantly underperformed on the environment front. According to the World Bank, China has accounted for a greater increase in carbon emissions since the beginning of this century than another country.[1] The choices China is making influence not only the health and well-being of the Chinese people but very future of the planet. How China's government will approach the problem of climate change will be a critical policy question for the coming decades.

Especially since the withdrawal of the United States from the Paris Agreement, which leaves a void in global climate politics, many have speculated about China's role in the global fight on climate change. Beijing could certainly use the United States' inactions as an excuse to backslide on its promises, but it doesn't seem to be the path it has chosen. Various Chinese government officials have repeatedly declared that China wants to take on more responsibility for climate policy at the international level. For example, China's President Xi Jinping stated at the 19th CPC congress held in October 2017 that his country would take the driving seat in international cooperation to respond to climate change[2]. More recently, he has also indicated that China is showing leadership on climate at home and on the

---

1 World Bank, 2015. "Carbon Pricing." http://www.worldbank.org/en/news/feature/2015/09/20/state-and-trends-of-carbon-pricing-2015

2 Somini Sengugta, 2017. "Why China Wants to lead on Climate, but Clings to Coal." *The New York Times*. November 14.

international sphere[1]. Indeed, Beijing has expressed interest in working not only with other major powers, such as the European Union, but also small island states and other vulnerable countries. And with regards to the least developed countries, many of which will be devastatingly impacted by climate change, China has expressed a willingness to provide financial and technical support.[2]

It has been argued that China has become the new biggest champion in the global fight about climate change[3]. In a recent global survey, when asked which country is doing more to "maintain peace", China beats the United States by 11%; when asked "who is doing more to address environmental issues", China beats the United States by 6%[4].

These developments point to the importance of understanding how China's policies on energy, climate change, and on the environment, are evolving. This paper aims at reviewing China's policy on climate change and its recent attitude toward climate negotiations in order to assess China's potential role as a "climate champion". It will help us better understand China's role in global governance and provide us with a window into its behavior and future intentions. It will first review the global issue of climate change and assess China's responsibility. It will then review China's energy policy and its action to fight climate change. Finally, it will evaluate China's commitment and actions.

I. What is Climate Change?

The term "climate change" refers to a broad range of global phenomena due to changes in the concentration levels of carbon dioxide (CO_2), methane (CH_4), nitrous oxide, and others gases - collectively referred to as "greenhouse gases" (GHG)

---

1 Louise Watt, 2017. "China's Xi slams unwillingness to combat climate change," *AP News*. https://apnews.com/6aa3c628308f48c1857735c698e84848
2 D.D. Wu, 2017. "What Did China Say After US Announced Exit From Paris Agreement?", *The Diplomat*. June 3 2017. https://thediplomat.com/2017/06/what-did-china-say-after-us-announced-exit-from-paris-agreement/
3 Bingqiang Ren and Huisheng Shou, 2013. China's Environmental Governance. P.1.
4 http://nationalpost.com/news/politics/more-than-two-thirds-of-canadians-support-a-free-trade-deal-with-china

within the atmosphere.¹ These phenomena include the increased temperature trends described by global warming, but also encompass changes such as sea level rise; ice mass loss in Greenland, Antarctica, the Arctic and mountain glaciers worldwide; shifts in flower/plant blooming; and extreme weather events.²

As there is clear evidence that levels of atmospheric CO_2 have been rising ever since the beginning of the industrial revolution, the most logical approach to the climate change problem is to significantly cut GHG emissions. But this task is not as simple as it appears, as CO_2 emissions are not evenly produced by countries.³ According to the Intergovernmental Panel on Climate Change (IPCC) the first major source of CO_2 is the burning of fossil fuels, since 80% of global CO_2 emissions comes from energy production, industrial process, and transport. These are not evenly distributed around the world because of the unequal distribution of industry and wealth, and because the developed nations have historically emitted much more than less developed countries, as they have been emitting them since the start of the industrial revolution in the latter half of the 18th century. But even if this historic carbon burden is important, according to International Energy Authority (IEA) projections, it is rapidly changing. Between 2015 and 2044 it is estimated that the world will put half a trillion tonnes of CO_2 into the atmosphere, which is the same amount that was emitted between 1750 and 2015. This is mostly because rapidly developing countries such as China, India, South Africa, Brazil, etc., are increasing their emissions of GHG at a huge rate.⁴

II. Global Environmental Governance and China's Climate Change Policy

After the Second World War and the global economic recovery it triggered,

---

1 IPCC, 2007. *Summary for Policy makers in Climate Change 2007: The Physical Science Basis. Contribution of Working Group 1 to fourth Assessment Report of the Intergovernmental Panel on Climate Change.* Cambridge: Cambridge University Press.
2 Mark Maslin, 2014. *Climate Change: A Very Short Introduction.* Oxford, Oxford University Press. p.7.
3 Mark Maslin, 2014. p.7.
4 Mark Maslin, 2014. p.10.

evidence of increasing harmful pollution became more and more apparent. Some international agreements were signed in the 1950's and 1960's to address mainly oil spills and discharges from tankers, but nothing was done on environmental protection. In 1968, the UN General Assembly agreed to convene what became the 1972 UN Conference on the Human Environment, which led to the creation of the United Nations Environment Programme (UNEP) and the establishment of environment departments by many governments. The success of the Conference was limited as the Soviet Union and other Warsaw Pact nations boycotted the conference due to the exclusion of East Germany. Divisions between developed and developing countries also emerged. The Chinese delegation took an hostile position regarding the United States condemning their actions in Vietnam and around the world. Doing so, China's position emboldened other developing countries who also issued statements against the United States.

Transnational pollution increasingly became a concern around the world and the scientific realization that some environmental problems were truly global in scale gained momentum. In 1988, the UN created the IPCC and gave it the mandate to prepare a comprehensive review and recommendations with respect to the state of knowledge of the science of climate change, the social and economic impact of climate change, and possible responses, strategies, and elements for inclusion in a possible future international convention on climate.[1] IPCC published its first assessment report in 1990, which concluded that continued accumulation of anthropogenic greenhouse gases in the atmosphere would lead to climate changes whose rate and magnitude were likely to have important impacts on natural and human systems.[2]

In addition to this increased awareness, the end of the cold war allowed for a second and more productive UN Conference: the UN Conference on Environment

---

1 Mark Maslin, 2014. p.15.
2 IPCC, 1990. *Climate Change: The IPCC Scientific Assessment (1990)* http://www.ipcc.ch/publications_and_data/publications_ipcc_first_assessment_1990_wg1.shtml

and Development (UNCED).¹ Coined the "Earth Summit" or the "Rio Conference", this conference launched the international cooperation to fight climate change with the signing of the United Nations Framework Convention on Climate Change (UNFCCC). The UNFCCC is an international framework put in place to combat global warming by limiting average global temperature increases and the resulting climate change. The Convention established a long-term objective of stabilizing greenhouse gas concentrations in the atmosphere at a level that would prevent dangerous anthropogenic interference with the climate system[2]. It came into force in March 1994 after a sufficient number of countries had ratified the Convention.

The parties to the convention began meeting annually from 1995 in Conferences of the Parties (COP) to assess progress in dealing with climate change. As a result, negotiations to strengthen the global response to climate change were launched at the first COP held in Berlin in 1995, which led to the adoption of the Kyoto Protocol in 1997. Recognizing that developed countries are principally responsible for the current high levels of GHG emissions in the atmosphere resulting in more than 150 years of industrial activity, the Protocol placed a heavier burden on developed nations under the principle of "common but differentiated responsibilities."

The notion of "common but differentiated responsibilities and respective capabilities" was a key principle in the founding of UNFCCC. This notion means that although all nations had to accept responsibility for the world's changing climate, it was developed nations that were immediately responsible because they had benefited from the industrialization which was generally regarded as the source of the excess carbon dioxide emissions that had caused mean temperature increases.[3] The UNFCCC indeed acknowledges that different countries have emitted different amount of GHGs and therefore need to make greater or lesser

---

1 John Vogler, 2014. "Environmental Issues." In *The Globalization of World Politics,* ed, John Baylis. Oxford University Press.
2 United Nations, 1992. *United Nations Framework Convention on Climate Change.* https://unfccc.int/resource/docs/convkp/conveng.pdf
3 Mark Maslin, 2014. p.30.

efforts to reduce their emissions. For example, in the 1990s, the USA emitted around 25% of global emissions but had only 4.5% of the world's population while China accounted for 14% of global emissions for about 20% of the world's population. At the negotiations three different groups of countries were formed. All the developed countries formed the Annex I countries and the rest formed the non-Annex I countries. The Annex I was subsequently divided in Annex I and Annex II when some countries argued that their economies were in transition. As a result, the richest countries were placed in the additional category, Annex II, and the rest remained in Annex I.

By 1995, countries had launched negotiations to strengthen the global response to climate change, which cumulated in 1997 at the COP 3, that took place in December 1997 in Kyoto, Japan. After intensive negotiations, the Kyoto Protocol was adopted. It outlined the greenhouse gas emissions reduction obligation for Annex I countries, along with what came to be known as Kyoto mechanisms such as emissions trading, clean development mechanism and joint implementation. Most industrialized countries and some central European economies in transition (all defined as Annex II countries) agreed to legally binding reductions in greenhouse gas emissions of an average of 6% to 8% below 1990 levels between the years 2008–2012, defined as the first emissions commitment period. But the Kyoto protocol drew a clear line between developed countries and developing ones. On the one hand, the United States, for example, was required to reduce its total emissions an average of 7% below 1990 levels. Developing countries including China on the other hand, were not required to take on legally binding GHG emissions targets under the principle of common but differentiated responsibilities.

The Protocol's first commitment period (2008-2012) was further extended to cover a second period that began on January 1st 2013 and will end in 2020. In line with the principle of differentiated responsibility, developed countries were assigned emissions reduction targets, while developing countries, including emerging economies such as China, were not required to cut emissions at all. This was to balance out the historic legacy of emissions by developed countries. It was assumed that developing countries would join the post-2012 agreement. The decision to limit emission targets to non-Annex countries in the first commitment period appears to have been largely a tactical move to delay dealing with the thorny issue of emissions limits for major developing countries such as India and China. During the Kyoto negotiations it was already clear that a climate change treaty that excluded China or India could not avert climate change, but neither countries would accept emissions limits that restricted their capacity to develop.[1]

Negotiations towards a "post-Kyoto" agreement that would cover the post-2012 period began at the COP13 in 2007 with the publication of the Bali Road Map. The main challenge was to find a way to include developing countries into the global efforts to cut GHG emissions. It was anticipated that this would lead to a formal agreement at the COP15 in 2009 at Copenhagen. If progress were made in some areas, the Copenhagen conference failed to deliver the much anticipated legally binding treaty to cover the post-Kyoto period. The tensions following the divide in responsibility between developed and developing countries had culminated and became evident at the negotiations in Copenhagen. For the first time China was blamed for dragging out international climate negotiations, while such blame had previously always been put on the United States.[2] French president Nicolas Sarkozy for example, publicly asserted that China had held back progress in the talks during the Copenhagen meeting.[3] In the lead-up to the conference, China had teamed up with India and other developing countries in order to try securing a deal to its advantage. If China was officially backed by India and Brazil, it was acknowledged that the negotiations had been China's battle.[4]

---

1 John Vogler, 2014.
2 Zongxiang Zhang, 2015. "China's role in Climate Negotiations." *Friedrich-Ebert-Stiftung*. http://library.fes.de/pdf-files/iez/12072.pdf
3 Tobias Rapp, 2009. "How China and India Sabotaged the UN Climate Summit," *Der Spiegel*. http://www.spiegel.de/international/world/the-copenhagen-protocol-how-china-and-india-sabotaged-the-un-climate-summit-a-692861.html
4 Zongxiang Zhang, 2015.

If the Copenhagen conference didn't lead to a strong legally binding global agreement, it at least blurred the distinction between developed and developing countries in terms of responsibilities and it reflected the beginning of what would become a consensus on the main elements of a future framework. Building on what has nonetheless been achieved in Copenhagen, the following Conferences held in Cancun and Durban helped to put back the discussions back on track, which led to the adoption of a timetable for a climate agreement that was supposed to be agreed in 2015, at the COP 21 in Paris.

At the Paris climate conference in December 2015, 195 countries adopted the first-ever universal, legally binding global climate deal. The agreement sets out a global action plan to put the world on track to avoid dangerous climate change by limiting global warming to well below 2°C and highlights the aim of limiting the increase to 1.5°C, as this would significantly reduce risks and the impacts of climate change. The Paris Agreement is a bridge between today's policies and climate-neutrality before the end of the century. It recognizes that the world needs to stop the increase of global GHG emissions as soon as possible but that this will take longer for developing countries.

Before and during the Paris conference, countries submitted comprehensive national climate action plans (INDCs). These are not yet enough to keep global warming below 2°C, but the agreement traces the way to achieving this target. For example, the Paris Agreement seeks to accelerate and intensify the actions and investment needed for a sustainable low carbon future. Its central aim is to strengthen the global response to the threat of climate change by keeping a global temperature rise this century well below 2°C above pre-industrial levels and to pursue efforts to limit the temperature increase even further to 1.5°C. The Agreement also aims to strengthen the ability of countries to deal with the impacts of climate change.[1] The Paris agreement produced an agreement hailed as historic, durable and ambitious and was

---

1　The Guardian, 2015. "Keeping temperature rises below below 1.5℃." https://www.theguardian.com/environment/2015/dec/12/paris-climate-deal-key-points

even claimed as the world's greatest diplomatic success.[1]

There is today an incredible awareness of climate change. According to a new Pew Research Center survey, people around the globe identify climate change as the second most important threats to national security, behind ISIS.[2] The United States under Donald Trump, however, withdrew from the Paris agreement, which caused widespread condemnation both internationally and domestically. China for example, criticized the American decision and said it would stick by its commitments to the Paris agreement.[3] As China is showing an emerging leadership on climate change, the next section will review its climate change policy and assess and evaluate China's commitment and actions.

III. China's Climate Change Policy

As for most countries, China started paying attention more seriously to the environment in the 1970s. There has been some environmental management before that period, but on a very small scale and environmental protection was linked to air and water pollution control.[4] China was also able to join the global environment movement more formally in the late 1970's after joining the United Nations in 1971 and reopening itself to the outside world following the reforms launched by Deng Xiaoping in 1978. China attended various environmental conferences and signed many international treaties. For example, China attended the 1972 UN Conference on the Human Environment, which is recognized as the beginning of environmental concepts that prompted environmental protection. China signed various treaties such as the Vienna Convention for the Protection of the Ozone Layer in 1989.

---

1 The Guardian, 2015. "Paris Climate Change Agreement." https://www.theguardian.com/environment/2015/dec/13/paris-climate-deal-cop-diplomacy-developing-united-nations
2 Pew Research Center, 2017. "Paris Climate Deal" http://www.pewglobal.org/2017/08/01/globally-people-point-to-isis-and-climate-change-as-leading-security-threats/
3 Laura Smith-Spark, 2017. "World's leaders condemn Trump's decision to quit Paris climate deal", *CNN*. http://www.cnn.com/2017/06/02/world/us-climate-world-reacts/index.html
4 Qui Zong and Guoqing Shi, 2011. "Environmental Consciousness Change". In *Environmental Protection Policy and Experience in the US and China's western regions*, dir Sujian Guo et al. (eds) Lexington, Lanham. p. 90.

Domestically, China held its first National Conference on Environmental Protection in 1973 and incorporated environmental concerns in its constitution in 1978. Three environmental disasters in 1972 sparked a new environmental consciousness in China and additional environmental protection laws. Climate change, however, was still a taboo subject in China as it was seen as part of a rising western eco-imperialism.[1] For example, at the 1972 UN Conference on the Human Environment, the Chinese delegation was highly skeptical of the issue and condemned what was it seen as Western attempts to intervene in its foreign affairs.[2] As a leading member of the G-77, China played an instrumental role in leading developing countries' desire not to pay the prices of developed countries industrial revolution and high rates of consumption.[3]

Climate change entered the public discourse in China in the late 1980's when the first Chinese National Climate Committee was created to coordinate climate change related research. Climate change was then only a concern to a fraction of high-level policy makers and was seen, especially at the local level, as a barrier to economic development. Some examples show that some Chinese were seeing the possibility to integrate environmental protection with economic development, but it is only two to three decades later that we would see a significant shift in rhetoric.[4] Indeed, the reforms launched in 1978 led to China's rise and rapid economic growth. If the reform of China's economy represents one of the greatest success stories of the 20th century, environmental protection efforts lagged and were superseded by economic growth.

After several years of economic reforms, local officials began to report wood shortages, altered ecosystems, soil erosion, riverbed deposits, flooding, and changing local climates.[5] By the 1990s' China started to pay more attention to

---

1   Miriam Schroder, 2012. *Local Climate Governance in China*. New York: Palgrave. p.21
2   Miriam Schroder, 2012. p.23
3   Judith Shapiro, 2011. *China's environmental challenges*. Malden: Polity Press. p. 62.
4   Miriam Schroder, 2012. p.21
5   Elizabeth Economy, 2004. *The Rivers Run Black*. Ithaca: Cornell University Press. p.65.

environmental protection, and it became more proactive when it joined with other developing countries the UNFCCC 1992 negotiations at the earth Summit in Rio de Janeiro. But if things were beginning to change in China, it kept the same position it had been holding for since the 1972 UN Conference. China articulated Five Principles of environmental protection, putting forward its right to development and the responsibility of developed countries.[1] To many observers, China was an inflexible obstructionist at the Rio Conference, allying developing countries against advanced industrialized nations to prevent an international agreement on climate change. China categorically refused to consider any targets or timetables for limiting its emissions, arguing, just like it had done in 1972, that, as a newly industrializing county, it bore little historical responsibility for the problem of climate change.[2] China kept its position during the negotiations for a first UNFCCC climate agreement, passed in Kyoto in 1997.

Domestically, however, China's participation at the Rio Conference triggered a number of changes in China. First, China formulated "Ten Measures for Environment and Development" and took the lead to issue China's Agenda 21, China's first White Paper on Population, Environment and Development in the 21st Century. Officials also began to incorporate sustainable development into their planning process.[3] Despite the rise of environmental issues in the political agenda, however, the deteriorating state of the environment suggested that China's leaders were not yet ready to bridge the gap between recognizing the importance of protecting the environment and acting to respond to the challenges.[4]

In the mid 1990s negotiations meant to lead to a first agreement to limit GHG emissions in order to address climate change, China held firmly to its position and helped put forward the principle of "common but differentiated responsibilities".

---

1 Elizabeth Economy, 2004. p.98.
2 Elizabeth Economy, 2004. p.98.
3 United Nations, *Institutional Aspects of Sustainable Development*. http://www.un.org/esa/agenda21/natlinfo/countr/china/inst.htm
4 Stephan Tsang and Ans Kolk, 2010. "The evolution of Chinese Policies and Governance structures on Environment, Energy and Climate." *Environmental Policy and Governance* 20, 186-196.

Indeed, in the Kyoto Protocol signed in December 1997, developed countries were legally obliged to cut their GHG emissions while developing countries were facing no restrictions on their emissions and were only encouraged to adopt policies aimed at promoting greener growth. Although the Kyoto Protocol represented a landmark diplomatic accomplishment, its success was doomed. Reports issued in the first two years after the treaty took effect indicated that most participants would fail to meet their emission targets. And even if the targets were met, the benefit to the environment would not be significant as China, the second leading emitter of greenhouse gases was not bound by the protocol. The United States, Canada, Russia and Japan cited the lack of wider participation by large emitters such as China as their rationale to abandon the treaty. Even if the treaty failed, one of its main values was that it exposed what didn't work, i.e. the splitting the world into two sides: one responsible for climate change and the other that was not. It also pointed to what needed to be fixed for the next international agreement to work.[1] Thus, in the negotiations to find a post-Kyoto climate regime, China, and other large emitting developed countries, came under significant pressure to commit to binding reduction targets.

During those negotiations, world leaders agreed to keep the rise in global surface temperature below 2 degrees above pre-industrialised levels, which laid the foundation for a post-Kyoto treaty. But negotiations derailed as developing countries wanted for developed countries to share most of the burden of GHG reduction. Particularly important was the deadlock between China and the U.S. at the Copenhagen conference of 2009, where each side refusing to commit to a meaningful reduction targets due to the lack of action by the other. This has been cited as one of the reasons for the unsuccessful outcome of the summit.[2] Based on the trends of the 1980s and 1990s, the U.S. Energy Information Administration had estimated that China's GHG emissions would not catch up with the United States'

---

1 Quirin Schiermeier, 2012. "The Kyoto Protocol: Hot air." *Nature* 491, 656–658.
2 ABC News, 2009. "India, China cooperated to torpedo climate deal". http://www.abc.net.au/news/2009-12-23/india-china-cooperated-to-torpedo-climate-deal/1188486

emission before 2030 because China had successfully quadrupled its GDP between 1980 and 2000 with only doubling its energy consumption. But China's energy use surged between 2000 and 2007. Despite similar growth rate as in the previous decades, its energy use during that period more than doubled, and China became the world's biggest GHG emitters in 2007.[1]

Up until the failure of the Copenhagen Conference, China's stance toward international climate negotiations has been evolving concurrent with changes in domestic and international contexts. While China had been very active in participating in international climate negotiations and formulating and undertaking domestic climate mitigation and adaptation measures since the early days of climate talks, there was a discrepancy between its domestic actions and its simultaneous reticence to act at the international level. But it was also a turning point where the Chinese leadership wanted to be an active participant on climate change issues. Other than the increasing international pressure, China began to realize the dire consequences of its own environmental problems after decades of neglect and the impact of global warming. With China turning into the number one CO_2 emitting country in recent years, there is growing realization that combating global warming trends must be a global effort and China must be a part of the solution.[2] China's particularly polluted air in major cities in 2011 was also an eye opener for the nation. Flights were grounded due to smog, children hospitalized, and it became clear that the country's growing middle class wanted solutions.[3]

The first major shift in Beijing's dealing of climate change came with the publication of its 12th Five-Year Plan (2011-2015). For the first time, China put green and low-carbon development as an important component of what was defined

---

1 Chris Bukley, 2017. "China's Role in Climate Change, and Possibly in Fighting It", *The New York Times*. https://www.nytimes.com/2017/06/02/world/asia/chinas-role-in-climate-change-and-possibly-in-fighting-it.html
2 Wenran Jiang, 2017. "China Takes Up Global Role on Climate Change", *Geopolitics of Energy*. http://iar2015.sites.olt.ubc.ca/files/2017/12/Geopolitics-of-Energy-November-December-2017.pdf
3 Li Shuo, 2017. "Can China Lead the World in Fighting Climate Change?", *The Diplomat*. https://thediplomat.com/2017/05/can-china-lead-the-world-in-fighting-climate-change/

as the "ecological civilization construction," and a crucial opportunity to accelerate "the shift in the country's economic development mode and promote the economic restructuring." In 2014, China launched the National Plan on Climate Change (2014-2020), presenting the major targets and tasks for addressing climate change by 2020. As agreed at the COP 19 in Lima, China also submitted its Intended Nationally Determined Contribution (INDC) document to the United Nations Framework Convention on Climate Change (UNFCCC) Secretariat. China's INDC specified a number of targets including reaching the peak in CO_2 emissions around 2030 if not earlier and proposed measures that will ensure the delivery of the targets. In terms of specific actions, China has taken measures to adjust its industrial structure, save energy, improve energy efficiency, optimize energy structure, and control emissions from non-energy related greenhouse gases.[1] For the first time China was committing to cap its carbon emissions, which sent a positive signal encouraging the remaining major economies to follow suit and this provided a big boost to the prospect of the coming Conference of Parties in Paris in 2015. China also actively discussed with the United States during the later years of the Obama Administration to put a strong US-China joint support to the Paris Conference process, pushing for its early approval through numerous multilateral and bilateral initiatives. At the Paris Conference China played a much more visible role, with President Xi Jinping speaking, and China setting ambitious emission targets, promising to reach the peak of emissions by 2030, and cutting CO_2 emissions per unit GDP by 60-65% from 2005 level. But when Donald Trump pulled the United States out of the Paris Climate Change process, Beijing wasted no time in expressing its firm commitment to the process, thus positioning itself as an emerging leader in the entire UN process. When President Xi Jinping gave the keynote speech at the Davos World Economic Forum in January 2017, all eyes were on China for global leadership, not just in the realm of climate change but also free trade and multilateralism.[2] Such a

---

1 UN Environment, Green Economy. http://web.unep.org/greeneconomy/sites/unep.org.greeneconomy/files/publications/greenisgold_en_20160519.pdf
2 Wenran Jiang, 2017. "China Takes Up Global Role on Climate Change", *Geopolitics of Energy*. http://iar2015.sites.olt.ubc.ca/files/2017/12/Geopolitics-of-Energy-November-December-2017.pdf

reverse role between the US and China was not even conceivable a couple of years ago, and yet China is now called upon to take the leadership role in the fight to stop global warming. And as reported, in the recently concluded COP23 in Bonn, China again played an active role in promoting collaboration among both developed and developing countries.[1]

IV. Conclusion

China's international stand on climate change has gone through dramatic changes in the past 10 years. For many years, China, together with other developing countries, insisted that Western industrialized countries were historically responsible for global warming and they should pay for the cost while claiming that developing economies have a right to continue to use more fossil fuels due to their early stages of development and industrialization. The Copenhagen conference has been a low point in international negotiations on climate change and also a turning point where the Chinese leadership wanted to be a more active participant on climate change issues. Other than the increasing international pressure, China had begun to realize the dire consequences of its own environmental problems after decades of neglect and the impact of global warming. With China turning into the number one CO_2 emitting country in recent years, there has been a growing realization that combating global warming trends must be a global effort and that China must not only be a part of the solution but must be a leading force in this global fight.

There are currently two visions on China's potential role as a global leader on climate change. The first vision highlights that China is already developing effective policies to fight pollution at home. For example, Changjian Wang and Fei Wang notes that after decades of low-carbon development, China's energy-related carbon emissions declined for the first time in 2015 by 0.1% and 0.7% in 2016 and that its consumption of coal has been declining continuously from 2014.[2] China has also

---

1 Carbon Brief, 2017. "COP23: Key outcomes agreed at the UN climate talks in Bonn", https://www.carbonbrief.org/cop23-key-outcomes-agreed-un-climate-talks-bonn
2 Jennifer Sills, 2016. "China can lead on climate change", *Science*. http://science.sciencemag.org/content/357/6353/764.1

been leading the way on renewables such as hydropower, wind and solar power. China also plans to form a nationwide carbon-trading scheme that will be bigger than the EU's, currently the world largest carbon system.[1] And with the United States withdrawal of the Paris agreement, China has been placed on the spotlight.

The second vision recognises China's new positive stance on climate negotiation but questions its intention. For example, Elisabeth Economy notes that China is still the largest emitter of CO_2 on the planet by a substantial margin and will remain so for the foreseeable future.[2] For example, the Climate Action Tracker, produced by three international research institutions, indicates that China's current emission reduction targets are not consistent with ensuring that the earth's warming remains below 2°C. More concerning, however, is that whatever positive steps China is taking at home are not being replicated in its behavior abroad. China is the world's largest exporter of coal-fired power plant finance and technology. Even as Xi is calling for an "international coalition for green development on the Belt and Road", Beijing is backing more than 100 new coal-fired power projects in the Belt and Road countries.[3] And beyond the clear limitations of China's climate policies at home and abroad, there is thus far no indication that China has plans to adopt any of leadership-worthy measures such as to rally other countries to adopt another round of more ambitious greenhouse gas reduction targets and to push forward to limit other harmful greenhouse gas emissions, such as methane.

As China's air, land, water, and other pollutions worsened in recent years, the public cry for a more balanced development approach has been growing, leading the Chinese government to take significant action. In the case of climate change, the world will have to wait to see if China will effectively take the lead. This study

---

1 UNDP, 2017. "The launch of the Environomist 2017 Carbon Market Research Report", http://www.cn.undp.org/content/china/en/home/presscenter/articles/2017/02/17/the-launch-of-the-environomist-2017-carbon-market-research-report.html
2 Elizabeth Economy, 2017. "Why China is no Climate Leader", *Politico*. https://www.politico.com/magazine/story/2017/06/12/why-china-is-no-climate-leader-215249
3 Lili Pike, 2017. "Will China's new Silk Road be green?", *China Dialogue*. https://www.chinadialogue.net/blog/9775-Explainer-Will-China-s-new-Silk-Road-be-green-/en

shows that China takes climate change seriously, but that it will not take priority over other national objectives. Indeed, it appears that if China can make climate change mitigation consistent with economic growth, China will act and potentially lead on the issue.